H

To Kay:

with love from her
devoted brother —

John.

Christmas, 1933

PLAYS AND POEMS OF
W. S. GILBERT

PLAYS & POEMS

OF

W. S. GILBERT

WITH A PREFACE BY DEEMS TAYLOR

INCLUDING

THE COMPLETE TEXT OF THE FOURTEEN
GILBERT AND SULLIVAN OPERAS
THREE OTHER GILBERT PLAYS

AND

ALL OF THE BAB BALLADS.
WITH ILLUSTRATIONS
BY THE AUTHOR

NEW YORK · RANDOM HOUSE

MCM XXXII

PRINTED AND BOUND IN THE UNITED STATES OF AMERICA
BY J. J. LITTLE & IVES COMPANY, NEW YORK
TYPOGRAPHY BY ROBERT S. JOSEPHY

FOR ASSISTANCE IN THE COMPILATION OF THIS VOLUME
THE PUBLISHERS MAKE GRATEFUL ACKNOWLEDGMENT
TO MR. JOHN R. MEEKER, MR. HARRY SCHERMAN,
AND MR. HERBERT A. WISE

CONTENTS

THE BAB BALLADS

THE LOST BAB BALLADS

CHRONOLOGICAL TABLE

Born in London November 18th, 1836

Became contributor to Fun 1861

Became Barrister-at-Law 1866. Practised to 1870

First play (*Dulcamara*) produced December 29th, 1866

Bab Ballads first published 1869

First meeting with Arthur Sullivan autumn of 1870

Palace of Truth produced November 19th, 1870

First Gilbert and Sullivan collaboration (*Thespis*) produced December 23rd, 1871

Trial by Jury (with Sullivan) produced March 25th, 1875

The Sorcerer (first D'Oyley Carte production, music by Sullivan) November 17th, 1877

H.M.S. Pinafore (with Sullivan) produced May 25th, 1878

The Pirates of Penzance (with Sullivan) produced April 3rd, 1880

Patience (with Sullivan) produced April 23rd, 1881

Iolanthe (with Sullivan) produced November 25th, 1882

Arthur Sullivan knighted, May 27th, 1883

Princess Ida (with Sullivan) produced January 5th, 1884

The Mikado (with Sullivan) produced March 14th, 1885

Ruddigore (with Sullivan) produced January 22nd, 1887

The Yeomen of the Guard (music by Sullivan) produced October 3rd, 1888

The Gondoliers (with Sullivan) December 7th, 1889

Breach between Gilbert and Sullivan 1889-1893

The Mountebanks (music by Alfred Cellier) produced January 4th, 1892

His Excellency (music by Osmond Carr) produced October 27th, 1894

Utopia Limited (music by Sullivan) produced October 7th, 1893

The Grand Duke (music by Sullivan) produced March 7th, 1896

Death of Sir Arthur Sullivan November 22nd, 1900

Wm. S. Gilbert knighted, June 30th, 1907

Drowned May 29th, 1911

A Preface by Deems Taylor

[1]

WE LIVED in a flat (there were no such things as apartments in those days) on West Tenth Street, New York. At the age of six, one is not given to observing such things, but as I look back I realize that we were not wealthy. The piano, for instance, the traditional result and symbol of affluence, was missing. We did, however, possess a parlor organ; a Mason & Hamlin, and a good one; and what time he was not teaching day or night school, my father used to play and sing a good deal.

One song of his I particularly liked. It announced that he was the Monarch of the Sea and the Ruler of the Queen's Navy. The last word bothered me, for he pronounced it "nah-*vee*." This, I knew, was utterly incorrect (I had made tactful inquiries at school); but since he was obviously perpetrating the barbarism in order to make some sort of rhyme with "sea," and seemed to derive pleasure therefrom, I humored him and let the error pass. Besides, I did like the song. I liked the tune, and the way the words went with it. There was a part at the end, about "his sisters and his cousins and his aunts," where the words went faster and faster, so that your tongue tripped over itself trying to get them out, that was particularly fascinating. I had no notion what it meant.

He used to sing another, too, about a poor little buttercup; and a very sad one, about some kind of little bird that died, and whose name was Tit Willow. Both delightful. Then, too, my parents had a number of mysterious jokes that were in some way connected with the songs. My father, for example, was fond of announcing that he had polished up the handle of the big front door —an obvious lie. It seemed to amuse my mother, which was more than my own small falsehoods did. Also, every once in a while, to some statement of my mother's my father would retort, "What, never?" Without even waiting for her to speak he would instantly answer himself, "Well, hardly ever!" and burst into laughter. My mother would laugh, too. It seemed to me almost unbearably silly for two such aged people to go on like that over a simple question and its perfectly satisfactory answer.

This, mind you, was in the very early nineties. *Pinafore,* even then, was thirteen years old, and *The Mikado* was seven. My parents were no exceptions. They were, I fancy, rather mild cases of a prevailing mania. All through America people were still chuckling and humming and quoting and generally making fools of themselves over the comic operas of two authors named Gilbert and Sullivan. Another smaller but equally rabid group went about declaiming stanzas from a series of *Bab Ballads* written by the Gilbert of the combination.

The mania had somewhat abated, of course. What it must have been like during the early eighties, at the height of the *Pinafore* madness, one can guess from a recital of the bare facts. We know, for instance, that *Pinafore* was performed professionally by nearly one hundred companies; that it was performed as well by countless amateur dramatic societies, in churches, in club rooms, and in private houses; that there were children's *Pinafore* companies, and blackface *Pinafore* companies; that it was done with men singing some of the women's rôles, and—Miss Rose Temple sang the rôle of *Ralph Rackstraw* at the first performance in America—vice versa; and that the style sheets of many an American newspaper of the period specifically forbade reporters to incorporate "What, never?" "Well, hardly ever!" in their news stories.

The wonder is that there is anything left of Gilbert and Sullivan today; that such a book as this one, for instance, can be published in the well justified expectation of finding readers. As a rule, any epidemic is its own eventual cure. Once it has run its course, it vanishes. If it is a disease, it may reappear after a generation; if it is a popular amusement, it usually passes forever. Considering the craze that they inspired, Gilbert and Sullivan ought to be as dead as tiddledewinks. On the contrary, as I write this, a New York company has just finished a prosperous summer series of Gilbert and Sullivan, and two Gilbert and Sullivan companies in Boston have been offering rival productions. The army of Gilbertians and Sullivanites is possibly not the *levée en masse* that it once was; nevertheless, its ranks are still serried and its colors still draw recruits.

In one respect these devotees are unique. They know the words. Not only the words of the solo numbers, but the words of the choruses, the openings and finales. Play "tum-de-UM, tum, tum, tum, *tum*-ta-dum" to a Gilbert and Sullivan addict, and he unhesitatingly begins, "Careful-LEE on tip-toe *stee*-hee-ling . . ." and what is more, goes through to the end. Start him on "I am the very model of a modern Major-General," and when he reaches the line—"About binomial theorem I'm teeming with a lot o' news"—he even knows that traditionally he must pause and say, "Lot o' news . . . lot o' news . . . now what's a good rime for lot o' news? . . . Ah! I have it! . . ." before continuing, triumphantly, "With many cheerful facts about the square of the hypotenuse."

He knows much of the spoken dialogue as well. Say to him, "I am the last person to insult a British sailor, Sir Joseph," and the chances are that he will reply, "You are the last person who did, Captain Corcoran." He can tell *Nanki-Poo* from *Pooh-Bah,* and *Pooh-Bah* from *Ko-Ko;* and he knows that the gallant captain of the *Pinafore* was resuscitated, fifteen years after his first terrestrial appearance, as a character in the last but one of the Savoy operas.

But what definitely makes him unique is his complete familiarity with the words of the songs; not only the first and tag lines of the lyrics, but all of them. It is that fact, plus the inspired nonsense of the libretti, that has kept the works of Gilbert and Sullivan alive, not only in memory, but in the theatre.

In the long run, it is not the music of an opera that keeps it on the active list, but the words. This is not to say that an opera with a bad score and a good book will survive. But no matter how superlative the music, the life of a musical work written for the stage is determined by the viability of the libretto. Incidentally, this is true of any kind of opera—the so-called "grand" variety as well as the lighter brand. If the libretti of *Fidelio* and *Euryanthe* and *The Magic Flute* had been up to the music, both works would be in the active operatic repertoire today, instead of leading a hand-to-mouth existence through the medium of sporadic revivals (blessed by the critics and damned by the box-office) and performances of the *Euryanthe* and third *Leonore* overtures at symphony concerts.

Consider the operettas of Victor Herbert, who is responsible for some of the most enchanting light opera music ever written. Herbert is still available over the air, to be sure. No composer is heard more frequently *via* the radio; there is no questioning the tremendous popular appeal of his music. Yet, of the forty-odd musical comedies and operettas that he wrote (as against Sullivan's fourteen), only a handful are ever revived; and even when they are, they are good, at the most, for a few weeks' run. Generally they are failures.

Why? Because even now, only seven years after their composer's death, their libretti "date" unbearably, and the flat commonplace of their lyrics cannot stand a rehearing. Even when the lyrics are somewhat better than doggerel, they seldom have distinction of style or individuality of form; there is little about them to stick in the mind. Three of his most popular airs, for instance, are "Kiss Me Again," "A Kiss in the Dark" (I should like to hear Gilbert's comments on those titles!), and "The Mascot of the Troop." Granted that you know and like their music, try singing one of them through, without missing a word. What is the plot of *Babes in Toyland?* Of *Mlle. Modiste?* Of *The Fortune Teller?* Of *Naughty Marietta?* Can you name a half dozen characters, offhand, from any of Herbert's operas? Who wrote the libretto of *It Happened in Nordland?* Of *The Princess Pat?* Of *Eileen?* Of *The Madcap Duchess?*

You will be similarly vague, I think, concerning even the most popular medodies of other modern composers of operetta. How many of the words of the *Merry Widow* waltz can you remember? What are the words of "My

Hero," from *The Chocolate Soldier*? "Come, come, I love you only . . ." Yes, and what then?

It is fairly safe to say that if Sullivan survives today on the stage, he has Gilbert to thank. I would go even further, and say that if Gilbert had never met Sullivan, if he had written the best of the Savoy operas with another composer, they would still be performed. The words might not have been set with such felicity (Sullivan's prime distinction is the fact that he is the first—and almost the only—composer to catch the distinctive rhythms of English speech, and translate them into terms of music), but they would still be Gilbert's words.

Had Sullivan chosen another librettist, he would still be remembered; it is permissible to wonder whether he would still be performed. Sullivan has several peers in his own field—Offenbach, Auber, Von Suppe, Herbert, Johann Strauss. Gilbert had none, and has none. He has been approached, upon occasion, as a writer of humorous verse and song lyrics—by Charles Stuart Calverly, Franklin P. Adams, Brian Hooker, Wallace Irwin, and P. G. Wodehouse, among others. But no successor has possessed quite his peculiar combination of gifts. As a librettist, as a deviser of entertaining plots, able to unfold them with equal effectiveness and charm both in prose and verse, he stands alone. There is only one Gilbert.

[2]

If this were the millennium, if everyone were wise, and comfortable, and gay, there would be few wits and no satirists. For satire is fundamentally a pointing out of what is wrong with life. Some men grow angry over man's injustice to man; some shed tears over it; the satirist chooses to laugh, and his laughter is an attack. If William Schwenk Gilbert had been less sensitive; if his childhood had had more laughter in it; if his formative years had involved less of a struggle to adjust himself to an ill-fitting environment and to find some not too uncongenial means of earning a living, he might have lived to a comfortable, contented, and intellectually barren old age. He is rated as a Victorian, and so far as outward conformity to the conventions of that haircloth epoch is concerned, he was one; yet the bulk of his work is an outburst of rebellion—a sometimes amused, sometimes savage revolt against the rather self-satisfied, unquestioning, parochial, and wholly unsmiling respectability of the age in which he found himself, and in which he was, in his soul, unhappy.

His father is the best clue to his career. Gilbert Senior, after a harmless flirtation with a naval career and a somewhat platonic liaison with medicine, had inherited enough money to make him independent, and had forthwith settled down to a life that was a long and futile pursuit of literature. As a naval officer he had written a blank verse tragedy, and as soon as he achieved leisured solvency he took up writing in deadly—very deadly—earnest. He turned out a mass of plays, novels, biographies, monographs, and pamphlets, none of which, apparently, gave forth even a feeble glow, and not all of which even saw the light of print. In 1863 he did publish a novel, *Shirley Hall Asylum,* and late in life he saw his translation of *Lucia di Lammermoor* (Scott at third hand, from Cammarano's libretto that Donizetti had set!) produced briefly at the Princess Theatre in London. He was a heavy man, with the utterly humorless mind that is frequently known as "serious," and it is difficult, offhand, to think of him as the immediate ancestor of one of the first wits of his time. Yet such a paternity was logical enough. The step from the dull nonsense written by William the First to the brilliant nonsense written by William the Second is a short one, the difference between them being one of intent. The almost inevitable reaction against the father's solemnity and morbidity would be the son's pursuit of humor and make-believe.

He was born in London, at No. 17 Southampton Street, on November 8, 1836. The family took him abroad almost immediately after his birth, travelling through Germany and Italy. In Naples, at the age of two, he was spirited away from his nurse, kidnapped by Italian brigands, and held for ransom. No wonder Gilbert was fond of plots involving stolen babies, nefarious nurses, changelings, potions, elixirs, outlaws, and similar legendary bric-a-brac! Impossible people and events were not so impossible, after all. Had they not figured in his own life? (The ransom, in case you are curious, was paid: one hundred twenty-five pounds sterling.)

At seven, he was shipped off to a boys' school at Boulogne, where, among other things—as several of the *Bab Ballads* testify—he acquired a reliable working knowledge of the French tongue. Six years later he was back in England, in a private school at Great Ealing. While he was no phenomenon of learning, he did exhibit faint symptoms of his later rhythmic virtuosity by carrying off most of the prizes for metrical translations of the Latin and Greek classics. Here, too, began the great passion of his life—the theatre. He wrote and directed school plays, and even acted in them. His acting ambitions—which were never to be realized—impelled him to run away from school when he was fifteen, go up to London, and make a timid attempt to join the company of which the great Charles Kean was the head. He was promptly bundled back to Great Ealing.

At sixteen, in 1852, he matriculated at King's College, Cambridge, where he was not particularly happy, until the outbreak of the Crimean War, in 1854, attracted his eager attention. The following year he had left Cambridge and was in London, cramming for his examination for a commission in the Royal Artillery. The war, however, ended, and there was no examination.

Gilbert's interest in military affairs, although temporarily thwarted, continued undiminished for many years. He became a militia officer in 1859, was commissioned lieutenant in the Royal Aberdeenshire Militia in 1865, and became a captain in 1868. He retained the last post for ten years.

The sword, nevertheless, was never more than an avocation. His pen was mightier. Prophetically enough, his first chance to write for public performance came shortly after the abrupt termination of the war had dashed his martial hopes. A friend of the Gilbert family, Madame Parepa, a concert singer (she was afterwards Mme. Carl Rosa), needed an English translation of a French laughing song that she was to sing at one of the London Promenade concerts, and asked young Gilbert (he was just twenty-one) to write it for her. As opportunities go, it was not a very golden one, but he grasped it eagerly nevertheless. The first appearance of that translation on the printed program was a historic occasion, but like many such occasions, passed unnoticed at the moment—except by Gilbert, who, as he himself relates, used to attend the concerts regularly in order to watch the promenaders reading his translation.

No avalanche of offers resulting from this preliminary sortie into the field of belles-lettres, young Gilbert was confronted by the necessity that has annoyed so many poets—that of making a living. Accordingly, in 1860, he took and passed another examination, and became an assistant clerk in the Education Department of the Privy Council Office. Here he passed four bored and miserable years. Freedom—or, at any rate, a reprieve—came in the form of a small inheritance. During his clerkship he had studied law at King's College in his leisure moments, so that at the time his windfall arrived he was ready to be called to the Bar. He paid the call, enrolled as a pupil in the chambers of Judge Watkin Wilkins, set himself up in Clement's Inn—and began to write for the papers.

He never was much of a lawyer—as a practicing one, that is. He made a few appearances in court, and in his later years he liked to sit as a justice of the peace. Throughout his life he exhibited a readiness for litigation that could be characteristic only of one totally ignorant of the law or reasonably conversant with it—which he was. But even at twenty-eight, when he was called to the Bar, his preoccupation with the writing craft overshadowed his nominal profession and the amateur military career that was concurrent with it.

[3]

For a time his writings, although voluminous, attracted no attention whatsoever. He tried everything—reporting, dramatic criticism, editorials, weekly news letters to provincial papers, political polemics, essays—all the forms of quotidian literature that flow from the pen of any young person who vaguely "wants to write" (a sentence that, appropriately, has no object). The results were financially negligible. Nor did he have the meagre satisfaction of knowing that there were those who were watching him, believing in him. Nobody was watching a young journalistic hack who was no different from scores of his fellows except that he combined a gift for saying cutting things with a complete inability to refrain from saying them.

But the door opened at last, not widely, but sufficiently ajar for him to get his foot in the crack—which was all he wanted. Periodicals, in that Arcadian epoch, were not launched with the pomp and solemnity, administrative and financial, that attend their inception today. "Circulation manager" was a title yet to be invented, and the advertising department was an incidental expense. You assembled a basketful of manuscripts—mostly your own—found a printer and wood engraver who would wait for their money, and hopefully began publication. Three months was a long span of life for the average literary or humorous weekly of those days. But in 1861 one Henry J. Byron, having found not only a printer, but a backer for his literary and editorial aspirations, started a weekly which he called *Fun*. It was an unblushing paraphrase of *Punch*, but it survived and prospered.

Its existence did not long remain a secret from young Gilbert, to whom the advent of a new weekly was as the advent of a new poultry-yard to a hawk. As promptly as might be he swooped down with an article and an accompanying half-page picture. Both were accepted, and Byron delighted and terrified him by inviting him to be a regular contributor, supplying a column of reading matter and a half-page drawing every week. Thus, some time between 1861 and 1864, began an association that lasted for a decade, and that saw the creation of the ballads that are still the most widely read comic verse in the English language.

His early contributions to *Fun* were much the same sort of stuff that he had hitherto turned out, except that it was all published. He reviewed plays and art exhibitions, covered politics, and wrote burlesques and parodies, including a quantity of verse. Some of the pictures were initialed; at first, "W.G.," and later "W.S.G." The text was generally anonymous. In 1865 Tom Hood, whose *The Rhymester* is still in everyone's library of rhyming dictionaries, succeeded Byron as editor, retaining Gilbert as staff contributor, both as author and artist.

Under Hood's editorship Gilbert began to give increasing attention to the humorous verses that were beginning to be one of the paper's weekly features. He illustrated them himself, and at first the drawings received quite as much notice as the rhymes they adorned. The non-committal signatory initials gave way to a pseudonym, "Bab," which had been Gilbert's pet name as a child.

The pictures that are now associated with the *Bab Ballads* are not those that accompanied them in the columns of *Fun*. The first were drawn directly on wood blocks, ready for the engraver, and because of the exigencies of time and woodcut technique were highly simplified, with a minimum of line and bold blacks and whites. Also, they had a fantastic quality, an element of outrageousness, that is not so conspicuous in the later drawings. For the ballads Gilbert invented a new race of people, creatures who were not so much caricatures of existing humans as a strange, autochthonous goblin species that was like nothing on land or sea. A few of them still survive (the illustrations for *John and Freddy* and *Sir Macklin* are good examples). As a rule, though, they were plucked by the hand that grew them. In 1898, when the collected edition of Gilbert's ballads and song-poems was published, his introduction announced, incredibly: "I have always felt that many of the original illustrations to *The Bab Ballads* erred gravely in the direction of unnecessary extravagance. This defect I have endeavored to correct through the medium of the two hundred new drawings which I have designed for this volume. I am afraid I cannot claim for them any other recommendation."

He was too modest, and too rash. The new drawings are charming, but they bear about the same relation to the originals that all the gallant endeavors of countless illustrators to enhance *Alice in Wonderland* have borne to Tenniel's old drawings. They simply are not the same thing.

But they are good. Gilbert, I think, is underrated as a draughtsman, his drawings usually being dismissed as amusing amateur efforts, with no more claim to technical merit than Lear's absurdities in *A Book of Nonsense*. On the contrary, he deserves to be ranked, if not with Du Maurier and Howard Pyle, certainly with Thackeray and Oliver Herford. For Gilbert could draw—"draw" in the technician's sense of the word. Examine the hands and feet of these little figures—always the downfall of the amateur draughtsman. They are beautifully done, anatomically correct, and never shirked. His line is clean, his foreshortening is excellent, and his proportions, however grotesque, are always convincing. Moreover, his people have faces that can be recognized from one drawing to another, and those faces mirror any kind or degree of emotion that the artist wills. He indicates colors and textures with great economy of means, and his action is always deft and vigorous. Although by no means a great illustrator, he is decidedly a professional.

The poems, however, soon overshadowed the illustrations. Long before they were titled *Bab Ballads* in print (*The Two Ogres,* in the issue of January 23, 1869, is the first official Bab Ballad), they had been so dubbed by a growing army of delighted readers. If Gilbert began his collaboration with the famous and popular Sullivan on equal terms, he had the *Bab Ballads* to thank. They hardly made him rich (his weekly pay check from *Fun* averaged about $25), but they made him known.

[4]

THE ballads are important, not only for their own entertaining sakes, but as a source-book of the Gilbert and Sullivan operettas. In one of his letters to Mathilde Wesendonk, Wagner wrote: "It is quite clear to me that I shall never create anything new again. That one highest peak of productiveness left me with such an abundance of fertile germs that I have now but to reach back and take one from my store, the cultivation being then an easy matter." This was not literally true of Wagner, and it is not literally true of Gilbert. He created new themes and characters long after his days on the staff of *Fun*. But it is quite true that in the *Bab Ballads* Gilbert reached a peak of inventiveness that he never again approached.

It is hardly a secret that he drew freely upon the ballads in writing the libretti of the Savoy operas. In Isaac Goldberg's admirable *The Story of Gilbert and Sullivan,* for instance, there is an exhaustive analysis of Gilbert's debt to that talented and resourceful alter ego, Bab. Yet it is hard to realize the full extent of that indebtedness, so multitudinous and intricate are his borrowings from himself. Confronted by the need of a plot, a situation, or a character, nine times out of ten he reaches back and takes one from his store of "fertile germs" in the back numbers of *Fun*. The motivating incident of *Iolanthe,* to cite one example, was related, years before the opera was dreamed of, in the ballad of *The Fairy Curate*. Or consider *H. M. S. Pinafore,* a notable instance of the way in which he would synthesize a whole new plot out of old material. *Captain Corcoran,* his right good crew, and his ship itself, are nothing but a reincarnation of *Captain Reece* and his frigate, *The Mantelpiece,* out of one of the early ballads.

> The sisters, cousins, aunts, and niece
> And widowed ma of Captain Reece

become, of course, the justly celebrated female relatives of *Sir Joseph Porter*. The changeling relationship of the *Captain* and *Ralph Rackstraw,* including the instant and unquestioning acceptance, by both, of their altered stations the moment the truth is revealed (without corroboration), is all set forth in the ballad, *General John*. The "great big D—" that the Captain hardly ever uses can be traced, direct, to—

> They growl with a big, big D——

from *The Bumboat Woman's Story,* while the bumboat woman, herself, becomes *Little Buttercup*. These are by no means all of the borrowings that can be found in *Pinafore*. For the really fanatical Savoyard I can recommend no more engrossing occupation for a long winter's evening (several of them, in fact) than tracking plots, incidents, and characters in the Savoy operas back to their *Bab Ballads* originals.

It is not, however, for such a purpose that thousands still purchase, read, and memorize the *Bab Ballads*. As to why they do, the shortest, and perhaps the best explanation is, "read them and see." They are, to begin with, nonsense rhymes; and nonsense rhymes have always been the weakness of the Anglo-Saxon. Offer him literary or dramatic entertainment whose chief excuse for being is its complete silliness, and he seizes it with a whole-souled delight that is likely to attract the perplexed stares of his Latin or Teutonic brothers. Particularly does he enjoy logical nonsense. Give him a completely ridiculous major premise, and develop it for him with perfect gravity and strict logic, and you make him very happy. In this particular species of insane reasonableness the *Bab Ballads* are surpassed only by the two *Alice* books.

Further, the ballads are good social satire. The smug inflexibility of established religion, the pomposities of small people in great estate, the pretensions of the well-born fool—these are a few of the balloons that he pricks. Even when the subject of his discourse is no longer of immediate interest we are diverted by the discourse itself. His, like all good satirical writing, defines and illuminates the thing it attacks; so that we do not need to believe in the Minotaur in order to enjoy watching Jason abolishing him.

A ballad is supposed to be a narrative in rhyme, and the *Bab Ballads* are generally faithful to the definition. There is hardly one that does not develop a microscopic plot, and some of them are extraordinarily good yarns that would be equally entertaining if told in prose. Indeed, some of them *were* eventually told in prose, as the Savoy operas testify.

Occasionally, in the ballads, he is serious, either in attack or defense, and results are almost invariably unfortunate. Gilbert always affected to regard the *Bab Ballads* as inconsequential trifles, and was even heard to refer to his operettas as "twaddle." While he was doubtless a good deal less indifferent to his humorous writings than he pretended to be, it is true that he took himself very solemnly as a serious thinker and dramatist, and resented the fact that neither his serious plays nor his serious thoughts were as much esteemed as his nonsense. Some of the serious ballads make it all too clear why his readers preferred being amused to being edified. *Only a Dancing Girl,* for instance, is almost unbelievable: Gilbert, of all people, heavily assuring us that theatrical cuties are good girls at heart, and kind to their parents! *The Haughty Actor* sounds more like the aftermath of a row at rehearsal than Gilbert poking genial fun at humanity's weaknesses. *Disillusioned* has been done a thousand times, and never more dully than Gilbert does it. *Old Paul and Young Tim,* both in subject-matter and temper, might express the sentiments of any bellicose stay-at-home in 1917; unfortunately it is not the sentiments that are the object of Gilbert's jibes.

One needs little space or time in which to mention these dull spots. To cite the brilliant ones would involve quoting most of the ballads in full. As a whole, they stand unmatched in their *genre* for fertility of invention, felicity of expression, and perfection of craftsmanship. The average writer of light verse does not get far beyond the comic *manner* of writing. Like a stage comedian working with poor material, he relies upon a humorous delivery to conceal the fact that what he has to say is not particularly funny. Gilbert's manner and matter are almost always commensurate. The ideas that his lines express are as amusing as the lines themselves. It is seldom that an ingenious mechanical twist of his does not serve as the vehicle of an equally ingenious turn of thought.

One needs to have written light verse—or tried to write it—in order fully to appreciate Gilbert's inimitable technical facility. Here is a brief sample, from *The Fairy Curate:*

He, resuming
Fairy pluming
(That's not English, is it?)
Oft would fly up,
To the sky up,
Pay Mamma a visit.

Simple enough, in its effortless flow—but how did he do it? He probably wrote the last line first; it is the point of the stanza. But then, with "is it" as about the only available rhyme for "visit," how did he manage to work it into a line that would not only excuse the clumsy participial rhyme of the first couplet (which he must have invented *after* conceiving the last line), but would be the most entertaining feature of the entire stanza?

Parenthetical clauses, like the one above, are among Gilbert's happiest conceits. He uses them freely, throwing one in as an added comic touch, a sort of literary *lagniappe* to reward the reader for his attention. The effect, that of the author's suddenly coming forward with a helpful comment of his own, is irresistible. The stage is set, the comedy has begun, when suddenly Gilbert's anxious face appears in the wings, casts an apprehensive glance at the audience, and is gone. One of my favorites among the ballads is *Emily, John, James, and I,* in which the author stolidly insists on tagging parenthetically along in the wake of three characters who are wholly unconscious of his presence:

> A very good girl was Emily Jane,
> Jimmy was good and true,
> And John was a very good man in the main

—whereupon, unasked, the author informs an indifferent public—

> (And I am a good man, too).

A little later, he is stuck for a rhyme:

> He noticed his Emily Jane with Jim,
> And envied the well-made elf;
> And people remarked that he muttered "Oh, dim!"

—and remarks, hastily—

> (I often say "dim!" myself).

It is such a pathetic lie; you pretend, at least, to believe it.

He can take a hackneyed joke and make it sound fresh. Even in his time there could not have been much novelty in the idea of using elaborate circumlocution in referring to indelicate objects. Yet, in *The Perils of Invisibility,* observe his diverting struggles to avoid saying "breeches":

Old Peter woke next day and dressed,
Put on his coat and shoes and vest,
His shirt and stock—but could not find
His only pair of—never mind!

. . .

"Now give them up, I beg of you—
You know what I'm referring to!"

. . .

But no; the cross old lady swore
She'd keep his—what I said before—

. . .

And Peter left his humble cot
To find a pair of—you know what.

And if there be any who think it is easy to combine such perfectly natural and logical phrases with equally simple and inevitable rhymes, let him try it.

There are other felicities. An analysis of humor is a solemn and disillusioning business, at best; it resolves itself, in the end, into saying, "I think this is funny—and this"; and if you disagree, there is no logic that will convert you. Myself, I take huge delight in Gilbert's feminine rhymes, usually as correct as they are unexpected—

"A fool is bent upon a twig, but wise men dread a bandit."
Which I think must have been clever, for I didn't understand it.

—his stock of proper nouns, as queer and appropriate as those of Dickens—

King Borria Bungalee Boo
Was a man-eating African swell;

. . .

Dalilah de Dardy adored
The very correctest of cards,
Lorenzo de Lardy, a lord—
He was one of Her Majesty's Guards.

. . .

Macphairson Clonglocketty Angus M'Clan
Was the son of an elderly labouring man.

. . .

Calamity Pop Von Peppermint Drop,
The King of Canoodle-Dum.

—and certain isolated lines, for no reason except their silliness—

"The French for 'Pooh!'" our Tommy cried,
"L'anglais pour 'Va!'" the Frenchman crowed.

—particularly the superb opening of *Gentle Alice Brown,* in which the scene is set, the characters introduced, and the author's intentions set forth, all in one deathless quatrain:

It was a robber's daughter, and her name was Alice Brown,
Her father was the terror of a small Italian town;
Her mother was a foolish, weak, but amiable old thing;
But it isn't of her parents that I'm going for to sing.

One feature of the ballads is significant. From the very earliest on, most of them are peculiarly *musical,* in rhyme, rhythm, and structure. They can be set to music, some of them, in fact, having been written, Kipling-wise, to existing popular tunes. Gilbert always claimed to have no ear for music. For "ear" substitute "appreciation," and the sentence is more exact. He always had the lyrist's ear, writing naturally in singable rhythms (he was always careful to give corresponding lines in two stanzas exactly the same number and kind of feet, a *sine qua non* when different verses are to go to the same tune), arranging his lines generally in the four- and eight-bar groups that are the easiest to set, and writing as much to be heard as to be read.

The *Bab Ballads,* therefore, aside from their intrinsic value, were an unconscious training for the vast number of song-poems that he was to write in the course of his career as librettist. The Savoy operas are two-thirds singing, and Gilbert was perfecting his technique of making them effective to sing.

[5]

Meanwhile he was busily acquiring a store of theatrical experience that was to be the background of the prose department of his future career. Curiously enough, the composer Donizetti, who was indirectly responsible, through one of his operas, for Gilbert Senior's solitary stage production, was in like wise involved in getting Gilbert Junior his first start in the theatre. Donizetti and T. W. Robinson, that is. The latter, an author of light comedies and burlesques, and one of the contributors to

Fun, was a crony of Gilbert's. They used to go to first nights together, and Robinson had upon occasion brought Gilbert with him to rehearsals of his plays. In 1866 the lessee of St. James's Theatre, a Miss Herbert, asked Robinson to write her something special for the Christmas holidays. He was too busy, and recommended Gilbert, who jumped at the chance.

Accordingly the Christmas season of 1866 saw Gilbert's debutant offering in the theatre—*Dr. Dulcamara; or, The Little Duck and the Great Quack,* a burlesque of Donizetti's *L'Elisir d'amore.* As such things went, it was a decided success, and Gilbert got thirty pounds for it. After what he had been thankfully receiving for the *Bab Ballads* this must have seemed high pay for ten days' work (and Miss Herbert's manager had told him never again to sell so good a piece for so little). While it would be hardly accurate to say that his subsequent theatrical activities were strictly commercial in motive, it is safe to assume that pure love of art was not the sole inspiration of his next works.

These were a series of burlesques and parodies of Italian and French grand opera, in the style of the initial *Dulcamara.* Some idea of how wraith-like their subtlety must have been can be gleaned from the title of his parody of *The Bohemian Girl,* as reported in Goldberg's book: *The Merry Zingara; or, The Pipsy-Wipsy and the Tipsy Gypsy.* In 1868 he was commissioned by John Hollingshead to write a piece for the opening of his new Gaiety Theatre, and obliged with a travesty of Meyerbeer's *Robert the Devil.* Another producer for whom he did considerable work was Thomas German Reed, who conducted what was discreetly called a "Gallery of Illustration" (it was a sort of polite burlesque show) in St. Martin's Hall.

Reed needed a rather more genteel form of entertainment than the rowdy goings-on that Hollingshead provided. Gilbert, in consequence, began to write sketches and fantasies of his own, in place of parodies of other men's work.

It was during the rehearsals of a piece of his called *Ages Ago,* with music by Frederic Clay (surely you remember his *I'll Sing Thee Songs of Araby!*), that Gilbert was introduced to a young composer named Arthur Sullivan, who had asked to meet him. The latter was already famous for his talent and versatility. His incidental music for *The Tempest,* performed when he was only nineteen, had attracted wide attention. In 1866, the year that Gilbert was writing *Dulcamara,* Sullivan's *In Memoriam* overture had been performed successfully at the Norwich Festival, and he had come to be looked upon as a sort of unofficial composer-laureate of England, without whose music no festival or official celebration was complete.

He had just scored a resounding theatrical success as well, with *Cox and Box,* a musical farce that he had written with F. C. Burnand as an amateur entertainment, and which had gone over so well that German Reed had eventually taken it over for the Gallery, where it had run for 300 nights. Sullivan and Burnand had written another that same year, *The Contrabandista,* which had been reasonably successful. Both Gilbert and Sullivan, then, were already provided with collaborators with whom they were well satisfied, and the first meeting between them was a purely social one. They were introduced, presumably passed the time of day, and went their respective ways.

Gilbert's way took him in the direction of a piece for German Reed, *Our Island Home,* in 1870, for which Reed himself provided the music. This opus, not very momentous in itself, is noteworthy for containing a pirate chieftain, whose parents had told his nurse to apprentice him to a pilot. If you know your *Pirates of Penzance* you will not have to be told that she misunderstood, and apprenticed him to a pirate. Also, the chieftain had a song, one stanza of which was to be the basis of a famous ditty from *H. M. S. Pinafore*. It goes:

I'm a hardy sailor, too;
I've a vessel and a crew.
When it doesn't blow a gale
I can reef a little sail.
I never go below
And I generally know
The weather from the "lee",
And I'm never sick at sea.

He likewise wrote two plays in verse, one a "respectful perversion" of Tennyson's *The Princess,* and the other *The Palace of Truth;* a melodrama or so, and *Pygmalion and Galatea.* Sullivan returned to his serious Muse, appropriately enough, with an oratorio, *The Prodigal Son,* for the Worcester Festival.

But their paths were converging. In 1871 Hollingshead went to Sullivan with a libretto of Gilbert's and asked him to write the music for it; and Sullivan accepted. *Thespis; or, The Gods Grown Old,* the first fruit of what was to prove a famous collaboration, was produced around Christmas time as an after-piece to a comedy by the same H. J. Byron who had accepted Gilbert's first contribution to *Fun.* It was not, apparently, a very ripe fruit, for it did not agree with the public. The idea—that of a company of stranded actors changing places with the gods of Olympus—was promising, but the piece lasted barely a month. The score, even though the popular Sullivan had written it, was not published, and the sole relic of it that survives (outside of probable borrowings in later scores) is the song, *Little Maid of Arcadee.* Hollingshead had no further commissions to offer, and the pair separated.

Thespis did, however, contain two Gilbertian ingredients that were to add much to the flavor of the later operettas. One was the autobiographical patter-song, in which a character, as though under Mime's spell, tells the truth about himself; the other was the Gilbert chorus. As Sullivan told his biographer:

"Until Gilbert took the matter in hand choruses were dummy concerns, and were practically nothing more than a part of the stage setting. It was in *Thespis* that Gilbert began to carry out his expressed determination to get the chorus to play its proper part in the performance. At this moment it seems difficult to realize that the idea of the chorus being anything more than a sort of stage audience was, at that time, a tremendous novelty. In consequence of this innovation, some of the incidents at the rehearsals of *Thespis* were rather amusing. I remember that, on one occasion, one of the principals became quite indignant and said, 'really, Mr. Gilbert, why should I stand here? I am not a chorus girl!' to which Gilbert replied curtly, 'No, madam, your voice is not strong enough, or no doubt you would be.'" A captivating fellow, this Gilbert!

[6]

For the next three years each was busy with his own affairs. Sullivan travelled on the Continent, wrote a Festival *Te Deum* to celebrate the recovery of the Prince of Wales from an attack of typhoid fever, and became conductor of the "Classical Nights" at the Covent Garden Promenade Concerts. He was appointed editor of *The Hymnal,* for which he wrote several hymns, including the perennial *Onward, Christian Soldiers.* In 1873 he wrote his oratorio, *The Light of the World,* for the Birmingham Festival. It was as successful as it was long, and was later (1876) to win him an honorary degree of Doctor of Music from Gilbert's ex-Alma Mater, Cambridge.

Gilbert himself was consolidating his position in the theatre. His play, *The Wicked World,* having been attacked as immoral, he countered with a burlesque of it, *The Happy Land,* and promptly got into trouble with the Lord Chamberlain on account of the too-realistic make-up of the actors who were impersonating three well known British statesmen (one of them was Gladstone). The make-up was altered, and the play, partly as a result of the censor's free advertising, ran for 200 nights. The year 1874 saw four more plays from his pen, including the still-performed *Sweethearts.* He was now a full-fledged man of the theatre, wholly dependent upon it for his support. Tom Hood had died, and Gilbert, characteristically, had lost little time in having a row with the new editor of *Fun,* and severing his connection with the paper in 1874.

Some years before, in April, 1868, he had published in *Fun* a miniature operetta, *Trial by Jury.* It filled just a page, with illustrations (by Bab), the entire text, including title and stage directions, being only 94 lines long. Taking a friend's advice, he had elaborated it, and had submitted the new version to Carl Rosa, husband of his old friend, Madame Parepa. Rosa, delighted with it, decided to produce it for his wife, and to write the music himself. Unhappily, Mme. Parepa-Rosa died shortly afterward, and the manuscript was returned.

Meanwhile the third character in the Gilbert and Sullivan drama appeared on the scene. Richard D'Oyly Carte was the son of a London musical instrument maker, and had begun his career as a composer of light opera, two of his pieces already having been produced, in '68 and '71 respectively. In 1875 he was acting manager of the Royalty Theatre, where Offenbach's *La Périchole* was running. Needing a curtain-raiser, he asked Gilbert to provide one, and suggested Sullivan as the composer. Gilbert outlined his revamped *Trial by Jury,* which Carte immediately accepted, and which Sullivan as promptly set to music. The latter is quoted as having said, later, that "the words and music were written, and the rehearsals completed, within the space of three weeks." So far as the words were concerned, this was inaccurate, as we know; but Sullivan and Carte undoubtedly did their share in record-breaking time.

The new work had its first performance on March 25, 1875 (as an after-piece, not a curtain-raiser), and was an instantaneous success, running for the balance of the year. Here was something new, and something wholly English. *Thespis* had been pure extravaganza; it might conceivably have been written by two clever Frenchmen. But *Trial by Jury* was satire—an English institution laughed at by Englishmen, in the same terms that had made the *Bab Ballads* irresistible. Even the music was satirical, with its Handelian choruses and burlesque Italian grand opera finale. Soon everybody was quoting the lines and humming the tunes. By the time the piece had finished its run, "Gilbert and Sullivan" was well on the way to being, not two names, but a trade-mark.

The partnership was still far from being considered a permanent and exclusive one, by either member of the firm. Gilbert promptly wrote an operetta with Frederic Clay, *Princess Toto,* which was produced in October, 1876. He further signalized the year by becoming involved in a plagiarism suit with one William Muskerry, who claimed that the farce, *Engaged,* had been stolen from a play of his (Gilbert was completely exonerated), and by staging a public controversy with Miss Henrietta Hodson, an actress with whom he had had several differences of opinion and who claimed that he had blacklisted her. The row came to no definite, legal conclusion, but the press was inclined to side with Miss Hodson.

Sullivan, after taking his degree at Cambridge, accepted the position of head of the new National Training School (later The Royal College) of Music. He took the post with many misgivings—he hated teaching—was never happy in the position, and resigned five years later. Early in '77 his brother Fred, who had created the rôle of the Judge in *Trial by Jury,* was taken suddenly ill, and died. It was by his deathbed that Sullivan wrote *The Lost Chord.*

It is not only possible, but highly probable, that the association between Gilbert and Sullivan would never have gone beyond the casual and occasional stage if the initiative had been left solely to them. Their major ambitions were widely divergent. Sullivan was bent on a career as composer of serious choral and orchestral works, while Gilbert, to whom music for its own sake meant little, wanted most to be recognized as a dramatist. Nor did their social orbits by any means overlap. Sullivan was easy-going, popular, and gregarious; Gilbert truculent, caustic, and inclined to misanthropy. Although they were to be intimately associated, professionally, for more than two decades, there is no evidence that the two men were ever close friends.

The initiative, however, was not left to them. D'Oyly Carte, enthusiastic over the success of *Trial by Jury,* conceived the idea of founding a permanent light opera company for the performance of original native works. At the time, French operetta (frequently in pirated form, incidentally) held the field in England as completely as Viennese operetta was to hold it in America in the days following *The Merry Widow.* Carte's dream was an all-English company, producing all-English works. It was not, as has been assumed, originally planned solely as an outlet for the activities of Gilbert and Sullivan. He planned to enlist the talents of several other librettists and composers, among them James Albey, F. C. Burnand, Alfred Cellier, and Frederic Clay. The authors of *Trial by Jury* were, however, his trump card, and it was from them that he obtained the promise of a new opera, and it was their names that figured most prominently in his interviews with prospective backers.

He obtained his capital, and leased the Opéra Comique —by no means the best theatre in London, nor the most favorably located, but the best he could get at the time. Then he faced the difficult task of assembling a company that could do justice to the new Gilbert and Sullivan opus. Present-day producers who lament the fact that it is so hard to find people who can both act and sing Gilbert and Sullivan seem to think that their troubles are something special and unique. They are not. They were D'Oyly Carte's troubles, too.

A few years ago, when Winthrop Ames was recruiting the company for his Gilbert and Sullivan revivals, he was compelled to take some of his cast from the concert halls, some from grand opera, some from the spoken stage, and virtually none at all from musical comedy. D'Oyly Carte's solution of the problem had been identical. His leading female "heavy," Mrs. Howard Paul, was an entertainer rather than an actress. His baritone "heavy" was Richard Temple, one of the few recruits from light opera. Rutland Barrington had been playing in melodrama. His principal comedian was George Grossmith, Jr., who had been doing pianologues and other forms of club entertaining before Y. M. C. A. gatherings or their equivalents. Carte's choice of these three men in particular proved to be a momentous one; for they were to be with him for many years, and it was for their voices that much of Sullivan's music was to be written, and for their styles and personalities that many of Gilbert's lines and situations were to be created. They were the framework about which the series was built, and without them it might have been a different series.

His company collected and rehearsed, D'Oyly Carte's Comedy Opera Company made its bow on November 17,

1877, in *The Sorcerer,* "an Entirely Original Modern Comic Opera, written by W. S. Gilbert, composed by Arthur Sullivan." Mrs. Paul played the rôle of *Lady Sangazure,* with Alice May as *Aline,* her daughter; Miss Everard was *Mrs. Partlett;* her daughter, *Constance,* being played by Giulia Warwick. The men included Richard Temple as *Sir Marmaduke Pointdextre,* George Bentham as *Alexis,* Rutland Barrington as *Dr. Daly,* and George Grossmith, Jr., as *John Wellington Wells.* The members of the chorus were mostly vocal students, and Alfred Cellier conducted.

The reception of the new piece was friendly. Although *The Sorcerer* had nothing like the success that some of the later works were to achieve, it ran for 175 performances. A few of the critics undertook to lecture Sullivan, the Cambridge Doctor of Music and composer of hymns and oratorios, for stooping to write comic opera tunes; and there were those who found in Gilbert's handling of *Dr. Daly,* the Vicar, more than a touch of irreverence, not to say sacrilege. This latter charge, with variations, was to become a familiar one. Most of Gilbert's jabs, however gentle—for him—were sure to be followed by anguished howls from some afflicted quarter. As for Sullivan, his serious-minded friends never ceased hounding him to quit this operetta piffle and do Big Things—with the unfortunate *Ivanhoe* as the ultimate result.

[7]

The Sorcerer closed on May 22, 1878. Five days later the Comedy Opera Company offered a new piece by Gilbert and Sullivan: *H.M.S. Pinafore; or, The Lass that Loved a Sailor,* "An Entirely Original Nautical Comic Opera in Two Acts." D'Oyly Carte never made any formal announcement of the change in his original policy; but from the time *The Sorcerer* opened there was no talk of producing operettas by other authors. He was the producer of Gilbert and Sullivan, and they were his authors; that was his platform for the ensuing two decades.

Of the men in the cast, the original triumvirate remained, with Grossmith as *Sir Joseph Porter,* Barrington as *Captain Corcoran,* and Temple as *Dick Deadeye.* There was a new leading tenor, George Power, singing *Ralph Rackstraw.* Miss Everard, as *Little Buttercup,* was the only surviving female member of the *Sorcerer* Company. Emma Howson (an inadvertently American member of this "all-English" company) created the rôle of *Josephine,* while Jessie Bond, destined to be the company's perennial ingénue lead, made her debut in the small part of *Hebe.*

Pinafore began by bringing the D'Oyly Carte Company to the verge of extinction, and left it a solidly established national institution. The opening night aroused considerable enthusiasm, but business was poor from the start, and grew steadily worse. Carte had been having trouble with his backers, and there was talk of closing the piece and abandoning the whole project. Not until the company offered to take a heavy cut in salary did the management decide to struggle on a bit longer. It was Sullivan who saved the situation. He was conducting the Covent Garden "Proms," and included a potpourri from *Pinafore* on his programs. It was an immediate hit, and the public began to flock to the Opéra Comique to see the show that had such a delightful score. Business picked up like magic, and the idea of closing was soon forgotten. Doctor Goldberg, in his book on Gilbert and Sullivan, contends that it was the success of *Pinafore* in America that attracted the attention of the British public to the piece; but the evidence hardly justifies the theory. News of the success of a British work in America would, I imagine, have been received by the average Englishman of the time very much as news of the success of an American work among the Head-hunters of Borneo would be received by an average American today: Interesting, but what of it? In the second place, Sullivan began conducting his *Pinafore* excerpts some time in August, 1878, while America did not see the work until November of that year. It seems probable that *Pinafore* would not have lasted the six months between May and November unless business had improved considerably.

Prosperity did not put an end to the exciting times ahead for all concerned. Carte's backers had insisted on closing the theatre for alterations from Christmas until February, and had nearly wrecked the run of the opera in consequence. On November 25, 1878, R. M. Field produced it at the Boston Museum, and in January, 1880, James C. Duff opened it at the Standard Theatre in New York. Both were pirated productions. They were wildly successful, and *Pinafore* became epidemic in America. The loss of a vast potential revenue was not to be borne with equanimity by Carte or his authors. Accordingly, early in July he sailed for the United States to see what could be done about protecting his rights.

During his absence the lease on the Opéra Comique expired, and the backers decided that he was not to renew it. On the night of July 31 they invaded the theatre with vans and movers, and attempted to carry off the scenery. Defeated in this attempt, and beaten in the courts, they excommunicated Carte and opened a *Pinafore* production of their own in the Olympic, almost next door to the Opéra Comique. The bootleg *Pinafore,* however, was not to the public's liking. After fruitless cruising from one theatre to another it finally went down with all on board, including the backers. From that time on, D'Oyly Carte played a lone hand.

When he returned from the campaign against the American pirates he held a council of war. The situation offered no legal redress, but an authorized *Pinafore* production in America, supervised by the authors, promised tempting returns. Accordingly, Gilbert and Sullivan sailed, taking with them the conductor, Alfred Cellier, and a few picked members of the English company, including Jessie Bond. They arrived in New York on November 5, 1879, and opened at the Fifth Avenue Theatre, to an enthusiastic house, on the first of December.

I believe that the *Pinafore* production was never more than a very good pretext for Gilbert and Sullivan's coming to America. They kept the piece running a day less than a month, despite good business, and from all the evidence never intended to keep it on any longer. It made, however, an excellent blind, to keep their real purpose a secret until the last possible moment.

What brought them here was their decision to protect their performing rights in the only way they could: by producing their next operetta in America first. The copyright situation was this: If a foreign author wrote a stage work and had it published, either abroad or in America, he lost all exclusive production rights; anyone who could obtain a printed copy was free to produce the work without paying any royalty. If, however, he kept the work in manuscript, it remained his personal property, and whoever stole or borrowed it could be prosecuted, under the common law, for theft. Gilbert and Sullivan had therefore decided to produce in New York, and not to publish the book or score of their new operetta until they had skimmed the cream of the American market.

(Parenthetically, as regards recorded music, we are no more scrupulous today. A composer can retain his recording rights by refusing to allow his music to be recorded at all; but if he grants permission to have it recorded by one phonograph company, every other phonograph company is automatically thereby free to record it also, without his permission. The pirate has only to pay him a statutory royalty, amounting to about three-quarters of one per cent of the price of the average record.)

On December 31, 1879, Gilbert and Sullivan opened at the Fifth Avenue Theatre with *The Pirates of Penzance*. The night before, in Paignton, England, it had been given a scratch performance, without special costumes or scenery, by a travelling *Pinafore* company, in order to secure the authors' rights at home. *The Pirates* is the one Gilbert-and-Sullivan operetta to which America can lay—partially at least—a proprietary claim. It is probable that Gilbert had finished most of the libretto before he sailed, his interviews to the contrary, in New York, notwithstanding; but Sullivan had composed only the music for the second act. He wrote the first act, and scored the entire opera, after his arrival.

Incidentally, he must have been a lightning-fast worker in an emergency. Since *The Pirates* opened in England on December 30th, the vocal score must have been ready not later than the first week of the month, to allow time for it to cross the Atlantic. The orchestration must have been finished by Christmas, to enable the orchestra to rehearse it for an opening six days later. Assuming that Sullivan set to work the day after his arrival—that is, November 6th—he must have composed the first act in a month, and scored the whole piece in a little less than a month; all this, while he was seeing *Pinafore* through the mill!

The New York production did not solve the publication problem, for under the American law anyone was entitled to publish whatever he could *remember* of someone's else's music, provided he said so. Accordingly, publishers hired expert arrangers to attend performances and take down the melodies as they were sung and played. The results were published as *Recollections of The Pirates of Penzance,* and were declared perfectly legal. So far as pirated productions were concerned, however, Gilbert and Sullivan had managed to protect themselves, at least for the time being. They saw the New York production off to a prosperous start, sent several companies out on the road, and returned to England in March, 1880.

Shortly after their arrival, *Pinafore* ended its phenomenal London run of more than 675 nights, and on April 3, 1880, *The Pirates of Penzance, or The Slave of Duty,* replaced it at the Opéra Comique. Grossmith, Temple, and Barrington were again in the cast, as *Major-General Stanley, The Pirate King,* and the *Sergeant of Police,* respectively. Miss Everard had gone (until Rosina Brandram's promotion to the post, there was great mortality among the female "heavies"), and in her place Emily Cross opened in the rôle of *Ruth.* (Alice Barnett, of the New York company, later replaced *her*). Julia Gwynne opened in the part of *Edith,* but was later transferred to *Kate,* in order to make room for Jessie Bond, upon her return from the States.

[8]

The Pirates of Penzance ran about a year. When it closed, Gilbert and Sullivan were ready with its successor, which opened on April 23, 1881. It was *Patience; or, Bunthorne's Bride,* "An Entirely New and Original Aesthetic Opera." Curiously enough, the libretto began life as a dramatization of Bab's ballad, *The Rival Curates;* but recollections of what had been said about his treatment of *Dr. Daly* seem to have given Gilbert pause. Besides, there was equally fair game close at hand. The aesthetic movement was beginning to creep over England, with Oscar Wilde trying to live up to his blue china, and being lampooned and caricatured—and liking it. Accordingly, Gilbert changed his two curates into two poets, and let it go at that. The cast at the opening was largely a familiar one. Grossmith, made up to look like Wilde, was *Bunthorne,* with Barrington, not in the least resembling Swinburne, as *Grosvenor.* Richard Temple was *Colonel Calverly,* Jessie Bond was *Lady Agatha,* and Julia Gwynne was *Lady Saphir.* Leonora Braham, a newcomer, was *Patience.*

It was during the run of *Patience* that D'Oyly Carte built and opened the Savoy Theatre, erected out of the profits of previous Gilbert and Sullivan successes, and designed to house their future ones. It was the last word in theatre planning in its day, and was the first theatre in London to be lighted throughout by electricity. (Carte inserted a reassuring note in the prospectus, pointing out the fact that the house was also piped with gas, in case the new lighting system should break down. So far as we know, it never did.) The Savoy was ready in October, and on the tenth of that month *Patience* moved into its new home at a gala performance conducted by Sullivan himself. All in all, the opera ran for 408 performances. The seating capacity of the theatre, by the way, was about 1300 persons, with an average possible revenue amounting to about as many dollars. This was twice as much as Carte's productions needed to keep them going. Those were happy days! A very modest musical production today must play to nearly twice thirteen hundred dollars a night in order to break even.

[9]

I WONDER what it must have felt like to be, not an old Savoyard, but a new one; to be going into the stalls of the Savoy, for instance, on the evening of November 25,

1882. Here were two authors who had thus far collaborated on six operettas, of which only one had been a failure, while another had scored one of the historic successes of the English theatre. They had a manager who produced no stage works but theirs, had organized a permanent company for them, and had just built a new theatre to be devoted exclusively to their output. There must have been more than a few well-wishers in the audience that evening who were just a bit apprehensive. What would the new piece be like? Could Gilbert and Sullivan keep it up? Wasn't this unbroken series of successes almost too good to be true? Was it not time, merely by the law of averages, for Gilbert and Sullivan to have a failure?

It was not. Fate must have thought that one of the partners had had trouble enough, without having to undergo any added distress of mind and spirit. In May, Sullivan's mother, whom he adored, had died, and it was with a grief-stricken heart that he had started work on one of the gayest of his scores. Furthermore, according to his friend Arthur Lawrence, on the very day of the opening of the new opera, the banking house of Cooper, Hall & Company, to whom his lifetime's savings had been entrusted, went bankrupt; and as he entered the orchestra pit of the Savoy that evening, to conduct the opening performance he had, beyond his current bank balance, not a farthing in the world.

However, the new piece, *Iolanthe; or, The Peer and the Peri,* fared as well as had its predecessors. The faithful three, Grossmith, Barrington, and Temple, were respectively *The Lord Chancellor, The Earl of Mountararat,* and *Strephon.* Jessie Bond was *Iolanthe,* Leonora Braham was *Phyllis,* and Alice Barnett was *The Fairy Queen.* The opera's reception was not unanimously favorable. *Punch* announced that it was "not within a mile of *Pinafore,*" and even the faithful Lawrence includes it "amongst the least appreciated of the operas." Nevertheless and notwithstanding, *Iolanthe* ran fourteen months.

During its run Sullivan was knighted (May, 1883) "in recognition of your distinguished talents as a composer and of the services which you have rendered to the promotion of the art of music generally in this country." Gilbert was not. It may be—it is probable, in fact—that the operettas were not taken into account in awarding Sullivan his knighthood. The mass of church music he had written was in itself almost a patent of nobility, his more frivolous output figuring as a mildly regrettable but pardonable misstep. But in Gilbert's case the operettas were the very things to be taken into account. His jabs at the clergy, in the *Bab Ballads* and *The Sorcerer,* and at the Peerage, in *Iolanthe,* undoubtedly had something to do with his being forced to wait so long for the honor.

No sooner was he "Sir" Arthur, than Sullivan's friends and commentators redoubled their efforts to make him ashamed of his most brilliant talent. *Grove's Dictionary* took the trouble to suggest that it was high time he applied his gifts to "a serious opera on some subject of abiding human or national [the distinction is Grove's] interest," while the *Musical Review,* in an article cited by two of his biographers, announced solemnly that it simply wouldn't do to see "Sir" Arthur Sullivan's name affixed to any more comic operas. Sullivan kept his head, but the council of the owls was yet to have its effect.

For his next libretto Gilbert turned to his blank-verse parody of Tennyson's *The Princess.* He rewrote the "respectful perversion" almost entirely, greatly improving it in the process, and turned it over to Sullivan. The result, *Princess Ida; or, Castle Adamant,* opened at the Savoy on January 5, 1884, with Grossmith as *King Gama,* Barrington as *King Hildebrand,* and Temple as *Arac.* Leonora Braham played the title rôle, with Jessie Bond as *Melissa.* Rosina Brandram, promoted to a leading rôle, was *Lady Blanche.* The opera had a run—nine months—that would have been considered excellent for a musical piece by any other authors, but was not what Gilbert and Sullivan had been taught to expect. When it closed, in October, they had nothing ready. Carte accordingly staged revivals of *Trial by Jury* and *The Sorcerer.* Both were successful, the latter surprisingly so.

From most accounts of the famous quarrel that broke the spirit, if not the back, of the Gilbert and Sullivan partnership, one would gather that the two squabbled, without preamble, over a piece of carpet, and forthwith parted. As a matter of fact, the seeds of that separation were planted, I should say, on the day that Sullivan was knighted. Gilbert was not a humble man, and he was a sensitive one; and it must have hurt his feelings abominably to be passed over in favor of his more popular collaborator, who, he must have thought, had achieved no more in music than he had in the theatre. Naturally the slight was no fault of Sullivan's, but as Gilbert was of a type that must have a culprit for every wrong, his feeling toward Sullivan must—however unconsciously—have become faintly tinged with resentment. Sullivan, moreover, could not be wholly unaffected by the incessant urgings of his highbrow friends to do "something serious" in the theatre—an exhortation that was in itself a disparagement of Gilbert. At intervals he was beginning to condescend, ever so little, to his librettist.

The first of these intervals occurred after the run of *Princess Ida*. Sullivan, suddenly declaring that he was at the end of his rope, announced that he could set no more supernatural, fairy, or topsy-turvy libretti. "I have rung all changes possible in the way of variety of rhythm. It has hitherto been word setting, I might almost say syllable setting, for I have looked upon the words as being of such importance that I have been continually keeping down the music in order that not one should be lost. . . . I want a chance for the music to act in its own proper sphere—to intensify the emotional element not only of the actual words but of the situation. I should like to set a story of human interest and probability, where the humorous words would come in a humorous (not serious) situation, and where, if the situation were a tender or dramatic one, the words would be of similar character."

The complaint was fair enough. Certainly Gilbert's libretti are not swept by any hurricanes of passion. Whether it was relevant or not is another matter. Sullivan's definition of what he would like to set would apply as well to the libretto of *Die Meistersinger von Nürnberg* as to that of an operetta. But conceding that his demands were reasonable, he might have couched them in terms that were somewhat less like an ultimatum. The tone of the entire letter (why "I should like," and "I want," instead of "could we not?") must have been galling to a man with whom he had been closely associated for ten years, and with whom he had already written seven comic operas. It would have been more tactful, not to say more courageous, to have waited to see Gilbert, and to have talked things out, instead of writing thus, rather stuffily, from Paris.

Gilbert behaved with surprising meekness. After a first indignant reply he had a meeting with Sullivan and tried to evolve a plot that would please him. He even talked of having Sullivan write an *ad interim* piece with someone else, before resuming their collaboration. Matters were at a standstill until Gilbert, in May, 1884, announced that he had the libretto Sullivan wanted: nothing supernatural, nothing improbable. Sullivan promptly agreed to set it.

Just how he reconciled his demands with the actual book that he set to music, is not for us to inquire. But he did; for in due course there opened at the Savoy, on March 14, 1885—if you do not know, you cannot guess! —*The Mikado; or, The Town of Titipu.* Grossmith was *Ko-Ko,* Barrington was *Pooh-Bah,* and Temple was *The Mikado,* with Durward Lely as *Nanki-Poo.* The rôles of *Yum-Yum, Pitti Sing,* and *Peep-Bo* were sung by Leonora Braham, Jessie Bond, and Sybil Grey, with the self-sacrificing Rosina Brandram as *Katisha.* The travail and argument that had attended its inception were a small price, measured by the magnitude of its success. *The Mikado* ran at the Savoy for 672 performances—nearly two years—and, figuratively at least, has never stopped. At this moment there is probably a *Mikado* production current somewhere.

The instantaneous success of the piece naturally did not go unnoticed in America, and D'Oyly Carte's old piratical friend, John C. Duff, promptly announced a forthcoming *Mikado* production. Sullivan's orchestration was out of his reach, but he had one made from the piano-vocal score. What thereupon happened is a twice-told tale: how Duff planned his opening for the early part of August, 1885; how, on the morning of August 18th, John B. Stetson, of the Fifth Avenue Theatre, went down to the pier to meet a Mr. Chapman, of London, who turned out to be D'Oyly Carte, with a complete English *Mikado* production and an English *Mikado* company; and how, on Tuesday evening, August 20th, the authorized version was produced at the Fifth Avenue Theatre, to the discomfiture of Duff, who could not open until the 25th.

Such is the universally accepted version of a famous *coup*. Yet there is contemporary evidence to show that Carte's dramatic arrival was less melodramatically satisfying than one might wish. Henry Krehbiel, then (and for nearly forty years thereafter) music critic of the New York *Tribune*, was in the habit of publishing an annual *Review of the New York Music Season*, listing every important musical event of the year, with appropriate comment. Here are extracts from the *Review* for 1885-86.

AUGUST

Wednesday, Nineteenth

Fifth Avenue Theatre. Production of Gilbert and Sullivan's opera, "The Mikado; or, The Town of Titipu," under the direction of Mr. R. D'Oyly Carte.

The opera had been given for ten days previously, in a vulgarized and perverted form, by a company of comedians of mediocre ability in the Union Square Theatre, but this was the first authorized representation in the United States, the performers, with the exception of Miss Ulmer [*Yum-Yum*], having come with Mr. Carte from England. In the Union Square performance, and those which followed in the Standard Theatre, under Mr. J. C. Duff, use was made of orchestral parts arranged from the published pianoforte and vocal scores.

Monday, Twenty-fourth

Standard Theatre. Production of "The Mikado" by Mr. Duff's Company.

In other words, according to the usually painfully accurate Krehbiel, Duff had produced *The Mikado* nine days before Carte's arrival, and merely moved his company from the Union Square Theatre to the Standard. Further, the date of Carte's opening was not Tuesday, the 20th, but Wednesday, the 19th (a calendar of 1885 would settle that point, I should think). According to the same chronicler, Carte later got Duff out of New York by leasing the Standard Theatre over his head; for the *Review,* under the heading, "NOVEMBER. *Saturday, Twenty-first,"* records:

> Standard Theatre. Gilbert and Sullivan's "Mikado" was withdrawn under an agreement between Mr. Duff and Mr. Stetson of the Fifth Avenue Theatre, who, having made contracts for the latter theatre, rented the Standard in order not to disturb the successful run of "The Mikado" at the Fifth Avenue. At the Standard the operetta received seventy-eight evening and thirteen afternoon representations. The company [that is, Duff's company] "went on the road."

[10]

SULLIVAN had gone to America ahead of the *Mikado* company—not, one hastens to add, as its advance man, but to wind up the affairs of his deceased sister-in-law (Frederick's widow, who had remarried) in Los Angeles. He returned East, saw the New York production at a gala performance (in the course of which he made a speech), and returned to England to work on his cantata, *The Golden Legend.* Also, to work on a new libretto of Gilbert's. The cantata was first performed at Leeds, in October, 1886, and was a terrific success. The new operetta, produced at the Savoy on January 22, 1887, was not. It was *Ruddygore; or, The Witch's Curse,* with a cast that included Grossmith and Barrington as *Robin* and *Sir Despard;* Lely as *Richard* (there was no part for Temple); Jessie Bond as *Mad Margaret;* Leonora Braham as *Rose Maybud;* and Rosina Brandram as *Dame Hannah.*

We have all travelled such a distance along the road of untrammelled vivacity of speech in and about the theatre, that it is hard for us profligates to realize how deeply the title of *Ruddygore* shocked London. The newspapers and the public pounced at once upon the fact that "ruddy" was really a synonym for "bloody"; and "bloody," to many an Englishman, even today, is on a par with the famous term that one American may not apply to another without smiling. Hark to the voice of the London *Graphic,* a week after the opening, as quoted by Goldberg: "The sterner and less mealy mouthed sex, safe in the club smoking-room, might pass such a name with a smile. But it is different in the case of ladies, to whom Savoy operas largely appeal, and on whose lips such a title would scarcely sound pretty." The management sought to appease the public wrath by excising the "y" in favor of "i", shortly after the opening; but there were still shocked grumblings.

Furthermore, the second act undeniably dragged, and both authors admitted it. Gilbert thought the music was inappropriately heavy, and Sullivan thought there were too many words. This was ominous, for never before had either of the pair ever had anything but praise for his collaborator's share in one of their completed works. What with one thing and another, *Ruddigore* was withdrawn on November 5, 1887, after 288 performances (it was destined to wait more than thirty years before being revived, with triumphant success, by the Hinshaw Opera Company in New York). Again a Gilbert and Sullivan work had had a run that would be the envy of most authors, and again it had been so brief—for a Savoy opera—that they had nothing ready to succeed it. Carte promptly staged a series of revivals of *Pinafore, The Pirates,* and *The Mikado*. Meanwhile, Sullivan again was hearing, and not unwillingly, the voice of the tempter. The Queen had heard *The Golden Legend,* and had told him that he ought to write a grand opera; and he was inclined to agree with her. He even got to the point of announcing, again, that he was through with comic opera.

It is a typically Gilbertian paradox of their relationship that whenever there was any patching up to be done between the two, it was usually the cantankerous Gilbert who bestirred himself to appease the easy-going Sullivan. This time he was once more into the breach. He would write Sullivan a really lyric and romantic libretto, offering plenty of opportunity for the musical and dramatic effects for which his collaborator yearned. Sullivan was delighted with it, and wrote for it what he always considered was his best score. It replaced the *Mikado* revival at the Savoy on October 3, 1888: *The Yeomen of the Guard; or, The Merryman and his Maid*. Temple was back, as *Sergeant Meryll,* and Grossmith was, of course, *Jack Point;* but Barrington was out. He had resigned from the Savoy Company to embark upon an ill-fated career as producer. Gilbert, in fact, had written him a melodrama, *Brantingham Hall,* earlier in the year, which was a prompt and inglorious failure. Leonora Braham was gone, too. In her place, singing *Elsie,* was Geraldine Ulmer, who had been the sole American member of the New York *Mikado* company. Jessie Bond was *Phoebe,* and the long-suffering Rosina Brandram was *Dame Carruthers.*

But although Gilbert was as pleased over his share of the work as Sullivan was over his, and although *The Yeomen* ran something over a year, there was thunder in the air. Sullivan was more restless than ever. He had tasted blood. Having at last had a—comparatively speaking—romantic libretto, he wanted more. He was tired of subordinating music to words, tired of setting fantastic plots, tired of having no voice in the musical construction of his libretti; and said so, almost in so many words. He wanted a wholly romantic story, not necessarily a humorous one at all, to which he could write serious music; he wanted, in short, to write a grand opera. Gilbert had no faith in the grand opera idea. He did not believe that he could write a grand opera libretto, and did not believe the public would take him seriously if he did. When Sullivan grew more pressing, he finally suggested another librettist, Julian Sturgis; and it was Sturgis who did write the libretto of *Ivanhoe.*

Carte, also, had become fired with the grand opera scheme, and had begun to formulate plans for an all-English grand opera company, in a theatre of its own, to parallel, on a more pretentious plane, the Savoy and the Comedy Opera Company. Gilbert, naturally, did not figure very largely in these plans, and Sullivan did. There were many points upon which Gilbert and his producer violently disagreed. The details of the grievance are not yet definitely known, but it undoubtedly had something to do with money matters, and was of long standing.

The Savoy Company had just sustained a heavy loss in

the resignation of George Grossmith, who had been one of its mainstays since the days of *The Sorcerer.* He had found the rôle of *Jack Point* too serious, and too heavy vocally, and wanted to get back to his pianologues. He left before the run of *The Yeomen* had ended, never to return. (When I was in high school, by the way, about 1900, I remember hearing him giving a pianologue in Mendelssohn Hall, New York, and being enchanted thereby. To this day I could, if urged, render an approximation of the one beginning, "This is the desert." [Chord]. "These" [plunk, plunk] "are two palm trees. And this" [plink] "is the evening star.")

Sullivan, temporarily pacified with his grand opera libretto, grew more amenable; and despite their increasing differences the two proceeded to turn out one of the gayest and most tuneful operettas of the entire series, *The Gondoliers; or, The King of Barataria.* It opened at the Savoy on December 7, 1889, and was a great success. Rutland Barrington, sadder, wiser, and back in the fold, played *Giuseppe,* with Courtice Pounds as *Marco.* Frank Wyatt, who had been in *The Yeomen,* was the *Duke of Plaza-Toro,* with Rosina Brandram as his *Duchess.* Jessie Bond was *Tessa,* Geraldine Ulmer was *Gianetta,* and Decima Moore was *Casilda.* It was the last unqualified success the famous duumvirate was to know.

[11]

THE historic quarrel, when it finally exploded, was set off by a disproportionately trivial cause. For some years the two authors, instead of leasing their works to Carte on a royalty basis had been operating the Savoy jointly with him, under a profit-sharing agreement whereby, of course, they shared operating expenses as well (just how the shares were apportioned we do not know). During the run of *The Gondoliers,* while Gilbert was away in India, D'Oyly Carte had bought a new carpet for the Savoy, and had charged Gilbert's share of the cost to his account. The details of the transaction are not clear. According to Carte's version, the total bill was £140 (about $700); Gilbert claimed that it was £1500 (about

$7500) for refurnishing the entire auditorium. In any case, Gilbert, returning, was furious, insisting that the expense was unwarranted and excessive. Sullivan had entered no protest, and was, up to this point, neutral; but when Gilbert demanded that he side either with or against him, he finally upheld Carte. Gilbert then drew up a new agreement under which the three partners were to operate, and when Sullivan refused to sign it, promptly wrote to Sullivan that the time had come to end their collaboration. "I am writing a letter to Carte (of which I enclose a copy), giving him notice that he is not to produce or perform any of my libretti after Christmas, 1890."

Obviously, whatever the justification for his indignation, the moral responsibility for the rupture was Gilbert's. Obviously too, the sum of money involved was hardly large enough to explain the fury into which he had worked himself. So tragically absurd was the whole business that commentators have always taken it for granted that there was "something behind it"; that the real cause of the break was not the apparent one, and that the full facts have never transpired. There are so many theories extant regarding the quarrel that I may as well contribute one more. If it is no better than the rest, it is at least no worse.

I believe that the Something behind the upheaval was the emotional state into which Gilbert had fallen, in his relation with Sullivan. He was much fonder of Sullivan than he is assumed to have been, much more genuinely attached to Sullivan than Sullivan was to him. There are so many stories of his sharp tongue and aggressive dogmatism that he is frequently regarded as having been a self-centered curmudgeon, incapable of much depth of feeling toward any person or any thing. But there are, after all, other stories, not so pointed and not nearly so entertaining to hear, of his kindness in the theatre and his patience with actors. He was forty-four years married; and no man whose wife can stand him for such a length of time may be set down as wholly impossible!

Since the vogue of psycho-analysis, the sensitive man with an unfortunate personality, whose only defense against the dislike he inspires is an accentuated disagreeableness, has become such a familiar figure that he is rather tiresome. Nevertheless, tiresome or not, such men do and did exist, and Gilbert was probably one of them. Sullivan girded at the lack of emotional depth in Gilbert's libretti. Even if such a quality had been desirable in the Savoy operas—which it was not—Gilbert had no ready flow of sentiment. But to assume that the mildly jeering tone of his opera books is the result of heartlessness—as some do—is a mistake. Read *Aline's* little aria—"Yet—yet we must part, Young heart!" from the first act of *The Sorcerer;* read the famous duet in the first act of *Iolanthe*—"Thou the tree and I the flower"; read *Phoebe's* song at the opening of *The Yeomen of the Guard*. These were not written by a man who was incapable of tenderness.

I think Gilbert's attitude toward Sullivan must have been one of affection and admiration—that, six years his senior, he looked upon him as a brilliantly gifted younger brother. Consider the fact that in every serious difference between them (after *Patience* and *The Yeomen,* for instance), Gilbert, the pig-headed and opinionated, never defended his case *in extremis,* always did everything possible to preserve their friendship and partnership, always—the carpet incident excepted—deferred to Sullivan's wishes. His letters to Sullivan are always fair, always courteous, never high-handed—which is more than can be said of some of Sullivan's letters to him. He stood out against Sullivan's grand opera aspirations as long as he could, because he honestly believed that they were ill-advised (his objections were not selfish, for Sullivan wanted a libretto from him); and when Sullivan insisted, and he saw that further argument was hopeless, he stepped aside without a trace of ill feeling, admitting that grand opera was beyond him, and even found Sullivan a librettist.

The cantatas and oratorios he did not mind. They were a part of Sullivan's career outside the theatre. But when he had stepped aside, the more fully the grand opera scheme began to work out, the more he saw Sullivan drifting away from him. Worse still, Carte was encouraging and backing Sullivan. The two were being drawn ever closer together, and he was being left out in the cold. He must have been hurt, and jealous. Then, to return from a long absence and find that apparently his wishes were not even to be consulted regarding the running of the Savoy, which his work, just as much as Sullivan's and Carte's, had helped to build—that must have been the final stab to his hurt feelings. Another man, more emotionally articulate, might have waxed reproachful or plaintive. For Gilbert there was nothing left but to see red. This, then, was the showdown. Was it to be Carte and Sullivan, or Gilbert and Sullivan? Did he count for anything in the combination, or not? Better to deliver an ultimatum, and find out once and for all, than to stand about any longer, waiting to be noticed.

It was a silly thing to do, of course. He took offense at something that was not, either in fact or intent, an affront; but a man does not always act sensibly when he is hurt. He asked for his answer, and he got it—the only answer his attitude made possible; and having trained his guns, had no choice but to stick by them. But when the answer was given, and the separation from Sullivan was a fact, Gilbert's, I think, was the heavier heart.

[12]

Plans for the new grand opera scheme were already in full swing. D'Oyly Carte had bought ground on Shaftsbury Avenue and was building a new opera house, and Sullivan was working day and night on the music of *Ivanhoe*. There was to be a permanent company, to give only English works; the whole enterprise was to be called The Royal English Opera. By the end of 1890 all was ready, and on January 31, 1891, *Ivanhoe,* libretto by Julian Sturgis, music by Sir Arthur Sullivan, opened the Royal English Opera. Sullivan sent tickets to Gilbert, who refused to attend—not, as so many have assumed, through rancor, but probably for the simpler and more human reason that he could not bear to go.

In Donald Ogden Stewart's fantastic tale, *The Crazy Fool,* the hero is a young man who inherits an insane asylum from his uncle. This latter worthy, it is explained, had started his career with nothing but "a few dollars, his bare hands, and one idiot." It was not an asylum that Carte had founded, but something even less rational, an opera company. And he started with an opera house, a complete double company—and one opera. *Ivanhoe* was put on exactly like a Savoy production—for a continuous run. Granted that it had justified Carte's faith, and had accomplished the impossible feat of running as long, say, as *The Yeomen of the Guard,* with what did he plan to follow it? Grand operas take time to write. Rossini may have written *The Barber of Seville* in less than a month, but the chances are that he had been thinking about it for a year. It seems incredible that the shrewd and far-seeing proprietor of the Savoy and the foolhardy entrepreneur of the Royal English Opera could have been one and the same person.

Inevitably enough, *Ivanhoe* ran nothing like a Savoy opera. It closed after 160 nights, the marvel being that it had run that long. I do not know the capacity of the Royal English Opera House, but it must have seated not less than 2000 persons. At that figure, *Ivanhoe* played to 320,000 people during its run; and the fact that more than a quarter of a million people in London were willing to attend a grand opera, if Sullivan had written it, is one of the most striking instances in musical history of a composer's hold upon the affections of his public (New York's opera-going public today is probably fifty or sixty thousand). *Ivanhoe* would, presumably, not have survived long, even in repertoire—it was never revived; but the whole venture was doomed from the start. After *Ivanhoe,* Carte produced Messager's *La Basoche* (which was anything but all-English), and shortly afterward sold the house to a vaudeville syndicate.

In the fall of 1891 Gilbert, as usual, took the first step toward a reconciliation, making peace overtures through the agency of Chappel, the music publisher. The two met, talked things over, and shook hands. But the old partnership was not yet resumed. Sullivan was working on the incidental music for Tennyson's *The Foresters,* which was first produced in New York, on March 25,

1892. In June of the same year Gilbert's operetta, *The Mountebanks,* with music by Alfred Cellier, was produced at the Lyric Theatre, with no great success. On September 24th Sullivan opened at the Savoy with *Haddon Hall,* for which Sydney Grundy had provided the libretto. It, too, languished and died.

But the day came when all London—all of England and a good deal of America, for that matter—thrilled to great news: Gilbert and Sullivan were at work together again! The opening of their new piece, *Utopia, Limited; or, The Flowers of Progress,* on October 3, 1893, was a gala night at the Savoy. The cast, however, held few familiar faces. Of the old company, only Barrington, as *King Paramount,* and Rosina Brandram, as *Lady Sophy,* were left. Nor did the opera, despite the sentimental interest of the reunion that it celebrated, and D'Oyly Carte's lavish production, long survive. It lasted for about seven months—245 performances—and then closed without a successor in sight. In July, 1894, Carte put on Messager's *Mirette* as a stop-gap. In December came *The Chieftain,* by Sullivan and Burnand, a revamped version of their old *Contrabandista.* This lasted only until April, 1895, when it was followed by a production of Humperdinck's *Hansel and Gretel.* When that closed, the Savoy was dark for a time. Gilbert, meanwhile, had written *His Excellency* with Osmond Carr. Its reception was not too cordial, and it soon went the way of all flesh.

In November there were fresh rumors of a new Gilbert and Sullivan collaboration, and renewed activity at the Savoy, where Carte staged another *Mikado* revival, which ran four months. Finally the new opera was ready, opening on March 7, 1896—*The Grand Duke; or, The Statutory Duel.* The faithful Barrington, as *Ludwig,* and Rosina Brandram, as *The Baroness,* were again the sole reminders of the old days. The production was elaborate, and the press was friendly; but the tale of *The Grand Duke* was the tale of *Utopia.* It closed after the shortest run since *Thespis*—123 performances. It was the last flicker of their combined lights. They never wrote together again.

Carte kept the Savoy open with revivals of former Gilbert and Sullivan successes until Sullivan was ready with a new piece—*The Beauty Stone,* written with Arthur Pinero and Comyns Carr. It opened on May 28, 1898, failed after seven weeks, and was followed by *The Gondoliers.* This, in turn, was followed by a revival of *The Sorcerer,* for which Sullivan conducted the opening performance. Gilbert was there, too, and both took a curtain call to a tremendous ovation. It was noticed, however, that the two did not speak. This was a pity; for it was the last time either was to see the other.

On November 29, 1899, The Savoy offered another work by Sullivan, *The Rose of Persia,* for which Basil Hood had written the libretto. Hood was an experienced librettist, and a good one, and seems to have had a happy effect upon Sullivan. Book and music were well received, and the opera had a very fair run of more than 200 performances. Sullivan's health, which had always been precarious, was failing rapidly. He began work on a new libretto by Hood, completed two numbers and sketched out fifteen others, but did not live to complete the score. It was finished by Edward German, and the opera, *The Emerald Isle,* opened on April 27, 1901. Sullivan was gone, a victim to a complication of bronchitis and heart trouble. He had died in London, on November 21, 1900, in his fifty-ninth year.

Gilbert had virtually retired, spending most of his time in his beautiful country home, Grim's Dyke. On June 30, 1907, he was knighted by Edward VII. He had made light of the honor, and grumbled, characteristically, because it was bestowed upon him as a "playwright" rather than a "dramatist"; but he accepted it, with satisfaction. His last operetta was written with Edward German—*Fallen Fairies,* produced on September 16, 1909. The libretto, founded on *The Wicked World,* was one that Sullivan had—rightly—refused. The piece did not last long.

On May 29, 1911, he had an engagement to give a swimming lesson to two young women friends in the lake at Grim's Dyke. As he came out of the house, one of them, who had already entered the water, slipped out of her depth, and called for help. He ran to the lake, plunged in, swam to her, told her to put her hand on his shoulder—and sank to the bottom. He was rescued, and frantically worked over, but he was dead; not by drowning, but from heart failure, brought on by over-exertion. He had lived seventy-four years and six months.

[13]

"I SHOULD like to set a story of human interest and probability, where the humorous words would come in a humorous (not serious) situation." How wisely Gilbert's angel guided him! For if he had assented, in his heart, to those words of Sullivan's, and had done his best, throughout their partnership, to write the sort of libretto the words prescribe, there would be no need to print this book. *The Mikado* would be as dead as *The Wicked World* and *Ivanhoe;* the Savoy operas would be a footnote, rather than a page, in England's theatrical history. For a story of human interest and probability was the one tale that neither of the two was fitted to tell.

Sullivan's genius was lyric. Of his "serious" music, only "The Lost Chord", one or two other songs, and some of the hymns, survive. The rest—the overtures and cantatas and oratorios, and the "grand" opera, are, if not yet forgotten, certainly gone. He was put here to sing—something gay, with a bit of skip to it; philosophy and drama were not in him. To expect to draw profound spiritual sustenance from his music is foolish; as well try to eat a buttercup.

Gilbert could do many things, but creating flesh and blood people was not one of them. The people in his serious plays pretend to be human, but we know better. They are not alive, and behind all that they do or say we see and hear the author. "That is not true," we say, watching them. "Live people do not talk or behave like that."

But the people of Gilbert's fairyland are a different matter. To complain that they are not human is to be guilty of irrelevance. They do not pretend to be. There is no question of plausibility involved in any of their acts. As Krehbiel put it, forty-six years ago, theirs is a world in which "everybody persists . . . in seeing everything upside down and refusing to believe that a pyramid can rest on anything else but its apex. The personages who affect to reason about anything pursue the line on which they start out, until the road runs out in a squirrel track, and this they follow up a tree, and accept the result with a perfectly grave complacency." Situations grow ever more complicated, the net of circumstance is drawn closer and closer, and there seems to be no way out. If this were a human drama, peopled with human characters and motivated by human emotions, the dramatist would give up, in despair. But this is nothing of the sort. The bumboat woman spins a preposterous yarn about two mixed babies, the young heir performs a few card tricks with logic, the executioner suddenly remembers that the victim is not dead, after all, the pirates turn out to be peers—and lo! the sky has cleared, the problems solve themselves, and everything has suddenly come out all right. Every fundamental axiom of human motive and conduct has been outraged, and we are delighted.

They are not sentimental, these people. Gilbert was not capable of writing romance, and he knew it. He was capable of writing sentimentality; and he knew that, too, and dreaded it. And so the humorous words come, not only in "the humorous (not serious) scenes", but in those that Sullivan would have liked to see uninterruptedly tender or dramatic. And their hard, unsentimental logic, that Sullivan so deplored, is one of the secrets of their longevity—and his.

Time is the death of romance. The "heart-interest" of one generation is perilously apt to become the laughingstock of the next. Nothing sours so quickly as a too-sweet drink. The swooning lushness of mid-Victorian sentimentality moves us, today, to nothing so polite as tears. Out of all their contemporaries, the Savoy people alone have survived. They slip, laughing, through Time's fingers. He cannot destroy, by making it ridiculous, a race that was never anything else.

If they are not human, it does not follow that they are

not living people. If they are not actual persons that we know, they are at least the quintessential essence of generations of persons that we know. *Sir Joseph* is no more Landlubber Smith, Victoria's First Lord of the Admiralty, than he is Landlubber Daniels, Wilson's Secretary of the Navy; yet he is what, in an ever so slightly more logical world, both would be. All the Smiths and Danielses that have ever lived, and shall live, have in their veins the blood of *Sir Joseph*. Oscar Wilde is dead, and the aesthetic movement in England is a dim memory. But capture this young something-ist poet, that young painter of what-isms. Put him in a strong light, and look carefully. Is that *Bunthorne's* shadow on the wall?

John Wellington Wells, Sir Joseph Porter, Little Buttercup, Ruth, Patience, Bunthorne, The Lord Chancellor, Phyllis, King Gama, Pooh-Bah, Yum-Yum, Robin, Jack Point, Phoebe, Marco, and *Giuseppe*—how many they are, and how alive, and how well we know them! It was romance that Gilbert was writing, all the time, if only he and Sullivan had noticed. For as this gay, silly, endearing crew skip upon the stage, the sum of all that they say is always the same thing; and it is a romantic thing: That the light of pure reason casts grotesque shadows; that a world in which there is nothing but the letter of the law, and the logical conclusion, and the inevitable deduction, and the axiomatic fact, and the rational course of conduct, is, in the last account, a ridiculous one. Looking at their world, in which there is everything but the truth that lies beyond logic, we perceive that it is, in more ways than one, an impossible world.

If we laugh at it, and them, they do not mind. They rather hoped we would. For our grandfathers laughed, and our fathers; and so, I think, will our children's children. For there is life in these fairy comedians. They are the Little People, and have no souls. And so they are deathless.

DEEMS TAYLOR

Hunting Ridge, Conn.

October, 1931

THESPIS

OR

THE GODS GROWN OLD

DRAMATIS PERSONÆ

GODS

JUPITER, APOLLO, MARS, DIANA — *Aged Deities*

MERCURY

THESPIANS

THESPIS	STUPIDAS
SILLIMON	SPARKEION
TIMIDON	NICEMIS
TIPSEION	PRETTEIA
PREPOSTEROS	DAPHNE

CYMON

ACT I

RUINED TEMPLE ON THE SUMMIT OF OLYMPUS

ACT II

THE SAME SCENE, WITH THE RUINS RESTORED

Produced at the Gaiety Theatre, under the management of J. Hollingshead, Tuesday, December 23rd, 1871.

THESPIS

OR

THE GODS GROWN OLD

ACT I

SCENE.—*The ruins of The Temple of the Gods on summit of Mount Olympus. Picturesque shattered columns, overgrown with ivy, etc.,* R. *and* L., *with entrances to temple (ruined)* R. *Fallen columns on the stage. Three broken pillars* 2 R. E. *At the back of stage is the approach from the summit of the mountain. This should be "practicable" to enable large numbers of people to ascend and descend. In the distance are the summits of adjacent mountains. At first all this is concealed by a thick fog, which clears presently. Enter (through fog) Chorus of Stars coming off duty, as fatigued with their night's work.*

CHORUS OF STARS

Throughout the night
  The constellations
Have given light
  From various stations.
When midnight gloom
  Falls on all nations,
We will resume
  Our occupations.

Solo.
Our light, it's true,
  Is not worth mention;
What can we do
  To gain attention,
When, night and noon,
  With vulgar glaring,
A great big Moon
  Is *always* flaring?

Chorus. Throughout the night, &c.

During Chorus Enter DIANA, *an elderly Goddess. She is carefully wrapped up in Cloaks, Shawls, etc. A Hood is over her head, a Respirator in her mouth, and Goloshes on her feet. During the chorus she takes these things off, and discovers herself dressed in the usual costume of the Lunar Diana, the Goddess of the Moon.*

DIA. (*shuddering*). Ugh! How cold the nights are! I don't know how it is, but I seem to feel the night air a great deal more than I used to. But it is time for the sun to be rising. (*Calls.*) Apollo.

AP. (*within*). Hollo!

DIA. I've come off duty—it's time for you to be getting up.

Enter APOLLO. *He is an elderly "buck" with an air of assumed juvenility, and is dressed in dressing gown and smoking cap.*

AP. (*yawning*). I shan't go out to-day. I was out yesterday and the day before and I want a little rest. I don't know how it is, but I seem to feel my work a great deal more than I used to.

DIA. I'm sure these short days can't hurt you. Why, you don't rise till six and you're in bed again by five: you should have a turn at *my* work and see how you like that—out all night!

AP. My dear sister, I don't envy you—though I remember when I did—but that was when I was a younger sun. I don't think I'm quite well. Perhaps a little change of air will do me good. I've a great mind to show myself in London this winter, they'll be very glad to see me. No! I shan't go out to-day. I shall send them this fine, thick wholesome fog and they won't miss me. It's the best substitute for a blazing sun—and like most substitutes, nothing at all like the real thing. (*To fog.*) Be off with you.

[*Fog clears away and discovers the scene described.*

Hurried Music. MERCURY *shoots up from behind precipice at back of stage. He carries several parcels afterwards described. He sits down, very much fatigued.*

MER. Home at last. A nice time I've had of it.

DIA. You young scamp you've been down all night again. This is the third time you've been out this week.

MER. Well *you're* a nice one to blow me up for that.

DIA. *I* can't help being out all night.

MER. And I can't help being down all night. The nature of Mercury requires that he should go down when the sun sets, and rise again, when the sun rises.

DIA. And what have you been doing?

MER. Stealing on commission. There's a set of false teeth and a box of Life Pills—that's for Jupiter—An invisible peruke and a bottle of hair dye—that's for Apollo—A respirator and a pair of goloshes—that's for Cupid—A full bottomed chignon, some auricomous fluid, a box of pearl-powder, a pot of rouge, and a hare's foot—that's for Venus.

DIA. Stealing! you ought to be ashamed of yourself!

MER. Oh, as the god of thieves I must do something to justify my position.

DIA *and* AP. (*contemptuously*). Your position!

MER. Oh I know it's nothing to boast of, even on earth. Up here, it's simply contemptible. Now that you gods are too old for your work, you've made me the miserable drudge of Olympus—groom, valet, postman, butler, commissionaire, maid of all work, parish beadle, and original dustman.

AP. Your Christmas boxes ought to be something considerable.

MER. They ought to be but they're not. I'm treated abominably. I make everybody and I'm nobody—I go everywhere and I'm nowhere—I do everything and I'm nothing. I've made thunder for Jupiter, odes for Apollo, battles for Mars, and love for Venus. I've married couples for Hymen, and six weeks afterwards, I've divorced them for Cupid—and in return I get all the kicks while they pocket the halfpence. And in compensation for robbing me of the halfpence in question, what have they done for me?

AP. Why they've—ha! ha! they've made you the god of thieves!

MER. Very self-denying of them—there isn't one of

them who hasn't a better claim to the distinction than I have.

SONG—MERCURY

Oh, I'm the celestial drudge,
  From morning to night I must stop at it,
On errands all day I must trudge,
  And I stick to my work till I drop at it!
In summer I get up at one
  (As a good-natured donkey I'm ranked for it),
Then I go and I light up the Sun,
  And Phœbus Apollo gets thanked for it!
    Well, well, it's the way of the world,
      And will be through all its futurity;
    Though noodles are baroned and earled,
      There's nothing for clever obscurity!

I'm the slave of the Gods, neck and heels,
  And I'm bound to obey, though I rate at 'em;
And I not only order their meals,
  But I cook 'em, and serve 'em, and wait at 'em.
Then I make all their nectar—I do—
  (Which a terrible liquor to rack us is)
And whenever I mix them a brew,
  Why all the thanksgivings are Bacchus's!
    Well, well, it's the way of the world, &c.

Then reading and writing I teach,
  And spelling-books many I've edited!
And for bringing those arts within reach,
  That donkey Minerva gets credited.
Then I scrape at the stars with a knife,
  And plate-powder the moon (on the days for it),
And I hear all the world and his wife
  Awarding Diana the praise for it!
    Well, well, it's the way of the world, &c.

[*After song—very loud and majestic music is heard.*

DIA. AND MER. (*looking off*). Why, who's this? Jupiter, by Jove!

Enter JUPITER, *an extremely old man, very decrepit, with very thin straggling white beard, he wears a long braided dressing-gown, handsomely trimmed, and a silk night-cap on his head.* MERCURY *falls back respectfully as he enters.*

JUP. Good day, Diana—ah Apollo—Well, well, well, what's the matter? what's the matter?

DIA. Why, that young scamp Mercury says that we do nothing, and leave all the duties of Olympus to him! Will you believe it, he actually says that our influence on earth is dropping down to *nil*.

JUP. Well, well—don't be hard on the lad—to tell you the truth, I'm not sure that he's very far wrong. Don't let it go any further, but, between ourselves, the sacrifices and votive offerings have fallen off terribly of late. Why, I can remember the time when people offered us human sacrifices—no mistake about it—human sacrifices! think of that!

DIA. Ah! those good old days!

JUP. Then it fell off to oxen, pigs, and sheep.

AP. Well, there are worse things than oxen, pigs, and sheep.

JUP. So I've found to my cost. My dear sir—between ourselves, it's dropped off from one thing to another until it has positively dwindled down to preserved Australian beef! What do you think of that?

AP. I don't like it at all.

JUP. You won't mention it—it might go further——

DIA. It couldn't fare worse.

JUP. In short, matters have come to such a crisis that there's no mistake about it—something must be done to restore our influence, the only question is, *What?*

QUARTETTE

MER. (*coming forward in great alarm*).

Enter MARS

Oh incident unprecedented!
I hardly can believe it's true!
MARS. Why, bless the boy, he's quite demented!
Why, what's the matter, sir, with you?
AP. Speak quickly, or you'll get a warming!

MER. Why, mortals up the mount are swarming,
Our temple on Olympus storming,
In hundreds—aye in thousands, too!

ALL. Goodness gracious,
How audacious;
Earth is spacious,
Why come here?
Our impeding
Their proceeding
Were good breeding,
That is clear.

DIA. Jupiter, hear my plea;
Upon the mount if *they* light,
There'll be an end of me,
I won't be seen by daylight!

AP. Tartarus is the place
These scoundrels you should send to—
Should they behold my face
My influence there's an end to!

JUP. (*looking over precipice*). What fools to give themselves so much exertion!

DIA. " " A government survey I'll make assertion!

AP. " " Perhaps the Alpine club at their diversion!

MER. " " They seem to be more like a "Cook's Excursion."

ALL. Goodness gracious, etc.

AP. If, mighty Jove, you value your existence,
Send them a thunderbolt with your regards!

JUP. My thunderbolts, though valid at a distance,
Are not effective at a hundred yards.

MER. Let the moon's rays, Diana, strike 'em flighty,
Make 'em all lunatics in various styles!

DIA. My Lunar rays unhappily are mighty
Only at many hundred thousand miles.

ALL. Goodness gracious, etc.

[*Exeunt* JUPITER, APOLLO, DIANA, *and* MERCURY *into ruined temple.*

Enter SPARKEION *and* NICEMIS *climbing mountain at back.*

SPARK. Here we are at last on the very summit, and we've left the others ever so far behind! Why, what's this?

NICE. A ruined palace! A palace on the top of a mountain. I wonder who lives here? Some mighty king, I dare say, with wealth beyond all counting, who came to live up here——

SP. To avoid his creditors! It's a lovely situation for a country house, though it's very much out of repair.

NICE. Very inconvenient situation.

SP. Inconvenient?

NICE. Yes—how are you to get butter, milk, and eggs up here? No pigs—no poultry—no postman. Why, I should go mad.

SP. What a dear little practical mind it is! What a wife you will make!

NICE. Don't be too sure—we are only partly married—the marriage ceremony lasts all day.

SP. I've no doubt at all about it. We shall be as happy as a king and queen, though we are only a strolling actor and actress.

NICE. It's very kind of Thespis to celebrate our marriage day by giving the company a pic-nic on this lovely mountain.

SP. And still more kind to allow us to get so much ahead of all the others. Discreet Thespis! [*Kissing her.*

NICE. There now, get away, do! Remember the marriage ceremony is not yet completed.

SP. But it would be ungrateful to Thespis's discretion not to take advantage of it by improving the opportunity.

NICE. Certainly not; get away.

SP. On second thoughts the opportunity's so good it don't admit of improvement. There! [*Kisses her.*

NICE. How dare you kiss me before we are quite married?

SP. Attribute it to the intoxicating influence of the mountain air.

NICE. Then we had better go down again. It is not right to expose ourselves to influences over which we have no control.

DUET.—SPARKEION *and* NICEMIS.

SP. Here far away from all the world,
Dissension and derision,
With Nature's wonders all unfurled
To our delighted vision,
With no one here
(At least in sight)
To interfere
With our delight,
And two fond lovers sever,
Oh do not free,
Thine hand from mine,
I swear to thee
My love is thine,
For ever and for ever!

NICE. On mountain top the air is keen,
And most exhilarating,
And we say things we do not mean
In moments' less elating.
So please to wait,
For thoughts that crop,
En tête-à-tête,
On mountain top,
May not exactly tally
With those that you
May entertain,
Returning to
The sober plain
Of yon relaxing valley.

SP. Very well—if you won't have anything to say to me, I know who will.

NICE. Who will?

SP. Daphne will.

NICE. Daphne would flirt with anybody.

SP. Anybody would flirt with Daphne. She is quite as pretty as you and has twice as much back-hair.

NICE. She has twice as much money, which may account for it.

SP. At all events, *she* has appreciation. *She* likes good looks.

NICE. We all like what we haven't got.

SP. *She* keeps her eyes open.

NICE. Yes—one of them.

SP. Which one?

NICE. The one she doesn't wink with.

SP. Well, I was engaged to her for six months and if she still makes eyes at me, you must attribute it to force of habit. Besides—remember—we are only half-married at present.

NICE. I suppose you mean that you are going to treat me as shamefully as you treated her. Very well, break it off if you like. *I* shall not offer any objection. Thespis used to be very attentive to me, and I'd just as soon be a manager's wife as a fifth-rate actor's!

Chorus heard, at first below, then enter DAPHNE, PRETTEIA, PREPOSTEROS, STUPIDAS, TIPSEION, CYMON, *and other members of* THESPIS' *company climbing over rocks at back. All carry small baskets.*

CHORUS—(*with dance*) *

Climbing over rocky mountain,
Skipping rivulet and fountain,
Passing where the willows quiver,
By the ever rolling river,
Swollen with the summer rain.
Threading long and leafy mazes,
Dotted with unnumbered daisies,
Scaling rough and rugged passes,
Climb the hardy lads and lasses,
Till the mountain-top they gain.

FIRST VOICE.
Fill the cup and tread the measure,
Make the most of fleeting leisure,
Hail it as a true ally,
Though it perish bye and bye!

SECOND VOICE.
Every moment brings a treasure
Of its own especial pleasure,
Though the moments quickly die,
Greet them gaily as they fly!

* *Afterwards transplanted to Act I of "The Pirates of Penzance."*

THIRD VOICE. Far away from grief and care,
High up in the mountain air,
Let us live and reign alone,
In a world that's all our own.

FOURTH VOICE. Here enthroned in the sky,
Far away from mortal eye,
We'll be gods and make decrees,
Those may honour them who please.

CHORUS. Fill the cup and tread the measure,
etc.

After CHORUS *and* COUPLETS *enter* THESPIS *climbing over rocks*

THES. Bless you, my people, bless you. Let the revels commence. After all, for thorough, unconstrained unconventional enjoyment give me a pic-nic.

PREP. (*very gloomily*). Give him a pic-nic somebody!

THES. Be quiet Preposteros—don't interrupt.

PREP. Ha! ha! shut up again! But no matter.

[STUPIDAS *endeavours, in pantomime, to reconcile him. Throughout the scene* PREP. *shows symptoms of breaking out into a furious passion, and* STUPIDAS *does all he can to pacify and restrain him.*

THES. The best of a pic-nic is that everybody contributes what he pleases, and nobody knows what anybody else has brought till the last moment. Now, unpack everybody, and let's see what there is for everybody.

NICE. I have brought you—a bottle of soda water—for the claret-cup.

DAPH. I have brought you—a lettuce for the lobster salad.

SP. A piece of ice—for the claret-cup.

PRETT. A bottle of vinegar—for the lobster-salad.

CYMON. A bunch of burrage for the claret-cup!

TIPS. A hard-boiled egg—for the lobster salad!

STUP. One lump of sugar for the claret-cup!

PREP. He has brought one lump of sugar for the claret-cup? Ha! Ha! Ha! [*Laughing melodramatically.*

STUP. Well, Preposteros, and what have *you* brought?

PREP. *I* have brought *two* lumps of the very best salt for the lobster salad.

THES. Oh—is that all?

PREP. All! Ha! Ha! He asks if it is all!

[STUPIDAS *consoles him.*

THES. But, I say—this is capital so far as it goes—nothing could be better, but it doesn't go far enough. The claret, for instance! I don't insist on claret—or a lobster—I don't insist on lobster, but a lobster salad without a lobster, why, it isn't lobster salad. Here, Tipseion!

TIPSEION (*a very drunken bloated fellow, dressed, however, with scrupulous accuracy and wearing a large medal round his neck*). My Master?

[*Falls on his knees to* THES. *and kisses his robe.*

THES. Get up—don't be a fool. Where's the claret? We arranged last week that you were to see to that?

TIPS. True, dear master. But then I was a drunkard!

THES. You were.

TIPS. You engaged me to play convivial parts on the strength of my personal appearance.

THES. I did.

TIPS. You then found that my habits interfered with my duties as low comedian.

THES. True——

TIPS. You said yesterday that unless I took the pledge you would dismiss me from your company.

THES. Quite so.

TIPS. Good. I have taken it. It is all I have taken since yesterday. My preserver! [*Embraces him.*

THES. Yes, but where's the wine?

TIPS. I left it behind, that I might not be tempted to violate my pledge.

PREP. Minion!

[*Attempts to get at him, is restrained by* STUPIDAS.

THES. Now, Preposteros, what *is* the matter with you?

PREP. It is enough that I am down-trodden in my profession. I will not submit to imposition out of it. It is enough that as your heavy villain I get the worst of it every night in a combat of six. I will *not* submit to insult in the day time. I have come out, ha! ha! to enjoy myself!

THES. But look here, you know—virtue only triumphs at night from seven to ten—vice gets the best of it during the other twenty-three hours. Won't that satisfy you?

[STUPIDAS *endeavours to pacify him.*

PREP. (*irritated to* STUP.). Ye are odious to my sight! get out of it!

STUP. (*in great terror*). What have I done?

THES. Now *what* is it, Preposteros, *what* is it?

PREP. I a—hate him and would have his life!

THES. (*to* STUP.). That's it—he hates you and would have your life. Now go and be merry.

STUP. Yes, but why does he hate me?

THES. Oh—exactly. (*To* PREP.) Why do you hate him?

PREP. Because he is a minion!

THES. He hates you because you are a minion. It explains itself. Now go and enjoy yourselves. Ha! ha! It is well for those who *can* laugh—let them do so—there is no extra charge. The light-hearted cup and the convivial jest for them—but for me—what is there for me?

SILLIMON. There is some claret-cup and lobster salad.

[*Handing some.*

THES. (*taking it*). Thank you. (*Resuming.*) What is there for me but anxiety—ceaseless gnawing anxiety that tears at my very vitals and rends my peace of mind asunder? There is nothing whatever for me but anxiety of the nature I have just described. The charge of these thoughtless revellers is my unhappy lot. It is not a small charge, and it is rightly termed a lot, because they are many. Oh why did the gods make me a manager?

SILL. (*as guessing a riddle*). *Why* did the gods make him a manager?

SP. Why did the *gods* make him a manager?

DAP. Why did the gods make *him* a manager?

PRETT. Why did the gods make him a *manager*?

THES. No—no—what are you talking about? what do you mean?

DAP. I've got it—don't tell us——

ALL. No—no—because—because——

THES. (*annoyed*). It isn't a conundrum—it's a misan thropical question. Why cannot I join you?

[*Retires up centre.*

DAP. (*who is sitting with* SPARKEION *to the annoyance of* NICEMIS *who is crying alone*). I'm sure I don't know. We do not want you. Don't distress yourself on our account—we are getting on very comfortably—aren't we, Sparkeion?

SPAR. We are so happy that we don't miss the lobster or the claret. What are lobster and claret compared with the society of those we love? [*Embracing* DAPHNE.

DAP. Why, Nicemis, love, you are eating nothing. Aren't you happy, dear?

NICE. (*spitefully*). *You* are *quite* welcome to *my* share of *everything. I* intend to console *myself* with the society of my manager. [*Takes* THESPIS' *arm affectionately.*

THES. Here I say—this won't do, you know—I can't allow it—at least before my company—besides, you are half-married to Sparkeion. Sparkeion, here's your half-wife impairing my influence before my company. Don't you know the story of the gentleman who undermined his influence by associating with his inferiors?

ALL. Yes, yes,—we know it.

PREP. (*furiously*). *I* do not know it! It's ever thus! Doomed to disappointment from my earliest years——

[STUPIDAS *endeavours to console him.*

THES. There—that's enough. Preposteros—you *shall* hear it.

SONG.—THESPIS

I once knew a chap who discharged a function
On the North South East West Diddlesex junction,
He was conspicu*ous* exceeding,
For his affable ways and his easy breeding.
Although a Chairman of Directors,
He was hand in glove with the ticket inspectors,
He tipped the guards with bran-new fivers,
And sang little songs to the engine drivers.
'Twas told to me with great compunction,
By one who had discharged with unction,
A Chairman of Directors' function,
On the North South East West Diddlesex junction.
Fol diddle, lol diddle, lol lol lay.

Each Christmas Day he gave each stoker
A silver shovel and a golden poker,
He'd button-hole flowers for the ticket sorters,
And rich Bath-buns for the outside porters.
He'd mount the clerks on his first-class hunters,
And he built little villas for the road-side shunters,
And if any were fond of pigeon shooting,
He'd ask them down to his place at Tooting.
'Twas told to me, etc.

In course of time there spread a rumour
That he did all this from a sense of humour,
So instead of signalling and stoking,
They gave themselves up to a course of joking.
Whenever they knew that he was riding,
They shunted his train on lonely siding,
Or stopped all night in the middle of a tunnel,
On the plea that the boiler was a-coming through the funnel.
'Twas told to me, etc.

If he wished to go to Perth or Stirling,
His train through several counties whirling,
Would set him down in a fit of larking,
At four a.m. in the wilds of Barking.
This pleased his whim and seemed to strike it,
But the general Public did not like it,
The receipts fell, after a few repeatings,
And he got it hot at the annual meetings,
'Twas told to me, etc.

He followed out his whim with vigour,
The shares went down to a nominal figure,
These are the sad results proceeding
From his affable ways and his easy breeding!
The line, with its rails and guards and peelers,
Was sold for a song to marine store dealers,
The shareholders are all in the work'us,
And he sells pipe-lights in the Regent Circus.
'Twas told to me with much compunction,
By one who had discharged with unction
A Chairman of Directors' function,

On the North South East West Diddlesex junction,
Fol diddle lol diddle lol lol lay!

[*After song.*

THES. It's very hard. As a man I am naturally of an easy disposition. As a manager, I am compelled to hold myself aloof, that my influence may not be deteriorated. As a man, I am inclined to fraternize with the pauper—as a manager I am compelled to walk about like this: Don't know yah! Don't know yah! Don't know yah!

[*Strides haughtily about the stage,* JUPITER, MARS, *and* APOLLO, *in full Olympian costume appear on the three broken columns. Thespians scream.*

JUPITER, MARS *and* APOLLO (*in recit.*). Presumptuous mortal!

THES. (*same business*). Don't know yah! Don't know yah!

JUP., MARS *and* APOLLO (*seated on three broken pillars, still in recit.*). Presumptuous mortal!

THES. I do not know you, I do not know you.

JUP., MARS *and* APOLLO (*standing on ground, recit.*). Presumptuous mortal!

THES. (*recit.*). Remove this person.

[STUP. *and* PREP. *seize* APOLL. *and* MARS.

JUP. (*speaking*). Stop, you evidently *don't* know me. Allow me to offer you my card. [*Throws flash paper.*

THES. Ah yes, it's very pretty, but we don't want any at present. When we do our Christmas piece I'll let you know. (*Changing his manner.*) Look here, you know, this is a private party and we haven't the pleasure of your acquaintance. There are a good many other mountains about, if you must have a mountain all to yourself. Don't make me let myself down before my company. (*Resuming.*) Don't know yah! Don't know yah!

JUP. I am Jupiter, the King of the Gods. This is Apollo. This is Mars. [*All kneel to them except* THESPIS.

THES. Oh! then as I'm a respectable man, and rather particular about the company I keep, I think I'll go.

JUP. No—no—stop a bit. We want to consult you on a matter of great importance. There! Now we are alone. Who are you?

THES. I am Thespis of the Thessalian Theatres.

JUP. The very man we want. Now as a judge of what the public likes, are you impressed with my appearance as the father of the gods?

THES. Well to be candid with you, I am not. In fact I'm disappointed.

JUP. Disappointed?

THES. Yes, you see you're so much out of repair. No, you don't come up to my idea of the part. Bless you, I've played you often.

JUP. You have!

THES. To be sure I have.

JUP. And how have you dressed the part?

THES. Fine commanding party in the prime of life. Thunderbolt—full beard—dignified manner—A good deal of this sort of thing "Don't know yah! Don't know yah! don't know yah!" [*Imitating, crosses* L.

JUP. (*much affected*). I—I'm very much obliged to you. It's very good of you. I—I—I used to be like that. I can't tell you how much I feel it. And do you find I'm an impressive character to play?

THES. Well no, I can't say you are. In fact we don't use you much out of burlesque.

JUP. Burlesque! [*Offended, walks up.*

THES. Yes, it's a painful subject, drop it, drop it. The fact is, you are not the gods you were—you're behind your age.

JUP. Well, but what are we to do? We feel that we ought to do something, but we don't know what.

THES. Why don't you all go down to Earth, incog., mingle with the world, hear and see what people think of you, and judge for yourselves as to the best means to take to restore your influence?

JUP. Ah, but what's to become of Olympus in the meantime?

THES. Lor bless you, don't distress yourself about that. I've a very good company, used to take long parts on the shortest notice. Invest us with your powers and we'll fill your places till you return.

JUP. (*aside*). The offer is tempting. But suppose you fail?

THES. Fail! Oh, we never fail in our profession. We've nothing but great successes!

JUP. Then it's a bargain?

THES. It's a bargain. [*They shake hands on it.*

JUP. And that you may not be entirely without assistance, we will leave you Mercury, and whenever you find yourself in a difficulty you can consult him.

Enter MERCURY (*trap* C.)

QUARTETTE

JUP. So that's arranged—you take my place, my boy,
While we make trial of a new existence.
At length I shall be able to enjoy
The pleasures I have envied from a distance.

MER. Compelled upon Olympus here to stop,
While other gods go down to play the hero,
Don't be surprised if on this mountain top
You find your Mercury is down at zero!

AP. To earth away to join in mortal acts,
And gather fresh materials to write on,
Investigate more closely several facts,
That I for centuries have thrown some light on!

DIAN. I, as the modest moon with crescent bow,
Have always shown a light to nightly scandal,
I must say I should like to go below,
And find out if the game is worth the candle!

Enter all the Thespians, summoned by MERCURY

MER. Here come your people!

THES. People better now!

AIR.—THESPIS

While mighty Jove goes down below
With all the other deities,
I fill his place and wear his "clo,"
The very part for me it is.
To mother earth to make a track,
They all are spurred and booted, too,
And you will fill, till they come back,
The parts you best are suited to.

CHORUS. Here's a pretty tale for future Iliads and Odysseys,
Mortals are about to personate the gods and goddesses.
Now to set the world in order, we will work in unity.
Jupiter's perplexity is Thespis's opportunity.

SOLO.—SPARKEON

Phœbus am I, with golden ray,
The god of day, the god of day,
When shadowy night has held her sway,
I make the goddess fly.
'Tis mine the task to wake the world,
In slumber curled, in slumber curled,
By me her charms are all unfurled,
The god of day am I!

CHORUS. The god of day, the god of day,
That part shall our Sparkeion play.
Ha! ha! &c.
The rarest fun and rarest fare,
That ever fell to mortal share!
Ha! ha! &c.

SOLO.—NICEMIS

I am the moon, the lamp of night.
I show a light—I show a light.
With radiant sheen I put to flight
The shadows of the sky.
By my fair rays, as you're aware,
Gay lovers swear—gay lovers swear,
While greybeards sleep away their care,
The lamp of night am I!

CHORUS. The lamp of night—the lamp of night,
Nicemis plays, to her delight.
Ha! ha! ha! ha!
The rarest fun and rarest fare,
That ever fell to mortal share.
Ha! ha! ha! ha!

SOLO.—TIMIDON

Mighty old Mars, the God of War,
I'm destined for—I'm destined for—
A terribly famous conqueror,
With sword upon his thigh.
When armies meet with eager shout,
And warlike rout, and warlike rout,
You'll find me there without a doubt.
The God of War am I!

CHORUS. The God of War, the God of War.
Great Timidon is destined for!
Ha! ha! ha! ha!
The rarest fun and rarest fare,
That ever fell to mortal share.
Ha! ha! ha! ha! &c.

SOLO.—DAPHNE

When, as the fruit of warlike deeds,
The soldier bleeds, the soldier bleeds,
Calliope crowns heroic deeds,
With immortality.
From mere oblivion I reclaim
The soldier's name, the soldier's name,
And write it on the roll of fame,
The muse of fame am I!

CHORUS. The muse of fame, the muse of fame,
Calliope is Daphne's name,
Ha! ha! ha! ha!
The rarest fun and rarest fare,
That ever fell to mortal share!
Ha! ha! ha! ha!

TUTTI. Here's a pretty tale!

Enter procession of old Gods, they come down very much astonished at all they see, then passing by, ascend the platform that leads to the descent at the back.

Gods (JUP., DIA., *and* APOLLO) *in corner are together.*

We will go,
Down below,
Revels rare,
We will share.
Ha! ha! ha!

With a gay
Holiday,
All unknown,
And alone.
Ha! ha! ha!

TUTTI. Here's a pretty tale!

[*The Gods, including those who have lately entered in procession, group themselves on rising ground at back. The Thespians (kneeling) bid them farewell.*

ACT II

SCENE.—*The same scene as in Act I with the exception that in place of the ruins that filled the foreground of the stage, the interior of a magnificent temple is seen, showing the background of the scene of Act I, through the columns of the portico at the back. High throne* L.U.E. *Low seats below it.*

All the substitute gods and goddesses (that is to say, Thespians) are discovered grouped in picturesque attitudes about the stage, eating, drinking, and smoking, and singing the following verses:—

CHORUS

Of all symposia,
The best by half,
Upon Olympus, here, await us,
We eat Ambrosia,
And nectar quaff—
It cheers but don't inebriate us.

We know the fallacies
 Of human food,
  So please to pass Olympian rosy,
We built up palaces,
 Where ruins stood,
  And find them much more snug and cosy.

SOLO—SILLIMON

To work and think, my dear,
 Up here, would be,
  The height of conscientious folly,
So eat and drink, my dear,
 I like to see,
  Young people gay—young people jolly.
Olympian food, my love,
 I'll lay long odds,
  Will please your lips—those rosy portals,
What is the good, my love
 Of being gods,
  If we must work like common mortals?

CHORUS. Of all symposia, &c.

[*Exeunt all but* NICEMIS, *who is dressed as* DIANA, *and* PRETTEIA, *who is dressed as* VENUS. *They take* SILLIMON'S *arm and bring him down.*

SILLIMON. Bless their little hearts, I can refuse them nothing. As the Olympian stage-manager I ought to be strict with them and make them do their duty, but I can't. Bless their little hearts, when I see the pretty little craft come sailing up to me with a wheedling smile on their pretty little figure-heads, I can't turn my back on 'em. I'm all bow, though I'm sure I try to be stern!

PRETT. You certainly are a dear old thing.

SILL. She says I'm a dear old thing! Deputy Venus says I'm a dear old thing!

NICE. It's her affectionate habit to describe everybody in those terms. *I* am more particular, but still even *I* am bound to admit that you are certainly a very dear old thing.

SILL. Deputy Venus says I'm a dear old thing, and

deputy Diana, who is much more particular, endorses it! Who could be severe with such deputy divinities?

PRETT. Do you know, I'm going to ask you a favour.

SILL. Venus is going to ask me a favour!

PRETT. You see, I am Venus.

SILL. No one who saw your face would doubt it.

NICE. (*aside*). No one who knew her *character* would.

PRETT. Well Venus, you know, is married to Mars.

SILL. To Vulcan, my dear, to Vulcan. The exact connubial relation of the different gods and goddesses is a point on which we must be extremely particular.

PRETT. I beg your pardon—Venus is married to Mars.

NICE. If she isn't married to Mars, she ought to be.

SILL. Then that decides it—call it married to Mars.

PRETT. Married to Vulcan or married to Mars, what does it signify?

SILL. My dear, it's a matter on which I have no personal feeling whatever.

PRETT. So that she is married to some one!

SILL. Exactly! so that she is married to some one. Call it married to Mars.

PRETT. Now here's my difficulty. Presumptios takes the place of Mars, and Presumptios is my father!

SILL. Then why object to Vulcan?

PRETT. Because Vulcan is my grandfather!

SILL. But, my dear, what an objection! You are playing a part till the real gods return. That's all! Whether you are supposed to be married to your father—or your grandfather, what does it matter? This passion for realism is the curse of the stage!

PRETT. That's all very well, but I can't throw myself into a part that has already lasted a twelvemonth, when I have to make love to my father. It interferes with my conception of the characters. It spoils the part.

SILL. Well, well, I'll see what can be done. (*Exit* PRETTEIA L.U.E.) That's always the way with beginners, they've no imaginative power. A true artist ought to be superior to such considerations. (NICEMIS *comes down* R.) Well, Nicemis—I should say Diana—what's wrong with you? Don't you like your part?

NICE. Oh, immensely! It's great fun.

SILL. Don't you find it lonely out by yourself all night?

NICE. Oh, but I'm *not* alone all night!

SILL. But—I don't want to ask any injudicious questions—but who accompanies you?

NICE. Who? why Sparkeion, of course.

SILL. Sparkeion? Well, but Sparkeion is Phœbus Apollo. (*Enter* SPARKEION) He's the Sun, you know.

NICE. Of course he is; I should catch my death of cold, in the night air, if he didn't accompany me.

SP. My dear Sillimon, it would never do for a young lady to be out alone all night. It wouldn't be respectable.

SILL. There's a good deal of truth in that. But still—the Sun—at night—I don't like the idea. The original Diana always went out alone.

NICE. I hope the original Diana is no rule for *me.* After all, what *does* it matter?

SILL. To be sure—what *does* it matter?

SP. The sun at night, or in the daytime!

SILL. So that he shines. That's all that's necessary. (*Exit* NICEMIS R.U.E.) But poor Daphne, what will she say to this?

SP. Oh, Daphne can console herself; young ladies soon get over this sort of thing. Did you never hear of the young lady who was engaged to Cousin Robin?

SILL. Never.

SP. Then I'll sing it to you.

SONG—SPARKEION

Little maid of Arcadee
Sat on Cousin Robin's knee,
Thought in form and face and limb,
Nobody could rival him.
He was brave and she was fair.
Truth, they made a pretty pair.
Happy little maiden, she—
Happy maid of Arcadee!

Moments fled as moments will
Happily enough, until,
After, say, a month or two,
Robin did as Robins do.

Weary of his lover's play,
Jilted her and went away.
Wretched little maiden, she—
Wretched maid of Arcadee!

To her little home she crept,
There she sat her down and wept,
Maiden wept as maidens will—
Grew so thin and pale—until
Cousin Richard came to woo!
Then again the roses grew!
Happy little maiden, she—
Happy maid of Arcadee!

[*Exit* SPARKEION.

SILL. Well, Mercury, my boy, you've had a year's experience of us here. How do we do it? I think we're rather an improvement on the original gods—don't you?

MER. Well, you see, there's a good deal to be said on both sides of the question; you are certainly younger than the original gods, and, therefore, more active. On the other hand, they are certainly older than you, and have, therefore, more experience. On the whole I prefer *you,* because your mistakes amuse me.

SONG.—MERCURY

Olympus is now in a terrible muddle,
 The deputy deities all are at fault;
They splutter and splash like a pig in a puddle,
 And dickens a one of 'em's earning his salt,
For Thespis as Jove is a terrible blunder,
 Too nervous and timid—too easy and weak—
Whenever he's called on to lighten or thunder,
 The thought of it keeps him awake for a week!

Then mighty Mars hasn't the pluck of a parrot,
 When left in the dark he will quiver and quail;
And Vulcan has arms that would snap like a carrot,
 Before he could drive in a tenpenny nail!
Then Venus's freckles are very repelling.
 And Venus should *not* have a squint in her eyes;
The learned Minerva is weak in her spelling,
 And scatters her h's all over the skies.

Then Pluto, in kindhearted tenderness erring,
  Can't make up his mind to let anyone die—
The *Times* has a paragraph ever recurring,
  "Remarkable instance of longevi*ty*."
On some it has come as a serious onus,
  To others it's quite an advantage—in short,
While ev'ry Life Office declares a big bonus,
  The poor undertakers are all in the court!

Then Cupid, the rascal, forgetting his trade is
  To make men and women impartially smart,
Will only shoot at pretty young ladies,
  And never takes aim at a bachelor's heart.
The results of this freak—or whatever you term it—
  Should cover the wicked young scamp with disgrace,
While ev'ry young man is as shy as a hermit,
  Young ladies are popping all over the place!

This wouldn't much matter—for bashful and shy men,
  When skilfully handled, are certain to fall,
But, alas! that determined young bachelor Hymen
  Refuses to wed anybody at all!
He swears that Love's flame is the vilest of arsons,
  And looks upon marriage as quite a mistake;
Now, what in the world's to become of the parsons,
  And what of the artist who sugars the cake?

In short, you will see from the facts that I'm showing,
  The state of the case is exceedingly sad;
If Thespis's people go on as they're going,
  Olympus will certainly go to the bad!
From Jupiter downwards there isn't a dab in it,
  All of 'em quibble and shuffle and shirk;
A premier in Downing Street, forming a Cabinet,
  Couldn't find people less fit for their work!

Enter THESPIS, L.U.E.

THES. Sillimon, you can retire.

SILL. Sir, I—

THES. Don't pretend you can't when I say you can. I've seen you do it—go! (*Exit* SILLIMON *bowing extravagantly,* THESPIS *imitates him.*) Well, Mercury, I've been in power one year to-day.

MER. One year to-day. How do you like ruling the world?

THES. Like it! Why it's as straightforward as possible. Why there hasn't been a hitch of any kind since we came up here. Lor! The airs you gods and goddesses give yourselves are perfectly sickening. Why it's mere child's play!

MER. Very simple, isn't it?

THES. Simple? Why I could do it on my head?

MER. Ah—I daresay you will do it on your head very soon.

THES. What do you mean by *that,* Mercury?

MER. I mean that when you've turned the world *quite* topsy-turvy you won't know whether you're standing on your head or your heels.

THES. Well, but, Mercury, it's all right at present.

MER. Oh yes—as far as we know.

THES. Well, but, you know, we know as much as anybody knows; you know, I believe, that the world's still going on.

MER. Yes—as far as we can judge—much as usual.

THES. Well, then, give the Father of the Drama his due, Mercury. Don't be envious of the Father of the Drama.

THES. Well, but you see you leave so much to accident.

MER. Well, Mercury, if I do, it's my principle. I am an easy man, and I like to make things as pleasant as possible. What did I do the day we took office? Why I called the company together and I said to them: "Here we are, you know, gods and goddesses, no mistake about it, the real thing. Well, we have certain duties to discharge, let's discharge them intelligently. Don't let us be hampered by routine and red tape and precedent, let's set the original gods an example, and put a liberal interpretation on our duties. If it occurs to any one to try an experiment in his own department, let him try it, if he fails there's no harm done, if he succeeds it is a distinct gain to society. Take it easy," I said, "and at the same time, make experiments. Don't hurry your work, do it slowly, and do it well." And here we are after a twelvemonth, and not a single complaint or a single petition has reached me.

MER. No—not yet.

THES. What do you mean by "no, not yet"?

MER. Well, you see, you don't understand these things. All the petitions that are addressed by men to Jupiter pass through my hands, and it's my duty to collect them and present them once a year.

THES. Oh, only once a year?

MER. Only once a year.

THES. And the year is up—?

MER. To-day.

THES. Oh, then I suppose there are *some* complaints?

MER. Yes, there *are some.*

THES (*disturbed*). Oh. Perhaps there are a good many?

MER. There are a good many.

THES. Oh. Perhaps there are a thundering lot?

MER. There are a thundering lot.

THES. (*very much disturbed*). Oh!

MER. You see you've been taking it so very easy—and so have most of your company.

THES. Oh, who has been taking it easy?

MER. Well, all except those who have been trying experiments.

THES. Well but I suppose the experiments are ingenious?

MER. Yes; they are ingenious, but on the whole ill-judged. But it's time to go and summon your court.

THES. What for?

MER. To hear the complaints. In five minutes they will be here. [*Exit.*

THES. (*very uneasy*). I don't know how it is, but there is something in that young man's manner that suggests that the Father of the Gods has been taking it *too* easy. Perhaps it would have been better if I hadn't given my company so much scope. I wonder what they've been doing. I think I will curtail their discretion, though none of them appear to have much of the article. It seems a pity to deprive 'em of what little they have.

Enter DAPHNE, *weeping.*

THES. Now then, Daphne, what's the matter with you?

DAPHNE. Well, you know how disgracefully Sparkeion——

THES. (*correcting her*). Apollo——

DAPHNE. Apollo, then—has treated me. He promised to marry me years ago, and now he's married to Nicemis.

THES. Now look here. I can't go into that. You're in Olympus now and must behave accordingly. Drop your Daphne—assume your Calliope.

DAP. Quite so. That's it! [*Mysteriously.*

THES. Oh—that is it? [*Puzzled.*

DAP. That is it, Thespis. I am Calliope, the Muse of Fame. Very good. This morning I was in the Olympian library, and I took down the only book there. Here it is.

THES. (*taking it*). Lemprière's Classical Dictionary. The Olympian Peerage.

DAP. Open it at Apollo.

THES. (*opens it*). It is done.

DAP. Read.

THES. "Apollo was several times married, among others to Issa, Bolina, Coronis, Chymene, Cyrene, Chione, Acacallis, and Calliope."

DAP. *And* Calliope.

THES. (*musing*). Ha! I didn't know he was *married* to them.

DAP. (*severely*). Sir! This is the Family Edition.

THES. Quite so.

DAP. You couldn't expect a lady to read any other?

THES. On no consideration. But in the original version——

DAP. I go by the Family Edition.

THES. Then by the Family Edition, Apollo is your husband.

Enter NICEMIS *and* SPARKEION.

NICE. Apollo your husband? He is my husband.

DAP. I beg your pardon. He is *my* husband.

NICE. Apollo is Sparkeion, and he's married to me.

DAP. Sparkeion is Apollo, and he's married to me.

NICE. He's my husband.

DAP. He's your brother.

THES. Look here, Apollo, whose husband are you? Don't let's have any row about it; whose husband are you?

SP. Upon my honour I don't know. I'm in a very delicate position, but I'll fall in with any arrangement Thespis may propose.

DAP. I've just found out that he's my husband, and yet he goes out every evening with that "thing"!

THES. Perhaps he's trying an experiment.

DAP. I don't like my husband to make such experiments. The question is, who are we all and what is our relation to each other.

QUARTETTE

SP. You're Diana, I'm Apollo—
And Calliope is she.
DAP. He's you're brother.
NICE. You're another.
He has fairly married me,
DAP. By the rules of this fair spot
I'm his wife, and you are not—
SP. *and* DAP. By the rules of this fair spot,
I'm / She's } his wife, and you are not.
NICE. By this golden wedding ring,
I'm his wife, and you're a "thing."
DAP., NICE. *and* SP. By this golden wedding ring,
I'm / She's } his wife, and you're a "thing."
ALL. Please will some one kindly tell us,
Who are our respective kin?
All of { us / them } are very jealous,
Neither of { us / them } will give in.
NICE. He's my husband I declare,
I espoused him properlee.
SP. That is true, for I was there,
And I saw her marry me.
DAP. He's you're brother—I'm his wife,
If we go by Lemprière,

SP. So she is, upon my life,
Really that seems very fair.
NICE. You're my husband and no other
SP. That is true enough I swear,
DAP. I'm his wife, and you're his brother,
SP. If we go by Lemprière.
NICE. It will surely be unfair,
To decide by Lemprière.
(*Crying.*)
DAP. I will surely be quite fair,
To decide by Lemprière,
SP. *and* THES. How you settle I don't care,
Leave it all to Lemprière.
(*Spoken.*) The Verdict.
As Sparkeion is Apollo
Up in this Olympian clime,
Why, Nicemis, it will follow,
He's *her* husband, for the time
—(*indicating* DAPHNE)
When Sparkeion turns to mortal,
Join once more the sons of men,
He may take *you* to his portal
(*indicating* NICEMIS)
He will be *your* husband then.
That oh that is my decision,
'Cording to my mental vision.
Put an end to all collision,
That oh that is my decision.
My decision—my decision,
ALL. That oh that is his decision,
His decision—his decision! &c.

[*Exeunt* THES., NICE., SPARK., *and* DAPHNE, SPARK. *with* DAPHNE, NICEMIS *weeping with* THESPIS.

Mysterious Music. Enter JUPITER, APOLLO, *and* MARS, *from below, at the back of stage. All wear cloaks as disguise and all are masked.*

RECIT

Oh rage and fury! Oh shame and sorrow!
We'll be resuming our ranks to-morrow,

Since from Olympus we have departed,
We've been distracted and brokenhearted,
Oh wicked Thespis! Oh villain scurvy;
Through him Olympus is topsy-turvy!
Compelled to silence to grin and bear it!
He's caused our sorrow, and he shall share it.
Where is the monster! Avenge his blunders,
He has awakened Olympian thunders.

Enter MERCURY

JUP. (*recit.*). Oh Monster!
AP. (*recit.*). Oh Monster!
MARS. (*recit.*). Oh Monster!

MER. (*in great terror*). Please sir, what have I done sir?

JUP. What did we leave you behind for?

MER. Please sir, that's the question I asked for when you went away.

JUP. Was it not that Thespis might consult you whenever he was in a difficulty?

MER. Well, here I've been, ready to be consulted, chockful of reliable information—running over with celestial maxims—advice gratis ten to four—after twelve ring the night bell in cases of emergency.

JUP. And hasn't he consulted you?

MER. Not he—he disagrees with me about everything.

JUP. He must have misunderstood me. I told him to consult you whenever he was in a fix.

MER. He must have thought you said *in*sult. Why whenever I opened my mouth he jumps down my throat. It isn't pleasant to have a fellow constantly jumping down your throat—especially when he always disagrees with you. It's just the sort of thing I can't digest.

JUP. (*in a rage*). Send him here, I'll talk to him.

Enter THESPIS. *He is much terrified*

JUP. (*recit.*). Oh Monster!
AP. (*recit.*). Oh Monster!
MARS (*recit.*) Oh Monster!

THESPIS *sings in great terror, which he endeavours to conceal.*

JUP. Well Sir, the year is up to-day.

AP. And a nice mess you've made of it.

MARS. You've deranged the whole scheme of society.

THES. (*aside*). There's going to be a row! (*Aloud and very familiarly.*) My dear boy—I do assure you——

JUP. (*in recit.*). Be respectful!

AP. (*in recit.*). Be respectful!

MARS (*in recit.*). Be respectful!

THES. I don't know what you allude to. With the exception of getting our scene-painter to "run up" this temple, because we found the ruins draughty, we haven't touched a thing.

JUP. (*in recit.*). Oh story teller!

AP. (*in recit.*). Oh story teller!

MARS. (*in recit.*). Oh story teller!

Enter THESPIANS

THES. My dear fellows, you're distressing yourselves unnecessarily. The court of Olympus is about to assemble to listen to the complaints of the year, if any. But there are none, or next to none. Let the Olympians assemble!

Enter THESPIANS

[THESPIS *takes chair.* JUP., AP. *and* MARS *sit below him.*

THES. Ladies and gentlemen. It seems that it is usual for the gods to assemble once a year to listen to mortal petitions. It doesn't seem to me to be a good plan, as work is liable to accumulate; but as I'm particularly anxious not to interfere with Olympian precedent, but to allow everything to go on as it has always been accustomed to go—why, we'll say no more about it. (*Aside.*) But how shall I account for your presence?

JUP. Say we are gentlemen of the press.

THES. That all our proceedings may be perfectly open and above-board I have communicated with the most influential members of the Athenian press, and I beg to introduce to your notice three of its most distinguished members. They bear marks emblematic of the anonymous character of modern journalism. (*Business of intro-*

duction. THESPIS *very uneasy.*) Now then, if you're all ready we will begin.

MER. (*brings tremendous bundles of petitions*). Here is the agenda.

THES. What's that. The petitions?

MER. Some of them. (*Opens one and reads.*) Ah, I thought there'd be a row about it.

THES. Why, what's wrong now?

MER. Why, it's been a foggy Friday in November for the last six months and the Athenians are tired of it.

THES. There's no pleasing some people. This craving for perpetual change is the curse of the country. Friday's a very nice day.

MER. So it is, but a Friday six months long!—it gets monotonous.

JUP., AP. *and* MARS (*in recit. rising*). It's perfectly ridiculous.

THES. (*calling them*). It shall be arranged. Cymon!

CYMON (*as Time with the usual attributes*). Sir!

THES. (*introducing him to* THREE GODS). Allow me—Father Time—rather young at present but even Time must have a beginning. In course of Time, Time will grow older. Now then, Father Time, what's this about a wet Friday in November for the last six months.

CYM. Well, the fact is, I've been trying an experiment. Seven days in the week is an awkward number. It can't be halved. Two's into seven won't go.

THES. (*tries it on his fingers*). Quite so—quite so.

CYM. So I abolished Saturday.

JUP., AP. *and* MARS. Oh but— [*Rising.*

THES. Do be quiet. He's a very intelligent young man and knows what he is about. So you abolished Saturday. And how did you find it answer?

CYM. Admirably.

THES. You hear? He found it answer admirably.

CYM. Yes, only Sunday refused to take its place.

THES. Sunday refused to take its place?

CYM. Sunday comes after Saturday—Sunday won't go on duty after Friday, Sunday's principles are very strict. That's where my experiment sticks.

THES. Well, but why November? come, why November?

CYM. December can't begin till November has finished. November can't finish because he's abolished Saturday. There again my experiment sticks.

THES. Well, but why wet? Come now, why wet?

CYM. Ah, that is your fault. You turned on the rain six months ago, and you forgot to turn it off again.

JUP., MARS *and* AP. (*rising—recitative*). Oh this is monstrous!

ALL. Order, order.

THES. Gentlemen, pray be seated. (*To the others.*) The liberty of the press, one can't help it. (*To the three gods.*) It is easily settled. Athens has had a wet Friday in November for the last six months. Let them have a blazing Tuesday in July for the next twelve.

JUP., MARS *and* AP. But——

ALL. Order, order.

THES. Now then, the next article.

MER. Here's a petition from the Peace Society. They complain that there are no more battles.

MARS (*springing up*). What!

THES. Quiet there! Good dog—soho; Timidon!

TIM. (*as* MARS). Here.

THES. What's this about there being no battles?

TIM. I've abolished battles; it's an experiment.

MARS (*springing up*). Oh come, I say——

THES. Quiet then! (*To* TIM.) Abolished battles?

TIM. Yes, you told us on taking office to remember two things, to try experiments and to take it easy. I found I couldn't take it easy while there are any battles to attend to, so I tried the experiment and abolished battles. And then I took it easy. The Peace Society ought to be very much obliged to me.

THES. Obliged to you! Why, confound it! since battles have been abolished war is universal.

TIM. War universal?

THES. To be sure it is! Now that nations can't fight, no two of 'em are on speaking terms. The dread of fighting was the only thing that kept them civil to each other. Let battles be restored and peace reign supreme.

MER. (*reads*). Here's a petition from the associated wine merchants of Mytilene.

THES. Well, what's wrong with the associated wine merchants of Mytilene? Are there no grapes this year?

MER. Plenty of grapes; more than usual.

THES. (*to the gods*). You observe, there is no deception; there are more than usual.

MER. There are plenty of grapes, only they are full of ginger beer.

THREE GODS. Oh, come I say.

[*Rising, they are put down by* THESPIS.

THES. Eh? what. (*Much alarmed.*) Bacchus?

TIPS. (*as* BACCHUS). Here!

THES. There seems to be something unusual with the grapes of Mytilene; they only grow ginger beer.

TIPS. And a very good thing too.

THES. It's very nice in its way, but it is not what one looks for from grapes.

TIPS. Beloved master, a week before we came up here, you insisted on my taking the pledge. By so doing you rescued me from my otherwise inevitable misery. I cannot express my thanks. Embrace me!

[*Attempts to embrace him.*

THES. Get out, don't be a fool. Look here, you know you're the god of wine.

TIPS. I am.

THES. (*very angry*). Well, do you consider it consistent with your duty as the god of wine to make the grapes yield nothing but ginger beer?

TIPS. Do you consider it consistent with my duty as a total abstainer to grow anything stronger than ginger beer?

THES. But your duty as the god of wine——

TIPS. In every respect in which my duty as the god of wine can be discharged consistently with my duty as a total abstainer, I will discharge it. But when the functions clash, everything must give way to the pledge. My preserver! [*Attempts to embrace him.*

THES. Don't be a confounded fool! This can be arranged. We can't give over the wine this year, but at least we can improve the ginger beer. Let all the ginger beer be extracted from it immediately.

JUP., MARS., AP. (*aside*). We can't stand this,
We can't stand this,
It's much too strong,
We can't stand this.
It would be wrong,
Extremely wrong,
If we stood this,
If we stand this,
If we stand this,
We can't stand this.

DAP., SPARK., NICE. Great Jove, this interference,
Is more than we can stand;
Of them make a clearance,
With your majestic hand.

JOVE. This cool audacity, it beats us hollow
(*removing mask*) I'm Jupiter!

MARS. I'm Mars!

AP. I'm Apollo!

Enter DIANA *and all the other gods and goddesses.*

ALL. (*kneeling with their foreheads on the ground*).
Jupiter, Mars and Apollo,
Have quitted the dwellings of men;
The other gods quickly will follow,
And what will become of us then.
Oh, pardon us, Jove and Apollo,
Pardon us, Jupiter, Mars;
Oh, see us in misery wallow,
Cursing our terrible stars.

Enter other gods.

CHORUS AND BALLET

ALL THE THESPIANS. Let us remain, we beg of you pleadingly!

THREE GODS. Let them remain, they beg of us pleadingly!

THES. Life on Olympus suits us exceedingly.

GODS. Life on Olympus suits them exceedingly.
THES. Let us remain, we pray in humility!
GODS. Let 'em remain, they pray in humility.
THES. If we have shown some little ability.
GODS. If they have shown some little ability.
Let us remain, etc.

JUPITER. Enough, your reign is ended;
Upon this sacred hill
Let him be apprehended,
And learn our awful will.
Away to earth, contemptible comedians,
And hear our curse, before we set you free;
You shall all be eminent tragedians,
Whom no one ever goes to see!

ALL. We go to earth, contemptible comedians,
We hear his curse before he sets us free,
We shall all be eminent tragedians,
Whom no one ever, ever goes to see!

SIL. Whom no one—
SP. Whom no one—
THES. Whom *no* one—
ALL. Ever, ever goes to see.

[*The Thespians are driven away by the gods, who group themselves in attitudes of triumph.*

THES. Now, here you see the arrant folly
Of doing your best to make things jolly.
I've ruled the world like a chap in his senses,
Observe the terrible consequences.
Great Jupiter, whom nothing pleases,
Splutters and swears, and kicks up breezes,
And sends us home in a mood avengin',
In double quick time, like a railroad engine.
And this he does without compunction,
Because I have discharged with unction
A highly complicated function,

Complying with his own injunction.
Fol, lol, lay.

CHORUS. All this he does, etc.

[*The gods drive the Thespians away. The Thespians prepare to descend the mountain as the curtain falls.*

TRIAL BY JURY

DRAMATIS PERSONÆ

THE LEARNED JUDGE

THE PLAINTIFF

THE DEFENDANT

COUNSEL FOR THE PLAINTIFF

USHER

FOREMAN OF THE JURY

ASSOCIATE

FIRST BRIDESMAID

First produced at the Royalty Theatre, March 25, 1875

TRIAL BY JURY

SCENE.—*A Court of Justice. Barristers, Attorneys, and Jurymen discovered.*

CHORUS

Hark, the hour of ten is sounding:
Hearts with anxious fears are bounding,
Hall of Justice crowds surrounding,
  Breathing hope and fear—
For to-day in this arena,
Summoned by a stern subpœna,
Edwin, sued by Angelina,
  Shortly will appear.

Enter USHER

SOLO—USHER

Now, Jurymen, hear my advice—
All kinds of vulgar prejudice
  I pray you set aside:
With stern judicial frame of mind

From bias free of every kind,
This trial must be tried.

CHORUS

From bias free of every kind,
This trial must be tried.

[*During Chorus,* USHER *sings fortissimo, "Silence in Court!"*

USHER. Oh, listen to the plaintiff's case:
Observe the features of her face—
The broken-hearted bride.
Condole with her distress of mind:
From bias free of every kind,
This trial must be tried!

CHORUS. From bias free, etc.

USHER. And when amid the plaintiff's shrieks,
The ruffianly defendant speaks—
Upon the other side;
What *he* may say you needn't mind—
From bias free of every kind,
This trial must be tried!

CHORUS. From bias free, etc.

Enter DEFENDANT

RECIT—DEFENDANT

Is this the Court of the Exchequer?
ALL. It is!
DEFENDANT (*aside*). Be firm, be firm, my pecker,
Your evil star's in the ascendant!
ALL. Who are you?
DEFENDANT. I'm the Defendant!

CHORUS OF JURYMEN (*shaking their fists*)

Monster, dread our damages.
We're the jury,
Dread our fury!

DEFENDANT. Hear me, hear me, if you please,
These are very strange proceedings—

For permit me to remark
  On the merits of my pleadings,
You're at present in the dark.

[DEFENDANT *beckons to* JURYMEN—*they leave the box and gather round him as they sing the following:*

That's a very true remark—
  On the merits of his pleadings
We're at present in the dark!
Ha! ha!—ha! ha!

SONG—DEFENDANT

When first my old, old love I knew,
  My bosom welled with joy;
My riches at her feet I threw—
  I was a love-sick boy!
No terms seemed too extravagant
  Upon her to employ—
I used to mope, and sigh, and pant,
  Just like a love-sick boy!
      Tink-a-Tank—Tink-a-Tank.

But joy incessant palls the sense;
  And love, unchanged, will cloy,
And she became a bore intense
  Unto her love-sick boy!

With fitful glimmer burnt my flame,
And I grew cold and coy,
At last, one morning, I became
Another's love-sick boy.
Tink-a-Tank—Tink-a-Tank.

CHORUS OF JURYMEN (*advancing stealthily*)

Oh, I was like that when a lad!
A shocking young scamp of a rover,
I behaved like a regular cad;
But that sort of thing is all over.
I'm now a respectable chap
And shine with a virtue resplendent
And, therefore, I haven't a scrap
Of sympathy with the defendant!
He shall treat us with awe,
If there isn't a flaw,
Singing so merrily—Trial-la-law!
Trial-la-law—Trial-la-law!
Singing so merrily—Trial-la-law!

[*They enter the Jury-box.*

RECIT—USHER (*on Bench*)

Silence in Court, and all attention lend.
Behold your Judge! In due submission bend!

Enter JUDGE *on Bench*

CHORUS

All hail great Judge!
To your bright rays
We never grudge
Ecstatic praise.
All hail!

May each decree
As statute rank
And never be
Reversed in banc.
All hail!

RECIT—JUDGE

For these kind words accept my thanks, I pray.
A Breach of Promise we've to try to-day.
But firstly, if the time you'll not begrudge,
I'll tell you how I came to be a Judge.

ALL. He'll tell us how he came to be a Judge!

SONG—JUDGE

When I, good friends, was called to the bar,
I'd an appetite fresh and hearty,
But I was, as many young barristers are,
An impecunious party.

I'd a swallow-tail coat of a beautiful blue—
A brief which I bought of a booby—
A couple of shirts and a collar or two,
And a ring that looked like a ruby!

CHORUS. A couple of shirts, etc.

JUDGE. In Westminster Hall I danced a dance,
Like a semi-despondent fury;
For I thought I should never hit on a chance
Of addressing a British Jury—
But I soon got tired of third-class journeys,
And dinners of bread and water;
So I fell in love with a rich attorney's
Elderly, ugly daughter.

CHORUS. So he fell in love, etc.

JUDGE. The rich attorney, he jumped with joy,
And replied to my fond professions:
"You shall reap the reward of your pluck, my boy
At the Bailey and Middlesex Sessions.
You'll soon get used to her looks," said he,
"And a very nice girl you'll find her!
She may very well pass for forty-three
In the dusk, with a light behind her!"

CHORUS. She may very well, etc.

JUDGE. The rich attorney was good as his word;
The briefs came trooping gaily,
And every day my voice was heard
At the Sessions or Ancient Bailey.
All thieves who could my fees afford
Relied on my orations,
And many a burglar I've restored
To his friends and his relations.

CHORUS. And many a burglar, etc.

JUDGE. At length I became as rich as the Gurneys—
An incubus then I thought her,
So I threw over that rich attorney's
Elderly, ugly daughter.
The rich attorney my character high
Tried vainly to disparage—
And now, if you please, I'm ready to try
This Breach of Promise of Marriage!

CHORUS. And now if you please, etc

JUDGE. For now I am a Judge!
ALL. And a good Judge too.
JUDGE. Yes, now I am a Judge!
ALL. And a good Judge too!
JUDGE. Though all my law is fudge,
Yet I'll never, never budge,
But I'll live and die a Judge!
ALL. And a good Judge too!
JUDGE (*pianissimo*). It was managed by a job—
ALL. And a good job too!
JUDGE. It was managed by a job!
ALL. And a good job too!
JUDGE. It is patent to the mob,
That my being made a nob
Was effected by a job.
ALL. And a good job too!

Enter COUNSEL *for* PLAINTIFF. *He takes his place in front row of Counsels' seats*

RECIT—COUNSEL

Swear thou the Jury!

USHER. Kneel, Jurymen, oh, kneel!

[*All the* JURY *kneel in the Jury-box, and so are hidden from audience.*

USHER. Oh, will you swear by yonder skies,
Whatever question may arise,
'Twixt rich and poor, 'twixt low and high,
That you will well and truly try?

JURY (*raising their hands, which alone are visible*)

To all of this we make reply
By the dull slate of yonder sky:
That we will well and truly try.

(*All rise with the last note*)

RECIT—COUNSEL

Where is the Plaintiff?
Let her now be brought.

RECIT—USHER

Oh, Angelina! Come thou into Court!
Angelina! Angelina!!

Enter the BRIDESMAIDS

CHORUS OF BRIDESMAIDS

Comes the broken flower—
Comes the cheated maid—
Though the tempest lower,
Rain and cloud will fade
Take, oh take these posies:
Though thy beauty rare
Shame the blushing roses,
They are passing fair!
Wear the flowers till they fade;
Happy be thy life, oh maid!

[*The* JUDGE, *having taken a great fancy to* FIRST BRIDESMAID, *sends her a note by* USHER, *which she reads, kisses rapturously, and places in her bosom.*

Enter PLAINTIFF

SOLO—PLAINTIFF

O'er the season vernal,
Time may cast a shade;
Sunshine, if eternal,
Makes the roses fade!
Time may do his duty;
Let the thief alone—
Winter hath a beauty,
That is all his own.
Fairest days are sun and shade:
I am no unhappy maid!

[*The* JUDGE *having by this time transferred his admiration to* PLAINTIFF, *directs the* USHER *to take the note from* FIRST BRIDESMAID *and hand it to* PLAINTIFF, *who reads it, kisses it rapturously, and places it in her bosom.*

CHORUS OF BRIDESMAIDS

Comes the broken flower, etc.

JUDGE. Oh, never, never, never, since I joined the
human race,
Saw I so exquisitely fair a face.

THE JURY (*shaking their forefingers at him*). Ah, sly dog! Ah, sly dog!

JUDGE (*to* JURY). How say you? Is she not designed for capture?

FOREMAN (*after consulting with the* JURY). We've but one word, my lord, and that is—Rapture.

PLAINTIFF (*curtseying*). Your kindness, gentleman, quite overpowers!

JURY. We love you fondly and would make you ours!

THE BRIDESMAIDS (*shaking their forefingers at* JURY)

Ah, sly dogs! Ah, sly dogs!

RECIT—COUNSEL *for* PLAINTIFF

May it please you, my lud!
Gentlemen of the jury!

ARIA

With a sense of deep emotion,
I approach this painful case;
For I never had a notion
That a man could be so base,
Or deceive a girl confiding,
Vows, *etcetera,* deriding.

ALL. He deceived a girl confiding,
Vows, *etcetera,* deriding.

[PLAINTIFF *falls sobbing on* COUNSEL'S *breast and remains there.*

COUNSEL. See my interesting client,
Victim of a heartless wile!
See the traitor all defiant
Wear a supercilious smile!
Sweetly smiled my client on him,
Coyly woo'd and gently won him.

ALL. Sweetly smiled, etc.

COUNSEL. Swiftly fled each honeyed hour
Spent with this unmanly male!
Camberwell became a bower,
Peckham an Arcadian Vale,
Breathing concentrated otto!—
An existence *à la* Watteau.

ALL. Bless, us, concentrated otto! etc.

COUNSEL. Picture, then, my client naming,
And insisting on the day:
Picture him excuses framing—
Going from her far away;
Doubly criminal to do so,
For the maid had bought her *trousseau!*

ALL. Doubly criminal, etc.

COUNSEL (*to* PLAINTIFF, *who weeps*)
Cheer up, my pretty—oh, cheer up!

JURY. Cheer up, cheer up, we love you!

[COUNSEL *leads* PLAINTIFF *fondly into Witness-box; he takes a tender leave of her, and resumes his place in Court.*

(PLAINTIFF *reels as if about to faint*)

JUDGE. That she is reeling
Is plain to see!

FOREMAN. If faint you're feeling
Recline on me!

[*She falls sobbing on to the* FOREMAN'S *breast.*

PLAINTIFF (*feebly*)
I shall recover
If left alone.

ALL (*shaking their fists at* DEFENDANT)

Oh, perjured lover,
Atone! atone!

FOREMAN. Just like a father
I wish to be. [*Kissing her.*

JUDGE (*approaching her*)
Or, if you'd rather,
Recline on me!

[*She jumps on to Bench, sits down by the* JUDGE, *and falls sobbing on his breast.*

COUNSEL. Oh! fetch some water
From far Cologne!

ALL. For this sad slaughter
Atone! atone!

JURY (*shaking fists at* DEFENDANT)
Monster, monster, dread our fury—
There's the Judge, and we're the Jury!
Come! Substantial damages,
Dam—

USHER. Silence in Court!

SONG—DEFENDANT

Oh, gentlemen, listen, I pray,
Though I own that my heart has been ranging,
Of nature the laws I obey,
For nature is constantly changing.
The moon in her phases is found,
The time and the wind and the weather,

The months in succession come round,
And you don't find two Mondays together.
Consider the moral, I pray,
Nor bring a young fellow to sorrow,
Who loves this young lady to-day,
And loves that young lady to-morrow.

BRIDESMAIDS (*rushing forward, and kneeling to* JURY)

Consider the moral, etc.
You cannot eat breakfast all day,
Nor is it the act of a sinner,
When breakfast is taken away,
To turn your attention to dinner;
And it's not in the range of belief,
That you could hold him as a glutton,
Who, when he is tired of beef,
Determines to tackle the mutton.
But this I am willing to say,
If it will appease her sorrow,
I'll marry this lady to-day,
And I'll marry that lady to-morrow!

BRIDESMAIDS (*rushing forward as before*)

But this he is willing to say, etc.

RECIT—JUDGE

That seems a reasonable proposition,
To which, I think, your client may agree.

COUNSEL

But, I submit, my lord, with all submission,
To marry two at once is Burglaree!
[*Referring to law book.*
In the reign of James the Second,
It was generally reckoned
As a very serious crime
To marry two wives at one time.
[*Hands book up to* JUDGE, *who reads it.*

ALL. Oh, man of learning!

QUARTETTE

JUDGE. A nice dilemma we have here,
That calls for all our wit:

COUNSEL. And at this stage, it don't appear
That we can settle it.

DEFENDANT (*in Witness-box*)
If I to wed the girl am loth
A breach 'twill surely be—

PLAINTIFF. And if he goes and marries both,
It counts as Burglaree!

ALL. A nice dilemma, etc.

DUET—PLAINTIFF *and* DEFENDANT

PLAINTIFF (*embracing him rapturously*)

I love him—I love him—with fervour unceasing
I worship and madly adore;
My blind adoration is always increasing,
My loss I shall ever deplore.
Oh, see what a blessing, what love and caressing
I've lost, and remember it, pray,
When you I'm addressing, are busy assessing
The damages Edwin must pay!

DEFENDANT (*repelling her furiously*)

I smoke like a furnace—I'm always in liquor,
  A ruffian—a bully—a sot;
I'm sure I should thrash her, perhaps I should kick her,
  I am such a very bad lot!
I'm not prepossessing, as you may be guessing,
  She couldn't endure me a day;
Recall my professing, when you are assessing
  The damages Edwin must pay!

[*She clings to him passionately; after a struggle, he throws her off into arms of* COUNSEL.

JURY. We would be fairly acting,
  But this is most distracting!

RECIT—JUDGE

The question, gentlemen—is one of liquor;
  You ask for guidance—this is my reply:
He says, when tipsy, he would thrash and kick her,
  Let's make him tipsy, gentlemen, and try!

COUNSEL. With all respect
  I do object!

PLAINTIFF. I do object!

DEFENDANT. I don't object!

ALL. With all respect
  We do object!

JUDGE (*tossing his books and papers about*)

All the legal furies seize you!
No proposal seems to please you,
I can't stop up here all day,
I must shortly go away.
Barristers, and you, attorneys,
Set out on your homeward journeys;
Gentle, simple-minded Usher,
Get you, if you like, to Russ*her;*
Put your briefs upon the shelf,
I will marry her myself!

[*He comes down from Bench to floor of Court. He embraces* ANGELINA.

FINALE

PLAINTIFF. Oh, joy unbounded,
With wealth surrounded,
The knell is sounded
Of grief and woe.

COUNSEL. With love devoted
On you he's doated
To castle moated
Away they go.

DEFENDANT. I wonder whether
They'll live together
In marriage tether
In manner true?

USHER. It seems to me, sir,
Of such as she, sir,
A judge is he, sir,
And a good judge too.

JUDGE. Yes, I am a Judge.

ALL. And a good Judge too!

JUDGE. Yes, I am a Judge.

ALL. And a good Judge too!

JUDGE. Though homeward as you trudge,
You declare my law is fudge.
Yet of beauty I'm a judge.

ALL. And a good Judge too!

CURTAIN

THE SORCERER

DRAMATIS PERSONÆ

SIR MARMADUKE POINTDEXTRE, *an Elderly Baronet*

ALEXIS, *of the Grenadier Guards—his Son*

DR. DALY, *Vicar of Ploverleigh*

NOTARY

JOHN WELLINGTON WELLS, *of J. W. Wells & Co., Family Sorcerers*

LADY SANGAZURE, *a Lady of Ancient Lineage*

ALINE, *her Daughter—betrothed to Alexis*

MRS. PARTLET, *a Pew-opener*

CONSTANCE, *her Daughter*

Chorus of Villagers

ACT I

EXTERIOR OF SIR MARMADUKE'S MANSION. MID-DAY

(*Twelve hours are supposed to elapse between Acts I and II*)

ACT II

EXTERIOR OF SIR MARMADUKE'S MANSION. MIDNIGHT

First produced at the Opéra Comique on November 17, 1877

THE SORCERER

ACT I

SCENE.—*Exterior of* SIR MARMADUKE'S *Elizabethan Mansion.*

CHORUS OF VILLAGERS

Ring forth, ye bells,
With clarion sound—
Forget your knells,
For joys abound.
Forget your notes
Of mournful lay,
And from your throats
Pour joy to-day.

For to-day young Alexis—young Alexis Pointdextre
Is betrothed to Aline—to Aline Sangazure,
And that pride of his sex is—of his sex is to be next her,
At the feast on the green—on the green, oh, be sure!

Ring forth, ye bells, etc.

[*Exeunt the men into house.*

Enter MRS. PARTLET *with* CONSTANCE, *her daughter*

RECITATIVE

MRS. P. Constance, my daughter, why this strange depression?
The village rings with seasonable joy,
Because the young and amiable Alexis,
Heir to the great Sir Marmaduke Pointdextre,
Is plighted to Aline, the only daughter
Of Annabella, Lady Sangazure.
You, you alone are sad and out of spirits;
What is the reason? Speak, my daughter, speak!

CON. Oh, mother, do not ask! If my complexion
From red to white should change in quick succession,
And then from white to red, oh, take no notice!
If my poor limbs should tremble with emotion,
Pay no attention, mother—it is nothing!
If long and deep-drawn sighs I chance to utter,
Oh, heed them not, their cause must ne'er be known!

[MRS. PARTLET *motions to* CHORUS *to leave her with* CONSTANCE. *Exeunt Ladies of* CHORUS.

ARIA—CONSTANCE

When he is here,
I sigh with pleasure—
When he is gone,
I sigh with grief.
My hopeless fear
No soul can measure—
His love alone
Can give my aching heart relief!

When he is cold,
I weep for sorrow—
When he is kind,
I weep for joy.
My grief untold
Knows no to-morrow—
My woe can find
No hope, no solace, no alloy!

MRS. P. Come, tell me all about it! Do not fear—
I, too, have loved; but that was long ago!
Who is the object of your young affections?
CON. Hush, mother! He is here!

Enter DR. DALY. *He is pensive and does not see them*

MRS. P. (*amazed*). Our reverend vicar!
CON. Oh, pity me, my heart is almost broken!

MRS. P. My child, be comforted. To such an union
I shall not offer any opposition.
Take him—he's yours! May you and he be happy!

CON. But, mother dear, he is not yours to give!

MRS. P. That's true, indeed!

CON. He might object!

MRS. P. He might.
But come—take heart—I'll probe him on the subject.
Be comforted—leave this affair to me.

RECITATIVE—DR. DALY

The air is charged with amatory numbers—
Soft madrigals, and dreamy lovers' lays.
Peace, peace, old heart! Why waken from its slumbers
The aching memory of the old, old days?

BALLAD

Time was when Love and I were well acquainted.
Time was when we walked ever hand in hand.

A saintly youth, with worldly thought untainted,
  None better-loved than I in all the land!
Time was, when maidens of the noblest station,
  Forsaking even military men,
Would gaze upon me, rapt in adoration—
  Ah me, I was a fair young curate then!

Had I a headache? sighed the maids assembled;
  Had I a cold? welled forth the silent tear;
Did I look pale? then half a parish trembled;
  And when I coughed all thought the end was near!
I had no care—no jealous doubts hung o'er me—
  For I was loved beyond all other men.
Fled gilded dukes and belted earls before me—
  Ah me, I was a pale young curate then!

[*At the conclusion of the ballad,* MRS. PARTLET *comes forward with* CONSTANCE.

MRS. P. Good day, reverend sir.

DR. D. Ah, good Mrs. Partlet, I am glad to see you. And your little daughter, Constance! Why, she is quite a little woman, I declare!

CON. (*aside*). Oh, mother, I cannot speak to him!

MRS. P. Yes, reverend sir, she is nearly eighteen, and

as good as girl as ever stepped. (*Aside to* DR. D.). Ah, sir, I'm afraid I shall soon lose her!

DR. D. (*aside to* MRS. P.). Dear me, you pain me very much. Is she delicate?

MRS. P. Oh no, sir—I don't mean that—but young girls look to get married.

DR. D. Oh, I take you. To be sure. But there's plenty of time for that. Four or five years hence, Mrs. Partlet, four or five years hence. But when the time *does* come, I shall have much pleasure in marrying her myself—

CON. (*aside*). Oh, mother!

DR. D. To some strapping young fellow in her own rank of life.

CON. (*in tears*). He does *not* love me!

MRS. P. I have often wondered, reverend sir (if you'll excuse the liberty), that *you* have never married.

DR. D. (*aside*). Be still, my fluttering heart!

MRS. P. A clergyman's wife does so much good in a village. Besides that, you are not as young as you were, and before very long you will want somebody to nurse you, and look after your little comforts.

DR. D. Mrs. Partlet, there is much truth in what you say. I am indeed getting on in years, and a helpmate would cheer my declining days. Time was when it might have been; but I have left it too long—I am an old fogy, now, am I not, my dear? (*to* CONSTANCE)—a very old fogy, indeed. Ha! ha! No, Mrs. Partlet, my mind is quite made up. I shall live and die a solitary old bachelor.

CON. Oh, mother, mother! (*Sobs on* MRS. PARTLET'S *bosom.*)

MRS. P. Come, come, dear one, don't fret. At a more fitting time we will try again—we will try again.

[*Exeunt* MRS. PARTLET *and* CONSTANCE.

DR. D. (*looking after them*). Poor little girl! I'm afraid she has something on her mind. She is rather comely. Time was when this old heart would have throbbed in double-time at the sight of such a fairy form! But tush! I am puling! Here comes the young Alexis with his proud and happy father. Let me dry this tell-tale tear!

Enter SIR MARMADUKE *and* ALEXIS

RECITATIVE

DR. D. Sir Marmaduke—my dear young friend, Alexis—
On this most happy, most auspicious plighting—
Permit me, as a true old friend, to tender
My best, my very best congratulations!

SIR M. Sir, you are most obleeging!

ALEXIS. Dr. Daly,
My dear old tutor, and my valued pastor,
I thank you from the bottom of my heart!

(*Spoken through music.*)

DR. D. May fortune bless you! may the middle distance
Of your young life be pleasant as the foreground—
The joyous foreground! and, when you have reached it,
May that which now is the far-off horizon
(But which will then become the middle distance),
In fruitful promise be exceeded only
By that which will have opened, in the meantime,
Into a new and glorious horizon!

SIR. M. Dear Sir, that is an excellent example
Of an old school of stately compliment
To which I have, through life, been much addicted.
Will you obleege me with a copy of it,
In clerkly manuscript, that I myself
May use it on appropriate occasions?

DR. D. Sir, you shall have a fairly-written copy
Ere Sol has sunk into his western slumbers!

[*Exit* DR. DALY.

SIR M. (*to* ALEXIS, *who is in a reverie*). Come, come,

my son—your *fiancée* will be here in five minutes. Rouse yourself to receive her.

ALEXIS. Oh rapture!

SIR M. Yes, you are a fortunate young fellow, and I will not disguise from you that this union with the House of Sangazure realizes my fondest wishes. Aline is rich, and she comes of a sufficiently old family, for she is the seven thousand and thirty-seventh in direct descent from Helen of Troy. True, there was a blot on the escutcheon of that lady—that affair with Paris—but where is the family, other than my own, in which there is no flaw? You are a lucky fellow, sir—a very lucky fellow!

ALEXIS. Father, I am welling over with limpid joy! No sicklying taint of sorrow overlies the lucid lake of liquid love, upon which, hand in hand, Aline and I are to float into eternity!

SIR M. Alexis, I desire that of your love for this young lady you do not speak so openly. You are always singing ballads in praise of her beauty, and you expect the very menials who wait behind your chair, to chorus your ecstasies. It is not delicate.

ALEXIS. Father, a man who loves as I love—

SIR. M. Pooh pooh, sir! fifty years ago I madly loved your future mother-in-law, the Lady Sangazure, and I have reason to believe that she returned my love. But were we guilty of the indelicacy of publicly rushing into each other's arms, exclaiming—

"Oh, my adored one!" "Beloved boy!"
"Ecstatic rapture!" "Unmingled joy!"

which seems to be the modern fashion of love-making? No! it was "Madam, I trust you are in the enjoyment of good health"—"Sir, you are vastly polite, I protest I am mighty well"—and so forth. Much more delicate—much more respectful. But see—Aline approaches—let us retire, that she may compose herself for the interesting ceremony in which she is to play so important a part.

[*Exeunt* SIR MARMADUKE *and* ALEXIS.

Enter ALINE, *on terrace, preceded by Chorus of Girls*

CHORUS OF GIRLS

With heart and with voice
  Let us welcome this mating:
To the youth of her choice,
  With a heart palpitating,
    Comes the lovely Aline!

May their love never cloy!
  May their bliss be unbounded!
With a halo of joy
  May their lives be surrounded!
    Heaven bless our Aline!

RECITATIVE—ALINE

My kindly friends, I thank you for this greeting,
And as you wish me every earthly joy,
I trust your wishes may have quick fulfilment!

ARIA—ALINE

Oh, happy young heart!
  Comes thy young lord a-wooing
With joy in his eyes,
  And pride in his breast—
Make much of thy prize,
  For he is the best
That ever came a-suing.
  Yet—yet we must part,
    Young heart!
  Yet—yet we must part!

Oh, merry young heart,
  Bright are the days of thy wooing!
But happier far
  The days untried—
No sorrow can mar,
  When Love has tied
The knot there's no undoing.
  Then, never to part,
    Young heart!
  Then, never to part!

Enter LADY SANGAZURE

RECITATIVE—LADY S

My child, I join in these congratulations:
Heed not the tear that dims this aged eye!
Old memories crowd upon me. Though I sorrow,
'Tis for myself, Aline, and not for thee!

Enter ALEXIS, *preceded by Chorus of Men*

CHORUS OF MEN AND WOMEN

With heart and with voice
Let us welcome this mating;
To the maid of his choice,
With a heart palpitating,
Comes Alexis the brave!

SIR MARMADUKE *enters.* LADY SANGAZURE *and he exhibit signs of strong emotion at the sight of each other, which they endeavour to repress.* ALEXIS *and* ALINE *rush into each other's arms.*

RECITATIVE

ALEXIS. Oh, my adored one!

ALINE. Beloved boy!

ALEXIS. Ecstatic rapture!

ALINE. Unmingled joy!

[*They retire up.*

DUET—SIR MARMADUKE *and* LADY SANGAZURE

SIR. M. (*with stately courtesy*)
Welcome joy, adieu to sadness!
As Aurora gilds the day,
So those eyes, twin orbs of gladness,
Chase the clouds of care away.
Irresistible incentive
Bids me humbly kiss your hand;
I'm your servant most attentive—
Most attentive to command!

(*Aside with frantic vehemence*)
Wild with adoration!
Mad with fascination!
To indulge my lamentation
No occasion do I miss!
Goaded to distraction
By maddening inaction,
I find some satisfaction
In apostrophe like this:
"Sangazure immortal,
"Sangazure divine,
"Welcome to my portal,
"Angel, oh be mine!"

(*Aloud with much ceremony*)
Irresistible incentive
Bids me humbly kiss your hand;
I'm your servant most attentive—
Most attentive to command!

LADY S. Sir, I thank you most politely
For your graceful courtesee;
Compliment more true and knightly
Never yet was paid to me!
Chivalry is an ingredient
Sadly lacking in our land—
Sir, I am your most obedient,
Most obedient to command!

(*Aside with great vehemence*)
Wild with adoration!
Mad with fascination!
To indulge my lamentation
No occasion do I miss!
Goaded to distraction
By maddening inaction,
I find some satisfaction
In apostrophe like this:
"Marmaduke immortal,
"Marmaduke divine,
"Take me to thy portal,
"Loved one, oh be mine!"

(*Aloud with much ceremony*)
Chivalry is an ingredient
Sadly lacking in our land;
Sir, I am your most obedient,
Most obedient to command!

[*During this the* NOTARY *has entered, with marriage contract.*

RECIT—NOTARY

All is prepared for sealing and for signing,
The contract has been drafted as agreed;
Approach the table, oh, ye lovers pining,
With hand and seal come execute the deed!

[ALEXIS *and* ALINE *advance and sign,* ALEXIS *supported by* SIR MARMADUKE, ALINE *by her Mother.*

CHORUS

See they sign, without a quiver, it—
Then to seal proceed.
They deliver it—they deliver it
As their Act and Deed!
ALEXIS. I deliver it—I deliver it
As my Act and Deed!
ALINE. I deliver it—I deliver it
As my Act and Deed!

CHORUS

With heart and with voice
Let us welcome this mating;
Leave them here to rejoice,
With true love palpitating,
Alexis the brave,
And the lovely Aline!

[*Exeunt all but* ALEXIS *and* ALINE.

ALEXIS. At last we are alone! My darling, you are now irrevocably betrothed to me. Are you not very, very happy?

ALINE. Oh, Alexis, can you doubt it? Do I not love

you beyond all on earth, and am I not beloved in return? Is not true love, faithfully given and faithfully returned, the source of every earthly joy?

ALEXIS. Of that there can be no doubt. Oh, that the world could be persuaded of the truth of that maxim! Oh, that the world would break down the artificial barriers of rank, wealth, education, age, beauty, habits, taste, and temper, and recognise the glorious principle, that in marriage alone is to be found the panacea for every ill!

ALINE. Continue to preach that sweet doctrine, and you will succeed, oh, evangel of true happiness!

ALEXIS. I hope so, but as yet the cause progresses but slowly. Still I have made some converts to the principle, that men and women should be coupled in matrimony without distinction of rank. I have lectured on the subject at Mechanics' Institutes, and the mechanics were unanimous in favour of my views. I have preached in workhouses, beershops and Lunatic Asylums, and I have been received with enthusiasm. I have addressed navvies on the advantages that would accrue to them if they married wealthy ladies of rank, and not a navvy dissented!

ALINE. Noble fellows! And yet there are those who hold that the uneducated classes are not open to argument! And what do the countesses say?

ALEXIS. Why, at present, it can't be denied, the aristocracy hold aloof.

ALINE. Ah, the working man is the true Intelligence after all!

ALEXIS. He is a noble creature when he is quite sober. Yes, Aline, true happiness comes of true love, and true love should be independent of external influences. It should live upon itself and by itself—in itself love should live for love alone!

BALLAD—ALEXIS

Love feeds on many kinds of food, I know,
Some love for rank, and some for duty:
Some give their hearts away for empty show,
And others love for youth and beauty.

To love for money all the world is prone:
Some love themselves, and live all lonely:
Give me the love that loves for love alone—
I love that love—I love it only!

What man for any other joy can thirst,
Whose loving wife adores him duly?
Want, misery, and care may do their worst,
If loving woman loves you truly.
A lover's thoughts are ever with his own—
None truly loved is ever lonely:
Give me the love that loves for love alone—
I love that love—I love it only!

ALINE. Oh, Alexis, those are noble principles!

ALEXIS. Yes, Aline, and I am going to take a desperate step in support of them. Have you ever heard of the firm of J. W. Wells & Co., the old-established Family Sorcerers in St. Mary Axe?

ALINE. I have seen their advertisement.

ALEXIS. They have invented a philtre, which, if report may be believed, is simply infallible. I intend to distribute it through the village, and within half an hour of my doing so there will not be an adult in the place who will not have learnt the secret of pure and lasting happiness. What do you say to that?

ALINE. Well, dear, of course a filter is a very useful thing in a house; but still I don't quite see that it is the sort of thing that places its possessor on the very pinnacle of earthly joy.

ALEXIS. Aline, you misunderstand me. I didn't say a filter—I said a philtre.

ALINE (*alarmed*). You don't mean a love-potion?

ALEXIS. On the contrary—I *do* mean a love-potion.

ALINE. Oh, Alexis! I don't think it would be right. I don't indeed. And then—a real magician! Oh, it would be downright wicked.

ALEXIS. Aline, is it, or is it not, a laudable object to steep the whole village up to its lips in love, and to couple them in matrimony without distinction of age, rank, or fortune?

ALINE. Unquestionably, but—

ALEXIS. Then unpleasant as it must be to have recourse to supernatural aid, I must nevertheless pocket my aversion, in deference to the great and good end I have in view. (*Calling*) Hercules.

Enter a PAGE *from tent*

PAGE. Yes, sir.

ALEXIS. Is Mr. Wells there?

PAGE. He's in the tent, sir—refreshing.

ALEXIS. Ask him to be so good as to step this way.

PAGE. Yes, sir. [*Exit* PAGE

ALINE. Oh, but, Alexis! A real Sorcerer! Oh, I shall be frightened to death!

ALEXIS. I trust my Aline will not yield to fear while the strong right arm of her Alexis is here to protect her.

ALINE. It's nonsense, dear, to talk of your protecting me with your strong right arm, in face of the fact that this Family Sorcerer could change me into a guinea-pig before you could turn round.

ALEXIS. He *could* change you into a guinea-pig, no doubt, but it is most unlikely that he would take such a liberty. It's a most respectable firm, and I am sure he would never be guilty of so untradesmanlike an act.

Enter MR. WELLS *from tent*

MR. W. Good day, sir. (ALINE *much terrified*)

ALEXIS. Good day—I believe you are a Sorcerer.

MR. W. Yes, sir, we practise Necromancy in all its branches. We've a choice assortment of wishing-caps, divining-rods, amulets, charms, and counter-charms. We can cast you a nativity at a low figure, and we have a horoscope at three-and-six that we can guarantee. Our Abudah chests, each containing a patent Hag who comes out and prophesies disasters, with spring complete, are strongly recommended. Our Aladdin lamps are very chaste, and our Prophetic Tablets, foretelling everything —from a change of Ministry down to a rise in Unified— are much enquired for. Our penny Curse—one of the cheapest things in the trade—is considered infallible. We have some very superior Blessings, too, but they're very little asked for. We've only sold one since Christmas—to a gentleman who bought it to send to his mother-in-law—but it turned out that he was afflicted in the head, and it's been returned on our hands. But our sale of penny Curses, especially on Saturday nights, is tremendous. We can't turn 'em out fast enough.

SONG—MR. WELLS

Oh! my name is John Wellington Wells,
I'm a dealer in magic and spells,
    In blessings and curses
    And ever-filled purses,
In prophecies, witches, and knells.

If you want a proud foe to "make tracks"—
If you'd melt a rich uncle in wax—

You've but to look in
On our resident Djinn,
Number seventy, Simmery Axe!

We've a first-class assortment of magic;
And for raising a posthumous shade
With effects that are comic or tragic,
There's no cheaper house in the trade.
Love-philtre—we've quantities of it;
And for knowledge if any one burns,
We keep an extremely small prophet, a prophet
Who brings us unbounded returns:

For he can prophesy
With a wink *of* his eye,
Peep with security
Into futurity,
Sum up your history,
Clear up a mystery,
Humour proclivity
For a nativity—for a nativity;
With mirrors so magical,
Tetrapods tragical,
Bogies spectacular,
Answers oracular,
Facts astronomical,
Solemn or comical,
And, if you want it, he
Makes a reduction on taking a quantity!
Oh!

If any one anything lacks,
He'll find it all ready in stacks,
If he'll only look in
On the resident Djinn,
Number seventy, Simmery Axe!

He can raise you hosts
Of ghosts,
And that without reflectors;
And creepy things
With wings,
And gaunt and grisly spectres.

He can fill you crowds
Of shrouds,
And horrify you vastly;
He can rack your brains
With chains,
And gibberings grim and ghastly!

Then, if you plan it, he
Changes organity,
With an urbanity,
Full of Satanity,
Vexes humanity
With an inanity
Fatal to vanity—
Driving your foes to the verge of insanity!

Barring tautology,
In demonology,
'Lectro-biology,
Mystic nosology,
Spirit philology,
High-class astrology,
Such is his knowledge, he
Isn't the man to require an apology!

Oh!
My name is John Wellington Wells,
I'm a dealer in magic and spells,
In blessings and curses
And ever-filled purses,
In prophecies, witches, and knells.

If any one anything lacks,
He'll find it all ready in stacks,
If he'll only look in
On the resident Djinn,
Number seventy, Simmery Axe!

ALEXIS. I have sent for you to consult you on a very important matter. I believe you advertise a Patent Oxy-Hydrogen Love-at-first-sight Philtre?

MR. W. Sir, it is our leading article. (*Producing a phial.*)

ALEXIS. Now I want to know if you can confidently guarantee it as possessing all the qualities you claim for it in your advertisement?

MR. W. Sir, we are not in the habit of puffing our goods. Ours is an old-established house with a large family connection, and every assurance held out in the advertisement is fully realised. (*Hurt.*)

ALINE (*aside*). Oh, Alexis, don't offend him! He'll change us into something dreadful—I know he will!

ALEXIS. I am anxious from purely philanthropical motives to distribute this philtre, secretly, among the inhabitants of this village. I shall of course require a quantity. How do you sell it?

MR. W. In buying a quantity, sir, we should strongly advise you taking it in the wood, and drawing it off as you happen to want it. We have it in four-and-a-half and nine gallon casks—also in pipes and hogsheads for laying down, and we deduct 10 per cent for prompt cash.

ALEXIS. I should mention that I am a Member of the Army and Navy Stores.

MR. W. In that case we deduct 25 per cent.

ALEXIS. Aline, the villagers will assemble to carouse in a few minutes. Go and fetch the tea-pot.

ALINE. But, Alexis—

ALEXIS. My dear, you must obey me, if you please. Go and fetch the tea-pot.

ALINE (*going*). I'm sure Dr. Daly would disapprove of it. [*Exit* ALINE.

ALEXIS. And how soon does it take effect?

MR. W. In twelve hours. Whoever drinks of it loses consciousness for that period, and on waking falls in love, as a matter of course, with the first lady he meets who has also tasted it, and his affection is at once returned. One trial will prove the fact.

Enter ALINE *with large tea-pot*

ALEXIS. Good: then, Mr. Wells, I shall feel obliged if you will at once pour as much philtre into this tea-pot as will suffice to affect the whole village.

ALINE. But bless me, Alexis, many of the villagers are married people!

MR. W. Madam, this philtre is compounded on the strictest principles. On married people it has no effect whatever. But are you quite sure that you have nerve enough to carry you through the fearful ordeal?

ALEXIS. In the good cause I fear nothing.

MR. W. Very good, then, we will proceed at once to the Incantation.

(*The stage grows dark.*)

INCANTATION

MR. W. Sprites of earth and air—
Fiends of flame and fire—
Demon souls,
Come here in shoals,
This dreadful deed inspire!
Appear, appear, appear.

MALE VOICES. Good master, we are here!

MR. W. Noisome hags of night—
Imps of deadly shade—
Pallid ghosts,
Arise in hosts,
And lend me all your aid.
Appear, appear, appear!

FEMALE VOICES. Good master, we are here!

ALEXIS (*aside*). Hark, they assemble,
These fiends of the night!

ALINE (*aside*). Oh, Alexis, I tremble,
Seek safety in flight!

ARIA—ALINE

Let us fly to a far-off land,
Where peace and plenty dwell—
Where the sigh of the silver strand
Is echoed in every shell
To the joy that land will give,
On the wings of Love we'll fly;
In innocence there to live—
In innocence there to die!

CHORUS OF SPIRITS

Too late—too late
It may not be!
That happy fate
Is not for thee!

ALEXIS, ALINE, *and* MR. WELLS

Too late—too late,
That may not be!
That happy fate
Is not for { me! / thee! }

MR. WELLS

Now shrivelled hags, with poison bags,
Discharge your loathsome loads!
Spit flame and fire, unholy choir!
Belch forth your venom, toads!
Ye demons fell, with yelp and yell,
Shed curses far afield—
Ye fiends of night, your filthy blight
In noisome plenty yield!

MR. WELLS (*pouring phial into tea-pot—flash*).
Number One!
CHORUS. It is done!
MR. W. (*same business*). Number Two! (*flash*).
CHORUS. One too few!
MR. W. (*same business*). Number Three! (*flash*).
CHORUS. Set us free!
Set us free—our work is done
Ha! ha! ha!
Set us free—our course is run!
Ha! ha! ha!

ALINE and ALEXIS (*aside*)

Let us fly to a far-off land,
Where peace and plenty dwell—
Where the sigh of the silver strand
Is echoed in every shell.

CHORUS OF FIENDS

Ha! ha! ha! ha! ha! ha! ha! ha! ha! ha!

[*Stage grows light.* MR. WELLS *beckons villagers. Enter villagers and all the dramatis personæ, dancing joyously.* MRS. PARTLET *and* MR. WELLS *then distribute tea-cups.*

CHORUS

Now to the banquet we press;
  Now for the eggs, the ham;
Now for the mustard and cress,
  Now for the strawberry jam!

Now for the tea of our host,
  Now for the rollicking bun,
Now for the muffin and toast,
  Now for the gay Sally Lunn!

WOMEN. The eggs and the ham, and the strawberry jam!

MEN. The rollicking bun, and the gay Sally Lunn!
  The rollicking, rollicking bun!

RECIT—SIR MARMADUKE

Be happy all—the feast is spread before ye;
  Fear nothing, but enjoy yourselves, I pray!
Eat, aye, and drink—be merry, I implore ye,
  For once let thoughtless Folly rule the day.

TEA-CUP BRINDISI

Eat, drink, and be gay,
  Banish all worry and sorrow,
Laugh gaily to-day,
  Weep, if you're sorry, to-morrow!
Come, pass the cup round—
  I will go bail for the liquor;
It's strong, I'll be bound,
  For it was brewed by the vicar!

CHORUS

None so knowing as he
At brewing a jorum of tea,
  Ha! ha!
A pretty stiff jorum of tea.

TRIO—MR. WELLS, ALINE, *and* ALEXIS (*aside*)

See—see—they drink—
  All thought unheeding,
The tea-cups clink,
  They are exceeding!
Their hearts will melt
  In half-an-hour—
Then will be felt
  The potion's power!

[*During this verse* CONSTANCE *has brought a small tea-pot, kettle, caddy, and cosy to* DR. DALY. *He makes tea scientifically.*

BRINDISI, 2nd Verse—DR. DALY (*with the tea-pot*)

Pain, trouble, and care,
  Misery, heart-ache, and worry,
Quick, out of your lair!
  Get you all gone in a hurry!
Toil, sorrow, and plot,
  Fly away quicker and quicker—
Three spoons to the pot—
  That is the brew of your vicar!

CHORUS

None so cunning as he
At brewing a jorum of tea,
  Ha! ha!
A pretty stiff jorum of tea!

ENSEMBLE—ALEXIS *and* ALINE (*aside*)

Oh love, true love—unworldly, abiding!
  Source of all pleasure—true fountain of joy,—
Oh love, true love—divinely confiding,
  Exquisite treasure that knows no alloy,—

O love, true love, rich harvest of gladness,
  Peace-bearing tillage—great garner of bliss,—
Oh love, true love, look down on our sadness—
  Dwell in this village—oh, hear us in this!

[*It becomes evident by the strange conduct of the characters that the charm is working. All rub their eyes, and stagger about the stage as if under the influence of a narcotic.*

TUTTI (*aside*)

Oh, marvellous illusion!
  Oh, terrible surprise!
What is this strange confusion
  That veils my aching eyes?
I must regain my senses,
  Restoring Reason's law,
Or fearful inferences
  Society will draw!

ALEXIS, MR. WELLS, *and* ALINE (*aside*)

A marvellous illusion!
  A terrible surprise
Excites a strange confusion
  Within their aching eyes—
They must regain their senses,
  Restoring Reason's law,
Or fearful inferences
  Society will draw!

[*Those who have partaken of the philtre struggle in vain against its effects, and, at the end of the chorus, fall insensible on the stage.*

END OF ACT I

ACT II

SCENE.—*Exterior of* SIR MARMADUKE'S *mansion by moonlight. All the peasantry are discovered asleep on the ground, as at the end of Act I.*

Enter MR. WELLS, *on tiptoe, followed by* ALEXIS *and* ALINE. MR. WELLS *carries a dark lantern.*

TRIO—ALEXIS, ALINE, *and* MR. WELLS

'Tis twelve, I think,
  And at this mystic hour
The magic drink
  Should manifest its power.
Oh, slumbering forms,
  How little have ye guessed

The fire that warms
Each apathetic breast!

ALEXIS. But stay, my father is not here!

ALINE. And pray where is my mother dear?

MR. WELLS. I did not think it meet to see
A dame of lengthy pedigree,
A Baronet and K.C.B.
A Doctor of Divinity,
And that respectable Q.C.,
All fast asleep, al-fresco-ly,
And so I had them taken home
And put to bed respectably!
I trust my conduct meets your approbation.

ALEXIS. Sir, you have acted with discrimination,
And shown more delicate appreciation
Than we expect in persons of your station.

MR. WELLS. But stay—they waken, one by one—
The spell has worked—the deed is done!
I would suggest that we retire
While Love, the Housemaid, lights her kitchen fire!

[*Exeunt* MR. WELLS, ALEXIS, *and* ALINE, *on tiptoe, as the villagers stretch their arms, yawn, rub their eyes, and sit up.*

MEN. Why, where be oi, and what be oi a doin',
A sleepin' out, just when the dews du rise?

GIRLS. Why, that's the very way your health to ruin,
And don't seem quite respectable likewise!

MEN (*staring at girls*). Eh, that's you!
Only think o' that now!

GIRLS (*coyly*). What may you be at, now?
Tell me, du!

MEN (*admiringly*). Eh, what a nose,
And eh, what eyes, miss!
Lips like a rose,
And cheeks likewise, miss!

GIRLS (*coyly*). Oi tell you true,
Which I've never done, sir,

Oi loike you
As I never loiked none, sir!

ALL. Eh, but oi du loike you!

MEN. If you'll marry me, I'll dig for you and rake for you!

GIRLS. If you'll marry me, I'll scrub for you and bake for you!

MEN. If you'll marry me, all others I'll forsake for you!

ALL. All this will I du, if you'll marry me!

GIRLS. If you'll marry me, I'll cook for you and brew for you!

MEN. If you'll marry me, I've guineas not a few for you!

GIRLS. If you'll marry me, I'll take you in and du for you!

ALL. All this will I du, if you'll marry me!
En, but oi du loike you!

Country dance

At end of dance, enter CONSTANCE *in tears, leading* NOTARY, *who carries an ear-trumpet*

ARIA—CONSTANCE

Dear friends, take pity on my lot,
My cup is not of nectar!
I long have loved—as who would not?—
Our kind and reverend rector.
Long years ago my love began
So sweetly—yet so sadly—
But when I saw this plain old man,
Away my old affection ran—
I found I loved him madly.
Oh!

(*To* NOTARY.) You very, very plain old man,
I love, I love you madly!

CHORUS. You very, very plain old man,
She loves, she loves you madly!

NOTARY. I am a very deaf old man,
And hear you very badly!

CONSTANCE. I know not why I love him so;
It is enchantment, surely!
He's dry and snuffy, deaf and slow
Ill-tempered, weak, and poorly!
He's ugly, and absurdly dressed,
And sixty-seven nearly,
He's everything that I detest,
But if the truth must be confessed,
I love him very dearly!
Oh!

(*To* NOTARY.) You're everything that I detest,
But still I love you dearly!

CHORUS. You're everything that girls detest,
But still she loves you dearly!

NOTARY. I caught that line, but for the rest,
I did not hear it clearly!

[*During this verse* ALINE *and* ALEXIS *have entered at back unobserved.*

ALINE *and* ALEXIS

ALEXIS. Oh joy! oh joy!
The charm works well,
And all are now united.

ALINE. The blind young boy
Obeys the spell,
Their troth they all have plighted!

ENSEMBLE

ALINE *and* ALEXIS	CONSTANCE	NOTARY
Oh joy! oh joy! The charm works well, And all are now united! The blind young boy Obeys the spell, Their troth they all have plighted.	Oh, bitter joy! No words can tell How my poor heart is blighted! They'll soon employ A marriage bell, To say that we're united.	Oh joy! oh joy! No words can tell My state of mind delighted. They'll soon employ A marriage bell, To say that we're united.

True happiness
Reigns everywhere,
And dwells with
both the sexes,
And all will bless
The thoughtful care
Of their beloved
Alexis.

I do confess
A sorrow rare
My humbled spirit
vexes,
And none will bless
Example rare
Of their beloved
Alexis!

True happiness
Reigns everywhere
And dwells with
both the sexes,
And all will bless
Example rare
Of their beloved
Alexis!

[*All, except* ALEXIS *and* ALINE, *exeunt lovingly.*

ALINE. How joyful they all seem in their new-found happiness! The whole village has paired off in the happiest manner. And yet not a match has been made that the hollow world would not consider ill-advised!

ALEXIS. But we are wiser—far wiser—than the world. Observe the good that will become of these ill-assorted unions. The miserly wife will check the reckless expenditure of her too frivolous consort, the wealthy husband will shower innumerable bonnets on his penniless bride, and the young and lively spouse will cheer the declining days of her aged partner with comic songs unceasing!

ALINE. What a delightful prospect for him!

ALEXIS. But one thing remains to be done, that my happiness may be complete. We must drink the philtre ourselves, that I may be assured of your love for ever and ever.

ALINE. Oh, Alexis, do you doubt me? Is it necessary that such love as ours should be secured by artificial means? Oh, no, no, no!

ALEXIS. My dear Aline, time works terrible changes, and I want to place our love beyond the chance of change.

ALINE. Alexis, it is already far beyond that chance. Have faith in me, for my love can never, never change!

ALEXIS. Then you absolutely refuse?

ALINE. I do. If you cannot trust me, you have no right to love me—no right to be loved *by* me.

ALEXIS. Enough, Aline, I shall know how to interpret this refusal.

BALLAD—ALEXIS

Thou hast the power thy vaunted love
To sanctify, all doubt above,

Despite the gathering shade:
To make that love of thine so sure
That, come what may, it must endure
Till time itself shall fade.
Thy love is but a flower
That fades within the hour!
If such thy love, oh, shame!
Call it by other name—
It is not love!

Thine is the power and thine alone,
To place me on so proud a throne
That kings might envy me!
A priceless throne of love untold,
More rare than orient pearl and gold.
But no! Thou wouldst be free!
Such love is like the ray
That dies within the day:
If such thy love, oh, shame!
Call it by other name—
It is not love!

Enter DR. DALY

DR. D. (*musing*). It is singular—it is very singular. It has overthrown all my calculations. It is distinctly opposed to the doctrine of averages. I cannot understand it.

ALINE. Dear Dr. Daly, what has puzzled you?

DR. D. My dear, this village has not hitherto been addicted to marrying and giving in marriage. Hitherto the youths of this village have not been enterprising, and the maidens have been distinctly coy. Judge then of my surprise when I tell you that the whole village came to me in a body just now, and implored me to join them in matrimony with as little delay as possible. Even your excellent father has hinted to me that before very long it is not unlikely that he also may change his condition.

ALINE. Oh, Alexis—do you hear that? Are you not delighted?

ALEXIS. Yes. I confess that a union between your mother and my father would be a happy circumstance indeed. (*Crossing to* DR. DALY.) My dear sir—the news that you bring us is very gratifying.

DR. D. Yes—still, in my eyes, it has its melancholy side. This universal marrying recalls the happy days—now, alas, gone for ever—when I myself might have—but tush! I am puling. I am too old to marry—and yet, within the last half-hour, I have greatly yearned for companionship. I never remarked it before, but the young maidens of this village are very comely. So likewise are the middle-aged. Also the elderly. All are comely—and (*with a deep sigh*) all are engaged!

ALINE. Here comes your father.

Enter SIR MARMADUKE *with* MRS. PARTLET, *arm-in-arm*

ALINE *and* ALEXIS (*aside*). Mrs. Partlet!

SIR M. Dr. Daly, give me joy. Alexis, my dear boy, you will, I am sure, be pleased to hear that my declining days are not unlikely to be solaced by the companionship of this good, virtuous, and amiable woman.

ALEXIS (*rather taken aback*). My dear father, this is not altogether what I expected. I am certainly taken somewhat by surprise. Still it can hardly be necessary to assure you that any wife of yours is a mother of mine. (*Aside to* ALINE.) It is not quite what I could have wished.

MRS. P. (*crossing to* ALEXIS). Oh, sir, I entreat your forgiveness. I am aware that socially I am noth everythink that could be desired, nor am I blessed with an abundance of worldly goods, but I can at least confer on your estimable father the great and priceless dowry of a true, tender, and lovin' 'art!

ALEXIS (*coldly*). I do not question it. After all, a faithful love is the true source of every earthly joy.

SIR M. I knew that my boy would not blame his poor father for acting on the impulse of a heart that has never yet misled him. Zorah is not perhaps what the world calls beautiful—

DR. D. Still she is comely—distinctly comely. (*Sighs.*)

ALINE. Zorah is very good, and very clean, and honest, and quite, quite sober in her habits: and that is worth far more than beauty, dear Sir Marmaduke.

DR. D. Yes; beauty will fade and perish, but personal

cleanliness is practically undying, for it can be renewed whenever it discovers symptoms of decay. My dear Sir Marmaduke, I heartily congratulate you. (*Sighs.*)

QUINTETTE

ALEXIS, ALINE, SIR MARMADUKE, ZORAH, *and* DR. DALY

ALEXIS. I rejoice that it's decided,
Happy now will be his life,
For my father is provided
With a true and tender wife.

ENSEMBLE

She will tend him, nurse him, mend him,
Air his linen, dry his tears;
Bless the thoughtful fates that send him
Such a wife to soothe his years!

ALINE. No young giddy thoughtless maiden,
Full of graces, airs, and jeers—
But a sober widow, laden
With the weight of fifty years!

SIR M. No high-born exacting beauty,
Blazing like a jewelled sun—
But a wife who'll do her duty,
As that duty should be done!

MRS. P. I'm no saucy minx and giddy—
Hussies such as them abound—
But a clean and tidy widdy
Well be-known for miles around!

DR. D. All the village now have mated,
All are happy as can be—
I to live alone am fated:
No one's left to marry me!

ENSEMBLE. She will tend him etc.

[*Exeunt* SIR MARMADUKE, MRS. PARTLET, *and* ALINE, *with* ALEXIS. DR. DALY *looks after them sentimentally, then exit with a sigh.*

Enter MR. WELLS

RECITATIVE—MR. WELLS

Oh, I have wrought much evil with my spells!
And ill I can't undo!
This is too bad of you, J. W. Wells—
What wrong have they done you?
And see—another love-lorn lady comes—
Alas, poor stricken dame!
A gentle pensiveness her life benumbs—
And mine, alone, the blame!

LADY SANGAZURE *enters. She is very melancholy*

LADY S. Alas, ah me! and well-a-day!
I sigh for love, and well I may,
For I am very old and grey.
But stay!

(*Sees* MR. WELLS, *and becomes fascinated by him.*)

RECITATIVE

LADY S. What is this fairy form I see before me?
MR. W. Oh, horrible!—she's going to adore me!
This last catastrophe is overpowering!
LADY S. Why do you glare at one with visage lowering?
For pity's sake recoil not thus from me!
MR. W. My lady, leave me—this may never be!

DUET—LADY SANGAZURE *and* MR. WELLS

MR. W. Hate me! I drop my H's—have through life!
LADY S. Love me! I'll drop them too!
MR. W. Hate me! I always eat peas with a knife!
LADY S. Love me! I'll eat like you!
MR. W. Hate me! I spend the day at Rosherville!
LADY S. Love me! that joy I'll share!
MR. W. Hate me! I often roll down One Tree Hill!
LADY S. Love me! I'll join you there!

LADY S. Love me! my prejudices I will drop!
MR. W. Hate me! that's not enough!
LADY S. Love me! I'll come and help you in the shop!
MR. W. Hate me! the life is rough!
LADY S. Love me! my grammar I will all forswear!
MR. W. Hate me! abjure my lot!

LADY S. Love me! I'll stick sunflowers in my hair!
MR. W. Hate me! they'll suit you not!

RECITATIVE—MR. WELLS

At what I am going to say be not enraged—
I may not love you—for I am engaged!

LADY S. (*horrified*). Engaged!
MR. W. Engaged!
To a maiden fair,
With bright brown hair,
And a sweet and simple smile,
Who waits for me
By the sounding sea,
On a South Pacific isle.

MR. W. (*aside*). A lie! No maiden waits me there!
LADY S. (*mournfully*). She has bright brown hair;
MR. W. (*aside*). A lie! No maiden smiles on me!
LADY S. (*mournfully*). By the sounding sea!

ENSEMBLE

LADY SANGAZURE

Oh, agony, rage, despair!
The maiden has bright brown hair,
And mine is as white as snow!
False man, it will be your fault,
If I go to my family vault,
And bury my life-long woe!

MR. WELLS

Oh, agony, rage, despair!
Oh, where will this end—oh, where?
I should like very much to know!
It will certainly be my fault,
If she goes to her family vault,
To bury her life-long woe!

BOTH. The family vault—the family vault.
It will certainly be {your / my} fault.
If {I go / she goes} to {my / her} family vault,
To bury {my / her} life-long woe!

[*Exit* LADY SANGAZURE, *in great anguish, accompanied by* MR. WELLS.

Enter ALINE, RECITATIVE

Alexis! Doubt me not, my loved one! See,
Thine uttered will is sovereign law to me!

All fear—all thought of ill I cast away!
It is my darling's will, and I obey!
(*She drinks the philtre.*)

The fearful deed is done,
My love is near!
I go to meet my own
In trembling ſear!
If o'er us aught of ill
Should cast a shade,
It was my darling's will,
And I obeyed!

[*As* ALINE *is going off, she meets* DR. DALY, *entering pensively. He is playing on a flageolet. Under the influence of the spell she at once becomes strangely fascinated by him, and exhibits every symptom of being hopelessly in love with him.*

SONG—DR. DALY

Oh, my voice is sad and low
And with timid step I go—
For with load of love o'erladen
I enquire of every maiden,
"Will you wed me, little lady?
Will you share my cottage shady?"
Little lady answers "No!
Thank you for your kindly proffer—
Good your heart, and full your coffer;
Yet I must decline your offer—
I'm engaged to So-and-so!"
So-and-so!
So-and-so! (*flageolet solo*)
She's engaged to So-and-so!
What a rogue young hearts to pillage;
What a worker on Love's tillage!
Every maiden in the village
Is engaged to So-and-so!
So-and-so!
So-and-so! (*flageolet solo*)
All engaged to So-and-so!

[*At the end of the song* DR. DALY *sees* ALINE, *and, under the influence of the potion, falls in love with her.*

ENSEMBLE—ALINE *and* DR. DALY

Oh, joyous boon! oh, mad delight;
Oh, sun and moon! oh, day and night!
Rejoice, rejoice with me!
Proclaim our joy, ye birds above—
Yet brooklets, murmur forth our love,
In choral ecstasy:

ALINE. Oh, joyous boon!
DR. D. Oh, mad delight!
ALINE. Oh, sun and moon!
DR. D. Oh, day and night!
BOTH. Ye birds, and brooks, and fruitful trees,
With choral joy delight the breeze—
Rejoice, rejoice with me!

Enter ALEXIS

ALEXIS (*with rapture*). Aline my only love, my happiness!

The philtre—you have tasted it?

ALINE (*with confusion*). Yes! Yes!

ALEXIS. Oh, joy, mine, mine for ever, and for aye! (*Embraces her.*)

ALINE. Alexis, don't do that—you must not!

(DR. DALY *interposes between them.*)

ALEXIS (*amazed*). Why?

DUET—ALINE *and* DR. DALY

ALINE. Alas! that lovers thus should meet:
Oh, pity, pity me!
Oh, charge me not with cold deceit;
Oh, pity, pity me!
You bade me drink—with trembling awe
I drank, and, by the potion's law,
I loved the very first I saw!
Oh, pity, pity me!

DR. D. My dear young friend, consolèd be—
We pity, pity you.

In this I'm not an agent free—
We pity, pity you.
Some most extraordinary spell
O'er us has cast its magic fell—
The consequence I need not tell.
We pity, pity you.

ENSEMBLE

Some most extraordinary spell
O'er {us / them} has cast its magic fell—
The consequence {we / they} need not tell.
{We / They} pity, pity {thee! / me.}

ALEXIS (*furiously*). False one, begone—I spurn thee,
To thy new lover turn thee!
Thy perfidy all men shall know.
ALINE (*wildly*). I could not help it!
ALEXIS (*calling off*). Come one, come all!
DR. D. We could not help it!
ALEXIS (*calling off*). Obey my call!
ALINE (*wildly*). I could not help it!
ALEXIS (*calling off*). Come hither, run!
DR. D. We could not help it!
ALEXIS (*calling off*). Come, every one!

Enter all the characters except LADY SANGAZURE *and* MR. WELLS

CHORUS

Oh, what is the matter, and what is the clatter?
He's glowering at her, and threatens a blow!
Oh, why does he batter the girl he did flatter?
And why does the latter recoil from him so?

RECITATIVE—ALEXIS

Prepare for sad surprises—
My love Aline despises!
No thought of sorrow shames her—
Another lover claims her!
Be his, false girl, for better or for worse—
But, ere you leave me, may a lover's curse——

DR. D. (*coming forward*). Hold! Be just. This poor child drank the philtre at your instance. She hurried off to meet you—but, most unhappily, she met me instead. As you had administered the potion to both of us, the result was inevitable. But fear nothing from me—I will be no man's rival. I shall quit the country at once—and bury my sorrow in the congenial gloom of a Colonial Bishopric.

ALEXIS. My excellent old friend! (*Taking his hand—then turning to* MR. WELLS, *who has entered with* LADY SANGAZURE.) Oh, Mr. Wells, what, what is to be done?

MR. W. I do not know—and yet—there is one means by which this spell may be removed.

ALEXIS. Name it—oh, name it!

MR. W. Or you or I must yield up his life to Ahrimanes. I would rather it were you. I should have no hesitation in sacrificing my own life to spare yours, but we take stock next week, and it would not be fair on the Co.

ALEXIS. True. Well, I am ready!

ALINE. No, no—Alexis—it must not be! Mr. Wells, if he must die that all may be restored to their old loves, what is to become of me? I should be left out in the cold, with no love to be restored to!

MR. W. True—I did not think of that. (*To the others.*) My friends, I appeal to you, and I will leave the decision in your hands.

FINALE

MR. W. Or I or he
Must die!
Which shall it be?
Reply!

SIR M. Die thou!
Thou art the cause of all offending!

DR. D. Die thou!
Yield thou to this decree unbending!

ALL. Die thou!

MR. W. So be it! I submit! My fate is sealed.
To public execration thus I yield!

(*Falls on trap.*)

Be happy all—leave me to my despair—
I go—it matters not with whom—or where!

(*Gong.*)

[*All quit their present partners, and rejoin their old lovers.* SIR MARMADUKE *leaves* MRS. PARTLET, *and goes to* LADY SANGAZURE. ALINE *leaves* DR. DALY, *and goes to* ALEXIS. DR. DALY *leaves* ALINE, *and goes to* CONSTANCE. NOTARY *leaves* CONSTANCE, *and goes to* MRS. PARTLET. *All the* CHORUS *make a corresponding change.*

ALL

GENTLEMEN. Oh, my adored one!
LADIES. Unmingled joy!
GENTLEMEN. Ecstatic rapture!
LADIES. Beloved boy!

(*They embrace.*)

SIR M. Come to my mansion, all of you! At least
We'll crown our rapture with another feast!

ENSEMBLE

SIR MARMADUKE, LADY SANGAZURE, ALEXIS, *and* ALINE

Now to the banquet we press—
Now for the eggs and the ham—
Now for the mustard and cress—
Now for the strawberry jam!

CHORUS. Now to the banquet, etc.

DR. DALY, CONSTANCE, NOTARY, *and* MRS. PARTLET

Now for the tea of our host—
Now for the rollicking bun—
Now for the muffin and toast—
Now for the gay Sally Lunn!

CHORUS. Now for the tea, etc.

(*General Dance.*)

[*During the symphony* MR. WELLS *sinks through trap, amid red fire.*

CURTAIN

H.M.S. PINAFORE

OR

THE LASS THAT LOVED A SAILOR

DRAMATIS PERSONÆ

THE RT. HON. SIR JOSEPH PORTER, K.C.B. (*First Lord of the Admiralty*).

CAPTAIN CORCORAN (*Commanding H.M.S. Pinafore*).

TOM TUCKER (*Midshipmite*).

RALPH RACKSTRAW (*Able Seaman*).

DICK DEADEYE (*Able Seaman*).

BILL BOBSTAY (*Boatswain's Mate*).

BOB BECKET (*Carpenter's Mate*).

JOSEPHINE (*the Captain's Daughter*).

HEBE (*Sir Joseph's First Cousin*).

MRS. CRIPPS (LITTLE BUTTERCUP) (*a Portsmouth Bumboat Woman*).

First Lord's Sisters, his Cousins, his Aunts, Sailors, Marines, etc.

Scene: QUARTER-DECK OF H.M.S. *Pinafore*, OFF PORTSMOUTH.

ACT I.—*Noon.* ACT II.—*Night.*

First produced at the Opéra Comique on May 25, 1878

H.M.S. PINAFORE

OR

THE LASS THAT LOVED A SAILOR

ACT I

SCENE.—*Quarter-deck of H.M.S. Pinafore. Sailors, led by* BOATSWAIN, *discovered cleaning brasswork, splicing rope, etc.*

CHORUS

We sail the ocean blue,
And our saucy ship's a beauty;
We're sober men and true,
And attentive to our duty.
When the balls whistle free
O'er the bright blue sea,
We stand to our guns all day;
When at anchor we ride
On the Portsmouth tide,
We have plenty of time to play.

Enter LITTLE BUTTERCUP, *with large basket on her arm*

RECIT

Hail, men-o'-war's men—safeguards of your nation,
Here is an end, at last, of all privation;
You've got your pay—spare all you can afford
To welcome Little Buttercup on board.

ARIA

For I'm called Little Buttercup—dear Little Buttercup,
Though I could never tell why,
But still I'm called Buttercup—poor little Buttercup,
Sweet Little Buttercup I!

I've snuff and tobaccy, and excellent jacky,
  I've scissors, and watches, and knives;
I've ribbons and laces to set off the faces
  Of pretty young sweethearts and wives.

I've treacle and toffee, I've tea and I've coffee,
  Soft tommy and succulent chops;
I've chickens and conies, and pretty polonies,
  And excellent peppermint drops.

Then buy of your Buttercup—dear Little Buttercup;
  Sailors should never be shy;
So, buy of your Buttercup—poor Little Buttercup;
  Come, of your Buttercup buy!

BOAT. Aye, Little Buttercup—and well called—for you're the rosiest, the roundest, and the reddest beauty in all Spithead.

BUT. Red, am I? and round—and rosy! Maybe, for I have dissembled well! But hark ye, my merry friend—hast ever thought that beneath a gay and frivolous exterior there may lurk a canker-worm which is slowly but surely eating its way into one's very heart?

BOAT. No, my lass, I can't say I've ever thought that.

Enter DICK DEADEYE. *He pushes through sailors, and comes down*

DICK. *I* have thought it often. (*All recoil from him.*)

BUT. Yes, you look like it! What's the matter with the man? Isn't he well?

BOAT. Don't take no heed of *him;* that's only poor Dick Deadeye.

DICK. I say—it's a beast of a name, ain't it—Dick Deadeye?

BUT. It's not a nice name.

DICK. I'm ugly too, ain't I?

BUT. You are certainly plain.

DICK. And I'm three-cornered too, ain't I?

BUT. You are rather triangular.

DICK. Ha! ha! That's it. I'm ugly, and they hate me for it; for you all hate me, don't you?

ALL. We do!

DICK. There!

BOAT. Well, Dick, we wouldn't go for to hurt any fellow-creature's feelings, but you can't expect a chap with such a name as Dick Deadeye to be a popular character—now can you?

DICK. No.

BOAT. It's asking too much, ain't it?

DICK. It is. From such a face and form as mine the noblest sentiments sound like the black utterances of a depraved imagination. It is human nature—I am resigned.

RECIT

BUT. (*looking down hatchway*).
But, tell me—who's the youth whose faltering feet
With difficulty bear him on his course?

BOAT. That is the smartest lad in all the fleet—
Ralph Rackstraw!

BUT. Ha! That name! Remorse! remorse!

Enter RALPH *from hatchway*

MADRIGAL—RALPH

The Nightingale
Sighed for the moon's bright ray,
And told his tale
In his own melodious way!
He sang "Ah, well-a-day!"

ALL. He sang "Ah, well-a-day!"

The lowly vale
For the mountain vainly sighed,
To his humble wail
The echoing hills replied.
They sang "Ah, well-a-day!"

ALL. They sang "Ah, well-a-day!"

RECIT

I know the value of a kindly chorus,
But choruses yield little consolation
When we have pain and sorrow too before us!
I love—and love, alas, above my station!

BUT. (*aside*). He loves—and loves a lass above his station!

ALL (*aside*). Yes, yes, the lass is much above his station!

[*Exit* LITTLE BUTTERCUP.

BALLAD—RALPH

A maiden fair to see,
The pearl of minstrelsy,
A bud of blushing beauty;
For whom proud nobles sigh,
And with each other vie
To do her menial's duty.
ALL. To do her menial's duty.

A suitor, lowly born,
With hopeless passion torn,
And poor beyond denying,
Has dared for her to pine
At whose exalted shrine
A world of wealth is sighing.
ALL. A world of wealth is sighing.

Unlearned he in aught
Save that which love has taught
(For love had been his tutor);
Oh, pity, pity me—
Our captain's daughter she,
And I that lowly suitor!
ALL. And he that lowly suitor!

BOAT. Ah, my poor lad, you've climbed too high: our worthy captain's child won't have nothin' to say to a poor chap like you. Will she, lads?

ALL. No, no.

DICK. No, no, captains' daughters don't marry foremast hands.

ALL (*recoiling from him*). Shame! shame!

BOAT. Dick Deadeye, them sentiments o' yourn are a disgrace to our common natur'.

RALPH. But it's a strange anomaly, that the daughter of a man who hails from the quarter-deck may not love another who lays out on the fore-yard arm. For a man is but a man, whether he hoists his flag at the main-truck or his slacks on the main-deck.

DICK. Ah, it's a queer world!

RALPH. Dick Deadeye, I have no desire to press hardly on you, but such a revolutionary sentiment is enough to make an honest sailor shudder.

BOAT. My lads, our gallant captain has come on deck; let us greet him as so brave an officer and so gallant a seaman deserves.

Enter CAPTAIN CORCORAN

RECIT

CAPT. My gallant crew, good morning.
ALL (*saluting*). Sir, good morning!
CAPT. I hope you're all quite well.
ALL (*as before*). Quite well; and you, sir?
CAPT. I am in reasonable health, and happy
To meet you all once more.
ALL (*as before*). You do us proud, sir!

SONG—CAPT.

CAPT. I am the Captain of the *Pinafore;*
ALL. And a right good captain, too!
CAPT. You're very, very good,
And be it understood,
I command a right good crew,
ALL. We're very, very good,
And be it understood,
He commands a right good crew.
CAPT. Though related to a peer,
I can hand, reef, and steer,
And ship a selvagee;
I am never known to quail
At the fury of a gale,
And I'm never, never sick at sea!
ALL. What, never?
CAPT. No, never!
ALL. What, *never*?
CAPT. Hardly ever!
ALL. He's hardly ever sick at sea!

Then give three cheers, and one cheer more,
For the hardy Captain of the *Pinafore*!'

CAPT. I do my best to satisfy you all—
ALL. And with you we're quite content.
CAPT. You're exceedingly polite,
And I think it only right
To return the compliment.
ALL. We're exceedingly polite,
And he thinks it's only right
To return the compliment.
CAPT. Bad language or abuse,
I never, never use,
Whatever the emergency;
Though "Bother it" I may
Occasionally say,
I never use a big, big D—
ALL. What, never?
CAPT. No, never!
ALL. What, *never*?
CAPT. Hardly ever!
ALL. Hardly ever swears a big, big D—
Then give three cheers, and one cheer more,
For the well-bred Captain of the *Pinafore*!
[*After song exeunt all but* CAPTAIN

Enter LITTLE BUTTERCUP

RECITATIVE

BUT. Sir, you are sad! The silent eloquence
Of yonder tear that trembles on your eyelash
Proclaims a sorrow far more deep than common;
Confide in me—fear not—I am a mother!

CAPT. Yes, Little Buttercup, I'm sad and sorry—
My daughter, Josephine, the fairest flower
That ever blossomed on ancestral timber,
Is sought in marriage by Sir Joseph Porter,
Our Admiralty's First Lord, but for some reason
She does not seem to tackle kindly to it.

BUT. (*with emotion*). Ah, poor Sir Joseph! Ah, I know too well

The anguish of a heart that loves but vainly!
But see, here comes your most attractive daughter.
I go—Farewell! [*Exit.*

CAPT. (*looking after her*). A plump and pleasing person! [*Exit.*

Enter JOSEPHINE, *twining some flowers which she carries in a small basket*

BALLAD—JOSEPHINE

Sorry her lot who loves too well,
Heavy the heart that hopes but vainly,
Sad are the sighs that own the spell,
Uttered by eyes that speak too plainly;
Heavy the sorrow that bows the head
When love is alive and hope is dead!

Sad is the hour when sets the sun—
Dark is the night to earth's poor daughters,
When to the ark the wearied one
Flies from the empty waste of waters!
Heavy the sorrow that bows the head
When love is alive and hope is dead!

Enter CAPTAIN

CAPT. My child, I grieve to see that you are a prey to melancholy. You should look your best to-day, for Sir Joseph Porter, K.C.B., will be here this afternoon to claim your promised hand.

JOS. Ah, father, your words cut me to the quick. I can esteem—reverence—venerate Sir Joseph, for he is a great and good man; but oh, I cannot love him! My heart is already given.

CAPT. (*aside*). It is then as I feared. (*Aloud.*) Given? And to whom? Not to some gilded lordling?

JOS. No, father—the object of my love is no lordling. Oh, pity me, for he is but a humble sailor on board your own ship!

CAPT. Impossible!

JOS. Yes, it is true—too true.

CAPT. A common sailor? Oh fie!

JOS. I blush for the weakness that allows me to cherish

such a passion. I hate myself when I think of the depth to which I have stooped in permitting myself to think tenderly of one so ignobly born, but I love him! I love him! I love him! (*Weeps.*)

CAPT. Come, my child, let us talk this over. In a matter of the heart I would not coerce my daughter—I attach but little value to rank or wealth, but the line must be drawn somewhere. A man in that station may be brave and worthy, but at every step he would commit solecisms that society would never pardon.

JOS. Oh, I have thought of this night and day. But fear not, father, I have a heart, and therefore I love; but I am your daughter, and therefore I am proud. Though I carry my love with me to the tomb, he shall never, never know it.

CAPT. You *are* my daughtei after all. But see, Sir Joseph's barge approaches, manned by twelve trusty oarsmen and accompanied by the admiring crowd of sisters, cousins, and aunts that attend him wherever he goes. Retire, my daughter, to your cabin—take this, his photograph, with you—it may help to bring you to a more reasonable frame of mind.

JOS. My own thoughtful father!

[*Exit* JOSEPHINE. CAPTAIN *remains and ascends the poop-deck.*

BARCAROLLE (*invisible*)

Over the bright blue sea
Comes Sir Joseph Porter, K.C.B.,
Wherever he may go
Bang-bang the loud nine-pounders go!
Shout o'er the bright blue sea
For Sir Joseph Porter, K.C.B.

[*During this the Crew have entered on tiptoe, listening attentively to the song.*

CHORUS OF SAILORS

Sir Joseph's barge is seen,
And its crowd of blushing beauties,

We hope he'll find us clean,
And attentive to our duties.
We sail, we sail the ocean blue,
And our saucy ship's a beauty.
We're sober, sober men and true
And attentive to our duty.
We're smart and sober men,
And quite devoid of fe-ar,
In all the Royal N.
None are so smart as we are.

Enter SIR JOSEPH'S FEMALE RELATIVES

(*They dance round stage*)

REL. Gaily tripping,
Lightly skipping,
Flock the maidens to the shipping.
SAILORS. Flags and guns and pennants dipping!
All the ladies love the shipping.
REL. Sailors sprightly
Always rightly
Welcome ladies so politely.
SAILORS. Ladies who can smile so brightly,
Sailors welcome most politely.
CAPT. (*from poop*). Now give three cheers, I'll lead the way
ALL. Hurrah! hurrah! hurrah! hurray!

Enter SIR JOSEPH *with* COUSIN HEBE

SONG—SIR JOSEPH

I am the monarch of the sea,
The ruler of the Queen's Navee,
Whose praise Great Britain loudly chants.
COUSIN HEBE. And we are his sisters, and his cousins and his aunts!
REL. And we are his sisters, and his cousins, and his aunts!
SIR JOSEPH. When at anchor here I ride,
My bosom swells with pride,
And I snap my fingers at a foeman's taunts;

COUSIN HEBE. And so do his sisters, and his cousins, and his aunts!

ALL. And so do his sisters, and his cousins, and his aunts!

SIR JOSEPH. But when the breezes blow,
I generally go below,
And seek the seclusion that a cabin grants;

COUSIN HEBE. And so do his sisters, and his cousins, and his aunts!

ALL. And so do his sisters, and his cousins, and his aunts!
His sisters and his cousins,
Whom he reckons up by dozens,
And his aunts!

SONG—SIR JOSEPH

When I was a lad I served a term
As office boy to an Attorney's firm.
I cleaned the windows and I swept the floor,
And I polished up the handle of the big front door.
I polished up that handle so carefullee
That now I am the Ruler of the Queen's Navee!

CHORUS.—He polished, etc.

As office boy I made such a mark
That they gave me the post of a junior clerk.
I served the writs with a smile so bland,
And I copied all the letters in a big round hand—
I copied all the letters in a hand so free,
That now I am the Ruler of the Queen's Navee!

CHORUS.—He copied, etc.

In serving writs I made such a name
That an articled clerk I soon became;
I wore clean collars and a brand-new suit
For the pass examination at the Institute,
And that pass examination did so well for me,
That now I am the Ruler of the Queen's Navee!

CHORUS.—And that pass examination, etc.

Of legal knowledge I acquired such a grip
That they took me into the partnership.
And that junior partnership, I ween,
Was the only ship that I ever had seen.
But that kind of ship so suited me,
That now I am the Ruler of the Queen's Navee!

CHORUS.—But that kind, etc.

I grew so rich that I was sent
By a pocket borough into Parliament.
I always voted at my party's call,
And I never thought of thinking for myself at all.
I thought so little, they rewarded me
By making me the Ruler of the Queen's Navee!

CHORUS.—He thought so little, etc.

Now landsmen all, whoever you may be,
If you want to rise to the top of the tree,
If your soul isn't fettered to an office stool,
Be careful to be guided by this golden rule—
Stick close to your desks and never go to sea,
And you all may be Rulers of the Queen's Navee!

CHORUS.—Stick close, etc.

SIR JOSEPH. You've a remarkably fine crew, Captain Corcoran.

CAPT. It *is* a fine crew, Sir Joseph.

SIR JOSEPH (*examining a very small midshipman*). A British sailor is a splendid fellow, Captain Corcoran.

CAPT. A splendid fellow indeed, Sir Joseph.

SIR JOSEPH. I hope you treat your crew kindly, Captain Corcoran.

CAPT. Indeed I hope so, Sir Joseph.

SIR JOSEPH. Never forget that they are the bulwarks of England's greatness, Captain Corcoran.

CAPT. So I have always considered them, Sir Joseph.

SIR JOSEPH. No bullying, I trust—no strong language of any kind, eh?

CAPT. Oh, never, Sir Joseph.

SIR JOSEPH. What, *never*?

CAPT. Hardly ever, Sir Joseph. They are an excellent crew, and do their work thoroughly without it.

SIR JOSEPH. Don't patronise them, sir—pray, don't patronise them.

CAPT. Certainly not, Sir Joseph.

SIR JOSEPH. That you are their captain is an accident of birth. I cannot permit these noble fellows to be patronised because an accident of birth has placed you above them and them below you.

CAPT. I am the last person to insult a British sailor, Sir Joseph.

SIR JOSEPH. You are the last person who did, Captain Corcoran. Desire that splendid seaman to step forward.

(DICK *comes forward.*)

SIR JOSEPH. No, no, the other splendid seaman.

CAPT. Ralph Rackstraw, three paces to the front—march!

SIR JOSEPH (*sternly*). If what?

CAPT. I beg your pardon—I don't think I understand you.

SIR JOSEPH. If you *please*.

CAPT. Oh, yes, of course. If you please. (RALPH *steps forward.*)

SIR JOSEPH. You're a remarkably fine fellow.

RALPH. Yes, your honour.

SIR JOSEPH. And a first-rate seaman, I'll be bound.

RALPH. There's not a smarter topman in the Navy, your honour, though I say it who shouldn't.

SIR JOSEPH. Not at all. Proper self-respect, nothing more. Can you dance a hornpipe?

RALPH. No, your honour.

SIR JOSEPH. That's a pity: all sailors should dance hornpipes. I will teach you one this evening, after dinner. Now tell me—don't be afraid—how does your captain treat you, eh?

RALPH. A better captain don't walk the deck, your honour.

ALL. Aye; Aye!

SIR JOSEPH. Good. I like to hear you speak well of your commanding officer; I daresay he don't deserve it, but still it does you credit. Can you sing?

RALPH. I can hum a little, your honour.

SIR JOSEPH. Then hum this at your leisure. (*Giving him MS. music.*) It is a song that I have composed for the use of the Royal Navy. It is designed to encourage independence of thought and action in the lower branches of the service, and to teach the principle that a British sailor is any man's equal, excepting mine. Now, Captain Corcoran, a word with you in your cabin, on a tender and sentimental subject.

CAPT. Aye, aye, Sir Joseph. (*Crossing.*) Boatswain, in commemoration of this joyous occasion, see that extra grog is served out to the ship's company at seven bells.

BOAT. Beg pardon. If what, your honour?

CAPT. If what? I don't think I understand you.

BOAT. If you *please,* your honour.

CAPT. What!

SIR JOSEPH. The gentleman is quite right. If you *please.*

CAPT. (*stamping his foot impatiently*). If you *please*!

[*Exit.*

SIR. JOSEPH. For I hold that on the seas
The expression, "if you please",
A particularly gentlemanly tone implants.

COUSIN HEBE. And so do his sisters, and his cousins, and his aunts!

ALL. And so do his sisters, and his cousins, and his aunts!

[*Exeunt* SIR JOSEPH *and* RELATIVES.

BOAT. Ah! Sir Joseph's true gentleman; courteous and considerate to the very humblest.

RALPH. True, Boatswain, but we are not the very humblest. Sir Joseph has explained our true position to us. As he says, a British seaman is any man's equal excepting his, and if Sir Joseph says that, is it not our duty to believe him?

ALL. Well spoke! well spoke!

DICK. You're on a wrong tack, and so is he. He means well, but he don't know. When people have to obey other people's orders, equality's out of the question.

ALL (*recoiling*). Horrible! horrible!

BOAT. Dick Deadeye, if you go for to infuriate this here ship's company too far, I won't answer for being able to hold 'em in. I'm shocked! that's what I am—shocked!

RALPH. Messmates, my mind's made up. I'll speak to the captain's daughter, and tell her, like an honest man, of the honest love I have for her.

ALL. Aye, aye!

RALPH. Is not my love as good as another's? Is not my heart as true as another's? Have I not hands and eyes and ears and limbs like another?

ALL. Aye, Aye!

RALPH. True, I lack birth——

BOAT. You've a berth on board this very ship.

RALPH. Well said—I had forgotten that. Messmates—what do you say? Do you approve my determination?

ALL. We do.

DICK. *I* don't.

BOAT. What is to be done with this here hopeless chap? Let us sing him the song that Sir Joseph has kindly composed for us. Perhaps it will bring this here miserable creetur to a proper state of mind.

GLEE—RALPH, BOATSWAIN, BOATSWAIN'S MATE, *and* CHORUS

A British tar is a soaring soul,
    As free as a mountain bird,

His energetic fist should be ready to resist
  A dictatorial word.
His nose should pant and his lip should curl,
His cheeks should flame and his brow should furl,
His bosom should heave and his heart should glow,
And his fist be ever ready for a knock-down blow.

CHORUS.—His nose should pant, etc.

His eyes should flash with an inborn fire,
  His brow with scorn be wrung;
He never should bow down to a domineering frown,
  Or the tang of a tyrant tongue.
His foot should stamp and his throat should growl,
His hair should twirl and his face should scowl;
His eyes should flash and his breast protrude,
And this should be his customary attitude—(*pose*).

CHORUS.—His foot should stamp, etc.

[*All dance off excepting* RALPH, *who remains, leaning pensively against bulwark.*

Enter JOSEPHINE *from cabin*

JOS. It is useless—Sir Joseph's attentions nauseate me. I know that he is a truly great and good man, for he told me so himself, but to me he seems tedious, fretful, and dictatorial. Yet his must be a mind of no common order, or he would not dare to teach my dear father to dance a hornpipe on the cabin table. (*Sees* RALPH.) Ralph Rackstraw! (*Overcome by emotion.*)

RALPH. Aye, lady—no other than poor Ralph Rackstraw!

JOS. (*aside*). How my heart beats! (*Aloud.*) And why poor, Ralph?

RALPH. I am poor in the essence of happiness, lady—rich only in never-ending unrest. In me there meet a combination of antithetical elements which are at eternal war with one another. Driven hither by objective influences—thither by subjective emotions—wafted one moment into blazing day, by mocking hope—plunged the next into the Cimmerian darkness of tangible despair, I am but a living ganglion of irreconcilable antagonisms. I hope I make myself clear, lady?

JOS. Perfectly. (*Aside.*) His simple eloquence goes to my heart. Oh, if I dared—but no, the thought is madness! (*Aloud.*) Dismiss these foolish fancies, they torture you but needlessly. Come, make one effort.

RALPH (*aside*). I will—one. (*Aloud.*) Josephine!

JOS. (*indignantly*). Sir!

RALPH. Aye, even though Jove's armoury were launched at the head of the audacious mortal whose lips, unhallowed by relationship, dared to breathe that precious word, yet would I breathe it once, and then perchance be silent evermore. Josephine, in one brief breath I will concentrate the hopes, the doubts, the anxious fears of six weary months. Josephine, I am a British sailor, and I love you!

JOS. Sir, this audacity! (*Aside.*) Oh, my heart, my beating heart! (*Aloud.*) This unwarrantable presumption on the part of a common sailor! (*Aside.*) Common! oh, the irony of the word! (*Crossing, aloud.*) Oh, sir, you forget the disparity in our ranks.

RALPH. I forget nothing, haughty lady. I love you desperately, my life is in your hand—I lay it at your feet! Give me hope, and what I lack in education and polite accomplishments, that I will endeavour to acquire. Drive me to despair, and in death alone I shall look for consolation. I am proud and cannot stoop to implore. I have spoken and I wait your word.

JOS. You shall not wait long. Your proffered love I haughtily reject. Go, sir, and learn to cast your eyes on some village maiden in your own poor rank— they should be lowered before your captain's daughter.

DUET—JOSEPHINE *and* RALPH

JOS. Refrain, audacious tar,
Your suit from pressing,
Remember what you are,
And whom addressing!
(*Aside.*) I'd laugh my rank to scorn
In union holy,
Were he more highly born
Or I more lowly!

RALPH. Proud lady, have your way,
Unfeeling beauty!
You speak and I obey,
It is my duty!
I am the lowliest tar
That sails the water,
And you, proud maiden, are
My captain's daughter!
(*Aside.*) My heart with anguish torn
Bows down before her,
She laughs my love to scorn,
Yet I adore her!

[*Repeat refrain, ensemble, then exit* JOSEPHINE *into cabin.*

RALPH (*Recit.*) Can I survive this overbearing
Or live a life of mad despairing,
My proffered love despised, rejected?
No, no, it's not to be expected!
(*Calling off.*)
Messmates, ahoy!
Come here! Come here!

Enter SAILORS, HEBE, *and* RELATIVES

ALL.
Aye, aye, my boy,
What cheer, what cheer?
Now tell us, pray,
Without delay,
What does she say—
What cheer, what cheer?

RALPH (*to* COUSIN HEBE).
The maiden treats my suit with scorn,
Rejects my humble gift, my lady;
She says I am ignobly born,
And cuts my hopes adrift, my lady.

ALL. Oh, cruel one.

DICK. She spurns your suit? Oho! Oho!
I told you so, I told you so.

SAILORS *and* RELATIVES.
Shall {we / they} submit? Are {we / they} but slaves?
Love comes alike to high and low—
Britannia's sailors rule the waves,
And shall they stoop to insult? No!

DICK. You must submit, you are but slaves;
A lady she! Oho! Oho!
You lowly toilers of the waves,
She spurns you all—I told you so!

RALPH. My friends, my leave of life I'm taking,
For oh, my heart, my heart is breaking.
When I am gone, oh, prithee tell
The maid that, as I died, I loved her well!

ALL (*turning away, weeping*).
Of life, alas! his leave he's taking,
For ah! his faithful heart is breaking;
When he is gone we'll surely tell
The maid that, as he died, he loved her well.

[*During Chorus* BOATSWAIN *has loaded pistol, which he hands to* RALPH.

RALPH. Be warned, my messmates all
Who love in rank above you—
For Josephine I fall!

[*Puts pistol to his head. All the sailors stop their ears.*

Enter JOSEPHINE *on deck*

JOS. Ah! stay your hand! I love you!
ALL. Ah! stay your hand—she loves you!
RALPH (*incredulously*). Loves me?
JOS. Loves you!
ALL. Yes, yes—ah, yes,—she loves you!

ENSEMBLE

SAILORS *and* RELATIVES *and* JOSEPHINE

Oh joy, oh rapture unforeseen,
For now the sky is all serene;
The god of day—the orb of love—
Has hung his ensign high above,
The sky is all ablaze.

With wooing words and loving song,
We'll chase the lagging hours along,
And if {I find / we find} the maiden coy,
{I'll / We'll} murmur forth decorous joy
In dreamy roundelays!

DICK DEADEYE

He thinks he's won his Josephine,
But though the sky is now serene,
A frowning thunderbolt above
May end their ill-assorted love
Which now is all ablaze.

Our captain, ere the day is gone,
Will be extremely down upon
The wicked men who art employ
To make his Josephine less coy
In many various ways. [*Exit* DICK.

JOS. This very night,
HEBE. With bated breath
RALPH. And muffled oar—
JOS. Without a light,
HEBE. As still as death,
RALPH. We'll steal ashore
JOS. A clergyman
RALPH. Shall make us one
BOAT. At half-past ten,
JOS. And then we can
RALPH. Return, for none
BOAT. Can part them then!
ALL. This very night, etc.

(DICK *appears at hatchway.*)

DICK. Forbear, nor carry out the scheme you've planned;
She is a lady—you a foremast hand!
Remember, she's your gallant captain's daughter,
And you the meanest slave that crawls the water!

ALL. Back, vermin, back,
Nor mock us!
Back, vermin, back,
You shock us!

[*Exit* DICK.

Let's give three cheers for the sailor's bride
Who casts all thought of rank aside—
Who gives up home and fortune too
For the honest love of a sailor true!
For a British tar is a soaring soul
As free as a mountain bird!
His energetic fist should be ready to resist
A dictatorial word!
His foot should stamp and his throat should growl,
His hair should twirl and his face should scowl,
His eyes should flash and his breast protrude,
And this should be his customary attitude—(*pose*).

GENERAL DANCE

END OF ACT I

ACT II

Same Scene. Night. Awning removed. Moonlight. CAPTAIN *discovered singing on poop-deck, and accompanying himself on a mandolin.* LITTLE BUTTERCUP *seated on quarter-deck, gazing sentimentally at him.*

SONG—CAPTAIN

Fair moon, to thee I sing,
Bright regent of the heavens,
Say, why is everything
Either at sixes or at sevens?
I have lived hitherto
Free from breath of slander,
Beloved by all my crew—
A really popular commander.
But now my kindly crew rebel,
My daughter to a tar is partial,
Sir Joseph storms, and, sad to tell,
He threatens a court martial!
Fair moon, to thee I sing,
Bright regent of the heavens,
Say, why is everything
Either at sixes or at sevens?

BUT. How sweetly he carols forth his melody to the unconscious moon! Of whom is he thinking? Of some high-born beauty? It may be! Who is poor Little Buttercup that she should expect his glance to fall on one so lowly! And yet if he knew—if he only knew!

CAPT. (*coming down*). Ah! Little Buttercup, still on board? That is not quite right, little one. It would have been more respectable to have gone on shore at dusk.

BUT. True, dear Captain—but the recollection of your sad pale face seemed to chain me to the ship. I would fain see you smile before I go.

CAPT. Ah! Little Buttercup, I fear it will be long before I recover my accustomed cheerfulness, for misfortunes crowd upon me, and all my old friends seem to have turned against me!

BUT. Oh no—do not say "all", dear Captain. That were unjust to one, at least.

CAPT. True, for you are staunch to me. (*Aside.*) If ever I gave my heart again, methinks it would be to such a one as this! (*Aloud.*) I am touched to the heart by your innocent regard for me, and were we differently situated, I think I could have returned it. But as it is, I fear I can never be more to you than a friend.

BUT. I understand! You hold aloof from me because you are rich and lofty—and I poor and lowly. But take care! The poor bumboat woman has gipsy blood in her veins, and she can read destinies.

CAPT. Destinies?

BUT. There is a change in store for you!

CAPT. A change?

BUT. Aye—be prepared!

DUET—LITTLE BUTTERCUP *and* CAPTAIN

BUT. Things are seldom what they seem,
Skim milk masquerades as cream;
Highlows pass as patent leathers;
Jackdaws strut in peacock's feathers.

CAPT. (*puzzled*). Very true,
So they do.

BUT. Black sheep dwell in every fold;
All that glitters is not gold;
Storks turn out to be but logs;
Bulls are but inflated frogs.

CAPT. (*puzzled*). So they be,
Frequentlee.

BUT. Drops the wind and stops the mill;
Turbot is ambitious brill;
Gild the farthing if you will,
Yet it is a farthing still.

CAPT. (*puzzled*). Yes, I know.
That is so.
Though to catch your drift I'm striving,
It is shady—it is shady;
I don't see at what you're driving,
Mystic lady—mystic lady,

(*Aside.*) Stern conviction's o'er me stealing,
That the mystic lady's dealing
In oracular revealing.

BUT. (*aside*). Stern conviction's o'er him stealing,
That the mystic lady's dealing
In oracular revealing.

BOTH. Yes, I know—
That is so!

CAPT. Though I'm anything but clever,
I could talk like that for ever:
Once a cat was killed by care;
Only brave deserve the fair.

BUT. Very true,
So they do.

CAPT. Wink is often good as nod;
Spoils the child who spares the rod;
Thirsty lambs run foxy dangers;
Dogs are found in many mangers.

BUT. Frequentlee,
I agree.

CAPT. Paw of cat the chestnut snatches;
Worn-out garments show new patches;
Only count the chick that hatches;
Men are grown-up catchy-catchies.

BUT. Yes, I know,
That is so.

(*Aside.*) Though to catch my drift he's striving,
I'll dissemble—I'll dissemble;
When he sees at what I'm driving,
Let him tremble—let him tremble!

ENSEMBLE

Though a mystic tone {I / you} borrow,
{You will / I shall} learn the truth with sorrow,
Here to-day and gone to-morrow;
Yes, I know—
That is so!

[*At the end exit* LITTLE BUTTERCUP *melodramatically*.

CAPT. Incomprehensible as her utterances are, I nevertheless feel that they are dictated by a sincere regard for me. But to what new misery is she referring? Time alone can tell!

Enter SIR JOSEPH

SIR JOSEPH. Captain Corcoran, I am much disappointed with your daughter. In fact, I don't think she will do.

CAPT. She won't do, Sir Joseph!

SIR JOSEPH. I'm afraid not. The fact is, that although I have urged my suit with as much eloquence as is consistent with an official utterance, I have done so hitherto without success. How do you account for this?

CAPT. Really, Sir Joseph, I hardly know. Josephine is of course sensible of your condescension.

SIR JOSEPH. She naturally would be.

CAPT. But perhaps your exalted rank dazzles her.

SIR JOSEPH. You think it does?

CAPT. I can hardly say; but she is a modest girl, and her social position is far below your own. It may be that she feels she is not worthy of you.

SIR JOSEPH. That is really a very sensible suggestion, and displays more knowledge of human nature than I had given you credit for.

CAPT. See, she comes. If your lordship would kindly reason with her and assure her officially that it is a standing rule at the Admiralty that love levels all ranks, her respect for an official utterance might induce her to look upon your offer in its proper light.

SIR JOSEPH. It is not unlikely. I will adopt your suggestion. But soft, she is here. Let us withdraw, and watch our opportunity.

Enter JOSEPHINE *from cabin.* FIRST LORD *and* CAPTAIN *retire*

SCENA—JOSEPHINE

The hours creep on apace,
My guilty heart is quaking!
Oh, that I might retrace
The step that I am taking!
Its folly it were easy to be showing,
What I am giving up and whither going.

On the one hand, papa's luxurious home,
  Hung with ancestral armour and old brasses,
Carved oak and tapestry from distant Rome,
  Rare "blue and white" Venetian finger-glasses,
Rich oriental rugs, luxurious sofa pillows,
And everything that isn't old, from Gillow's.
And on the other, a dark and dingy room,
  In some back street with stuffy children crying,
Where organs yell, and clacking housewives fume.
  And clothes are hanging out all day a-drying.
With one cracked looking-glass to see your face in,
And dinner served up in a pudding basin!

A simple sailor, lowly born,
  Unlettered and unknown,
Who toils for bread from early morn
  Till half the night has flown!
No golden rank can he impart—
  No wealth of house or land—
No fortune save his trusty heart
  And honest brown right hand!
And yet he is so wondrous fair
That love for one so passing rare,
So peerless in his manly beauty,
Were little else than solemn duty!
Oh, god of love, and god of reason, say,
Which of you twain shall my poor heart obey!

SIR JOSEPH *and* CAPTAIN *enter*

SIR JOSEPH. Madam, it has been represented to me that you are appalled by my exalted rank. I desire to convey to you officially my assurance, that if your hesitation is attributable to that circumstance, it is uncalled for.

JOS. Oh! then your lordship is of opinion that married happiness is *not* inconsistent with discrepancy in rank?

SIR JOSEPH. I am officially of that opinion.

JOS. That the high and the lowly may be truly happy together, provided that they truly love one another?

SIR JOSEPH. Madam, I desire to convey to you officially my opinion that love is a platform upon which all ranks meet.

JOS. I thank you, Sir Joseph. I *did* hesitate, but I will hesitate no longer. (*Aside.*) He little thinks how eloquently he has pleaded his rival's cause!

TRIO

FIRST LORD, CAPTAIN, *and* JOSEPHINE

CAPT. Never mind the why and wherefore,
Love can level ranks, and therefore,
Though his lordship's station's mighty,
Though stupendous be his brain,
Though your tastes are mean and flighty
And your fortune poor and plain,
CAPT. *and* SIR JOSEPH. Ring the merry bells on board-ship,
Rend the air with warbling wild,
For the union of {his / my} lordship
With a humble captain's child!
CAPT. For a humble captain's daughter—
JOS. For a gallant captain's daughter—
SIR JOSEPH. And a lord who rules the water—
JOS. (*aside*). And a *tar* who ploughs the water!
ALL. Let the air with joy be laden,
Rend with songs the air above,
For the union of a maiden
With the man who owns her love!
SIR JOSEPH. Never mind the why and wherefore,
Love can level ranks, and therefore,
Though your nautical relation (*alluding to* CAPT.)
In my set could scarcely pass—
Though you occupy a station
In the lower middle class—
CAPT. *and* SIR JOSEPH. Ring the merry bells on board-ship,
Rend the air with warbling wild,
For the union of {my / his} lordship
With a humble captain's child!
CAPT. For a humble captain's daughter—
JOS. For a gallant captain's daughter—
SIR JOSEPH. And a lord who rules the water—
JOS. (*aside*). And a *tar* who ploughs the water!

ALL. Let the air with joy be laden,
Rend with songs the air above,
For the union of a maiden
With the man who owns her love!

JOS. Never mind the why and wherefore,
Love can level ranks, and therefore
I admit the jurisdiction;
Ably have you played your part;
You have carried firm conviction
To my hesitating heart.

CAPT. *and* SIR JOSEPH. Ring the merry bells on board-ship,
Rend the air with warbling wild,
For the union of {my / his} lordship
With a humble captain's child!

CAPT. For a humble captain's daughter—
JOS. For a gallant captain's daughter—
SIR JOSEPH. And a lord who rules the water—
JOS. (*aside*). And a *tar* who ploughs the water!
(*Aloud.*) Let the air with joy be laden.
CAPT. *and* SIR JOSEPH. Ring the merry bells on board-ship—
JOS. For the union of a maiden—
CAPT. *and* SIR JOSEPH. For her union with his lordship.
ALL. Rend with songs the air above
For the man who owns her love!

[*Exit* JOS.

CAPT. Sir Joseph, I cannot express to you my delight at the happy result of your eloquence. Your argument was unanswerable.

SIR JOSEPH. Captain Corcoran, it is one of the happiest characteristics of this glorious country that official utterances are invariably regarded as unanswerable.

[*Exit* SIR JOSEPH.

CAPT. At last my fond hopes are to be crowned. My only daughter is to be the bride of a Cabinet Minister. The prospect is Elysian. (*During this speech* DICK DEADEYE *has entered.*)

DICK. Captain.

CAPT. Deadeye! You here? Don't! (*Recoiling from him.*)

DICK. Ah, don't shrink from me, Captain. I'm unpleasant to look at, and my name's agin me, but I ain't as bad as I seem.

CAPT. What would you with me?

DICK (*mysteriously*). I'm come to give you warning.

CAPT. Indeed! do you propose to leave the Navy then?

DICK. No, no, you misunderstand me; listen!

DUET

CAPTAIN *and* DICK DEADEYE

DICK. Kind Captain, I've important information,
Sing hey, the kind commander that you are,
About a certain intimate relation,
Sing hey, the merry maiden and the tar.

BOTH. The merry maiden and the tar.

CAPT. Good fellow, in conundrums you are speaking,
Sing hey, the mystic sailor that you are;
The answer to them vainly I am seeking;
Sing hey, the merry maiden and the tar.

BOTH. The merry maiden and the tar.

DICK. Kind Captain, your young lady is a-sighing,
Sing hey, the simple captain that you are,
This very night with Rackstraw to be flying;
Sing hey, the merry maiden and the tar.

BOTH. The merry maiden and the tar.

CAPT. Good fellow, you have given timely warning,
Sing hey, the thoughtful sailor that you are,
I'll talk to Master Rackstraw in the morning:
Sing hey, the cat-o'-nine-tails and the tar.
(*Producing a "cat".*)

BOTH. The merry cat-o'-nine-tails and the tar!

CAPT. Dick Deadeye—I thank you for your warning—I will at once take means to arrest their flight. This boat cloak will afford me ample disguise—So! (*Envelops himself in a mysterious cloak, holding it before his face.*)

DICK. Ha, ha! They are foiled—foiled—foiled!

Enter Crew on tiptoe, with RALPH *and* BOATSWAIN *meeting* JOSEPHINE, *who enters from cabin on tiptoe, with bundle of necessaries, and accompanied by* LITTLE BUTTERCUP.

ENSEMBLE

Carefully on tiptoe stealing,
Breathing gently as we may,
Every step with caution feeling,
We will softly steal away.

(CAPTAIN *stamps.*)—*Chord.*

ALL (*much alarmed*). Goodness me—
Why, what was that?
DICK. Silent be,
It was the cat!
ALL (*reassured*). It was—it was the cat!
CAPT. (*producing cat-o'-nine-tails*). They're right, it was the cat!

ALL. Pull ashore, in fashion steady,
Hymen will defray the fare,
For a clergyman is ready
To unite the happy pair!

(*Stamp as before, and Chord.*)

ALL. Goodness me,
Why, what was that?
DICK. Silent be,
Again the cat!
ALL. It was again that cat!
CAPT. (*aside*). They're right, it was the cat!
CAPT. (*throwing off cloak*). Hold! (*All start.*)
Pretty daughter of mine,
I insist upon knowing
Where you may be going
With these sons of the brine,
For my excellent crew,
Though foes they could thump any,
Are scarcely fit company,
My daughter, for you.
CREW. Now, hark at that, do!
Though foes we could thump any,

We are scarcely fit company
For a lady like you!

RALPH. Proud officer, that haughty lip uncurl!
Vain man, suppress that supercilious sneer,
For I have dared to love your matchless girl,
A fact well known to all my messmates here!

CAPT. Oh, horror!

RALPH *and* JOS. {I, / He,} humble, poor, and lowly born,
The meanest in the port division—
The butt of epauletted scorn—
The mark of quarter-deck derision—
{Have / Has} dare to raise {my / his} wormy eyes
Above the dust to which you'd mould {me / him}
In manhood's glorious pride to rise,
{I am / He is} an Englishman—behold {me! / him!}

ALL. He is an Englishman!

BOAT. He is an Englishman!
For he himself has said it,
And it's greatly to his credit,
That he is an Englishman!

ALL. That he is an Englishman!
BOAT. For he might have been a Roosian,
A French, or Turk, or Proosian,
Or perhaps Itali-an!

ALL. Or perhaps Itali-an!
BOAT. But in spite of all temptations
To belong to other nations,
He remains an Englishman!

ALL. For in spite of all temptations, etc.

CAPT. (*trying to repress his anger*).
In uttering a reprobation
To any British tar,
I try to speak with moderation,
But you have gone too far.
I'm very sorry to disparage
A humble foremast lad,
But to seek your captain's child in marriage,
Why damme, it's too bad!

[*During this,* COUSIN HEBE *and* FEMALE RELATIVES *have entered.*

ALL (*shocked*). Oh!
CAPT. Yes, damme, it's too bad!
ALL. Oh!
CAPT. *and* DICK DEADEYE. Yes, damme, it's too bad.

[*During this,* SIR JOSEPH *has appeared on poop-deck. He is horrified at the bad language.*

HEBE. Did you hear him—did you hear him?
Oh, the monster overbearing!
Don't go near him—don't go near him—
He is swearing—he is swearing!
SIR JOSEPH. My pain and my distress,
I find it is not easy to express;

My amazement—my surprise—
You may learn from the expression of my eyes!

CAPT. My lord—one word—the facts are not before you
The word was injudicious, I allow—
But hear my explanation, I implore you,
And you will be indignant too, I vow!

SIR JOSEPH. I will hear of no defence,
Attempt none if you're sensible.
That word of evil sense
Is wholly indefensible.
Go, ribald, get you hence
To your cabin with celerity.
This is the consequence
Of ill-advised asperity!

[*Exit* CAPTAIN, *disgraced, followed by* JOSEPHINE

ALL. This is the consequence,
Of ill-advised asperity!

SIR JOSEPH. For I'll teach you all, ere long,
To refrain from language strong
For I haven't any sympathy for ill-bred taunts!

HEBE. No more have his sisters, nor his cousins, nor his aunts.

ALL. For he is an Englishman, etc.

SIR JOSEPH. Now, tell me, my fine fellow—for you *are* a fine fellow——

RALPH. Yes, your honour.

SIR JOSEPH. How came your captain so far to forget himself? I am quite sure you had given him no cause for annoyance.

RALPH. Please your honour, it was thus-wise. You see I'm only a topman—a mere foremast hand——

SIR JOSEPH. Don't be ashamed of that. Your position as a topman is a very exalted one.

RALPH. Well, your honour, love burns as brightly in the fo'c'sle as it does on the quarter-deck, and Josephine is the fairest bud that ever blossomed upon the tree of a poor fellow's wildest hopes.

Enter JOSEPHINE; *she rushes to* RALPH'S *arms*

JOS. Darling! (SIR JOSEPH *horrified.*)

RALPH. She is the figurehead of my ship of life—the bright beacon that guides me into my port of happiness—that the rarest, the purest gem that ever sparkled on a poor but worthy fellow's trusting brow!

ALL. Very pretty, very pretty!

SIR JOSEPH. Insolent sailor, you shall repent this outrage. Seize him!

(*Two Marines seize him and handcuff him.*)

JOS. Oh, Sir Joseph, spare him, for I love him tenderly.

SIR JOSEPH. Pray, don't. I will teach this presumptuous mariner to discipline his affections. Have you such a thing as a dungeon on board?

ALL. We have!

DICK. They have!

SIR JOSEPH. Then load him with chains and take him there at once!

OCTETTE

RALPH. Farewell, my own,
Light of my life, farewell!
For crime unknown
I go to a dungeon cell.

JOS. I will atone.
In the meantime farewell!
And all alone
Rejoice in your dungeon cell!

SIR JOSEPH. A bone, a bone
I'll pick with this sailor fell;
Let him be shown
At once to his dungeon cell.

BOATSWAIN, DICK DEADEYE, *and* COUSIN HEBE

He'll hear no tone
Of the maiden he loves so well!
No telephone
Communicates with his cell!

BUT. (*mysteriously*). But when is known
The secret I have to tell,
Wide will be thrown
The door of his dungeon cell.

ALL. For crime unknown
He goes to a dungeon cell!

[RALPH *is led off in custody.*

SIR JOSEPH. My pain and my distress
Again it is not easy to express.
My amazement, my surprise,
Again you may discover from my eyes.

ALL. How terrible the aspect of his eyes!

BUT. Hold! Ere upon your loss
You lay much stress,
A long-concealèd crime
I would confess.

SONG—BUTTERCUP

A many years ago,
When I was young and charming,
As some of you may know,
I practised baby-farming.

ALL. Now this is most alarming!
When she was young and charming,
She practised baby-farming,
A many years ago.

BUT. Two tender babes I nussed:
One was of low condition,
The other, upper crust,
A regular patrician.

ALL (*explaining to each other*).
Now, this is the position:
One was of low condition,
The other a patrician,
A many years ago.

BUT. Oh, bitter is my cup!
However could I do it?
I mixed those children up,
And not a creature knew it!

ALL. However could you do it?
Some day, no doubt, you'll rue it,
Although no creature knew it,
So many years ago.

BUT. In time each little waif
Forsook his foster-mother,
The well-born babe was Ralph—
Your captain was the other!!!

ALL. They left their foster-mother,
The one was Ralph, our brother,
Our captain was the other,
A many years ago.

SIR JOSEPH. Then I am to understand that Captain Corcoran and Ralph were exchanged in childhood's happy hour—that Ralph is really the Captain, and the Captain is Ralph?

BUT. That is the idea I intended to convey, officially!

SIR JOSEPH. And very well you have conveyed it.

BUT. Aye! aye! yer 'onour.

SIR JOSEPH. Dear me! Let them appear before me, at once!

RALPH *enters as* CAPTAIN; CAPTAIN *as a common sailor.* JOSEPHINE *rushes to his arms*

JOS. My father—a common sailor!

CAPT. It is hard, is it not, my dear?

SIR JOSEPH. This is a very singular occurrence; I congratulate you both. (*To* RALPH.) Desire that remarkably fine seaman to step forward.

RALPH. Corcoran. Three paces to the front—march!

CAPT. If what?

RALPH. If what? I don't think I understand you.

CAPT. If you please.

SIR JOSEPH. The gentleman is quite right. If you *please.*

RALPH. Oh! If you *please.* (CAPTAIN *steps forward.*)

SIR JOSEPH (*to* CAPTAIN). You are an extremely fine fellow.

CAPT. Yes, your honour.

SIR JOSEPH. So it seems that you were Ralph, and Ralph was you.

CAPT. So it seems, your honour.

SIR JOSEPH. Well, I need not tell you that after this change in your condition, a marriage with your daughter will be out of the question.

CAPT. Don't say that, your honour—love levels all ranks.

SIR JOSEPH. It does to a considerable extent, but it does not level them as much as that. (*Handing* JOSEPHINE *to* RALPH.) Here—take her, sir, and mind you treat her kindly.

RALPH *and* JOS. Oh bliss, oh rapture!

CAPT. *and* BUT. Oh rapture, oh bliss!

SIR JOSEPH. Sad my lot and sorry,
What shall I do? I cannot live alone!

HEBE. Fear nothing—while I live I'll not desert you.
I'll soothe and comfort your declining days.

SIR JOSEPH. No, don't do that.

HEBE. Yes, but indeed I'd rather—

SIR JOSEPH (*resigned*). To-morrow morn our vows shall all be plighted,
Three loving pairs on the same day united!

QUARTETTE

JOSEPHINE, HEBE, RALPH, *and* DEADEYE

Oh joy, oh rapture unforeseen,
The clouded sky is now serene,
The god of day—the orb of love,
Has hung his ensign high above,
The sky is all ablaze.

With wooing words and loving song,
We'll chase the lagging hours along,
And if {he finds / I find} the maiden coy,
We'll murmur forth decorous joy,
In dreamy roundelay.

CAPT. For he's the Captain of the *Pinafore*.
ALL. And a right good captain too!
CAPT. And though before my fall
I was captain of you all,
I'm a member of the crew.

ALL. Although before his fall, etc.

CAPT. I shall marry with a wife,
In my humble rank of life! (*turning to* BUT.)
And you, my own, are she—
I must wander to and fro;
But wherever I may go,
I shall never be untrue to thee!

ALL. What, never?

CAPT. No, never!

ALL. What, *never*?

CAPT. Hardly ever!

ALL. Hardly ever be untrue to thee.
Then give three cheers, and one cheer more
For the former Captain of the *Pinafore*.

BUT. For he loves Little Buttercup, dear Little Buttercup,
Though I could never tell why;
But still he loves Buttercup, poor Little Buttercup,
Sweet Little Buttercup, aye!

ALL. For he loves, etc.

SIR JOSEPH. I'm the monarch of the sea,
And when I've married thee (*to* HEBE),
I'll be true to the devotion that my love implants,

HEBE. Then good-bye to his sisters, and his cousins, and his aunts,
Especially his cousins,
Whom he reckons up by dozens,
His sisters, and his cousins, and his aunts!

ALL. For he is an Englishman,
And he himself hath said it,
And it's greatly to his credit
That he is an Englishman!

CURTAIN

THE PIRATES OF PENZANCE

OR

THE SLAVE OF DUTY

DRAMATIS PERSONÆ

MAJOR-GENERAL STANLEY

THE PIRATE KING

SAMUEL (*his Lieutenant*)

FREDERIC (*the Pirate Apprentice*)

SERGEANT OF POLICE

MABEL, EDITH, KATE, ISABEL (*General Stanley's Daughters*)

RUTH (*a Pirate Maid of all Work*)

Chorus of Pirates, Police, and General Stanley's Daughters

ACT I

A ROCKY SEA-SHORE ON THE COAST OF CORNWALL

ACT II

A RUINED CHAPEL BY MOONLIGHT

First produced at the Opéra Comique on April 3, 1880

THE PIRATES OF PENZANCE

OR

THE SLAVE OF DUTY

ACT I

SCENE.—*A rocky sea-shore on the coast of Cornwall. In the distance is a calm sea, on which a schooner is lying at anchor. As the curtain rises groups of pirates are discovered—some drinking, some playing cards.* SAMUEL, *the Pirate Lieutenant, is going from one group to another, filling the cups from a flask.* FREDERIC *is seated in a despondent attitude at the back of the scene.*

OPENING CHORUS

Pour, oh, pour the pirate sherry;
Fill, oh, fill the pirate glass;
And, to make us more than merry,
Let the pirate bumper pass.

SAM. For to-day our pirate 'prentice
Rises from indenture freed;
Strong his arm and keen his scent is,
He's a pirate now indeed!

ALL. Here's good luck to Frederic's ventures!
Frederic's out of his indentures.

SAM. Two-and-twenty now he's rising,
And alone he's fit to fly,
Which we're bent on signalizing
With unusual revelry.

ALL. Here's good luck to Frederic's ventures!
Frederic's out of his indentures.
Pour, oh, pour the pirate sherry, etc.

FREDERIC *rises and comes forward with* PIRATE KING, *who enters*

KING. Yes, Frederic, from to-day you rank as a full-blown member of our band.

ALL. Hurrah.

FRED. My friends, I thank you all, from my heart, for your kindly wishes. Would that I could repay them as they deserve!

KING. What do you mean?

FRED. To-day I am out of my indentures, and to-day I leave you for ever.

KING. But this is quite unaccountable; a keener hand at scuttling a Cunarder or cutting out a P. & O. never shipped a handspike.

FRED. Yes, I have done my best for you. And why? It was my duty under my indentures, and I am the slave of duty. As a child I was regularly apprenticed to your band. It was through an error—no matter, the mistake was ours, not yours, and I was in honour bound by it.

SAM. An error? What error?

RUTH *enters*

FRED. I may not tell you; it would reflect upon my well-loved Ruth.

RUTH. Nay, dear master, my mind has long been gnawed by the cankering tooth of mystery. Better have it out at once.

SONG—RUTH

When Frederic was a little lad he proved so brave and daring,
His father thought he'd 'prentice him to some career seafaring.
I was, alas! his nurserymaid, and so it fell to *my* lot
To take and bind the promising boy apprentice to a *pilot*—
A life not bad for a hardy lad, though surely not a high lot,
Though I'm a nurse, you might do worse than make your boy a pilot.

I was a stupid nurserymaid, on breakers always steering,
And I did not catch the word aright, through being hard
of hearing;
Mistaking my instructions, which within my brain did
gyrate,
I took and bound this promising boy apprentice to a
pirate.
A sad mistake it was to make and doom him to a vile lot.
I bound him to a pirate—you—instead of to a pilot.

I soon found out, beyond all doubt, the scope of this
disaster,
But I hadn't the face to return to my place, and break
it to my master.
A nurserymaid is not afraid of what you people *call*
work,
So I made up my mind to go as a kind of piratical maid-
of-all-work.
And that is how you find me now, a member of your
shy lot,
Which you wouldn't have found, had he been bound
apprentice to a pilot.

RUTH. Oh, pardon! Frederic, pardon! (*Kneels.*)

FRED. Rise, sweet one, I have long pardoned you.

RUTH (*rises*). The two words were so much alike!

FRED. They were. They still are, though years have rolled over their heads. But this afternoon my obligation ceases. Individually, I love you all with affection unspeakable, but, collectively, I look upon you with a disgust that amounts to absolute detestation. Oh! pity me, my beloved friends, for such is my sense of duty that, once out of my indentures, I shall feel myself bound to devote myself heart and soul to your extermination!

ALL. Poor lad—poor lad! (*All weep.*)

KING. Well, Frederic, if you conscientiously feel that it is your duty to destroy us, we cannot blame you for acting on that conviction. Always act in accordance with the dictates of your conscience, my boy, and chance the consequences.

SAM. Besides, we can offer you but little temptation

to remain with us. We don't seem to make piracy pay. I'm sure I don't know why, but we don't.

FRED. *I* know why, but, alas! I mustn't tell you; it wouldn't be right.

KING. Why not, my boy? It's only half-past eleven, and you are one of us until the clock strikes twelve.

SAM. True, and until then you are bound to protect our interests.

ALL. Hear, hear!

FRED. Well, then, it is my duty, as a pirate, to tell you that you are too tender-hearted. For instance, you make a point of never attacking a weaker party than yourselves, and when you attack a stronger party you invariably get thrashed.

KING. There is some truth in that.

FRED. Then, again, you make a point of never molesting an orphan!

SAM. Of course: we are orphans ourselves, and know what it is.

FRED. Yes, but it has got about, and what is the consequence? Every one we capture says he's an orphan. The last three ships we took proved to be manned entirely by orphans, and so we had to let them go. One would think that Great Britain's mercantile navy was recruited solely from her orphan asylums—which we know is not the case.

SAM. But, hang it all! you wouldn't have us absolutely merciless?

FRED. There's my difficulty; until twelve o'clock I would, after twelve I wouldn't. Was ever a man placed in so delicate a situation.

RUTH. And Ruth, your own Ruth, whom you love so well, and who has won her middle-aged way into your boyish heart, what is to become of *her*?

KING. Oh, he will take you with him.

FRED. Well, Ruth, I feel some little difficulty about you. It is true that I admire you very much, but I have been constantly at sea since I was eight years old, and yours is the only woman's face I have seen during that time. I think it is a sweet face.

RUTH. It is—oh, it is!

FRED. I say I *think* it is; that is my impression. But as I have never had an opportunity of comparing you with other women, it is just possible I may be mistaken.

KING. True.

FRED. What a terrible thing it would be if I were to marry this innocent person, and then find out that she is, on the whole, plain!

KING. Oh, Ruth, is very well, very well indeed.

SAM. Yes, there are the remains of a fine woman about Ruth.

FRED. Do you really think so?

SAM. I do.

FRED. Then I will not be so selfish as to take her from you. In justice to her, and in consideration for you, I will leave her behind. (*Hands* RUTH *to* KING.)

KING. No, Frederic, this must not be. We are rough men who lead a rough life, but we are not so utterly heartless as to deprive thee of thy love. I think I am right in saying that there is not one here who would rob thee of this inestimable treasure for all the world holds dear.

ALL (*loudly*). Not one!

KING. No, I thought there wasn't. Keep thy love, Frederic, keep thy love. (*Hands her back to* FREDERIC.)

FRED. You're very good, I'm sure. [*Exit* RUTH.

KING. Well, it's the top of the tide, and we must be off. Farewell, Frederic. When your process of extermination begins, let our deaths be as swift and painless as you can conveniently make them.

FRED. I will! By the love I have for you, I swear it! Would that you could render this extermination unnecessary by accompanying me back to civilization!

KING. No, Frederic, it cannot be. I don't think much of our profession, but, contrasted with respectability, it is comparatively honest. No, Frederic, I shall live and die a Pirate King.

SONG—PIRATE KING

Oh better far to live and die
Under the brave black flag I fly,
Than play a sanctimonious part,

With a pirate head and a pirate heart.
Away to the cheating world go you,
Where pirates all are well-to-do;
But I'll be true to the song I sing,
And live and die a Pirate King.
For I am a Pirate King.

ALL. You are!
Hurrah for our Pirate King!

KING. And it is, it is a glorious thing
To be a Pirate King.

ALL. Hurrah!
Hurrah for our Pirate King!

KING. When I sally forth to seek my prey
I help myself in a royal way:
I sink a few more ships, it's true,
Than a well-bred monarch ought to do;
But many a king on a first-class throne,
If he wants to call his crown his own,
Must manage somehow to get through
More dirty work than ever *I* do,
Though I am a Pirate King.

ALL. You are!
Hurrah for our Pirate King!

KING. And it is, it is a glorious thing
To be a Pirate King!

ALL. It is!
Hurrah for our Pirate King!

[*Exeunt all except* FREDERIC.

Enter RUTH

RUTH. Oh, take me with you! I cannot live if I am left behind.

FRED. Ruth, I will be quite candid with you. You are very dear to me, as you know, but I must be circumspect. You see, you are considerably older than I. A lad of twenty-one usually looks for a wife of seventeen.

RUTH. A wife of seventeen! You will find me a wife of a thousand!

FRED. No, but I shall find you a wife of forty-seven, and that is quite enough. Ruth, tell me candidly, and without reserve: compared with other women—how are *you?*

RUTH. I will answer you truthfully, master—I have a slight cold, but otherwise I am quite well.

FRED. I am sorry for your cold, but I was referring rather to your personal appearance. Compared with other women, are you beautiful?

RUTH (*bashfully*). I have been told so, dear master.

FRED. Ah, but lately?

RUTH. Oh, no, years and years ago.

FRED. What do you think of yourself?

RUTH. It is a delicate question to answer, but I think I am a fine woman.

FRED. That is your candid opinion?

RUTH. Yes, I should be deceiving you if I told you otherwise.

FRED. Thank you, Ruth, I believe you, for I am sure you would not practise on my inexperience; I wish to do the right thing, and if—I say *if*—you are really a fine woman, your age shall be no obstacle to our union! (*Chorus of Girls heard in the distance.*) Hark! Surely I hear voices! Who has ventured to approach our all but inaccessible lair? Can it be Custom House? No, it does not sound like Custom House.

RUTH (*aside*). Confusion! it is the voices of young girls! If he should see them I am lost.

FRED. (*looking off*). By all that's marvellous, a bevy of beautiful maidens!

RUTH (*aside*). Lost! lost! lost!

FRED. How lovely! how surpassingly lovely is the plainest of them! What grace—what delicacy—what refinement! And Ruth—Ruth told me she was beautiful!

RECIT

FRED. Oh, false one, you have deceived me!
RUTH. I have deceived you?
FRED. Yes, deceived me!
(*Denouncing her.*)

DUET—FRED. *and* RUTH

FRED. You told me you were fair as gold!

RUTH (*wildly*). And, master, am I not so?
FRED. And now I see you're plain and old.
RUTH. I am sure I am not a jot so.
FRED. Upon my innocence you play.
RUTH. I'm not the one to plot so.
FRED. Your face is lined, your hair is grey.
RUTH. It's gradually got so.
FRED. Faithless woman, to deceive me,
I who trusted so!
RUTH. Master, master, do not leave me!
Hear me, ere you go!
My love without reflecting,
Oh, do not be rejecting.
Take a maiden tender—her affection raw and green,
At very highest rating,
Has been accumulating
Summers seventeen—summers seventeen.
Don't, beloved master,
Crush me with disaster.
What is such a dower to the dower I have here?
My love unabating
Has been accumulating
Forty-seven year—forty-seven year!

ENSEMBLE

RUTH	FRED
Don't, beloved master,	Yes, your former master
Crush me with disaster.	Saves you from disaster.
What is such a dower to the dower I have here?	Your love would be uncomfortably fervid, it is clear,
My love unabating	If, as you are stating,
Has been accumulating	It's been accumulating
Forty-seven year — forty-seven year!	Forty-seven year — forty-seven year!

[*At the end he renounces her, and she goes off in despair.*

RECIT—FRED.

What shall I do? Before these gentle maidens
I dare not show in this alarming costume.
No, no, I must remain in close concealment
Until I can appear in decent clothing!

(*Hides in cave as they enter climbing over the rocks.*)

GIRLS. Climbing over rocky mountain,
Skipping rivulet and fountain,
Passing where the willows quiver
By the ever-rolling river,
Swollen with the summer rain;
Threading long and leafy mazes
Dotted with unnumbered daisies;
Scaling rough and rugged passes,
Climb the hardy little lasses,
Till the bright sea-shore they gain!

EDITH. Let us gaily tread the measure,
Make the most of fleeting leisure;
Hail it as a true ally,
Though it perish by and by.

ALL. Hail it as a true ally,
Though it perish by and by.

EDITH. Every moment brings a treasure
Of its own especial pleasure,
Though the moments quickly die,
Greet them gaily as they fly.

KATE. Far away from toil and care,
Revelling in fresh sea air,
Here we live and reign alone
In a world that's all our own.
Here in this our rocky den,
Far away from mortal men,
We'll be queens, and make decrees—
They may honour them who please.

ALL. Let us gaily tread the measure, etc.

KATE. What a picturesque spot! I wonder where we are!

EDITH. And I wonder where papa is. We have left him ever so far behind.

ISABEL. Oh, he will be here presently! Remember poor papa is not as young as we are, and we have come over a rather difficult country.

KATE. But how thoroughly delightful it is to be so entirely alone! Why, in all probability we are the first human beings who ever set foot on this enchanting spot.

ISABEL. Except the mermaids—it's the very place for mermaids.

KATE. Who are only human beings down to the waist!

EDITH. And who can't be said strictly to set *foot* anywhere. Tails they may, but feet they *cannot.*

KATE. But what shall we do until papa and the servants arrive with the luncheon?

EDITH. We are quite alone, and the sea is as smooth as glass. Suppose we take off our shoes and stockings and paddle?

ALL. Yes, yes! The very thing! (*They prepare to carry out the suggestion. They have all taken off one shoe, when* FREDERIC *comes forward from cave.*)

FRED. (*recitative*). Stop, ladies, pray!
ALL (*hopping on one foot*). A man!
FRED. I had intended
Not to intrude myself upon your notice
In this effective but alarming costume,
But under these peculiar circumstances
It is my bounden duty to inform you
That your proceedings will not be unwitnessed!
EDITH. But who are you, sir? Speak! (*All hopping.*)
FRED. I am a pirate!
ALL (*recoiling, hopping*). A pirate! Horror!
FRED. Ladies, do not shun me!
This evening I renounce my wild profession;
And to that end, oh, pure and peerless maidens!
Oh, blushing buds of ever-blooming beauty!
I, sore at heart, implore your kind assistance.
EDITH. How pitiful his tale!
KATE. How rare his beauty!
ALL. How pitiful his tale! How rare his beauty!

SONG—FRED.

Oh, is there not one maiden breast
Which does not feel the moral beauty
Of making worldly interest
Subordinate to sense of duty?

Who would not give up willingly
All matrimonial ambition,
To rescue such a one as I
From his unfortunate position?

ALL. Alas! there's not one maiden breast
Which seems to feel the moral beauty
Of making worldly interest
Subordinate to sense of duty!

FRED. Oh, is there not one maiden here
Whose homely face and bad complexion
Have caused all hopes to disappear
Of ever winning man's affection?
To such a one, if such there be,
I swear by Heaven's arch above you,
If you will cast your eyes on me—
However plain you be—I'll love you!

ALL. Alas! there's not one maiden here
Whose homely face and bad complexion
Have caused all hope to disappear
Of ever winning man's affection!

FRED. (*in despair*). Not one?
ALL. No, no—not one!
FRED. Not one?
ALL. No, no!

MABEL *enters*

MABEL. Yes, one!
ALL. 'Tis Mabel!
MABEL. Yes, 'tis Mabel!

RECIT—MABEL

Oh, sisters, deaf to pity's name,
For shame!
It's true that he has gone astray,
But pray
Is that a reason good and true
Why you
Should all be deaf to pity's name?

ALL (*aside*). The question is, had he not been
A thing of beauty,
Would she be swayed by quite as keen
A sense of duty?

MABEL. For shame, for shame, for shame!

SONG—MABEL

Poor wandering one!
Though thou hast surely strayed,
Take heart of grace,
Thy steps retrace,
Poor wandering one!
Poor wandering one!
If such poor love as mine
Can help thee find
True peace of mind—
Why, take it, it is thine!
Take heart, fair days will shine;
Take any heart—take mine!

ALL. Take heart; no danger lowers;
Take any heart—but ours!

[*Exeunt* MABEL *and* FREDERIC.

(EDITH *beckons her sisters, who form in a semicircle around her.*)

EDITH

What ought we to do,
Gentle sisters, say?
Propriety, we know,
Says we ought to stay;
While sympathy exclaims,
"Free them from your tether—
Play at other games—
Leave them here together."

KATE

Her case may, any day,
Be yours, my dear, or mine.

Let her make her hay
  While the sun doth shine.
Let us compromise,
  (Our hearts are not of leather.)
Let us shut our eyes,
  And talk about the weather.

GIRLS. Yes, yes, let's talk about the weather.

Chattering chorus

How beautifully blue the sky,
The glass is rising very high,
Continue fine I hope it may,
And yet it rained but yesterday.
To-morrow it may pour again
(I hear the country wants some rain),
Yet people say, I know not why,
That we shall have a warm July.

Enter MABEL *and* FREDERIC

[*During* MABEL'S *solo the* GIRLS *continue chatter pianissimo, but listening eagerly all the time.*

SOLO—MABEL

Did ever maiden wake
  From dream of homely duty,
To find her daylight break
  With such exceeding beauty?
Did ever maiden close
  Her eyes on waking sadness,
To dream of such exceeding gladness?

FRED. Oh, yes! ah, yes! this is exceeding gladness.
GIRLS. How beautifully blue the sky, etc.

SOLO—FRED

[*During this,* GIRLS *continue their chatter pianissimo as before, but listening intently all the time.*

Did ever pirate roll
  His soul in guilty dreaming,
And wake to find that soul
  With peace and virtue beaming?

ENSEMBLE

MABEL	FRED	GIRLS
Did ever maiden wake, etc.	Did ever pirate roll, etc.	How beautifully blue the sky, etc.

RECIT—FRED

Stay, we must not lose our senses;
Men who stick at no offences
Will anon be here.
Piracy their dreadful trade is
Pray you, get you hence, young ladies,
While the coast is clear.
[FREDERIC *and* MABEL *retire.*

GIRLS. No, we must not lose our senses,
If they stick at no offences
We should not be here.
Piracy their dreadful trade is—
Nice companions for the young ladies!
Let us disappear.

[*During this chorus the* PIRATES *have entered stealthily, and formed in a semicircle behind the* GIRLS. *As the* GIRLS *move to go off each* PIRATE *seizes a girl.* KING *seizes* EDITH *and* ISABEL, SAMUEL *seizes* KATE.

ALL. Too late!
PIRATES. Ha! Ha!
ALL. Too late!
PIRATES. Ha! Ha!
Ha! ha! ha! ha! Ha! ha! ha! ha!

ENSEMBLE

(*Pirates pass in front of Girls.*)	(*Girls pass in front of Pirates.*)
PIRATES	GIRLS
Here's a first-rate opportunity	We have missed our opportunity
To get married with impunity,	Of escaping with impunity;
And indulge in the felicity	So farewell to the felicity
Of unbounded domesticity.	Of our maiden domesticity!
You shall quickly be parsonified,	We shall quickly be parsonified,
Conjugally matrimonified,	Conjugally matrimonified,
By a doctor of divinity,	By a doctor of divinity,
Who resides in this vicinity.	Who resides in this vicinity.

MABEL (*coming forward*).

RECIT

Hold, monsters! Ere your pirate caravanserai
Proceed, against our will, to wed us all,
Just bear in mind that we are Wards in Chancery,
And father is a Major-General!

SAM. (*cowed*). We'd better pause, or danger may befall,
Their father is a Major-General.

GIRLS. Yes, yes; he is a Major-General!

The MAJOR-GENERAL *has entered unnoticed, on rock*

GEN. Yes, I am a Major-General!
SAM. For he is a Major-General!
ALL. He is! Hurrah for the Major-General!
GEN. And it is—it is a glorious thing
To be a Major-General!
ALL. It is! Hurrah for the Major-General!

SONG—MAJOR-GENERAL

I am the very model of a modern Major-General,
I've information vegetable, animal, and mineral,
I know the kings of England, and I quote the fights historical,
From Marathon to Waterloo, in order categorical;
I'm very well acquainted too with matters mathematical,
I understand equations, both the simple and quadratical,
About binomial theorem I'm teeming with a lot o' news—
With many cheerful facts about the square of the hypotenuse.

ALL. With many cheerful facts, etc.

GEN. I'm very good at integral and differential calculus,
I know the scientific names of beings animalculous;
In short, in matters vegetable, animal, and mineral,
I am the very model of a modern Major-General.

ALL. In short, in matters vegetable, animal, and mineral,
He is the very model of a modern Major-General.

GEN. I know our mythic history, King Arthur's and Sir Caradoc's,
I answer hard acrostics, I've a pretty taste for paradox,
I quote in elegiacs all the crimes of Heliogabalus,
In conics I can floor peculiarities parabolous.
I can tell undoubted Raphaels from Gerard Dows and Zoffanies,
I know the croaking chorus from the *Frogs* of Aristophanes,
Then I can hum a fugue of which I've heard the music's din afore,
And whistle all the airs from that infernal nonsense *Pinafore*.

ALL. And whistle all the airs, etc.

GEN. Then I can write a washing bill in Babylonic cuneiform,
And tell you every detail of Caractacus's uniform;
In short, in matters vegetable, animal, and mineral,
I am the very model of a modern Major-General.

ALL. In short, in matters vegetable, animal, and mineral,
He is the very model of a modern Major-General.

GEN. In fact, when I know what is meant by "mamelon" and "ravelin,"
When I can tell at sight a chassepôt rifle from a javelin,
When such affairs as sorties and surprises I'm more wary at,
And when I know precisely what is meant by "commissariat",
When I have learnt what progress has been made in modern gunnery,
When I know more of tactics than a novice in a nunnery:
In short, when I've a smattering of elemental strategy,
You'll say a better Major-Gener*al* has never *sat* a gee—

ALL. You'll say a better, etc.

GEN. For my military knowledge, though I'm plucky and adventury,
Has only been brought down to the beginning of the century;
But still in matters vegetable, animal, and mineral,
I am the very model of a modern Major-General.

ALL. But still in matters vegetable, animal, and mineral,
He is the very model of a modern Major-General.

GEN. And now that I've introduced myself I should like to have some idea of what's going on.

KATE. Oh, papa—we——

SAM. Permit me, I'll explain in two words: we propose to marry your daughters.

GEN. Dear me!

GIRLS. Against our wills, papa—against our wills!

GEN. Oh, but you mustn't do that! May I ask—this is a picturesque uniform, but I'm not familiar with it. What are you?

KING. We are all single gentlemen.

GEN. Yes, I gathered that—anything else?

KING. No, nothing else.

EDITH. Papa, don't believe them; they are pirates—the famous Pirates of Penzance!

GEN. The Pirates of Penzance! I have often heard of them.

MABEL. All except this gentleman—(*indicating* FREDERIC)—who was a pirate once, but who is out of his indentures to-day, and who means to lead a blameless life evermore.

GEN. But wait a bit. I object to pirates as sons-in-law.

KING. We object to Major-Generals as fathers-in-law. But we waive that point. We do not press it. We look over it.

GEN. (*aside*). Hah! an idea! (*Aloud*). And do you mean to say that you would deliberately rob me of these, the sole remaining props of my old age, and leave me to go through the remainder of my life unfriended, unprotected, and alone?

KING. Well, yes, that's the idea.

GEN. Tell me, have you ever known what it is to be an orphan?

PIRATES (*disgusted*). Oh, dash it all!

KING. Here we are again!

GEN. I ask you, have you ever known what it is to be an orphan?

KING. Often!

GEN. Yes, orphan. Have you ever known what it is to be one?

KING. I say, often.

ALL (*disgusted*). Often, often, often. (*Turning away.*)

GEN. I don't think we quite understand one another. I ask you, have you ever known what it is to be an orphan, and you say "orphan". As I understand you, you are merely repeating the word "orphan" to show that you understand me.

KING. I didn't repeat the word often.

GEN. Pardon me, you did indeed.

KING. I only repeated it once.

GEN. True, but you repeated it.

KING. But not often.

GEN. Stop: I think I see where we are getting confused. When you said "orphan", did you mean "orphan" —a person who has lost his parents, or "often"—frequently?

KING. Ah! I beg pardon—I see what you mean—frequently.

GEN. Ah! you said often—frequently.

KING. No, only once.

GEN. (*irritated*). Exactly—you said often, frequently, only once.

RECIT—GENERAL

Oh, men of dark and dismal fate,
Forgo your cruel employ,
Have pity on my lonely state,
I am an orphan boy!

KING *and* SAM. An orphan boy?
GEN. An orphan boy!
PIRATES. How sad—an orphan boy.

SOLO—GENERAL

These children whom you see
Are all that I can call my own!
PIRATES. Poor fellow!
GEN. Take them away from me
And I shall be indeed alone.
PIRATES. Poor fellow!
GEN. If pity you can feel,
Leave me my sole remaining joy—
See, at your feet they kneel;
Your hearts you cannot steel
Against the sad, sad tale of the lonely orphan boy!
PIRATES (*sobbing*). Poor fellow!
See at our feet they kneel;
Our hearts we cannot steel
Against the sad, sad tale of the lonely orphan boy!

KING. The orphan boy!

SAM. The orphan boy!

ALL. The lonely orphan boy! Poor fellow!

ENSEMBLE

GENERAL (*aside*)	GIRLS (*aside*)	PIRATES (*aside*)
I'm telling a terrible story	He's telling a terrible story,	If he's telling a terrible story,
But it doesn't diminish my glory;	Which will tend to diminish his glory;	He shall die by a death that is gory,
For they would have taken my daughters	Though they would have taken his daughters	One of the cruellest slaughters
Over the billowy waters,	Over the billowy waters.	That ever were known in these waters;
If I hadn't, in elegant diction,	It's easy, in elegant diction,	And we'll finish his moral affliction
Indulged in an innocent fiction;	To call it an innocent fiction,	By a very complete malediction,
Which is not in the same categ*ory*	But it comes in the same categ*ory*	As a compliment valedict*ory*,
As a regular terrible story.	As a regular terrible story.	If he's telling a terrible story.

KING. Although our dark career
Sometimes involves the crime of stealing,
We rather think that we're
Not altogether void of feeling.
Although we live by strife,
We're always sorry to begin it,
For what, we ask, is life
Without a touch of Poetry in it?

ALL (*kneeling*).
Hail, Poetry, thou heaven-born maid!
Thou gildest e'en the pirate's trade:
Hail, flowing fount of sentiment!
All hail, Divine Emollient! (*All rise.*)

KING. You may go, for you're at liberty, our pirate rules protect you,
And honorary members of our band we do elect you!

SAM. For he is an orphan boy.

CHORUS. He is! Hurrah for the orphan boy.
GEN. And it sometimes is a useful thing
To be an orphan boy.
CHORUS. It is! Hurrah for the orphan boy!

Oh, happy day, with joyous glee
They will away and married be;
Should it befall auspiciously,
Our sisters all will bridesmaids be!

RUTH *enters and comes down to* FREDERIC

RUTH. Oh, master, hear one word, I do implore you!
Remember Ruth, your Ruth, who kneels before you!
CHORUS. Yes, yes, remember Ruth, who kneels before you!
FRED. (PIRATES *threaten* RUTH.) Away, you did deceive me!
CHORUS. Away, you did deceive him!

RUTH. Oh, do not leave me!
CHORUS. Oh, do not leave her!

FRED. Away, you grieve me!
CHORUS. Away, you grieve him!
FRED. I wish you'd leave me!

(FREDERIC *casts* RUTH *from him.*)

CHORUS. We wish you'd leave him!

ENSEMBLE

Pray observe the magnanimity
{We / They} display to lace and dimity!
Never was such opportunity
To get married with impunity,
But {we / they} give up the felicity
Of unbounded domesticity,
Though a doctor of divinity
Resides in this vicinity.

[GIRLS *and* GENERAL *go up rocks, while* PIRATES *indulge in a wild dance of delight on stage. The* GENERAL *produces a British flag, and the* PIRATE KING *produces a black flag with skull and cross-bones. Enter* RUTH, *who makes a final appeal to* FREDERIC, *who casts her from him.*

END OF ACT I

ACT II

SCENE.—*A Ruined Chapel by Moonlight. Ruined Gothic windows at back.* GENERAL STANLEY *discovered seated pensively, surrounded by his daughters.*

CHORUS

Oh, dry the glistening tear
  That dews that martial cheek;
Thy loving children hear,
  In them thy comfort seek.
With sympathetic care
  Their arms around thee creep,
For oh, they cannot bear
  To see their father weep!

Enter MABEL

SOLO—MABEL

Dear father, why leave your bed
  At this untimely hour,
When happy daylight is dead,
  And darksome dangers lower?
See heaven has lit her lamp,
  The midnight hour is past,
The chilly night air is damp,
  And the dews are falling fast!

Dear father, why leave your bed
When happy daylight is dead?

FREDERIC *enters*

MABEL. Oh, Frederic, cannot you, in the calm excellence of your wisdom, reconcile it with your conscience to say something that will relieve my father's sorrow?

FRED. I will try, dear Mabel. But why does he sit, night after night, in this draughty old ruin?

GEN. Why do I sit here? To escape from the pirates' clutches, I described myself as an orphan, and, heaven help me, I am no orphan! I come here to humble myself before the tombs of my ancestors, and to implore their pardon for having brought dishonour on the family escutcheon.

FRED. But you forget, sir, you only bought the property a year ago, and the stucco in your baronial hall is scarcely dry.

GEN. Frederic, in this chapel are ancestors: you cannot deny that. With the estate, I bought the chapel and its contents. I don't know whose ancestors they *were,* but I know whose ancestors they *are,* and I shudder to think that their descendant by purchase (if I may so describe myself) should have brought disgrace upon what, I have no doubt, was an unstained escutcheon.

FRED. Be comforted. Had you not acted as you did, these reckless men would assuredly have called in the nearest clergyman, and have married your large family on the spot.

GEN. I thank you for your proffered solace, but it is unavailing. I assure you, Frederic, that such is the anguish and remorse I feel at the abominable falsehood by which I escaped these easily deluded pirates, that I would go to their simple-minded chief this very night and confess all, did I not fear that the consequences would be most disastrous to myself. At what time does your expedition march against these scoundrels?

FRED. At eleven, and before midnight I hope to have atoned for my involuntary association with the pestilent scourges by sweeping them from the face of the earth—and then, dear Mabel, you will be mine!

GEN. Are your devoted followers at hand?
FRED. They are, they only wait my orders.

RECIT—GENERAL

Then, Frederic, let your escort lion-hearted
Be summoned to receive a General's blessing,
Ere they depart upon their dread adventure.

FRED. Dear sir, they come.

Enter POLICE, *marching in single file. They form in line, facing audience*

SONG—SERGEANT

When the foeman bares his steel,
Tarantara! tarantara!
We uncomfortable feel,
Tarantara!
And we find the wisest thing,
Tarantara! tarantara!
Is to slap our chests and sing
Tarantara!
For when threatened with emeutes,
Tarantara! tarantara!
And your heart is in your boots,
Tarantara!
There is nothing brings it round,
Tarantara! tarantara!
Like the trumpet's martial sound,
Tarantara! tarantara!
Tarantara-ra-ra-ra-ra!

ALL. Tarantara-ra-ra-ra-ra!

MABEL. Go, ye heroes, go to glory,
Though you die in combat gory,
Ye shall live in song and story.
Go to immortality!
Go to death, and go to slaughter;
Die, and every Cornish daughter
With her tears your grave shall water.
Go, ye heroes, go and die!

ALL. Go, ye heroes, go and die!

POLICE. Though to us it's evident,
Tarantara! tarantara!
These intentions are well meant,
Tarantara!
Such expressions don't appear,
Tarantara! tarantara!
Calculated men to cheer,
Tarantara!
Who are going to meet their fate
In a highly nervous state,
Tarantara!
Still to us it's evident
These intentions are well meant.
Tarantara!

EDITH. Go and do your best endeavour,
And before all links we sever,
We will say farewell for ever.
Go to glory and the grave!

GIRLS. For your foes are fierce and ruthless,
False, unmerciful, and truthless.
Young and tender, old and toothless,
All in vain their mercy crave.

SERG. We observe too great a stress,
On the risks that on us press,
And of reference a lack
To our chance of coming back.
Still, perhaps it would be wise
Not to carp or criticise,
For it's very evident
These attentions are well meant.

ALL. Yes, to them it's evident
Our attentions are well meant.
Tarantara-ra-ra-ra-ra!
Go, ye heroes, go to glory, etc.

ENSEMBLE

Chorus of all but Police

Go and do your best endeavour,
And before all links we sever
We will say farewell for ever.
Go to glory and the grave!
For your foes are fierce and ruthless,
False, unmerciful, and truthless.
Young and tender, old and toothless,
All in vain their mercy crave.

Chorus of Police

Such expressions don't appear,
Tarantara, tarantara!
Calculated men to cheer,
Tarantara!
Who are going to their fate,
Tarantara, tarantara!
In a highly nervous state—
Tarantara!
We observe too great a stress,
Tarantara, tarantara!
On the risks that on us press,
Tarantara!
And of reference a lack,
Tarantara, tarantara!
To our chance of coming back,
Tarantara!

GEN. Away, away!
POLICE (*without moving*). Yes, yes, we go.
GEN. These pirates slay.
POLICE. Tarantara!
GEN. Then do not stay.
POLICE. Tarantara!
GEN. Then why this delay?
POLICE. All right—we go.
Yes, forward on the foe!
GEN. Yes, but you *don't* go!
POLICE. We go, we go!
Yes, forward on the foe!
GEN. Yes, but you *don't* go!
ALL. At last they really go.

[MABEL *tears herself from* FREDERIC *and exit, followed by her sisters, consoling her. The* GENERAL *and others follow.* FREDERIC *remains.*

RECIT—FRED

Now for the pirates' lair! Oh, joy unbounded!
Oh, sweet relief! Oh, rapture unexampled!
At last I may atone, in some slight measure,
For the repeated acts of theft and pillage
Which, at a sense of duty's stern dictation,
I, circumstance's victim, have been guilty.

(KING *and* RUTH *appear at the window, armed.*)

KING. Young Frederic! (*Covering him with pistol.*)
FRED. Who calls?
KING. Your late commander!
RUTH. And I, your little Ruth! (*Covering him with pistol.*)
FRED. Oh, mad intruders,
How dare ye face me? Know ye not, oh rash ones,
That I have doomed you to extermination?

(KING *and* RUTH *hold a pistol to each ear.*)

KING. Have mercy on us, hear us, ere you slaughter.
FRED. I do not think I ought to listen to you.
Yet, mercy should alloy our stern resentment,
And so I will be merciful—say on!

TRIO—RUTH, KING, *and* FRED

RUTH. When you had left our pirate fold
We tried to raise our spirits faint,
According to our customs old,
With quips and quibbles quaint.
But all in vain the quips we heard,
We lay and sobbed upon the rocks,
Until to somebody occurred
A startling paradox.
FRED. A paradox?
KING (*laughing*). A paradox!
RUTH. A most ingenious paradox!
We've quips and quibbles heard in flocks,
But none to beat this paradox!
Ha! ha! ha! ha! Ho! ho! ho! ho!
KING. We knew your taste for curious quips,
For cranks and contradictions queer,
And with the laughter on our lips,
We wished you there to hear.
We said, "If we could tell it him,
How Frederic would the joke enjoy!"
And so we've risked both life and limb
To tell it to our boy.

FRED. (*interested*). That paradox? That paradox?

KING and RUTH (*laughing*). That most ingenious paradox!

We've quips and quibbles heard in flocks,
But none to beat that paradox!
Ha! ha! ha! ha! Ho! ho! ho! ho!

CHANT—KING

For some ridiculous reason, to which, however, I've no desire to be disloyal,
Some person in authority, I don't know who, very likely the Astronomer Royal,
Has decided that, although for such a beastly month as February, twenty-eight days as a rule are plenty.
One year in every four his days shall be reckoned as nine-and-twenty.
Through some singular coincidence—I shouldn't be surprised if it were owing to the agency of an ill-natured fairy—
You are the victim of this clumsy arrangement, having been born in leap-year, on the twenty-ninth of Febru*a*ry,
And so, by a simple arithmetical process, you'll easily discover,
That though you've lived twenty-one years, yet, if we go by birthdays, you're only five and a little bit over!

RUTH. Ha! ha! ha! ha!
KING. Ho! ho! ho! ho!
FRED. Dear me!
Let's see! (*counting on fingers*).
Yes, yes; with yours my figures do agree!
ALL. Ha! ha! ha! Ho! ho! ho! ho! (FREDERIC *more amused than any.*)
FRED. How quaint the ways of Paradox!
At common sense she gaily mocks!
Though counting in the usual way,
Years twenty-one I've been alive,
Yet, reckoning by my natal day,
I am a little boy of five!

ALL. He is a little boy of five! Ha! ha!
A paradox, a paradox,
A most ingenious paradox!
Ha! ha! ha! ha! Ho! ho! ho! ho! (RUTH *and* KING *throw themselves back on seats, exhausted with laughter.*)

FRED. Upon my word, this is most curious—most absurdly whimsical. Five-and-a-quarter! No one would think it to look at me!

RUTH. You are glad now, I'll be bound, that you spared us. You would never have forgiven yourself when you discovered that you had killed *two of your comrades.*

FRED. My comrades?

KING (*rises*). I'm afraid you don't appreciate the delicacy of your position. You were apprenticed to us——

FRED. Until I reached my twenty-first year.

KING. No, until you reached your twenty-first *birthday* (*producing document*), and, going by birthdays, you are as yet only five-and-a-quarter.

FRED. You don't mean to say you are going to hold me to that?

KING. No, we merely remind you of the fact, and leave the rest to your sense of duty.

RUTH. Your sense of duty!

FRED. (*wildly*). Don't put it on that footing! As I was merciful to you just now, be merciful to me! I implore you not to insist on the letter of your bond just as the cup of happiness is at my lips!

RUTH. We insist on nothing; we content ourselves with pointing out to you *your duty.*

KING. Your duty!

FRED. (*after a pause*). Well, you have appealed to my sense of duty, and my duty is only too clear. I abhor your infamous calling; I shudder at the thought that I have ever been mixed up with it; but duty is before all —at any price I will do my duty.

KING. Bravely spoken! Come, you are one of us once more.

FRED. Lead on, I follow. (*Suddenly.*) Oh, horror!

KING. }
RUTH. } What is the matter?

FRED. Ought I to tell you? No, no, I cannot do it; and yet, as one of your band——

KING. Speak out, I charge you by that sense of conscientiousness to which we have never yet appealed in vain.

FRED. General Stanley, the father of my Mabel——

KING. }
RUTH. } Yes, yes!

FRED. He escaped from you on the plea that he was an orphan!

KING. He did!

FRED. It breaks my heart to betray the honoured father of the girl I adore, but as your apprentice I have no alternative. It is my duty to tell you that General Stanley is no orphan!

KING. }
RUTH. } What!

FRED. More than that, he never was one!

KING. Am I to understand that, to save his contemptible life, he dared to practise on our credulous simplicity? (FREDERIC *nods as he weeps.*) Our revenge shall be swift and terrible. We will go and collect our band and attack Tremorden Castle this very night.

FRED. But—stay——

KING. Not a word! He is doomed!

TRIO

KING *and* RUTH

Away, away! my heart's on fire,
I burn this base deception to repay,
This very night my vengeance dire
Shall glut itself in gore. Away, away!

FRED

Away, away! ere I expire—
I find my duty hard to do to-day!
My heart is filled with anguish dire,
It strikes me to the core. Away, away!

KING.

With falsehood foul
He tricked us of our brides.
Let vengeance howl;
The Pirate so decides.
Our nature stern
He softened with his lies,
And, in return,
To-night the traitor dies.

ALL. Yes, yes! to-night the traitor dies.

RUTH. To-night he dies!
KING. Yes, or early to-morrow.
FRED. His girls likewise?
RUTH. They will welter in sorrow.
KING. The one soft spot
FRED. In their natures they cherish—
RUTH. And all who plot
KING. To abuse it shall perish!
ALL. Yes, all who plot
To abuse it shall perish!
Away, away! etc.

[*Exeunt* KING *and* RUTH.

Enter MABEL

RECIT—MABEL

All is prepared, your gallant crew await you.
My Frederic in tears? It cannot be
That lion-heart quails at the coming conflict?

FRED. No, Mabel, no. A terrible disclosure
Has just been made! Mabel, my dearly-loved one,
I bound myself to serve the pirate captain
Until I reached my one-and-twentieth birthday—

MABEL. But you *are* twenty-one?

FRED. I've just discovered
That I was born in leap-year, and that birthday
Will not be reached by me till 1940.

MABEL. Oh, horrible! catastrophe appalling!

FRED. And so, farewell!

MABEL. No, no! Ah, Frederic, hear me.

DUET—MABEL *and* FRED

MABEL. Stay, Frederic, stay!
They have no legal claim,
No shadow of a shame
Will fall upon thy name.
Stay, Frederic, stay!

FRED. Nay, Mabel, nay!
To-night I quit these walls,
The thought my soul appals,
But when stern Duty calls,
I must obey.

MABEL. Stay, Frederic, stay!
FRED. Nay, Mabel, nay!
MABEL. They have no claim—
FRED. But Duty's name!
The thought my soul appals,
But when stern Duty calls,
I must obey.

BALLAD—MABEL

Ah, leave me not to pine
Alone and desolate;
No fate seemed fair as mine,
No happiness so great!
And nature, day by day,
Has sung, in accents clear,
This joyous roundelay,
"He loves thee—he is here.
Fa-la, fa-la, fa-la."

FRED. Ah, must I leave thee here
In endless night to dream,
Where joy is dark and drear,
And sorrow all supreme!
Where nature, day by day,
Will sing, in altered tone,
This weary roundelay,
"He loves thee—he is gone.
Fa-la, fa-la, fa-la."

FRED. In 1940 I of age shall be,
I'll then return, and claim you—I declare it!
MABEL. It seems so long!
FRED. Swear that, till then, you will be true to me.
MABEL. Yes, I'll be strong!
By all the Stanleys dead and gone, I swear it!

ENSEMBLE

Oh, here is love, and here is truth,
And here is food for joyous laughter.
He / She will be faithful to his / her sooth
Till we are wed, and even after.

[FREDERIC *rushes to window and leaps out*

MABEL (*almost fainting*). No, I am brave! Oh, family descent,
How great thy charm, thy sway how excellent!
Come, one and all, undaunted men in blue,
A crisis, now, affairs are coming to!

Enter Police, marching in single file

SERG. Though in body and in mind,
Tarantara, tarantara!
We are timidly inclined,
Tarantara!
And anything but blind,
Tarantara, tarantara!
To the danger that's behind,
Tarantara!
Yet, when the danger's near,
Tarantara, tarantara!
We manage to appear,
Tarantara!
As insensible to fear
As anybody here.
Tarantara, tarantara-ra-ra-ra-ra!

MABEL. Sergeant, approach! Young Frederic was to have led you to death and glory.

ALL. That is not a pleasant way of putting it.

MABEL. No matter; he will not so lead you, for he has allied himself once more with his old associates.

ALL. He has acted shamefully!

MABEL. You speak falsely. You know nothing about it. He has acted nobly.

ALL. He has acted nobly!

MABEL. Dearly as I loved him before, his heroic sacrifice to his sense of duty has endeared him to me tenfold. He has done his duty. I will do mine. Go ye and do yours. [*Exit* MABEL.

ALL. Right oh!

SERG. This is perplexing.

ALL. We cannot understand it at all.

SERG. Still, as he is actuated by a sense of duty——

ALL. That makes a difference, of course. At the same time we repeat, we cannot understand it at all.

SERG. No matter; our course is clear. We must do our best to capture these pirates alone. It is most distressing to us to be the agents whereby our erring fellow-creatures are deprived of that liberty which is so dear to all—but we should have thought of that before we joined the Force.

ALL. We should!

SERG. It is too late now!

ALL. It is!

SONG—SERGEANT

SERG. When a felon's not engaged in his employment—
ALL. His employment,
SERG. Or maturing his felonious little plans—
ALL. Little plans,
SERG. His capacity for innocent enjoyment—
ALL. 'Cent enjoyment

SERG. Is just as great as any honest man's—
ALL. Honest man's.
SERG. Our feelings we with difficulty smother—
ALL. 'Culty smother
SERG. When constabulary duty's to be done—
ALL. To be done.
SERG. Ah, take one consideration with another—
ALL. With another,
SERG. A policeman's lot is not a happy one.
ALL. When constabulary duty's to be done—
To be done,
The policeman's lot is not a happy one.

SERG. When the enterprising burglar's not a-burgling—
ALL. Not a-burgling,
SERG. When the cut-throat isn't occupied in crime—
ALL. 'Pied in crime,
SERG. He loves to hear the little brook a-gurgling—
ALL. Brook a-gurgling,
SERG. And listen to the merry village chime—
ALL. Village chime.
SERG. When the coster's finished jumping on his mother—
ALL. On his mother,
SERG. He loves to lie a-basking in the sun—
ALL. In the sun.
SERG. Ah, take one consideration with another—
ALL. With another,
SERG. The policeman's lot is not a happy one.
ALL. When constabulary duty's to be done—
To be done,
The policeman's lot is not a happy one—
Happy one.

(*Chorus of Pirates without, in the distance.*)

A rollicking band of pirates we,
Who, tired of tossing on the sea,
Are trying their hand at a burglaree,
With weapons grim and gory.

SERG. Hush, hush! I hear them on the manor poaching,
With stealthy step the pirates are approaching.

(*Chorus of Pirates, resumed nearer.*)

We are not coming for plate or gold—
A story General Stanley's told—
We seek a penalty fifty-fold,
For General Stanley's story.

POLICE. They seek a penalty—
PIRATES (*without*). Fifty-fold,
We seek a penalty—
POLICE. Fifty-fold,
ALL. We / They } seek a penalty fifty-fold,
For General Stanley's story.
SERG. They come in force, with stealthy stride,
Our obvious course is now—to hide.

[*Police conceal themselves. As they do so, the Pirates are seen appearing at ruined window. They enter cautiously, and come down stage.* SAMUEL *is laden with burglarious tools and pistols, etc.*

CHORUS—PIRATES (*very loud*)

With cat-like tread,
Upon our prey we steal,
In silence dread
Our cautious way we feel.
No sound at all,
We never speak a word,
A fly's foot-fall
Would be distinctly heard—

POLICE (*pianissimo*). Tarantara, tarantara!
PIRATES. So stealthily the pirate creeps,
While all the household soundly sleeps.
Come, friends, who plough the sea,
Truce to navigation,
Take another station;
Let's vary piracee
With a little burglaree!
POLICE (*pianissimo*). Tarantara, tarantara!
SAM. (*distributing implements to various members of the gang*).
Here's your crowbar and your centrebit,
Your life-preserver—you may want to hit;

Your silent matches, your dark lantern seize,
Take your file and your skeletonic keys.

Enter KING, FREDERIC, *and* RUTH

ALL (*fortissimo*). With cat-like tread, etc.

RECIT

FRED. Hush, hush, not a word! I see a light inside!
The Major-General comes, so quickly hide!
PIRATES. Yes, yes, the Major-General comes!

[*Exeunt* KING, FREDERIC, SAMUEL, *and* RUTH.

POLICE. Yes, yes, the Major-General comes!

GEN. (*entering in dressing-gown, carrying a light*).
Yes, yes, the Major-General comes!

SOLO—GENERAL

Tormented with the anguish dread
Of falsehood unatoned,
I lay upon my sleepless bed,
And tossed and turned and groaned.
The man who finds his conscience ache
No peace at all enjoys,
And as I lay in bed awake
I thought I heard a noise.

PIRATES. } He thought he heard a noise—ha! ha!
POLICE. } He thought he heard a noise—ha! ha! (*Very loud.*)

GEN. No, all is still
In dale, on hill;
My mind is set at ease.
So still the scene—
It must have been
The sighing of the breeze.

BALLAD—GENERAL

Sighing softly to the river
Comes the loving breeze,
Setting nature all a-quiver,
Rustling through the trees—

ALL. Through the trees.

GEN. And the brook, in rippling measure,
Laughs for very love,
While the poplars, in their pleasure,
Wave their arms above.

POLICE. and PIRATES. Yes, the trees, for very love,
Wave their leafy arms above,
River, river, little river,
May thy loving prosper ever.
Heaven speed thee, poplar tree,
May thy wooing happy be.

GEN. Yet, the breeze is but a rover;
When he wings away,
Brook and poplar mourn a lover!
Sighing well-a-day!

ALL. Well-a-day!

GEN. Ah! the doing and undoing,
That the rogue could tell!
When the breeze is out a-wooing,
Who can woo so well?

POLICE. and PIRATES. Shocking tales the rogue could tell
Nobody can woo so well.
Pretty brook, thy dream is over,
For thy love is but a rover!

Sad the lot of poplar trees,
Courted by the fickle breeze!

[*Enter the* GENERAL'S *daughters, all in white peignoirs and night-caps, and carrying lighted candles*

GIRLS. Now what is this, and what is that, and why does father leave his rest
At such a time of night as this, so very incompletely dressed?
Dear father is, and always was, the most methodical of men!
It's his invariable rule to go to bed at half-past ten.
What strange occurrence can it be that calls dear father from his rest
At such a time of night as this, so very incompletely dressed?

Enter KING, SAMUEL, *and* FREDERIC

KING. Forward, my men, and seize that General there!
(*They seize the* GENERAL.)
GIRLS. The pirates! the pirates! Oh, despair!
PIRATES. Yes, we're the pirates, so despair!
GEN. Frederic here! Oh, joy! Oh, rapture!
Summon your men and effect their capture!
MABEL. Frederic, save us!
FRED. Beautiful Mabel,
I would if I could, but I am not able.
PIRATES. He's telling the truth, he is not able.
KING. With base deceit
You worked upon our feelings!
Revenge is sweet,
And flavours all our dealings!
With courage rare
And resolution manly,
For death prepare,
Unhappy General Stanley.

MABEL (*wildly*). Is he to die, unshriven—unannealed?
GIRLS. Oh, spare him!
MABEL. Will no one in his cause a weapon wield?
GIRLS. Oh, spare him!

POLICE (*springing up*). Yes, we are here, though hitherto concealed!
GIRLS. Oh, rapture!
POLICE. So to the Constabulary, pirates, yield!
GIRLS. Oh, rapture!

[*A struggle ensues between Pirates and Police. Eventually the Police are overcome, and fall prostrate, the Pirates standing over them with drawn swords.*

CHORUS OF POLICE AND PIRATES

You/We triumph now, for well we trow
Our mortal career's cut short,
No pirate band will take its stand
At the Central Criminal Court.

SERG. To gain a brief advantage you've contrived.
But your proud triumph will not be long-lived
KING. Don't say you are orphans, for we know that game.
SERG. On your allegiance we've a stronger claim—
We charge you yield, in Queen Victoria's name!
KING (*baffled*). You do!
POLICE. We do!
We charge you yield, in Queen Victoria's name!

[*Pirates kneel, Police stand over them triumphantly.*

KING. We yield at once, with humbled mien,
Because, with all our faults, we love our Queen
POLICE. Yes, yes, with all their faults, they love their Queen.
GIRLS. Yes, yes, with all, etc.

[*Police, holding Pirates by the collar, take out handkerchiefs and weep.*

GEN. Away with them, and place them at the bar!

Enter RUTH

RUTH. One moment! let me tell you who they are.
They are no members of the common throng;
They are all noblemen who have gone wrong!

GEN. No Englishman unmoved that statement hears,
Because, with all our faults, we love our House
of Peers.

RECIT—GENERAL

I pray you, pardon me, ex-Pirate King,
Peers will be peers, and youth will have its fling.
Resume your ranks and legislative duties,
And take my daughters, all of whom are beauties.

FINALE

Poor wandering ones!
Though ye have surely strayed,
Take heart of grace.
Your steps retrace,
Poor wandering ones!

Poor wandering ones!
If such poor love as ours
Can help you find
True peace of mind,
Why, take it, it is yours!
Poor wandering ones! etc.

CURTAIN

PATIENCE

OR

BUNTHORNE'S BRIDE

DRAMATIS PERSONÆ

COLONEL CALVERLEY MAJOR MURGATROYD LIEUT. THE DUKE OF DUNSTABLE	(*Officers of Dragoon Guards*)

REGINALD BUNTHORNE (*a Fleshly Poet*)

ARCHIBALD GROSVENOR (*an Idyllic Poet*)

MR. BUNTHORNE'S SOLICITOR

THE LADY ANGELA THE LADY SAPHIR THE LADY ELLA THE LADY JANE	(*Rapturous Maidens*)

PATIENCE (*a Dairy Maid*)

Chorus of Rapturous Maidens and Officers of Dragoon Guards

ACT I

EXTERIOR OF CASTLE BUNTHORNE

ACT II

A GLADE

First produced at the Opéra Comique on April 23, 1881

PATIENCE

OR

BUNTHORNE'S BRIDE

ACT I

SCENE.—*Exterior of Castle Bunthorne. Entrance to Castle by drawbridge over moat. Young ladies dressed in æsthetic draperies are grouped about the stage. They play on lutes, mandolins, etc., as they sing, and all are in the last stage of despair.* ANGELA, ELLA, *and* SAPHIR *lead them.*

CHORUS

Twenty love-sick maidens we,
Love-sick all against our will.
Twenty years hence we shall be
Twenty love-sick maidens still.
Twenty love-sick maidens we,
And we die for love of thee.

SOLO—ANGELA

Love feeds on hope, they say, or love will die—

ALL. Ah, miserie!

Yet my love lives, although no hope have I!

ALL. Ah, miserie!

Alas, poor heart, go hide thyself away—
To weeping concords tune thy roundelay!
Ah, miserie!

CHORUS

All our love is all for one,
Yet that love he heedeth not.

He is coy and cares for none,
  Sad and sorry is our lot!
                Ah, miserie!

SOLO—ELLA

Go, breaking heart,
  Go, dream of love requited;
Go, foolish heart,
  Go, dream of lovers plighted;
Go, madcap heart,
  Go, dream of never waking;
And in thy dream
  Forget that thou art breaking!

CHORUS. Ah, miserie!

ELLA. Forget that thou art breaking!

CHORUS. Twenty love-sick maidens, etc.

ANG. There is a strange magic in this love of ours! Rivals as we all are in the affections of our Reginald, the very hopelessness of our love is a bond that binds us to one another!

SAPH. Jealousy is merged in misery. While he, the very cynosure of our eyes and hearts, remains icy insensible—what have we to strive for?

ELLA. The love of maidens is, to him, as interesting as the taxes!

SAPH. Would that it were! He pays his taxes.

ANG. And cherishes the receipts!

Enter LADY JANE

SAPH. Happy receipts!

JANE (*suddenly*). Fools!

ANG. I beg your pardon?

JANE. Fools and blind! The man loves—wildly loves!

ANG. But whom? None of us!

JANE. No, none of us. His weird fancy has lighted, for the nonce, on Patience, the village milkmaid!

SAPH. On Patience? Oh, it cannot be!

JANE. Bah! But yesterday I caught him in her dairy, eating fresh butter with a tablespoon. To-day he is not well!

SAPH. But Patience boasts that she has never loved—that love is, to her, a sealed book! Oh, he cannot be serious!

JANE. 'Tis but a fleeting fancy—'twill quickly pass away. (*Aside.*) Oh, Reginald, if you but knew what a wealth of golden love is waiting for you, stored up in this rugged old bosom of mine, the milkmaid's triumph would be short indeed!

PATIENCE *appears on an eminence. She looks down with pity on the despondent Ladies*

RECIT—PATIENCE

Still brooding on their mad infatuation!
I thank thee, Love, thou comest not to me!
Far happier I, free from thy ministration,
Than dukes or duchesses who love can be!

SAPH. (*looking up*). 'Tis Patience—happy girl! Loved by a Poet!

PA. Your pardon, ladies. I intrude upon you. (*Going.*)

ANG. Nay, pretty child, come hither. Is it true
That you have never loved?

PA. Most true indeed.

SOPRANOS. Most marvellous!

CONTRALTOS. And most deplorable!

SONG—PATIENCE

I cannot tell what this love may be
That cometh to all, but not to me.
It cannot be kind as they'd imply,
Or why do these ladies sigh?
It cannot be joy and rapture deep,
Or why do these gentle ladies weep?
It cannot be blissful as 'tis said,
Or why are their eyes so wondrous red?

Though everywhere true love I see
A-coming to all, but not to me
I cannot tell what this love may be!
For I am blithe and I am gay,
While they sit sighing night and day

Think of the gulf 'twixt them and me,
"Fal la la la!"—and "Miserie!"

CHORUS. Yes, she is blithe, etc.

PA. If love is a thorn, they show no wit
Who foolishly hug and foster it.
If love is a weed, how simple they
Who gather it, day by day!
If love is a nettle that makes you smart,
Then why do you wear it next your heart?
And if it be none of these, say I,
Ah, why do you sit and sob and sigh?
Though everywhere, etc.

CHORUS. For she is blithe, etc.

ANG. Ah, Patience, if you have never loved, you have never known true happiness! (*All sigh.*)

PA. But the truly happy always seem to have so much on their minds. The truly happy never seem quite well.

JANE. There is a transcendentality of delirium—an acute accentuation of a supremest ecstasy—which the earthy might easily mistake for indigestion. But it is *not* indigestion—it is æsthetic transfiguration! (*To the others.*) Enough of babble. Come!

PA. But stay, I have some news for you. The 35th Dragoon Guards have halted in the village, and are even now on their way to this very spot.

ANG. The 35th Dragoon Guards!

SAPH. They are fleshly men, of full habit!

ELLA. We care nothing for Dragoon Guards!

PA. But, bless me, you were all engaged to them a year ago!

SAPH. A year ago!

ANG. My poor child, you don't understand these things. A year ago they were very well in our eyes, but since then our tastes have been etherealized, our perceptions exalted. (*To others.*) Come, it is time to lift up our voices in morning carol to our Reginald. Let us to his door.

[*The Ladies go off, two and two, into the Castle, singing refrain of "Twenty love-sick maidens we," and accompanying themselves on harps and mandolins.* PATIENCE *watches them in surprise, as she climbs the rock by which she entered.*

March. Enter Officers of Dragoon Guards, led by MAJOR

CHORUS OF DRAGOONS

The soldiers of our Queen
  Are linked in friendly tether;
Upon the battle scene
  They fight the foe together.
There every mother's son
  Prepared to fight and fall is;
The enemy of one
  The enemy of all is!

Enter COLONEL

SONG—COLONEL

If you want a receipt for that popular mystery.
  Known to the world as a Heavy Dragoon,
Take all the remarkable people in history,
  Rattle them off to a popular tune.
The pluck of Lord Nelson on board of the
    Victory—
  Genius of Bismarck devising a plan—
The humour of Fielding (which sounds contra-
    dictory)—

Coolness of Paget about to trepan—
The science of Jullien, the eminent musico—
Wit of Macaulay, who wrote of Queen Anne—
The pathos of Paddy, as rendered by Boucicault—
Style of the Bishop of Sodor and Man—
The dash of a D'Orsay, divested of quackery—
Narrative powers of Dickens and Thackeray—
Victor Emmanuel—peak-haunting Peveril—
Thomas Aquinas, and Doctor Sacheverell—
Tupper and Tennyson—Daniel Defoe—
Anthony Trollope and Mr. Guizot!

Take of these elements all that is fusible,
Melt them all down in a pipkin or crucible,
Set them to simmer and take off the scum,
And a Heavy Dragoon is the residuum!

CHORUS. Yes! yes! yes! yes!
A Heavy Dragoon is the residuum!

COL. If you want a receipt for this soldier-like paragon,
Get at the wealth of the Czar (if you can)—
The family pride of a Spaniard from Aragon—
Force of Mephisto pronouncing a ban—
A smack of Lord Waterford, reckless and rollicky—
Swagger of Roderick, heading his clan—
The keen penetration of Paddington Pollaky—
Grace of an Odalisque on a divan—
The genius strategic of Cæsar or Hannibal—
Skill of Sir Garnet in thrashing a cannibal—
Flavour of Hamlet—the Stranger, a touch of him—
Little of Manfred (but not very much of him)—
Beadle of Burlington—Richardson's show—
Mr. Micawber and Madame Tussaud!
Take of these elements all that is fusible,
Melt them all down in a pipkin or crucible,
Set them to simmer and take off the scum,
And a Heavy Dragoon is the residuum!

ALL. Yes! yes! yes! yes!
A Heavy Dragoon is the residuum!

COL. Well, here we are once more on the scene of our former triumphs. But where's the Duke?

Enter DUKE, *listlessly, and in low spirits*

DUKE. Here I am! (*Sighs.*)

COL. Come, cheer up, don't give way!

DUKE. Oh, for that, I'm as cheerful as a poor devil can be expected to be who has the misfortune to be a duke, with a thousand a day!

MAJ. Humph! Most men would envy you!

DUKE. Envy *me?* Tell me, Major, are you fond of toffee?

MAJ. Very!

COL. We are all fond of toffee.

ALL. We are!

DUKE. Yes, and toffee in moderation is a capital thing. But to *live* on toffee—toffee for breakfast, toffee for dinner, toffee for tea—to have it supposed that you care for nothing *but* toffee, and that you would consider yourself insulted if anything but toffee were offered to you —how would you like *that?*

COL. I can quite believe that, under those circumstances, even toffee would become monotonous.

DUKE. For "toffee" read flattery, adulation, and abject deference, carried to such a pitch that I began, at last, to think that man was born bent at an angle of forty-five degrees! Great Heavens, what is there to adulate in me! Am I particularly intelligent, or remarkably studious, or excruciatingly witty, or unusually accomplished, or exceptionally virtuous?

COL. You're about as commonplace a young man as ever I saw.

ALL. You are!

DUKE. Exactly! That's it exactly! That describes me to a T! Thank you all very much! Well, I couldn't stand it any longer, so I joined this second-class cavalry regiment. In the Army, thought I, I shall be occasionally snubbed, perhaps even bullied, who knows? The thought was rapture, and here I am.

COL. (*looking off*). Yes, and here are the ladies!

DUKE. But who is the gentleman with the long hair?

COL. I don't know.

DUKE. He seems popular!

COL. He *does* seem popular!

BUNTHORNE *enters, followed by Ladies, two and two, singing and playing on harps as before. He is composing a poem, and quite absorbed. He sees no one, but walks across the stage, followed by Ladies. They take no notice of Dragoons—to the surprise and indignation of those Officers.*

CHORUS OF LADIES

In a doleful train
    Two and two we walk all day—
For we love in vain!
    None so sorrowful as they
        Who can only sigh and say,
        Woe is me, alackaday!

CHORUS OF DRAGOONS

Now is not this ridiculous—and is not this preposterous?
A thorough-paced absurdity—explain it if you can.
Instead of rushing eagerly to cherish us and foster us,
They all prefer this melancholy literary man.
Instead of slyly peering at us,
Casting looks endearing at us,
Blushing at us, flushing at us—flirting with a fan;
They're actually sneering at us, fleering at us, jeering at us!
Pretty sort of treatment for a military man!
Pretty sort of treatment for a military man!

ANG. Mystic poet, hear our prayer,
Twenty love-sick maidens we—
Young and wealthy, dark and fair—
All of county family.
And we die for love of thee—
Twenty love-sick maidens we!

CHORUS OF LADIES.
Yes, we die for love of thee—
Twenty love-sick maidens we!

BUN. (*aside—slyly*). Though my book I seem to scan
In a rapt ecstatic way,
Like a literary man
Who despises female clay,
I hear plainly all they say,
Twenty love-sick maidens they!

OFFICERS (*to each other*). He hears plainly, etc.

SAPH. Though so excellently wise,
For a moment mortal be,
Deign to raise thy purple eyes
From thy heart-drawn poesy.
Twenty love-sick maidens see—
Each is kneeling on her knee! (*All kneel.*)

CHORUS OF LADIES. Twenty love-sick, etc.

BUN. (*aside*). Though, as I remarked before,
Any one convinced would be
That some transcendental lore
Is monopolizing me,
Round the corner I can see
Each is kneeling on her knee!

OFFICERS (*to each other*).
Round the corner, etc.

ENSEMBLE

OFFICERS	LADIES
Now is not this ridiculous, etc.	Mystic poet, hear our prayer, etc.

COL. Angela! what is the meaning of this?

ANG. Oh, sir, leave us; our minds are but ill-tuned to light love-talk.

MAJ. But what in the world has come over you all?

JANE. Bunthorne! *He* has come over us. He has come among us, and he has idealized us.

DUKE. Has he succeeded in idealizing *you?*

JANE. He has!

DUKE. Good old Bunthorne!

JANE. My eyes are open; I droop despairingly; I am soulfully intense; I am limp and I cling!

[*During this* BUNTHORNE *is seen in all the agonies of composition. The Ladies are watching him intently as he writhes. At last he hits on the word he wants and writes it down. A general sense of relief.*

BUN. Finished! At last! Finished!

[*He staggers, overcome with the mental strain, into arms of* COLONEL

COL. Are you better now?

BUN. Yes,—oh, it's you—I am better now. The poem is finished, and my soul had gone out into it. That was all. It was nothing worth mentioning, it occurs three times a day. (*Sees* PATIENCE, *who has entered during this scene.*) Ah, Patience! Dear Patience! (*Holds her hand; she seems frightened.*)

ANG. Will it please you to read it to us, sir?

SAPH. This we supplicate. (*All kneel.*)

BUN. Shall I?

ALL THE DRAGOONS. No!

BUN. (*annoyed*—to PATIENCE). I will read it if *you* bid me!

PA. (*much frightened*). You can if you like!

BUN. It is a wild, weird, fleshly thing; yet very tender, very yearning, very precious. It is called, "Oh, Hollow! Hollow! Hollow!"

PA. Is it a hunting song?

BUN. A hunting song? No, it is *not* a hunting song. It is the wail of the poet's heart on discovering that everything is commonplace. To understand it, cling passionately to one another and think of faint lilies. (*They do so as he recites*)—

"OH, HOLLOW! HOLLOW! HOLLOW!"

What time the poet hath hymned
The writhing maid, lithe-limbed,
  Quivering on amaranthine asphodel,
How can he paint her woes,
Knowing, as well he knows,
  That all can be set right with calomel?

When from the poet's plinth
The amorous colocynth
  Yearns for the aloe, faint with rapturous thrills,
How can he hymn their throes
Knowing, as well he knows,
  That they are only uncompounded pills?

Is it, and can it be,
Nature hath this decree,
  Nothing poetic in the world shall dwell?
Or that in all her works
Something poetic lurks,
  Even in colocynth and calomel?
                I cannot tell.

[*Exit* BUNTHORNE.

ANG. How purely fragrant!

SAPH. How earnestly precious!

PA. Well, it seems to me to be nonsense.

SAPH. Nonsense, yes, perhaps—but oh, what precious nonsense!

COL. This is all very well, but you seem to forget that you are engaged to us.

SAPH. It can never be. You are not Empyrean. You are not Della Cruscan. You are not even Early English. Oh, be Early English ere it is too late! (*Officers look at each other in astonishment.*)

JANE (*looking at uniform*). Red and yellow! Primary colours! Oh, South Kensington!

DUKE. We didn't design our uniforms, but we don't see how they could be improved.

JANE. No, you wouldn't. Still, there *is* a cobwebby grey velvet, with a tender bloom like cold gravy, which, made Florentine fourteenth-century, trimmed with Venetian leather and Spanish altar lace, and surmounted with something Japanese—it matters not what—would at least be Early English! Come, maidens.

[*Exeunt Maidens, two and two, singing refrain of "Twenty love-sick maidens we". The Officers watch them off in astonishment.*

DUKE. Gentlemen, this is an insult to the British uniform——

COL. A uniform that has been as successful in the courts of Venus as on the field of Mars!

SONG—COLONEL

When I first put this uniform on,
I said, as I looked in the glass,
"It's one to a million
That any civilian
My figure and form will surpass.
Gold lace has a charm for the fair,
And I've plenty of that, and to spare,
While a lover's professions,
When uttered in Hessians,
Are eloquent everywhere!"
A fact that I counted upon,
When I first put this uniform on!

CHORUS OF DRAGOONS

By a simple coincidence, few
Could ever have counted upon,
The same thing occurred to me, too,
When I first put this uniform on!

COL. I said, when I first put it on,
"It is plain to the veriest dunce
That every beauty
Will feel it her duty
To yield to its glamour at once.
They will see that I'm freely gold-laced
In a uniform handsome and chaste"—
But the peripatetics

Of long-haired æsthetics
Are very much more to their taste—
Which I never counted upon,
When I first put this uniform on!

CHORUS. By a simple coincidence, few
Could ever have reckoned upon,
I didn't anticipate that,
When I first put this uniform on!

[*The Dragoons go off angrily.*

Enter BUNTHORNE, *who changes his manner and becomes intensely melodramatic*

RECIT AND SONG—BUNTHORNE

Am I alone,
And unobserved? I am!
Then let me own
I'm an æsthetic sham!

This air severe
Is but a mere
Veneer!

This cynic smile
Is but a wile
Of guile!

This costume chaste
Is but good taste
Misplaced!

Let me confess!
A languid love for lilies does *not* blight me!
Lank limbs and haggard cheeks do *not* delight me!
I do *not* care for dirty greens
By any means.
I do *not* long for all one sees
That's Japanese.
I am *not* fond of uttering platitudes
In stained-glass attitudes.
In short, my mediævalism's affectation,
Born of a morbid love of admiration!

SONG

If you're anxious for to shine in the high æsthetic line as a man of culture rare,
You must get up all the germs of the transcendental terms, and plant them everywhere.

You must lie upon the daisies and discourse in novel phrases of your complicated state of mind,
The meaning doesn't matter if it's only idle chatter of a transcendental kind.
And every one will say,
As you walk your mystic way,

"If this young man expresses himself in terms too deep for *me,*
Why, what a very singularly deep young man this deep young man must be!"

Be eloquent in praise of the very dull old days which have long since passed away,
And convince 'em, if you can, that the reign of good Queen Anne was Culture's palmiest day.
Of course you will pooh-pooh whatever's fresh and new, and declare it's crude and mean,
For Art stopped short in the cultivated court of the Empress Josephine.
And every one will say,
As you walk your mystic way,
"If that's not good enough for him which is good enough for *me,*
Why, what a very cultivated kind of youth this kind of youth must be!"

Then a sentimental passion of a vegetable fashion must excite your languid spleen,
An attachment *à la* Plato for a bashful young potato, or a not-too-French French bean!
Though the Philistines may jostle, you will rank as an apostle in the high æsthetic band,
If you walk down Piccadilly with a poppy or a lily in your mediæval hand.
And every one will say,
As you walk your flowery way,
"If he's content with a vegetable love which would certainly not suit *me,*
Why, what a most particularly pure young man this pure young man must be!"

At the end of his song PATIENCE *enters. He sees her*

BUN. Ah! Patience, come hither. I am pleased with thee. The bitter-hearted one, who finds all else hollow, is pleased with thee. For you are not hollow. *Are* you?

PA. No, thanks, I have dined; but—I beg your pardon —I interrupt you.

BUN. Life is made up of interruptions. The tortured

soul, yearning for solitude, writhes under them. Oh, but my heart is a-weary! Oh, I am a cursed thing! Don't go.

PA. Really, I'm very sorry——

BUN. Tell me, girl, do you ever yearn?

PA. (*misunderstanding him*). I earn my living.

BUN. (*impatiently*). No, no! Do you know what it is to be heart-hungry? Do you know what it is to yearn for the Indefinable, and yet to be brought face to face, daily, with the Multiplication Table? Do you know what it is to seek oceans and to find puddles?—to long for whirlwinds and yet to have to do the best you can with the bellows? That's my case. Oh, I am a cursed thing! Don't go.

PA. If you please, I don't understand you—you frighten me!

BUN. Don't be frightened—it's only poetry.

PA. Well, if that's poetry, I don't like poetry.

BUN. (*eagerly*). Don't you? (*Aside.*) Can I trust her? (*Aloud.*) Patience, you don't like poetry—well, between you and me, *I* don't like poetry. It's hollow, unsubstantial—unsatisfactory. What's the use of yearning for Elysian Fields when you know you can't get 'em, and would only let 'em out on building leases if you had 'em?

PA. Sir, I——

BUN. Patience, I have long loved you. Let me tell you a secret. I am not as bilious as I look. If you like, I will cut my hair. There is more innocent fun within me than a casual spectator would imagine. You have never seen me frolicsome. Be a good girl—a very good girl—and one day you shall. If you are fond of touch-and-go jocularity—this is the shop for it.

PA. Sir, I will speak plainly. In the matter of love I am untaught. I have never loved but my great-aunt. But I am quite certain, under any circumstances, I couldn't possibly love *you*.

BUN. Oh, you think not?

PA. I'm quite sure of it. Quite sure. Quite.

BUN. Very good. Life is henceforth a blank. I don't care what becomes of me. I have only to ask that you will not abuse my confidence; though *you* despise me, I am extremely popular with the other young ladies.

PA. I only ask that you will leave me and never renew the subject.

BUN. Certainly. Broken-hearted and desolate, I go. (*Recites.*)

"Oh, to be wafted away
From this black Aceldama of sorrow,
Where the dust of an earthy to-day
Is the earth of a dusty to-morrow!"

It is a little thing of my own. I call it "Heart Foam". I shall not publish it. Farewell! Patience, Patience, farewell!

[*Exit* BUNTHORNE

PA. What on earth does it all mean? Why does he love me? Why does he expect me to love him? He's not a relation! It frightens me!

Enter ANGELA

ANG. Why, Patience, what is the matter?

PA. Lady Angela, tell me two things. Firstly, what on earth is this love that upsets everybody; and, secondly, how is it to be distinguished from insanity?

ANG. Poor blind child! Oh, forgive her, Eros! Why, love is of all passions the most essential! It is the embodiment of purity, the abstraction of refinement! It is the one unselfish emotion in this whirlpool of grasping greed!

PA. Oh, dear, oh! (*Beginning to cry.*)

ANG. Why are you crying?

PA. To think that I have lived all these years without having experienced this ennobling and unselfish passion! Why, what a wicked girl I must be! For it *is* unselfish, isn't it?

ANG. Absolutely! Love that is tainted with selfishness is no love. Oh, try, try, try to love! It really isn't difficult if you give your whole mind to it.

PA. I'll set about it at once. I won't go to bed until I'm head over ears in love with somebody.

ANG. Noble girl! But is it possible that you have never loved anybody?

PA. Yes, one.

ANG. Ah! Whom?

PA. My great-aunt——

ANG. Great-aunts don't count.

PA. Then there's nobody. At least—no, nobody. Not since I was a baby. But *that* doesn't count, I suppose.

ANG. I don't know. Tell me all about it.

DUET—PATIENCE *and* ANGELA

Long years ago—fourteen, maybe—
When but a tiny babe of four,
Another baby played with me,
My elder by a year or more;
A little child of beauty rare,
With marvellous eyes and wondrous hair,
Who, in my child-eyes, seemed to me
All that a little child should be!
Ah, how we loved, that child and I!
How pure our baby joy!
How true our love—and, by the by,
He was a little boy!

ANG. Ah, old, old tale of Cupid's touch!
I thought as much—I thought as much!
He *was* a little boy!

PA. (*shocked*). Pray don't misconstrue what I say—
Remember, pray—remember, pray,
He was a *little* boy!

ANG. No doubt! Yet, spite of all your pains,
The interesting fact remains—
He was a little *boy!*

ENSEMBLE. { Ah, yes, in / No doubt! Yet } spite of all { my / your } pains, etc.

[*Exit* ANGELA.

PA. It's perfectly dreadful to think of the appalling state I must be in! I had no idea that love was a duty. No wonder they all look so unhappy! Upon my word, I hardly like to associate with myself. I don't think I'm respectable. I'll go at once and fall in love with—— (*Enter* GROSVENOR.) A stranger!

DUET—PATIENCE *and* GROSVENOR

GROS. Prithee, pretty maiden—prithee, tell me true,
(Hey, but I'm doleful, willow willow waly)
Have you e'er a lover a-dangling after you?
Hey willow waly O!
I would fain discover
If you have a lover?
Hey willow waly O!

PA. Gentle sir, my heart is frolicsome and free—
(Hey, but he's doleful, willow willow waly!)
Nobody I care for comes a-courting me—
Hey willow waly O!
Nobody I care for
Comes a-courting—therefore,
Hey willow waly O!

GROS. Prithee, pretty maiden, will you marry me?
(Hey, but I'm hopeful, willow willow waly!)

I may say, at once, I'm a man of propertee—
Hey willow waly O!
Money, I despise it;
Many people prize it,
Hey willow waly O!

PA. Gentle sir, although to marry I design—
(Hey, but he's hopeful, willow willow waly!)
As yet I do not know you, and so I must decline.
Hey willow waly O!
To other maidens go you—
As yet I do not know you,
Hey willow waly O!

GROS. Patience! Can it be that you don't recognise me?

PA. Recognise you? No, indeed I don't!

GROS. Have fifteen years so greatly changed me?

PA. Fifteen years? What do you mean?

GROS. Have you forgotten the friend of your youth, your Archibald?—your little playfellow? Oh, Chronos, Chronos, this is too bad of you!

PA. Archibald! Is it possible? Why, let me look! It is! It is! It must be! Oh, how happy I am! I thought we should never meet again! And how you've grown!

GROS. Yes, Patience, I am much taller and much stouter than I was.

PA. And how you've improved!

GROS. Yes, Patience, I am very beautiful! (*Sighs.*)

PA. But surely *that* doesn't make you unhappy.

GROS. Yes, Patience. Gifted as I am with a beauty which probably has not its rival on earth, I am, nevertheless, utterly and completely miserable.

PA. Oh—but why?

GROS. My child-love for you has never faded. Conceive, then, the horror of my situation when I tell you that it is my hideous destiny to be madly loved at first sight by every woman I come across!

PA. But why do you make yourself so picturesque? Why not disguise yourself, disfigure yourself, anything to escape this persecution?

GROS. No, Patience, that may not be. These gifts—irksome as they are—were given to me for the enjoyment and delectation of my fellow-creatures. I am a trustee for Beauty, and it is my duty to see that the conditions of my trust are faithfully discharged.

PA. And you, too, are a Poet?

GROS. Yes, I am the Apostle of Simplicity. I am called "Archibald the All-Right"—for I am infallible!

PA. And is it possible that you condescend to love such a girl as I?

GROS. Yes, Patience, is it not strange? I have loved you with a Florentine fourteenth-century frenzy for full fifteen years!

PA. Oh, marvellous! I have hitherto been deaf to the voice of love. I seem now to know what love is! It has been revealed to me—it is Archibald Grosvenor!

GROS. Yes, Patience, it is!

PA. (*as in a trance*). We will never, never part!

GROS. We will live and die together!

PA. I swear it!

GROS. We both swear it!

PA. (*recoiling from him*). But—oh, horror!

GROS. What's the matter?

PA. Why, you are perfection! A source of endless ecstasy to all who know you!

GROS. I know I am. Well?

PA. Then, bless my heart, there can be nothing unselfish in loving *you*!

GROS. Merciful powers! I never thought of that!

PA. To monopolize those features on which all women love to linger! It would be unpardonable!

GROS. Why, so it would! Oh, fatal perfection, again you interpose between me and my happiness!

PA. Oh, if you were but a thought less beautiful than you are!

GROS. Would that I were; but candour compels me to admit that I'm not!

PA. Our duty is clear; we must part, and for ever!

GROS. Oh, misery! And yet I cannot question the propriety of your decision. Farewell, Patience!

PA. Farewell, Archibald! But stay!

GROS. Yes, Patience?

PA. Although I may not love *you*—for you are perfection—there is nothing to prevent your loving *me*. I am plain, homely, unattractive!

GROS. Why, that's true!

PA. The love of such a man as you for such a girl as I must be unselfish!

GROS. Unselfishness itself!

DUET—PATIENCE *and* GROSVENOR

PA. Though to marry you would very selfish be—
GROS. Hey, but I'm doleful—willow willow waly!
PA. You may, all the same, continue loving me—
GROS. Hey willow waly O!
BOTH. All the world ignoring,
You'll / I'll } go on adoring—
Hey willow waly O!

[*At the end, exeunt despairingly, in opposite directions.*

FINALE—ACT I

Enter BUNTHORNE, *crowned with roses and hung about with garlands, and looking very miserable. He is led by* ANGELA *and* SAPHIR (*each of whom holds an end of the rose-garland by which he is bound*), *and accompanied by procession of Maidens. They are dancing classically, and playing on cymbals, double pipes, and other archaic instruments.*

CHORUS

Let the merry cymbals sound,
Gaily pipe Pandæan pleasure,
With a Daphnephoric bound
Tread a gay but classic measure.
Every heart with hope is beating,
For at this exciting meeting
Fickle Fortune will decide
Who shall be our Bunthorne's bride!

Enter Dragoons, led by COLONEL, MAJOR, *and* DUKE. *They are surprised at proceedings*

CHORUS OF DRAGOONS

Now tell us, we pray you,
Why thus they array you—
Oh, poet, how say you—
What is it you've done?

DUKE. Of rite sacrificial,
By sentence judicial,
This seems the initial,
Then why don't you run?

COL. They cannot have led you
To hang or behead you,
Nor may they *all* wed you,
Unfortunate one!

CHORUS OF DRAGOONS

Then tell us, we pray you,
Why thus they array you—
Oh, poet, how say you—
What is it you've done?

RECIT—BUNTHORNE

Heart-broken at my Patience's barbarity,
By the advice of my solicitor
(*introducing his* SOLICITOR),
In aid—in aid of a deserving charity,
I've put myself up to be raffled for!

MAIDENS. By the advice of his solicitor
He's put himself up to be raffled for!

DRAGOONS. Oh, horror! urged by his solicitor,
He's put himself up to be raffled for!

MAIDENS. Oh, heaven's blessing on his solicitor!

DRAGOONS. A hideous curse on his solicitor!

[*The* SOLICITOR, *horrified at the Dragoons' curse, rushes off*.

COL. Stay, we implore you,
Before our hopes are blighted;
You see before you
The men to whom you're plighted!

CHORUS OF DRAGOONS

Stay we implore you,
For we adore you;
To us you're plighted
To be united—
Stay, we implore you!

SOLO—DUKE

Your maiden hearts, ah, do not steel
To pity's eloquent appeal,
Such conduct British soldiers feel.
(*Aside to Dragoons.*) Sigh, sigh, all sigh!
(*They all sigh.*)

To foeman's steel we rarely see
A British soldier bend the knee,
Yet, one and all, they kneel to ye—
(*Aside to Dragoons.*) Kneel, kneel, all kneel!
(*They all kneel.*)

Our soldiers very seldom cry,
And yet—I need not tell you why—
A tear-drop dews each martial eye!
(*Aside to Dragoons.*) Weep, weep, all weep!
(*They all weep.*)

ENSEMBLE

Our soldiers very seldom cry,
And yet—I need not tell you why—
A tear-drop dews each manly eye!
Weep, weep, all weep!

BUNTHORNE (*who has been impatient during this appeal*).

Come, walk up, and purchase with avidity,
Overcome your diffidence and natural timidity,
Tickets for the raffle should be purchased with avidity,
Put in half a guinea and a husband you may gain—
Such a judge of blue-and-white and other kinds of pottery—
From early Oriental down to modern terra-cotta-ry—
Put in half a guinea—you may draw him in a lottery—
Such an opportunity may not occur again.

CHORUS. Such a judge of blue-and-white, etc.

[MAIDENS *crowd up to purchase tickets; during this* DRAGOONS *dance in single file round stage, to express their indifference.*

DRAGOONS. We've been thrown over, we're aware,
But we don't care—but we don't care!
There's fish in the sea, no doubt of it,
As good as ever came out of it,
And some day we shall get our share,
So we don't care—so we don't care!

[*During this the* MAIDENS *have been buying tickets. At last* JANE *presents herself.* BUNTHORNE *looks at her with aversion.*

RECIT

BUN. And are *you* going a ticket for to buy?
JANE (*surprised*). Most certainly I am; why shouldn't I?
BUN. (*aside*). Oh, Fortune, this is hard! (*Aloud.*) Blindfold your eyes;
Two minutes will decide who wins the prize! (MAIDENS *blindfold themselves.*)

CHORUS OF MAIDENS

Oh, Fortune, to my aching heart be kind!
Like us, thou art blindfolded, but not blind; (*Each uncovers one eye.*)
Just raise your bandage, thus, that you may see,
And give the prize, and give the prize to me! (*They cover their eyes again.*)

BUN. Come, Lady Jane, I pray you draw the first!
JANE (*joyfully*). He loves me best!
BUN. (*aside*). I want to know the worst!

[JANE *puts hand in bag to draw ticket.* PATIENCE *enters and prevents her doing so.*

PA. Hold! Stay your hand!
ALL (*uncovering their eyes*). What means this interference?
Of this bold girl I pray you make a clearance!
JANE. Away with you, and to your milk-pails go!

BUN. (*suddenly*). She wants a ticket! Take a dozen!

PA. No!

SOLO—PATIENCE (*kneeling to* BUNTHORNE)

If there be pardon in your breast
For this poor penitent,
Who, with remorseful thought opprest,
Sincerely doth repent;
If you, with one so lowly, still
Desire to be allied,
Then you may take me, if you will,
For I will be your bride!

ALL. Oh, shameless one!
Oh, bold-faced thing!
Away you run,
Go, take you wing,
You shameless one!
You bold-faced thing!

BUN. How strong is love! For many and many a week
She's loved me fondly and has feared to speak
But Nature, for restraint too mighty far,
Has burst the bonds of Art—and here we are!

PA. No, Mr. Bunthorne, no—you're wrong again;
Permit me—I'll endeavour to explain!

SONG—PATIENCE

PA. True love must single-hearted be—
BUN. Exactly so!
PA. From every selfish fancy free—
BUN. Exactly so!
PA. No idle thought of gain or joy
A maiden's fancy should employ—
True love must be without alloy.
ALL. Exactly so!

PA. Imposture to contempt must lead—
COL. Exactly so!
PA. Blind vanity's dissension's seed—
MAJ. Exactly so!
PA. It follows, then, a maiden who

Devotes herself to loving you (*indicating* BUNTHORNE)
Is prompted by no selfish view—

ALL. Exactly so!

SAPH. Are you resolved to wed this shameless one?

ANG. Is there no chance for any other?

BUN. (*decisively*). None! (*Embraces* PATIENCE.)

[*Exeunt* PATIENCE *and* BUNTHORNE.

[ANGELA, SAPHIR, *and* ELLA *take* COLONEL, DUKE, *and* MAJOR *down, while* GIRLS *gaze fondly at other* OFFICERS.

SEXTETTE

I hear the soft note of the echoing voice
Of an old, old love, long dead—
It whispers my sorrowing heart "rejoice"—
For the last sad tear is shed—
The pain that is all but a pleasure will change
For the pleasure that's all but pain,
And never, oh never, this heart will range
From that old, old love again!
(GIRLS *embrace* OFFICERS.)

CHORUS. Yes, the pain that is all, etc. (*Embrace.*)

Enter PATIENCE *and* BUNTHORNE

[*As the* DRAGOONS *and* GIRLS *are embracing, enter* GROSVENOR, *reading. He takes no notice of them, but comes slowly down, still reading. The* GIRLS *are all strangely fascinated by him, and gradually withdraw from* DRAGOONS.

ANG. But who is this, whose god-like grace
Proclaims he comes of noble race?
And who is this, whose manly face
Bears sorrow's interesting trace?

ENSEMBLE—TUTTI

Yes, who is this, etc.

GROS. I am a broken-hearted troubadour,
Whose mind's æsthetic and whose tastes are pure!

ANG. Æsthetic! He is æsthetic!
GROS. Yes, yes—I am æsthetic
And poetic!
ALL THE LADIES. Then, we love you!

[*The* GIRLS *leave* DRAGOONS *and group, kneeling, around* GROSVENOR. *Fury of* BUNTHORNE, *who recognizes a rival.*

DRAGOONS. They love him! Horror!
BUN. *and* PA. They love him! Horror!
GROS. They love me! Horror! Horror! Horror!

ENSEMBLE—TUTTI

GIRLS

Oh, list while we a love confess
That words imperfectly express.
Those shell-like ears, ah, do not close
To blighted love's distracting woes!

GROSVENOR

Again my cursed comeliness
Spreads hopeless anguish and distress!
Thine ears, oh Fortune, do not close
To my intolerable woes.

PATIENCE

List, Reginald, while I confess
A love that's all unselfishness;
That it's unselfish, goodness knows,
You won't dispute it, I suppose?

BUNTHORNE

My jealousy I can't express,
Their love they openly confess;
His shell-like ears he does not close
To their recital of their woes.

DRAGOONS. Now is not this ridiculous, etc.

END OF ACT I

ACT II

SCENE.—*A glade.* JANE *is discovered leaning on a violoncello, upon which she presently accompanies herself. Chorus of* MAIDENS *are heard singing in the distance.*

JANE. The fickle crew have deserted Reginald and sworn allegiance to his rival, and all, forsooth, because he has glanced with passing favour on a puling milkmaid! Fools! of that fancy he will soon weary—and then

I, who alone am faithful to him, shall reap my reward. But do not dally too long, Reginald, for my charms are ripe, Reginald, and already they are decaying. Better secure me ere I have gone too far!

RECIT—JANE

Sad is that woman's lot who, year by year,
Sees, one by one, her beauties disappear,
When Time, grown weary of her heart-drawn sighs,
Impatiently begins to "dim her eyes"!
Compelled, at last, in life's uncertain gloamings,
To wreathe her wrinkled brow with well-saved "combings",
Reduced, with rouge, lip-salve, and pearly grey,
To "make up" for lost time as best she may!

SONG—JANE

Silvered is the raven hair,
Spreading is the parting straight,
Mottled the complexion fair,
Halting is the youthful gait,
Hollow is the laughter free,
Spectacled the limpid eye—
Little will be left of me
In the coming by and by!

Fading is the taper waist,
Shapeless grows the shapely limb,

And although severely laced,
  Spreading is the figure trim!
Stouter than I used to be,
  Still more corpulent grow I—
There will be too much of me
  In the coming by and by!

[*Exit* JANE.

Enter GROSVENOR, *followed by* MAIDENS, *two and two, each playing on an archaic instrument, as in Act I. He is reading abstractedly, as* BUNTHORNE *did in Act I, and pays no attention to them.*

CHORUS OF MAIDENS

Turn, oh, turn in this direction,
  Shed, oh, shed a gentle smile,
With a glance of sad perfection
  Our poor fainting hearts beguile!
On such eyes as maidens cherish
  Let thy fond adorers gaze,
Or incontinently perish
  In their all-consuming rays!

[*He sits—they group around him.*

GROS. (*aside*). The old, old tale. How rapturously these maidens love me, and how hopelessly! Oh, Patience, Patience, with the love of thee in my heart, what have I for these poor mad maidens but an unvalued pity? Alas, they will die of hopeless love for me, as I shall die of hopeless love for thee!

ANG. Sir, will it please you read to us?

GROS. (*sighing*). Yes, child, if you will. What shall I read?

ANG. One of your own poems.

GROS. One of my own poems? Better not, my child. *They* will not cure thee of thy love.

ELLA. Mr. Bunthorne used to read us a poem of his own every day.

SAPH. And, to do him justice, he read them extremely well.

GROS. Oh, did he so? Well, who am I that I should take upon myself to withhold my gifts from you? What am I but a trustee? Here is a decalet—a pure and simple thing, a very daisy—a babe might understand it. To appreciate it, it is not necessary to think of anything at all.

ANG. Let us think of nothing at all!

GROSVENOR *recites*

Gentle Jane was good as gold,
She always did as she was told;
She never spoke when her mouth was full,
Or caught bluebottles their legs to pull,
Or spilt plum jam on her nice new frock,
Or put white mice in the eight-day clock,
Or vivisected her last new doll,
Or fostered a passion for alcohol.
And when she grew up she was given in marriage
To a first-class earl who keeps his carriage!

GROS. I believe I am right in saying that there is not one word in that decalet which is calculated to bring the blush of shame to the cheek of modesty.

ANG. Not one; it is purity itself.

GROS. Here's another.

Teasing Tom was a very bad boy,
A great big squirt was his favourite toy;
He put live shrimps in his father's boots,
And sewed up the sleeves of his Sunday suits;
He punched his poor little sisters' heads,
And cayenne-peppered their four-post beds,
He plastered their hair with cobbler's wax,
And dropped hot halfpennies down their backs.
The consequence was he was lost tot*a*lly,
And married a girl in the *corps de bally!*

ANG. Marked you how grandly—how relentlessly—the damning catalogue of crime strode on, till Retribution, like a poisèd hawk, came swooping down upon the Wrong-Doer? Oh, it was terrible!

ELLA. Oh, sir, you are indeed a true poet, for you touch our hearts, and they go out to you!

GROS. (*aside*). This is simply cloying. (*Aloud.*) Ladies, I am sorry to appear ungallant, but this is Saturday, and you have been following me about ever since Monday. I should like the usual half-holiday. I shall take it as a personal favour if you will kindly allow me to close early to-day.

SAPH. Oh, sir, do not send us from you!

GROS. Poor, poor girls! It is best to speak plainly. I know that I am loved by you, but I never can love you in return, for my heart is fixed elsewhere! Remember the fable of the Magnet and the Churn.

ANG. (*wildly*). But we don't know the fable of the Magnet and the Churn!

GROS. Don't you? Then I will sing it to you.

SONG—GROSVENOR

A magnet hung in a hardware shop,
And all around was a loving crop
Of scissors and needles, nails and knives,
Offering love for all their lives;
But for iron the magnet felt no whim,
Though he charmed iron, it charmed not him;
From needles and nails and knives he'd turn,
For he'd set his love on a Silver Churn!

ALL. A Silver Churn?

GROS. A Silver Churn!

His most æsthetic,
Very magnetic
Fancy took this turn—
"If I can wheedle
A knife or a needle,
Why not a Silver Churn?"

CHORUS. His most æsthetic, etc.

GROS. And Iron and Steel expressed surprise,
The needles opened their well-drilled eyes,
The penknives felt "shut up", no doubt,
The scissors declared themselves "cut out",
The kettles they boiled with rage, 'tis said,
While every nail went off its head,
And hither and thither began to roam,
Till a hammer came up—and drove them home.

ALL. It drove them home?
GROS. It drove them home!

While this magnetic,
Peripatetic
Lover he lived to learn,
By no endeavour
Can magnet ever
Attract a Silver Churn!

ALL. While this magnetic, etc.

[*They go off in low spirits, gazing back at him from time to time.*

GROS. At last they are gone! What is this mysterious fascination that I seem to exercise over all I come across? A curse on my fatal beauty, for I am sick of conquests!

PATIENCE *appears*

PA. Archibald!

GROS. (*turns and sees her*). Patience!

PA. I have escaped with difficulty from my Reginald. I wanted to see you so much that I might ask you if you still love me as fondly as ever?

GROS. Love you? If the devotion of a lifetime—— (*Seizes her hand.*)

PA. (*indignantly*). Hold! Unhand me, or I scream! (*He releases her.*) If you are a gentleman, pray remember that I am another's! (*Very tenderly.*) But you *do* love me, don't you?

GROS. Madly, hopelessly, despairingly!

PA. That's right! I never can be yours; but that's right!

GROS. And you love this Bunthorne?

PA. With a heart-whole ecstasy that withers, and scorches, and burns, and stings! (*Sadly.*) It is my duty.

GROS. Admirable girl! But you are not happy with him?

PA. Happy? I am miserable beyond description!

GROS. That's right! I never can be yours; but that's right!

PA. But go now. I see dear Reginald approaching. Farewell, dear Archibald; I cannot tell you how happy it has made me to know that you still love me.

GROS. Ah, if I only dared—— (*Advances towards her.*)

PA. Sir! this language to one who is promised to another! (*Tenderly.*) Oh, Archibald, think of me sometimes, for my heart is breaking! He is so unkind to me, and you would be so loving!

GROS. Loving! (*Advances towards her.*)

PA. Advance one step, and as I am a good and pure woman, I scream! (*Tenderly.*) Farewell, Archibald! (*Sternly.*) Stop there! (*Tenderly.*) Think of me sometimes! (*Angrily.*) Advance at your peril! Once more, adieu!

[GROSVENOR *sighs, gazes sorrowfully at her, sighs deeply, and exit. She bursts into tears*

Enter BUNTHORNE, *followed by* JANE. *He is moody and preoccupied*

JANE *sings*

In a doleful train,
One and one I walk all day;
For I love in vain—
None so sorrowful as they
Who can only sigh and say,
Woe is me, alackaday!

BUN. (*seeing* PATIENCE). Crying, eh? What are you crying about?

PA. I've only been thinking how dearly I love you!

BUN. Love me! Bah!

JANE. Love him! Bah!

BUN. (*to* JANE). Don't you interfere.

JANE. He always crushes me!

PA. (*going to him*). What is the matter, dear Reginald? If you have any sorrow, tell it to me, that I may share it with you. (*Sighing.*) It is my duty!

BUN. (*snappishly*). Whom were you talking with just now?

PA. With dear Archibald.

BUN. (*furiously*). With dear Archibald! Upon my honour, this is too much!

JANE. A great deal too much!

BUN. (*angrily to* JANE). Do be quiet!

JANE. Crushed again!

PA. I think he is the noblest, purest, and most perfect being I have ever met. But I don't love him. It is true that he is devotedly attached to me, but indeed I don't love *him*. Whenever he grows affectionate, I scream. It is my duty! (*Sighing.*)

BUN. I dare say!

JANE. So do I! *I* dare say!

PA. Why, how could I love him and love you too? You can't love two people at once!

BUN. Oh, can't you, though!

PA. No, you can't; I only wish you could.

BUN. I don't believe you know what love is!

PA. (*sighing*). Yes, I do. There was a happy time when I didn't, but a bitter experience has taught me.

[*Exeunt* BUNTHORNE *and* JANE.

BALLAD—PATIENCE

Love is a plaintive song,
  Sung by a suffering maid,
Telling a tale of wrong,
  Telling of hope betrayed;
Tuned to each changing note,
  Sorry when *he* is sad,
Blind to his every mote,
  Merry when he is glad!
    Love that no wrong can cure,
      Love that is always new,
    Love is the love that's pure,
      That is the love that's true!

Rendering good for ill,
  Smiling at every frown,
Yielding your own self-will,
  Laughing your tear-drops down;
Never a selfish whim,
  Trouble, or pain to stir;
Everything for him,
  Nothing at all for her!
    Love that will aye endure,
      Though the rewards be few,
    That is the love that's pure,
      That is the love that's true!

[*At the end of ballad exit* PATIENCE, *weeping.*

Enter BUNTHORNE *and* JANE

BUN. Everything has gone wrong with me since that smug-faced idiot came here. Before that I was admired—I may say, loved.

JANE. Too mild—adored!

BUN. Do let a poet soliloquize! The damozels used to follow me wherever I went; now they all follow him!

JANE. Not all! *I* am still faithful to you.

BUN. Yes, and a pretty damozel *you* are!

JANE. No, not pretty. Massive. Cheer up! I will never leave you, I swear it!

BUN. Oh, thank you! I know what it is; it's his confounded mildness. They find me too highly spiced, if you please! And no doubt I *am* highly spiced.

JANE. Not for my taste!

BUN. (*savagely*). No, but I am for theirs. But I will show the world I can be as mild as he. If they want insipidity, they shall have it. I'll meet this fellow on his own ground and beat him on it.

JANE. You shall. And I will help you.

BUN. You will? Jane, there's a good deal of good in you, after all!

DUET—BUNTHORNE *and* JANE

JANE. So go to him and say to him, with compliment ironical—

BUN. Sing "Hey to you—
Good day to you"—
And that's what I shall say!

JANE. "Your style is much too sanctified—your cut is too canonical"—

BUN. Sing "Bah to you—
Ha! ha! to you"—
And that's what I shall say!

JANE. "I was the beau ideal of the morbid young æsthetical—
To doubt my inspiration was regarded as heretical—
Until you cut me out with your placidity emetical."—

BUN. Sing "Booh to you—
Pooh, pooh to you"—
And that's what I shall say!

BOTH. Sing "Hey to you—good day to you"—
Sing "Bah to you—ha! ha! to you"—
Sing "Booh to you—pooh, pooh to you"—
And that's what {you / I} shall say!

BUN. I'll tell him that unless he will consent to be more jocular—

JANE. Sing "Booh to you—
Pooh, pooh to you"—
And that's what you should say!

BUN. To cut his curly hair, and stick an eyeglass in his ocular—

JANE. Sing "Bah to you—
Ha! ha! to you"—
And that's what you should say!

BUN. To stuff his conversation full of quibble and of quiddity—
To dine on chops and roly-poly pudding with avidity—
He'd better clear away with all convenient rapidity.

JANE. Sing "Hey to you—
Good day to you"—
And that's what you should say!

BOTH. Sing "Booh to you—pooh, pooh to you"—
Sing "Bah to you—ha! ha! to you"—
Sing "Hey to you—good day to you"—
And that's what {I / you} shall say!

[*Exeunt* JANE *and* BUNTHORNE *together.*

Enter DUKE, COLONEL, *and* MAJOR. *They have abandoned their uniforms, and are dressed and made up in imitation of Æsthetics. They have long hair, and other outward signs of attachment to the brotherhood. As they sing they walk in stiff, constrained, and angular attitudes—a grotesque exaggeration of the attitudes adopted by* BUNTHORNE *and the young Ladies in Act I.*

TRIO—DUKE, COLONEL, *and* MAJOR

It's clear that mediæval art alone retains its zest,
To charm and please its devotees we've done our little best.

We're not quite sure if all we do has the Early English ring;
But, as far as we can judge, it's something like this sort of thing:
You hold yourself like this (*attitude*),
You hold yourself like that (*attitude*),
By hook and crook you try to look both angular and flat (*attitude*).
We venture to expect
That what we recollect,
Though but a part of true High Art, will have its due effect.

If this is not exactly right, we hope you won't upbraid;
You can't get high Æsthetic tastes, like trousers, ready made.
True views on Mediævalism Time alone will bring,
But, as far as we can judge, it's something like this sort of thing:
You hold yourself like this (*attitude*),
You hold yourself like that (*attitude*),
By hook and crook you try to look both angular and flat (*attitude*).
To cultivate the trim
Rigidity of limb,
You ought to get a Marionette, and form your style on him (*attitude*).

COL. (*attitude*). Yes, it's quite clear that our only chance of making a lasting impression on these young ladies is to become as æsthetic as they are.

MAJ. (*attitude*). No doubt. The only question is how far we've succeeded in doing so. I don't know why, but I've an idea that this is not quite right.

DUKE. (*attitude*). *I* don't like it. I never did. I don't see what it means. I do it, but I don't like it.

COL. My good friend, the question is not whether we like it, but whether they do. They understand these things—we don't. Now I shouldn't be surprised if this is effective enough—at a distance.

MAJ. I can't help thinking, we're a little stiff at it. It would be extremely awkward if we were to be "struck" so!

COL. I don't think we shall be struck so. Perhaps we're a little awkward at first—but everything must have a beginning. Oh, here they come! 'Tention!

They strike fresh attitudes, as ANGELA *and* SAPHIR *enter*

ANG. (*seeing them*). Oh, Saphir—see—see! The immortal fire has descended on them, and they are of the Inner Brotherhood—perceptively intense and consummately utter. (*The* OFFICERS *have some difficulty in maintaining their constrained attitudes.*)

SAPH. (*in admiration*). How Botticellian! How Fra Angelican! Oh, Art, we thank thee for this boon!

COL. (*apologetically*). I'm afraid we're not quite right.

ANG. Not supremely, perhaps, but oh, so, all-but! (*To* SAPHIR.) Oh, Saphir, are they not quite too all-but?

SAPHIR. They are indeed jolly utter!

MAJ. (*in agony*). I wonder what the Inner Brotherhood usually recommend for cramp?

COL. Ladies, we will not deceive you. We are doing this at some personal inconvenience with a view of expressing the extremity of our devotion to you. We trust that it is not without its effect.

ANG. We will not deny that we are much moved by this proof of your attachment.

SAPH. Yes, your conversion to the principles of Æsthetic Art in its highest development has touched us deeply.

ANG. And if Mr. Grosvenor should remain obdurate—

SAPH. Which we have every reason to believe he will—

MAJ. (*aside, in agony*). I wish they'd make haste.

ANG. We are not prepared to say that our yearning hearts will not go out to you.

COL. (*as giving a word of command*). By sections of threes—Rapture! (*All strike a fresh attitude, expressive of æsthetic rapture.*)

SAPH. Oh, it's extremely good—for beginners it's admirable.

MAJ. The only question is, who will take who?

COL. Oh, the Duke chooses first, as a matter of course.

DUKE. Oh, I couldn't think of it—you are really too good!

COL. Nothing of the kind. You are a great matrimonial

fish, and it's only fair that each of these ladies should have a chance of hooking you. It's perfectly simple. Observe, suppose you choose Angela, I take Saphir, Major takes nobody. Suppose you choose Saphir, Major takes Angela, I take nobody. Suppose you choose neither, I take Angela, Major takes Saphir. Clear as day!

QUINTET

DUKE, COLONEL, MAJOR, ANGELA, *and* SAPHIR

DUKE (*taking* SAPHIR)

If Saphir I choose to marry,
  I shall be fixed up for life;
Then the Colonel need not tarry,
  Angela can be his wife.

[DUKE *dances with* SAPHIR, COLONEL *with* ANGELA, MAJOR *dances alone.*

MAJOR (*dancing alone*)

In that case unprecedented,
  Single I shall live and die—
I shall have to be contented
  With their heartfelt sympathy!

ALL (*dancing as before*)

He will have to be contented
  With our heartfelt sympathy!

DUKE (*taking* ANGELA)

If on Angy I determine,
  At my wedding she'll appear
Decked in diamonds and in ermine,
  Major then can take Saphir!

(DUKE *dances with* ANGELA, MAJOR *with* SAPHIR, COLONEL *dances alone.*)

COLONEL (*dancing*)

In that case unprecedented,
  Single I shall live and die—
I shall have to be contented
  With their heartfelt sympathy!

ALL (*dancing as before*)

He will have to be contented
  With our heartfelt sympathy!

DUKE (*taking both* ANGELA *and* SAPHIR)

After some debate internal,
  If on neither I decide,
Saphir then can take the Colonel,
(*Handing* SAPHIR *to* COLONEL.)
  Angy be the Major's bride!
(*Handing* ANGELA *to* MAJOR.)

(COLONEL *dances with* SAPHIR, MAJOR *with* ANGELA, DUKE *dances alone.*)

DUKE (*dancing*)

In that case unprecedented,
  Single I must live and die—
I shall have to be contented
  With their heartfelt sympathy!

ALL (*dancing as before*)

He will have to be contented
  With our heartfelt sympathy.

[*At the end,* DUKE, COLONEL, *and* MAJOR, *and two girls dance off arm-in-arm.*

Enter GROSVENOR

GROS. It is very pleasant to be alone. It is pleasant to be able to gaze at leisure upon those features which all others may gaze upon at their good will! (*Looking at his reflection in hand-mirror*). Ah, I am a very Narcissus!

Enter BUNTHORNE, *moodily*

BUN. It's no use; I can't live without admiration. Since Grosvenor came here, insipidity has been at a premium. Ah, he is there!

GROS. Ah, Bunthorne! come here—look! Very graceful, isn't it!

BUN. (*taking hand-mirror*). Allow me; I haven't seen it. Yes, it is graceful.

GROS. (*re-taking hand-mirror*). Oh, good gracious! not that—this——

BUN. You don't mean that! Bah! I am in no mood for trifling.

GROS. And what is amiss?

BUN. Ever since you came here, you have entirely monopolized the attentions of the young ladies. I don't like it, sir!

GROS. My dear sir, how can I help it? They are the plague of my life. My dear Mr. Bunthorne, with your personal disadvantages, you can have no idea of the inconvenience of being madly loved, at first sight, by every woman you meet.

BUN. Sir, until you came here I was adored!

GROS. Exactly—until I came here. That's my grievance. I cut everybody out! I assure you, if you could only suggest some means whereby, consistently with my duty to society, I could escape these inconvenient attentions, you would earn my everlasting gratitude.

BUN. I will do so at once. However popular it may be with the world at large, your personal appearance is highly objectionable to *me*.

GROS. It is? (*Shaking his hand.*) Oh, thank you! thank you! How can I express my gratitude?

BUN. By making a complete change at once. Your conversation must henceforth be perfectly matter-of-fact. You must cut your hair, and have a back parting. In appearance and costume you must be absolutely commonplace.

GROS. (*decidedly*). No. Pardon me, that's impossible.

BUN. Take care! When I am thwarted I am very terrible.

GROS. I can't help that. I am a man with a mission. And that mission must be fulfilled.

BUN. I don't think you quite appreciate the consequences of thwarting me.

GROS. I don't care what they are.

BUN. Suppose—I won't go so far as to say that I will do it—but suppose for one moment I were to curse you? (GROSVENOR *quails.*) Ah! Very well. Take care.

GROS. But surely you would never do that? (*In great alarm.*)

BUN. I don't know. It would be an extreme measure, no doubt. Still——

GROS. (*wildly*). But you would not do it—I am sure you would not. (*Throwing himself at* BUNTHORNE'S *knees, and clinging to him.*) Oh, reflect, reflect! You had a mother once.

BUN. Never!

GROS. Then you had an aunt! (BUNTHORNE *affected.*) Ah! I see you had! By the memory of that aunt, I implore you to pause ere you resort to this last fearful expedient. Oh, Mr. Bunthorne, reflect, reflect! (*Weeping.*)

BUN. (*aside, after a struggle with himself*). I must not allow myself to be unmanned! (*Aloud.*) It is useless. Consent at once, or may a nephew's curse——

GROS. Hold! Are you absolutely resolved?

BUN. Absolutely.

GROS. Will nothing shake you?

BUN. Nothing. I am adamant.

GROS. Very good. (*Rising.*) Then I yield.

BUN. Ha! You swear it?

GROS. I do, cheerfully. I have long wished for a reasonable pretext for such a change as you suggest. It has come at last. I do it on compulsion!

BUN. Victory! I triumph!

DUET—BUNTHORNE *and* GROSVENOR

BUN. When I go out of door,
Of damozels a score
(All sighing and burning,
And clinging and yearning)
Will follow me as before.
I shall, with cultured taste,
Distinguish gems from paste,
And "High diddle diddle"
Will rank as an idyll,
If I pronounce it chaste!

BOTH. A most intense young man,
A soulful-eyed young man,

An ultra-poetical, super-æsthetical,
Out-of-the-way young man!

GROS. Conceive me, if you can,
An every-day young man:
A commonplace type,
With a stick and a pipe,
And a half-bred black-and-tan;
Who thinks suburban "hops"
More fun than "Monday Pops",
Who's fond of his dinner,
And doesn't get thinner
On bottled beer and chops.

BOTH. A commonplace young man,
A matter-of-fact young man,
A steady and stolid-y, jolly Bank-holiday
Every-day young man!

BUN. A Japanese young man,
A blue-and-white young man,
Francesca da Rimini, miminy, piminy,
Je-ne-sais-quoi young man!

GROS. A Chancery Lane young man,
A Somerset House young man,
A very delectable, highly respectable,
Threepenny-bus young man!

BUN. A pallid and thin young man,
A haggard and lank young man,
A greenery-yallery, Grosvenor Gallery,
Foot-in-the-grave young man!

GROS. A Sewell & Cross young man,
A Howell & James young man,
A pushing young particle—"What's the next article?"—
Waterloo-House young man!

ENSEMBLE

BUN.	GROS.
Conceive me, if you can,	Conceive me, if you can,
A crotchety, cracked young man,	A matter-of-fact young man,
An ultra-poetical, super-æsthetical,	An alphabetical, arithmetical,
Out-of-the-way young man!	Every-day young man!

[*At the end,* GROSVENOR *dances off.* BUNTHORNE *remains.*

BUN. It is all right! I have committed my last act of ill-nature, and henceforth I'm a changed character. (*Dances about stage, humming refrain of last air.*)

Enter PATIENCE. *She gazes in astonishment at him*

PA. Reginald! Dancing! And—what in the world is the matter with you?

BUN. Patience, I'm a changed man. Hitherto I've been gloomy, moody, fitful—uncertain in temper and selfish in disposition—

PA. You have, indeed! (*Sighing.*)

BUN. All that is changed. I have reformed. I have modelled myself upon Mr. Grosvenor. Henceforth I am mildly cheerful. My conversation will blend amusement with instruction. I shall still be æsthetic; but my æstheticism will be of the most pastoral kind.

PA. Oh, Reginald! Is all this true?

BUN. Quite true. Observe how amiable I am. (*Assuming a fixed smile.*)

PA. But, Reginald, how long will this last?

BUN. With occasional intervals for rest and refreshment, as long as I do.

PA. Oh, Reginald, I'm so happy! (*In his arms.*) Oh, dear, dear Reginald, I cannot express the joy I feel at this change. It will no longer be a duty to love you, but a pleasure—a rapture—an ecstasy!

BUN. My darling!

PA. But—oh, horror! (*Recoiling from him.*)

BUN. What's the matter?

PA. Is it quite certain that you have absolutely reformed—that you are henceforth a perfect being—utterly free from defect of any kind?

BUN. It is quite certain. I have sworn it.

PA. Then I never can be yours!

BUN. Why not?

PA. Love, to be pure, must be absolutely unselfish, and there can be nothing unselfish in loving so perfect a being as you have now become!

BUN. But, stop a bit! I don't want to change—I'll relapse—I'll be as I was—interrupted!

Enter GROSVENOR, *followed by all the young Ladies, who are followed by Chorus of Dragoons. He has had his hair cut, and is dressed in an ordinary suit of dittoes and a pot hat. They all dance cheerfully round the stage in marked contrast to their former languor.*

CHORUS—GROSVENOR *and* GIRLS

GROS.	GIRLS
I'm a Waterloo House young man,	We're Swears & Wells young girls,
A Sewell & Cross young man,	We're Madame Louise young girls,
A steady and stolid-y, jolly Bank-holiday,	We're prettily pattering, cheerily chattering,
Every-day young man!	Every-day young girls!

BUN. Angela—Ella—Saphir—what—what does this mean?

ANG. It means that Archibald the All-Right cannot be all-wrong; and if the All-Right chooses to discard æstheticism, it proves that æstheticism ought to be discarded.

PA. Oh, Archibald! Archibald! I'm shocked—surprised—horrified!

GROS. I can't help it. I'm not a free agent. I do it on compulsion.

PA. This is terrible. Go! I shall never set eyes on you again. But—oh, joy!

GROS. What is the matter?

PA. Is it quite, quite certain that you will always be a commonplace young man?

GROS. Always—I've sworn it.

PA. Why, then, there's nothing to prevent my loving you with all the fervour at my command!

GROS. Why, that's true.

PA. My Archibald!

GROS. My Patience! (*They embrace.*)

BUN. Crushed again!

Enter JANE

JANE (*who is still æsthetic*). Cheer up! I am still here. I have never left you, and I never will!

BUN. Thank you, Jane. After all, there is no denying it, you're a fine figure of a woman!

JANE. My Reginald!

BUN. My Jane!

Flourish. Enter COLONEL, DUKE, *and* MAJOR

COL. Ladies, the Duke has at length determined to select a bride! (*General excitement.*)

DUKE. I have a great gift to bestow. Approach such of you as are truly lovely. (*All come forward, bashfully, except* JANE *and* PATIENCE.) In personal appearance you have all that is necessary to make a woman happy. In common fairness, I think I ought to choose the only one among you who has the misfortune to be distinctly plain. (*Girls retire disappointed.*) Jane!

JANE (*leaving* BUNTHORNE'S *arms*). Duke! (JANE *and* DUKE *embrace.* BUNTHORNE *is utterly disgusted.*)

BUN. Crushed again!

FINALE

DUKE. After much debate internal,
I on Lady Jane decide,
Saphir now may take the Colonel,
Angy be the Major's bride!

[SAPHIR *pairs off with* COLONEL, ANGELA *with* MAJOR, ELLA *with* SOLICITOR

BUN. In that case unprecedented,
Single I must live and die—
I shall have to be contented
With a tulip or li*ly!*

(*Takes a lily from button-hole and gazes affectionately at it.*)

ALL. He will have to be contented
With a tulip or li*ly!*

Greatly pleased with one another,
To get married we decide.
Each of us will wed the other,
Nobody be Bunthorne's Bride!

DANCE

CURTAIN

IOLANTHE

OR

THE PEER AND THE PERI

DRAMATIS PERSONÆ

THE LORD CHANCELLOR

EARL OF MOUNTARARAT

EARL TOLLOLLER

PRIVATE WILLIS *(of the Grenadier Guards)*

STREPHON *(an Arcadian Shepherd)*

QUEEN OF THE FAIRIES

IOLANTHE *(a Fairy, Strephon's Mother)*

CELIA }
LEILA } *Fairies*
FLETA }

PHYLLIS *(an Arcadian Shepherdess and Ward in Chancery)*

Chorus of Dukes, Marquises, Earls, Viscounts, Barons, and Fairies

ACT I

AN ARCADIAN LANDSCAPE

ACT II

PALACE YARD, WESTMINSTER

First produced at the Savoy Theatre, November 25, 1882

IOLANTHE

OR

THE PEER AND THE PERI

ACT I

SCENE.—*An Arcadian Landscape. A river runs around the back of the stage. A rustic bridge crosses the river.*

Enter Fairies, led by LEILA, CELIA, *and* FLETA. *They trip around the stage, singing as they dance*

CHORUS

Tripping hither, tripping thither,
Nobody knows why or whither;
We must dance and we must sing
Round about our fairy ring!

SOLO—CELIA

We are dainty little fairies,
  Ever singing, ever dancing;
We indulge in our vagaries
  In a fashion most entrancing.
If you ask the special function
  Of our never-ceasing motion,
We reply, without compunction,
  That we haven't any notion!

CHORUS

No, we haven't any notion!
  Tripping hither, etc.

SOLO—LEILA

If you ask us how we live,
Lovers all essentials give—

We can ride on lovers' sighs,
Warm ourselves in lovers' eyes,
Bathe ourselves in lovers' tears,
Clothe ourselves with lovers' fears,
Arm ourselves with lovers' darts,
Hide ourselves in lovers' hearts.
When you know us, you'll discover
That we almost live on lover!

CHORUS

Tripping hither, etc.
(*At the end of Chorus, all sigh wearily.*)

CELIA. Ah, it's all very well, but since our Queen banished Iolanthe, fairy revels have not been what they were!

LEILA. Iolanthe was the life and soul of Fairyland. Why, she wrote all our songs and arranged all our dances! We sing her songs and we trip her measures, but we don't enjoy ourselves!

FLETA. To think that five-and-twenty years have elapsed since she was banished! What could she have done to have deserved so terrible a punishment?

LEILA. Something awful! She married a mortal!

FLETA. Oh! Is it injudicious to marry a mortal?

LEILA. Injudicious? It strikes at the root of the whole fairy system! By our laws, the fairy who marries a mortal dies!

CELIA. But Iolanthe didn't die!

Enter FAIRY QUEEN

QUEEN. No, because your Queen, who loved her with a surpassing love, commuted her sentence to penal servitude for life, on condition that she left her husband and never communicated with him again!

LEILA. That sentence of penal servitude she is now working out, on her head, at the bottom of that stream!

QUEEN. Yes, but when I banished her, I gave her all the pleasant places of the earth to dwell in. I'm sure I never intended that she should go and live at the bottom of a stream! It makes me perfectly wretched to think of the discomfort she must have undergone!

LEILA. Think of the damp! And her chest was always delicate.

QUEEN. And the frogs! Ugh! I never shall enjoy any peace of mind until I know why Iolanthe went to live among the frogs!

FLETA. Then why not summon her and ask her?

QUEEN. Why? Because if I set eyes on her I should forgive her at once!

CELIA. Then why not forgive her? Twenty-five years—it's a long time!

LEILA. Think how we loved her!

QUEEN. Loved her? What was your love to mine? Why, she was invaluable to me! Who taught me to curl myself inside a buttercup? Iolanthe! Who taught me to swing upon a cobweb? Iolanthe! Who taught me to dive into a dewdrop—to nestle in a nutshell—to gambol upon gossamer? Iolanthe!

LEILA. She certainly did surprising things!

FLETA. Oh, give her back to us, great Queen, for your sake if not for ours! (*All kneel in supplication.*)

QUEEN (*irresolute*). Oh, I should be strong, but I am weak! I should be marble, but I am clay! Her punishment has been heavier than I intended. I did not mean that she should live among the frogs—and—well, well, it shall be as you wish—it shall be as you wish!

INVOCATION—QUEEN

Iolanthe!
From thy dark exile thou art summoned!
Come to our call—
Come, Iolanthe!

CELIA. Iolanthe!

LEILA. Iolanthe!

ALL. Come to our call,
Come, Iolanthe!

[IOLANTHE *rises from the water. She is clad in water-weeds. She approaches the* QUEEN *with head bent and arms crossed.*

IOLANTHE. With humbled breast
And every hope laid low,
To thy behest,
Offended Queen, I bow!

QUEEN. For a dark sin against our fairy laws
We sent thee into life-long banishment;
But mercy holds her sway within our hearts—
Rise—thou art pardoned!

IOL. Pardoned!

ALL. Pardoned!

[*Her weeds fall from her, and she appears clothed as a fairy. The* QUEEN *places a diamond coronet on her head, and embraces her. The others also embrace her.*

CHORUS

Welcome to our hearts again,
Iolanthe! Iolanthe!
We have shared thy bitter pain,
Iolanthe! Iolanthe!

Every heart, and every hand
In our loving little band
Welcomes thee to Fairyland,
Iolanthe!

QUEEN. And now, tell me, with all the world to choose from, why on earth did you decide to live at the bottom of that stream?

IOL. To be near my son, Strephon.

QUEEN. Bless my heart, I didn't know you had a son.

IOL. He was born soon after I left my husband by your royal command—but he does not even know of his father's existence.

FLETA. How old is he?

IOL. Twenty-four.

LEILA. Twenty-four! No one, to look at you, would think you had a son of twenty-four! But that's one of the advantages of being immortal. We never grow old! Is he pretty?

IOL. He's extremely pretty, but he's inclined to be stout.

ALL (*disappointed*). Oh!

QUEEN. I see no objection to stoutness, in moderation.

CELIA. And what is he?

IOL. He's an Arcadian shepherd—and he loves Phyllis, a Ward in Chancery.

CELIA. A mere shepherd! and he half a fairy!

IOL. He's a fairy down to the waist—but his legs are mortal.

ALL. Dear me!

QUEEN. I have no reason to suppose that I am more curious than other people, but I confess I should like to see a person who is fairy down to the waist, but whose legs are mortal.

IOL. Nothing easier, for here he comes!

Enter STREPHON, *singing and dancing and playing on a flageolet. He does not see the Fairies, who retire up stage as he enters.*

SONG—STREPHON

Good morrow, good mother!
Good mother, good morrow!
By some means or other,
Pray banish your sorrow!
With joy beyond telling
My bosom is swelling,
So join in a measure
Expressive of pleasure,
For I'm to be married to-day—to-day—
Yes, I'm to be married to-day!

CHORUS (*aside*). Yes, he's to be married to-day—to-day—
Yes, he's to be married to-day!

IOL. Then the Lord Chancellor has at last given his consent to your marriage with his beautiful ward, Phyllis?

STREPH. Not he, indeed. To all my tearful prayers he answers me, "A shepherd lad is no fit helpmate for a Ward of Chancery." I stood in court, and there I sang him songs of Arcadee, with flageolet accompaniment—in vain. At first he seemed amused, so did the Bar; but quickly wearying of my song and pipe, bade me get out. A servile usher then, in crumpled bands and rusty bombazine, led me, still singing, into Chancery Lane! I'll go no more; I'll marry her to-day, and brave the upshot, be it what it may! (*Sees Fairies.*) But who are these?

IOL. Oh, Strephon! rejoice with me, my Queen has pardoned me!

STREPH. Pardoned you, mother? This is good news indeed.

IOL. And these ladies are my beloved sisters.

STREPH. Your sisters! Then they are—my aunts!

QUEEN. A pleasant piece of news for your bride on her wedding day!

STREPH. Hush! My bride knows nothing of my fairyhood. I dare not tell her, lest it frighten her. She thinks me mortal, and prefers me so.

LEILA. Your fairyhood doesn't seem to have done you much good.

STREPH. Much good! My dear aunt! it's the curse of my existence! What's the use of being half a fairy? My body can creep through a keyhole, but what's the good of that when my legs are left kicking behind? I can make myself invisible down to the waist, but that's of no use when my legs remain exposed to view? My brain is a fairy brain, but from the waist downwards I'm a gibbering idiot. My upper half is immortal, but my lower half grows older every day, and some day or other must die of old age. What's to become of my upper half when I've buried my lower half I really don't know!

FAIRIES. Poor fellow!

QUEEN. I see your difficulty, but with a fairy brain you should seek an intellectual sphere of action. Let me see. I've a borough or two at my disposal. Would you like to go into Parliament?

IOL. A fairy Member! That would be delightful!

STREPH. I'm afraid I should do no good there—you see, down to the waist, I'm a Tory of the most determined description, but my legs are a couple of confounded Radicals, and, on a division, they'd be sure to take me into the wrong lobby. You see, they're two to one, which is a strong working majority.

QUEEN. Don't let that distress you; you shall be returned as a Liberal-Unionist, and your legs shall be our peculiar care.

STREPH. (*bowing*). I see your Majesty does not do things by halves.

QUEEN. No, we are fairies down to the feet.

ENSEMBLE

QUEEN. Fare thee well, attractive stranger.
FAIRIES. Fare thee well, attractive stranger.
QUEEN. Shouldst thou be in doubt or danger,
Peril or perplexitee,
Call us, and we'll come to thee!
FAIRIES. Call us, and we'll come to thee!
Tripping hither, tripping thither,
Nobody knows why or whither;
We must now be taking wing
To another fairy ring!

[*Fairies and* QUEEN *trip off,* IOLANTHE, *who takes an affectionate farewell of her son, going off last.*

Enter PHYLLIS, *singing and dancing, and accompanying herself on a flageolet*

SONG—PHYLLIS

Good morrow, good lover!
Good lover, good morrow!
I prithee discover,
Steal, purchase, or borrow
Some means of concealing
The care you are feeling,
And join in a measure
Expressive of pleasure,
For we're to be married to-day—to-day!
For we're to be married to-day!

BOTH. Yes, we're to be married, etc.

STREPH. (*embracing her*). My Phyllis! And to-day we are to be made happy for ever.

PHYL. Well, we're to be married.

STREPH. It's the same thing.

PHYL. I suppose it is. But oh, Strephon, I tremble at the step I'm taking! I believe it's penal servitude for life to marry a Ward of Court without the Lord Chancellor's consent! I shall be of age in two years. Don't you think you could wait two years?

STREPH. Two years. Have you ever looked in the glass?

PHYL. No, never.

STREPH. Here, look at that (*showing her a pocket mirror*), and tell me if you think it rational to expect me to wait two years?

PHYL. (*looking at herself*). No. You're quite right—it's asking too much. One must be reasonable.

STREPH. Besides, who knows what will happen in two years? Why, you might fall in love with the Lord Chancellor himself by that time!

PHYL. Yes. He's a clean old gentleman.

STREPH. As it is, half the House of Lords are sighing at your feet.

PHYL. The House of Lords are certainly extremely attentive.

STREPH. Attentive? I should think they were! Why did five-and-twenty Liberal Peers come down to shoot over your grass-plot last autumn? It couldn't have been the sparrows. Why did five-and-twenty Conservative Peers come down to fish your pond? Don't tell me it was the gold-fish! No, no—delays are dangerous, and if we are to marry, the sooner the better.

DUET—STREPHON *and* PHYLLIS

PHYLLIS. None shall part us from each other,
One in life and death are we:
All in all to one another—
I to thee and thou to me!

BOTH. Thou the tree and I the flower—
Thou the idol; I the throng—
Thou the day and I the hour—
Thou the singer; I the song!

STREPH. All in all since that fond meeting
When in joy, I woke to find

Mine the heart within thee beating,
Mine the love that heart enshrined!

BOTH. Thou the stream and I the willow—
Thou the sculptor; I the clay—
Thou the ocean; I the billow—
Thou the sunrise; I the day!

[*Exeunt* STREPHON *and* PHYLLIS *together.*

March. Enter Procession of Peers

CHORUS

Loudly let the trumpet bray!
Tantantara!
Proudly bang the sounding brasses!
Tzing! Boom!
As upon its lordly way
This unique procession passes,
Tantantara! Tzing! Boom!
Bow, bow, ye lower middle classes!
Bow, bow, ye tradesmen, bow, ye masses!
Blow the trumpets, bang the brasses!
Tantantara! Tzing! Boom!
We are peers of highest station,
Paragons of legislation,
Pillars of the British nation!
Tantantara! Tzing! Boom!

Enter the LORD CHANCELLOR, *followed by his train-bearer*

SONG—LORD CHANCELLOR

The Law is the true embodiment
Of everything that's excellent.
It has no kind of fault or flaw,
And I, my Lords, embody the Law.
The constitutional guardian I
Of pretty young Wards in Chancery,
All very agreeable girls—and none
Are over the age of twenty-one.
A pleasant occupation for
A rather susceptible Chancellor!

ALL. A pleasant, etc.

LORD CH. But though the compliment implied
Inflates me with legitimate pride,
It nevertheless can't be denied
That it has its inconvenient side.

For I'm not so old, and not so plain,
And I'm quite prepared to marry again,
But there'd be the deuce to pay in the Lords
If I fell in love with one of my Wards!
Which rather tries my temper, for
I'm *such* a susceptible Chancellor!

ALL. Which rather, etc.

And every one who'd marry a Ward
Must come to me for my accord,
And in my court I sit all day,
Giving agreeable girls away,
With one for him—and one for he—
And one for you—and one for ye—
And one for thou—and one for thee—
But never, oh, never a one for me!

Which is exasperating for
A highly susceptible Chancellor!

ALL. Which is, etc.

Enter LORD TOLLOLLER

LORD TOLL. And now, my Lords, to the business of the day.

LORD CH. By all means. Phyllis, who is a Ward of Court, has so powerfully affected your Lordships, that you have appealed to me in a body to give her to whichever one of you she may think proper to select, and a noble Lord has just gone to her cottage to request her immediate attendance. It would be idle to deny that I, myself, have the misfortune to be singularly attracted by this young person. My regard for her is rapidly undermining my constitution. Three months ago I was a stout man. I need say no more. If I could reconcile it with my duty, I should unhesitatingly award her to myself, for I can conscientiously say that I know no man who is so well fitted to render her exceptionally happy. (*Peers*: Hear, hear!) But such an award would be open to misconstruction, and therefore, at whatever personal inconvenience, I waive my claim.

LORD TOLL. My Lord, I desire, on the part of this House, to express its sincere sympathy with your Lordship's most painful position.

LORD. CH. I thank your Lordships. The feelings of a Lord Chancellor who is in love with a Ward of Court are not to be envied. What is his position? Can he give his own consent to his own marriage with his own Ward? Can he marry his own Ward without his own consent? And if he marries his own Ward without his own consent, can he commit himself for contempt of his own Court? And if he commit himself for contempt of his own Court, can he appear by counsel before himself, to move for arrest of his own judgment? Ah, my Lords, it is indeed painful to have to sit upon a woolsack which is stuffed with such thorns as these!

Enter LORD MOUNTARARAT

LORD MOUNT. My Lords, I have much pleasure in announcing that I have succeeded in inducing the young person to present herself at the Bar of this House.

Enter PHYLLIS

RECIT—PHYLLIS

My well-loved Lord and Guardian dear,
You summoned me, and I am here!

CHORUS OF PEERS

Oh, rapture, how beautiful!
How gentle—how dutiful!

SOLO—LORD TOLLOLLER

Of all the young ladies I know
This pretty young lady's the fairest;
Her lips have the rosiest show,
Her eyes are the richest and rarest.
Her origin's lowly, it's true,
But of birth and position I've plenty;
I've grammar and spelling for two,
And blood and behaviour for twenty!
Her origin's lowly, it's true,
I've grammar and spelling for two;

CHORUS. Of birth and position he's plenty,
With blood and behaviour for twenty!

SOLO—LORD MOUNTARARAT

Though the views of the House have diverged
On every conceivable motion,
All questions of Party are merged
In a frenzy of love and devotion;
If you ask us distinctly to say
What Party we claim to belong to,
We reply, without doubt or delay,
The Party I'm singing this song to!

SOLO—PHYLLIS

I'm very much pained to refuse,
But I'll stick to my pipes and my tabors;
I can spell all the words that I use,
And my grammar's as good as my neighbours'.
As for birth—I was born like the rest,
My behaviour is rustic but hearty,
And I know where to turn for the best,
When I want a particular Party!

CHORUS. Though her station is none of the best,
I suppose she was born like the rest;
And she knows where to look for her hearty,
When she wants a particular Party!

RECIT—PHYLLIS

Nay, tempt me not.
To rank I'll not be bound;
In lowly cot
Alone is virtue found!

CHORUS. No, no; indeed high rank will never hurt you,
The Peerage is not destitute of virtue.

BALLAD—LORD TOLLOLLER

Spurn not the nobly born
With love affected,
Nor treat with virtuous scorn
The well-connected.
High rank involves no shame—
We boast an equal claim

With him of humble name
To be respected!
Blue blood! blue blood!
When virtuous love is sought
Thy power is naught,
Though dating from the Flood,
Blue blood!

CHORUS. Blue blood! blue blood! etc.

Spare us the bitter pain
Of stern denials,
Nor with low-born disdain
Augment our trials.
Hearts just as pure and fair
May beat in Belgrave Square
As in the lowly air
Of Seven Dials!
Blue blood! Blue blood!
Of what avail art thou
To serve us now?
Though dating from the Flood,
Blue blood!

CHORUS. Blue blood! blue blood! etc.

RECIT—PHYLLIS

My Lords, it may not be.
With grief my heart is riven!
You waste your time on me,
For ah! my heart is given!

ALL. Given!
PHYL. Yes, given!
ALL. Oh, horror!!!

RECIT—LORD CHANCELLOR

And who has dared to brave our high displeasure,
And thus defy our definite command?

Enter STREPHON

STREPH. 'Tis I—young Strephon! mine this priceless treasure!
Against the world I claim my darling's hand!

[PHYLLIS *rushes to his arms.*

A shepherd I—
ALL. A shepherd he!
STREPH. Of Arcady—
ALL. Of Arcadee!
STREPH. Betrothed are we!
ALL. Betrothed are they—
STREPH. And mean to be—
ALL. Espoused to-day!

ENSEMBLE

STREPH.	THE OTHERS
A shepherd I	A shepherd he
Of Arcady,	Of Arcadee,
Betrothed are we,	Betrothed is he,
And mean to be	And means to be
Espoused to-day!	Espoused to-day!

DUET—LORD MOUNTARARAT *and* LORD TOLLOLLER
(*aside to each other*)

'Neath this blow,
Worse than stab of dagger—
Though we mo-
Mentarily stagger,
In each heart
Proud are we innately—
Let's depart,
Dignified and stately!

ALL. Let's depart,
Dignified and stately!

CHORUS OF PEERS

Though our hearts she's badly bruising,
In another suitor choosing,
Let's pretend it's most amusing.
Ha! ha! ha! Tan-ta-ra!

[*Exeunt all the Peers, marching round stage with much dignity.* LORD CHANCELLOR *separates* PHYLLIS *from* STREPHON *and orders her off. She follows Peers. Manent* LORD CHANCELLOR *and* STREPHON.

LORD CH. Now, sir, what excuse have you to offer for having disobeyed an order of the Court of Chancery?

STREPH. My Lord, I know no Courts of Chancery; I go by Nature's Acts of Parliament. The bees—the breeze—the seas—the rooks—the brooks—the gales—the vales—the fountains and the mountains cry, "You love this maiden—take her, we command you!" 'Tis writ in heaven by the bright barbèd dart that leaps forth into lurid light from each grim thundercloud. The very rain pours forth her sad and sodden sympathy! When chorused Nature bids me take my love, shall I reply, "Nay, but a certain Chancellor forbids it"? Sir, you are England's Lord High Chancellor, but are you Chancellor of birds and trees, King of the winds and Prince of thunderclouds?

LORD CH. No. It's a nice point. I don't know that I ever met it before. But my difficulty is that at present there's no evidence before the Court that chorused Nature has interested herself in the matter.

STREPH. No evidence! You have my word for it. I tell you that she bade me take my love.

LORD CH. Ah! but, my good sir, you mustn't tell us what she told you—it's not evidence. Now an affidavit from a thunderstorm, or a few words on oath from a heavy shower, would meet with all the attention they deserve.

STREPH. And have you the heart to apply the prosaic rules of evidence to a case which bubbles over with poetical emotion?

LORD CH. Distinctly. I have always kept my duty strictly before my eyes, and it is to that fact that I owe my advancement to my present distinguished position.

SONG—LORD CHANCELLOR

When I went to the Bar as a very young man,
(Said I to myself—said I),
I'll work on a new and original plan
(Said I to myself—said I),

I'll never assume that a rogue or a thief
Is a gentleman worthy implicit belief,
Because his attorney has sent me a brief
(Said I to myself—said I!).

Ere I go into court I will read my brief through
(Said I to myself—said I).
And I'll never take work I'm unable to do
(Said I to myself—said I),
My learned profession I'll never disgrace
By taking a fee with a grin on my face,
When I haven't been there to attend to the case
(Said I to myself—said I!).

I'll never throw dust in a juryman's eyes
(Said I to myself—said I),
Or hoodwink a judge who is not over-wise
(Said I to myself—said I),
Or assume that the witnesses summoned in force
In Exchequer, Queen's Bench, Common Pleas, or
Divorce,
Have perjured themselves as a matter of course
(Said I to myself—said I!).

In other professions in which men engage
(Said I to myself—said I),
The Army, the Navy, the Church, and the Stage
(Said I to myself—said I),
Professional license, if carried too far,
Your chance of promotion will certainly mar—
And I fancy the rule might apply to the Bar
(Said I to myself—said I!).

[*Exit* LORD CHANCELLOR.

Enter IOLANTHE

STREPH. Oh, Phyllis, Phyllis! To be taken from you just as I was on the point of making you my own! Oh, it's too much—it's too much!

IOL. (*to* STREPHON, *who is in tears*). My son in tears—and on his wedding day!

STREPH. My wedding day! Oh, mother, weep with me, for the Law has interposed between us, and the Lord Chancellor has separated us for ever!

IOL. The Lord Chancellor! (*Aside.*) Oh, if he did but know!

STREPH. (*overhearing her*). If he did but know what?

IOL. No matter! The Lord Chancellor has no power over you. Remember you are half a fairy. You can defy him—down to the waist.

STREPH. Yes, but from the waist downwards he can commit me to prison for years! Of what avail is it that my body is free, if my legs are working out seven years' penal servitude?

IOL. True. But take heart—our Queen has promised you her special protection. I'll go to her and lay your peculiar case before her.

STREPH. My beloved mother! how can I repay the debt I owe you?

FINALE—QUARTET

As it commences, the Peers appear at the back, advancing unseen and on tiptoe. LORD MOUNTARARAT *and* LORD TOLLOLLER *lead* PHYLLIS *between them, who listens in horror to what she hears.*

STREPH. (*to* IOLANTHE). When darkly looms the day,
And all is dull and grey,
To chase the gloom away,
On thee I'll call!

PHYL. (*speaking aside to* LORD MOUNTARARAT). What was that?

LORD MOUNT. (*aside to* PHYLLIS).
I think I heard him say,
That on a rainy day,
To while the time away,
On her he'd call!

CHORUS. We think we heard him say, etc.

[PHYLLIS *much agitated at her lover's supposed faithlessness.*

IOL. (*to* STREPHON). When tempests wreck thy bark,
And all is drear and dark,
If thou shouldst need an Ark,
I'll give thee one!

PHYL. (*speaking aside to* LORD TOLLOLLER). What was that?

LORD TOLL. (*aside to* PHYLLIS).
I heard the minx remark,
She'd meet him after dark,
Inside St. James's Park,
And give him one!

PHYL.
The prospect's very bad,
My heart so sore and sad
Will never more be glad
As summer's sun.

IOL., LORD TOLL., STREPH., LORD MOUNT.
The prospect's not so bad,
{My / Thy} heart so sore and sad
May very soon be glad
As summer's sun;

PHYL., IOL., LORD TOLL., STREPH., LORD MOUNT.
For when the sky is dark
And tempests wreck {my / thy / his} bark,
If {he should / I should / thou shouldst} need an Ark,
{She'll / I'll} give {him / me / thee} one!

PHYL. (*revealing herself*). Ah!

[IOLANTHE *and* STREPHON *much confused.*

PHYL.
Oh, shameless one, tremble!
Nay, do not endeavour
Thy fault to dissemble,
We part—and for ever!
I worshipped him blindly,
He worships another—

STREPH.
Attend to me kindly,
This lady's my mother!

.TOLL. This lady's his *what*?
STREPH. This lady's my mother!
TENORS. This lady's his *what*?
BASSES. He says she's his mother!

[*They point derisively to* IOLANTHE, *laughing heartily at her. She goes for protection to* STREPHON.

Enter LORD CHANCELLOR. IOLANTHE *veils herself*

LORD CH. What means this mirth unseemly,
That shakes the listening earth?

LORD TOLL. The joke is good extremely,
And justifies our mirth.

LORD MOUNT. This gentleman is seen,
With a maid of seventeen;
A-taking of his *dolce far niente*;
And wonders he'd achieve,
For he asks us to believe
She's his mother—and he's nearly five-and-twenty!

LORD CH. (*sternly*). Recollect yourself, I pray,
And be careful what you say—
As the ancient Romans said, *festina lente.*
For I really do not see
How so young a girl could be
The mother of a man of five-and-twenty.

ALL. Ha! ha! ha! ha! ha!

STREPH. My Lord, of evidence I have no dearth—
She is—has been—my mother from my birth!

BALLAD

In babyhood
Upon her lap I lay,
With infant food
She moistenèd my clay;
Had she withheld
The succour she supplied,
By hunger quelled,
Your Strephon might have died!

LORD CH. (*much moved*).
Had that refreshment been denied,
Indeed our Strephon might have died!

ALL (*much affected*).
Had that refreshment been denied,
Indeed our Strephon might have died!

LORD MOUNT. But as she's not
His mother, it appears,
Why weep these hot
Unnecessary tears?
And by what laws
Should we so joyously
Rejoice, because
Our Strephon did not die?
Oh, rather let us pipe our eye
Because our Strephon did not die!

ALL. That's very true—let's pipe our eye
Because our Strephon did not die!

[*All weep.* IOLANTHE, *who has succeeded in hiding her face from* LORD CHANCELLOR, *escapes unnoticed.*

PHYL. Go, traitorous one—for ever we must part:
To one of you, my Lords, I give my heart!

ALL. Oh, rapture!

STREPH. Hear me, Phyllis, ere you leave me.

PHYL. Not a word—you did deceive me.

ALL. Not a word—you did deceive her.

[*Exit* STREPHON.

BALLAD—PHYLLIS

For riches and rank I do not long—
Their pleasures are false and vain;
I gave up the love of a lordly throng
For the love of a simple swain.
But now that simple swain's untrue,
With sorrowful heart I turn to you—

A heart that's aching,
Quaking, breaking,
As sorrowful hearts are wont to do!

The riches and rank that you befall
Are the only baits you use,
So the richest and rankiest of you all
My sorrowful heart shall choose.
As none are so noble—none so rich
As this couple of lords, I'll find a niche
In my heart that's aching,
Quaking, breaking,
For one of you two—and I don't care which!

ENSEMBLE

PHYL. (*to* LORD MOUNTARARAT *and* LORD TOLLOLLER).
To you I give my heart so rich!
ALL (*puzzled*). To which?
PHYL. I do not care!
To you I yield—it is my doom!
ALL. To whom?
PHIL. I'm not aware!
I'm yours for life if you but choose.
ALL. She's whose?
PHYL. That's your affair!
I'll be a countess, shall I not?
ALL. Of what?
PHYL. I do not care!
ALL. Lucky little lady!
Strephon's lot is shady;
Rank, it seems, is vital,
"Countess" is the title,
But of what I'm not aware;

Enter STREPHON

STREPH. Can I inactive see my fortunes fade?
No, no!
Mighty protectress, hasten to my aid!

Enter Fairies, tripping, headed by CELIA, LEILA, *and* FLETA, *and followed by* QUEEN

CHORUS OF FAIRIES
Tripping hither, tripping thither,
Nobody knows why or whither;
Why you want us we don't know,
But you've summoned us, and so
Enter all the little fairies
To their usual tripping measure!
To oblige you all our care is—
Tell us, pray, what is your pleasure!

STREPH. The lady of my love has caught me talking to another—
PEERS. Oh, fie! our Strephon is a rogue!
STREPH. I tell her very plainly that the lady is my mother—
PEERS. Taradiddle, taradiddle, tol lol lay!
STREPH. She won't believe my statement, and declares we must be parted,
Because on a career of double-dealing I have started,
Then gives her hand to one of these, and leaves me broken-hearted—
PEERS. Taradiddle, taradiddle, tol lol lay!
QUEEN. Ah, cruel ones, to separate two lovers from each other!
FAIRIES. Oh, fie! our Strephon's not a rogue!
QUEEN. You've done him an injustice, for the lady *is* his mother!
FAIRIES. Taradiddle, taradiddle, tol lol lay!
LORD CH. That fable perhaps may serve his turn as well as any other.
(*Aside.*) I didn't see her face, but if they fondled one another,
And she's but seventeen—I don't believe it was his mother!
Taradiddle, taradiddle.
ALL. Tol lol lay!
LORD TOLL. I have often had a use
For a thorough-bred excuse
Of a sudden (which is English for "*repente*"),
But of all I ever heard
This is much the most absurd,
For she's seventeen, and he is five-and-twenty!

ALL. Though she is seventeen, and he's four or five-and-twenty!
Oh, fie! our Strephon is a rogue!

LORD MOUNT Now, listen, pray to me,
For this paradox will be
Carried, nobody at all *contradicente.*
Her age, upon the date
Of his birth, was *minus* eight,
If she's seventeen, and he is five-and-twenty!

ALL. To say she is his mother is an utter bit of folly!
Oh, fie! our Strephon is a rogue!
Perhaps his brain is addled, and it's very melancholy!
Taradiddle, taradiddle, tol lol lay!
I wouldn't say a word that could be reckoned as injurious,
But to find a mother younger than her son is very curious,
And that's a kind of mother that is usually spurious.
Taradiddle, taradiddle, tol lol lay!

LORD CH. Go away, madam;
I should say, madam,
You display, madam,
Shocking taste.

It is rude, madam,
To intrude, madam,
With your brood, madam,
Brazen-faced!

You come here, madam,
Interfere, madam,
With a peer, madam.
(I am one.)

You're aware, madam,
What you dare, madam,
So take care, madam,
And begone!

ENSEMBLE

FAIRIES (*to* QUEEN)

Let us stay, madam;
I should say, madam,
They display, madam,
Shocking taste.

It is rude, madam,
To allude, madam,
To your brood, madam,
Brazen-faced!

We don't fear, madam,
Any peer, madam,
Though, my dear madam,
This is one.

They will stare, madam,
When aware, madam,
What they dare, madam—
What they've done!

PEERS

Go away, madam;
I should say, madam,
You display, madam,
Shocking taste.

It is rude, madam,
To intrude, madam,
With your brood, madam,
Brazen-faced!

You come here, madam,
Interfere, madam,
With a peer, madam,
(I am one.)

You're aware, madam,
What you dare, madam,
So take care, madam,
And begone!

QUEEN. (*furious*).
Bearded by these puny mortals!
I will launch from fairy portals
All the most terrific thunders
In my armory of wonders!

PHYL. (*aside*).
Should they launch terrific wonders,
All would then repent their blunders.
Surely these must be immortals.

[*Exit* PHYLLIS.

QUEEN.
Oh! Chancellor unwary
It's highly necessary
Your tongue to teach
Respectful speech—
Your attitude to vary!

Your badinage so airy,
Your manner arbitrary,
Are out of place
When face to face
With an influential Fairy.

ALL THE PEERS (*aside*).
We never knew
We were talking to
An influential Fairy!

LORD CH.
A plague on this vagary,
I'm in a nice quandary!
Of hasty tone
With dames unknown
I ought to be more chary;
It seems that she's a fairy
From Andersen's lib*ra*ry,
And I took her for
The proprietor
Of a Ladies' Seminary!

PEERS.
We took her for
The proprietor
Of a Ladies' Seminary!

QUEEN.
When next your Houses do assemble,
You may tremble!

CELIA.
Our wrath, when gentlemen offend us,
Is tremendous!

LEILA.
They meet, who underrate our calling,
Doom appalling!

QUEEN.
Take down our sentence as we speak it,
And *he* shall wreak it!
[*Indicating* STREPHON.

PEERS.
Oh, spare us!

QUEEN.
Henceforth, Strephon, cast away
Crooks and pipes and ribbons so gay—
Flocks and herds that bleat and low;
Into Parliament you shall go!

ALL.
Into Parliament he shall go!
Backed by our supreme authority,
He'll command a large majority!
Into Parliament he shall go!

QUEEN.
In the Parliamentary hive,
Liberal or Conservative—

Whig or Tory—I don't know—
But into Parliament you shall go!

FAIRIES. Into Parliament, etc.

QUEEN (*speaking through music*)

Every bill and every measure
That may gratify his pleasure,
Though your fury it arouses,
Shall be passed by both your Houses!

PEERS. Oh!

You shall sit, if he sees reason,
Through the grouse and salmon season;

PEERS. No!

He shall end the cherished rights
You enjoy on Friday nights:

PEERS. No!

He shall prick that annual blister,
Marriage with deceased wife's sister:

PEERS. Mercy!

Titles shall ennoble, then,
All the Common Councilmen:

PEERS. Spare us!

Peers shall teem in Christendom,
And a Duke's exalted station
Be attainable by Com-
Petitive Examination!

PEERS	FAIRIES *and* PHYLLIS
Oh, horror!	Their horror They can't dissemble Nor hide the fear that makes them tremble!

ENSEMBLE

PEERS	FAIRIES, PHYLLIS *and* STREPHON
Young Strephon is the kind of lout We do not care a fig about! We cannot say What evils may Result in consequence.	With Strephon for your foe, no doubt, A fearful prospect opens out, And who shall say What evils may Result in consequence?

But lordly vengeance will pursue
All kinds of common people who
Oppose our views,
Or boldly choose
To offer us offence.

He'd better fly at humbler game,
Or our forbearance he must claim,
If he'd escape
In any shape
A very painful wrench!

Your powers we dauntlessly pooh-pooh:
A dire revenge will fall on you,
If you besiege
Our high *prestige*—
(The word "*prestige*" is French).

A hideous vengeance will pursue
All noblemen who venture to
Oppose his views,
Or boldly choose
To offer him offence.

'Twill plunge them into grief and shame;
His kind forbearance they must claim,
If they'd escape
In any shape
A very painful wrench.

Although our threats you now pooh-pooh,
A dire revenge will fall on you,
Should he besiege
Your high *prestige*—
(The word "*prestige*" is French).

PEERS. Our lordly style
You shall not quench
With base *canaille*!
FAIRIES. (That word is French.)
PEERS. Distinction ebbs
Before a herd
Of vulgar *plebs*!
FAIRIES. (A Latin word.)
PEERS. 'Twould fill with joy,
And madness stark
The *οἱ πολλοί*!
FAIRIES. (A Greek remark.)

PEERS. One Latin word, one Greek remark,
And one that's French.

FAIRIES. Your lordly style
We'll quickly quench
With base *canaille*!
PEERS. (That word is French.)
FAIRIES. Distinction ebbs
Before a herd
Of vulgar *plebs*!
PEERS. (A Latin word.)
FAIRIES. 'Twill fill with joy
And madness stark
The *οἱ πολλοί*!

PEERS. (A Greek remark.)

FAIRIES. One Latin word, one Greek remark,
And one that's French.

PEERS	FAIRIES
You needn't wait:	We will not wait:
Away you fly!	We go sky-high!
Your threatened hate	Our threatened hate
We won't defy!	You won't defy!

[FAIRIES *threaten* PEERS *with their wands.* PEERS *kneel as begging for mercy.* PHYLLIS *implores* STREPHON *to relent. He casts her from him, and she falls fainting into the arms of* LORD MOUNTARARAT *and* LORD TOLLOLLER.

END OF ACT I

ACT II

SCENE.—*Palace Yard, Westminster. Westminster Hall,* L. *Clock tower up,* R.C. PRIVATE WILLIS *discovered on sentry,* R. *Moonlight.*

SONG—PRIVATE WILLIS

When all night long a chap remains
On sentry-go, to chase monotony
He exercises of his brains,
That is, assuming that he's got any.
Though never nurtured in the lap
Of luxury, yet I admonish you,
I am an intellectual chap,
And think of things that would astonish you.
I often think it's comical—Fal, lal, la!
Now Nature always does contrive—Fal, lal, la!
That every boy and every gal
That's born into the world alive
Is either a little Liberal
Or else a little Conservative!
Fal, lal, la!

When in that House M.P.'s divide,
  If they've a brain and cerebellum, too,
They've got to leave that brain outside,
  And vote just as their leaders tell 'em to.
But then the prospect of a lot
  Of dull M.P.'s in close proximity,
All thinking for themselves, is what
  No man can face with equanimity.
    Then let's rejoice with loud Fal la—Fal lal la!
    That Nature always does contrive—Fal lal la!
      That every boy and every gal
        That's born into the world alive
      Is either a little Liberal
        Or else a little Conservative!
            Fal lal la!

Enter FAIRIES, *with* CELIA, LEILA, *and* FLETA. *They trip round stage*

CHORUS OF FAIRIES

Strephon's a Member of Parliament!
Carries every Bill he chooses.
To his measures all assent—
  Showing that fairies have their uses.
    Whigs and Tories
    Dim their glories,
Giving an ear to all his stories—
Lords and Commons are both in the blues!
Strephon makes them shake in their shoes!
    Shake in their shoes!
    Shake in their shoes!
Strephon makes them shake in their shoes!

Enter PEERS *from Westminster Hall*

CHORUS OF PEERS

Strephon's a Member of Parliament!
  Running a-muck of all abuses.
His unqualified assent
  Somehow nobody now refuses.
    Whigs and Tories
    Dim their glories,

Giving an ear to all his stories
Carrying every Bill he may wish:
Here's a pretty kettle of fish!
    Kettle of fish!
    Kettle of fish!
Here's a pretty kettle of fish!

Enter LORD MOUNTARARAT *and* LORD TOLLOLLER *from Westminster Hall*

CELIA. You seem annoyed.

LORD MOUNT. Annoyed! I should think so! Why, this ridiculous *protégé* of yours is playing the deuce with everything! To-night is the second reading of his Bill to throw the Peerage open to Competitive Examination!

LORD TOLL. And he'll carry it, too!

LORD MOUNT. Carry it? Of course he will! He's a Parliamentary Pickford—he carries everything!

LEILA. Yes. If you please, that's our fault!

LORD MOUNT. The deuce it is!

CELIA. Yes; we influence the members, and compel them to vote just as he wishes them to.

LEILA. It's our system. It shortens the debates.

LORD TOLL. Well, but think what it all means. I don't so much mind for myself, but with a House of Peers with no grandfathers worth mentioning, the country must go to the dogs!

LEILA. I suppose it must!

LORD MOUNT. I don't want to say a word against brains—I've a great respect for brains—I often wish I had some myself—but with a House of Peers composed exclusively of people of intellect, what's to become of the House of Commons?

LEILA. I never thought of that!

LORD MOUNT. This comes of women interfering in politics. It so happens that if there is an insitution in Great Britain which is not susceptible of any improvement at all, it is the House of Peers!

SONG—LORD MOUNTARARAT

When Britain really ruled the waves—
  (In good Queen Bess's time)

The House of Peers made no pretence
To intellectual eminence,
  Or scholarship sublime;
Yet Britain won her proudest bays
In good Queen Bess's glorious days!

CHORUS. Yes, Britain won, etc.

When Wellington thrashed Bonaparte,
  As every child can tell,
The House of Peers, throughout the war,
Did nothing in particular,
  And did it very well:
Yet Britain set the world ablaze
In good King George's glorious days!

CHORUS. Yes, Britain set, etc.

And while the House of Peers withholds
  Its legislative hand,
And noble statesmen do not itch
To interfere with matters which
  They do not understand,

As bright will shine Great Britain's rays
As in King George's glorious days!

CHORUS. As bright will shine, etc.

LEILA (*who has been much attracted by the* PEERS *during this song*). Charming persons, are they not?

CELIA. Distinctly. For self-contained dignity, combined with airy condescension, give me a British Representative Peer!

LORD TOLL. Then pray stop this *protégé* of yours before it's too late. Think of the mischief you're doing!

LEILA (*crying*). But we *can't* stop him now. (*Aside to* CELIA.) Aren't they lovely! (*Aloud.*) Oh, why did you go and defy us, you great geese!

DUET—LEILA *and* CELIA

LEILA. In vain to us you plead—
Don't go!
Your prayers we do not heed—
Don't go!
It's true we sigh,
But don't suppose
A tearful eye
Forgiveness shows.
Oh, no!

We're very cross indeed—
Don't go!

FAIRIES. It's true we sigh, etc.

CELIA. Your disrespectful sneers—
Don't go!
Call forth indignant tears—
Don't go!
You break our laws—
You are our foe:
We cry because
We hate you so!
You know!
You very wicked Peers!
Don't go!

FAIRIES	LORDS MOUNT. *and* TOLL.
You break our laws—	Our disrespectful sneers,
You are our foe:	Ha, ha!
We cry because	Call forth indignant tears,
We hate you so!	Ha, ha!
You know!	If that's the case, my dears—
You very wicked peers!	FAIRIES. Don't go!
Don't go!	PEERS. We'll go!

[*Exeunt* LORD MOUNTARARAT, LORD TOLLOLLER, *and* PEERS. FAIRIES *gaze wistfully after them.*

Enter FAIRY QUEEN

QUEEN. Oh, shame—shame upon you! Is this your fidelity to the laws you are bound to obey? Know ye not that it is death to marry a mortal?

LEILA. Yes, but it's not death to *wish* to marry a mortal!

FLETA. If it were, you'd have to execute us all!

QUEEN. Oh, this is weakness! Subdue it!

CELIA. We know it's weakness, but the weakness is so strong!

LEILA. We are not all as tough as you are!

QUEEN. Tough! Do you suppose that I am insensible to the effect of manly beauty? Look at that man! (*Referring to* SENTRY.) A perfect picture! (*To* SENTRY.) Who are you, sir?

WILLIS (*coming to "attention"*). Private Willis, B Company, 1st Grenadier Guards.

QUEEN. You're a very fine fellow, sir.

WILLIS. I am generally admired.

QUEEN. I can quite understand it. (*To* FAIRIES.) Now here is a man whose physical attributes are simply godlike. That man has a most extraordinary effect upon me. If I yielded to a natural impulse, I should fall down and worship that man. But I mortify this inclination; I wrestle with it, and it lies beneath my feet! That is how I treat my regard for that man!

SONG—FAIRY QUEEN

Oh, foolish fay,
  Think you, because
His brave array
  My bosom thaws,
I'd disobey
  Our fairy laws?
Because I fly
  In realms above,
In tendency
  To fall in love,
Resemble I
  The amorous dove?

(*Aside.*) Oh, amorous dove!
Type of Ovidius Naso!
This heart of mine
Is soft as thine,
Although I dare not say so!

CHORUS. Oh, amorous dove, etc.

On fire that glows
With heat intense
I turn the hose
Of common sense,
And out it goes
At small expense!
We must maintain
Our fairy law;
That is the main
On which to draw—
In that we gain
A Captain Shaw!

(*Aside.*) Oh, Captain Shaw!
Type of true love kept under!
Could thy Brigade
With cold cascade
Quench my great love, I wonder!

CHORUS. Oh, Captain Shaw! etc.

[*Exeunt* FAIRIES *and* FAIRY QUEEN, *sorrowfully*.

Enter PHYLLIS

PHYL. (*half crying*). I can't think why I'm not in better spirits. I'm engaged to two noblemen at once. That ought to be enough to make any girl happy. But I'm miserable! Don't suppose it's because I care for Strephon, for I hate him! No girl *could* care for a man who goes about with a mother considerably younger than himself!

Enter LORD MOUNTARARAT *and* LORD TOLLOLLER

LORD MOUNT. Phyllis! My darling!

LORD TOLL. Phyllis! My own!

PHYL. Don't! How dare you? Oh, but perhaps you're the two noblemen I'm engaged to?

LORD MOUNT. I am one of them.

LORD TOLL. I am the other.

PHYL. Oh, then, my darling! (*to* LORD MOUNTARARAT). My own! (*to* LORD TOLLOLLER). Well, have you settled which it's to be?

LORD TOLL. Not altogether. It's a difficult position. It would be hardly delicate to toss up. On the whole we would rather leave it to you.

PHYL. How can it possibly concern me? You are both Earls, and you are both rich, and you are both plain.

LORD MOUNT. So we are. At least I am.

LORD TOLL. So am I.

LORD MOUNT. No, no!

LORD TOLL. I am indeed. Very plain.

LORD MOUNT. Well, well—perhaps you are.

PHYL. There's really nothing to choose between you. If one of you would forgo his title, and distribute his estates among his Irish tenantry, why, then, I should then see a reason for accepting the other.

LORD MOUNT. Tolloller, are you prepared to make this sacrifice.

LORD TOLL. No!

LORD MOUNT. Not even to oblige a lady?

LORD TOLL. No! not even to oblige a lady.

LORD MOUNT. Then, the only question is, which of us shall give way to the other? Perhaps, on the whole, she would be happier with me. I don't know. I may be wrong.

LORD TOLL. No. I don't know that you are. I really believe she would. But the awkward part of the thing is that if you rob me of the girl of my heart, we must fight, and one of us must die. It's a family tradition that I have sworn to respect. It's a painful position, for I have a very strong regard for you, George.

LORD MOUNT. (*much affected*). My dear Thomas!

LORD TOLL. You are very dear to me, George. We were boys together—at least *I* was. If I were to survive you, my existence would be hopelessly embittered.

LORD MOUNT. Then, my dear Thomas, you must not do it. I say it again and again—if it will have this effect upon you, you must not do it. No, no. If one of us is to destroy the other, let it be me!

LORD TOLL. No, no!

LORD MOUNT. Ah, yes!—by our boyish friendship I implore you!

LORD TOLL. (*much moved*). Well, well, be it so. But, no—no!—I cannot consent to an act which would crush you with unavailing remorse.

LORD MOUNT. But it would not do so. I should be very sad at first—oh, who would not be?—but it would wear off. I like you *very much*—but not, perhaps, as much as you like me.

LORD TOLL. George, you're a noble fellow, but that telltale tear betrays you. No, George; you are very fond of me, and I cannot consent to give you a week's uneasiness on my account.

LORD MOUNT. But, dear Thomas, it would not last a week! Remember, you lead the House of Lords! on your demise I shall take your place! Oh, Thomas, it would not last a day!

PHYL. (*coming down*). Now, I do hope you're not going to fight about me, because it's really not worth while.

LORD TOLL. (*looking at her*). Well, I don't believe it is!

LORD MOUNT. Nor I. The sacred ties of Friendship are paramount.

QUARTETTE—LORD MOUNTARARAT

LORD TOLLOLLER, PHYLLIS, *and* PRIVATE WILLIS

LORD TOLL. Though p'r'aps I may incur your blame,
The things are few
I would not do
In Friendship's name!

LORD MOUNT. And I may say I think the same;
Not even love
Should rank above
True Friendship's name!

PHYL. Then free me, pray; be mine the blame;
Forget your craze
And go your ways
In Friendship's name!

ALL. Oh, many a man, in Friendship's name,
Has yielded fortune, rank, and fame!
But no one yet, in the world so wide,
Has yielded up a promised bride!

WILLIS. Accept, O Friendship, all the same,

ALL. This sacrifice to thy dear name!

[*Exeunt* LORD MOUNTARARAT *and* LORD TOLLOLLER, *lovingly, in one direction, and* PHYLLIS *in another. Exit* SENTRY.

Enter LORD CHANCELLOR, *very miserable*

RECIT—LORD CHANCELLOR

Love, unrequited, robs me of my rest:
Love, hopeless love, my ardent soul encumbers:
Love, nightmare-like, lies heavy on my chest,
And weaves itself into my midnight slumbers!

SONG—LORD CHANCELLOR

When you're lying awake with a dismal headache, and repose is taboo'd by anxiety,
I conceive you may use any language you choose to indulge in, without impropriety;

For your brain is on fire—the bedclothes conspire of usual slumber to plunder you:
First your counterpane goes, and uncovers your toes, and your sheet slips demurely from under you;
Then the blanketing tickles—you feel like mixed pickles —so terribly sharp is the pricking,
And you're hot, and you're cross, and you tumble and toss till there's nothing 'twixt you and the ticking.
Then the bedclothes all creep to the ground in a heap, and you pick 'em all up in a tangle;
Next your pillow resigns and politely declines to remain at its usual angle!
Well, you get some repose in the form of a doze, with hot eye-balls and head ever aching,
But your slumbering teems with such horrible dreams that you'd very much better be waking;
For you dream you are crossing the Channel, and tossing about in a steamer from Harwich—
Which is something between a large bathing machine and a very small second-class carriage—
And you're giving a treat (penny ice and cold meat) to a party of friends and relations—
They're a ravenous horde—and they all came on board at Sloane Square and South Kensington Stations.
And bound on that journey you find your attorney (who started that morning from Devon);
He's a bit undersized, and you don't feel surprised when he tells you he's only eleven.
Well, you're driving like mad with this singular lad (by the by, the ship's now a four-wheeler),
And you're playing round games, and he calls you bad names when you tell him that "ties pay the dealer";
But this you can't stand, so you throw up your hand, and you find you're as cold as an icicle,
In your shirt and your socks (the black silk with gold clocks), crossing Salisbury Plain on a bicycle:
And he and the crew are on bicycles too—which they've somehow or other invested in—
And he's telling the tars all the particu*lars* of a company he's interested in—

It's a scheme of devices, to get at low prices all goods
from cough mixtures to cables
(Which tickled the sailors), by treating retailers as
though they were all vege*ta*bles—

You get a good spadesman to plant a small tradesman
(first take off his boots with a boot-tree),
And his legs will take root, and his fingers will shoot,
and they'll blossom and bud like a fruit-tree—
From the greengrocer tree you get grapes and green pea,
cauliflower, pineapple, and cranberries,
While the pastrycook plant cherry brandy will grant,
apple puffs, and three-corners, and Banburys—
The shares are a penny, and ever so many are taken by
Rothschild and Baring,
And just as a few are allotted to you, you awake with a
shudder despairing—

You're a regular wreck, with a crick in your neck, and no wonder you snore, for your head's on the floor, and you've needles and pins from your soles to your shins, and your flesh is a-creep, for your left leg's asleep, and you've cramp in your toes, and a fly on your nose, and some fluff in your lung, and a feverish tongue, and a thirst that's intense, and a general sense that you haven't been sleeping in clover;
But the darkness has passed, and it's daylight at last, and the night has been long—ditto ditto my song—and thank goodness they're both of them over!

[LORD CHANCELLOR *falls exhausted on a seat.*

LORDS MOUNTARARAT *and* TOLLOLLER *come forward*

LORD MOUNT. I am much distressed to see your Lordship in this condition.

LORD CH. Ah, my Lords, it is seldom that a Lord Chancellor has reason to envy the position of another, but I am free to confess that I would rather be two Earls engaged to Phyllis than any other half-dozen noblemen upon the face of the globe.

LORD TOLL. (*without enthusiasm*). Yes. It's an enviable position when you're the only one.

LORD MOUNT. Oh yes, no doubt—most enviable. At the same time, seeing you thus, we naturally say to ourselves, "This is very sad. His Lordship is constitutionally as blithe as a bird—he trills upon the bench like a thing of song and gladness. His series of judgments in F sharp minor, given *andante* in six-eight time, are among the most remarkable effects ever produced in a Court of Chancery. He is, perhaps, the only living instance of a judge whose decrees have received the honour of a double *encore*. How can we bring ourselves to do that which will deprive the Court of Chancery of one of its most attractive features?"

LORD CH. I feel the force of your remarks, but I am here in two capacities, and they clash, my Lord, they clash! I deeply grieve to say that in declining to entertain my last application to myself, I presumed to address myself in terms which render it impossible for me ever to apply to myself again. It was a most painful scene, my Lord—most painful!

LORD TOLL. This is what it is to have two capacities! Let us be thankful that we are persons of no capacity whatever.

LORD MOUNT. Come, come. Remember you are a very just and kindly old gentleman, and you need have no hesitation in approaching yourself, so that you do so respectfully and with a proper show of deference.

LORD CH. Do you really think so?

LORD MOUNT. I do.

LORD CH. Well, I will nerve myself to another effort, and, if that fails, I resign myself to my fate!

TRIO—LORD CHANCELLOR, LORDS MOUNTARARAT *and* TOLLOLLER

LORD MOUNT. If you go in
You're sure to win—
Yours will be the charming maidie:
Be your law
The ancient saw,
"Fain heart never won fair lady!"

ALL. Faint heart never won fair lady!
Every journey has an end—
When at the worst affairs will mend—
Dark the dawn when day is nigh—
Hustle your horse and don't say die!

LORD TOLL. He who shies
At such a prize
Is not worth a maravedi,
Be so kind
To bear in mind—
Faint heart never won fair lady!

ALL. Faint heart never won fair lady!
While the sun shines make your hay—
Where a will is, there's a way—
Beard the lion in his lair—
None but the brave deserve the fair!

LORD CH.
I'll take heart
And make a start—
Though I fear the prospect's shady—
Much I'd spend
To gain my end—
Faint heart never won fair lady!

ALL.
Faint heart never won fair lady!
Nothing venture, nothing win—
Blood is thick, but water's thin—
In for a penny, in for a pound—
It's Love that makes the world go round!

[*Dance, and exeunt arm-in-arm together.*

Enter STREPHON, *in very low spirits*

STREPH. I suppose one ought to enjoy oneself in Parliament, when one leads both Parties, as I do! But I'm miserable, poor, broken-hearted fool that I am! Oh, Phyllis, Phyllis!——

Enter PHYLLIS

PHYL. Yes.

STREPH. (*surprised*). Phyllis! But I suppose I should say "My Lady". I have not yet been informed which title your ladyship has pleased to select?

PHYL. I—I haven't quite decided. You see *I* have no *mother* to advise *me*!

STREPH. No. I have.

PHYL. Yes; a *young* mother.

STREPH. Not very—a couple of centuries or so.

PHYL. Oh! She wears well.

STREPH. She does. She's a fairy.

PHYL. I beg your pardon—a what?

STREPH. Oh, I've no longer any reason to conceal the fact—she's a fairy.

PHYL. A fairy! Well, but—that would account for a good many things! Then—I suppose *you're* a fairy?

STREPH. I'm half a fairy.

PHYL. Which half?

STREPH. The upper half—down to the waistcoat.

PHYL. Dear me! (*Prodding him with her fingers.*) There is nothing to show it!

STREPH. Don't do that.

PHYL. But why didn't you tell me this before?

STREPH. I thought you would take a dislike to me. But as it's all off, you may as well know the truth—I'm only half a mortal!

PHYL. (*crying*). But I'd rather have half a mortal I do love, than have a dozen I don't!

STREPH. (*crying.*) But I think not—go to your half-dozen.

PHYL. (*crying*). It's only two! and I hate 'em! Please forgive me!

STREPH. I don't think I ought to. Besides, all sorts of difficulties will arise. You know, my grandmother looks quite as young as my mother. So do all my aunts.

PHYL. I quite understand. Whenever I see you kissing a very young lady, I shall know it's an elderly relative.

STREPH. You will? Then, Phyllis, I think we shall be very happy! (*Embracing her.*)

PHYL. We won't wait long.

STREPH. No. We might change our minds. We'll get married first.

PHYL. And change our minds afterwards?

STREPH. That's the usual course.

DUET—STREPHON *and* PHYLLIS

STREPH.
If we're weak enough to tarry
Ere we marry,
You and I,
Of the feeling I inspire
You may tire
By and by,
For peers with flowing coffers
Press their offers—
That is why
I am sure we should not tarry
Ere we marry,
You and I!

PHYL.
If we're weak enough to tarry
Ere we marry,
You and I,

With a more attractive maiden,
Jewel-laden,
You may fly.
If by chance we should be parted,
Broken-hearted
I should die—
So I think we will not tarry
Ere we marry,
You and I.

PHYL. But does your mother know you're— I mean, is she aware of our engagement?

Enter IOLANTHE

IOL. She is; and thus she welcomes her daughter-in-law! (*Kisses her.*)

PHYL. She kisses just like other people! But the Lord Chancellor?

STREPH. I forgot him! Mother, none can resist your fairy eloquence; you will go to him and plead for us?

IOL. (*much agitated*). No, no; impossible!

STREPH. But our happiness—our very lives—depend upon our obtaining his consent!

PHYL. Oh, madam, you cannot refuse to do this!

IOL. You know not what you ask! The Lord Chancellor is—my husband!

STREPH. *and* PHYL. Your husband!

IOL. My husband and your father! (*Addressing* STREPHON, *who is much moved.*)

PHYL. Then our course is plain; on his learning that Strephon is his son, all objection to our marriage will be at once removed!

IOL. No; he must never know! He believes me to have died childless, and, dearly as I love him, I am bound, under penalty of death, not to undeceive him. But see—he comes! Quick—my veil!

[IOLANTHE *veils herself*. STREPHON *and* PHYLLIS *go off on tiptoe.*

Enter LORD CHANCELLOR

LORD CH. Victory! Victory! Success has crowned my efforts, and I may consider myself engaged to Phyllis!

At first I wouldn't hear of it—it was out of the question. But I took heart. I pointed out to myself that I was no stranger to myself; that, in point of fact, I had been personally acquainted with myself for some years. This had its effect. I admitted that I had watched my professional advancement with considerable interest, and I handsomely added that I yielded to no one in admiration for my private and professional virtues. This was a great point gained. I then endeavoured to work upon my feelings. Conceive my joy when I distinctly perceived a tear glistening in my own eye! Eventually, after a severe struggle with myself, I reluctantly—most reluctantly—consented.

[IOLANTHE *comes down veiled.*

RECIT—IOLANTHE

My lord, a suppliant at your feet I kneel,
Oh, listen to a mother's fond appeal!
Hear me to-night! I come in urgent need—
'Tis for my son, young Strephon, that I plead!

BALLAD—IOLANTHE

He loves! If in the bygone years
  Thine eyes have ever shed
Tears—bitter, unavailing tears,
  For one untimely dead—
If, in the eventide of life,
  Sad thoughts of her arise,
Then let the memory of thy wife
  Plead for my boy—he dies!

He dies! If fondly laid aside
  In some old cabinet,
Memorials of thy long-dead bride
  Lie, dearly treasured yet,
Then let her hallowed bridal dress—
  Her little dainty gloves—
Her withered flowers—her faded tress—
  Plead for my boy—he loves!

[*The* LORD CHANCELLOR *is moved by this appeal. After a pause.*

LORD CH. It may not be—for so the fates decide!
Learn thou that Phyllis is my promised bride.

IOL. (*in horror*). Thy bride! No! no!

LORD CH. It shall be so!
Those who would separate us woe betide!

IOL. My doom thy lips have spoken—
I plead in vain!

CHORUS OF FAIRIES (*without*). Forbear! forbear!

IOL. A vow already broken
I break again!

CHORUS OF FAIRIES (*without*). Forbear! forbear!

IOL. For him—for her—for thee
I yield my life.
Behold—it may not be!
I am thy wife.

CHORUS OF FAIRIES (*without*). Aiaiah! Aiaiah! Willaloo!

LORD CH. (*recognizing her*). Iolanthe! thou livest?

IOL. Aye!
I live! Now let me die!

Enter FAIRY QUEEN *and* FAIRIES. IOLANTHE *kneels to her*

QUEEN. Once again thy vows are broken:
Thou thyself thy doom hast spoken!

CHORUS OF FAIRIES. Aiaiah! Aiaiah!
Willahalah! Willaloo!
Willahalah! Willaloo!

QUEEN. Bow thy head to Destiny:
Death thy doom, and thou shalt die!

CHORUS OF FAIRIES. Aiaiah! Aiaiah! etc.

PEERS *and* SENTRY *enter. The* QUEEN *raises her spear*

LEILA. Hold! If Iolanthe must die, so must we all; for, as she has sinned, so have we!

QUEEN. What?

CELIA. We are all fairy duchesses, marchionesses, countesses, viscountesses, and baronesses.

LORD MOUNT. It's our fault. They couldn't help themselves.

QUEEN. It seems they *have* helped themselves, and pretty freely, too! (*After a pause.*) You have all incurred death; but I can't slaughter the whole company! And yet (*unfolding a scroll*) the law is clear—every fairy must die who marries a mortal!

LORD CH. Allow me, as an old Equity draftsman, to make a suggestion. The subtleties of the legal mind are equal to the emergency. The thing is really quite simple—the insertion of a single word will do it. Let it stand that every fairy shall die who doesn't marry a mortal, and there you are, out of your difficulty at once!

QUEEN. We like your humour. Very well! (*Altering the MS. in pencil.*) Private Willis!

SENTRY (*coming forward*). Ma'am!

QUEEN. To save my life, it is necessary that I marry at once. How should you like to be a fairy guardsman?

SENTRY. Well, m'am, I don't think much of the British soldier who wouldn't ill-convenience himself to save a female in distress.

QUEEN. You are a brave fellow. You're a fairy from this moment. (*Wings spring from* SENTRY'S *shoulders.*) And you, my Lords, how say you, will you join our ranks?

[FAIRIES *kneel to* PEERS *and implore them to do so*

PHYLLIS *and* STREPHON *enter*

LORD MOUNT. (*to* LORD TOLLOLLER). Well, now that the Peers are to be recruited entirely from persons of intelligence, I really don't see what use *we* are, down here, do you, Tolloller?

LORD TOLL. None whatever.

QUEEN. Good (*Wings spring from shoulders of* PEERS). Then away we go to Fairyland.

FINALE

PHYL. Soon as we may,
Off and away!
We'll commence our journey airy—

Happy are we—
As you can see,
Every one is now a fairy!

ALL. Every one is now a fairy!

IOL., QUEEN, *and* PHYL. Though as a general rule we know
Two strings go to every bow,
Make up your minds that grief 'twill bring,
If you've two beaux to every string.

ALL. Though as a general rule, etc.

LORD CH. Up in the sky,
Ever so high,
Pleasures come in endless series;
We will arrange
Happy exchange—
House of Peers for House of Peris!

ALL. House of Peers for House of Peris!

LORDS CH., MOUNT., *and* TOLL. Up in the air, sky-high, sky-high,
Free from Wards in Chancery,
{I / He} will be surely happier, for
{I'm / He's} such a susceptible Chancellor.

ALL. Up in the air, etc.

CURTAIN

PRINCESS IDA

OR

CASTLE ADAMANT

DRAMATIS PERSONÆ

KING HILDEBRAND

HILARION (*his Son*)

CYRIL } (*Hilarion's Friends*)
FLORIAN }

KING GAMA

ARAC }
GURON } (*his Sons*)
SCYNTHIUS }

PRINCESS IDA (*Gama's Daughter*)

LADY BLANCHE (*Professor of Abstract Science*)

LADY PSYCHE (*Professor of Humanities*)

MELISSA (*Lady Blanche's Daughter*)

SACHARISSA }
CHLOE } (*Girl Graduates*)
ADA }

Soldiers, Courtiers, "Girl Graduates", "Daughters of the Plough", etc.

ACT I

PAVILION IN KING HILDEBRAND'S PALACE

ACT II

GARDENS OF CASTLE ADAMANT

ACT III

COURTYARD OF CASTLE ADAMANT

First produced at the Savoy Theatre, January 5, 1884

PRINCESS IDA

OR

CASTLE ADAMANT

ACT I

SCENE.—*Pavilion attached to* KING HILDEBRAND'S PALACE. *Soldiers and Courtiers discovered looking out through opera-glasses, telescopes, etc.,* FLORIAN *leading.*

CHORUS Search throughout the panorama
For a sign of royal Gama,
Who to-day should cross the water
With his fascinating daughter—
Ida is her name.

Some misfortune evidently
Has detained them—consequently
Search throughout the panorama
For the daughter of King Gama,
Prince Hilarion's flame!

SOLO

FLOR. Will Prince Hilarion's hopes be sadly blighted?
ALL. Who can tell?
FLOR. Will Ida break the vows that she has plighted?
ALL. Who can tell?
FLOR. Will she back out, and say she did not mean them?
ALL. Who can tell?
FLOR. If so, there'll be the deuce to pay between them!

ALL. No, no—we'll not despair,
For Gama would not dare
To make a deadly foe
Of Hildebrand, and so,
Search throughout, etc.

Enter KING HILDEBRAND, *with* CYRIL

HILD. See you no sign of Gama?

FLOR. None, my liege!

HILD. It's very odd indeed. If Gama fail
To put in an appearance at our Court
Before the sun has set in yonder west,
And fail to bring the Princess Ida here
To whom our son Hilarion was betrothed
At the extremely early age of one,
There's war between King Gama and ourselves!
(*Aside to* CYRIL.) Oh, Cyril, how I dread this interview
It's twenty years since he and I have met.
He was a twisted monster—all awry—
As though Dame Nature, angry with her work,
Had crumpled it in fitful petulance!

CYR. But, sir, a twisted and ungainly trunk
Often bears goodly fruit. Perhaps he was
A kind, well-spoken gentleman?

HILD. Oh, no!
For, adder-like, his sting lay in his tongue.
(His "sting" is present, though his "stung" is past.)

FLOR. (*looking through glass*). But stay, my liege; o'er yonder mountain's brow
Comes a small body, bearing Gama's arms;
And now I look more closely at it, sir,
I see attached to it King Gama's legs;
From which I gather this corollary
That that small body must be Gama's own!

HILD. Ha! Is the Princess with him?

FLOR. Well, my liege,
Unless her highness is full six feet high,
And wears mustachios too—and smokes cigars—
And rides *en cavalier* in coat of steel—
I do not think she is.

HILD. One never knows.
She's a strange girl, I've heard, and does odd things!
Come, bustle there!
For Gama place the richest robes we own—

For Gama place the coarsest prison dress—
For Gama let our best spare bed be aired—
For Gama let our deepest dungeon yawn—
For Gama lay the costliest banquet out—
For Gama place cold water and dry bread!
For as King Gama brings the Princess here,
Or brings her not, so shall King Gama have
Much more than everything—much less than nothing!

SONG AND CHORUS

HILD. Now hearken to my strict command
On every hand, on every hand—

CHORUS To your command,
On every hand,
We dutifully bow!

HILD. If Gama bring the Princess here,
Give him good cheer, give him good cheer.

CHORUS If she come here
We'll give him a cheer,
And we will show you how.
Hip, hip, hurrah! hip, hip, hurrah!
Hip, hip, hurrah! hurrah! hurrah!
We'll shout and sing
Long live the King,
And his daughter, too, I trow!
Then shout ha! ha! hip, hip, hurrah!
Hip, hip, hip, hip, hurrah!
For the fair Princess and her good papa,
Hurrah! hurrah!

HILD. But if he fail to keep his troth,
Upon our oath, we'll trounce them both!

CHORUS He'll trounce them both,
Upon his oath,
As sure as quarter-day!

HILD. We'll shut him up in a dungeon cell,
And toll his knell on a funeral bell.

CHORUS From his dungeon cell,
His funeral knell
Shall strike him with dismay!
Hip, hip, hurrah! hip, hip, hurrah!
Hip, hip, hurrah! hurrah! hurrah!
As up we string
The faithless King,
In the old familiar way!
We'll shout ha! ha! hip, hip, hurrah!
Hip, hip, hip, hip, hurrah!
As we make an end of her false papa,
Hurrah! hurrah!

[*Exeunt all.*

Enter HILARION

RECIT—HILARION

To-day we meet, my baby bride and I—
But ah, my hopes are balanced by my fears!
What transmutations have been conjured by
The silent alchemy of twenty years!

BALLAD—HILARION

Ida was a twelvemonth old,
Twenty years ago!
I was twice her age, I'm told,
Twenty years ago!
Husband twice as old as wife
Argues ill for married life
Baleful prophecies were rife,
Twenty years ago!

Still, I was a tiny prince
Twenty years ago.
She has gained upon me, since
Twenty years ago.
Though she's twenty-one, it's true,
I am barely twenty-two—
False and foolish prophets you,
Twenty years ago!

Enter HILDEBRAND

HIL. Well, father, is there news for me at last?
HILD. King Gama is in sight, but much I fear
With no Princess!
HIL. Alas, my liege, I've heard
That Princess Ida has forsworn the world,
And, with a band of women, shut herself
Within a lonely country house, and there
Devotes herself to stern philosophies!
HILD. Then I should say the loss of such a wife
Is one to which a reasonable man
Would easily be reconciled.
HIL. Oh, no!
Or I am not a reasonable man.
She *is* my wife—has been for twenty years!
(*Holding glass.*) I think I see her now.
HILD. Ha! let me look!
HIL. In my mind's eye, I mean—a blushing bride,
All bib and tucker, frill and furbelow!
How exquisite she looked as she was borne,
Recumbent, in her foster-mother's arms!
How the bride wept—nor would be comforted
Until the hireling mother-for-the-nonce
Administered refreshment in the vestry.
And I remember feeling much annoyed
That she should weep at marrying with me.
But then I thought, "These brides are all alike.
You cry at marrying me? How much more cause
You'd have to cry if it were broken off!"
These were my thoughts; I kept them to myself,
For at that age I had not learned to speak.

[*Exeunt.*

Enter Courtiers

CHORUS From the distant panorama
Come the sons of royal Gama.
They are heralds evidently,
And are sacred consequently,
Sons of Gama, hail! oh, hail!

Enter ARAC, GURON, *and* SCYNTHIUS

SONG—ARAC

We are warriors three,
Sons of Gama, Rex.
Like most sons are we,
Masculine in sex.

ALL THREE. Yes, yes, yes,
Masculine in sex.

ARAC. Politics we bar,
They are not our bent;
On the whole we are
Not intelligent.

ALL THREE. No, no, no,
Not intelligent.

ARAC. But with doughty heart,
And with trusty blade
We can play our part—
Fighting is our trade.

ALL THREE. Yes, yes, yes,
Fighting is our trade.

ALL THREE. Bold, and fierce, and strong, ha! ha!
For a war we burn,
With its right or wrong, ha! ha!
We have no concern.
Order comes to fight, ha! ha!
Order is obeyed,
We are men of might, ha! ha!
Fighting is our trade.
Yes, yes, yes,
Fighting is our trade, ha! ha!

CHORUS They are men of might, ha! ha!
Fighting is their trade.
Order comes to fight, ha! ha!
Order is obeyed, ha! ha!
Fighting is their trade!

Enter KING GAMA

SONG—GAMA

If you give me your attention, I will tell you what I am:
I'm a genuine philanthropist—all other kinds are sham.
Each little fault of temper and each social defect
In my erring fellow-creatures I endeavour to correct.
To all their little weaknesses I open people's eyes;
And little plans to snub the self-sufficient I devise;
I love my fellow-creatures—I do all the good I can—
Yet everybody says I'm such a disagreeable man!
And I can't think why!

To compliments inflated I've a withering reply;
And vanity I always do my best to mortify;
A charitable action I can skilfully dissect;
And interested motives I'm delighted to detect;
I know everybody's income and what everybody earns;
And I carefully compare it with the income tax returns;
But to benefit humanity however much I plan,
Yet everybody says I'm such a disagreeable man!
And I can't think why!

I'm sure I'm no ascetic; I'm as pleasant as can be;
You'll always find me ready with a crushing repartee,
I've an irritating chuckle, I've a celebrated sneer,
I've an entertaining snigger, I've a fascinating leer.
To everybody's prejudice I know a thing or two;
I can tell a woman's age in half a minute—and I do.

But although I try to make myself as pleasant as I can,
Yet everybody says I am a disagreeable man!
And I can't think why!

Enter HILDEBRAND, HILARION, CYRIL, *and* FLORIAN

GAMA. So this is Castle Hildebrand? Well, well!
Dame Rumour whispered that the place was grand;
She told me that your taste was exquisite,
Superb, unparalleled!

HILD. (*gratified*). Oh, really, King!

GAMA. But she's a liar! Why, how old you've grown!
Is this Hilarion? Why, you've changed too—
You were a singularly handsome child!
(*To* FLOR.) Are you a courtier? Come, then, ply your trade,
Tell me some lies. How do you like your King?
Vile rumour says he's all but imbecile.
Now, that's not true?

FLOR. My lord, we love our King.
His wise remarks are valued by his court
As precious stones.

GAMA. And for the self-same cause.
Like precious stones, his sensible remarks
Derive their value from their scarcity!
Come now, be honest, tell the truth for once!
Tell it of me. Come, come, I'll harm you not.
This leg is crooked—this foot is ill-designed—
This shoulder wears a hump! Come, out with it!
Look, here's my face! Now, am I not the worst
Of Nature's blunders?

CYR. Nature never errs.
To those who know the workings of your mind,
Your face and figure, sir, suggest a book
Appropriately bound.

GAMA (*enraged*). Why, harkye, sir,
How dare you bandy words with me?

CYR. No need
To bandy aught that appertains to you.

GAMA (*furiously*). Do you permit this, King?

HILD. We are in doubt

Whether to treat you as an honoured guest
Or as a traitor knave who plights his word
And breaks it.

GAMA (*quickly*). If the casting vote's with me,
I give it for the former!

HILD. We shall see.
By the terms of our contract, signed and sealed,
You're bound to bring the Princess here to-day:
Why is she not with you?

GAMA. Answer me this:
What think you of a wealthy purse-proud man,
Who, when he calls upon a starving friend,
Pulls out his gold and flourishes his notes,
And flashes diamonds in the pauper's eyes?
What name have you for such an one?

HILD. A snob.

GAMA. Just so. The girl has beauty, virtue, wit,
Grace, humour, wisdom, charity, and pluck.
Would it be kindly, think you, to parade
These brilliant qualities before *your* eyes?
Oh no, King Hildebrand, I am no snob!

HILD. (*furiously*). Stop that tongue,
Or you shall lose the monkey head that holds it!

GAMA. Bravo! your King deprives me of my head,
That he and I may meet on equal terms!

HILD. Where is she now?

GAMA. In Castle Adamant,
One of my many country houses. There
She rules a woman's University,
With full a hundred girls, who learn of her.

CYR. A hundred girls! A hundred ecstasies!

GAMA. But no mere girls, my good young gentleman;
With all the college learning that you boast,
The youngest there will prove a match for *you*.

CYR. With all my heart, if she's the prettiest!
(*To* FLOR.) Fancy, a hundred matches—all alight!—
That's if I strike them as I hope to do!

GAMA. Despair your hope; their hearts are dead to men.
He who desires to gain their favour must
Be qualified to strike their teeming brains,

And not their hearts. They're safety matches, sir,
And they light only on the knowledge box—
So *you've* no chance!

FLOR. And there are no males whatever in those walls?

GAMA. None, gentlemen, excepting letter mails—
And they are driven (as males often are
In other large communities) by women.
Why, bless my heart, she's so particular
She'll scarcely suffer Dr. Watts's hymns—
And all the animals she owns are "hers"!
The ladies rise at cockcrow every morn—

CYR. Ah, then they have male poultry?

GAMA. Not at all,
(*Confidentially.*) The crowing's done by an accomplished hen!

DUET—GAMA *and* HILDEBRAND

GAMA. Perhaps if you address the lady
Most politely, most politely—
Flatter and impress the lady,
Most politely, most politely—
Humbly beg and humbly sue—
She may deign to look on you,
But your doing you must do
Most politely, most politely!

ALL. Humbly beg and humbly sue, etc.

HILD. Go you, and inform the lady,
Most politely, most politely,
If she don't, we'll storm the lady
Most politely, most politely!

(*To* GAMA.) You'll remain as hostage here;
Should Hilarion disappear,
We will hang you, never fear,
Most politely, most politely!

ALL. He'll / I'll / You'll } remain as hostage here, etc.

[GAMA, ARAC, GURON, *and* SCYNTHIUS *are marched off in custody,* HILDEBRAND *following.*

RECIT—HILARION

Come, Cyril, Florian, our course is plain,
To-morrow morn fair Ida we'll engage;
But we will use no force her love to gain,
Nature has armed us for the war we wage!

TRIO—HILARION, CYRIL, *and* FLORIAN

HIL. Expressive glances
Shall be our lances,
And pops of Sillery
Our light artillery.
We'll storm their bowers
With scented showers
Of fairest flowers
That we can buy!

CHORUS. Oh, dainty triolet!
Oh, fragrant violet!
Oh, gentle heigho-let
(Or little sigh).
On sweet urbanity,
Though mere inanity,
To touch their vanity
We will rely!

CYR. When day is fading,
With serenading
And such frivolity
We'll prove our quality.
A sweet profusion
Of soft allusion
This bold intrusion
Shall justify.

CHORUS. Oh, dainty triolet, etc.

FLOR. We'll charm their senses
With verbal fences,
With ballads amatory
And declamatory.

Little heeding
Their pretty pleading,
Our love exceeding
We'll justify!

CHORUS. Oh, dainty triolet, etc.

Re-enter GAMA, ARAC, GURON, *and* SCYNTHIUS *heavily ironed*

RECIT

GAMA. Must we, till then, in prison cell be thrust?
HILD. You must!
GAMA. This seems unnecessarily severe!
ARAC, GURON, and SCYNTHIUS. Hear, hear!

TRIO—ARAC, GURON, *and* SCYNTHIUS

For a month to dwell
In a dungeon cell;
Growing thin and wizen
In a solitary prison,
Is a poor look-out
For a soldier stout,
Who is longing for the rattle
Of a complicated battle—
For the rum-tum-tum
Of the military drum
And the guns that go boom! boom!

ALL. The rum-tum-tum
Of the military drum, etc.

HILD. When Hilarion's bride
Has at length complied
With the just conditions
Of our requisitions,
You may go in haste
And indulge your taste
For the fascinating rattle
Of a complicated battle—
For the rum-tum-tum,
Of the military drum,
And the guns that go boom! boom!

ALL. For the rum-tum-tum
Of the military drum, etc.

ALL. But till that time {we'll / you'll} here remain,
And bail {they / we} will not entertain,
Should she {his / our} mandate disobey,
{Our / Your} lives the penalty will pay!

[GAMA, ARAC, GURON, *and* SCYNTHIUS *are marched off.*

END OF ACT I

ACT II

Gardens in Castle Adamant. A river runs across the back of the stage, crossed by a rustic bridge. Castle Adamant in the distance.

Girl graduates discovered seated at the feet of LADY PSYCHE

CHORUS Towards the empyrean heights
Of every kind of lore,
We've taken several easy flights,
And mean to take some more.
In trying to achieve success
No envy racks our heart,
And all the knowledge we possess,
We mutually impart.

SONG—MELISSA

Pray, what authors should she read
Who in Classics would succeed?

PSYCHE

If you'd climb the Helicon,
You should read Anacreon,
Ovid's *Metamorphoses,*
Likewise Aristophanes,
And the works of Juvenal:
These are worth attention, all;
But, if you will be advised,
You will get them Bowdlerized!

CHORUS Ah! we will get them Bowdlerized!

SOLO—SACHARISSA

Pray you, tell us, if you can,
What's the thing that's known as Man?

PSYCHE

Man will swear and Man will storm—
Man is not at all good form—
Man is of no kind of use—
Man's a donkey—Man's a goose—
Man is coarse and Man is plain—
Man is more or less insane—
Man's a ribald—Man's a rake,
Man is Nature's sole mistake!

CHORUS We'll a memorandum make—
Man is Nature's sole mistake!

And thus to empyrean height
Of every kind of lore,
In search of wisdom's pure delight,
Ambitiously we soar.
In trying to achieve success
No envy racks our heart,
For all we know and all we guess,
We mutually impart!

Enter LADY BLANCHE. *All stand up demurely*

BLA. Attention, ladies, while I read to you
The Princess Ida's list of punishments.
The first is Sacharissa. She's expelled!

ALL. Expelled!

BLA. Expelled, because although she knew
No man of any kind may pass our walls,
She dared to bring a set of chessmen here!

SACH. (*crying*). I meant no harm; they're only men of wood!

BLA. They're men with whom you give each other mate,
And that's enough! The next is Chloe.

CHLOE. Ah!

BLA. Chloe will lose three terms, for yesterday,
When looking through her drawing-book, I found
A sketch of a perambulator!

ALL (*horrified*). Oh!

BLA. *Double* perambulator, shameless girl!
That's all at present. Now, attention, pray;
Your Principal the Princess comes to give
Her usual inaugural address
To those young ladies who joined yesterday.

CHORUS Mighty maiden with a mission,
Paragon of common sense,
Running fount of erudition,
Miracle of eloquence,
We are blind, and we would see;
We are bound, and would be free;
We are dumb, and we would talk;
We are lame, and we would walk.

Enter the PRINCESS

Mighty maiden with a mission—
Paragon of common sense;
Running fount of erudition—
Miracle of eloquence!

PRIN. (*Recit.*). Minerva, oh, hear me!

ARIA

Oh, goddess wise
That lovest light
Endow with sight
Their unillumined eyes.

At this my call,
A fervent few
Have come to woo
The rays that from thee fall.

Let fervent words and fervent thoughts be mine,
That I may lead them to thy sacred shrine!

Women of Adamant, fair Neophytes—
Who thirst for such instruction as we give,
Attend, while I unfold a parable.
The elephant is mightier than Man,
Yet Man subdues him. Why? The elephant
Is elephantine everywhere but here (*tapping her forehead*),
And Man, whose brain is to the elephant's
As Woman's brain to Man's—(that's rule of three),—
Conquers the foolish giant of the woods,
As Woman, in her turn, shall conquer Man.
In Mathematics, Woman leads the way:
The narrow-minded pedant still believes
That two and two make four! Why, we can prove,
We women—household drudges as we are—
That two and two make five—or three—or seven;
Or five-and-twenty, if the case demands!
Diplomacy? The wiliest diplomat
Is absolutely helpless in our hands,
He wheedles monarchs—woman wheedles him!
Logic? Why, tyrant Man himself admits
It's waste of time to argue with a woman!
Then we excel in social qualities:
Though Man professes that he holds our sex
In utter scorn, I venture to believe
He'd rather pass the day with one of you,
Than with five hundred of his fellow-men!
In all things we excel. Believing this,
A hundred maidens here have sworn to place
Their feet upon his neck. If we succeed,
We'll treat him better than he treated us:

But if we fail, why, then let hope fail too!
Let no one care a penny how she looks—
Let red be worn with yellow—blue with green—
Crimson with scarlet—violet with blue!
Let all your things misfit, and you yourselves
At inconvenient moments come undone!
Let hair-pins lose their virtue: let the hook
Disdain the fascination of the eye—
The bashful button modestly evade
The soft embraces of the button-hole!
Let old associations all dissolve,
Let Swan secede from Edgar—Gask from Gask,
Sewell from Cross—Lewis from Allenby!
In other words—let Chaos come again!
(*Coming down.*) Who lectures in the Hall of Arts to-day?

BLA. I, madam, on Abstract Philosophy.
There I propose considering, at length,
Three points—The Is, the Might Be, and the Must.
Whether the Is, from being actual fact,
Is more important than the vague Might Be,
Or the Might Be, from taking wider scope,
Is for that reason greater than the Is:
And lastly, how the Is and Might Be stand
Compared with the inevitable Must!

PRIN. The subject's deep—how do you treat it, pray?

BLA. Madam, I take three possibilities,
And strike a balance, then, between the three:
As thus: The Princess Ida Is our head,
The Lady Psyche Might Be,—Lady Blanche,
Neglected Blanche, inevitably Must.
Given these three hypotheses—to find
The actual betting against each of them!

PRIN. Your theme's ambitious: pray you, bear in mind
Who highest soar fall farthest. Fare you well,
You and your pupils! Maidens, follow me.

[*Exeunt* PRINCESS *and Maidens singing refrain of chorus, "And thus to empyrean heights", etc. Manet* LADY BLANCHE.

BLA. I should command here—I was born to rule,
But do I rule? I don't. Why? I don't know.

I shall some day. Not yet. I bide my time.
I once was Some One—and the Was Will Be.
The Present as we speak becomes the Past,
The Past repeats itself, and so is Future!
This sounds involved. It's not. It's right enough.

SONG—LADY BLANCHE

Come, mighty Must!
Inevitable Shall!
In thee I trust.
Time weaves my coronal!
Go, mocking Is!
Go, disappointing Was!
That I am this
Ye are the cursed cause!
Yet humble second shall be first,
I ween;
And dead and buried be the curst
Has Been!

Oh, weak Might Be!
Oh, May, Might, Could, Would, Should!
How powerless ye
For evil or for good!
In every sense
Your moods I cheerless call,
Whate'er your tense
Ye are Imperfect, all!
Ye have deceived the trust I've shown
In ye!
Away! The Mighty Must alone
Shall be!

[*Exit* LADY BLANCHE.

Enter HILARION, CYRIL, *and* FLORIAN, *climbing over wall, and creeping cautiously among the trees and rocks at the back of the stage.*

TRIO—HILARION, CYRIL, FLORIAN

Gently, gently,
Evidently
We are safe so far,
After scaling
Fence and paling,
Here, at last, we are!
In this college
Useful knowledge
Everywhere one finds,
And already,
Growing steady,
We've enlarged our minds.

CYR. We've learnt that prickly cactus
Has the power to attract us
When we fall.

ALL. When we fall!

HIL. That nothing man unsettles
Like a bed of stinging nettles,
Short or tall.

ALL. Short or tall!

FLOR. That bull-dogs feed on throttles—
That we don't like broken bottles
On a wall.

ALL. On a wall!

HIL. That spring-guns breathe defiance!
And that burglary's a science
After all!

ALL. After all!

RECIT—FLORIAN

A Woman's college! maddest folly going!
What can girls learn within its walls worth knowing?
I'll lay a crown (the Princess shall decide it)
I'll teach them twice as much in half-an-hour outside it.

HILARION

Hush, scoffer; ere you sound your puny thunder,
List to their aims, and bow your head in wonder!

They intend to send a wire
To the moon—to the moon;
And they'll set the Thames on fire
Very soon—very soon;
Then they learn to make silk purses
With their rigs—with their rigs,
From the ears of Lady Circe's
Piggy-wigs—piggy-wigs.
And weasels at their slumbers
They trepan—they trepan;
To get sunbeams from cu*cum*bers,
They've a plan—they've a plan.
They've a firmly rooted notion
They can cross the Polar Ocean,
And they'll find Perpetual Motion,
If they can—if they can.

ALL. These are the phenomena
That every pretty domina

Is hoping we shall see
At her Universitee!

CYR. As for fashion, they forswear it,
So they say—so they say;
And the circle—they will square it
Some fine day—some fine day;
Then the little pigs they're teaching
For to fly—for to fly;
And the niggers they'll be bleaching,
By and by—by and by!
Each newly-joined aspirant
To the clan—to the clan—
Must repudiate the tyrant
Known as Man—known as Man.
They mock at him and flout him,
For they do not care about him,
And they're "going to do without him"
If they can—if they can!

ALL. These are the phenomena, etc.

In this college
Useful knowledge
Ev'rywhere one finds,
And already growing steady
We've enlarg'd our minds.

HIL. So that's the Princess Ida's castle! Well,
They must be lovely girls, indeed, if it requires
Such walls as those to keep intruders off!

CYR. To keep men off is only half their charge,
And that the easier half. I much suspect
The object of these walls is not so much
To keep men off as keep the maidens in!

FLOR. But what are these? (*Examining some Collegiate robes.*)

HIL. (*looking at them*). Why, Academic robes,
Worn by the lady undergraduates
When they matriculate. Let's try them on.
(*They do so.*)
Why, see,—we're covered to the very toes.
Three lovely lady undergraduates

Who, weary of the world and all its wooing—
FLOR. And penitent for deeds there's no undoing—
CYR. Looked at askance by well-conducted maids—
ALL. Seek sanctuary in these classic shades!

TRIO—HILARION, CYRIL, FLORIAN

HIL. I am a maiden, cold and stately,
Heartless I, with a face divine.
What do I want with a heart, innately?
Every heart I meet is mine!

ALL. Haughty, humble, coy, or free,
Little care I what maid may be.
So that a maid is fair to see,
Every maid is the maid for me!
(*Dance.*)

CYR. I am a maiden frank and simple,
Brimming with joyous roguery;
Merriment lurks in every dimple,
Nobody breaks more hearts than I!

ALL. Haughty, humble, coy, or free,
Little care I what maid may be.
So that a maid is fair to see,
Every maid is the maid for me!
(*Dance.*)

FLOR. I am a maiden coyly blushing,
Timid am I as a startled hind;
Every suitor sets me flushing:
I am the maid that wins mankind!

ALL. Haughty, humble, coy, or free,
Little care I what maid may be.
So that a maid is fair to see,
Every maid is the maid for me!

Enter the PRINCESS *reading. She does not see them*

FLOR. But who comes here? The Princess, as I live! What shall we do?

HIL. (*aside*). Why, we must brave it out!
(*Aloud.*) Madam, accept our humblest reverence.

[*They bow, then, suddenly recollecting themselves, curtsey.*

PRIN. (*surprised*). We greet you, ladies. What would you with us?

HIL. (*aside*). What shall I say? (*Aloud.*) We are three students, ma'am,
Three well-born maids of liberal estate,
Who wish to join this University.

[HILARION *and* FLORIAN *curtsey again.* CYRIL *bows extravagantly, then, being recalled to himself by* FLORIAN, *curtseys.*

PRIN. If, as you say, you wish to join our ranks,
And will subscribe to all our rules, 'tis well.

FLOR. To all your rules we cheerfully subscribe.

PRIN. You say you're noblewomen. Well, you'll find
No sham degrees for noblewomen here.
You'll find no sizars here, or servitors,
Or other cruel distinctions, meant to draw
A line 'twixt rich and poor: you'll find no tufts
To mark nobility, except such tufts
As indicate nobility of brain.
As for your fellow-students, mark me well:
There are a hundred maids within these walls,
All good, all learned, and all beautiful:
They are prepared to love you: will you swear
To give the fullness of your love to them?

HIL. Upon our words and honours, ma'am, we will!

PRIN. But we go further: will you undertake
That you will never marry any man?

FLOR. Indeed we never will!

PRIN. Consider well,
You must prefer our maids to all mankind!

HIL. To all mankind we much prefer your maids!

CYR. We should be dolts indeed, if we did not,
Seeing how fair——

HIL. (*aside to* CYRIL). Take care—that's rather strong!

PRIN. But have you left no lovers at your home
Who may pursue you here?

HIL. No, madam, none.
We're homely ladies, as no doubt you see,

And we have never fished for lover's love.
We smile at girls who deck themselves with gems,
False hair, and meretricious ornament,
To chain the fleeting fancy of a man,
But do not imitate them. What we have
Of hair, is all our own. Our colour, too,
Unladylike, but not unwomanly,
Is Nature's handiwork, and man has learnt
To reckon Nature an impertinence.

PRIN. Well, beauty counts for naught within these walls;
If all you say is true, you'll pass with us
A happy, happy time!

CYR. If, as you say,
A hundred lovely maidens wait within,
To welcome us with smiles and open arms,
I think there's very little doubt we shall!

QUARTETTE—PRINCESS, HILARION, CYRIL, FLORIAN

PRIN. The world is but a broken toy,
Its pleasure hollow—false its joy,
Unreal its loveliest hue,
Alas!
Its pains alone are true,
Alas!
Its pains alone are true.

HIL. The world is everything you say,
The world we think has had its day.
Its merriment is slow,
Alas!
We've tried it, and we know.
Alas!
We've tried it and we know.

TUTTI

PRINCESS	HILARION, CYRIL, FLORIAN
The world is but a broken toy,	The world is but a broken toy,
Its pleasure hollow—false its joy,	We freely give it up with joy,
Unreal its loveliest hue,	Unreal its loveliest hue,
Alas!	Alas!
Its pains alone are true,	Its pains alone are true,
Alas!	Alas!
Its pains alone are true!	Its pains alone are true!

[*Exit* PRINCESS. *The three gentlemen watch her off.* LADY PSYCHE *enters, and regards them with amazement.*

HIL. I'faith, the plunge is taken, gentlemen!
For, willy-nilly, we are maidens now,
And maids against our will we must remain!
(*All laugh heartily.*)

PSY. (*aside*). These ladies are unseemly in their mirth.

[*The gentlemen see her, and, in confusion, resume their modest demeanour.*

FLOR. (*aside*). Here's a catastrophe, Hilarion!
This is my sister! She'll remember me,
Though years have passed since she and I have met!

HIL. (*aside to* FLORIAN). Then make a virtue of necessity,
And trust our secret to her gentle care.

FLOR. (*to* PSYCHE, *who has watched* CYRIL *in amazement*). Psyche!
Why, don't you know me? Florian!

PSY. (*amazed*). Why, Florian!

FLOR. My sister (*embraces her*).

PSY. Oh, my dear!
What are you doing here—and who are these?

HIL. I am that Prince Hilarion to whom
Your Princess is betrothed. I come to claim
Her plighted love. Your brother Florian
And Cyril came to see me safely through.

PSY. The Prince Hilarion? Cyril too? How strange!
My earliest playfellows!

HIL. Why, let me look!
Are you that learned little Psyche who
At school alarmed her mates because she called
A buttercup "ranunculus bulbosus"?

CYR. Are you indeed that Lady Psyche, who
At children's parties drove the conjuror wild,
Explaining all his tricks before he did them?

HIL. Are you that learned little Psyche, who
At dinner parties, brought in to dessert,
Would tackle visitors with "You don't know
Who first determined longitude—I do—

Hipparchus 'twas—B.C. one sixty-three!"
Are you indeed that small phenomenon?

PSY. That small phenomenon indeed am I!
But, gentlemen, 'tis death to enter here:
We have all promised to renounce mankind!

FLOR. Renounce mankind? On what ground do you base
This senseless resolution?

PSY. Senseless? No.
We are all taught, and, being taught, believe
That Man, sprung from an Ape, is Ape at heart.

CYR. That's rather strong.

PSY. The truth is always strong!

SONG—LADY PSYCHE

A Lady fair, of lineage high,
Was loved by an Ape, in the days gone by.
The Maid was radiant as the sun,
The Ape was a most unsightly one—
So it would not do—
His scheme fell through,
For the Maid, when his love took formal shape,
Expressed such terror
At his monstrous error,
That he stammered an apology and made his 'scape,
The picture of a disconcerted Ape.

With a view to rise in the social scale,
He shaved his bristles, and he docked his tail,
He grew mustachios, and he took his tub,
And he paid a guinea to a toilet club—
But it would not do,
The scheme fell through—
For the Maid was Beauty's fairest Queen,
With golden tresses,
Like a real princess's,
While the Ape, despite his razor keen,
Was the apiest Ape that ever was seen!
He bought white ties, and he bought dress suits,
He crammed his feet into bright tight boots—

And to start in life on a brand-new plan,
He christened himself Darwinian Man!

But it would not do,
The scheme fell through—
For the Maiden fair, whom the monkey craved,
Was a radiant Being,
With a brain far-seeing—
While a Darwinian Man, though well-behaved,
At best is only a monkey shaved!

ALL. While Darwinian Man, etc.

During this MELISSA *has entered unobserved; she looks on in amazement*

MEL. (*coming down*). Oh, Lady Psyche!

PSY. (*terrified*). What! you heard us then?
Oh, all is lost!

MEL. Not so! I'll breathe no word!
(*Advancing in astonishment to* FLORIAN.)

How marvellously strange! and are you then
Indeed young men?

FLOR. Well, yes, just now we are—
But hope by dint of study to become,
In course of time, young women.

MEL. (*eagerly*). No, no, no—
Oh, don't do that! Is this indeed a man?
I've often heard of them, but, till to-day,
Never set eyes on one. They told me men
Were hideous, idiotic, and deformed!
They're quite as beautiful as women are!
As beautiful, they're infinitely more so!
Their cheeks have not that pulpy softness which
One gets so weary of in womankind:
Their features are more marked—and—oh, their chins!
How curious! (*Feeling his chin.*)

FLOR. I fear it's rather rough.

MEL. (*eagerly*). Oh, don't apologize—I like it so!

QUINTETTE—PSYCHE, MELISSA, HILARION, CYRIL, FLORIAN

PSY. The woman of the wisest wit
May sometimes be mistaken, O!
In Ida's views, I must admit,
My faith is somewhat shaken, O!

CYR. On every other point than this
Her learning is untainted, O!
But Man's a theme with which she is
Entirely unacquainted, O!
—acquainted, O!
—acquainted, O!
Entirely unacquainted, O!

ALL. Then jump for joy and gaily bound,
The truth is found—the truth is found!
Set bells a-ringing through the air—
Ring here and there and everywhere—
And echo forth the joyous sound,
The truth is found—the truth is found!
(*Dance.*)

MEL. My natural instinct teaches me
(And instinct is important, O!)
You're everything you ought to be,
And nothing that you oughtn't, O!

HIL. That fact was seen at once by you
In casual conversation, O!
Which is most creditable to
Your powers of observation, O!
—servation, O!
—servation, O!
Your powers of observation, O!

ALL. Then jump for joy, etc.

[*Exeunt* PSYCHE, HILARION, CYRIL, *and* FLORIAN. MELISSA *going*.

Enter LADY BLANCHE

BLA. Melissa!
MEL. (*returning*). Mother!
BLA. Here—a word with you.
Those are the three new students?
MEL. (*confused*). Yes, they are.
They're charming girls.
BLA. Particularly so.
So graceful, and so very womanly!
So skilled in all a girl's accomplishments!
MEL. (*confused*). Yes—very skilled.
BLA. They sing so nicely too!
MEL. They *do* sing nicely!
BLA. Humph! It's very odd.
Two are tenors, one is a baritone!
MEL. (*much agitated*). They've all got colds!
BLA. Colds! Bah! D'ye think I'm blind?
These "girls" are men disguised!
MEL. Oh no—indeed!
You wrong these gentlemen—I mean—why, see,
Here is an *étui* dropped by one of them (*picking up an étui*).
Containing scissors, needles, and——
BLA. (*opening it*). Cigars!

Why, these *are* men! And you knew this, you minx!

MEL. Oh, spare them—they are gentlemen indeed.
The Prince Hilarion (married years ago
To Princess Ida) with two trusted friends!
Consider, mother, he's her husband now,
And has been, twenty years! Consider, too,
You're only second here—you should be first.
Assist the Prince's plan, and when he gains
The Princess Ida, why, you *will* be first.
You will design the fashions—think of that—
And always serve out all the punishments!
The scheme is harmless, mother—wink at it!

BLA. (*aside*). The prospect's tempting! Well, well, well, I'll try—
Though I've not winked at anything for years!
'Tis but one step towards my destiny—
The mighty Must! the inevitable Shall!

DUET—MELISSA *and* LADY BLANCHE

MEL. Now wouldn't you like to rule the roast,
And guide this University?

BLA. I must agree
'Twould pleasant be.
(Sing hey, a Proper Pride!)

MEL. And wouldn't you like to clear the coast
Of malice and perversity?

BLA. Without a doubt
I'll bundle 'em out,
Sing hey, when I preside!

BOTH. Sing, hoity, toity! Sorry for some!
Sing marry, come up and {my / her} day will come!
Sing, Proper Pride
Is the horse to ride,
And Happy-go-lucky, my Lady, O!

BLA. For years I've writhed beneath her sneers,
Although a born Plantagenet!

MEL. You're much too meek,
Or you would speak.
(Sing hey, I'll say no more!)

BLA. Her elder I, by several years,
Although you'd ne'er imagine it.

MEL. Sing, so I've heard
But never a word
Have I e'er believed before!

BOTH. Sing, hoity, toity! Sorry for some!
Sing, marry come up and {my / her} day will come!

Sing, she shall learn
That a worm will turn.
Sing Happy-go-lucky, my Lady, O!

[*Exit* LADY BLANCHE.

MEL. Saved for a time, at least!

Enter FLORIAN, *on tiptoe*

FLOR. (*whispering*). Melissa—come!
MEL. Oh, sir! you must away from this at once—
My mother guessed your sex! It was my fault—
I blushed and stammered so that she exclaimed,
"Can these be men?" Then, seeing this, "Why these——"
"*Are men*", she would have added, but "*are men*"
Stuck in her throat! She keeps your secret, sir,
For reasons of her own—but fly from this
And take me with you—that is—no—not that!
FLOR. I'll go, but not without you! (*Bell.*) Why, what's that?
MEL. The luncheon bell.
FLOR. I'll wait for luncheon then!

Enter HILARION *with* PRINCESS, CYRIL *with* PSYCHE, LADY BLANCHE *and* LADIES. *Also "Daughters of the Plough" bearing luncheon.*

CHORUS Merrily ring the luncheon bell!
Here in meadow of asphodel,
Feast we body and mind as well,
So merrily ring the luncheon bell!

SOLO—BLANCHE

Hunger, I beg to state,
Is highly indelicate,
This is a fact profoundly true,
So learn your appetites to subdue.

ALL. Yes, yes,
We'll learn our appetites to subdue!

SOLO—CYRIL (*eating*)

Madame, your words so wise,
Nobody should despise,
Cursed with appetite keen I am
And I'll subdue it—
And I'll subdue it—
And I'll subdue it with cold roast lamb!

ALL. Yes—yes—
We'll subdue it with cold roast lamb!

CHORUS. Merrily ring, etc.

PRIN. You say you know the court of Hildebrand?
There is a Prince there—I forget his name—

HIL. Hilarion?

PRIN. Exactly—is he well?

HIL. If it be well to droop and pine and mope,
To sigh "Oh, Ida! Ida!" all day long,
"Ida! my love! my life! Oh, come to me!"
If it be well, I say, to do all this,
Then Prince Hilarion is very well.

PRIN. He breathes *our* name? Well, it's a common one!
And is the booby comely?

HIL. Pretty well.
I've heard it said that if I dressed myself
In Prince Hilarion's clothes (supposing this

Consisted with my maiden modesty),
I might be taken for Hilarion's self.
But what is this to you or me, who think
Of all mankind with undisguised contempt?

PRIN. Contempt? Why, damsel, when I think of man,
Contempt is not the word.

CYR. (*getting tipsy*). I'm sure of that,
Or if it is, it surely should not be!

HIL. (*aside to* CYRIL). Be quiet, idiot, or they'll find us out.

CYR. The Prince Hilarion's a goodly lad!

PRIN. *You* know him then?

CYR. (*tipsily*). I rather think I do!
We are inseparables!

PRIN. Why, what's this?
You love him then?

CYR. We do indeed—all three!

HIL. Madam, she jests! (*Aside to* CYRIL.) Remember where you are!

CYR. Jests? Not at all! Why, bless my heart alive,
You and Hilarion, when at the Court,
Rode the same horse!

PRIN. (*horrified*). Astride?

CYR. Of course! Why not?
Wore the same clothes—and once or twice, I think,
Got tipsy in the same good company!

PRIN. Well, these are nice young ladies, on my word!

CYR. (*tipsy*). Don't you remember that old kissing-song
He'd sing to blushing Mistress Lalage,
The hostess of the Pigeons? Thus it ran:

SONG—CYRIL

[*During symphony* HILARION *and* FLORIAN *try to stop* CYRIL. *He shakes them off angrily*

Would you know the kind of maid
Sets my heart aflame-a?
Eyes must be downcast and staid,
Cheeks must flush for shame-a!
She may neither dance nor sing,
But, demure in everything,

Hang her head in modest way,
With pouting lips that seem to say,
"Oh, kiss me, kiss me, kiss me, kiss me,
Though I die of shame-a!"
Please you, that's the kind of maid
Sets my heart aflame-a!

When a maid is bold and gay
With a tongue goes clang-a,
Flaunting it in brave array,
Maiden may go hang-a
Sunflower gay and hollyhock
Never shall my garden stock;
Mine the blushing rose of May,
With pouting lips that seem to say,
"Oh, kiss me, kiss me, kiss me, kiss me,
Though I die for shame-a!"
Please you, that's the kind of maid
Sets my heart aflame-a!

PRIN. Infamous creature, get you hence away!

[HILARION, *who has been with difficulty restrained by* FLORIAN *during this song, breaks from him and strikes* CYRIL *furiously on the breast.*

HIL. Dog! there is something more to sing about!
CYR. (*sobered*). Hilarion, are you mad?
PRIN. (*horrified*). Hilarion? Help!
Why, these are men! Lost! lost! betrayed, undone! (*Running on to bridge.*)
Girls, get you hence! Man-monsters, if you dare
Approach one step, I—— Ah!

(*Loses her balance, and falls into the stream.*)

PSY. Oh! save her, sir!

BLA. It's useless, sir,—you'll only catch your death!

(HILARION *springs in.*)

SACH. He catches her!

MEL. And now he lets her go!
Again she's in his grasp—

PSY. And now she's not.
He seizes her back hair!

BLA. (*not looking*). And it comes off!

PSY. No, no! She's saved!—she's saved!—she's saved!—she's saved!

FINALE

CHORUS OF LADIES

Oh! joy, our chief is saved,
And by Hilarion's hand;
The torrent fierce he braved,
And brought her safe to land!
For his intrusion we must own
This doughty deed may well atone!

PRIN. Stand forth ye three,
Whoe'er ye be,
And hearken to our stern decree!

HIL., CYR., *and* FLOR. Have mercy, lady,—disregard your oaths!

PRIN. I know not mercy, men in women's clothes!
The man whose sacrilegious eyes
Invade our strict seclusion, dies.
Arrest these coarse intruding spies!

[*They are arrested by the "Daughters of the Plough".*

FLOR., CYR., *and* LADIES. Have mercy, lady—disregard your oaths!

PRIN. I know not mercy, men in women's clothes!

[CYRIL *and* FLORIAN *are bound.*

SONG—HILARION

Whom thou hast chained must wear his chain,
Thou canst not set him free,

He wrestles with his bonds in vain
  Who lives by loving thee!
If heart of stone for heart of fire,
  Be all thou hast to give,
If dead to me my heart's desire,
  Why should I wish to live?

FLOR., CYR., *and* LADIES. Have mercy, O lady!

No word of thine—no stern command
  Can teach my heart to rove,
Then rather perish by thy hand,
  Than live without thy love!
A loveless life apart from thee
  Were hopeless slavery,
If kindly death will set me free,
  Why should I fear to die?

[*He is bound by two of the attendants, and the three gentlemen are marched off.*

Enter MELISSA.

MEL. Madam, without the castle walls
  An armed band
Demand admittance to our halls
  For Hildebrand!

ALL. Oh, horror!

PRIN. Deny them!
  We will defy them!

ALL. Too late—too late!
  The castle gate
  Is battered by them!

[*The gate yields.* SOLDIERS *rush in.* ARAC, GURON, *and* SCYNTHIUS *are with them, but with their hands handcuffed.*

ENSEMBLE

GIRLS

Rend the air with wailing,
  Shed the shameful tear!
Walls are unavailing,
  Man has entered here!

MEN

Walls and fences scaling,
  Promptly we appear;
Walls are unavailing,
  We have entered here.

Shame and desecration
Are his staunch allies,
Let your lamentation
Echo to the skies!

Female execration
Stifle if you're wise,
Stop your lamentation,
Dry your pretty eyes!

Enter HILDEBRAND

RECIT

PRIN. Audacious tyrant, do you dare
To beard a maiden in her lair?

HILD. Since you inquire,
We've no desire
To beard a maiden here, or anywhere!

SOL. No, no—we've no desire
To beard a maiden here, or anywhere!

SOLO—HILDEBRAND

Some years ago
No doubt you know
(And if you don't I'll tell you so)
You gave your troth
Upon your oath
To Hilarion my son.
A vow you make
You must not break,
(If you think you may, it's a great mistake),
For a bride's a bride
Though the knot were tied
At the early age of one!
And I'm a peppery kind of King,
Who's indisposed for parleying
To fit the wit of a bit of a chit,
And that's the long and the short of it!

SOL. For he's a peppery kind of King, etc.

If you decide
To pocket your pride
And let Hilarion claim his bride,
Why, well and good,
It's understood
We'll let bygones go by—

But if you choose
To sulk in the blues
I'll make the whole of you shake in your shoes.
I'll storm your walls,
And level your halls,
In the twinkling of an eye!
For I'm a peppery Potentate,
Who's little inclined his claim to bate,
To fit the wit of a bit of a chit,
And that's the long and the short of it!

SOL. For he's a peppery kind of King, etc.

TRIO—ARAC, GURON, *and* SCYNTHIUS

We may remark, though nothing can
Dismay us,
That if you thwart this gentleman,
He'll slay us.
We don't fear death, of course—we're taught
To shame it;
But still upon the whole we thought
We'd name it.

(*To each other.*) Yes, yes, yes, better perhaps to name it.

Our interests we would not press
With chatter,
Three hulking brothers more or less
Don't matter;
If you'd pooh-pooh this monarch's plan,
Pooh-pooh it,
But when he says he'll hang a man,
He'll do it.

(*To each other.*) Yes, yes, yes, devil doubt he'll do it.

PRIN. (*Recit.*) Be reassured, nor fear his anger blind,
His menaces are idle as the wind.
He dares not kill you—vengeance lurks behind!

AR., GUR., SCYN. *We* rather think he dares, but never mind!
No, no,—never, never mind!

HILD. I rather think I dare, but never, never mind!
Enough of parley—as a special boon,
We give you till to-morrow afternoon;
Release Hilarion, then, and be his bride,
Or you'll incur the guilt of fratricide!

ENSEMBLE

PRINCESS

To yield at once to such a foe
With shame were rife;
So quick! away with him, although
He saved my life!
That he is fair, and strong, and tall,
Is very evident to all,
Yet I will die before I call
Myself his wife!

THE OTHERS

Oh! yield at once, 'twere better so
Than risk a strife!
And let the Prince Hilarion go—
He saved thy life!
Hilarion's fair, and strong, and tall—
A worse misfortune might befall—
It's not so dreadful, after all,
To be his wife!

SOLO—PRINCESS

Though I am but a girl,
Defiance thus I hurl,
Our banners all
On outer wall
We fearlessly unfurl.

ALL. Though she is but a girl, etc.

PRINCESS

That he is fair, etc.

THE OTHERS

Hilarion's fair, etc.

[*The* PRINCESS *stands, surrounded by girls kneeling.* HILDEBRAND *and soldiers stand on built rocks at back and sides of stage. Picture.*

CURTAIN

END OF ACT II

ACT III

SCENE.—*Outer Walls and Courtyard of Castle Adamant.* MELISSA, SACHARISSA, *and ladies discovered, armed with battleaxes.*

CHORUS
Death to the invader!
Strike a deadly blow,
As an old Crusader
Struck his Paynim foe!
Let our martial thunder
Fill his soul with wonder,
Tear his ranks asunder,
Lay the tyrant low!

SOLO—MELISSA

Thus our courage, all untarnished,
We're instructed to display:
But to tell the truth unvarnished,
We are more inclined to say,
"Please you, do not hurt us."

ALL. "Do not hurt us, if it please you!"
MEL. "Please you let us be."
ALL. "Let us be—let us be!"
MEL. "Soldiers disconcert us."
ALL. "Disconcert us, if it please you!"
MEL. "Frightened maids are we!"
ALL. "Maids are we—maids are we!"

MELISSA

But 'twould be an error
To confess our terror,
So, in Ida's name,
Boldly we exclaim:

CHORUS
Death to the invader!
Strike a deadly blow,
As an old Crusader
Struck his Paynim foe!

Flourish. Enter PRINCESS, *armed, attended by* BLANCHE *and* PSYCHE

PRIN. I like your spirit, girls! We have to meet
Stern bearded warriors in fight to-day:
Wear naught but what is necessary to
Preserve your dignity before their eyes,
And give your limbs full play.

BLA. One moment, ma'am,
Here is a paradox we should not pass
Without inquiry. We are prone to say,
"This thing is Needful—that, Superfluous"—
Yet they invariably co-exist!
We find the Needful comprehended in
The circle of the grand Superfluous,
Yet the Superfluous cannot be bought
Unless you're amply furnished with the Needful.
These singular considerations are—

PRIN. Superfluous, yet not Needful—so you see
The terms may independently exist.
(*To Ladies.*) Women of Adamant, we have to show
That women, educated to the task,
Can meet Man, face to face, on his own ground,
And beat him there. Now let us set to work:
Where is our lady surgeon?

SAC. Madam, here!

PRIN. We shall require your skill to heal the wounds
Of those that fall.

SAC. (*alarmed*). What, heal the wounded?

PRIN. Yes!

SAC. And cut off real live legs and arms?

PRIN. Of course!

SAC. I wouldn't do it for a thousand pounds!

PRIN. Why, how is this? Are you faint-hearted, girl?
You've often cut them off in theory!

SAC. In theory I'll cut them off again
With pleasure, and as often as you like,
But not in practice.

PRIN. Coward! get you hence,
I've craft enough for that, and courage too,
I'll do your work! My fusiliers, advance!

Why, you are armed with axes! Gilded toys!
Where are your rifles, pray?

CHLOE. Why, please you, ma'am,
We left them in the armoury, for fear
That in the heat and turmoil of the fight,
They might go off!

PRIN. "They might!" Oh, craven souls!
Go off yourselves! Thank heaven, I have a heart
That quails not at the thought of meeting men;
I will discharge your rifles! Off with you!
Where's my bandmistress?

ADA. Please you, ma'am, the band
Do not feel well, and can't come out to-day!

PRIN. Why, this is flat rebellion! I've no time
To talk to them just now. But, happily,
I can play several instruments at once,
And I will drown the shrieks of those that fall
With trumpet music, such as soldiers love!
How stand we with respect to gunpowder?
My Lady Psyche—you who superintend
Our lab'ratory—are you well prepared
To blow these bearded rascals into shreds?

PSY. Why, madam—

PRIN. Well?

PSY. Let us try gentler means.
We can dispense with fulminating grains
While we have eyes with which to flash our rage!
We can dispense with villainous saltpetre
While we have tongues with which to blow them up!
We can dispense, in short, with all the arts
That brutalize the practical polemist!

PRIN. (*contemptuously*). I never knew a more dispensing chemist!
Away, away—I'll meet these men alone
Since all my women have deserted me!

[*Exeunt all but* PRINCESS, *singing refrain of "Please you, do not hurt us", pianissimo.*

PRIN. So fail my cherished plans—so fails my faith—
And with it hope, and all that comes of hope!

SONG—PRINCESS

I built upon a rock,
But ere Destruction's hand
Dealt equal lot
To Court and cot,
My rock had turned to sand!
I leant upon an oak,
But in the hour of need,
Alack-a-day,
My trusted stay
Was but a bruisèd reed!
Ah, faithless rock,
My simple faith to mock!
Ah, trait'rous oak,
Thy worthlessness to cloak.
I drew a sword of steel,
But when to home and hearth
The battle's breath
Bore fire and death,
My sword was but a lath!
I lit a beacon fire,
But on a stormy day
Of frost and rime,
In wintertime,
My fire had died away!
Ah, coward steel,
That fear can unanneal!
False fire indeed,
To fail me in my need!

She sinks on a seat. Enter CHLOE *and all the ladies*

CHLOE. Madam, your father and your brothers claim
An audience!

PRIN. What do they do here?

CHLOE. They come
To fight for you!

PRIN. Admit them!

BLA. Infamous!
One's brothers, ma'am, are men!

PRIN. So I've heard.
But all my women seem to fail me when
I need them most. In this emergency,
Even one's brothers may be turned to use.

Enter GAMA, *quite pale and unnerved*

GAMA. My daughter!

PRIN. Father! thou art free!

GAMA. Aye, free!
Free as a tethered ass! I come to thee
With words from Hildebrand. Those duly given
I must return to blank captivity.
I'm free so far.

PRIN. Your message.

GAMA. Hildebrand
Is loth to war with women. Pit my sons,
My three brave sons, against these popinjays,
These tufted jack-a-dandy featherheads,
And on the issue let thy hand depend!

PRIN. Insult on insult's head! Are we a stake
For fighting men? What fiend possesses thee,
That thou hast come with offers such as these
From such as he to such an one as I?

GAMA. I am possessed
By the pale devil of a shaking heart!
My stubborn will is bent. I dare not face
That devilish monarch's black malignity!
He tortures me with torments worse than death,
I haven't anything to grumble at!
He finds out what particular meats I love,
And gives me them. The very choicest wines,
The costliest robes—the richest rooms are mine:
He suffers none to thwart my simplest plan,
And gives strict orders none should contradict me!
He's made my life a curse! (*weeps*).

PRIN. My tortured father!

SONG—GAMA

Whene'er I poke
Sarcastic joke
Replete with malice spiteful,
This people mild
Politely smiled,
And voted me delightful!

Now when a wight
Sits up all night
Ill-natured jokes devising,
And all his wiles
Are met with smiles
It's hard, there's no disguising!

O, don't the days seem lank and long
When all goes right and nothing goes wrong,
And isn't your life extremely flat
With nothing whatever to grumble at!

When German bands
From music stands
Played Wagner imper*fect*ly—
I bade them go —
They didn't say no,
But off they went directly!

The organ boys
They stopped their noise
With readiness surprising,
And grinning herds
Of hurdy-gurds
Retired apologising!
Oh, don't the days seem lank and long, etc.

I offered gold
In sums untold
To all who'd contradict me—
I said I'd pay
A pound a day
To any one who kicked me—
I bribed with toys
Great vulgar boys
To utter something spiteful,
But, bless you, no!
They *would* be so
Confoundedly politeful!

In short, these aggravating lads,
They tickle my tastes, they feed my fads,
They give me this and they give me that,
And I've nothing whatever to grumble at!

[*He bursts into tears, and falls sobbing on a seat.*

PRIN. My poor old father! How he must have suffered!
Well, well, I yield!

GAMA (*hysterically*). She yields! I'm saved, I'm saved!
[*Exit.*

PRIN. Open the gates—admit these warriors,
Then get you all within the castle walls. [*Exit.*

[*The gates are opened, and the girls mount the battlements as soldiers enter. Also* ARAC, GURON, *and* SCYNTHIUS.

CHORUS OF SOLDIERS

When anger spreads his wing,
And all seems dark as night for it,
There's nothing but to fight for it,
But ere you pitch your ring,

Select a pretty site for it,
(This spot is suited quite for it),
And then you gaily sing,

"Oh, I love the jolly rattle
Of an ordeal by battle,
There's an end of tittle-tattle
When your enemy is dead.
It's an arrant molly-coddle
Fears a crack upon his noddle
And he's only fit to swaddle
In a downy feather-bed!"—

ALL. For a fight's a kind of thing
That I love to look upon,
So let us sing,
Long live the King,
And his son Hilarion!

[*During this,* HILARION, FLORIAN, *and* CYRIL *are brought out by the "Daughters of the Plough". They are still bound and wear the robes. Enter* GAMA.

GAMA. Hilarion! Cyril! Florian! dressed as women!
Is this indeed Hilarion?

HIL. Yes, it is!

GAMA. Why, you look handsome in your women's clothes!
Stick to 'em! men's attire becomes you not!
(*To* CYRIL *and* FLORIAN). And you, young ladies, will you please to pray
King Hildebrand to set me free again?
Hang on his neck and gaze into his eyes,
He never could resist a pretty face!

HIL. You dog, you'll find, though I wear woman's garb,
My sword is long and sharp!

GAMA. Hush, pretty one!
Here's a virago! Here's a termagant!
If length and sharpness go for anything,
You'll want no sword while you can wag your tongue!

CYR. What need to waste your words on such as he?
He's old and crippled.

GAMA. Aye, but I've three sons,
Fine fellows, young, and muscular, and brave,
They're well worth talking to! Come, what d'ye say?

ARAC. Aye, pretty ones, engage yourselves with us,
If three rude warriors affright you not!

HIL. Old as you are, I'd wring your shrivelled neck
If you were not the Princess Ida's father,

GAMA. If I were not the Princess Ida's father,
And so had not her brothers for my sons,
No doubt you'd wring my neck—in safety too!
Come, come, Hilarion, begin, begin!
Give them no quarter—they will give you none.
You've this advantage over warriors
Who kill their country's enemies for pay,—
You know what you are fighting for—look there!

(*Pointing to Ladies on the battlements.*)

[*Exit* GAMA. HILARION, FLORIAN, *and* CYRIL *are led off.*

SONG—ARAC

This helmet, I suppose,
Was meant to ward off blows,
It's very hot,
And weighs a lot,
As many a guardsman knows,
So off that helmet goes.

ALL. Yes, yes, yes,
So off that helmet goes!

(*Giving their helmets to attendants.*)

ARAC. This tight-fitting cuirass
Is but a useless mass,
It's made of steel,
And weighs a deal,

A man is but an ass
Who fights in a cuirass,
So off goes that cuirass.

ALL. Yes, yes, yes,
So off goes that cuirass!
(*Removing cuirasses.*)

ARAC. These brassets, truth to tell,
May look uncommon well,
But in a fight
They're much too tight,
They're like a lobster shell!

ALL. Yes, yes, yes,
They're like a lobster shell.
(*Removing their brassets.*)

ARAC. These things I treat the same (*indicating leg pieces*).
(I quite forget their name)
They turn one's legs
To cribbage pegs—
Their aid I thus disclaim,
Though I forget their name!

ALL. Yes, yes, yes,
Their aid { we / they } thus disclaim!

[*They remove their leg pieces and wear close-fitting shape suits.*

Enter HILARION, FLORIAN, *and* CYRIL

[*Desperate fight between the three Princes and the three Knights, during which the Ladies on the battlements and the Soldiers on the stage sing the following chorus.*

This is our duty plain towards
Our Princess all immaculate,
We ought to bless her brothers' swords
And piously ejaculate:
Oh, Hungary!
Oh, Hungary!
Oh, doughty sons of Hungary!

May all success
Attend and bless
Your warlike ironmongery!

Hilarion! Hilarion! Hilarion!

[*By this time,* ARAC, GURON, *and* SCYNTHIUS *are on the ground, wounded*—HILARION, CYRIL, *and* FLORIAN *stand over them.*

PRIN. (*entering through gate and followed by Ladies,* HILDEBRAND, *and* GAMA). Hold! stay your hands—we yield ourselves to you!
Ladies, my brothers all lie bleeding there!
Bind up their wounds—but look the other way.
(*Coming down*). Is this the end? (*bitterly to* LADY BLANCHE). How say you, Lady Blanche—
Can I with dignity my post resign?
And if I do, will you then take my place?

BLA. To answer this, it's meet that we consult
The great Potential Mysteries; I mean
The five Subjunctive Possibilities—
The May, the Might, the Would, the Could, the Should.
Can you resign? The prince May claim you; if
He Might, you Could—and if you Should, I Would!

PRIN. I thought as much! Then, to my fate I yield—
So ends my cherished scheme! Oh, I had hoped
To band all women with my maiden throng,
And make them all abjure tyrannic Man!

HILD. A noble aim!

PRIN. You ridicule it now!
But if I carried out this glorious scheme,
At my exalted name Posterity
Would bow in gratitude!

HILD. But pray reflect—
If you enlist all women in your cause,
And make them all abjure tyrannic Man,
The obvious question then arises, "How
Is this Posterity to be provided?"

PRIN. I never thought of that! My Lady Blanche,
How do you solve the riddle?

BLA. Don't ask me—
Abstract Philosophy won't answer it.
Take him—he is your Shall. Give in to Fate!
PRIN. And you desert me. I alone am staunch!
HIL. Madam, you placed your trust in Woman—well,
Woman has failed you utterly—try Man,
Give him one chance, it's only fair—besides,
Women are far too precious, too divine,
To try unproven theories upon.
Experiments, the proverb says, are made
On humble subjects—try our grosser clay,
And mould it as you will!
CYR. Remember, too,
Dear Madam, if at any time you feel
A-weary of the Prince, you can return
To Castle Adamant, and rule your girls
As heretofore, you know.
PRIN. And shall I find
The Lady Psyche here?
PSY. If Cyril, ma'am,
Does not behave himself, I think you will.
PRIN. And you, Melissa, shall I find *you* here?
MEL. Madam, however Florian turns out,
Unhesitatingly I answer, No!
GAMA. Consider this, my love, if your mamma
Had looked on matters from your point of view
(I wish she had), why where would you have been?
BLA. There's an unbounded field of speculation,
On which I could discourse for hours!
PRIN. No doubt!
We will not trouble you. Hilarion,
I have been wrong—I see my error now.
Take me, Hilarion—"We will walk the world
Yoked in all exercise of noble end!
And so through those dark gates across the wild
That no man knows! Indeed, I love thee—
Come!"

FINALE

PRIN. With joy abiding,
Together gliding

Through life's variety,
In sweet society,
And thus enthroning
The love I'm owning,
On this atoning
I will rely!

CHORUS.
It were profanity
For poor humanity
To treat as vanity
The sway of Love.
In no locality
Or principality
Is our mortality
Its sway above!

HILARION.
When day is fading,
With serenading
And such frivolity
Of tender quality—
With scented showers
Of fairest flowers,
The happy hours
Will gaily fly!

CHORUS.
It were profanity, etc.

CURTAIN

THE MIKADO

OR

THE TOWN OF TITIPU

DRAMATIS PERSONÆ

THE MIKADO OF JAPAN

NANKI-POO (*his Son, disguised as a wandering minstrel, and in love with* YUM-YUM)

KO-KO (*Lord High Executioner of Titipu*)

POOH-BAH (*Lord High Everything Else*)

PISH-TUSH (*a Noble Lord*)

YUM-YUM, PITTI-SING, PEEP-BO — *Three Sisters—Wards of* KO-KO

KATISHA (*an elderly Lady, in love with* NANKI-POO)

Chorus of School-girls, Nobles, Guards, and Coolies

ACT I

COURTYARD OF KO-KO'S OFFICIAL RESIDENCE.

ACT II

KO-KO'S GARDEN.

First produced at the Savoy Theatre on March 14, 1885

THE MIKADO

OR

THE TOWN OF TITIPU

ACT I

SCENE.—*Courtyard of* KO-KO's *Palace in Titipu. Japanese nobles discovered standing and sitting in attitudes suggested by native drawings.*

CHORUS OF NOBLES

If you want to know who we are,
    We are gentlemen of Japan;
On many a vase and jar—
    On many a screen and fan,
        We figure in lively paint:
        Our attitude's queer and quaint—
        You're wrong if you think it ain't, oh!

If you think we are worked by strings,
    Like a Japanese marionette,
You don't understand these things:
    It is simply Court etiquette.
        Perhaps you suppose this throng
        Can't keep it up all day long?
        If that's your idea, you're wrong, oh!

Enter NANKI-POO *in great excitement. He carries a native guitar on his back and a bundle of ballads in his hand.*

RECIT—NANKI-POO

Gentlemen, I pray you tell me
Where a gentle maiden dwelleth,
Named Yum-Yum, the ward of Ko-Ko?
In pity speak—oh, speak, I pray you!

A NOBLE. Why, who are you who ask this question?

NANK. Come gather round me, and I'll tell you.

SONG AND CHORUS—NANKI-POO

A wandering minstrel I—
A thing of shreds and patches,
Of ballads, songs and snatches,
And dreamy lullaby!

My catalogue is long,
Through every passion ranging,
And to your humours changing
I tune my supple song!

Are you in sentimental mood?
I'll sigh with you,
Oh, sorrow, sorrow!
On maiden's coldness do you brood?
I'll do so, too—
Oh, sorrow, sorrow!
I'll charm your willing ears
With songs of lovers' fears,
While sympathetic tears
My cheeks bedew—
Oh, sorrow, sorrow!

But if patriotic sentiment is wanted,
I've patriotic ballads cut and dried;
For where'er our country's banner may be planted,
All other local banners are defied!
Our warriors, in serried ranks assembled,
Never quail—or they conceal it if they do—
And I shouldn't be surprised if nations trembled
Before the mighty troops of Titipu!

CHORUS. We shouldn't be surprised, etc.

NANK. And if you call for a song of the sea,
We'll heave the capstan round,
With a yeo heave ho, for the wind is free,
Her anchor's a-trip and her helm's a-lee,
Hurrah for the homeward bound!

CHORUS. Yeo-ho—heave ho—
Hurrah for the homeward bound!

To lay aloft in a howling breeze
May tickle a landsman's taste,
But the happiest hour a sailor sees
Is when he's down
At an inland town,
With his Nancy on his knees, yeo ho!
And his arm around her waist!

CHORUS. Then man the capstan—off we go,
As the fiddler swings us round,
With a yeo heave ho,
And a rumbelow,
Hurrah for the homeward bound!

A wandering minstrel I, etc.

Enter PISH-TUSH

PISH. And what may be your business with Yum-Yum?

NANK. I'll tell you. A year ago I was a member of the Titipu town band. It was my duty to take the cap round for contributions. While discharging this delicate office, I saw Yum-Yum. We loved each other at once, but she was betrothed to her guardian Ko-Ko, a cheap tailor, and I saw that my suit was hopeless. Overwhelmed with despair, I quitted the town. Judge of my delight when I heard, a month ago, that Ko-Ko had been condemned to death for flirting! I hurried back at once, in the hope of finding Yum-Yum at liberty to listen to my protestations.

PISH. It is true that Ko-Ko was condemned to death for flirting, but he was reprieved at the last moment, and raised to the exalted rank of Lord High Executioner under the following remarkable circumstances:

SONG—PISH-TUSH *and* CHORUS

Our great Mikado, virtuous man,
When he to rule our land began,
Resolved to try
A plan whereby
Young men might best be steadied.

So he decreed, in words succinct,
That all who flirted, leered or winked
(Unless connubially linked),
Should forthwith be beheaded.

And I expect you'll all agree
That he was right to so decree.
And I am right,
And you are right,
And all is right as right can be!

CHORUS. And you are right,
And we are right, etc.

This stern decree, you'll understand,
Caused great dismay throughout the land!
For young and old
And shy and bold
Were equally affected.
The youth who winked a roving eye,
Or breathed a non-connubial sigh,
Was thereupon condemned to die—
He usually objected.

And you'll allow, as I expect,
That he was right to so object.
And I am right,
And you are right,
And everything is quite correct!

CHORUS. And you are right,
And we are right, etc.

And so we straight let out on bail,
A convict from the county jail,
Whose head was next
On some pretext
Condemnëd to be mown off,
And made *him* Headsman, for we said,
"Who's next to be decapited
Cannot cut off another's head
Until he's cut his own off."

And we are right, I think you'll say,
To argue in this kind of way;

And I am right,
And you are right,
And all is right—too-looral-lay!

CHORUS. And you are right,
And we are right, etc.

[*Exeunt* CHORUS.

Enter POOH-BAH

NANK. Ko-Ko, the cheap tailor, Lord High Executioner of Titipu! Why, that's the highest rank a citizen can attain!

POOH. It is. Our logical Mikado, seeing no moral difference between the dignified judge who condemns a criminal to die, and the industrious mechanic who carries out the sentence, has rolled the two offices into one, and every judge is now his own executioner.

NANK. But how good of you (for I see that you are a nobleman of the highest rank) to condescend to tell all this to me, a mere strolling minstrel!

POOH. Don't mention it. I am, in point of fact, a particularly haughty and exclusive person, of pre-Adamite ancestral descent. You will understand this when I tell you that I can trace my ancestry back to a protoplasmal primordial atomic globule. Consequently, my family pride is something inconceivable. I can't help it. I was born sneering. But I struggle hard to overcome this defect. I mortify my pride continually. When all the great officers of State resigned in a body, because they were too proud to serve under an ex-tailor, did I not unhesitatingly accept all their posts at once?

PISH. And the salaries attached to them? You did.

POOH. It is consequently my degrading duty to serve this upstart as First Lord of the Treasury, Lord Chief Justice, Commander-in-Chief, Lord High Admiral, Master of the Buckhounds, Groom of the Back Stairs, Archbishop of Titipu, and Lord Mayor, both acting and elect, all rolled into one. And at a salary! A Pooh-Bah paid for his services! I a salaried minion! But I do it! It revolts me, but I do it!

NANK. And it does you credit.

POOH. But I don't stop at that. I go and dine with middle-class people on reasonable terms. I dance at cheap suburban parties for a moderate fee. I accept refreshment at any hands, however lowly. I also retail State secrets at a very low figure. For instance, any further information about Yum-Yum would come under the head of a State secret. (NANKI-POO *takes the hint, and gives him money.*) (*Aside.*) Another insult, and, I think, a light one!

SONG—POOH-BAH *with* NANKI-POO *and* PISH-TUSH

Young man, despair,
Likewise go to,
Yum-Yum the fair
You must not woo.
It will not do:
I'm sorry for you,
You very imperfect ablutioner!
This very day
From school Yum-Yum
Will wend her way,
And homeward come,
With beat of drum
And a rum-tum-tum,
To wed the Lord High Executioner!
And the brass will crash,
And the trumpets bray,
And they'll cut a dash
On their wedding day.
She'll toddle away, as all aver,
With the Lord High Executioner!

NANK. *and* POOH. And the brass will crash, etc.

It's a hopeless case,
As you may see,
And in your place
Away I'd flee;
But don't blame me—
I'm sorry to be
Of your pleasure a diminutioner.
They'll vow their pact

Extremely soon,
In point of fact
This afternoon.
Her honeymoon
With that buffoon
At seven commences, so *you* shun her!

ALL. And the brass will crash, etc.

[*Exit* PISH-TUSH.

RECIT NANKI-POO *and* POOH-BAH

NANK. And I have journeyed for a month, or nearly,
To learn that Yum-Yum, whom I love so dearly,
This day to Ko-Ko is to be united!

POOH. The fact appears to be as you've recited:
But here he comes, equipped as suits his station;
He'll give you any further information.

[*Exeunt* POOH-BAH *and* NANKI-POO.

Enter CHORUS OF NOBLES

Behold the Lord High Executioner
A personage of noble rank and title—
A dignified and potent officer,
Whose functions are particularly vital!
Defer, defer,
To the Lord High Executioner!

Enter KO-KO *attended*

SOLO—KO-KO

Taken from the county jail
By a set of curious chances;
Liberated then on bail,
On my own recognizances;
Wafted by a favouring gale
As one sometimes is in trances,
To a height that few can scale,
Save by long and weary dances;
Surely, never had a male
Under such like circumstances
So adventurous a tale
Which may rank with most romances.

CHORUS. Defer, defer,
To the Lord High Executioner, etc.

KO. Gentlemen, I'm much touched by this reception. I can only trust that by strict attention to duty I shall ensure a continuance of those favours which it will ever be my study to deserve. If I should ever be called upon to act professionally, I am happy to think that there will be no difficulty in finding plenty of people whose loss will be a distinct gain to society at large.

SONG—KO-KO *with* CHORUS OF MEN

As some day it may happen that a victim must be found,
I've got a little list—I've got a little list
Of society offenders who might well be underground,
And who never would be missed—who never would be missed!
There's the pestilential nuisances who write for autographs—
All people who have flabby hands and irritating laughs—
All children who are up in dates, and floor you with 'em flat—
All persons who in shaking hands, shake hands with you like *that*—
And all third persons who on spoiling *tête-à-têtes* insist—
They'd none of 'em be missed—they'd none of 'em be missed!

CHORUS. He's got 'em on the list—he's got 'em on the list;
And they'll none of 'em be missed—they'll none of 'em be missed.

There's the nigger serenader, and the others of his race,
And the piano-organist—I've got him on the list!
And the people who eat peppermint and puff it in your face,
They never would be missed—they never would be missed!
Then the idiot who praises, with enthusiastic tone,
All centuries but this, and every country but his own;
And the lady from the provinces, who dresses like a guy,

And who "doesn't think she waltzes, but would rather like to try";
And that singular anomaly, the lady novelist—
I don't think she'd be missed—I'm *sure* she'd not be missed!

CHORUS. He's got her on the list—he's got her on the list;
And I don't think she'll be missed—I'm *sure* she'll not be missed!

And that *Nisi Prius* nuisance, who just now is rather rife,
The Judicial humorist—I've got *him* on the list!
All funny fellows, comic men, and clowns of private life—
They'd none of 'em be missed—they'd none of 'em be missed.
And apologetic statesmen of a compromising kind,
Such as—What d'ye call him—Thing'em-bob, and likewise—Never-mind,
And 'St—'st—'st—and What's-his-name, and also You-know-who—
The task of filling up the blanks I'd rather leave to *you*.
But it really doesn't matter whom you put upon the list,
For they'd none of 'em be missed—they'd none of 'em be missed!

CHORUS. You may put 'em on the list—you may put 'em on the list;
And they'll none of 'em be missed—they'll none of 'em be missed!

Enter POOH-BAH

KO. Pooh-Bah, it seems that the festivities in connection with my approaching marriage must last a week. I should like to do it handsomely, and I want to consult you as to the amount I ought to spend upon them.

POOH. Certainly. In which of my capacities? As First Lord of the Treasury, Lord Chamberlain, Attorney-General, Chancellor of the Exchequer, Privy Purse, or Private Secretary?

KO. Suppose we say as Private Secretary.

POOH. Speaking as your Private Secretary, I should say that, as the city will have to pay for it, don't stint yourself, do it well.

KO. Exactly—as the city will have to pay for it. That is your advice.

POOH. As Private Secretary. Of course you will understand that, as Chancellor of the Exchequer, I am bound to see that due economy is observed.

KO. Oh! But you said just now "Don't stint yourself, do it well".

POOH. As Private Secretary.

KO. And now you say that due economy must be observed.

POOH. As Chancellor of the Exchequer.

KO. I see. Come over here, where the Chancellor can't hear us. (*They cross the stage.*) Now, as my Solicitor, how do you advise me to deal with this difficulty?

POOH. Oh, as your Solicitor, I should have no hesitation in saying "Chance it——"

KO. Thank you. (*Shaking his hand.*) I will.

POOH. If it were not that, as Lord Chief Justice, I am bound to see that the law isn't violated.

KO. I see. Come over here where the Chief Justice can't hear us. (*They cross the stage.*) Now, then, as First Lord of the Treasury?

POOH. Of course, as First Lord of the Treasury, I could propose a special vote that would cover all expenses, if it were not that, as Leader of the Opposition, it would be my duty to resist it, tooth and nail. Or, as Paymaster-General, I could so cook the accounts that, as Lord High Auditor, I should never discover the fraud. But then, as Archbishop of Titipu, it would be my duty to denounce my dishonesty and give myself into my own custody as First Commissioner of Police.

KO. That's extremely awkward.

POOH. I don't say that all these distinguished people couldn't be squared; but it is right to tell you that they wouldn't be sufficiently degraded in their own estimation unless they were insulted with a very considerable bribe.

KO. The matter shall have my careful consideration. But my bride and her sisters approach, and any little compliment on your part, such as an abject grovel in a characteristic Japanese attitude, would be esteemed a favour.

[*Exeunt together.*

Enter procession of YUM-YUM'S *schoolfellows, heralding* YUM-YUM, PEEP-BO, *and* PITTI-SING

CHORUS OF GIRLS

Comes a train of little ladies
 From scholastic trammels free,
Each a little bit afraid is,
 Wondering what the world can be!

Is it but a world of trouble—
  Sadness set to song?
Is its beauty but a bubble
  Bound to break ere long?

Are its palaces and pleasures
  Fantasies that fade?
And the glory of its treasures
  Shadow of a shade?

Schoolgirls we, eighteen and under,
  From scholastic trammels free,
And we wonder—how we wonder!—
  What on earth the world can be!

TRIO

YUM-YUM, PEEP-BO, *and* PITTI-SING, *with* CHORUS OF GIRLS

THE THREE. Three little maids from school are we,
Pert as a school-girl well can be,
Filled to the brim with girlish glee,
    Three little maids from school!
YUM-YUM. Everything is a source of fun. (*Chuckle.*)
PEEP-BO. Nobody's safe, for we care for none! (*Chuckle.*)
PITTI-SING. Life is a joke that's just begun! (*Chuckle.*)
THE THREE. Three little maids from school!
ALL (*dancing*). Three little maids who, all unwary,
Come from a ladies' seminary,
Freed from its genius tutelary—
THE THREE (*suddenly demure*). Three little maids from school!

YUM-YUM. One little maid is a bride, Yum-Yum—
PEEP-BO. Two little maids in attendance come—
PITTI-SING. Three little maids is the total sum.
THE THREE. Three little maids from school!
YUM-YUM. From three little maids take one away.
PEEP-BO. Two little maids remain, and they—
PITTI-SING. Won't have to wait very long, they say—
THE THREE. Three little maids from school!
ALL. (*dancing*). Three little maids who, all unwary,
Come from a ladies' seminary,
Freed from its genius tutelary—

THE THREE (*suddenly demure*). Three little maids from school!

Enter KO-KO *and* POOH-BAH

KO. At last, my bride that is to be! (*About to embrace her.*)

YUM. You're not going to kiss me before all these people?

KO. Well, that was the idea.

YUM. (*aside to* PEEP-BO). It seems odd, doesn't it?

PEEP. It's rather peculiar.

PITTI. Oh, I expect it's all right. Must have a beginning, you know.

YUM. Well, of course I know nothing about these things; but I've no objection if it's usual.

KO. Oh, it's quite usual, I think. Eh, Lord Chamberlain? (*Appealing to* POOH-BAH.)

POOH. I have known it done. (KO-KO *embraces her.*)

YUM. Thank goodness that's over! (*Sees* NANKI-POO, *and rushes to him.*) Why, that's never you? (*The Three Girls rush to him and shake his hands, all speaking at once.*)

YUM. Oh, I'm so glad! I haven't seen you for ever so long, and I'm right at the top of the school, and I've got three prizes, and I've come home for good, and I'm not going back any more!

PEEP. And have you got an engagement?—Yum-Yum's got one, but she doesn't like it, and she'd ever so much rather it was you! I've come home for good, and I'm not going back any more!

PITTI. Now tell us all the news, because you go about everywhere, and we've been at school, but, thank goodness, that's all over now, and we've come home for good, and we're not going back any more!

(*These three speeches are spoken together in one breath.*)

KO. I beg your pardon. Will you present me?

YUM. Oh, this is the musician who used—
PEEP. Oh, this is the gentleman who used—
PITTI. Oh, it is only Nanki-Poo who used—

KO. One at a time, if you please.

YUM. Oh, if you please, he's the gentleman who used to play so beautifully on the—on the——

PITTI. On the Marine Parade.

YUM. Yes, I think that was the name of the instrument.

NANK. Sir, I have the misfortune to love your ward, Yum-Yum—oh, I know I deserve your anger!

KO. Anger! not a bit, my boy. Why, I love her myself. Charming little girl, isn't she? Pretty eyes, nice hair. Taking little thing, altogether. Very glad to hear my opinion backed by a competent authority. Thank you very much. Good-bye. (*To* PISH-TUSH.) Take him away. (PISH-TUSH *removes him.*)

PITTI (*who has been examining* POOH-BAH). I beg your pardon, but what is this? Customer come to try on?

KO. That is a Tremendous Swell.

PITTI. Oh, it's alive. (*She starts back in alarm.*)

POOH. Go away, little girls. Can't talk to little girls like you. Go away, there's dears.

KO. Allow me to present you, Pooh-Bah. These are my three wards. The one in the middle is my bride elect.

POOH. What do you want me to do to them? Mind, I *will not* kiss them.

KO. No, no, you shan't kiss them; a little bow—a mere nothing—you needn't mean it, you know.

POOH. It goes against the grain. They are not young ladies, they are young persons.

KO. Come, come, make an effort, there's a good nobleman.

POOH. (*aside to* KO-KO). Well, I shan't mean it. (*With a great effort.*) How de do, little girls, how de do? (*Aside.*) Oh, my protoplasmal ancestor!

KO. That's very good. (*Girls indulge in suppressed laughter.*)

POOH. I see nothing to laugh at. It is very painful to me to have to say "How de do, little girls, how de do?" to young persons. I'm not in the habit of saying "How de do, little girls, how de do?" to anybody under the rank of a Stockbroker.

KO. (*aside to girls*). Don't laugh at him, he can't help it—he's under treatment for it. (*Aside to* POOH-BAH.) Never mind them, they don't understand the delicacy of your position.

POOH. We know how delicate it is, don't we?

KO. I should think we did! How a nobleman of your importance can do it at all is a thing I never can, never shall understand.

[KO-KO *retires up and goes off.*

QUARTET AND CHORUS OF GIRLS

YUM-YUM, PEEP-BO, PITTI-SING, *and* POOH-BAH

YUM., PEEP. *and* PITTI. So please you, Sir, we much regret
If we have failed in etiquette
Towards a man of rank so high—
We shall know better by and by.

YUM. But youth, of course, must have its fling,
So pardon us,
So pardon us,

PITTI. And don't, in girlhood's happy spring,
Be hard on us,
Be hard on us,
If we're inclined to dance and sing.
Tra la la, etc. (Dancing.)

CHORUS OF GIRLS. But youth, of course, etc.

POOH. I think you ought to recollect
You cannot show too much respect
Towards the highly titled few;
But nobody does, and why should you?
That youth at us should have its fling,
Is hard on us,
Is hard on us;
To our prerogative we cling—
So pardon us,
So pardon us,
If we decline to dance and sing.
Tra la la, etc. (*Dancing.*)

CHORUS OF GIRLS. But youth, of course, must have its fling, etc.

[*Exeunt all but* YUM-YUM.

Enter NANKI-POO

NANK. Yum-Yum, at last we are alone! I have sought you night and day for three weeks, in the belief that your guardian was beheaded, and I find that you are about to be married to him this afternoon!

YUM. Alas, yes!

NANK. But you do not love him?

YUM. Alas, no!

NANK. Modified rapture! But why do you not refuse him?

YUM. What good would that do? He's my guardian, and he wouldn't let me marry you!

NANK. But I would wait until you were of age!

YUM. You forget that in Japan girls do not arrive at years of discretion until they are fifty.

NANK. True; from seventeen to forty-nine are considered years of indiscretion.

YUM. Besides—a wandering minstrel, who plays a wind instrument outside tea-houses, is hardly a fitting husband for the ward of a Lord High Executioner.

NANK. But—— (*Aside.*) Shall I tell her? Yes! She will not betray me! (*Aloud.*) What if it should prove that, after all, I am no musician?

YUM. There! I was certain of it, directly I heard you play!

NANK. What if it should prove that I am no other than the son of his Majesty the Mikado?

YUM. The son of the Mikado! But why is your Highness disguised? And what has your Highness done? And will your Highness promise never to do it again?

NANK. Some years ago I had the misfortune to captivate Katisha, an elderly lady of my father's Court. She misconstrued my customary affability into expressions of affection, and claimed me in marriage, under my father's law. My father, the Lucius Junius Brutus of his race, ordered me to marry her within a week, or perish ignominiously on the scaffold. That night I fled his Court, and, assuming the disguise of a Second Trombone, I joined the band in which you found me when I had the happiness of seeing you! (*Approaching her.*)

YUM (*retreating*). If you please, I think your Highness had better not come too near. The laws against flirting are excessively severe.

NANK. But we are quite alone, and nobody can see us.

YUM. Still, that doesn't make it right. To flirt is capital.

NANK. It *is* capital!

YUM. And we must obey the law.

NANK. Deuce take the law!

YUM. I wish it would, but it won't!

NANK. If it were not for that, how happy we might be!

YUM. Happy indeed!

NANK. If it were not for the law, we should now be sitting side by side, like that. (*Sits by her.*)

YUM. Instead of being obliged to sit half a mile off, like that. (*Crosses and sits at other side of stage.*)

NANK. We should be gazing into each other's eyes, like that. (*Gazing at her sentimentally.*)

YUM. Breathing sighs of unutterable love—like that. (*Sighing and gazing lovingly at him.*)

NANK. With our arms round each other's waists, like that. (*Embracing her.*)

YUM. Yes, if it wasn't for the law.

NANK. If it wasn't for the law.

YUM. As it is, of course we couldn't do anything of the kind.

NANK. Not for worlds!

YUM. Being engaged to Ko-Ko, you know!

NANK. Being engaged to Ko-Ko!

DUET—YUM-YUM *and* NANKI-POO

NANK. Were you not to Ko-Ko plighted,
I would say in tender tone,
"Loved one, let us be united—
Let us be each other's own!"
I would merge all rank and station,
Worldly sneers are nought to us,
And, to mark my admiration,
I would kiss you fondly thus—
(*Kisses her.*)

BOTH. {I / He} would kiss {you / me} fondly thus— (*Kiss.*)

YUM. But as I'm engaged to Ko-Ko,
To embrace you thus, *con fuoco,*
Would be distinctly no *giuoco,*
And for yam I should get toko—

BOTH. Toko, toko, toko, toko!

NANK. So, in spite of all temptation,
Such a theme I'll not discuss,
And on no consideration
Will I kiss you fondly thus—
(*Kissing her.*)
Let me make it clear to you,
This is what I'll never do!
This, oh, this, oh, this, oh, this—
(*Kissing her.*)

TOGETHER. This, oh, this, etc.

[*Exeunt in opposite directions.*

Enter KO-KO

KO. (*looking after* YUM-YUM). There she goes! To think how entirely my future happiness is wrapped up in that little parcel! Really, it hardly seems worth while! Oh, matrimony!— (*Enter* POOH-BAH *and* PISH-TUSH.) Now then, what is it? Can't you see I'm soliloquizing? You have interrupted an apostrophe, sir!

PISH. I am the bearer of a letter from his Majesty the Mikado.

KO. (*taking it from him reverentially*). A letter from the Mikado! What in the world can he have to say to me? (*Reads letter.*) Ah, here it is at last! I thought it would come sooner or later! The Mikado is struck by the fact that no executions have taken place in Titipu for a year and decrees that unless somebody is beheaded within one month the post of Lord High Executioner shall be abolished, and the city reduced to the rank of a village!

PISH. But that will involve us all in irretrievable ruin!

KO. Yes. There is no help for it, I shall have to execute somebody at once. The only question is, who shall it be?

POOH. Well, it seems unkind to say so, but as you're already under sentence of death for flirting, everything seems to point to *you*.

KO. To me? What are you talking about? I can't execute myself.

POOH. Why not?

KO. Why not? Because, in the first place, self-decapitation is an extremely difficult, not to say dangerous, thing to attempt; and, in the second, it's suicide, and suicide is a capital offence.

POOH. That is so, no doubt.

PISH. We might reserve that point.

POOH. True, it could be argued six months hence, before the full Court.

KO. Besides, I don't see how a man *can* cut off his own head.

POOH. A man might try.

PISH. Even if you only succeeded in cutting it half off, that would be something.

POOH. It would be taken as an earnest of your desire to comply with the Imperial will.

KO. No. Pardon me, but there I am adamant. As official Headsman, my reputation is at stake, and I can't consent to embark on a professional operation unless I see my way to a successful result.

POOH. This professional conscientiousness is highly creditable to *you*, but it places us in a very awkward position.

KO. My good sir, the awkwardness of your position is grace itself compared with that of a man engaged in the act of cutting off his own head.

PISH. I am afraid that, unless you can obtain a substitute——

KO. A substitute? Oh, certainly—nothing easier. (*To* POOH-BAH.) I appoint you Lord High Substitute.

POOH. I should be delighted. Such an appointment would realize my fondest dreams. But no, at any sacrifice, I must set bounds to my insatiable ambition!

TRIO

KO-KO

My brain it teems
With endless schemes
Both good and new
For Titipu;
But if I flit,
The benefit
That I'd diffuse
The town would lose!
Now every man
To aid his clan
Should plot and plan
As best he can,
And so,
Although
I'm ready to go,
Yet recollect
'Twere disrespect
Did I neglect
To thus effect
This aim direct,
So I object—
So I object—
So I object—

POOH-BAH

I am so proud,
If I allowed
My family pride
To be my guide,
I'd volunteer
To quit this sphere
Instead of you,
In a minute or two.
But family pride
Must be denied,
And set aside,
And mortified.
And so,
Although
I wish to go,
And greatly pine
To brightly shine,
And take the line
Of a hero fine,
With grief condign
I must decline—
I must decline—
I must decline—

PISH-TUSH

I heard one day
A gentleman say
That criminals who
Are cut in two
Can hardly feel
The fatal steel,
And so are slain
Without much pain.
If this is true,
It's jolly for you;
Your courage screw
To bid us adieu,
And go
And show
Both friend and foe
How much you dare.
I'm quite aware
It's your affair,
Yet I declare
I'd take your share,
But I don't much care—
I don't much care—
I don't much care—

ALL. To sit in solemn silence in a dull, dark dock,
In a pestilential prison, with a life-long lock,
Awaiting the sensation of a short, sharp shock,
From a cheap and chippy chopper on a big black block!

[*Exeunt* POOH. *and* PISH.

KO. This is simply appalling! I, who allowed myself to be respited at the last moment, simply in order to benefit my native town, am now required to die within a month, and that by a man whom I have loaded with honours! Is this public gratitude? Is this—— (*Enter* NANKI-POO, *with a rope in his hands.*) Go away, sir! How dare you? Am I never to be permitted to soliloquize?

NANK. Oh, go on—don't mind me.

KO. What are you going to do with that rope?

NANK. I am about to terminate an unendurable existence.

KO. Terminate your existence? Oh, nonsense! What for?

NANK. Because you are going to marry the girl I adore.

KO. Nonsense, sir. I won't permit it. I am a humane man, and if you attempt anything of the kind I shall order your instant arrest. Come, sir, desist at once or I summon my guard.

NANK. That's absurd. If you attempt to raise an alarm, I instantly perform the Happy Despatch with this dagger.

KO. No, no, don't do that. This is horrible! (*Suddenly.*) Why, you cold-blooded scoundrel, are you aware that, in taking your life, you are committing a crime which —which—which is—— Oh! (*Struck by an idea.*) Substitute!

NANK. What's the matter?

KO. Is it *absolutely certain* that you are resolved to die?

NANK. Absolutely!

KO. Will *nothing* shake your resolution?

NANK. Nothing.

KO. Threats, entreaties, prayers—all useless?

NANK. All! My mind is made up.

KO. Then, if you really mean what you say, and if you are absolutely resolved to die, and if nothing whatever will shake your determination—don't spoil yourself by committing suicide, but be beheaded handsomely at the hands of the Public Executioner!

NANK. I don't see how that would benefit me.

KO. You don't? Observe: you'll have a month to live, and you'll live like a fighting-cock at my expense. When the day comes there'll be a grand public ceremonial—you'll be the central figure—no one will attempt to deprive you of that distinction. There'll be a procession—bands—dead march—bells tolling—all the girls in tears—Yum-Yum distracted—then, when it's all over, general rejoicings, and a display of fireworks in the evening. *You* won't see them, but they'll be there all the same.

NANK. Do you think Yum-Yum would really be distracted at my death?

KO. I am convinced of it. Bless you, she's the most tender-hearted little creature alive.

NANK. I should be sorry to cause her pain. Perhaps,

after all, if I were to withdraw from Japan, and travel in Europe for a couple of years, I might contrive to forget her.

KO. Oh, I don't think you could forget Yum-Yum so easily; and, after all, what is more miserable than a love-blighted life?

NANK. True.

KO. Life without Yum-Yum—why, it seems absurd!

NANK. And yet there are a good many people in the world who have to endure it.

KO. Poor devils, yes! You are quite right not to be of their number.

NANK. (*suddenly*). I *won't* be of their number!

KO. Noble fellow!

NANK. I'll tell you how we'll manage it. Let me marry Yum-Yum to-morrow, and in a month you may behead me.

KO. No, no. I draw the line at Yum-Yum.

NANK. Very good. If you can draw the line, so can I. (*Preparing rope.*)

KO. Stop, stop—listen one moment—be reasonable. How can I consent to your marrying Yum-Yum if I'm going to marry her myself?

NANK. My good friend, she'll be a widow in a month, and you can marry her then.

KO. That's true, of course. I quite see that. But, dear me! my position during the next month will be most unpleasant—most unpleasant.

NANK. Not half so unpleasant as my position at the end of it.

KO. But—dear me!—well—I agree—after all, it's only putting off my wedding for a month. But you won't prejudice her against me, will you? You see, I've educated her to be my wife; she's been taught to regard me as a wise and good man. Now I shouldn't like her views on that point disturbed.

NANK. Trust me, she shall never learn the truth from me.

FINALE

Enter CHORUS, POOH-BAH, *and* PISH-TUSH

CHORUS

With aspect stern
  And gloomy stride,
We come to learn
  How you decide.

Don't hesitate
  Your choice to name,
A dreadful fate
  You'll suffer all the same.

POOH. To ask you what you mean to do we punctually appear.

KO. Congratulate me, gentlemen, I've found a Volunteer!

ALL. The Japanese equivalent for Hear, Hear, Hear!

KO. (*presenting him*). 'Tis Nanki-Poo!

ALL. Hail, Nanki-Poo!

KO. I think he'll do?

ALL. Yes, yes, he'll do!

He yields his life if I'll Yum-Yum surrender.
Now I adore that girl with passion tender,
And could not yield her with a ready will,
  Or her allot
  If I did not
Adore myself with passion tenderer still!

Enter YUM-YUM, PEEP-BO, *and* PITTI-SING

ALL. Ah, yes!
He loves himself with passion tenderer still!

KO. (*to* NANKI-POO). Take her—she's yours!

[*Exit* KO-KO.

ENSEMBLE

NANKI-POO. The threatened cloud has passed away,
YUM-YUM. And brightly shines the dawning day;
NANKI-POO. What though the night may come too soon,
YUM-YUM. There's yet a month of afternoon!

NANKI-POO, POOH-BAH, YUM-YUM, PITTI-SING, *and* PEEP-BO

Then let the throng
Our joy advance,
With laughing song
And merry dance,

CHORUS. With joyous shout and ringing cheer,
Inaugurate our brief career!

PITTI-SING. A day, a week, a month, a year—
YUM. Or far or near, or far or near,
POOH. Life's eventime comes much too soon,
PITTI-SING. You'll live at least a honeymoon!

ALL. Then let the throng, etc.

CHORUS. With joyous shout, etc.

SOLO—POOH-BAH

As in a month you've got to die,
If Ko-Ko tells us true,
'Twere empty compliment to cry
"Long life to Nanki-Poo!"
But as one month you have to live
As fellow-citizen,
This toast with three times three we'll give—
"Long life to you—till then!"

[*Exit* POOH-BAH.

CHORUS. May all good fortune prosper you,
May you have health and riches too,
May you succeed in all you do!
Long life to you—till then!

(*Dance.*)

Enter KATISHA *melodramatically*

KAT. Your revels cease! Assist me, all of you!
CHORUS. Why, who is this whose evil eyes
Rain blight on our festivities?
KAT. I claim my perjured lover, Nanki-Poo!
Oh, fool! to shun delights that never cloy!
CHORUS. Go, leave thy deadly work undone!
KAT. Come back, oh, shallow fool! come back to joy!
CHORUS. Away, away! ill-favoured one!

NANK. (*aside to* YUM-YUM). Ah!
'Tis Katisha!
The maid of whom I told you. (*About to go.*)

KAT. (*detaining him*). No!
You shall not go,
These arms shall thus enfold you!

SONG—KATISHA

KAT. (*addressing* NANKI-POO).
Oh fool, that fleest
My hallowed joys!
Oh blind, that seest
No equipoise!
Oh rash, that judgest
From half, the whole!
Oh base, that grudgest
Love's lightest dole!
Thy heart unbind,
Oh fool, oh blind!
Give me my place,
Oh rash, oh base!

CHORUS. If she's thy bride, restore her place,
Oh fool, oh blind, oh rash, oh base!

KAT. (*addressing* YUM-YUM).
Pink cheek, that rulest
Where wisdom serves!
Bright eye, that foolest
Heroic nerves!
Rose lip, that scornest
Lore-laden years!
Smooth tongue, that warnest
Who rightly hears!
Thy doom is nigh,
Pink cheek, bright eye!
Thy knell is rung,
Rose lip, smooth tongue!

CHORUS. If true her tale, thy knell is rung,
Pink cheek, bright eye, rose lip, smooth tongue!

PITTI-SING. Away, nor prosecute your quest—
From our intention, well expressed,
You cannot turn us!
The state of your connubial views
Towards the person you accuse
Does not concern us!
For he's going to marry Yum-Yum—

ALL. Yum-Yum!

PITTI. Your anger pray bury,
For all will be merry,
I think you had better succumb—

ALL. Cumb—cumb!

PITTI. And join our expressions of glee.
On this subject I pray you be dumb—

ALL. Dumb—dumb.

PITTI. You'll find there are many
Who'll wed for a penny—
The word for your guidance is "Mum"—

ALL. Mum—mum!

PITTI. There's lots of good fish in the sea!

ALL. On this subject we pray you be dumb, etc.

SOLO—KATISHA

The hour of gladness
Is dead and gone;
In silent sadness
I live alone!
The hope I cherished
All lifeless lies,
And all has perished
Save love, which never dies!
Oh, faithless one, this insult you shall rue!
In vain for mercy on your knees you'll sue.
I'll tear the mask from your disguising!

NANK. (*aside*). Now comes the blow!

KAT. Prepare yourselves for new surprising!

NANK. (*aside*). How foil my foe?

KAT. No minstrel he, despite bravado!

YUM. (*aside, struck by an idea*). Ha! ha! I know!

KAT. He is the son of your——

[NANKI-POO, YUM-YUM, *and* CHORUS, *interrupting, sing Japanese words, to drown her voice.*

O ni! bikkuri shakkuri to!
KAT. In vain you interrupt with this tornado!
He is the only son of your——
ALL. O ni! bikkuri shakkuri to!
KAT. I'll spoil——
ALL. O ni! bikkuri shakkuri to!
KAT. Your gay gambado!
He is the son——
ALL. O ni! bikkuri shakkuri to!
KAT. Of your——
ALL. O ni! bikkuri shakkuri to!
KAT. The son of your——
ALL. O ni! bikkuri shakkuri to! oya! oya!

ENSEMBLE

KATISHA	THE OTHERS
Ye torrents roar!	We'll hear no more,
Ye tempests howl!	Ill-omened owl,
Your wrath outpour	To joy we soar,
With angry growl!	Despite your scowl!
Do ye your worst, my vengeance call	The echoes of our festival
Shall rise triumphant over all!	Shall rise triumphant over all!
Prepare for woe,	Away you go,
Ye haughty lords,	Collect your hordes;
At once I go	Proclaim your woe
Mikado-wards,	In dismal chords;
My wrongs with vengeance shall be crowned!	We do not heed their dismal sound,
My wrongs with vengeance shall be crowned!	For joy reigns everywhere around.

[KATISHA *rushes furiously up stage, clearing the crowd away right and left, finishing on steps at the back of stage.*

END OF ACT I

ACT II

SCENE.—KO-KO'S *Garden*

YUM-YUM *discovered seated at her bridal toilet, surrounded by maidens, who are dressing her hair and painting her face and lips, as she judges of the effect in a mirror.*

SOLO—PITTI-SING *and* CHORUS OF GIRLS

CHORUS.
Braid the raven hair—
  Weave the supple tress—
Deck the maiden fair,
  In her loveliness—
Paint the pretty face—
  Dye the coral lip—
Emphasize the grace
  Of her ladyship!
Art and nature, thus allied,
Go to make a pretty bride.

SOLO—PITTI-SING

Sit with downcast eye—
  Let it brim with dew—
Try if you can cry—
  We will do so, too.
When you're summoned, start

Like a frightened roe—
Flutter, little heart,
Colour, come and go!
Modesty at marriage-tide
Well becomes a pretty bride!

CHORUS

Braid the raven hair, etc.

[*Exeunt* PITTI-SING, PEEP-BO, *and* CHORUS.

YUM. Yes, I am indeed beautiful! Sometimes I sit and wonder, in my artless Japanese way, why it is that I am so much more attractive than anybody else in the whole world. Can this be vanity? No! Nature is lovely and rejoices in her loveliness. I am a child of Nature, and take after my mother.

SONG—YUM-YUM

The sun, whose rays
Are all ablaze
With ever-living glory,
Does not deny
His majesty—
He scorns to tell a story!
He don't exclaim,
"I blush for shame,
So kindly be indulgent."
But, fierce and bold,
In fiery gold,
He glories all effulgent!

I mean to rule the earth,
As he the sky—
We really know our worth,
The sun and I!

Observe his flame,
That placid dame,
The moon's Celestial Highness;
There's not a trace
Upon her face
Of diffidence or shyness:

She borrows light
That, through the night,
Mankind may all acclaim her!
And, truth to tell,
She lights up well,
So I, for one, don't blame her!

Ah, pray make no mistake,
We are not shy;
We're very wide awake,
The moon and I!

Enter PITTI-SING *and* PEEP-BO

YUM. Yes, everything seems to smile upon me. I am to be married to-day to the man I love best, and I believe I am the very happiest girl in Japan!

PEEP. The happiest girl indeed, for she is indeed to be envied who has attained happiness in all but perfection.

YUM. In "all but" perfection?

PEEP. Well, dear, it can't be denied that the fact that your husband is to be beheaded in a month is, in its way, a drawback. It does seem to take the top off it, you know.

PITTI. I don't know about that. It all depends!

PEEP. At all events, *he* will find it a drawback.

PITTI. Not necessarily. Bless you, it all depends!

YUM. (*in tears*). I think it very indelicate of you to

refer to such a subject on such a day. If my married happiness *is* to be—to be——

PEEP. Cut short.

YUM. Well, cut short—in a month, can't you let me forget it? (*Weeping.*)

Enter NANKI-POO, *followed by* PISH-TUSH

NANK. Yum-Yum in tears—and on her wedding morn!

YUM. (*sobbing*). They've been reminding me that in a month you're to be beheaded! (*Bursts into tears.*)

PITTI. Yes, we've been reminding her that you're to be beheaded. (*Bursts into tears.*)

PEEP. It's quite true, you know, you *are* to be beheaded! (*Bursts into tears.*)

NANK. (*aside*). Humph! Now, some bridegrooms would be depressed by this sort of thing! (*Aloud.*) A month? Well, what's a month? Bah! These divisions of time are purely arbitrary. Who says twenty-four hours make a day?

PITTI. There's a popular impression to that effect.

NANK. Then we'll efface it. We'll call each second a minute—each minute an hour—each hour a day—and each day a year. At that rate we've about thirty years of married happiness before us!

PEEP. And, at that rate, this interview has already lasted four hours and three-quarters!

[*Exit* PEEP-BO.

YUM. (*still sobbing*). Yes. How time flies when one is thoroughly enjoying oneself.

NANK. That's the way to look at it! Don't let's be downhearted! There's a silver lining to every cloud.

YUM. Certainly. Let's—let's be perfectly happy! (*Almost in tears.*)

PISH-TUSH. By all means. Let's—let's thoroughly enjoy ourselves.

PITTI. It's—it's absurd to cry. (*Trying to force a laugh.*)

YUM. Quite ridiculous! (*Trying to laugh.*)

[*All break into a forced and melancholy laugh.*

MADRIGAL

YUM-YUM, PITTI-SING, NANKI-POO, *and* PISH-TUSH

Brightly dawns our wedding day;
    Joyous hour, we give thee greeting!
    Whither, whither art thou fleeting?
Fickle moment, prithee stay!
    What though mortal joys be hollow?
    Pleasures come, if sorrows follow:
Though the tocsin sound, ere long,
    Ding dong! Ding dong!
Yet until the shadows fall
Over one and over all,
Sing a merry madrigal—
                A madrigal!

Fal-la—fal-la! etc. (*Ending in tears.*)

Let us dry the ready tear,
    Though the hours are surely creeping
    Little need for woeful weeping,
Till the sad sundown is near.
    All must sip the cup of sorrow—
    I to-day and thou to-morrow;
This the close of every song—
    Ding dong! Ding dong!
What, though solemn shadows fall,
Sooner, later, over all?
Sing a merry madrigal—
                A madrigal!

Fal-la—fal-la! etc. (*Ending in tears.*)

[*Exeunt* PITTI-SING *and* PISH-TUSH.

[NANKI-POO *embraces* YUM-YUM. *Enter* KO-KO. NANKI-POO *releases* YUM-YUM.

KO. Go on—don't mind me.

NANK. I'm afraid we're distressing you.

KO. Never mind, I must get used to it. Only please do it by degrees. Begin by putting your arm round her waist. (NANKI-POO *does so.*) There; let me get used to that first.

YUM. Oh, wouldn't you like to retire? It must pain you to see us so affectionate together!

KO. No, I must learn to bear it! Now oblige me by allowing her head to rest on your shoulder.

NANK. Like that? (*He does so.* KO-KO *much affected.*)

KO. I am much obliged to you. Now—kiss her! (*He does so.* KO-KO *writhes with anguish.*) Thank you—it's simple torture!

YUM. Come, come, bear up. After all, it's only for a month.

KO. No. It's no use deluding oneself with false hopes.

NANK. }
YUM. } What do you mean?

KO. (*to* YUM-YUM). My child—my poor child! (*Aside.*) How shall I break it to her? (*Aloud.*) My little bride that was to have been?

YUM. (*delighted*). *Was* to have been?

KO. Yes, you never can be mine!

NANK. } (*in ecstasy.*) { What!
YUM. } { I'm so glad!

KO. I've just ascertained that, by the Mikado's law, when a married man is beheaded his wife is buried alive.

NANK. }
YUM. } Buried alive!

KO. Buried alive. It's a most unpleasant death.

NANK. But whom did you get that from?

KO. Oh, from Pooh-Bah. He's my Solicitor.

YUM. But he may be mistaken!

KO. So I thought; so I consulted the Attorney-General, the Lord Chief Justice, the Master of the Rolls, the Judge Ordinary, and the Lord Chancellor. They're all of the same opinion. Never knew such unanimity on a point of law in my life!

NANK. But stop a bit! This law has never been put in force.

KO. Not yet. You see, flirting is the only crime punishable with decapitation, and married men never flirt.

NANK. Of course, they don't. I quite forgot that! Well, I suppose I may take it that my dream of happiness is at an end!

YUM. Darling—I don't want to appear selfish, and I love you with all my heart—I don't suppose I shall ever love anybody else half as much—but when I agreed to marry you—my own—I had no idea—pet—that I should have to be buried alive in a month!

NANK. Nor I! It's the very first I've heard of it!

YUM. It—it makes a difference, doesn't it?

NANK. It *does* make a difference, of course.

YUM. You see—burial alive—it's such a stuffy death!

NANK. I call it a beast of a death.

YUM. You see my difficulty, don't you?

NANK. Yes, and I see my own. If I insist on your carrying out your promise, I doom you to a hideous death: if I release you, you marry KO-KO at once!

TRIO.—YUM-YUM, NANKI-POO, *and* KO-KO

YUM
Here's a how-de-do!
If I marry you,
When your time has come to perish,
When the maiden whom you cherish
Must be slaughtered, too!
Here's a how-de-do!

NANK.
Here's a pretty mess!
In a month, or less,
I must die without a wedding!
Let the bitter tears I'm shedding
Witness my distress,
Here's a pretty mess!

KO.
Here's a state of things!
To her life she clings!
Matrimonial devotion
Doesn't seem to suit her notion—
Burial it brings!
Here's a state of things!

ENSEMBLE

YUM-YUM *and* NANKI-POO
With a passion that's intense
I worship and adore,
But the laws of common sense
We oughtn't to ignore.
If what he says is true,
'Tis death to marry you!
Here's a pretty state of things!
Here's a pretty how-de-do!

KO-KO
With a passion that's intense
You worship and adore,
But the laws of common sense
You oughtn't to ignore.
If what I say is true,
'Tis death to marry you!
Here's a pretty state of things!
Here's a pretty how-de-do!

[*Exeunt* YUM-YUM.

KO. (*going up to* NANKI-POO). My poor boy, I'm really very sorry for you.

NANK. Thanks, old fellow. I'm sure you are.

KO. You see I'm quite helpless.

NANK. I quite see that.

KO. I can't conceive anything more distressing than to have one's marriage broken off at the last moment. But you shan't be disappointed of a wedding—you shall come to mine.

NANK. It's awfully kind of you, but that's impossible.

KO. Why so?

NANK. To-day I die.

KO. What do you mean?

NANK. I can't live without Yum-Yum. This afternoon I perform the Happy Despatch.

KO. No, no—pardon me—I can't allow that.

NANK. Why not?

KO. Why, hang it all, you're under contract to die by the hand of the Public Executioner in a month's time! If you kill yourself, what's to become of me? Why, I shall have to be executed in your place!

NANK. It would certainly seem so!

Enter POOH-BAH

KO. Now then, Lord Mayor, what is it?

POOH. The Mikado and his suite are approaching the city, and will be here in ten minutes.

KO. The Mikado! He's coming to see whether his orders have been carried out! (*To* NANKI-POO.) Now look here, you know—this is getting serious—a bargain's a bargain, and you really mustn't frustrate the ends of justice by committing suicide. As a man of honour and a gentleman, you are bound to die ignominiously by the hands of the Public Executioner.

NANK. Very well, then—behead me.

KO. What, now?

NANK. Certainly; at once.

POOH. Chop it off! Chop it off!

KO. My good sir, I don't go about prepared to execute gentlemen at a moment's notice. Why, I never even killed a blue-bottle!

POOH. Still, as Lord High Executioner——

KO. My good sir, as Lord High Executioner, I've got to behead him in a month. I'm not ready yet. I don't know how it's done. I'm going to take lessons. I mean to begin with a guinea pig, and work my way through the animal kingdom till I come to a Second Trombone. Why, you don't suppose that, as a humane man, I'd have accepted the post of Lord High Executioner if I hadn't thought the duties were purely nominal? I *can't* kill you—I can't kill anything! I can't kill anybody! (*Weeps.*)

NANK. Come, my poor fellow, we all have unpleasant duties to discharge at times; after all, what is it? If I don't mind, why should you? Remember, sooner or later it must be done.

KO. (*springing up suddenly.*) *Must it?* I'm not so sure about that!

NANK. What do you mean?

KO. Why should I kill you when making an affidavit that you've been executed will do just as well? Here are plenty of witnesses—the Lord Chief Justice, Lord High Admiral, Commander-in-Chief, Secretary of State for the Home Department, First Lord of the Treasury, and Chief Commissioner of Police.

NANK. But where are they?

KO. There they are. They'll all swear to it—won't you? (*To* POOH-BAH.)

POOH. Am I to understand that all of us high Officers of State are required to perjure ourselves to ensure your safety?

KO. Why not? You'll be grossly insulted, as usual.

POOH. Will the insult be cash down, or at a date?

KO. It will be a ready-money transaction.

POOH. (*Aside.*) Well, it will be a useful discipline. (*Aloud.*) Very good. Choose your fiction, and I'll endorse it! (*Aside.*) Ha! ha! Family Pride, how do you like *that,* my buck?

NANK. But I tell you that life without Yum-Yum——

KO. Oh, Yum-Yum, Yum-Yum! Bother Yum-Yum! Here, Commissionaire (*to* POOH-BAH), go and fetch Yum-Yum. (*Exit* POOH-BAH.) Take Yum-Yum and marry

Yum-Yum, only go away and never come back again. (*Enter* POOH-BAH *with* YUM-YUM.) Here she is. Yum-Yum, are you particularly busy?

YUM. Not particularly.

KO. You've five minutes to spare?

YUM. Yes.

KO. Then go along with his Grace the Archbishop of Titipu; he'll marry you at once.

YUM. But if I'm to be buried alive?

KO. Now, don't ask any questions, but do as I tell you, and Nanki-Poo will explain all.

NANK. But one moment——

KO. Not for worlds. Here comes the Mikado, no doubt to ascertain whether I've obeyed his decree, and if he finds you alive I shall have the greatest difficulty in persuading him that I've beheaded you. (*Exeunt* NANKI-POO *and* YUM-YUM, *followed by* POOH-BAH.) Close thing that, for here he comes! [*Exit* KO-KO

March.—Enter procession, heralding MIKADO, *with* KATISHA

Entrance of MIKADO *and* KATISHA

(*"March of the Mikado's troops."*)

CHORUS.
Miya sama, miya sama,
On n'm-ma no mayé ni
Pira-Pira suru no wa
Nan gia na
Toko tonyaré tonyaré na?

DUET—MIKADO *and* KATISHA

MIK.
From every kind of man
Obedience I expect;
I'm the Emperor of Japan—

KAT.
And I'm his daughter-in-law elect!
He'll marry his son
(He's only got one)
To his daughter-in-law elect.

MIK.
My morals have been declared
Particularly correct;

KAT. But they're nothing at all, compared
With those of his daughter-in-law elect!
Bow—Bow—
To his daughter-in-law elect!

ALL. Bow—Bow—
To his daughter-in-law elect.

MIK. In a fatherly kind of way
I govern each tribe and sect,
All cheerfully own my sway—

KAT. Except his daughter-in-law elect!
As tough as a bone,
With a will of her own,
Is his daughter-in-law elect!

MIK. My nature is love and light—
My freedom from all defect—

KAT. Is insignificant quite,
Compared with his daughter-in-law elect!
Bow—Bow—
To his daughter-in-law elect!

ALL. Bow—Bow—
To his daughter-in-law elect!

SONG—MIKADO *and* CHORUS

A more humane Mikado never
Did in Japan exist,
To nobody second,
I'm certainly reckoned
A true philanthropist.
It is my very humane endeavour
To make, to some extent,
Each evil liver
A running river
Of harmless merriment.

My object all sublime
I shall achieve in time—
To let the punishment fit the crime—
The punishment fit the crime;

And make each prisoner pent
Unwillingly represent
A source of innocent merriment!
Of innocent merriment!

All prosy dull society sinners,
Who chatter and bleat and bore,
Are sent to hear sermons
From mystical Germans
Who preach from ten till four.
The amateur tenor, whose vocal villainies
All desire to shirk,
Shall, during off-hours,
Exhibit his powers
To Madame Tussaud's waxwork.

The lady who dyes a chemical yellow
Or stains her grey hair puce,
Or pinches her figger,
Is blacked like a nigger

With permanent walnut juice.
The idiot who, in railway carriages,
Scribbles on window-panes,
We only suffer
To ride on a buffer
In Parliamentary trains.

My object all sublime, etc.

CHORUS. His object all sublime, etc.

The advertising quack who wearies
With tales of countless cures,
His teeth, I've enacted,
Shall all be extracted
By terrified amateurs.
The music-hall singer attends a series
Of masses and fugues and "ops"
By Bach, interwoven
With Spohr and Beethoven,
At classical Monday Pops.

The billiard sharp whom any one catches,
His doom's extremely hard—
He's made to dwell—
In a dungeon cell
On a spot that's always barred.
And there he plays extravagant matches
In fitless finger-stalls
On a cloth untrue,
With a twisted cue
And elliptical billiard balls!

My object all sublime, etc.

CHORUS. His object all sublime, etc.

Enter POOH-BAH, KO-KO, *and* PITTI-SING. *All kneel*

(POOH-BAH *hands a paper to* KO-KO.)

KO. I am honoured in being permitted to welcome your Majesty. I guess the object of your Majesty's visit—your wishes have been attended to. The execution has taken place.

MIK. Oh, you've had an execution, have you?

KO. Yes. The Coroner has just handed me his certificate.

POOH. I am the Coroner. (KO-KO *hands certificate to* MIKADO.)

MIK. And this is the certificate of his death. (*Reads.*) "At Titipu, in the presence of the Lord Chancellor, Lord Chief Justice, Attorney-General, Secretary of State for the Home Department, Lord Mayor, and Groom of the Second Floor Front——"

POOH. They were all present, your Majesty. I counted them myself.

MIK. Very good house. I wish I'd been in time for the performance.

KO. A tough fellow he was, too—a man of gigantic strength. His struggles were terrific. It was really a remarkable scene.

MIK. Describe it.

TRIO AND CHORUS

KO-KO, PITTI-SING, POOH-BAH *and* CHORUS

KO. The criminal cried, as he dropped him down,
In a state of wild alarm—
With a frightful, frantic, fearful frown,
I bared my big right arm.
I seized him by his little pig-tail,
And on his knees fell he,
As he squirmed and struggled,
And gurgled and guggled,
I drew my snickersnee!
Oh, never shall I
Forget the cry,
Or the shriek that shriekèd he,
As I gnashed my teeth,
When from its sheath
I drew my snickersnee!

CHORUS

We know him well,
He cannot tell
Untrue or groundless tales—

He always tries
To utter lies,
And every time he fails.

PITTI. He shivered and shook as he gave the sign
For the stroke he didn't deserve;
When all of a sudden his eye met mine,
And it seemed to brace his nerve;
For he nodded his head and kissed his hand,
And he whistled an air, did he,
As the sabre true
Cut cleanly through
His cervical vertebræ!

When a man's afraid,
A beautiful maid
Is a cheering sight to see;
And it's oh, I'm glad
That moment sad
Was soothed by sight of me!

CHORUS

Her terrible tale
You can't assail,
With truth it quite agrees:
Her taste exact
For faultless fact
Amounts to a disease.

POOH. Now though you'd have said that head was dead
(For its owner dead was he),
It stood on its neck, with a smile well-bred,
And bowed three times to me!
It was none of your impudent off-hand nods,
But as humble as could be;
For it clearly knew
The deference due
To a man of pedigree!
And it's oh, I vow,
This deathly bow
Was a touching sight to see;
Though trunkless, yet

It couldn't forget
The deference due to me!

CHORUS

This haughty youth,
He speaks the truth
Whenever he finds it pays:
And in this case
It all took place
Exactly as he says!

[*Exeunt* CHORUS.

MIK. All this is very interesting, and I should like to have seen it. But we came about a totally different matter. A year ago my son, the heir to the throne of Japan, bolted from our Imperial Court.

KO. Indeed! Had he any reason to be dissatisfied with his position?

KAT. None whatever. On the contrary, I was going to marry him—yet he fled!

POOH. I am surprised that he should have fled from one so lovely!

KAT. That's not true.

POOH. No!

KAT. You hold that I am not beautiful because my face is plain. But you know nothing; you are still unenlightened. Learn, then, that it is not in the face alone that beauty is to be sought. My face is unattractive!

POOH. It is.

KAT. But I have a left shoulder-blade that is a miracle of loveliness. People come miles to see it. My right elbow has a fascination that few can resist.

POOH. Allow me!

KAT. It is on view Tuesdays and Fridays, on presentation of visiting card. As for my circulation, it is the largest in the world.

KO. And yet he fled!

MIK. And is now masquerading in this town, disguised as a Second Trombone.

KO.
POOH. } A Second Trombone!
PITTI.

MIK. Yes; would it be troubling you too much if I asked you to produce him? He goes by the name of——

KAT. Nanki-Poo.

MIK. Nanki-Poo.

KO. It's quite easy. That is, it's rather difficult. In point of fact, he's gone abroad!

MIK. Gone abroad! His address.

KO. Knightsbridge!

KAT. (*who is reading certificate of death*). Ha!

MIK. What's the matter?

KAT. See here—his name—Nanki-Poo—beheaded this morning. Oh, where shall I find another? Where shall I find another?

[KO-KO, POOH-BAH, *and* PITTI-SING *fall on their knees.*

MIK. (*looking at paper*). Dear, dear, dear! this is very tiresome. (*To* KO- KO.) My poor fellow, in your anxiety to carry out my wishes you have beheaded the heir to the throne of Japan!

KO. I beg to offer an unqualified apology.

POOH. I desire to associate myself with that expression of regret.

PITTI. We really hadn't the least notion——

MIK. Of course you hadn't. How could you? Come, come, my good fellow, don't distress yourself—it was no fault of yours. If a man of exalted rank chooses to disguise himself as a Second Trombone, he must take the consequences. It really distresses me to see you take on so. I've no doubt he thoroughly deserved all he got. (*They rise.*)

KO. We are infinitely obliged to your Majesty——

PITTI. Much obliged, your Majesty.

POOH. Very much obliged, your Majesty.

MIK. Obliged? not a bit. Don't mention it. How *could* you tell?

POOH. No, of course we couldn't tell who the gentleman really was.

PITTI. It wasn't written on his forehead, you know.

KO. It might have been on his pocket-handkerchief, but Japanese don't use pocket-handkerchiefs! Ha! ha! ha!

MIK. Ha! ha! ha! (*To* KATISHA.) I forget the punishment for compassing the death of the Heir Apparent.

KO. / POOH. / PITTI. } Punishment. (*They drop down on their knees again.*)

MIK. Yes. Something lingering, with boiling oil in it, I fancy. Something of that sort. I think boiling oil occurs in it, but I'm not sure. I know it's something humorous, but lingering, with either boiling oil or melted lead. Come, come, don't fret—I'm not a bit angry.

KO. (*in abject terror*). If your Majesty will accept our assurance, we had no idea——

MIK. Of course——

PITTI. I knew nothing about it.

POOH. I wasn't there.

MIK. That's the pathetic part of it. Unfortunately, the fool of an Act says "compassing the death of the Heir Apparent." There's not a word about a mistake——

KO., PITTI., *and* POOH. No!

MIK. Or not knowing——

KO. No!

MIK. Or having no notion——

PITTI. No!

MIK. Or not being there——

POOH. No!

MIK. There should be, of course——

KO., PITTI., *and* POOH. Yes!

MIK. But there isn't.

KO., PITTI., *and* POOH. Oh!

MIK. That's the slovenly way in which these Acts are always drawn. However, cheer up, it'll be all right. I'll have it altered next session. Now, let's see about your execution—will after luncheon suit you? Can you wait till then?

KO., PITTI., *and* POOH. Oh, yes—we can wait till then!

MIK. Then we'll make it after luncheon.

POOH. I don't want any lunch.

MIK. I'm really very sorry for you all, but it's an unjust world, and virtue is triumphant only in theatrical performances.

GLEE

PITTI-SING, KATISHA, KO-KO, POOH-BAH, *and* MIKADO

MIK. See how the Fates their gifts allot,
For A is happy—B is not.
Yet B is worthy, I dare say,
Of more prosperity than A!

KO., POOH., *and* PITTI. *Is* B more worthy?

KAT. I should say
He's worth a great deal more than A

ENSEMBLE.
Yet A is happy!
Oh, so happy!
Laughing, Ha! ha!
Chaffing, Ha! ha!
Nectar quaffing, Ha! ha! ha!
Ever joyous, ever gay,
Happy, undeserving A!

KO., POOH., *and* PITTI.
If I were Fortune—which I'm not—
B should enjoy A's happy lot,
And A should die in miserie—
That is, assuming I am B.

MIK. *and* KAT. But *should* A perish?

KO., POOH., *and* PITTI. That should he
(Of course, assuming I am B).
B should be happy!
Oh, so happy!
Laughing, Ha! ha!
Chaffing, Ha! ha!
Nectar quaffing, Ha! ha! ha!
But condemned to die is he,
Wretched meritorious B!

[*Exeunt* MIKADO *and* KATISHA.

KO. Well, a nice mess you've got us into, with your nodding head and the deference due to a man of pedigree!

POOH. Merely corroborative detail, intended to give artistic verisimilitude to an otherwise bald and unconvincing narrative.

PITTI. Corroborative detail indeed! Corroborative fiddlestick!

KO. And you're just as bad as he is with your cock-and-a-bull stories about catching his eye and his whistling an air. But that's so like you! You must put in your oar!

POOH. But how about your big right arm?

PITTI. Yes, and your snickersnee!

KO. Well, well, never mind that now. There's only one thing to be done. Nanki-Poo hasn't started yet—he must come to life again at once. (*Enter* NANKI-POO *and* YUM-YUM *prepared for journey.*) Here he comes. Here, Nanki-Poo, I've good news for you—you're reprieved.

NANK. Oh, but it's too late. I'm a dead man, and I'm off for my honeymoon.

KO. Nonsense! A terrible thing has just happened. It seems you're the son of the Mikado.

NANK. Yes, but that happened some time ago.

KO. Is this a time for airy persiflage? Your father is here, and with Katisha!

NANK. My father! And with Katisha!

KO. Yes, he wants you particularly.

POOH. So does she.

YUM. Oh, but he's married now.

KO. But, bless my heart! what has that to do with it?

NANK. Katisha claims me in marriage, but I can't marry her because I'm married already—consequently she will insist on my execution, and if I'm executed, my wife will have to be buried alive.

YUM. You see our difficulty.

KO. Yes. I don't know what's to be done.

NANK. There's one chance for you. If you could persuade Katisha to marry you, she would have no further claim on me, and in that case I could come to life without any fear of being put to death.

KO. I marry Katisha!

YUM. I really think it's the only course.

KO. But, my good girl, have you seen her? She's something appalling!

PITTI. Ah! that's only her face. She has a left elbow which people come miles to see!

POOH. I am told that her right heel is much admired by connoisseurs.

KO. My good sir, I decline to pin my heart upon any lady's right heel.

NANK. It comes to this: While Katisha is single, I prefer to be a disembodied spirit. When Katisha is married, existence will be as welcome as the flowers in spring.

DUET—NANKI-POO *and* KO-KO
(*With* YUM-YUM, PITTI-SING, *and* POOH-BAH)

NANK. The flowers that bloom in the spring,
Tra la,
Breathe promise of merry sunshine—
As we merrily dance and we sing,
Tra la,
We welcome the hope that they bring,
Tra la,
Of a summer of roses and wine.
And that's what we mean when we say that a thing
Is welcome as flowers that bloom in the spring.
Tra la la la la la, etc.

ALL. Tra la la la, etc.

KO. The flowers that bloom in the spring,
Tra la,
Have nothing to do with the case.
I've got to take under my wing,
Tra la,
A most unattractive old thing,
Tra la,
With a caricature of a face
And that's what I mean when I say, or I sing,
"Oh, bother the flowers that bloom in the spring."
Tra la la la la la, etc.

ALL. Tra la la la, Tra la la la, etc.

[*Dance and exeunt* NANKI-POO, YUM-YUM, POOH-BAH, PITTI-SING, *and* KO-KO.

Enter KATISHA

RECITATIVE *and* SONG—KATISHA

Alone, and yet alive! Oh, sepulchre!
My soul is still my body's prisoner!
Remote the peace that Death alone can give—
My doom, to wait! my punishment, to live!

SONG

Hearts do not break!
They sting and ache
For old love's sake,
But do not die,
Though with each breath
They long for death
As witnesseth
The living I!
Oh, living I!
Come, tell me why,
When hope is gone,
Dost thou stay on?
Why linger here,
Where all is drear?
Oh, living I!
Come, tell me why,
When hope is gone,
Dost thou stay on?
May not a cheated maiden die?

KO. (*entering and approaching her timidly*). Katisha!

KAT. The miscreant who robbed me of my love! But vengeance pursues—they are heating the cauldron!

KO. Katisha—behold a suppliant at your feet! Katisha—mercy!

KAT. Mercy? Had you mercy on him? See here, you! You have slain my love. He did not love *me,* but he would have loved me in time. I am an acquired taste—only the educated palate can appreciate *me*. I was educating *his* palate when he left me. Well, he is dead, and where shall I find another? It takes years to train a man to love me. Am I to go through the weary round again, and, at the same time, implore mercy for you who robbed me of my prey—I mean my pupil—just as his education was on the point of completion? Oh, where shall I find another?

KO. (*suddenly, and with great vehemence*). Here!—Here!

KAT. What!!!

KO. (*with intense passion*). Katisha, for years I have loved you with a white-hot passion that is slowly but surely consuming my very vitals! Ah, shrink not from me! If there is aught of woman's mercy in your heart, turn not away from a love-sick suppliant whose every fibre thrills at your tiniest touch! True it is that, under a poor mask of disgust, I have endeavoured to conceal a passion whose inner fires are broiling the soul within me! But the fire will not be smothered—it defies all attempts at extinction, and, breaking forth, all the more eagerly for its long restraint, it declares itself in words that will not be weighed—that cannot be schooled—that should not be too severely criticised. Katisha, I dare not hope for your love—but I will not live without it! Darling!

KAT. You, whose hands still reek with the blood of my betrothed, dare to address words of passion to the woman you have so foully wronged!

KO. I do—accept my love, or I perish on the spot!

KAT. Go to! Who knows so well as I that no one ever yet died of a broken heart!

KO. You know not what you say. Listen!

SONG—KO-KO

On a tree by a river a little tom-tit
Sang "Willow, titwillow, titwillow!"
And I said to him, "Dicky-bird, why do you sit
Singing 'Willow, titwillow, titwillow'?"
"Is it weakness of intellect, birdie?" I cried,
"Or a rather tough worm in your little inside?"
With a shake of his poor little head, he replied,
"Oh, willow, titwillow, titwillow!"

He slapped at his chest, as he sat on that bough,
Singing "Willow, titwillow, titwillow!"
And a cold perspiration bespangled his brow,
Oh, willow, titwillow, titwillow!
He sobbed and he sighed, and a gurgle he gave,
Then he plunged himself into the billowy wave,
And an echo arose from the suicide's grave—
"Oh, willow, titwillow, titwillow!"

Now I feel just as sure as I'm sure that my name
Isn't Willow, titwillow, titwillow,
That 'twas blighted affection that made him exclaim
"Oh, willow, titwillow, titwillow!"
And if you remain callous and obdurate, I
Shall perish as he did, and you will know why,
Though I probably shall not exclaim as I die,
"Oh, willow, titwillow, titwillow!"

[*During this song* KATISHA *has been greatly affected, and at the end is almost in tears.*

KAT. (*whimpering*). Did he really die of love?

KO. He really did.

KAT. All on account of a cruel little hen?

KO. Yes.

KAT. Poor little chap!

KO. It's an affecting tale, and quite true. I knew the bird intimately.

KAT. Did you? He must have been very fond of her.

KO. His devotion was something extraordinary.

KAT. (*still whimpering*). Poor little chap! And—and if I refuse you, will you go and do the same?

KO. At once.

KAT. No, no—you mustn't! Anything but that! (*Falls on his breast.*) Oh, I'm a silly little goose!

KO. (*making a wry face*). You are!

KAT. And you won't hate me because I'm just a little teeny weeny wee bit bloodthirsty, will you?

KO. Hate you? Oh, Katisha! is there not beauty even in bloodthirstiness?

KAT. My idea exactly.

DUET—KATISHA *and* KO-KO

KAT. There is beauty in the bellow of the blast,
There is grandeur in the growling of the gale,
There is eloquent outpouring
When the lion is a-roaring,
And the tiger is a-lashing of his tail!
KO. Yes, I like to see a tiger
From the Congo or the Niger,
And especially when lashing of his tail!
KAT. Volcanoes have a splendour that is grim,
And earthquakes only terrify the dolts,
But to him who's scientific
There's nothing that's terrific
In the falling of a flight of thunderbolts!
KO. Yes, in spite of all my meekness,
If I have a little weakness,
It's a passion for a flight of thunderbolts!

BOTH. If that is so,
Sing derry down derry!
It's evident, very,
Our tastes are one.
Away we'll go,
And merrily marry,
Nor tardily tarry
Till day is done!

KO. There is beauty in extreme old age—
Do you fancy you are elderly enough?
Information I'm requesting
On a subject interesting:
Is a maiden all the better when she's tough?
KAT. Throughout this wide dominion
It's the general opinion
That she'll last a good deal longer when she's tough.
KO. Are you old enough to marry, do you think?
Won't you wait till you are eighty in the shade?
There's a fascination frantic
In a ruin that's romantic;
Do you think you are sufficiently decayed?

KAT. To the matter that you mention
I have given some attention,
And I think I am sufficiently decayed.

BOTH. If that is so,
Sing derry down derry!
It's evident, very,
Our tastes are one!
Away we'll go,
And merrily marry,
Nor tardily tarry
Till day is done!

[*Exeunt together.*

Flourish. Enter the MIKADO, *attended by* PISH-TUSH *and Court*

MIK. Now then, we've had a capital lunch, and we're quite ready. Have all the painful preparations been made?

PISH. Your Majesty, all is prepared.

MIK. Then produce the unfortunate gentleman and his two well-meaning but misguided accomplices.

Enter KO-KO, KATISHA, POOH-BAH, *and* PITTI-SING. *They throw themselves at the* MIKADO'S *feet*

KAT. Mercy! Mercy for Ko-Ko! Mercy for Pitti-Sing! Mercy even for Pooh-Bah!

MIK. I beg your pardon, I don't think I quite caught that remark.

POOH. Mercy even for Pooh-Bah.

KAT. Mercy! My husband that was to have been is dead, and I have just married this miserable object.

MIK. Oh! You've not been long about it!

KO. We were married before the Registrar.

POOH. *I* am the Registrar.

MIK. I see. But my difficulty is that, as you have slain the Heir Apparent——

Enter NANKI-POO *and* YUM-YUM. *They kneel*

NANKI. The Heir Apparent is *not* slain.

MIK. Bless my heart, my son!

YUM. And your daughter-in-law elected!

KAT. (*seizing* KO-KO). Traitor, you have deceived me!

MIK. Yes, you are entitled to a little explanation, but I think he will give it better whole than in pieces.

KO. Your Majesty, it's like this: It is true that I stated that I had killed Nanki-Poo——

MIK. Yes, with most affecting particulars.

POOH. Merely corroborative detail intended to give artistic verisimilitude to a bald and——

KO. *Will* you refrain from putting in your oar? (*To* MIKADO.) It's like this: When your Majesty says, "Let a thing be done," it's as good as done—practically, it *is* done—because your Majesty's will is law. Your Majesty says, "Kill a gentleman," and a gentleman is told off to be killed. Consequently, that gentleman is as good as dead—practically, he *is* dead—and if he is dead, why not say so?

MIK. I see. Nothing could possibly be more satisfactory!

FINALE

PITTI. For he's gone and married Yum-Yum—
ALL. Yum-Yum!
PITTI. Your anger pray bury,
For all will be merry,
I think you had better succumb—
ALL. Cumb—cumb!
PITTI. And join our expressions of glee!
KO. On this subject I pray you be dumb—
ALL. Dumb—dumb!
KO. Your notions, though many,
Are not worth a penny,
The word for your guidance is "Mum"—
ALL. Mum—Mum!
KO. You've a very good bargain in me.
ALL. On this subject we pray you be dumb—
Dumb—dumb!
We think you had better succumb—
Cumb—cumb!
You'll find there are many
Who'll wed for a penny,
There are lots of good fish in the sea.

YUM. *and* NANK. The threatened cloud has passed away,
And brightly shines the dawning day;
What though the night may come too soon,
We've years and years of afternoon!

ALL.
Then let the throng
Our joy advance,
With laughing song
And merry dance,
With joyous shout and ringing cheer,
Inaugurate our new career!
Then let the throng, etc.

CURTAIN

RUDDIGORE

OR

THE WITCH'S CURSE

DRAMATIS PERSONÆ

MORTALS

SIR RUTHVEN MURGATROYD (*disguised as Robin Oakapple, a Young Farmer*)

RICHARD DAUNTLESS (*his Foster-Brother—a Man-o'-war's-man*)

SIR DESPARD MURGATROYD, OF RUDDIGORE (*a Wicked Baronet*)

OLD ADAM GOODHEART (*Robin's Faithful Servant*)

ROSE MAYBUD (*a Village Maiden*)

MAD MARGARET

DAME HANNAH (*Rose's Aunt*)

ZORAH }
RUTH } (*Professional Bridesmaids*)

GHOSTS

SIR RUPERT MURGATROYD (*the First Baronet*)

SIR JASPER MURGATROYD (*the Third Baronet*)

SIR LIONEL MURGATROYD (*the Sixth Baronet*)

SIR CONRAD MURGATROYD (*the Twelfth Baronet*)

SIR DESMOND MURGATROYD (*the Sixteenth Baronet*)

SIR GILBERT MURGATROYD (*the Eighteenth Baronet*)

SIR MERVYN MURGATROYD (*the Twentieth Baronet*)

AND

SIR RODERIC MURGATROYD (*the Twenty-first Baronet*)

Chorus of Officers, Ancestors, Professional Bridesmaids, and Villagers

ACT I

THE FISHING VILLAGE OF REDERRING, IN CORNWALL

ACT II

THE PICTURE GALLERY IN RUDDIGORE CASTLE

TIME

EARLY IN THE 19TH CENTURY

First produced at the Savoy Theatre on January 22, 1887

RUDDIGORE

OR

THE WITCH'S CURSE

ACT I

SCENE.—*The fishing village of Rederring (in Cornwall). ROSE MAYBUD's cottage is seen L.*

Enter Chorus of Bridesmaids. They range themselves in front of ROSE's cottage

CHORUS OF BRIDESMAIDS

Fair is Rose as the bright May-day;
Soft is Rose as the warm west-wind;
Sweet is Rose as the new-mown hay—
Rose is the queen of maiden-kind!
Rose, all glowing
With virgin blushes, say—
Is anybody going
To marry you to-day?

SOLO—ZORAH

Every day, as the days roll on,
Bridesmaids' garb we gaily don,
Sure that a maid so fairly famed
Can't long remain unclaimed.
Hour by hour and day by day,
Several months have passed away,
Though she's the fairest flower that blows,
No one has married Rose!

CHORUS

Rose, all glowing
With virgin blushes, say—

Is anybody going
To marry you to-day?

Enter DAME HANNAH, *from cottage*

HANNAH. Nay, gentle maidens, you sing well but vainly, for Rose is still heart-free, and looks but coldly upon her many suitors.

ZORAH. It's very disappointing. Every young man in the village is in love with her, but they are appalled by her beauty and modesty, and won't declare themselves; so, until she makes her own choice, there's no chance for anybody else.

RUTH. This is, perhaps, the only village in the world that possesses an endowed corps of professional bridesmaids who are bound to be on duty every day from ten to four—and it is at least six months since our services were required. The pious charity by which we exist is practically wasted!

ZOR. We shall be disendowed—that will be the end of it! Dame Hannah—you're a nice old person—*you* could marry if you liked. There's old Adam—Robin's faithful servant—he loves you with all the frenzy of a boy of fourteen.

HAN. Nay—that may never be, for I am pledged!

ALL. To whom?

HAN. To an eternal maidenhood! Many years ago I was betrothed to a god-like youth who woo'd me under an assumed name. But on the very day upon which our wedding was to have been celebrated, I discovered that he was no other than Sir Roderic Murgatroyd, one of the bad Baronets of Ruddigore, and the uncle of the man who now bears that title. As a son of that accursed race he was no husband for an honest girl, so, madly as I loved him, I left him then and there. He died but ten years since, but I never saw him again.

ZOR. But why should you not marry a bad Baronet of Ruddigore?

RUTH. All baronets are bad; but was he worse than other baronets?

HAN. My child, he was accursed.

ZOR. But who cursed him? Not you, I trust!

HAN. The curse is on all his line and has been, ever since the time of Sir Rupert, the first Baronet. Listen, and you shall hear the legend:

LEGEND—HANNAH

Sir Rupert Murgatroyd
His leisure and his riches
He ruthlessly employed
In persecuting witches.
With fear he'd make them quake—
He'd duck them in his lake—
He'd break their bones
With sticks and stones,
And burn them at the stake!

CHORUS. This sport he much enjoyed,
Did Rupert Murgatroyd—
No sense of shame
Or pity came
To Rupert Murgatroyd!

Once, on the village green,
A palsied hag he roasted,
And what took place, I ween,
Shook his composure boasted;
For, as the torture grim
Seized on each withered limb,
The writhing dame
'Mid fire and flame
Yelled forth this curse on him:

"Each lord of Ruddigore,
Despite his best endeavour,
Shall do one crime, or more,
Once, every day, for ever!
This doom he can't defy,
However he may try,
For should he stay
His hand, that day
In torture he shall die!"

The prophecy came true:
Each heir who held the title

Had, every day, to do
Some crime of import vital;
Until, with guilt o'erplied,
"I'll sin no more!" he cried,
And on the day
He said that say,
In agony he died!

CHORUS. And thus, with sinning cloyed,
Has died each Murgatroyd,
And so shall fall,
Both one and all,
Each coming Murgatroyd!

[*Exeunt Chorus of Bridesmaids.*

Enter ROSE MAYBUD *from cottage, with small basket on her arm*

HAN. Whither away, dear Rose? On some errand of charity, as is thy wont?

ROSE. A few gifts, dear aunt, for deserving villagers. Lo, here is some peppermint rock for old gaffer Gadderby, a set of false teeth for pretty little Ruth Rowbottom, and a pound of snuff for the poor orphan girl on the hill.

HAN. Ah, Rose, pity that so much goodness should not help to make some gallant youth happy for life! Rose, why dost thou harden that little heart of thine? Is there none hereaway whom thou couldst love?

ROSE. And if there were such an one, verily it would ill become me to tell him so.

HAN. Nay, dear one, where true love is, there is little need of prim formality.

ROSE. Hush, dear aunt, for thy words pain me sorely. Hung in a plated dish-cover to the knocker of the workhouse door, with naught that I could call mine own, save a change of baby-linen and a book of etiquette, little wonder if I have always regarded that work as a voice from a parent's tomb. This hallowed volume (*producing a book of etiquette*), composed, if I may believe the title-page, by no less an authority than the wife of a Lord Mayor, has been, through life, my guide and monitor.

By its solemn precepts I have learnt to test the moral worth of all who approach me. The man who bites his bread, or eats peas with a knife, I look upon as a lost creature, and he who has not acquired the proper way of entering and leaving a room is the object of my pitying horror. There are those in this village who bite their nails, dear aunt, and nearly all are wont to use their pocket combs in public places. In truth I could pursue this painful theme much further, but behold, I have said enough.

HAN. But is there not one among them who is faultless, in thine eyes? For example—young Robin. He combines the manners of a Marquis with the morals of a Methodist. Couldst thou not love *him?*

ROSE. And even if I could, how should I confess it unto him? For lo, he is shy, and sayeth naught!

BALLAD—ROSE

If somebody there chanced to be
Who loved me in a manner true,
My heart would point him out to me,
And I would point him out to you.
(*Referring to book.*) But here it says of those who point—
Their manners must be out of joint—
You *may* not point—
You *must* not point—
It's manners out of joint, to point!
Had I the love of such as he,
Some quiet spot he'd take me to,
Then he could whisper it to me,
And I could whisper it to you.
(*Referring to book.*) But whispering, I've somewhere met,
Is contrary to etiquette:
Where can it be? (*Searching book.*)
Now let me see—(*Finding reference.*)
Yes, yes!
It's contrary to etiquette!

(*Showing it to* HANNAH)

If any well-bred youth I knew,
Polite and gentle, neat and trim,

Then I would hint as much to you,
And you could hint as much to him.
(*Referring to book.*) But here it says, in plainest print,
"It's most unladylike to hint"—
You *may* not hint,
You *must* not hint—
It says you mustn't hint, in print!
And if I loved him through and through—
(True love and not a passing whim),
Then I could speak of it to you,
And you could speak of it to him.
(*Referring to book.*) But here I find it doesn't do
To speak until you're spoken to.
Where can it be? (*Searching book.*)
Now let me see—(*Finding reference.*)
Yes, yes!
"Don't speak until you're spoken to!"

[*Exit* HANNAH.

ROSE. Poor aunt! Little did the good soul think, when she breathed the hallowed name of Robin, that he would do even as well as another. But he resembleth all the youths in this village, in that he is unduly bashful in my presence, and lo, it is hard to bring him to the point. But soft, he is here!

[ROSE *is about to go when* ROBIN *enters and calls her.*

ROBIN. Mistress Rose!

ROSE. (*Surprised.*) Master Robin!

ROB. I wished to say that—it is fine.

ROSE. It is passing fine.

ROB. But we do want rain.

ROSE. Aye, sorely! Is that all?

ROB. (*Sighing.*) That is all.

ROSE. Good day, Master Robin!

ROB. Good day, Mistress Rose! (*Both going—both stop.*)

ROSE. } I crave pardon, I——
ROB. } I beg pardon, I——

ROSE. You were about to say?——

ROB. I would fain consult you——

ROSE. Truly?
ROB. It is about a friend.
ROSE. In truth I have a friend myself.
ROB. Indeed? I mean, of course——
ROSE. And I would fain consult you——
ROB. (*Anxiously.*) About him?
ROSE. (*Prudishly.*) About *her*.
ROB. (*Relieved.*) Let us consult one another.

DUET—ROBIN *and* ROSE

ROB. I know a youth who loves a little maid—
(Hey, but his face is a sight for to see!)
Silent is he, for he's modest and afraid—
(Hey, but he's timid as a youth can be!)

ROSE. I know a maid who loves a gallant youth,
(Hey, but she sickens as the days go by!)
She cannot tell him all the sad, sad truth—
(Hey, but I think that little maid will die!)

ROB. Poor little man!

ROSE. Poor little maid!

ROB. Poor little man!

ROSE. Poor little maid!

BOTH. Now tell me pray, and tell me true,
What in the world should the {young man / maiden} do?

ROB. He cannot eat and he cannot sleep—
(Hey, but his face is a sight for to see!)
Daily he goes for to wail—for to weep
(Hey, but he's wretched as a youth can be!)

ROSE. She's very thin and she's very pale—
(Hey, but she sickens as the days go by!)
Daily she goes for to weep—for to wail—
(Hey, but I think that little maid will die!)

ROB. Poor little maid!

ROSE. Poor little man!

ROB. Poor little maid!

ROSE. Poor little man!

BOTH. Now tell me pray, and tell me true,
What in the world should the {young man / maiden} do?

ROSE. If I were the youth I should offer her my name—
(Hey, but her face is a sight for to see!)
ROB. If I were the maid I should fan his honest flame—
(Hey, but he's bashful as a youth can be!)
ROSE. If I were the youth I should speak to her to-day—
(Hey, but she sickens as the days go by!)
ROB. If I were the maid I should meet the lad half way—
(For I really do believe that timid youth will die!)

ROSE. Poor little man!

ROB. Poor little maid!

ROSE. Poor little man!

ROB. Poor little maid!

BOTH. I thank you, {miss, / sir,} for your counsel true;
I'll tell that {youth / maid} what {he / she} ought to do!

[*Exit* ROSE.

ROB. Poor child! I sometimes think that if she wasn't quite so particular I might venture—but no, no—even then I should be unworthy of her!

He sits desponding. Enter OLD ADAM

ADAM. My kind master is sad! Dear Sir Ruthven Murgatroyd——

ROB. Hush! As you love me, breathe not that hated name. Twenty years ago, in horror at the prospect of inheriting that hideous title, and with it the ban that compels all who succeed to the baronetcy to commit at least one deadly crime per day, for life, I fled my home, and concealed myself in this innocent village under the name of Robin Oakapple. My younger brother, Despard, believing me to be dead, succeeded to the title and its attendant curse. For twenty years I have been dead and buried. Don't dig me up now.

ADAM. Dear master, it shall be as you wish, for have I not sworn to obey you for ever in all things? Yet, as we are here alone, and as I belong to that particular description of good old man to whom the truth is a refreshing novelty, let me call you by your own right title once more! (ROBIN *assents.*) Sir Ruthven Murgatroyd! Baronet! Of Ruddigore! Whew! It's like eight hours at the seaside!

ROB. My poor old friend! Would there were more like you!

ADAM. Would there were indeed! But I bring you good tidings. Your foster-brother, Richard, has returned from sea—his ship the *Tom-Tit* rides yonder at anchor, and he himself is even now in this very village!

ROB. My beloved foster-brother? No, no—it cannot be!

ADAM. It is even so—and see, he comes this way!

[*Exeunt together.*

Enter Chorus of Bridesmaids

CHORUS

From the briny sea
Comes young Richard, all victorious!
Valorous is he—
His achievements all are glorious
Let the welkin ring
With the news we bring
Sing it—shout it—
Tell about it—
Safe and sound returneth he,
All victorious from the sea!

Enter RICHARD. *The girls welcome him as he greets old acquaintances*

BALLAD—RICHARD

I shipped, d'ye see, in a Revenue sloop,
And, off Cape Finistere,
A merchantman we see,
A Frenchman, going free,
So we made for the bold Mounseer,
D'ye see?
We made for the bold Mounseer.
But she proved to be a Frigate—and she up with her ports,
And fires with a thirty-two!
It come uncommon near,
But we answered with a cheer,
Which paralysed the Parley-voo,
D'ye see?
Which paralysed the Parley-voo!
Then our Captain he up and he says, says he,
"That chap we need not fear,—
We can take her, if we like,
She is sartin for to strike,

For she's only a darned Mounseer,
D'ye see?
She's only a darned Mounseer!
But to fight a French fal-lal—it's like hittin' of a gal—
It's a lubberly thing for to do;
For we, with our faults,
Why we're sturdy British salts,
While she's only a Parley-voo,
D'ye see?
While she's only a Parley-voo!"

So we up with our helm, and we scuds before the breeze
As we gives a compassionating cheer;
Froggee answers with a shout
As he sees us go about,
Which was grateful of the poor Mounseer,
D'ye see?
Which was grateful of the poor Mounseer!
And I'll wager in their joy they kissed each other's cheek
(Which is what them furriners do),

And they blessed their lucky stars
We were hardy British tars
Who had pity on a poor Parley-voo,
D'ye see?
Who had pity on a poor Parley-voo!

(HORNPIPE)

[*Exeunt* CHORUS.

Enter ROBIN

ROB. Richard!

RICH. Robin!

ROB. My beloved foster-brother, and very dearest friend, welcome home again after ten long years at sea! It is such deeds as yours that cause our flag to be loved and dreaded throughout the civilized world!

RICH. Why, lord love ye, Rob, that's but a trifle to what we *have* done in the way of sparing life! I believe I may say, without exaggeration, that the marciful little *Tom-Tit* has spared more French frigates than any craft afloat! But 'taint for a British seaman to brag, so I'll just stow my jawin' tackle and belay. (ROBIN *sighs.*) But 'vast heavin', messmate, what's brought *you* all a-cockbill?

ROB. Alas, Dick, I love Rose Maybud, and love in vain!

RICH. *You* love in vain? Come, that's too good! Why, you're a fine strapping muscular young fellow—tall and strong as a to'-gall'n'-m'st—taut as a forestay—aye, and a barrowknight to boot, if all had their rights!

ROB. Hush, Richard—not a word about my true rank, which none here suspect. Yes, I know well enough that few men are better calculated to win a woman's heart than I. I'm a fine fellow, Dick, and worthy any woman's love—happy the girl who gets me, say I. But I'm timid, Dick; shy—nervous—modest—retiring—diffident—and I cannot tell her, Dick, I cannot tell her! Ah, you've no idea what a poor opinion I have of myself, and how little I deserve it.

RICH. Robin, do you call to mind how, years ago, we swore that, come what might, we would always act upon our hearts' dictates?

ROB. Aye, Dick, and I've always kept that oath. In doubt, difficulty, and danger I've always asked my heart what I should do, and it has never failed me.

RICH. Right! Let your heart be your compass, with a clear conscience for your binnacle light, and you'll sail ten knots on a bowline, clear of shoals, rocks, and quicksands! Well, now, what does my heart say in this here difficult situation? Why, it says, "Dick," it says—(it calls me Dick acos it's known me from a babby)—"Dick," it says, "*you* ain't shy—*you* ain't modest—speak you up for him as is!" Robin, my lad, just you lay me alongside, and when she's becalmed under my lee, I'll spin her a yarn that shall sarve to fish you two together for life!

ROB. Will you do this thing for me? Can you, do you think? Yes (*feeling his pulse*). There's no false modesty about *you*. Your—what I would call bumptious self-assertiveness (I mean the expression in its complimentary sense) has already made you a bos'n's mate, and it will make an admiral of you in time, if you work it properly, you dear, incompetent old impostor! My dear fellow, I'd give my right arm for one tenth of your modest assurance!

SONG—ROBIN

My boy, you may take it from me,
That of all the afflictions accurst
With which a man's saddled
And hampered and addled,
A diffident nature's the worst.
Though clever as clever can be—
A Crichton of early romance—
You must stir it and stump it,
And blow your own trumpet,
Or, trust me, you haven't a chance!

If you wish in the world to advance,
Your merits you're bound to enhance,
You must stir it and stump it,
And blow your own trumpet,
Or, trust me, you haven't a chance!

Now take, for example, *my* case:
I've a bright intellectual brain—
In all London city
There's no one so witty—
I've though so again and again.
I've a highly intelligent face—
My features cannot be denied—
But, whatever I try, sir,
I fail in—and why, sir?
I'm modesty personified!

If you wish in the world to advance, etc.

As a poet, I'm tender and quaint—
I've passion and fervour and grace—
From Ovid and Horace
To Swinburne and Morris,
They all of them take a back place.
Then I sing and I play and I paint:
Though none are accomplished as I,
To say so were treason:
You ask me the reason?
I'm diffident, modest, and shy!

If you wish in the world to advance, etc.

[*Exit* ROBIN.

RICH. (*looking after him*). Ah, it's a thousand pities he's such a poor opinion of himself, for a finer fellow don't walk! Well, I'll do my best for him. "Plead for him as though it was for your own father"—that's what my heart's a-remarkin' to me just now. But here she comes! Steady! Steady it is! (*Enter* ROSE—*he is much struck by her.*) By the Port Admiral, but she's a tight little craft! Come, come, she's not for you, Dick, and yet—she's fit to marry Lord Nelson! By the Flag of Old England, I can't look at her unmoved.

ROSE. Sir, you are agitated——

RICH. Aye, aye, my lass, well said! I am agitated, true enough!—took flat aback, my girl; but 'tis naught—'twill pass. (*Aside.*) This here heart of mine's a-dictatin' to me like anythink. Question is, Have I a right to disregard its promptings?

ROSE. Can I do aught to relieve thine anguish, for it seemeth to me that thou art in sore trouble? This apple—(*offering a damaged apple*).

RICH. (*looking at it and returning it*). No, my lass, 'taint that: I'm—I'm took flat aback—I never see anything like you in all my born days. Parbuckle me, if you ain't the loveliest gal I've ever set eyes on. There—I can't say fairer than that, can I?

ROSE. No. (*Aside.*) The question is, Is it meet that an utter stranger should thus express himself? (*Refers to book.*) Yes—"Always speak the truth."

RICH. I'd no thoughts of sayin' this here to you on my own account, for, truth to tell, I was chartered by another; but when I see you my heart it up and it says, says it, "This is the very lass for *you,* Dick"—"speak up to her, Dick," it says—it calls me Dick acos we was at school together)—"tell her all, Dick," it says, "never sail under false colours—it's mean!" *That's* what my heart tells me to say, and in my rough, common-sailor fashion, I've said it, and I'm a-waiting for your reply. I'm a-tremblin', miss. Lookye here—(*holding out his hand*). That's narvousness!

ROSE (*aside*). Now, how should a maiden deal with such an one? (*Consults book.*) "Keep no one in unnecessary suspense." (*Aloud.*) Behold, I will not keep you in unnecessary suspense. (*Refers to book.*) "In accepting an offer of marriage, do so with apparent hesitation." (*Aloud.*) I take you, but with a certain show of reluctance. (*Refers to book.*) "Avoid any appearance of eagerness." (*Aloud.*) Though you will bear in mind that I am far from anxious to do so. (*Refers to book.*) "A little show of emotion will not be misplaced!" (*Aloud.*) Pardon this tear! (*Wipes her eye.*)

RICH. Rose, you've made me the happiest blue-jacket in England! I wouldn't change places with the Admiral of the Fleet, no matter who he's a-huggin' of at this present moment! But, axin' your pardon, miss (*wiping his lips with his hand*), might I be permitted to salute the flag I'm goin' to sail under?

ROSE (*referring to book*). "An engaged young lady should not permit too many familiarities." (*Aloud.*) Once! (RICHARD *kisses her.*)

DUET—RICHARD *and* ROSE

RICH. The battle's roar is over,
O my love!
Embrace thy tender lover,
O my love!
From tempests' welter,
From war's alarms,
O give me shelter
Within those arms!
Thy smile alluring,
All heart-ache curing,
Gives peace enduring,
O my love!

ROSE. If heart both true and tender,
O my love!
A life-love can engender,
O my love!
A truce to sighing
And tears of brine,
For joy undying
Shall aye be mine,
And thou and I, love,
Shall live and die, love,
Without a sigh, love—
My own, my love!

Enter ROBIN, *with* CHORUS OF BRIDESMAIDS

CHORUS

If well his suit has sped,
Oh, may they soon be wed!
Oh, tell us, tell us, pray,
What doth the maiden say?
In singing are we justified,
Hail the Bridegroom—hail the Bride!
Let the nuptial knot be tied:
In fair phrases,
Hymn their praises,
Hail the Bridegroom—hail the Bride?

ROB. Well—what news? Have you spoken to her?

RICH. Aye, my lad, I have—so to speak—spoke her.

ROB. And she refuses?

RICH. Why, no, I can't truly say she do.

ROB. Then she accepts! My darling! (*Embraces her.*)

BRIDESMAIDS

Hail the Bridegroom—hail the Bride! etc.

ROSE (*aside, referring to her book*). Now, what should a maiden do when she is embraced by the wrong gentleman?

RICH. Belay, my lad, belay. You don't understand.

ROSE. Oh, sir, belay, I beseech you!

RICH. You see, it's like this: she accepts—but it's *me!*

ROB. You! (RICHARD *embraces* ROSE.)

BRIDESMAIDS

Hail the Bridegroom—hail the Bride!
When the nuptial knot is tied——

ROB. (*interrupting angrily*). Hold your tongues, will you! Now then, what does this mean?

RICH. My poor lad, my heart grieves for thee, but it's like this: the moment I see her, and just as I was a-goin' to mention your name, my heart it up and it says, says it—"Dick, you've fell in love with her yourself," it says; "Be honest and sailor-like—don't skulk under false colours—speak up," it says, "take her, you dog, and with her my blessin'!"

BRIDESMAIDS

Hail the Bridegroom—hail the Bride!——

ROB. Will you be quiet! Go away! (CHORUS *make faces at him and exeunt.*) Vulgar girls!

RICH. What could I do? I'm bound to obey my heart's dictates.

ROB. Of course—no doubt. It's quite right—I don't mind—that is, not particularly—only it's—it *is* disappointing, you know.

ROSE (*to* ROBIN). Oh, but, sir, I knew not that thou didst seek me in wedlock, or in very truth I should not have hearkened unto this man, for behold, he is but a lowly mariner, and very poor withal, whereas thou art a tiller of the land, and thou hast fat oxen, and many sheep and swine, a considerable dairy farm and much corn and oil!

RICH. That's true, my lass, but it's done now, ain't it, Rob?

ROSE. Still it may be that I should not be happy in thy love. I am passing young and little able to judge. Moreover, as to thy character I know naught!

ROB. Nay, Rose, I'll answer for that. Dick has won thy love fairly. Broken-hearted as I am, I'll stand up for Dick through thick and thin!

RICH. (*with emotion*). Thankye, messmate! that's well said. That's spoken honest. Thankye, Rob! (*Grasps his hand.*)

ROSE. Yet methinks I have heard that sailors are but worldly men, and little prone to lead serious and thoughtful lives!

ROB. And what then? Admit that Dick is *not* a steady character, and that when he's excited he uses language that would make your hair curl. Grant that—he does. It's the truth, and I'm not going to deny it. But look at his *good* qualities. He's as nimble as a pony, and his hornpipe is the talk of the Fleet!

RICH. Thankye, Rob! That's well spoken. Thankye, Rob!

ROSE. But it may be that he drinketh strong waters which do bemuse a man, and make him even as the wild beasts of the desert!

ROB. Well, suppose he does, and I don't say he don't, for rum's his bane, and ever has been. He *does* drink—I won't deny it. But what of that? Look at his arms—tattooed to the shoulder! (RICH. *rolls up his sleeves.*) No, no—I won't hear a word against Dick!

ROSE. But they say that mariners are but rarely true to those whom they profess to love!

ROB. Granted—granted—and I don't say that Dick isn't as bad as any of 'em. (RICH. *chuckles.*) You are, you know you are, you dog! a devil of a fellow—a regular out-and-out Lothario! But what then? You can't have everything, and a better hand at turning-in a dead-eye don't walk a deck! And what an accomplishment *that* is in a family man! No, no—not a word against Dick. I'll stick up for him through thick and thin!

RICH. Thankye, Rob, thankye. You're a true friend. I've acted accordin' to my heart's dictates, and such orders as them no man should disobey.

ENSEMBLE—RICHARD, ROBIN, ROSE

In sailing o'er life's ocean wide
Your heart should be your only guide;
With summer sea and favouring wind,
Yourself in port you'll surely find.

SOLO—RICHARD

My heart says, "To this maiden strike—
She's captured you.
She's just the sort of girl you like—
You know you do.
If other man her heart should gain,
I shall resign."
That's what it says to me quite plain,
This heart of mine.

SOLO—ROBIN

My heart says, "You've a prosperous lot,
With acres wide;
You mean to settle all you've got
Upon your bride."

It don't pretend to shape my acts
By word or sign;
It merely states these simple facts,
This heart of mine!

SOLO—ROSE

Ten minutes since my heart said "white"—
It now says "black".
It then said "left"—it now says "right"—
Hearts often tack.

I must obey its latest strain—
You tell me so. (*To* RICHARD.)
But should it change its mind again,
I'll let you know.

(*Turning from* RICHARD *to* ROBIN, *who embraces her.*)

ENSEMBLE

In sailing o'er life's ocean wide
No doubt the heart should be your guide;
But it is awkward when you find
A heart that does not know its mind!

[*Exeunt* ROBIN *with* ROSE L., *and* RICHARD *weeping,* R.

Enter MAD MARGARET. *She is wildly dressed in picturesque tatters, and is an obvious caricature of theatrical madness.*

SCENA—MARGARET

Cheerily carols the lark
Over the cot.
Merrily whistles the clerk
Scratching a blot.
But the lark
And the clerk,
I remark,
Comfort me not!

Over the ripening peach
Buzzes the bee.

Splash on the billowy beach
  Tumbles the sea.
    But the peach
    And the beach
    They are each
  Nothing to me!
    And why?
    Who am I?
Daft Madge! Crazy Meg!
Mad Margaret! Poor Peg!
  He! he! he! he! he! (*chuckling*).

  Mad, I?
    Yes, very!
  But why?
    Mystery!
      Don't call!
        Whisht! whisht!
  No crime—
    'Tis only
  That I'm
      Love—lonely!
        That's all!

BALLAD

To a garden full of posies
  Cometh one to gather flowers,
  And he wanders through its bowers
Toying with the wanton roses,
  Who, uprising from their beds,
  Hold on high their shameless heads
With their pretty lips a-pouting,
Never doubting—never doubting
  That for Cytherean posies
  He would gather aught but roses!

In a nest of weeds and nettles
  Lay a violet, half-hidden,
  Hoping that his glance unbidden
Yet might fall upon her petals.
  Though she lived alone, apart,
  Hope lay nestling at her heart,

But, alas, the cruel awaking
Set her little heart a-breaking,
For he gathered for his posies
Only roses—only roses!

(*Bursts into tears.*)

Enter ROSE

ROSE. A maiden, and in tears? Can I do aught to soften thy sorrow? This apple—(*offering apple*).

MAR. (*Examines it and rejects it.*) No! (*Mysteriously.*) Tell me, are you mad?

ROSE. I? No! That is, I think not.

MAR. That's well! Then you don't love Sir Despard Murgatroyd? All mad girls love him. *I* love him. I'm poor Mad Margaret—Crazy Meg—Poor Peg! He! he! he! he! (*chuckling*).

ROSE. Thou lovest the bad Baronet of Ruddigore? Oh, horrible—too horrible!

MAR. You pity me? Then be my mother! The squirrel had a mother, but she drank and the squirrel fled! Hush! They sing a brave song in our parts—it runs somewhat thus: (*Sings.*)

"The cat and the dog and the little puppee
Sat down in a—down in a—in a——"

I forget what they sat down in, but so the song goes! Listen—I've come to pinch her!

ROSE. Mercy, whom?

MAR. You mean "who".

ROSE. Nay! it is the accusative after the verb.

MAR. True. (*Whispers melodramatically.*) I have come to pinch Rose Maybud!

ROSE. (*Aside, alarmed.*) Rose Maybud!

MAR. Aye! I love him—he loved me once. But that's all gone, Fisht! He gave me an Italian glance—thus (*business*)—and made me his. He will give *her* an Italian glance, and make *her* his. But it shall not be, for I'll stamp on her—stamp on her—stamp on her! Did you ever kill anybody? No? Why not? Listen—I killed a fly this morning! It buzzed, and I wouldn't have it. So it died—pop! So shall she!

ROSE. But, behold, *I* am Rose Maybud, and I would fain not die "pop".

MAR. You are Rose Maybud?

ROSE. Yes, sweet Rose Maybud!

MAR. Strange! They told me she was beautiful. And *he* loves *you!* No, no! If I thought that, I would treat you as the auctioneer and land-agent treated the lady-bird—I would rend you asunder!

ROSE. Nay, be pacified, for behold I am pledged to another, and lo, we are to be wedded this very day!

MAR. Swear me that! Come to a Commissioner and let me have it on affidavit! *I* once made an affidavit—but it died—it died—it died! But, see, they come—Sir Despard and his evil crew! Hide, hide—they are all mad—quite mad!

ROSE. What makes you think that?

MAR. Hush! They sing choruses in public. That's mad enough, I think! Go—hide away, or they will seize you! Hush! Quite softly—quite, quite softly!

[*Exeunt together, on tiptoe.*

Enter Chorus of Bucks and Blades, heralded by Chorus of Bridesmaids

CHORUS OF BRIDESMAIDS

Welcome, gentry,
For your entry
Sets our tender hearts a-beating.
Men of station,
Admiration
Prompts this unaffected greeting.
Hearty greeting offer we!

CHORUS OF BUCKS AND BLADES

When thoroughly tired
Of being admired
By ladies of gentle degree—degree,
With flattery sated,
High-flown and inflated,
Away from the city we flee—we flee!

From charms intramural
To prettiness rural
The sudden transition
Is simply Elysian,
So come, Amaryllis,
Come, Chloe and Phyllis,
Your slaves, for the moment, are we!

ALL. From charms intramural, etc.

CHORUS OF BRIDESMAIDS

The sons of the tillage
Who dwell in this village
Are people of lowly degree—degree.
Though honest and active,
They're most unattractive,
And awkward as awkward can be—can be.
They're clumsy clodhoppers
With axes and choppers,
And shepherds and ploughmen
And drovers and cowmen
And hedgers and reapers
And carters and keepers,
And never a lover for me!

BRIDESMAIDS

So, welcome, gentry, etc.

BUCKS AND BLADES

When thoroughly tired, etc.

Enter SIR DESPARD MURGATROYD

SONG AND CHORUS—SIR DESPARD

SIR D. Oh, why am I moody and sad?
CH. Can't guess!
SIR D. And why am I guiltily mad?
CH. Confess!
SIR D. Because I am thoroughly bad!
CH. Oh yes—
SIR D. You'll see it at once in my face.
Oh, why am I husky and hoarse?
CH. Ah, why?

SIR D. It's the workings of conscience, of course.
CH. Fie, fie!
SIR D. And huskiness stands for remorse,
CH. Oh my!
SIR D. At least it does so in my case!
SIR D. When in crime one is fully employed—
CH. Like you—
SIR D. Your expression gets warped and destroyed:
CH. It do.
SIR D. It's a penalty none can avoid;
CH. How true!
SIR D. I once was a nice-looking youth;
But like stone from a strong catapult—
CH. (*explaining to each other*). A trice—
SIR D. I rushed at my terrible cult—
CH. (*explaining to each other*). That's vice—
SIR D. Observe the unpleasant result!
CH. Not nice.
SIR D. Indeed I am telling the truth!
SIR D. Oh, innocent, happy though poor!
CH. That's we—
SIR D. If I had been virtuous, I'm sure—
CH. Like me—
SIR D. I should be as nice-looking as you're!
CH. May be.
SIR D. You are very nice-looking indeed!
Oh, innocents, listen in time—
CH. We *doe,*
SIR D. Avoid an existence of crime—
CH. Just so—
SIR D. Or you'll be as ugly as I'm—
CH. (*loudly*). No! No!
SIR D. And now, if you please, we'll proceed.

[*All the Girls express their horror of* SIR DESPARD. *As he approaches them they fly from him, terror-stricken, leaving him alone on the stage.*

SIR D. Poor children, how they loathe me—me whose hands are certainly steeped in infamy, but whose heart is as the heart of a little child. But what *is* a poor baronet to do, when a whole picture gallery of ancestors step down from their frames and threaten him with an excruciating death if he hesitate to commit his daily crime? But ha! ha! I am even with them! (*Mysteriously.*) I get my crime over the first thing in the morning, and then, ha! ha! for the rest of the day I do good—I do good—I do good! (*Melodramatically.*) Two days since, I stole a child and built an orphan asylum. Yesterday I robbed a bank and endowed a bishopric. To-day I carry off Rose Maybud and atone with a cathedral! This is what it is to be the sport and toy of a Picture Gallery! But I will be bitterly revenged upon them! I will give them all to the Nation, and nobody shall ever look upon their faces again!

Enter RICHARD

RICH. Ax your honour's pardon, but——

SIR. D. Ha! observed! And by a mariner! What would you with me, fellow?

RICH. Your honour, I'm a poor man-o'-war's man, becalmed in the doldrums——

SIR D. I don't know them.

RICH. And I make bold to ax your honour's advice. Does your honour know what it is to have a heart?

SIR D. My honour knows what it is to have a complete apparatus for conducting the circulation of the blood through the veins and arteries of the human body.

RICH. Aye, but has your honour a heart that ups and looks you in the face, and gives you quarter-deck orders that it's life and death to disobey?

SIR D. I have not a heart of that description, but I have a Picture Gallery that presumes to take that liberty.

RICH. Well, your honour, it's like this—Your honour had an elder brother——

SIR D. It had.

RICH. Who should have inherited your title and, with it, its cuss.

SIR D. Aye, but he died. Oh, Ruthven!——

RICH. He didn't.

SIR D. He did *not?*

RICH. He didn't. On the contrary, he lives in this here very village, under the name of Robin Oakapple, and he's a-going to marry Rose Maybud this very day.

SIR. D. Ruthven alive, and going to marry Rose Maybud! Can this be possible?

RICH. Now the question I was going to ask your honour is—Ought I to tell your honour this?

SIR D. I don't know. It's a delicate point. I think you ought. Mind, I'm not sure, but I think so.

RICH. That's what my heart says. It says, "Dick," it says (it calls me Dick acos it's entitled to take that liberty), "that there young gal would recoil from him if she knowed what he really were. Ought you to stand off and on, and let this young gal take this false step and never fire a shot across her bows to bring her to? No," it says, "you did *not* ought." And I won't ought, accordin'.

SIR D. Then you really feel yourself at liberty to tell me that my elder brother lives—that I may charge him with his cruel deceit, and transfer to his shoulders the hideous thraldom under which I have laboured for so many years! Free—free at last! Free to live a blameless life, and to die beloved and regretted by all who knew me!

DUET—SIR DESPARD *and* RICHARD

RICH. You understand?
SIR D. I think I do;
With vigour unshaken
This step shall be taken.
It's neatly planned.
RICH. I think so too;
I'll readily bet it
You'll never regret it!

BOTH. For duty, duty must be done;
The rule applies to every one,
And painful though that duty be,
To shirk the task were fiddle-de-dee!

SIR D. The bridegroom comes—
RICH. Likewise the bride—
The maidens are very
Elated and merry;
They are her chums.

SIR D. To lash their pride
Were almost a pity,
The pretty committee!

BOTH. But duty, duty must be done;
The rule applies to every one,
And painful though that duty be,
To shirk the task were fiddle-de-dee!

[*Exeunt* RICHARD *and* SIR DESPARD.

Enter Chorus of Bridesmaids and Bucks

CHORUS OF BRIDESMAIDS

Hail the bride of seventeen summers:
In fair phrases
Hymn her praises;
Lift your song on high, all comers.
She rejoices
In your voices.
Smiling summer beams upon her,
Shedding every blessing on her:
Maidens greet her—
Kindly treat her—
You may all be brides some day!

CHORUS OF BUCKS

Hail the bridegroom who advances,
Agitated,
Yet elated.
He's in easy circumstances,
Young and lusty,
True and trusty.

Enter ROBIN, *attended by* RICHARD *and* OLD ADAM, *meeting* ROSE, *attended by* ZORAH *and* DAME HANNAH. ROSE *and* ROBIN *embrace.*

MADRIGAL

ROSE. When the buds are blossoming,
Smiling welcome to the spring,
Lovers choose a wedding day—
Life is love in merry May!

GIRLS. Spring is green—Fal lal la!
Summer's rose—Fal lal la!
ALL. It is sad when summer goes,
Fal la!
MEN. Autumn's gold—Fal lal la!
Winter's grey—Fal lal la!

ALL. Winter still is far away—
Fal la!

Leaves in autumn fade and fall,
Winter is the end of all.
Spring and summer teem with glee:
Spring and summer, then, for me!
Fal la!

HANNAH. In the spring-time seed is sown:
In the summer grass is mown:
In the autumn you may reap:
Winter is the time for sleep.

GIRLS. Spring is hope—Fal lal la!
Summer's joy—Fal lal la!
ALL. Spring and summer never cloy.
Fal la!
MEN. Autumn, toil—Fal lal la!
Winter, rest—Fal lal la!

ALL. Winter, after all, is best—
Fal la!

ALL. Spring and summer pleasure you,
Autumn, aye, and winter too—
Every season has its cheer,
Life is lovely all the year!
Fal la!

(*Gavotte*)

After Gavotte, enter SIR DESPARD

SIR D. Hold, bride and bridegroom, ere you wed each other,
I claim young Robin as my elder brother!
His rightful title I have long enjoyed:
I claim him as Sir Ruthven Murgatroyd!

ALL. O wonder!
ROSE (*wildly*). Deny the falsehood, Robin, as you should,
It is a plot!
ROB. I would, if conscientiously I could,
But I cannot!
ALL. Ah, base one!

SOLO—ROBIN

As pure and blameless peasant,
I cannot, I regret,
Deny a truth unpleasant,
I am that Baronet!

ALL. He is that Baronet!

But when completely rated
Bad Baronet am I,
That I am what he's stated
I'll recklessly deny!

ALL. He'll recklessly deny!

ROB. When I'm a bad Bart. I will tell taradiddles!
ALL. He'll tell taradiddles when he's a bad Bart.
ROB. I'll play a bad part on the falsest of fiddles.

ALL. On very false fiddles he'll play a bad part!
ROB. But until that takes place I must be conscientious—
ALL. He'll be conscientious until that takes place.
ROB. Then adieu with good grace to my morals sententious!
ALL. To morals sententious adieu with good grace!

ZOR. Who is the wretch who hath betrayed thee?
Let him stand forth!
RICH. (*coming forward*). 'Twas I!
ALL. Die, traitor!
RICH. Hold! my conscience made me!
Withhold your wrath!

SOLO—RICHARD

Within this breast there beats a heart
Whose voice can't be gainsaid.
It bade me thy true rank impart,
And I at once obeyed.
I knew 'twould blight thy budding fate—
I knew 'twould cause thee anguish great—
But did I therefore hesitate?
No! I at once obeyed!
ALL. Acclaim him who, when his true heart
Bade him young Robin's rank impart,
Immediately obeyed!

SOLO—ROSE (*addressing* ROBIN)

Farewell!
Thou hadst my heart—
'Twas quickly won!
But now we part—
Thy face I shun!
Farewell!

Go bend the knee
At Vice's shrine,
Of life with me
All hope resign.
Farewell!

(*To* SIR DESPARD.) Take me—I am thy bride!

BRIDESMAIDS

Hail the Bridegroom—hail the Bride!
When the nuptial knot is tied;
Every day will bring some joy
That can never, never cloy!

Enter MARGARET, *who listens*

SIR D. Excuse me, I'm a virtuous person now—
ROSE. That's why I wed you!
SIR D. And I to Margaret must keep my vow!
MAR. Have I misread you?
Oh, joy! with newly kindled rapture warmed,
I kneel before you! (*Kneels.*)
SIR D. I once disliked you; now that I've reformed,
How I adore you! (*They embrace.*)

BRIDESMAIDS

Hail the Bridegroom—hail the Bride!
When the nuptial knot is tied;
Every day will bring some joy
That can never, never cloy!

ROSE. Richard, of him I love bereft,
Through thy design,
Thou art the only one that's left,
So I am thine! (*They embrace.*)

BRIDESMAIDS

Hail the Bridegroom—hail the Bride!
Let the nuptial knot be tied!

DUET—ROSE *and* RICHARD

Oh, happy the lily
When kissed by the bee;
And, sipping tranquilly,
Quite happy is he;
And happy the filly
That neighs in her pride;
But happier than any,
A pound to a penny,
A lover is, when he
Embraces his bride!

DUET—SIR DESPARD *and* MARGARET

Oh, happy the flowers
That blossom in June,
And happy the bowers
That gain by the boon,
But happier by hours
The man of descent,
Who, folly regretting,
Is bent on forgetting
His bad baronetting,
And means to repent!

TRIO—HANNAH, ADAM, *and* ZORAH

Oh, happy the blossom
That blooms on the lea,
Likewise the opossum
That sits on a tree,
But when you come across 'em,
They cannot compare
With those who are treading
The dance at a wedding,
While people are spreading
The best of good fare!

SOLO—ROBIN

Oh, wretched the debtor
Who's signing a deed!
And wretched the letter
That no one can read!
But very much better
Their lot it must be
Than that of the person
I'm making this verse on,
Whose head there's a curse on—
Alluding to me!

Repeat ensemble with Chorus
(Dance)

[*At the end of the dance* ROBIN *falls senseless on the stage. Picture.*

END OF ACT I

ACT II

SCENE.—*Picture Gallery in Ruddigore Castle. The walls are covered with full-length portraits of the Baronets of Ruddigore from the time of* JAMES I.—*the first being that of* SIR RUPERT, *alluded to in the legend; the last that of the last deceased Baronet,* SIR RODERIC.

Enter ROBIN *and* ADAM *melodramatically. They are greatly altered in appearance,* ROBIN *wearing the haggard aspect of a guilty roué;* ADAM, *that of the wicked steward to such a man.*

DUET—ROBIN *and* ADAM

ROB. I once was as meek as a new-born lamb,
I'm now Sir Murgatroyd—ha! ha!
With greater precision
(Without the elision),
Sir Ruthven Murgatroyd—ha! ha!

ADAM. And I, who was once his *valley-de-sham,*
As steward I'm now employed—ha! ha!
The dickens may take him—
I'll never forsake him!
As steward I'm now employed—ha! ha!

BOTH. How dreadful when an innocent heart
Becomes, perforce, a bad young Bart.,
And still more hard on old Adam,
His former faithful *valley-de-sham!*

ROB. This is a painful state of things, old Adam!

ADAM. Painful, indeed! Ah, my poor master, when I swore that, come what would, I would serve you in all things for ever, I little thought to what a pass it would bring me! The confidential adviser to the greatest villain unhung! Now, sir, to business. What crime do you propose to commit to-day?

ROB. How should I know? As my confidential adviser, it's your duty to suggest something.

ADAM. Sir, I loathe the life you are leading, but a good old man's oath is paramount, and I obey. Richard Dauntless is here with pretty Rose Maybud, to ask your consent to their marriage. Poison their beer.

ROB. No—not that—I know I'm a bad Bart., but I'm not as bad a Bart. as all that.

ADAM. Well, there you are, you see! It's no use my making suggestions if you don't adopt them.

ROB. (*melodramatically*). How would it be, do you think, were I to lure him here with cunning wile—bind him with good stout rope to yonder post—and then, by making hideous faces at him, curdle the heart-blood in his arteries, and freeze the very marrow in his bones? How say you, Adam, is not the scheme well planned?

ADAM. It would be simply rude—nothing more. But soft—they come!

ADAM *and* ROBIN *retire up as* RICHARD *and* ROSE *enter, preceded by Chorus of Bridesmaids*

DUET—RICHARD *and* ROSE

RICH. Happily coupled are we,
You see—
I am a jolly Jack Tar,
My star,
And you are the fairest,
The richest and rarest
Of innocent lasses you are,
By far—
Of innocent lasses you are!
Fanned by a favouring gale,
You'll sail
Over life's treacherous sea
With me,
And as for bad weather,
We'll brave it together,
And you shall creep under my lee,
My wee!
And you shall creep under my lee!

For you are such a smart little craft—
Such a neat little, sweet little craft,
  Such a bright little, tight little,
  Slight little, light little,
Trim little, prim little craft!

CHORUS. For she is such, etc.

ROSE. My hopes will be blighted, I fear,
          My dear;
In a month you'll be going to sea,
          Quite free,
  And all of my wishes
  You'll throw to the fishes
As though they were never to be;
          Poor me!
As though they were never to be.
And I shall be left all alone
          To moan,
And weep at your cruel deceit,
          Complete;
  While you'll be asserting
  Your freedom by flirting
With every woman you meet,
          You cheat—
With every woman you meet!

Though I am such a smart little craft—
Such a neat little, sweet little craft,
  Such a bright little, tight little,
  Slight little, light little,
Trim little, prim little craft!

CHORUS. Though she is such, etc.

Enter ROBIN

ROB. Soho! pretty one—in my power at last, eh? Know ye not that I have those within my call who, at my lightest bidding, would immure ye in an uncomfortable dungeon? (*Calling.*) What ho! within there!

RICH. Hold—we are prepared for this (*producing a Union Jack*). Here is a flag that none dare defy (*all kneel*), and while this glorious rag floats over Rose Maybud's head, the man does not live who would dare to lay unlicensed hand upon her!

ROB. Foiled—and by a Union Jack! But a time will come, and then——

ROSE. Nay, let me plead with him. (*To* ROBIN.) Sir Ruthven, have pity. In my book of etiquette the case of a maiden about to be wedded to one who unexpectedly turns out to be a baronet with a curse on him is not considered. Time was when you loved me madly. Prove that this was no selfish love by according your consent to my marriage with one who, if he be not you yourself, is the next best thing—your dearest friend!

BALLAD—ROSE

In bygone days I had thy love—
　　Thou hadst my heart.
But Fate, all human vows above,
　　Our lives did part!
By the old love thou hadst for me—
By the fond heart that beat for thee—
By joys that never now can be,
　　Grant thou my prayer!

ALL (*kneeling*). Grant thou her prayer!

ROB. (*recit.*). Take her—I yield!

ALL (*recit.*). Oh, rapture!

CHORUS. Away to the parson we go—
　　Say we're solicitous very
That he will turn two into one—
　　Singing hey, derry down derry!

RICH. For she *is* such a smart little craft—
ROSE. Such a neat little, sweet little craft—
RICH. Such a bright little—
ROSE. Tight little—
RICH. Slight little—
ROSE. Light little—
BOTH. Trim little, slim little craft!

CHORUS. For she *is* such a smart little craft, etc.

[*Exeunt all but* ROBIN.

ROB. For a week I have fulfilled my accursed doom! I have duly committed a crime a day! Not a great crime, I trust, but still, in the eyes of one as strictly regulated as I used to be, a crime. But will my ghostly ancestors be satisfied with what I have done, or will they regard it as an unworthy subterfuge? (*Addressing Pictures.*) Oh, my forefathers, wallowers in blood, there came at last a day when, sick of crime, you, each and every, vowed to sin no more, and so, in agony, called welcome Death to free you from your cloying guiltiness. Let the sweet psalm of that repentant hour soften your long-dead hearts, and tune your souls to mercy on your poor posterity! (*kneeling*).

[*The stage darkens for a moment. It becomes light again, and the Pictures are seen to have become animated.*

CHORUS OF FAMILY PORTRAITS

Painted emblems of a race,
All accurst in days of yore,
Each from his accustomed place
Steps into the world once more.

[*The Pictures step from their frames and march round the stage.*

Baronet of Ruddigore,
Last of our accursèd line,
Down upon the oaken floor—
Down upon those knees of thine.

Coward, poltroon, shaker, squeamer,
Blockhead, sluggard, dullard, dreamer,
Shirker, shuffler, crawler, creeper,
Sniffler, snuffler, wailer, weeper,
Earthworm, maggot, tadpole, weevil!
Set upon thy course of evil,
Lest the King of Spectre-Land
Set on thee his grisly hand!

[*The Spectre of* SIR RODERIC *descends from his frame.*

SIR ROD. Beware! beware! beware!

ROB. Gaunt vision, who art thou
That thus, with icy glare
And stern relentless brow,
Appearest, who knows how?

SIR ROD. I am the spectre of the late
Sir Roderic Murgatroyd,
Who comes to warn thee that thy fate
Thou canst not now avoid.

ROB. Alas, poor ghost!

SIR ROD. The pity you
Express for nothing goes:
We spectres are a jollier crew
Than you, perhaps, suppose!

CHORUS. We spectres are a jollier crew
Than you, perhaps, suppose!

SONG—SIR RODERIC

When the night wind howls in the chimney cowls, and the bat in the moonlight flies,
And inky clouds, like funeral shrouds, sail over the mid night skies—
When the footpads quail at the night-bird's wail, and black dogs bay at the moon,
Then is the spectres' holiday—then is the ghosts' high-noon!

CHORUS. Ha! ha!
Then is the ghosts' high-noon!

As the sob of the breeze sweeps over the trees, and the mists lie low on the fen,
From grey tomb-stones are gathered the bones that once were women and men,
And away they go, with a mop and a mow, to the revel that ends too soon,
For cockcrow limits our holiday—the dead of the night's high-noon!

CHORUS. Ha! ha!
The dead of the night's high-noon!

And then each ghost with his ladye-toast to their church-yard beds takes flight,
With a kiss, perhaps, on her lantern chaps, and a grisly grim "good-night";
Till the welcome knell of the midnight bell rings forth its jolliest tune,
And ushers in our next high holiday—the dead of the night's high-noon!

CHORUS. Ha! ha!
The dead of the night's high-noon!

ROB. I recognize you now—you are the picture that hangs at the end of the gallery.

SIR ROD. In a bad light. I am.

ROB. Are you considered a good likeness?

SIR ROD. Pretty well. Flattering.

ROB. Because as a work of art you are poor.

SIR ROD. I am crude in colour, but I have only been painted ten years. In a couple of centuries I shall be an Old Master, and then you will be sorry you spoke lightly of me.

ROB. And may I ask why you have left your frames?

SIR ROD. It is our duty to see that our successors commit their daily crimes in a conscientious and workmanlike fashion. It is our duty to remind you that you are evading the conditions under which you are permitted to exist.

ROB. Really, I don't know what you'd have. I've only been a bad baronet a week, and I've committed a crime punctually every day.

SIR ROD. Let us inquire into this. Monday?

ROB. Monday was a Bank Holiday.

SIR ROD. True. Tuesday?

ROB. On Tuesday I made a false income-tax return.

ALL. Ha! ha!

1ST GHOST. That's nothing.

2ND GHOST. Nothing at all.

3RD GHOST. Everybody does that.

4TH GHOST. It's expected of you.

SIR ROD. Wednesday?

ROB. (*melodramatically*). On Wednesday I forged a will.

SIR ROD. Whose will?

ROB. My own.

SIR ROD. My good sir, you can't forge your own will!

ROB. Can't I, though! I like that! I *did*! Besides, if a man can't forge his own will, whose will can be forge?

1ST GHOST. There's something in that.

2ND GHOST. Yes, it seems reasonable.

3RD GHOST. At first sight it does.

4TH GHOST. Fallacy somewhere, I fancy!

ROB. A man can do what he likes with his own?

SIR ROD. I suppose he can.

ROB. Well, then, he can forge his own will, stoopid! On Thursday I shot a fox.

1ST GHOST. Hear, hear!

SIR ROD. That's better (*addressing Ghosts*). Pass the fox, I think? (*They assent.*) Yes, pass the fox. Friday?

ROB. On Friday I forged a cheque.

SIR ROD. Whose cheque?

ROB. Old Adam's.

SIR ROD. But Old Adam hasn't a banker.

ROB. I didn't say I forged his banker—I said I forged his cheque. On Saturday I disinherited my only son.

SIR ROD. But you haven't got a son.

ROB. No—not yet. I disinherited him in advance, to save time. You see—by this arrangement—he'll be born ready disinherited.

SIR ROD. I see. But I don't think you can do that.

ROB. My good sir, if I can't disinherit my own unborn son, whose unborn son can I disinherit?

SIR ROD. Humph! These arguments sound very well, but I can't help thinking that, if they were reduced to syllogistic form, they wouldn't hold water. Now quite understand us. We are foggy, but we don't permit our fogginess to be presumed upon. Unless you undertake to—well, suppose we say, carry off a lady? (*Addressing Ghosts.*) Those who are in favour of his carrying off a lady? (*All hold up their hands except a Bishop.*) Those of the contrary opinion? (*Bishop holds up his hands.*) Oh, you're never satisfied! Yes, unless you undertake to carry off a lady at once—I don't care what lady—any lady—choose your lady—you perish in inconceivable agonies.

ROB. Carry off a lady? Certainly not, on any account. I've the greatest respect for ladies, and I wouldn't do anything of the kind for worlds! No, no. I'm not that kind of baronet, I assure you! If that's all you've got to say, you'd better go back to your frames.

SIR ROD. Very good—then let the agonies commence.

[*Ghosts make passes.* ROBIN *begins to writhe in agony.*

ROB. Oh! Oh! Don't do that! I can't stand it!

SIR ROD. Painful, isn't it? It gets worse by degrees.

ROB. Oh—Oh! Stop a bit! Stop it, will you? I want to speak.

[SIR RODERIC *makes signs to Ghosts, who resume their attitudes.*

SIR ROD. Better?

ROB. Yes—better now! Whew!

SIR ROD. Well, do you consent?

ROB. But it's such an ungentlemanly thing to do!

SIR ROD. As you please. (*To Ghosts.*) Carry on!

ROB. Stop—I can't stand it! I agree! I promise! It shall be done!

SIR ROD. To-day?

ROB. To-day!

SIR ROD. At once?

ROB. At once! I retract! I apologize! I had no idea it was anything like that!

CHORUS

He yields! He answers to our call!
We do not ask for more.
A sturdy fellow, after all,
This latest Ruddigore!
All perish in unheard-of woe
Who dare our wills defy;
We want your pardon, ere we go.
For having agonized you so—
So pardon us—
So pardon us—
So pardon us—
Or die!

ROB. I pardon you!
I pardon you!

ALL. He pardons us—
Hurrah!

[*The Ghosts return to their frames.*

CHORUS. Painted emblems of a race,
All accurst in days of yore,

Each to his accustomed place
Steps unwillingly once more!

[*By this time the Ghosts have changed to pictures again.* ROBIN *is overcome by emotion.*

Enter ADAM

ADAM. My poor master, you are not well——

ROB. Gideon Crawle, it won't do—I've seen 'em—all my ancestors—they're just gone. They say that I must do something desperate at once, or perish in horrible agonies. Go—go to yonder village—carry off a maiden—bring her here at once—any one—I don't care which—

ADAM. But——

ROB. Not a word, but obey! Fly!

[*Exit* ADAM.

RECIT. *and* SONG—ROBIN

Away, Remorse!
Compunction, hence!
Go, Moral Force!
Go, Penitence!
To Virtue's plea
A long farewell—
Propriety,
I ring your knell!
Come, guiltiness of deadliest hue!
Come, desperate deeds of derring-do!

Henceforth all the crimes that I find in the *Times,*
I've promised to perpetrate daily;
To-morrow I start, with a petrified heart,
On a regular course of Old Bailey.
There's confidence tricking, bad coin, pocket-picking,
And several other disgraces—
There's postage-stamp prigging, and then, thimble-rigging,
The three-card delusion at races!
Oh! a baronet's rank is exceedingly nice,
But the title's uncommonly dear at the price!

Ye well-to-do squires, who live in the shires,
Where petty distinctions are vital,

Who found Athenæums and local museums,
With views to a baronet's title—
Ye butchers and bakers and candlestick makers
Who sneer at all things that are tradey—
Whose middle-class lives are embarrassed by wives
Who long to parade as "My Lady",
Oh! allow me to offer a word of advice,
The title's uncommonly dear at the price!

Ye supple M.P.'s, who go down on your knees,
Your precious identity sinking,
And vote black or white as your leaders indite
(Which saves you the trouble of thinking),
For your country's good fame, her repute, or her shame,
You don't care the snuff of a candle—
But you're paid for your game when you're told that your name
Will be graced by a baronet's handle—
Oh! allow me to give *you* a word of advice—
The title's uncommonly dear at the price!

[*Exit* ROBIN.

Enter DESPARD *and* MARGARET. *They are both dressed in sober black of formal cut, and present a strong contrast to their appearance in Act I.*

DUET

DES. I once was a very abandoned person—
MAR. Making the most of evil chances.
DES. Nobody could conceive a worse 'un—
MAR. Even in all the old romances.
DES. I blush for my wild extravagances,
But be so kind
To bear in mind,
MAR. We were the victims of circumstances!

(*Dance.*)

That is one of our blameless dances.

MAR. I was once an exceedingly odd young lady—
DES. Suffering much from spleen and vapours.
MAR. Clergymen thought my conduct shady—
DES. She didn't spend much upon linen-drapers.

MAR. It certainly entertained the gapers.
My ways were strange
Beyond all range—
DES. Paragraphs got into all the papers.
(*Dance.*)

DES. We only cut respectable capers.

DES. I've given up all my wild proceedings.
MAR. My taste for a wandering life is waning.
DES. Now I'm a dab at penny readings.
MAR. They are not remarkably entertaining.
DES. A moderate livelihood we're gaining.
MAR. In fact we rule
A National School.
DES. The duties are dull, but I'm not complaining.
(*Dance.*)

This sort of thing takes a deal of training!

DES. We have been married a week.

MAR. One happy, happy week!

DES. Our new life—

MAR. Is delightful indeed!

DES. So calm!

MAR. So unimpassioned! (*wildly*). Master, all this I owe to you! See, I am no longer wild and untidy. My hair is combed. My face is washed. My boots fit!

DES. Margaret, don't. Pray restrain yourself. Remember, you are now a district visitor.

MAR. A gentle district visitor!

DES. You are orderly, methodical, neat; you have your emotions well under control.

MAR. I have! (*wildly*). Master, when I think of all you have done for me, I fall at your feet. I embrace your ankles. I hug your knees! (*Doing so.*)

DES. Hush. This is not well. This is calculated to provoke remark. Be composed, I beg!

MAR. Ah! you are angry with poor little Mad Margaret!

DES. No, not angry; but a district visitor should learn to eschew melodrama. Visit the poor, by all means, and give them tea and barley-water, but don't do it as if you were administering a bowl of deadly nightshade. It upsets them. Then when you nurse sick people, and find them not as well as could be expected, why go into hysterics?

MAR. Why not?

DES. Because it's too jumpy for a sick-room.

MAR. How strange! Oh, Master! Master!—how shall I express the all-absorbing gratitude that—(*about to throw herself at his feet*).

DES. Now! (*warningly*).

MAR. Yes, I know, dear—it shan't occur again. (*He is seated—she sits on the ground by him.*) Shall I tell you one of poor Mad Margaret's odd thoughts? Well, then, when I am lying awake at night, and the pale moonlight streams through the latticed casement, strange fancies crowd upon my poor mad brain, and I sometimes think that if we could hit upon some word for you to use whenever I am about to relapse—some word that teems with hidden meaning—like "Basingstoke"—it might recall me to my saner self. For, after all, I am only Mad Margaret! Daft Meg! Poor Meg! He! he! he!

DES. Poor child, she wanders! But soft—some one comes—Margaret—pray recollect yourself—Basingstoke, I beg! Margaret, if you don't Basingstoke at once, I shall be seriously angry.

MAR. (*recovering herself*). Basingstoke it is!

DES. Then make it so.

Enter ROBIN. *He starts on seeing them*

ROB. Despard! And his young wife! This visit is unexpected.

MAR. Shall I fly at him? Shall I tear him limb from limb? Shall I rend him asunder? Say but the word and——

DES. Basingstoke!

MAR. (*suddenly demure*). Basingstoke it is!

DES. (*aside*). Then make it so. (*Aloud.*) My brother—I call you brother still, despite your horrible profligacy—we have come to urge you to abandon the evil courses to which you have committed yourself, and at any cost to become a pure and blameless ratepayer.

ROB. But I've done no wrong yet.

MAR. (*wildly*). No wrong! He has done no wrong! Did you hear that!

DES. Basingstoke!

MAR. (*recovering herself*). Basingstoke it is!

DES. My brother—I still call you brother, you observe—you forget that you have been, in the eye of the law, a Bad Baronet of Ruddigore for ten years—and you are therefore responsible—in the eye of the law—for all the misdeeds committed by the unhappy gentleman who occupied your place.

ROB. I see! Bless my heart, I never thought of that! Was I very bad?

DES. Awful. Wasn't he? (*to* MARGARET).

ROB. And I've been going on like this for how long?

DES. Ten years! Think of all the atrocities you have committed—by attorney as it were—during that period. Remember how you trifled with this poor child's affections—how you raised her hopes on high (don't cry, my love—Basingstoke, you know), only to trample them in the dust when they were at the very zenith of their fullness. Oh fie, sir, fie—she trusted you!

ROB. Did she? What a scoundrel I must have been! There, there—don't cry, my dear (*to* MARGARET, *who is sobbing on* ROBIN's *breast*), it's all right now. Birmingham, you know—Birmingham——

MAR. (*sobbing*). It's Ba—Ba—Basingstoke!

ROB. Basingstoke! of course it is—Basingstoke.

MAR. Then make it so!

ROB. There, there—it's all right—he's married you now—that is, *I've* married you (*turning to* DESPARD)—I say, which of us has married her?

DES. Oh, *I've* married her.

ROB. (*aside*). Oh, I'm glad of that. (*To* MARGARET.) Yes, *he's* married you now (*passing her over to* DESPARD), and anything more disreputable than my conduct seems to have been I've never even heard of. But my mind is made up—I *will* defy my ancestors. I *will* refuse to obey their behests, thus, by courting death, atone in some degree for the infamy of my career!

MAR. I knew it—I knew it—God bless you—(*hysterically*).

DES. Basingstoke!

MAR. Basingstoke it is! (*Recovers herself.*)

PATTER-TRIO

ROBIN, DESPARD, *and* MARGARET

ROB. My eyes are fully open to my awful situation—
I shall go at once to Roderic and make him an oration.
I shall tell him I've recovered my forgotten moral senses,
And I don't care twopence-halfpenny for any consequences.
Now I do not want to perish by the sword or by the dagger,
But a martyr may indulge a little pardonable swagger,
And a word or two of compliment my vanity would flatter,
But I've got to die to-morrow, so it really doesn't matter!

DES. So it really doesn't matter—

MAR. So it really doesn't matter—

ALL. So it really doesn't matter, matter, matter, matter, matter!

MAR. If I were not a little mad and generally silly
I should give you my advice upon the subject, willy-nilly;
I should show you in a moment how to grapple with the question,
And you'd really be astonished at the force of my suggestion.
On the subject I shall write you a most valuable letter,
Full of excellent suggestions when I feel a little better,
But at present I'm afraid I am as mad as any hatter,
So I'll keep 'em to myself, for my opinion doesn't matter!

DES. Her opinion doesn't matter—

ROB. Her opinion doesn't matter—

ALL. Her opinion doesn't matter, matter, matter, matter, matter!

DES. If I had been so lucky as to have a steady brother
Who could talk to me as we are talking now to one another—
Who could give me good advice when he discovered I was erring
(Which is just the very favour which on you I am conferring),
My story would have made a rather interesting idyll,
And I might have lived and died a very decent indiwiddle.
This particularly rapid, unintelligible patter
Isn't generally heard, and if it is it doesn't matter!

ROB. If it is it doesn't matter—

MAR. If it ain't it doesn't matter—

ALL. If it is it doesn't matter, matter, matter, matter, matter!

[*Exeunt* DESPARD *and* MARGARET.

Enter ADAM

ADAM (*guiltily*). Master—the deed is done!

ROB. What deed?

ADAM. She is here—alone, unprotected——

ROB. Who?

ADAM. The maiden. I've carried her off—I had a hard task, for she fought like a tiger-cat!

ROB. Great heaven, I had forgotten her! I had hoped to have died unspotted by crime, but I am foiled again—and by a tiger-cat! Produce her—and leave us!

[ADAM *introduces* DAME HANNAH, *very much excited, and exit.*

ROB. Dame Hannah! This is—this is not what I expected.

HAN. Well, sir, and what would you with me? Oh, you have begun bravely—bravely indeed! Unappalled by the calm dignity of blameless womanhood, your minion has torn me from my spotless home, and dragged me, blindfold and shrieking, through hedges, over stiles, and across a very difficult country, and left me, helpless and trembling, at your mercy! Yet not helpless, coward sir, for approach one step—nay, but the twentieth part of one poor inch—and this poniard (*produces a very small dagger*) shall teach ye what it is to lay unholy hands on old Stephen Trusty's daughter!

ROB. Madam, I am extremely sorry for this. It is not at all what I intended—anything more correct—more deeply respectful than my intentions towards you, it would be impossible for any one—however particular—to desire.

HAN. Bah, I am not to be tricked by smooth words, hypocrite! But be warned in time, for there are, without, a hundred gallant hearts whose trusty blades would hack him limb from limb who dared to lay unholy hands on old Stephen Trusty's daughter!

ROB. And this is what it is to embark upon a career of unlicensed pleasure!

[HANNAH, *who has taken a formidable dagger from one of the armed figures, throws her small dagger to* ROBIN.

HAN. Harkye, miscreant, you have secured me, and I am your poor prisoner; but if you think I cannot take care of myself you are very much mistaken. Now then, it's one to one, and let the best man win!

[*Making for him.*

ROB. (*in an agony of terror*). Don't! don't look at me like that! I can't bear it! Roderic! Uncle! Save me!

RODERIC *enters, from his picture. He comes down the stage*

ROD. What is the matter? Have you carried her off?

ROB. I have—she is there—look at her—she terrifies me!

ROD. (*looking at* HANNAH). Little Nannikin!

HAN. (*amazed*). Roddy-doddy!

ROD. My own old love! Why, how came *you* here?

HAN. This brute—he carried me off! Bodily! But I'll show him! (*about to rush at* ROBIN).

ROD. Stop! (*To* ROB.) What do you mean by carrying off this lady? Are you aware that once upon a time she was engaged to be married to me? I'm very angry—very angry indeed.

ROB. Now I hope this will be a lesson to you in future not to——

ROD. Hold your tongue, sir.

ROB. Yes, uncle.

ROD. Have you given him any encouragement?

HAN. (*to* ROB.). Have I given you any encouragement? Frankly now, have I?

ROB. No. Frankly, you have not. Anything more scrupulously correct than your conduct, it would be impossible to desire.

ROD. You go away.

ROB. Yes, uncle. [*Exit* ROBIN.

ROD. This is a strange meeting after so many years!

HAN. Very. I thought you were dead.

ROD. I am. I died ten years ago.

HAN. And are you pretty comfortable?

ROD. Pretty well—that is—yes, pretty well.

HAN. You don't deserve to be, for I loved you all the while, dear; and it made me dreadfully unhappy to hear of all your goings-on, you bad, bad boy!

BALLAD—HANNAH

There grew a little flower
'Neath a great oak tree:
When the tempest 'gan to lower
Little heeded she:
No need had she to cower,
For she dreaded not its power—
She was happy in the bower
Of her great oak tree!
Sing hey,
Lackaday!

Let the tears fall free
For the pretty little flower and the great oak tree!

BOTH. Sing hey,
Lackaday, etc.

When she found that he was fickle,
Was that great oak tree,
She was in a pretty pickle,
As she well might be—
But his gallantries were mickle,
For Death followed with his sickle,
And her tears began to trickle
For her great oak tree!

BOTH. Sing hey,
Lackaday! etc.

Said she, "He loved me never,
Did that great oak tree,
But I'm neither rich nor clever,
And so why should he?
But though fate our fortunes sever,
To be constant I'll endeavour,
Aye, for ever and for ever,
To my great oak tree!"

BOTH. Sing hey,
Lackaday! etc.

[*Falls weeping on* RODERIC'S *bosom.*

Enter ROBIN, *excitedly, followed by all the characters and Chorus of Bridesmaids*

ROB. Stop a bit—both of you.

ROD. This intrusion is unmannerly.

HAN. I'm surprised at you.

ROB. I can't stop to apologize—an idea has just occurred to me. A Baronet of Ruddigore can only die through refusing to commit his daily crime.

ROD. No doubt.

ROB. Therefore, to refuse to commit a daily crime is tantamount to suicide!

ROD. It would seem so.

ROB. But suicide is, itself, a crime—and so, by your own showing, you ought never to have died at all!

ROD. I see—I understand! Then I'm practically alive!

ROB. Undoubtedly! (SIR RODERIC *embraces* HANNAH.) Rose, when you believed that I was a simple farmer, I believe you loved me?

ROSE. Madly, passionately!

ROB. But when I became a bad baronet, you very properly loved Richard instead?

ROSE. Passionately, madly!

ROB. But if I should turn out *not* to be a bad baronet after all, how would you love me then?

ROSE. Madly, passionately!

ROB. As before?

ROSE. Why, of course!

ROB. My darling! (*They embrace.*)

RICH. Here, I say, belay!

ROSE. Oh sir, belay, if it's absolutely necessary!

ROB. Belay? Certainly not!

FINALE

ROB. Having been a wicked baronet a week.
Once again a modest livelihood I seek,
Agricultural employment
Is to me a keen enjoyment,
For I'm naturally diffident and meek!

ROSE. When a man has been a naughty baronet,
And expresses his repentance and regret,
You should help him, if you're able,
Like the mousie in the fable,
That's the teaching of my Book of Etiquette.

RICH. If you ask me why I do not pipe my eye,
Like an honest British sailor, I reply,
That with Zorah for my missis,
There'll be bread and cheese and kisses,
Which is just the sort of ration I enjye!

DES. *and* MAR. Prompted by a keen desire to evoke,
All the blessed calm of matrimony's yoke,
We shall toddle off to-morrow,

From this scene of sin and sorrow,
For to settle in the town of Basingstoke!

ALL. For happy the lily
That's kissed by the bee;
And, sipping tranquilly,
Quite happy is he;
And happy the filly
That neighs in her pride;
But happier than any,
A pound to a penny,
A lover is, when he
Embraces his bride!

CURTAIN

THE YEOMEN OF THE GUARD

OR

THE MERRYMAN AND HIS MAID

DRAMATIS PERSONÆ

SIR RICHARD CHOLMONDELEY (*Lieutenant of the Tower*)

COLONEL FAIRFAX (*under sentence of death*)

SERGEANT MERYLL (*of the Yeomen of the Guard*)

LEONARD MERYLL (*his Son*)

JACK POINT (*a Strolling Jester*)

WILFRED SHADBOLT (*Head Jailer and Assistant Tormentor*)

THE HEADSMAN

FIRST YEOMAN

SECOND YEOMAN

FIRST CITIZEN

SECOND CITIZEN

ELSIE MAYNARD (*a Strolling Singer*)

PHŒBE MERYLL (*Sergeant Meryll's Daughter*)

DAME CARRUTHERS (*Housekeeper to the Tower*)

KATE (*her Niece*)

Chorus of Yeomen of the Guard, Gentlemen, Citizens, etc.

SCENE.—*Tower Green.*

Date, 16th Century.

First produced at the Savoy Theatre on October 3, 1888

THE YEOMEN OF THE GUARD

OR

THE MERRYMAN AND HIS MAID

ACT I

SCENE.—*Tower Green*

PHŒBE *discovered spinning*

SONG—PHŒBE

When maiden loves, she sits and sighs,
She wanders to and fro;
Unbidden tear-drops fill her eyes,
And to all questions she replies
With a sad "heigho!"
'Tis but a little word—"heigho!"
So soft, 'tis scarcely heard—"heigho!"
An idle breath—
Yet life and death
May hang upon a maid's "heigho!"

When maiden loves, she mopes apart,
As owl mopes on a tree;
Although she keenly feels the smart,
She cannot tell what ails her heart,
With its sad "Ah me!"
'Tis but a foolish sigh—"Ah me!"
Born but to droop and die—"Ah me!"
Yet all the sense
Of eloquence
Lies hidden in a maid's "Ah me!" (*Weeps.*)

Enter WILFRED

WIL. Mistress Meryll!

PHŒ. (*looking up*). Eh! Oh! it's you, is it? You may go away, if you like. Because I don't want you, you know.

WIL. Haven't you anything to say to me?

PHŒ. Oh yes! Are the birds all caged? The wild beasts all littered down? All the locks, chains, bolts, and bars in good order? Is the Little Ease sufficiently uncomfortable? The racks, pincers, and thumbscrews all ready for work? Ugh! you brute!

WIL. These allusions to my professional duties are in doubtful taste. I didn't become a head-jailer because I like head-jailing. I didn't become an assistant-tormentor because I like assistant-tormenting. We can't *all* be sorcerers, you know. (PHŒBE, *annoyed*.) Ah! you brought that upon yourself.

PHŒ. Colonel Fairfax is *not* a sorcerer. He's a man of science and an alchemist.

WIL. Well, whatever he is, he won't be one long, for he's to be beheaded to-day for dealings with the devil. His master nearly had him last night, when the fire broke out in the Beauchamp Tower.

PHŒ. Oh! how I wish he had escaped in the confusion! But take care; there's still time for a reply to his petition for mercy.

WIL. Ah! I'm content to chance that. This evening at half-past seven—ah!

PHŒ. You're a cruel monster to speak so unfeelingly of the death of a young and handsome soldier.

WIL. Young and handsome! How do *you* know he's young and handsome?

PHŒ. Because I've seen him every day for weeks past taking his exercise on the Beauchamp Tower.

WIL. Curse him!

PHŒ. There, I believe you're jealous of *him,* now. Jealous of a man I've never spoken to! Jealous of a poor soul who's to die in an hour!

WIL. I am! I'm jealous of everybody and everything. I'm jealous of the very words I speak to you—because they reach your ears—and I mustn't go near 'em!

PHŒ. How unjust you are! Jealous of the words you

speak to me! Why, you know as well as I do that I don't even like them.

WIL. You used to like 'em.

PHŒ. I used to *pretend* I liked them. It was mere politeness to comparative strangers.

[*Exit* PHŒBE, *with spinning wheel.*

WIL. I don't believe you know what jealousy is! I don't believe you know how it eats into a man's heart—and disorders his digestion—and turns his interior into boiling lead. Oh, you are a heartless jade to trifle with the delicate organization of the human interior!

[*Exit* WILFRED.

Enter Crowd of Men and Women, followed by Yeomen of the Guard.

CHORUS (*as Yeomen march on*)

Tower Warders,
Under orders,
Gallant pikemen, valiant sworders!
Brave in bearing,
Foemen scaring,
In their bygone days of daring!
Ne'er a stranger
There to danger—
Each was o'er the world a ranger;
To the story
Of our glory
Each a bold contributory!

CHORUS OF YEOMEN

In the autumn of our life,
Here at rest in ample clover,
We rejoice in telling over
Our impetuous May and June.
In the evening of our day,
With the sun of life declining,
We recall without repining
All the heat of bygone noon.

SOLO—2ND YEOMAN

This the autumn of our life,
  This the evening of our day;
Weary we of battle strife,
  Weary we of mortal fray.
But our year is not so spent,
  And our days are not so faded,
But that we with one consent,
  Were our lovèd land invaded,
    Still would face a foreign foe,
    As in days of long ago.

CHORUS. Still would face a foreign foe,
    As in days of long ago.

PEOPLE.	YEOMEN.
tower warders,	This the autumn of our life, etc.
under orders, etc.	

[*Exeunt Crowd. Manent Yeomen.*

Enter DAME CARRUTHERS

DAME. A good day to you!

2ND YEOMAN. Good day, Dame Carruthers. Busy to-day?

DAME. Busy, aye! the fire in the Beauchamp last night has given me work enough. A dozen poor prisoners—Richard Colfax, Sir Martin Byfleet, Colonel Fairfax, Warren the preacher-poet, and half-a-score others—all packed into one small cell, not six feet square. Poor Colonel Fairfax, who's to die to-day, is to be removed to No. 14 in the Cold Harbour that he may have his last hour alone with his confessor; and I've to see to that.

2ND YEO. Poor gentleman! He'll die bravely. I fought under him two years since, and he valued his life as it were a feather!

PHŒ. He's the bravest, the handsomest, and the best young gentleman in England! He twice saved my father's life; and it's a cruel thing, a wicked thing, and a barbarous thing that so gallant a hero should lose his head—for it's the handsomest head in England!

DAME. For dealings with the devil. Aye! if all were

beheaded who dealt with *him,* there'd be busy doings on Tower Green.

PHŒ. You know very well that Colonel Fairfax is a student of alchemy—nothing more, and nothing less; but this wicked Tower, like a cruel giant in a fairy-tale, must be fed with blood, and that blood must be the best and bravest in England, or it's not good enough for the old Blunderbore. Ugh!

DAME. Silence, you silly girl; you know not what you say. I was born in the old keep, and I've grown grey in it, and, please God, I shall die and be buried in it; and there's not a stone in its walls that is not as dear to me as my own right hand.

SONG WITH CHORUS—DAME CARRUTHERS *and* YEOMEN

When our gallant Norman foes
 Made our merry land their own,
  And the Saxons from the Conqueror were flying,
At his bidding it arose,
 In its panoply of stone,
  A sentinel unliving and undying.

Insensible, I trow,
 As a sentinel should be,
  Though a queen to save her head should come a-suing,
There's a legend on its brow
 That is eloquent to me,
  And it tells of duty done and duty doing.

  "The screw may twist and the rack may turn,
  And men may bleed and men may burn,
  O'er London town and its golden hoard
  I keep my silent watch and ward!"

CHORUS. The screw may twist, etc.

Within its wall of rock
 The flower of the brave
  Have perished with a constancy unshaken.
From the dungeon to the block,
 From the scaffold to the grave,
  Is a journey many gallant hearts have taken.

And the wicked flames may hiss
  Round the heroes who have fought
    For conscience and for home in all its beauty,
But the grim old fortalice
  Takes little heed of aught
    That comes not in the measure of its duty.

"The screw may twist and the rack may turn,
And men may bleed and men may burn,
O'er London town and its golden hoard
I keep my silent watch and ward!"

CHORUS. The screw may twist, etc.

[*Exeunt all but* PHŒBE. *Enter* SERGEANT MERYLL.

PHŒ. Father! Has no reprieve arrived for the poor gentleman?

MER. No, my lass; but there's one hope yet. Thy brother Leonard, who, as a reward for his valour in saving his standard and cutting his way through fifty foes who would have hanged him, has been appointed a Yeoman of the Guard, will arrive to-day; and as he comes straight from Windsor, where the Court is, it may be—it *may* be—that he will bring the expected reprieve with him.

PHŒ. Oh, that he may!

MER. Amen to that! For the Colonel twice saved my life, and I'd give the rest of my life to save his! And wilt thou not be glad to welcome thy brave brother, with the fame of whose exploits all England is a-ringing?

PHŒ. Aye, truly, if he brings the reprieve.

MER. And not otherwise?

PHŒ. Well, he's a brave fellow indeed, and I love brave men.

MER. *All* brave men?

PHŒ. Most of them, I verily believe! But I hope Leonard will not be too strict with me—they say he is a very dragon of virtue and circumspection! Now, my dear old father is kindness itself, and——

MER. And leaves thee pretty well to thine own ways, eh? Well, I've no fears for thee; thou hast a feather-brain, but thou'rt a good lass.

PHŒ. Yes, that's all very well, but if Leonard is going

to tell me that I may not do this and I may not do that, and I must not talk to this one, or walk with that one, but go through the world with my lips pursed up and my eyes cast down, like a poor nun who has renounced mankind—why, as I have *not* renounced mankind, and don't mean to renounce mankind, I won't have it—there!

MER. Nay, he'll not check thee more than is good for thee, Phœbe! He's a brave fellow, and bravest among brave fellows, and yet it seems but yesterday that he robbed the Lieutenant's orchard.

Enter LEONARD MERYLL

LEON. Father!

MER. Leonard! my brave boy! I'm right glad to see thee, and so is Phœbe!

PHŒ. Aye—hast thou brought Colonel Fairfax's reprieve?

LEON. Nay, I have here a despatch for the Lieutenant, but no reprieve for the Colonel!

PHŒ. Poor gentleman! poor gentleman!

LEON. Aye, I would I had brought better news. I'd give my right hand—nay, my body—my life, to save his!

MER. Dost thou speak in earnest, my lad?

LEON. Aye, father—I'm no braggart. Did he not save thy life? and am I not his foster-brother?

MER. Then hearken to me. Thou hast come to join the Yeomen of the Guard!

LEON. Well?

MER. None has seen thee but ourselves?

LEON. And a sentry, who took but scant notice of me.

MER. Now to prove thy words. Give me the despatch, and get thee hence at once! Here is money, and I'll send thee more. Lie hidden for a space, and let no one know. I'll convey a suit of Yeoman's uniform to the Colonel's cell—he shall shave off his beard, so that none shall know him, and I'll own him as my son, the brave Leonard Meryll, who saved his flag and cut his way through fifty foes who thirsted for his life. He will be welcomed without question by my brother-Yeomen, I'll warrant that. Now, how to get access to the Colonel's cell? (*To* PHŒBE.) The key is with thy sour-faced admirer, Wilfred Shadbolt.

PHŒ. (*demurely*). I think—I say, I *think*—I can get anything I want from Wilfred. I think—mind I say, I *think*—you may leave that to me.

MER. Then get thee hence at once, lad—and bless thee for this sacrifice.

PHŒ. And take my blessing, too, dear, dear Leonard!

LEON. And thine, eh? Humph! Thy love is newborn; wrap it up carefully, lest it take cold and die.

TRIO—PHŒBE, LEONARD, MERYLL

PHŒ. Alas! I waver to and fro!
Dark danger hangs upon the deed!

ALL. Dark danger hangs upon the deed!

LEON. The scheme is rash and well may fail,
But ours are not the hearts that quail,
The hands that shrink, the cheeks that pale
In hours of need!

ALL. No, ours are not the hearts that quail,
The hands that shrink, the cheeks that pale
In hours of need!

MER. The air I breathe to him I owe:
My life is his—I count it naught!

PHŒ. *and* LEON. That life is his—so count it naught!

MER. And shall I reckon risks I run
When services are to be done
To save the life of such an one?
Unworthy thought!

PHŒ. *and* LEON. And shall we reckon risks we run
To save the life of such an one?

ALL. Unworthy thought!
We may succeed—who can foretell?
May heaven help our hope—farewell!

[LEONARD *embraces* MERYLL *and* PHŒBE, *and then exit.* PHŒBE *weeping.*

MER. Nay, lass, be of good cheer, we may save him yet.

PHŒ. Oh! see, father—they bring the poor gentleman from the Beauchamp! Oh, father! his hour is not yet come?

MER. No, no,—they lead him to the Cold Harbour Tower to await his end in solitude. But softly—the Lieutenant approaches! He should not see thee weep.

Enter FAIRFAX, *guarded. The* LIEUTENANT *enters, meeting him.*

LIEUT. Halt! Colonel Fairfax, my old friend, we meet but sadly.

FAIR. Sir, I greet you with all good-will; and I thank you for the zealous care with which you have guarded me from the pestilent dangers which threaten human life outside. In this happy little community, Death, when he comes, doth so in punctual and business-like fashion; and, like a courtly gentleman, giveth due notice of his advent, that one may not be taken unawares.

LIEUT. Sir, you bear this bravely, as a brave man should.

FAIR. Why, sir, it is no light boon to die swiftly and surely at a given hour and in a given fashion! Truth to tell, I would gladly have my life; but if that may not be, I have the next best thing to it, which is death. Believe me, sir, my lot is not so much amiss!

PHŒ. (*aside to* MERYLL). Oh, father, father, I cannot bear it!

MER. My poor lass!

FAIR. Nay, pretty one, why weepest thou? Come, be comforted. Such a life as mine is not worth weeping for. (*Sees* MERYLL.) Sergeant Meryll, is it not? (*To* LIEUT.) May I greet my old friend? (*Shakes* MERYLL'S *hand.*) Why, man, what's all this? Thou and I have faced the grim old king a dozen times, and never has his majesty come to me in such goodly fashion. Keep a stout heart, good fellow—we are soldiers, and we know how to die, thou and I. Take my word for it, it is easier to die well than to live well—for, in sooth, I have tried both.

BALLAD—FAIRFAX

Is life a boon?
If so, it must befall,
That Death, whene'er he call,
Must call too soon.
Though fourscore years he give,
Yet one would pray to live
Another moon!
What kind of plaint have I,
Who perish in July?
I might have had to die,
Perchance, in June!

Is life a thorn?
Then count it not a whit!
Man is well done with it;
Soon as he's born
He should all means essay
To put the plague away;
And I, war-worn,
Poor captured fugitive,
My life most gladly give—
I might have had to live
Another morn!

[*At the end,* PHŒBE *is led off, weeping, by* MERYLL.

FAIR. And now, Sir Richard, I have a boon to beg. I am in this strait for no better reason than because my kinsman, Sir Clarence Poltwhistle, one of the Secretaries of State, has charged me with sorcery, in order that he may succeed to my estate, which devolves to him provided I die unmarried.

LIEUT. As thou wilt most surely do.

FAIR. Nay, as I will most surely *not* do, by your worship's grace! I have a mind to thwart this good cousin of mine.

LIEUT. How?

FAIR. By marrying forthwith, to be sure!

LIEUT. But heaven ha' mercy, whom wouldst thou marry?

FAIR. Nay, I am indifferent on that score. Coming Death hath made of me a true and chivalrous knight, who holds all womankind in such esteem that the oldest, and the meanest, and the worst-favoured of them is good enough for him. So, my good Lieutenant, if thou wouldst serve a poor soldier who has but an hour to live, find me the first that comes—my confessor shall marry us, and her dower shall be my dishonoured name and a hundred crowns to boot. No such poor dower for an hour of matrimony!

LIEUT. A strange request. I doubt that I should be warranted in granting it.

FAIR. There never was a marriage fraught with so little of evil to the contracting parties. In an hour she'll be a widow, and I—a bachelor again for aught I know!

LIEUT. Well, I will see what can be done, for I hold thy kinsman in abhorrence for the scurvy trick he has played thee.

FAIR. A thousand thanks, good sir; we meet again on this spot in an hour or so. I shall be a bridegroom then, and your worship will wish me joy. Till then, farewell. (*To Guard.*) I am ready, good fellows.

[*Exit with Guard into Cold Harbour Tower.*

LIEUT. He is a brave fellow, and it is a pity that he should die. Now, how to find him a bride at such short notice? Well, the task should be easy! [*Exit.*

Enter JACK POINT *and* ELSIE MAYNARD, *pursued by a crowd of men and women.* POINT *and* ELSIE *are much terrified;* POINT, *however, assuming an appearance of self-possession.*

CHORUS

Here's a man of jollity,
Jibe, joke, jollify!
Give us of your quality,
Come, fool, follify!

If you vapour vapidly,
River runneth rapidly,
Into it we fling
Bird who doesn't sing!

Give us an experiment
In the art of merriment;
    Into it we throw
    Cock who doesn't crow!

Banish your timidity,
And with all rapidity
Give us quip and quiddity—
    Willy-nilly, O!

River none can mollify;—
  Into it we throw
Fool who doesn't follify,
  Cock who doesn't crow!

POINT (*alarmed*). My masters, I pray you bear with us, and we will satisfy you, for we are merry folk who would make all merry as ourselves. For, look you, there is humour in all things, and the truest philosophy is that which teaches us to find it and to make the most of it.

ELSIE (*struggling with one of the crowd*). Hands off, I say, unmannerly fellow!

POINT (*to 1st Citizen*). Ha! Didst thou hear her say, "Hands off"?

1ST CIT. Aye, I heard her say it, and I felt her do it! What then?

POINT. Thou dost not see the humour of that?

1ST CIT. Nay, if I do, hang me!

POINT. Thou dost not? Now observe. She said, "Hands off!" Whose hands? Thine. Off whom? Off *her*. Why? Because she is a woman. Now, had she *not* been a woman, thine hands had not been set upon her at all. So the reason for the laying on of hands is the reason for the taking off of hands, and herein is contradiction contradicted! It is the very marriage of *pro* with *con;* and no such lopsided union either, as times go, for *pro* is not more unlike *con* than man is unlike woman—yet men and women marry every day with none to say, "Oh, the pity of it!" but I and fools like me! Now wherewithal shall we please you? We can rhyme you couplet, triolet, quatrain, sonnet, rondolet, ballade, what you will. Or we can dance you saraband, gondolet, carole, pimpernel, or Jumping Joan.

ELSIE. Let us give them the singing farce of the Merryman and his Maid—therein is song and dance too.

ALL. Aye, the Merryman and his Maid!

DUET—ELSIE *and* POINT

POINT. I have a song to sing, O!

ELSIE. Sing me your song, O!

POINT. It is song to the moon
By a love-lorn loon,
Who fled from the mocking throng, O!
It's a song of a merryman, moping mum,
Whose soul was sad, and whose glance was glum,
Who sipped no sup, and who craved no crumb,
As he sighed for the love of a ladye.
Heighdy! heighdy!
Misery me, lackadaydee!
He sipped no sup, and he craved no crumb,
As he sighed for the love of a ladye.

ELSIE. I have a song to sing, O!

POINT. What is your song, O?

ELSIE. It is sung with the ring
Of the songs maids sing
Who love with a love life-long, O!
It's the song of a merrymaid, peerly proud,
Who loved a lord and who laughed aloud
At the moan of the merryman, moping mum,
Whose soul was sad, and whose glance was glum,
Who sipped no sup, and who craved no crumb,
As he sighed for the love of a ladye.
Heighdy! heighdy!
Misery me, lackadaydee!
He sipped no sup, etc.

POINT. I have a song to sing, O!

ELSIE. Sing me your song, O!

POINT. It is sung to the knell
Of a churchyard bell,
And a doleful dirge, ding dong, O!
It's a song of a popinjay, bravely born,
Who turned up his noble nose with scorn
At the humble merrymaid, peerly proud,
Who loved a lord, and who laughed aloud
At the moan of a merryman, moping mum,
Whose soul was sad, and whose glance was glum,
Who sipped no sup, and who craved no crumb,
As he sighed for the love of a ladye.

BOTH. Heighdy! heighdy!
Misery me, lackadaydee!
He sipped no sup, etc.

ELSIE. I have a song to sing, O!

POINT. Sing me your song, O!

ELSIE. It is sung with a sigh
And a tear in the eye,
For it tells of a righted wrong, O!
It's a song of the merrymaid, once so gay,
Who turned on her heel and tripped away
From the peacock popinjay, bravely born,
Who turned up his noble nose with scorn

At the humble heart that he did not prize:
So she begged on her knees, with downcast eyes,
For the love of the merryman, moping mum,
Whose soul was sad, and whose glance was glum,
Who sipped no sup, and who craved no crumb,
As he sighed for the love of a ladye.

BOTH. Heighdy! heighdy!
Misery me, lackadaydee!
His pains were o'er, and he sighed no more,
For he lived in the love of a ladye.

1ST CIT. Well sung and well danced!

2ND CIT. A kiss for that, pretty maid!

ALL. Aye, a kiss all round.

ELSIE (*drawing dagger*). Best beware! I am armed!

POINT. Back, sirs—back! This is going too far.

2ND CIT. Thou dost not see the humour of it, eh? Yet there is humour in all things—even in this. (*Trying to kiss her.*)

ELSIE. Help! help!

Enter LIEUTENANT *with Guard. Crowd falls back*

LIEUT. What is this pother?

ELSIE. Sir, we sang to these folk, and they would have repaid us with gross courtesy, but for your honour's coming.

LIEUT. (*to Mob*). Away with ye! Clear the rabble. (*Guards push Crowd off, and go off with them.*) Now, my girl, who are you, and what do you here?

ELSIE. May it please you, sir, we are two strolling players, Jack Point and I, Elsie Maynard, at your worship's service. We go from fair to fair, singing, and dancing, and playing brief interludes; and so we make a poor living.

LIEUT. You two, eh? Are ye man and wife?

POINT. No, sir; for though I'm a fool, there is a limit to my folly. Her mother, old Bridget Maynard, travels with us (for Elsie is a good girl), but the old woman is a-bed with fever, and we have come here to pick up some silver to buy an electuary for her.

LIEUT. Hark ye, my girl! Your mother is ill?

ELSIE. Sorely ill, sir.

LIEUT. And needs good food, and many things that thou canst not buy?

ELSIE. Alas! sir, it is too true.

LIEUT. Wouldst thou earn an hundred crowns?

ELSIE. An hundred crowns! They might save her life!

LIEUT. Then listen! A worthy but unhappy gentleman is to be beheaded in an hour on this very spot. For sufficient reasons, he desires to marry before he dies, and he hath asked me to find him a wife. Wilt thou be that wife?

ELSIE. The wife of a man I have never seen!

POINT. Why, sir, look you, I am concerned in this; for though I am not yet wedded to Elsie Maynard, time works wonders, and there's no knowing what may be in store for us. Have we your worship's word for it that this gentleman will die to-day?

LIEUT. Nothing is more certain, I grieve to say.

POINT. And that the maiden will be allowed to depart the very instant the ceremony is at an end?

LIEUT. The very instant. I pledge my honour that it shall be so.

POINT. An hundred crowns?

LIEUT. An hundred crowns!

POINT. For my part, I consent. It is for Elsie to speak.

TRIO—ELSIE, POINT, *and* LIEUTENANT

LIEUT. How say you, maiden, will you wed
A man about to lose his head?
For half an hour
You'll be a wife,
And then the dower
Is yours for life.
A headless bridegroom why refuse?
If truth the poets tell,
Most bridegrooms, ere they marry, lose
Both head and heart as well!

ELSIE. A strange proposal you reveal,
It almost makes my senses reel.
Alas! I'm very poor indeed,
And such a sum I sorely need.

My mother, sir, is like to die,
This money life may bring.
Bear this in mind, I pray, if I
Consent to do this thing!

POINT. Though as a general rule of life
I don't allow my promised wife,
My lovely bride that is to be,
To marry any one but me,
Yet if the fee is promptly paid,
And he, in well-earned grave,
Within the hour is duly laid,
Objection I will waive!
Yes, objection I will waive!

ALL. Temptation, oh, temptation,
Were we, I pray, intended
To shun, whate'er our station,
Your fascinations splendid;
Or fall, whene'er we view you,
Head over heels into you?
Temptation, oh, temptation, etc.

[*During this, the* LIEUTENANT *has whispered to* WILFRED (*who has entered*). WILFRED *binds* ELSIE'S *eyes with a kerchief, and leads her into the Cold Harbour Tower.*

LIEUT. And so, good fellow, you are a jester?

POINT. Aye, sir, and like some of my jests, out of place.

LIEUT. I have a vacancy for such an one. Tell me, what are your qualifications for such a post?

POINT. Marry, sir, I have a pretty wit. I can rhyme you extempore; I can convulse you with quip and conundrum; I have the lighter philosophies at my tongue's tip; I can be merry, wise, quaint, grim, and sardonic, one by one, or all at once; I have a pretty turn for anecdote; I know all the jests—ancient and modern—past, present, and to come; I can riddle you from dawn of day to set of sun, and, if that content you not, well on to midnight and the small hours. Oh, sir, a pretty wit, I warrant you—a pretty, pretty wit!

RECITATIVE AND SONG—POINT

I've jibe and joke
And quip and crank
For lowly folk
And men of rank.
I ply my craft
And know no fear,
But aim my shaft
At prince or peer.
At peer or prince—at prince or peer,
I aim my shaft and know no fear!

I've wisdom from the East and from the West,
That's subject to no academic rule;
You may find it in the jeering of a jest,
Or distil it from the folly of a fool.
I can teach you with a quip, if I've a mind;
I can trick you into learning with a laugh;
Oh, winnow all my folly, and you'll find
A grain or two of truth among the chaff!

I can set a braggart quailing with a quip,
  The upstart I can wither with a whim;
He may wear a merry laugh upon his lip,
  But his laughter has an echo that is grim!
When they're offered to the world in merry guise,
  Unpleasant truths are swallowed with a will—
For he who'd make his fellow-creatures wise
  Should always gild the philosophic pill!

LIEUT. And how came you to leave your last employ?

POINT. Why, sir it was in this wise. My Lord was the Archbishop of Canterbury, and it was considered that one of my jokes was unsuited to His Grace's family circle. In truth, I ventured to ask a poor riddle, sir—Wherein lay the difference between His Grace and poor Jack Point? His Grace was pleased to give it up, sir. And thereupon I told him that whereas His Grace was paid £10,000 a year for being good, poor Jack Point was good—for nothing. 'Twas but a harmless jest, but it offended His Grace, who whipped me and set me in the stocks for a scurril rogue, and so we parted. I had as lief not take post again with the dignified clergy.

LIEUT. But I trust you are very careful not to give offence. I have daughters.

POINT. Sir, my jests are most carefully selected, and anything objectionable is expunged. If your honour pleases, I will try them first on your honour's chaplain.

LIEUT. Can you give me an example? Say that I had sat me down hurriedly on something sharp?

POINT. Sir I should say that you had sat down on the spur of the moment.

LIEUT. Humph! I don't think much of that. Is that the best you can do?

POINT. It has always been much admired, sir, but we will try again.

LIEUT. Well, then, I am at dinner, and the joint of meat is but half cooked.

POINT. Why then, sir, I should say that what is *underdone* cannot be helped.

LIEUT. I see. I think that manner of thing would be somewhat irritating.

POINT. At first, sir, perhaps; but use is everything, and you would come in time to like it.

LIEUT. We will suppose that I caught you kissing the kitchen wench under my very nose.

POINT. Under *her* very nose, good sir—not under yours! *That* is where *I* would kiss her. Do you take me? Oh, sir, a pretty wit—a pretty, pretty wit!

LIEUT. The maiden comes. Follow me, friend, and we will discuss this matter at length in my library.

POINT. I am your worship's servant. That is to say, I trust I soon shall be. But, before proceeding to a more serious topic, can you tell me, sir, why a cook's brain-pan is like an overwound clock?

LIEUT. A truce to this fooling—follow me.

POINT. Just my luck; my best conundrum wasted!

[*Exeunt.*

Enter ELSIE *from Tower, led by* WILFRED, *who removes the bandage from her eyes, and exit*

RECITATIVE AND SONG—ELSIE

'Tis done! I am a bride! Oh, little ring,
That bearest in thy circlet all the gladness
That lovers hope for, and that poets sing,
What bringest thou to me but gold and sadness?
A bridegroom all unknown, save in this wise,
To-day he dies! To-day, alas, he dies!

Though tear and long-drawn sigh
Ill fit a bride,
No sadder wife than I
The whole world wide!
Ah me! Ah me!
Yet maids there be
Who would consent to lose
The very rose of youth,
The flower of life,
To be, in honest truth,
A wedded wife,
No matter whose!

Ah me! what profit we,
O maids that sigh,
Though gold, though gold should live
If wedded love must die?

Ere half an hour has rung,
A widow I!
Ah, heaven, he is too young,
Too brave to die!
Ah me! Ah me!
Yet wives there be
So weary worn, I trow,
That they would scarce complain,
So that they could
In half an hour attain
To widowhood,
No matter how!

O weary wives
Who widowhood would win,
Rejoice that ye have time
To weary in.

[*Exit* ELSIE *as* WILFRED *re-enters.*

WIL. (*looking after* ELSIE). 'Tis an odd freak, for a dying man and his confessor to be closeted alone with a strange singing girl. I would fain have espied them, but they stopped up the keyhole. *My* keyhole!

Enter PHŒBE *with* MERYLL. MERYLL *remains in the background, unobserved by* WILFRED

PHŒ. (*aside*). Wilfred—and alone!

WIL. Now what could he have wanted with her? That's what puzzles me!

PHŒ. (*aside*). Now to get the keys from him. (*Aloud.*) Wilfred—has no reprieve arrived?

WIL. None. Thine adored Fairfax is to die.

PHŒ. Nay, thou knowest that I have naught but pity for the poor condemned gentleman.

WIL. I know that he who is about to die is more to thee than I, who am alive and well.

PHŒ. Why, that were out of reason, dear Wilfred. Do they not say that a live ass is better than a dead lion? No, I don't mean that!

WIL. Oh, they say that, do they?

PHŒ. It's unpardonably rude of them, but I believe they put it in that way. Not that it applies to thee, who art clever beyond all telling!

WIL. Oh yes, as an assistant-tormentor.

PHŒ. Nay, as a wit, as a humorist, as a most philosophic commentator on the vanity of human resolution.

[PHŒBE *slyly takes bunch of keys from* WILFRED's *waistband and hands them to* MERYLL, *who enters the Tower, unnoticed by* WILFRED.

WIL. Truly, I have seen great resolution give way under my persuasive methods (*working a small thumbscrew*). In the nice regulation of a thumbscrew—in the hundredth part of a single revolution lieth all the difference between stony reticence and a torrent of impulsive unbosoming that the pen can scarcely follow. Ha! ha! I am a mad wag.

PHŒ. (*with a grimace*). Thou art a most light-hearted and delightful companion, Master Wilfred. Thine anecdotes of the torture-chamber are the prettiest hearing.

WIL. I'm a pleasant fellow an I choose. I believe I am the merriest dog that barks. Ah, we might be passing happy together——

PHŒ. Perhaps. I do not know.

WIL. For thou wouldst make a most tender and loving wife.

PHŒ. Aye, to one whom I really loved. For there is a

wealth of love within this little heart—saving up for—I wonder whom? Now, of all the world of men, I wonder whom? To think that he whom I am to wed is now alive and somewhere! Perhaps far away, perhaps close at hand! And I know him not! It seemeth that I am wasting time in not knowing him.

WIL. Now say that it is I—nay! suppose it for the nonce. Say that we are wed—suppose it only—say that thou art my very bride, and I thy cheery, joyous, bright, frolicsome husband—and that, the day's work being done, and the prisoners stored away for the night, thou and I are alone together—with a long, long evening before us!

PHŒ. (*with a grimace*). It is a pretty picture—but I scarcely know. It cometh so unexpectedly—and yet—and yet—*were* I thy bride——

WIL. Aye!—wert thou my bride——?

PHŒ. Oh, how I would love thee!

SONG—PHŒBE

Were I thy bride,
Then all the world beside
Were not too wide
To hold my wealth of love—
Were I thy bride!

Upon thy breast
My loving head would rest,
As on her nest
The tender turtle dove—
Were I thy bride!

This heart of mine
Would be one heart with thine,
And in that shrine
Our happiness would dwell—
Were I thy bride!

And all day long
Our lives should be a song:
No grief, no wrong
Should make my heart rebel—
Were I thy bride!

The silvery flute,
The melancholy lute,
Were night-owl's hoot
To my low-whispered coo—
Were I thy bride!

The skylark's trill
Were but discordance shrill
To the soft thrill
Of wooing as I'd woo—
Were I thy bride!

MERYLL *re-enters; gives keys to* PHŒBE, *who replaces them at* WILFRED'S *girdle, unnoticed by him. Exit* MERYLL.

The rose's sigh
Were as a carrion's cry
To lullaby
Such as I'd sing to thee,
Were I thy bride!

A feather's press
Were leaden heaviness
To my caress.
But then, of course, you see,
I'm not thy bride!

[*Exit* PHŒBE.

WIL. No, thou'rt not—not yet! But, Lord, how she woo'd! I should be no mean judge of wooing, seeing that I have been more hotly woo'd than most men. I have been woo'd by maid, widow, and wife. I have been woo'd boldly, timidly, tearfully, shyly—by direct assault, by suggestion, by implication, by inference, and by innuendo. But this wooing is not of the common order: it is the wooing of one who must needs woo me, if she die for it!

[*Exit* WILFRED.

Enter MERYLL, *cautiously, from Tower*

MER. (*looking after them*). The deed is, so far, safely accomplished. The slyboots, how she wheedled him! What a helpless ninny is a love-sick man! He is but as a lute in a woman's hands—she plays upon him whatever tune she will. But the Colonel comes. I' faith, he's just in time, for the Yeomen parade here for his execution in two minutes!

Enter FAIRFAX, *without beard and moustache, and dressed in Yeoman's uniform*

FAIR. My good and kind friend, thou runnest a grave risk for me!

MER. Tut, sir, no risk. I'll warrant none here will recognise you. You make a brave Yeoman, sir! So—this ruff is too high; so—and the sword should hang thus. Here is your halbert, sir; carry it thus. The Yeomen come. Now remember, you are my brave son, Leonard Meryll.

FAIR. If I may not bear mine own name, there is none other I would bear so readily.

MER. Now, sir, put a bold face on it, for they come.

FINALE—ACT I

Enter Yeomen of the Guard

CHORUS

Oh, Sergeant Meryll, is it true—
  The welcome news we read in orders?
Thy son, whose deeds of derring-do
Are echoed all the country through,

Has come to join the Tower Warders?
If so, we come to meet him,
That we may fitly greet him,
And welcome his arrival here
With shout on shout and cheer on cheer.
Hurrah! Hurrah! Hurrah!

RECITATIVE—SERGEANT MERYLL

Ye Tower Warders, nursed in war's alarms,
Suckled on gunpowder, and weaned on glory,
Behold my son, whose all-subduing arms
Have formed the theme of many a song and story!
Forgive his aged father's pride; nor jeer
His aged father's sympathetic tear!

(*Pretending to weep.*)

CHORUS

Leonard Meryll!
Leonard Meryll!
Dauntless he in time of peril!
Man of power,
Knighthood's flower,
Welcome to the grim old Tower,
To the Tower, welcome thou!

RECITATIVE—FAIRFAX

Forbear, my friends, and spare me this ovation,
I have small claim to such consideration;
The tales that of my prowess are narrated
Have been prodigiously exaggerated!

CHORUS

'Tis ever thus!
Wherever valour true is found,
True modesty will there abound.

COUPLETS

1ST YEOMAN. Didst thou not, oh, Leonard Meryll!
Standard lost in last campaign,
Rescue it at deadly peril—
Bear it safely back again?

CHORUS. Leonard Meryll, at his peril,
Bore it safely back again!

2ND YEOMAN. Didst thou not, when prisoner taken,
And debarred from all escape,
Face, with gallant heart unshaken,
Death in most appalling shape?

CHORUS. Leonard Meryll, faced his peril,
Death in most appalling shape!

FAIR. (*aside*). Truly I was to be pitied,
Having but an hour to live,
I reluctantly submitted,
I had no alternative!

(*Aloud.*) Oh! the tales that are narrated
Of my deeds of derring-do
Have been much exaggerated,
Very much exaggerated,
Scarce a word of them is true!

CHORUS. They are not exaggerated, etc.

Enter PHŒBE. *She rushes to* FAIRFAX. *Enter* WILFRED

RECITATIVE

PHŒ. Leonard!
FAIR. (*puzzled*). I beg your pardon?
PHŒ. Don't you know me?
I'm little Phœbe!
FAIR. (*still puzzled*). Phœbe? Is this Phœbe?
What! little Phœbe? (*Aside.*) Who the deuce may *she* be?
It can't be Phœbe, surely?
WIL. Yes, 'tis Phœbe——
Your sister Phœbe! Your own little sister!
ALL. Aye, he speaks the truth;
'Tis Phœbe!
FAIR. (*pretending to recognise her*). Sister Phœbe!
PHŒ. Oh, my brother!
FAIR. Why, how you've grown! I did not recognise you!
PHŒ. So many years! Oh, brother!

FAIR. Oh, my sister!

WIL. Aye, hug him, girl! There are three thou mayst hug——
Thy father and thy brother and—myself!

FAIR. Thyself, forsooth? And who art thou thyself?

WIL. Good sir, we are betrothed. (FAIRFAX *turns inquiringly to* PHŒBE.)

PHŒ. Or more or less——
But rather less than more!

WIL. To thy fond care
I do commend thy sister. Be to her
An ever-watchful guardian—eagle-eyed!
And when she feels (as sometimes she does feel)
Disposed to indiscriminate caress,
Be thou at hand to take those favours from her!

ALL. Be thou at hand to take those favours from her!

PHŒ. Yes, yes.
Be thou at hand to take those favours from me!

TRIO—WILFRED, FAIRFAX, AND PHŒBE

WIL. To thy fraternal care
Thy sister I commend;
From every lurking snare
Thy lovely charge defend:
And to achieve this end,
Oh! grant, I pray, this boon—
She shall not quit thy sight:
From morn to afternoon—
From afternoon to night—
From seven o'clock to two—
From two to eventide—
From dim twilight to 'leven at night
She shall not quit thy side!

ALL. From morn to afternoon, etc.

PHŒ. So amiable I've grown,
So innocent as well,
That if I'm left alone
The consequences fell
No mortal can foretell.

So grant, I pray, this boon—
  I shall not quit thy sight:
From morn to afternoon—
  From afternoon to night—
From seven o'clock to two—
  From two to eventide—
From dim twilight to 'leven at night
  I shall not quit thy side.

ALL. From morn to afternoon, etc.

FAIR. With brotherly readiness,
  For my fair sister's sake,
At once I answer "Yes"—
  That task I undertake—
  My word I never break.
I freely grant that boon,
  And I'll repeat my plight.
From morn to afternoon— (*kiss*)
  From afternoon to night— (*kiss*)
From seven o'clock to two— (*kiss*)
  From two to evening meal— (*kiss*)
From dim twilight to 'leven at night
  That compact I will seal. (*kiss*)

ALL. From morn to afternoon, etc.

[*The bell of St. Peter's begins to toll. The Crowd enters; the block is brought on to the stage, and the Headsman takes his place. The Yeomen of the Guard form up. The* LIEUTENANT *enters and takes his place, and tells off* FAIRFAX *and two others to bring the prisoner to execution.* WILFRED, FAIRFAX, *and two Yeomen exeunt to Tower.*

CHORUS (*to tolling accompaniment*)

The prisoner comes to meet his doom;
The block, the headsman, and the tomb.
The funeral bell begins to toll—
May Heaven have mercy on his soul!

SOLO—ELSIE, *with* CHORUS

Oh, Mercy, thou whose smile has shone
  So many a captive heart upon;

Of all immured within these walls,
To-day the very worthiest falls!

Enter FAIRFAX *and two other Yeomen from Tower in great excitement*

FAIR. My lord! I know not how to tell
The news I bear!
I and my comrades sought the prisoner's cell—
He is not there!

ALL. He is not there!
They sought the prisoner's cell—he is not there!

TRIO—FAIRFAX *and two Yeomen*

As escort for the prisoner
We sought his cell, in duty bound;
The double gratings open were,
No prisoner at all we found!

We hunted high, we hunted low,
We hunted here, we hunted there—
The man we sought with anxious care
Had vanished into empty air!

[*Exit* LIEUTENANT.

GIRLS. Now, by my troth, the news is fair,
The man has vanished into air!

ALL. As escort for the prisoner
They sought his cell in duty bound, etc.

Enter WILFRED, *followed by* LIEUTENANT

LIEUT. Astounding news! The prisoner fled!
(*To* WILFRED.) Thy life shall forfeit be instead!

(WILFRED *is arrested.*)

WIL. My lord, I did not set him free,
I hate the man—my rival he!

(WILFRED *is taken away.*)

MER. The prisoner gone—I'm all agape!
Who could have helped him to escape?

PHŒ. Indeed I can't imagine who!
I've no idea at all—have you?

Enter JACK POINT

DAME. Of his escape no traces lurk,
Enchantment must have been at work!

ELSIE (*aside to* POINT).
What have I done! Oh, woe is me!
I am his wife, and he is free!

POINT. Oh, woe is *you?* Your anguish sink!
Oh, woe is *me,* I rather think!
Oh, woe is *me,* I rather think!
Yes, woe is *me,* I rather think!
Whate'er betide
You are his bride,
And I am left
Alone—bereft!
Yes, woe is *me,* I rather think!
Yes, woe is *me,* I rather think!

ENSEMBLE—LIEUTENANT *and* CHORUS

All frenzied with despair I rave,
The grave is cheated of its due.
Who is the misbegotten knave
Who hath contrived this deed to do?
Let search be made throughout the land,
Or {his / my} vindictive anger dread—
A thousand marks to him {he'll / I'll} hand
Who brings him here, alive or dead.

[*At the end,* ELSIE *faints in* FAIRFAX'*s arms; all the Yeomen and populace rush off the stage in different directions, to hunt for the fugitive, leaving only the Headsman on the stage, and* ELSIE *insensible in* FAIRFAX'*s arms.*

END OF ACT I

ACT II

SCENE.—*The same.—Moonlight*

Two days have elapsed

Women and Yeomen of the Guard discovered

CHORUS

Night has spread her pall once more,
And the prisoner still is free:
Open is his dungeon door,
Useless now his dungeon key!
He has shaken off his yoke—
How, no mortal man can tell!
Shame on loutish jailer-folk—
Shame on sleepy sentinel!

Enter DAME CARRUTHERS *and* KATE

SOLO—DAME CARRUTHERS

Warders are ye?
Whom do ye ward?
Bolt, bar, and key,
Shackle and cord,
Fetter and chain,
Dungeon of stone,
All are in vain—
Prisoner's flown!
Spite of ye all, he is free—he is free!
Whom do ye ward? Pretty warders are ye!

CHORUS OF WOMEN. Pretty warders are ye, etc.

CHORUS

YEOMEN. Up and down, and in and out,
Here and there, and round about;
Every chamber, every house,
Every chink that holds a mouse,

Every crevice in the keep,
Where a beetle black could creep,
Every outlet, every drain,
Have we searched, but all in vain.

WOMEN. Warders are ye?
Whom do ye ward? etc.

[*Exeunt all.*

Enter JACK POINT, *in low spirits, reading from a huge volume*

POINT (*reads*). "The Merrie Jestes of Hugh Ambrose. No. 7863. The Poor Wit and the Rich Councillor. A certayne poor wit, being an-hungered, did meet a well-fed councillor. 'Marry, fool,' quoth the councillor, 'whither away?' 'In truth,' said the poor wag, 'in that I have eaten naught these two dayes, I do wither away, and that right rapidly!' The councillor laughed hugely, and gave him a sausage." Humph! the councillor was easier to please than my new master the Lieutenant. I would like to take post under that councillor. Ah! 'tis but melancholy mumming when poor heart-broken, jilted Jack Point must needs turn to Hugh Ambrose for original light humour!

Enter WILFRED, *also in low spirits*

WIL. (*sighing*). Ah, Master Point!

POINT (*changing his manner*). Ha! friend jailer! Jailer that wast—jailer that never shalt be more! Jailer that jailed not, or that jailed, if jail he did, so unjailerly that 'twas but jerry-jailing, or jailing in joke—though no joke to him who, by unjailerlike jailing, did so jeopardise his jailership. Come, take heart, smile, laugh, wink, twinkle, thou tormentor that tormentest none—thou racker that rackest not—thou pincher out of place—come, take heart, and be merry, as I am!—(*aside, dolefully*)—as I am!

WIL. Aye, it's well for thee to laugh. Thou hast a good post, and hast cause to be merry.

POINT (*bitterly*). Cause? Have we not all cause? Is not the world a big butt of humour, into which all who will may drive a gimlet? See, I am a salaried wit; and is there aught in nature more ridiculous? A poor, dull, heart-broken man, who must needs be merry, or he will be whipped; who must rejoice, lest he starve; who must jest you, jibe you, quip you, crank you, wrack you, riddle you, from hour to hour, from day to day, from year to year, lest he dwindle, perish, starve, pine, and die! Why, when there's naught else to laugh at, I laugh at myself till I ache for it!

WIL. Yet I have often thought that a jester's calling would suit me to a hair.

POINT. Thee? Would suit *thee,* thou death's head and cross-bones?

WIL. Aye, I have a pretty wit—a light, airy, joysome wit, spiced with anecdotes of prison cells and the torture chamber. Oh, a very delicate wit! I have tried it on many a prisoner, and there have been some who smiled. Now it is not easy to make a prisoner smile. And it should not be difficult to be a good jester, seeing that thou art one.

POINT. Difficult? Nothing easier. Nothing easier. Attend, and I will prove it to thee!

SONG—POINT

Oh! a private buffoon is a light-hearted loon,
  If you listen to popular rumour;
From the morn to the night he's so joyous and bright,
  And he bubbles with wit and good humour!
He's so quaint and so terse, both in prose and in verse;
  Yet though people forgive his transgression,
There are one or two rules that all family fools
  Must observe, if they love their profession.
            There are one or two rules,
              Half a dozen, may be,
            That all family fools,
              Of whatever degree,
        Must observe, if they love their profession.

If you wish to succeed as a jester, you'll need
  To consider each person's auricular:
What is all right for B would quite scandalise C
  (For C is so very particular);

And D may be dull, and E's very thick skull
  Is as empty of brains as a ladle;
While F is F sharp, and will cry with a carp
  That he's known your best joke from his cradle!
      When your humour they flout,
        You can't let yourself go;
      And it *does* put you out
        When a person says, "Oh,
  I have known that old joke from my cradle!"

If your master is surly, from getting up early
  (And tempers are short in the morning),
An inopportune joke is enough to provoke
  Him to give you, at once, a month's warning.
Then if you refrain, he is at you again,
  For he likes to get value for money;
He'll ask then and there, with an insolent stare,
  "If you know that you're paid to be funny?"
      It adds to the tasks
        Of a merryman's place,
      When your principal asks,
        With a scowl on his face,
  If you know that you're paid to be funny?

Comes a Bishop, maybe, or a solemn D.D.—
  Oh, beware of his anger provoking!
Better not pull his hair—don't stick pins in his chair;
  He don't understand practical joking.
If the jests that you crack have an orthodox smack,
  You may get a bland smile from these sages;
But should they, by chance, be imported from France,
  Half-a-crown is stopped out of your wages!
    It's a general rule,
      Though your zeal it may quench,
    If the family fool
      Tells a joke that's too French,
  Half-a-crown is stopped out of his wages!

Though your head it may rack with a bilious attack,
  And your senses with toothache you're losing,
Don't be mopy and flat—they don't fine you for that,
  If you're properly quaint and amusing!
Though your wife ran away with a soldier that day,
  And took with her your trifle of money;
Bless your heart, they don't mind—they're exceedingly kind—
  They don't blame you—as long as you're funny!
    It's a comfort to feel,
      If your partner should flit,
    Though *you* suffer a deal,
      They don't mind it a bit—
  They don't blame you—so long as you're funny!

POINT. And so thou wouldst be a jester eh?

WIL. Aye!

POINT. Now, listen! My sweetheart, Elsie Maynard, was secretly wed to this Fairfax half an hour ere he escaped.

WIL. She did well.

POINT. She did nothing of the kind, so hold thy peace and perpend. Now, while he liveth she is dead to me and I to her, and so, my jibes and jokes notwithstanding, I am the saddest and the sorriest dog in England!

WIL. Thou art a very dull dog indeed.

POINT. Now, if thou wilt swear that thou didst shoot this Fairfax while he was trying to swim across the river

—it needs but the discharge of an arquebus on a dark night—and that he sank and was seen no more, I'll make thee the very Archbishop of jesters, and that in two days' time! Now, what sayest thou?

WIL. I am to lie?

POINT. Heartily. But thy lie must be a lie of circumstancc, which I will support with the testimony of eyes, ears, and tongue.

WIL. And thou wilt qualify me as a jester?

POINT. As a jester among jesters. I will teach thee all my original songs, my self-constructed riddles, my own ingenious paradoxes; nay, more, I will reveal to thee the source whence I get them. Now, what sayest thou?

WIL. Why, if it be but a lie thou wantest of me, I hold it cheap enough, and I say yes, it is a bargain!

DUET—POINT *and* WILFRED

BOTH. Hereupon we're both agreed,
All that we two
Do agree to
We'll secure by solemn deed,
To prevent all
Error mental.

POINT. You on Elsie are to call
With a story
Grim and gory;

WIL. How this Fairfax died, and all
I declare to
You're to swear to.

BOTH. Tell a tale of cock and bull,
Of convincing detail full
Talc tremendous,
Heaven defend us!
What a tale of cock and bull!

BOTH. In return for {your / my} own part
{You are / I am} making
Undertaking

To instruct {me / you} in the art
(Art amazing,
Wonder raising)

POINT. Of a jester, jesting free.
Proud position—
High ambition!

WIL. And a lively one I'll be,
Wag-a-wagging,
Never flagging!

BOTH. Tell a tale of cock and bull, etc.
[*Exeunt together.*

Enter FAIRFAX

FAIR. Two days gone, and no news of poor Fairfax. The dolts! They seek him everywhere save within a dozen yards of his dungeon. So I am free! Free, but for the cursed haste with which I hurried headlong into the bonds of matrimony with—Heaven knows whom! As far as I remember, she should have been young; but even had not her face been concealed by her kerchief, I doubt whether, in my then plight, I should have taken much note of her. Free? Bah! The Tower bonds were but a thread of silk compared with these conjugal fetters which I, fool that I was, placed upon mine own hands. From the one I broke readily enough—how to break the other!

BALLAD—FAIRFAX

Free from his fetters grim—
Free to depart;
Free both in life and limb—
In all but heart!
Bound to an unknown bride
For good and ill;
Ah, is not one so tied
A prisoner still?

Free, yet in fetters held
Till his last hour,
Gyves that no smith can weld,
No rust devour!

Although a monarch's hand
Had set him free,
Of all the captive band
The saddest he!

Enter MERYLL

FAIR. Well, Sergeant Meryll, and how fares thy pretty charge, Elsie Maynard?

MER. Well enough, sir. She is quite strong again, and leaves us to-night.

FAIR. Thanks to Dame Carruthers' kind nursing, eh?

MER. Aye, deuce take the old witch! Ah, 'twas but a sorry trick you played me, sir, to bring the fainting girl to me. It gave the old lady an excuse for taking up her quarters in my house, and for the last two years I've shunned her like the plague. Another day of it and she would have married me! (*Enter* DAME CARRUTHERS *and* KATE.) Good Lord, here she is again! I'll e'en go. (*Going.*)

DAME. Nay, Sergeant Meryll, don't go. I have something of grave import to say to thee.

MER. (*aside*). It's coming.

FAIR. (*laughing*). I'faith, I think I'm not wanted here. (*Going.*)

DAME. Nay, Master Leonard, I've naught to say to thy father that his son may not hear.

FAIR. (*aside*). True. I'm one of the family; I had forgotten!

DAME. 'Tis about this Elsie Maynard. A pretty girl, Master Leonard.

FAIR. Aye, fair as a peach blossom—what then?

DAME. She hath a liking for thee, or I mistake not.

FAIR. With all my heart. She's as dainty a little maid as you'll find in a midsummer day's march.

DAME. Then be warned in time, and give not thy heart to her. Oh, *I* know what it is to give my heart to one who will have none of it!

MER. (*aside*). Aye, *she* knows all about that. (*Aloud.*) And why is my boy to take heed of her? She's a good girl, Dame Carruthers.

DAME. Good enough, for aught I know. But she's no girl. She's a married woman.

MER. A married woman! Tush, old lady—she's promised to Jack Point, the Lieutenant's new jester.

DAME. Tush in thy teeth, old man! As my niece Kate sat by her bedside to-day, this Elsie slept, and as she slept she moaned and groaned, and turned this way and that way—and, "How shall I marry one I have never seen?" quoth she—then, "An hundred crowns!" quoth she—then, "Is it certain he will die in an hour?" quoth she—then, "I love him not, and yet I am his wife," quoth she! Is it not so, Kate?

KATE. Aye, aunt, 'tis even so.

FAIR. Art thou sure of all this?

KATE. Aye, sir, for I wrote it all down on my tablets.

DAME. Now, mark my words: it was of this Fairfax she spake, and he is her husband, or I'll swallow my kirtle!

MER. (*aside*). Is it true, sir?

FAIR. (*aside to* MERYLL). True? Why, the girl was raving! (*Aloud.*) Why should she marry a man who had but an hour to live?

DAME. Marry? There be those who would marry but for a minute, rather than die old maids.

MER. (*aside*). Aye, I know one of them!

QUARTET—FAIRFAX, SERGEANT MERYLL, DAME CARRUTHERS, *and* KATE

Strange adventure! Maiden wedded
To a groom she's never seen—
Never, never, never seen!
Groom about to be beheaded,
In an hour on Tower Green!
Tower, Tower, Tower Green!
Groom in dreary dungeon lying,
Groom as good as dead, or dying,
For a pretty maiden sighing—
Pretty maid of seventeen!
Seven—seven—seventeen!

Strange adventure that we're trolling:
Modest maid and gallant groom—
Gallant, gallant, gallant groom!—

While the funeral bell is tolling,
Tolling, tolling, Bim-a-boom!
Bim-a, Bim-a, Bim-a-boom!
Modest maiden will not tarry;
Though but sixteen years she carry,
She must marry, she must marry,
Though the altar be a tomb—
Tower—Tower—Tower tomb!

[*Exeunt* DAME CARRUTHERS, MERYLL, *and* KATE.

FAIR. So my mysterious bride is no other than this winsome Elsie! By my hand, 'tis no such ill plunge in Fortune's lucky bag! I might have fared worse with my eyes open! But she comes. Now to test her principles. 'Tis not every husband who has a chance of wooing his own wife!

Enter ELSIE

FAIR. Mistress Elsie!

ELSIE. Master Leonard!

FAIR. So thou leavest us to-night?

ELSIE. Yes, Master Leonard. I have been kindly tended, and I almost fear I am loth to go.

FAIR. And this Fairfax. Wast thou glad when he escaped?

ELSIE. Why, truly, Master Leonard, it is a sad thing that a young and gallant gentleman should die in the very fullness of his life.

FAIR. Then when thou didst faint in my arms, it was for joy at his safety?

ELSIE. It may be so. I was highly wrought, Master Leonard, and I am but a girl, and so, when I am highly wrought, I faint.

FAIR. Now, dost thou know, I am consumed with a parlous jealousy?

ELSIE. Thou? And of whom?

FAIR. Why, of this Fairfax, surely!

ELSIE. Of Colonel Fairfax?

FAIR. Aye. Shall I be frank with thee? Elsie—I love thee, ardently, passionately! (ELSIE *alarmed and surprised.*) Elsie, I have loved thee these two days—which is a long time—and I would fain join my life to thine!

ELSIE. Master Leonard! Thou art jesting!

FAIR. Jesting? May I shrivel into raisins if I jest! I love thee with a love that is a fever—with a love that is a frenzy—with a love that eateth up my heart! What sayest thou? Thou wilt not let my heart be eaten up?

ELSIE. (*aside*). Oh, mercy! What am I to say?

FAIR. Dost thou love me, or hast thou been insensible these two days?

ELSIE. I love all brave men.

FAIR. Nay, there is love in excess. I thank heaven there are many brave men in England; but if thou lovest them all, I withdraw my thanks.

ELSIE. I love the bravest best. But, sir, I may not listen —I am not free—I—I am a wife!

FAIR. Thou a wife? Whose? His name? His hours are numbered—nay, his grave is dug and his epitaph set up! Come, his name?

ELSIE. Oh, sir! keep my secret—it is the only barrier that Fate could set up between us. My husband is none other than Colonel Fairfax!

FAIR. The greatest villain unhung! The most ill-favoured, ill-mannered, ill-natured, ill-omened, ill-tempered dog in Christendom!

ELSIE. It is very like. He is naught to me—for I never saw him. I was blindfolded, and he was to have died within the hour; and he did not die—and I am wedded to him, and my heart is broken!

FAIR. He was to have died, and he did *not* die? The scoundrel! The perjured, traitorous villain! Thou shouldst have insisted on his dying first, to make sure. 'Tis the only way with these Fairfaxes.

ELSIE. I now wish I had!

FAIR. (*aside*). Bloodthirsty little maiden! (*Aloud.*) A fig for this Fairfax! Be mine—he will never know—he dares not show himself; and if he dare, what art thou to him? Fly with me, Elsie—we will be married to-morrow, and thou shalt be the happiest wife in England!

ELSIE. Master Leonard! I am amazed! Is it thus that brave soldiers speak to poor girls? Oh! for shame, for shame! I am wed—not the less because I love not my husband. I am a wife, sir, and I have a duty, and—oh, sir!—thy words terrify me—they are not honest—they are wicked words, and unworthy thy great and brave heart! Oh, shame upon thee! shame upon thee!

FAIR. Nay, Elsie, I did but jest. I spake but to try thee—— (*Shot heard.*)

Enter MERYLL *hastily*

MER. (*recit.*). Hark! What was that, sir?
FAIR. Why, an arquebus—
Fired from the wharf, unless I much mistake.
MER. Strange—and at such an hour! What can it mean?

Enter CHORUS

CHORUS

Now what can that have been—
A shot so late at night,
Enough to cause a fright!
What can the portent mean?

Are foemen in the land?
Is London to be wrecked?
What are we to expect?
What danger is at hand?
Let us understand
What danger is at hand!

LIEUTENANT *enters, also* POINT *and* WILFRED

RECITATIVE

LIEUT. Who fired that shot? At once the truth declare!
WIL. My lord, 'twas I—to rashly judge forbear!
POINT. My lord, 'twas he—to rashly judge forbear!

DUET *and* CHORUS—WILFRED *and* POINT

WIL. Like a ghost his vigil keeping—
POINT. Or a spectre all-appalling—
WIL. I beheld a figure creeping—
POINT. I should rather call it crawling—
WIL. He was creeping—
POINT. He was crawling—
WIL. He was creeping, creeping—
POINT. Crawling!

WIL. He was creeping—
POINT. He was crawling—
WIL. He was creeping, creeping—
POINT. Crawling!

WIL. Not a moment's hesitation—
I myself upon him flung,
With a hurried exclamation
To his draperies I hung;
Then we closed with one another
In a rough-and-tumble smother;
Colonel Fairfax and no other
Was the man to whom I clung!

ALL. Colonel Fairfax and no other
Was the man to whom he clung!

WIL. After mighty tug and tussle—
POINT. It resembled more a struggle—
WIL. He, by dint of stronger muscle—
POINT. Or by some infernal juggle—
WIL. From my clutches quickly sliding—
POINT. I should rather call it slipping—
WIL. With a view, no doubt, of hiding—
POINT. Or escaping to the shipping—
WIL. With a gasp, and with a quiver—
POINT. I'd describe it as a shiver—
WIL. Down he dived into the river,
And, alas, I cannot swim.

ALL. It's enough to make one shiver—
With a gasp and with a quiver,
Down he dived into the river;
It was very brave of him!

WIL. Ingenuity is catching;
With the view my king of pleasing,
Arquebus from sentry snatching—
POINT. I should rather call it seizing—
WIL. With an ounce or two of lead
I despatched him through the head!

ALL. With an ounce or two of lead
He despatched him through the head!

WIL. I discharged it without winking,
Little time I lost in thinking,
Like a stone I saw him sinking—

POINT. I should say a lump of lead.

ALL. He discharged it without winking,
Little time he lost in thinking.

WIL. Like a stone I saw him sinking—

POINT. I should say a lump of lead.

WIL. Like a stone, my boy, I said—

POINT. Like a heavy lump of lead.

WIL. Anyhow, the man is dead,
Whether stone or lump of lead!

ALL. Anyhow, the man is dead,
Whether stone or lump of lead!
Arquebus from sentry seizing,
With the view his king of pleasing,
Wilfred shot him through the head,
And he's very, very dead.
And it matters very little whether stone or lump of lead;
It is very, very certain that he's very, very dead!

RECITATIVE—LIEUTENANT

The river must be dragged—no time be lost;
The body must be found, at any cost.
To this attend without undue delay;
So set to work with what despatch ye may!

[*Exit.*

ALL. Yes, yes,
We'll set to work with what despatch we may!

[*Four men raise* WILFRED, *and carry him off on their shoulders.*

CHORUS

Hail the valiant fellow who
Did this deed of derring-do!

Honours wait on such an one;
By my head, 'twas bravely done!
Now, by my head, 'twas bravely done!

[*Exeunt all but* ELSIE, POINT, FAIRFAX, *and* PHŒBE.

POINT (*to* ELSIE, *who is weeping*). Nay, sweetheart, be comforted. This Fairfax was but a pestilent fellow, and, as he had to die, he might as well die thus as any other way. 'Twas a good death.

ELSIE. Still, he was my husband, and had he not been, he was nevertheless a living man, and now he is dead; and so, by your leave, my tears may flow unchidden, Master Point.

FAIR. And thou didst see all this?

POINT. Aye, with both eyes at once—this and that. The testimony of one eye is naught—he may lie. But when it is corroborated by the other, it is good evidence that none may gainsay. Here are both present in court, ready to swear to him!

PHŒ. But art thou sure it was Colonel Fairfax? Saw you his face?

POINT. Aye, and a plaguey ill-favoured face too. A very hang-dog face—a felon face—a face to fright the headsman himself, and make him strike awry. Oh, a plaguey, bad face, take my word for 't. (PHŒBE *and* FAIRFAX *laugh.*) How they laugh! 'Tis ever thus with simple folk—an accepted wit has but to say "Pass the mustard," and they roar their ribs out!

FAIR. (*aside*). If ever I come to life again, thou shalt pay for this, Master Point!

POINT. Now, Elsie, thou art free to choose again, so behold me: I am young and well-favoured. I have a pretty wit. I can jest you, jibe you, quip you, crank you, wrack you, riddle you——

FAIR. Tush, man, thou knowest not how to woo. 'Tis not to be done with time-worn jests and thread-bare sophistries; with quips, conundrums, rhymes, and paradoxes. 'Tis an art in itself, and must be studied gravely and conscientiously.

TRIO—ELSIE, PHŒBE, *and* FAIRFAX

FAIR. A man who would woo a fair maid
Should 'prentice himself to the trade,
And study all day,
In methodical way,
How to flatter, cajole, and persuade;

He should 'prentice himself at fourteen,
And practise from morning to e'en;
And when he's of age,
If he will, I'll engage,
He may capture the heart of a queen!

ALL It is purely a matter of skill,
Which all may attain if they will:
But every Jack,
He must study the knack
If he wants to make sure of his Jill!

ELSIE. If he's made the best use of his time,
His twig he'll so carefully lime
That every bird
Will come down at his word,
Whatever its plumage or clime.

He must learn that the thrill of a touch
May mean little, or nothing, or much:
It's an instrument rare,
To be handled with care,
And ought to be treated as such.

ALL. It is purely a matter of skill, etc.

PHŒ. Then a glance may be timid or free,
It will vary in mighty degree,
From an impudent stare
To a look of despair
That no maid without pity can see!
And a glance of despair is no guide—
It may have its ridiculous side;
It may draw you a tear
Or a box on the ear;
You can never be sure till you've tried!

ALL. It is purely a matter of skill, etc.

FAIR. (*aside to* POINT). Now, listen to me—'tis done thus—(*aloud*)—Mistress Elsie, there is one here who, as thou knowest, loves thee right well!

POINT (*aside*). That he does—right well!

FAIR. He is but a man of poor estate, but he hath a loving, honest heart. He will be a true and trusty husband to thee, and if thou wilt be his wife, thou shalt lie curled up in his heart, like a little squirrel in its nest!

POINT (*aside*). 'Tis a pretty figure. A maggot in a nut lies closer, but a squirrel will do.

FAIR. He knoweth that thou wast a wife—an unloved and unloving wife, and his poor heart was near to breaking. But now that thine unloving husband is dead, and thou art free, he would fain pray that thou wouldst hearken unto him, and give him hope that thou wouldst one day be his!

PHŒ. (*alarmed*). He presses her hands—and he whispers in her ear! Ods bodikins, what does it mean?

FAIR. Now, sweetheart, tell me—wilt thou be this poor good fellow's wife?

ELSIE. If the good, brave man—*is* he a brave man?

FAIR. So men say.

POINT (*aside*). That's not true, but let it pass.

ELSIE. If the brave man will be content with a poor, penniless, untaught maid——

POINT (*aside*). Widow—but let *that* pass.

ELSIE. I will be his true and loving wife, and that with my heart of hearts!

FAIR. My own dear love! (*Embracing her.*)

PHŒ. (*in great agitation*). Why, what's all this? Brother—brother—it is not seemly!

POINT (*also alarmed, aside*). Oh, I can't let *that* pass! (*Aloud.*) Hold, enough, Master Leonard! An advocate should have his fee, but methinks thou art over-paying thyself!

FAIR. Nay, that is for Elsie to say. I promised thee I would show thee how to woo, and herein lies the proof of the virtue of my teaching. Go thou, and apply it elsewhere! (PHŒBE *bursts into tears.*)

QUARTET—ELSIE, PHŒBE, FAIRFAX, *and* POINT

ELSIE *and* FAIR. When a wooer
Goes a-wooing,
Naught is truer
Than his joy.
Maiden hushing
All his suing—
Boldly blushing—
Bravely coy!

ALL. Oh, the happy days of doing!
Oh, the sighing and the suing!
When a wooer goes a-wooing,
Oh, the sweets that never cloy!

PHŒ. (*weeping*) When a brother
Leaves his sister
For another,
Sister weeps.
Tears that trickle,
Tears that blister—
'Tis but mickle
Sister reaps!

ALL. Oh, the doing and undoing,
Oh, the sighing and the suing,
When a brother goes a-wooing,
And a sobbing sister weeps!

POINT. When a jester
Is outwitted,
Feelings fester,
Heart is lead!
Food for fishes
Only fitted,
Jester wishes
He was dead!

ALL. Oh, the doing and undoing,
Oh, the sighing and the suing,
When a jester goes a-wooing,
And he wishes he was dead!

[*Exeunt all but* PHŒBE, *who remains weeping.*

PHŒ. And I helped that man to escape, and I've kept his secret, and pretended that I was his dearly loving sister, and done everything I could think of to make folk believe I *was* his loving sister, and this is his gratitude! Before I pretend to be sister to anybody again, I'll turn nun, and be sister to everybody—one as much as another!

Enter WILFRED

WIL. In tears, eh? What a plague art thou grizzling for now?

PHŒ. Why am I grizzling? Thou hast often wept for jealousy—well, 'tis for jealousy I weep now. Aye, yellow, bilious, jaundiced jealousy. So make the most of that, Master Wilfred.

WIL. But I have never given thee cause for jealousy. The Lieutenant's cook-maid and I are but the merest gossips!

PHŒ. Jealous of thee! Bah! I'm jealous of no craven cock-on-a-hill, who crows about what he'd do an he dared! I am jealous of another and a better man than thou—set that down, Master Wilfred. And he is to marry Elsie Maynard, the little pale fool—set that down, Master

Wilfred—and my heart is wellnigh broken! There, thou hast it all! Make the most of it!

WIL. The man thou lovest is to marry Elsie Maynard? Why, that is no other than thy brother, Leonard Meryll!

PHŒ. (*aside*). Oh, mercy! what have I said?

WIL. Why, what manner of brother is this, thou lying little jade? Speak! Who is this man whom thou hast called brother, and fondled, and coddled, and kissed!—with my connivance, too! Oh Lord! with my connivance! Ha! should it be this Fairfax! (PHŒBE *starts.*) It is! It is this accursed Fairfax! It's Fairfax! Fairfax, who——

PHŒ. Whom thou hast just shot through the head, and who lies at the bottom of the river!

WIL. A—I—I may have been mistaken. We are but fallible mortals, the best of us. But I'll make sure—I'll make sure. (*Going.*)

PHŒ. Stay—one word. I think it cannot be Fairfax—mind, I say I *think*—because thou hast just slain Fairfax. But whether he be Fairfax or no Fairfax, he is to marry Elsie—and—and—as thou hast shot him through the head, and he is dead, be content with that, and I will be thy wife!

WIL. Is that sure?

PHŒ. Aye, sure enough, for there's no help for it! Thou art a very brute—but even brutes must marry, I suppose.

WIL. My beloved! (*Embraces her.*)

PHŒ. (*aside*). Ugh!

Enter LEONARD, *hastily*

LEON. Phœbe, rejoice, for I bring glad tidings. Colonel Fairfax's reprieve was signed two days since, but it was foully and maliciously kept back by Secretary Poltwhistle, who designed that it should arrive after the Colonel's death. It hath just come to hand, and it is now in the Lieutenant's possession!

PHŒ. Then the Colonel is free? Oh, kiss me, kiss me, my dear! Kiss me, again, and again!

WIL. (*dancing with fury*). Ods bobs, death o' my life! Art thou mad? Am *I* mad? Are we *all* mad?

PHŒ. Oh, my dear—my dear, I'm wellnigh crazed with joy! (*Kissing* LEONARD.)

WIL. Come away from him, thou hussy—thou jade—thou kissing, clinging cockatrice! And as for thee, sir, devil take thee, I'll rip thee like a herring for this! I'll skin thee for it! I'll cleave thee to the chine! I'll—oh! Phœbe! Phœbe! Who is this man?

PHŒ. Peace, fool. He is my brother!

WIL. Another brother! Are there any more of them? Produce them all at once, and let me know the worst!

PHŒ. This is the real Leonard, dolt; the other was but his substitute. The *real* Leonard, I say—my father's own son.

WIL. How do I know this? Has he "brother" writ large on his brow? I mistrust thy brothers! Thou art but a false jade! [*Exit* LEONARD

PHŒ. Now, Wilfred, be just. Truly I did deceive thee before—but it was to save a precious life—and to save it, not for me, but for another. They are to be wed this very day. Is not this enough for thee? Come—I am thy Phœbe—thy very own—and we will be wed in a year—or two—or three, at the most. Is not that enough for thee?

Enter MERYLL, *excitedly, followed by* DAME CARRUTHERS (*who listens, unobserved*)

MER. Phœbe, hast thou heard the brave news?

PHŒ. (*still in* WILFRED's *arms*). Aye, father.

MER. I'm nigh mad with joy! (*Seeing* WILFRED.) Why, what's all this?

PHŒ. Oh, father, he discovered our secret through my folly, and the price of his silence is——

WIL. Phœbe's heart.

PHŒ. Oh dear, no—Phœbe's hand.

WIL. It's the same thing!

PHOE. *Is* it? [*Exeunt* WILFRED *and* PHŒBE.

MER. (*looking after them*). 'Tis pity, but the Colonel had to be saved at any cost, and as thy folly revealed our secret, thy folly must e'en suffer for it! (DAME CARRUTHERS *comes down*.) Dame Carruthers!

DAME. So this is a plot to shield this arch-fiend, and I have detected it. A word from me, and three heads besides his would roll from their shoulders!

MER. Nay, Colonel Fairfax is reprieved. (*Aside.*) Yet, if my complicity in his escape were known! Plague on the old meddler! There's nothing for it—(*aloud*)—Hush, pretty one! Such bloodthirsty words ill become those cherry lips! (*Aside.*) Ugh!

DAME (*bashfully*). Sergeant Meryll!

MER. Why, look ye, chuck—for many a month I've—I've thought to myself—"There's snug love saving up in that middle-aged bosom for some one, and why not for thee—that's me—so take heart and tell her—that's thee—that thou—that's me—lovest her—thee—and—and—well, I'm a miserable old man, and I've done it—and that's me!" But not a word about Fairfax! The price of thy silence is——

DAME. Meryll's heart?

MER. No, Meryll's *hand*.

DAME. It's the same thing!

MER. *Is* it!

DUET—DAME CARRUTHERS *and* SERGEANT MERYLL

DAME.
Rapture, rapture
When love's votary,
Flushed with capture,
Seeks the notary,
Joy and jollity
Then is polity;
Reigns frivolity!
Rapture, rapture!

MER.
Doleful, doleful!
When humanity
With its soul full
Of satanity,
Courting privity,
Down declivity
Seeks captivity!
Doleful, doleful!

DAME.
Joyful, joyful!
When virginity
Seeks, all coyful,
Man's affinity;

Fate all flowery,
Bright and bowery,
Is her dowery!
Joyful, joyful!

MER. Ghastly, ghastly!
When man, sorrowful,
Firstly, lastly,
Of to-morrow full,
After tarrying,
Yields to harrying—
Goes a-marrying.
Ghastly, ghastly!

BOTH. Rapture, etc.

[*Exeunt* DAME *and* MERYLL.

FINALE

Enter Yeomen and Women

CHORUS OF WOMEN

(ELEGIACS)

Comes the pretty young bride, a-blushing, timidly shrinking—
Set all thy fears aside—cheerily, pretty young bride!
Brave is the youth to whom thy lot thou art willingly linking!
Flower of valour is he—loving as loving can be!
Brightly thy summer is shining,
Fair as the dawn of the day;
Take him, be true to him—
Tender his due to him—
Honour him, love and obey!

Enter DAME, PHŒBE, *and* ELSIE *as Bride*

TRIO—PHŒBE, ELSIE, *and* DAME CARRUTHERS

'Tis said that joy in full perfection
Comes only once to womankind—
That, other times, on close inspection,
Some lurking bitter we shall find.

If this be so, and men say truly,
My day of joy has broken duly.
With happiness {my / her} soul is cloyed—
This is {my / her} joy-day unalloyed!

ALL. Yes, yes, with happiness her soul is cloyed!
This is her joy-day unalloyed!

Flourish. Enter LIEUTENANT

LIEUT. Hold, pretty one! I bring to thee
News—good or ill, it is for thee to say.
Thy husband lives—and he is free,
And comes to claim his bride this very day!

ELSIE. No! no! recall those words—it cannot be!

ENSEMBLE

KATE *and* CHORUS

Oh, day of terror! Day of tears!
Who is the man who, in his pride,
Claims thee as his bride?

DAME CARRUTHERS and PHŒBE

Oh, day of terror! Day of tears!
The man to whom thou art allied
Appears to claim thee as his bride.

LIEUT., MERYLL, *and* WILFRED

Come, dry these unbecoming tears,
Most joyful tidings greet thine ears,
The man to whom thou art allied
Appears to claim thee as his bride.

ELSIE

Oh, Leonard, come thou to my side,
And claim me as thy loving bride!
Oh, day of terror! Day of tears!

Flourish. Enter COLONEL FAIRFAX, *handsomely dressed, and attended by other Gentlemen*

FAIR. (*sternly*). All thought of Leonard Meryll set aside.
Thou art mine own! I claim thee as my bride.

ALL. Thou art his own! Alas! he claims thee as his bride.

ELSIE. A suppliant at thy feet I fall;
Thine heart will yield to pity's call!

FAIR. Mine is a heart of massive rock,
Unmoved by sentimental shock!

ALL. Thy husband he!

ELSIE (*aside*). Leonard, my loved one—come to me.
They bear me hence away!
But though they take me far from thee,
My heart is thine for aye!
My bruised heart,
My broken heart,
Is thine, my own, for aye!
(*To* FAIRFAX.) Sir, I obey!
I am thy bride;
But ere the fatal hour
I said the say
That placed me in thy power
Would I had died!
Sir, I obey!
I am thy bride!

(*Looks up and recognises* FAIRFAX.) Leonard!

FAIR. My own!

ELSIE. Ah! (*Embrace.*)

ELSIE *and* FAIR. With happiness my soul is cloyed,
This is our joy-day unalloyed!

ALL. Yes, yes!
With happiness their souls are cloyed,
This is their joy-day unalloyed!

Enter JACK POINT

POINT. Oh, thoughtless crew!
Ye know not what ye do!
Attend to me, and shed a tear or two—
For I have a song to sing, O!

ALL. Sing me your song, O!

POINT. It is sung to the moon
By a love-lorn loon,
Who fled from the mocking throng, O!
It's the song of a merryman, moping mum,
Whose soul was sad, and whose glance was glum,
Who sipped no sup, and who craved no crumb,
As he sighed for the love of a ladye!

ALL. Heighdy! heighdy!
Misery me, lackadaydee!
He sipped no sup, and he craved no crumb,
As he sighed for the love of a ladye!

ELSIE. I have a song to sing, O!

ALL. What is your song, O?

ELSIE. It is sung with the ring
Of the songs maids sing
Who love with a love life-long, O!
It's the song of a merrymaid, nestling near,
Who loved her lord—but who dropped a tear
At the moan of the merryman, moping mum,
Whose soul was sad, and whose glance was glum,
Who sipped no sup, and who craved no crumb,
As he sighed for the love of a ladye!

ALL. Heighdy! heighdy!
Misery me, lackadaydee!
He sipped no sup, and he craved no crumb,
As he sighed for the love of a ladye!

[FAIRFAX *embraces* ELSIE *as* POINT *falls insensible at their feet.*

CURTAIN

THE GONDOLIERS

OR

THE KING OF BARATARIA

DRAMATIS PERSONÆ

THE DUKE OF PLAZA-TORO (*a Grandee of Spain*)

LUIZ (*his Attendant*)

DON ALHAMBRA DEL BOLERO (*the Grand Inquisitor*)

MARCO PALMIERI
GIUSEPPE PALMIERI
ANTONIO
FRANCESCO
GIORGIO
ANNIBALE
} (*Venetian Gondoliers*)

THE DUCHESS OF PLAZA-TORO

CASILDA (*her Daughter*)

GIANETTA
TESSA
FIAMETTA
VITTORIA
GIULIA
} (*Contadine*)

INEZ (*the King's Foster-mother*)

Chorus of Gondoliers and Contadine, Men-at-Arms, Heralds, and Pages

Act I: THE PIAZZETTA, VENICE

Act II: PAVILION IN THE PALACE OF BARATARIA

(*An interval of three months is supposed to elapse between Acts I and II*)

Date 1750

First produced at the Savoy Theatre on December 7, 1889

THE GONDOLIERS

OR

THE KING OF BARATARIA

ACT I

SCENE.—*The Piazzetta, Venice. The Ducal Palace on the right*

FIAMETTA, GIULIA, VITTORIA, *and other Contadine discovered, each tying a bouquet of roses*

CHORUS OF CONTADINE

List and learn, ye dainty roses,
    Roses white and roses red,
Why we bind you into posies
    Ere your morning bloom has fled.
By a law of maiden's making,
Accents of a heart that's aching,
Even though that heart be breaking,
    Should by maiden be unsaid:
Though they love with love exceeding,
They must seem to be unheeding—
Go ye then and do their pleading,
    Roses white and roses red!

FIAMETTA

Two there are for whom in duty,
    Every maid in Venice sighs—
Two so peerless in their beauty
    That they shame the summer skies.
We have hearts for them, in plenty,
    They have hearts, but all too few,
We, alas, are four-and-twenty!
    They, alas, are only two!
We, alas!

CHORUS. Alas!

FIA. Are four-and-twenty,
They, alas!

CHORUS. Alas!

FIA. Are only two.

CHORUS. They, alas, are only two, alas!
Now ye know, ye dainty roses,
Why we bind you into posies,
Ere your morning bloom has fled,
Roses white and roses red!

[*During this chorus* ANTONIO, FRANCESCO, GIORGIO, *and other Gondoliers have entered unobserved by the Girls—at first two, then two more, then four, then half a dozen, then the remainder of the Chorus.*

SOLI

FRANC. Good morrow, pretty maids; for whom prepare ye
These floral tributes extraordinary?

FIA. For Marco and Giuseppe Palmieri,
The pink and flower of all the Gondolieri.

GIU. They're coming here, as we have heard but lately,
To choose two brides from us who sit sedately.

ANT. Do all you maidens love them?

ALL. Passionately!

ANT. These gondoliers are to be envied greatly!

GIOR. But what of us, who one and all adore you?
Have pity on our passion, we implore you!

FIA. These gentlemen must make their choice before you;

VIT. In the meantime we tacitly ignore you.

GIU. When they have chosen two that leaves you plenty—
Two dozen we, and ye are four-and-twenty.

FIA *and* VIT. Till then, enjoy your *dolce far niente*.

ANT. With pleasure, nobody *contradicente!*

SONG—ANTONIO *and* CHORUS

For the merriest fellows are we, tra la,
That ply on the emerald sea, tra la;
With loving and laughing,
And quipping and quaffing,
We're happy as happy can be, tra la—
As happy as happy can be!

With sorrow we've nothing to do, tra la,
And care is a thing to pooh-pooh, tra la;
And Jealousy yellow,
Unfortunate fellow,
We drown in the shimmering blue, tra la—
We drown in the shimmering blue!

FIA. (*looking off*). See, see, at last they come to make their choice—
Let us acclaim them with united voice.

[MARCO *and* GIUSEPPE *appear in gondola at back.*

CHORUS (*Girls*). Hail, hail! gallant gondolieri, ben venuti!
Accept our love, our homage, and our duty.

[MARCO *and* GIUSEPPE *jump ashore—the Girls salute them.*

DUET—MARCO *and* GIUSEPPE,
with CHORUS OF GIRLS

MAR. *and* GIU. Buon' giorno, signorine!

GIRLS. Gondolieri carissimi!
Siamo contadine!

MAR. *and* GIU. (*bowing*) Servitori umilissimi!
Per chi questi fiori—
Questi fiori bellissimi?

GIRLS. Per voi, bei signori
O eccellentissimi!

[*The Girls present their bouquets to* MARCO *and* GIUSEPPE, *who are overwhelmed with them, and carry them with difficulty.*

MAR. *and* GIU. (*their arms full of flowers*). O ciel'!

GIRLS. Buon' giorno, cavalieri!

MAR. *and* GIU. (*deprecatingly*). Siamo gondolieri.

(*To* FIA. *and* VIT.) Signorina, io t' amo!

GIRLS (*deprecatingly*). Contadine siamo.

MAR. *and* GIU. Signorine!

GIRLS (*deprecatingly*). Contadine!

(*Curtseying to* MAR. *and* GIU.) Cavalieri.

MAR. *and* GIU. (*deprecatingly*). Gondolieri!
Poveri gondolieri!

CHORUS. Buon' giorno, signorine, etc.

DUET—MARCO *and* GIUSEPPE

We're called *gondolieri,*
But that's a vagary,
It's quite honorary
The trade that we ply.
For gallantry noted
Since we were short-coated,
To beauty devoted,
Giuseppe / Are Marco } and I;

When morning is breaking,
Our couches forsaking,
To greet their awaking
With carols we come.
At summer day's nooning,
When weary lagooning,
Our mandolins tuning,
We lazily thrum.

When vespers are ringing,
To hope ever clinging,
With songs of our singing
A vigil we keep,

When daylight is fading,
Enwrapt in night's shading,
With soft serenading
We sing them to sleep.

We're called *gondolieri,* etc.

RECIT.—MARCO *and* GIUSEPPE

MAR. And now to choose our brides!

GIU. As all are young and fair,
And amiable besides,

BOTH. We really do not care
A preference to declare.

MAR. A bias to disclose
Would be indelicate—

GIU. And therefore we propose
To let impartial Fate
Select for us a mate!

ALL. Viva!

GIRLS. A bias to disclose
Would be indelicate—

MEN. But how do they propose
To let impartial Fate
Select for them a mate?

GIU. These handkerchiefs upon our eyes be good enough to bind,

MAR. And take good care that both of us are absolutely blind;

BOTH. Then turn us round—and we, with all convenient despatch,
Will undertake to marry any two of you we catch!

ALL. Viva!

They undertake to marry any two of {us they catch! / them they catch!}

[*The Girls prepare to bind their eyes as directed.*

FIA. (*to* MARCO). Are you peeping?
Can you see me?

MAR. Dark I'm keeping,
Dark and dreamy!

(MARCO *slyly lifts bandage.*)

VIT. (*to* GIUSEPPE). If you're blinded
Truly, say so.

GIU. All right-minded
Players play so! (*slyly lifts bandage*).

FIA. (*detecting* MARCO). Conduct shady!
They are cheating!
Surely they de-
Serve a beating! (*replaces bandage*).

VIT. (*detecting* GIUSEPPE).
This too much is;
Maidens mocking—
Conduct such is
Truly shocking! (*replaces bandage*).

ALL. You can spy, sir!
Shut your eye, sir!
You may use it by and by, sir!
You can see, sir!
Don't tell me, sir!
That will do—now let it be, sir!

CHORUS OF GIRLS. My papa he keeps three horses,
Black, and white, and dapple grey, sir;
Turn three times, then take your courses,
Catch whichever girl you may, sir!

CHORUS OF MEN. My papa, etc.

[MARCO *and* GIUSEPPE *turn round, as directed, and try to catch the girls. Business of blind-man's buff. Eventually* MARCO *catches* GIANETTA, *and* GIUSEPPE *catches* TESSA. *The two girls try to escape, but in vain. The two men pass their hands over the girls' faces to discover their identity.*

GIU. I've at length achieved a capture!
(*Guessing.*) This is Tessa! (*removes bandage*). Rapture, rapture!

MAR. (*guessing*). To me Gianetta fate has granted!
(*removes bandage*).
Just the very girl I wanted!

GIU. (*politely to* MAR.). If you'd rather change——

TESS. My goodness!
This indeed is simple rudeness.

MAR. (*politely to* GIU.). I've no preference whatever—

GIA. Listen to him! Well, I never!
(*Each man kisses each girl.*)

GIA. Thank you, gallant *gondolieri!*
In a set and formal measure
It is scarcely necessary
To express our pleasure.
Each of us to prove a treasure,
Conjugal and monetary,
Gladly will devote our leisure,
Gay and gallant *gondolieri.*
Tra, la, la, la, la, la, etc.

TESS. Gay and gallant *gondolieri,*
Take us both and hold us tightly,
You have luck extraordinary;
We might both have been unsightly!
If we judge your conduct rightly,
'Twas a choice involuntary;
Still we thank you most politely,
Gay and gallant *gondolieri*!
Tra, la, la, la, la, la, etc.

CHORUS OF GIRLS. Thank you, gallant *gondolieri;*
In a set and formal measure,
It is scarcely necessary
To express our pleasure.
Each of us to prove a treasure
Gladly will devote our leisure,
Gay and gallant *gondolieri*!
Tra, la, la, la, la, la, etc.

ALL. Fate in this has put his finger—
Let us bow to Fate's decree,
Then no longer let us linger,
To the altar hurry we!

[*They all dance off two and two*—GIANETTA *with* MARCO, TESSA *with* GIUSEPPE.

Flourish. A gondola arrives at the Piazzetta steps, from which enter the DUKE OF PLAZA-TORO, *the* DUCHESS, *their daughter* CASILDA, *and their attendant* LUIZ, *who carries a drum. All are dressed in pompous but old and faded clothes.*

Entrance of DUKE, DUCHESS, CASILDA, *and* LUIZ

DUKE. From the sunny Spanish shore,
The Duke of Plaza-Tor!—

DUCH. And His Grace's Duchess true—

CAS. And His Grace's daughter, too—

LUIZ. And His Grace's private drum
To Venetia's shores have come:

ALL. If ever, ever, ever
They get back to Spain,
They will never, never, never
Cross the sea again—

DUKE. Neither that Grandee from the Spanish shore,
The noble Duke of Plaza Tor'—

DUCH. Nor His Grace's Duchess, staunch and true—

CAS. You may add, His Grace's daughter, too—

LUIZ. Nor His Grace's own particular drum
To Venetia's shores will come:

ALL. If ever, ever, ever
They get back to Spain,
They will never, never, never
Cross the sea again!

DUKE. At last we have arrived at our destination. This is the Ducal Palace, and it is here that the Grand Inquisitor resides. As a Castilian hidalgo of ninety-five quarterings, I regret that I am unable to pay my state visit on a horse. As a Castilian hidalgo of that description, I should have preferred to ride through the streets of Venice; but owing, I presume, to an unusually wet season, the streets are in such a condition that equestrian exercise is impracticable. No matter. Where is our suite?

LUIZ (*coming forward*). Your Grace, I am here.

DUCH. Why do you not do yourself the honour to kneel when you address His Grace?

DUKE. My love, it is so small a matter! (*To* LUIZ.) Still, you may as well do it. (LUIZ *kneels*.)

CAS. The young man seems to entertain but an imperfect appreciation of the respect due from a menial to a Castilian hidalgo.

DUKE. My child, you are hard upon our suite.

CAS. Papa, I've no patience with the presumption of persons in his plebeian position. If he does not appreciate that position, let him be whipped until he does.

DUKE. Let us hope the omission was not intended as a slight. I should be much hurt if I thought it was. So would he. (*To* LUIZ.) Where are the halberdiers who were to have had the honour of meeting us here, that our visit to the Grand Inquisitor might be made in becoming state?

LUIZ. Your Grace, the halberdiers are mercenary people who stipulated for a trifle on account.

DUKE. How tiresome! Well, let us hope the Grand Inquisitor is a blind gentleman. And the band who were to have had the honour of escorting us? I see no band!

LUIZ. Your Grace, the band are sordid persons who required to be paid in advance.

DUCH. That's so like a band!

DUKE (*annoyed*). Insuperable difficulties meet me at every turn!

DUCH. But surely they know His Grace?

LUIZ. Exactly—they know His Grace.

DUKE. Well let us hope that the Grand Inquisitor is a deaf gentleman. A cornet-à-piston would be something. You do not happen to possess the accomplishment of tootling like a cornet-à-piston?

LUIZ. Alas, no, Your Grace! But I can imitate a farmyard.

DUKE (*doubtfully*). I don't see how that would help us. I don't see how we could bring it in.

CAS. It would not help us in the least. We are not a parcel of graziers come to market, dolt!

DUKE. My love, our suite's feelings! (*To* LUIZ.) Be so good as to ring the bell and inform the Grand Inquisitor that his Grace the Duke of Plaza-Toro, Count Matadoro, Baron Picadoro——

DUCH. And suite—

DUKE. And suite—have arrived at Venice, and seek——

CAS. Desire—

DUCH. Demand!

DUKE. And demand an audience.

LUIZ. Your Grace has but to command. (*Rising.*)

DUKE (*much moved*). I felt sure of it—I felt sure of it! (*Exit* LUIZ *into Ducal Palace.*) And now my love—(*aside to* DUCHESS) Shall we tell her? I think so—(*aloud to* CASILDA) And now, my love, prepare for a magnificent surprise. It is my agreeable duty to reveal to you a secret which should make you the happiest young lady in Venice!

CAS. A secret?

DUCH. A secret which, for state reasons, it has been necessary to preserve for twenty years.

DUKE. When you were a prattling babe of six months old you were married by proxy to no less a personage than the infant son and heir of His Majesty the immeasurably wealthy King of Barataria!

CAS. Married to the infant son of the King of Barataria? Was I consulted? (DUKE *shakes his head.*) Then it was a most unpardonable liberty!

DUKE. Consider his extreme youth and forgive him. Shortly after the ceremony that misguided monarch abandoned the creed of his forefathers, and became a Wesleyan Methodist of the most bigoted and persecuting type. The Grand Inquisitor, determined that the innovation should not be perpetuated in Barataria, caused your smiling and unconscious husband to be stolen and conveyed to Venice. A fortnight since the Methodist

Monarch and all his Wesleyan Court were killed in an insurrection, and we are here to ascertain the whereabouts of your husband, and to hail you, our daughter, as Her Majesty, the reigning Queen of Barataria! (*Kneels.*)

During this speech LUIZ *re-enters*

DUCH. Your Majesty! (*Kneels.*)

DUKE. It is at such moments as these that one feels how necessary it is to travel with a full band.

CAS. I, the Queen of Barataria! But I've nothing to wear! We are practically penniless!

DUKE. That point has not escaped me. Although I am unhappily in straitened circumstances at present, my social influence is something enormous; and a Company, to be called the Duke of Plaza-Toro, Limited, is in course of formation to work me. An influential directorate has been secured, and I shall myself join the Board after allotment.

CAS. Am I to understand that the Queen of Barataria may be called upon at any time to witness her honoured sire in process of liquidation?

DUCH. The speculation is not exempt from that drawback. If your father should stop, it will, of course, be necessary to wind him up.

CAS. But it's so undignified—it's so degrading! A Grandee of Spain turned into a public company? Such a thing was never heard of!

DUKE. My child, the Duke of Plaza-Toro does not follow fashions—he leads them. He always leads everybody. When he was in the army he led his regiment. He occasionally led them into action. He invariably led them out of it.

SONG—DUKE OF PLAZA-TORO

In enterprise of martial kind,
    When there was any fighting,
He led his regiment from behind—
    He found it less exciting.
But when away his regiment ran,
    His place was at the fore, O—

That celebrated,
Cultivated,
Underrated
Nobleman,
The Duke of Plaza-Toro!

ALL. In the first and foremost flight, ha, ha!
You always found that knight, ha, ha!
That celebrated,
Cultivated,
Underrated
Nobleman,
The Duke of Plaza-Toro!

When, to evade Destruction's hand,
To hide they all proceeded,
No soldier in that gallant band
Hid half as well as he did.
He lay concealed throughout the war,
And so preserved his gore, O!
That unaffected,
Undetected,
Well-connected
Warrior,
The Duke of Plaza-Toro!

ALL. In every doughty deed, ha, ha!
He always took the lead, ha, ha!
That unaffected,
Undetected,
Well-connected
Warrior,
The Duke of Plaza-Toro!

When told that they would all be shot
Unless they left the service,
That hero hesitated not,
So marvellous his nerve is.
He sent his resignation in,
The first of all his corps, O!
That very knowing,
Overflowing,
Easy-going
Paladin,
The Duke of Plaza-Toro!

ALL. To men of grosser clay, ha, ha!
He always showed the way, ha, ha!
That very knowing,
Overflowing,
Easy-going
Paladin,
The Duke of Plaza-Toro!

[*Exeunt* DUKE *and* DUCHESS *into Grand Ducal Palace. As soon as they have disappeared,* LUIZ *and* CASILDA *rush to each other's arms.*

RECIT. AND DUET—CASILDA *and* LUIZ

O rapture, when alone together
Two loving hearts and those that bear them
May join in temporary tether,
Though Fate apart should rudely tear them.

CAS. Necessity, Invention's mother,
Compelled me to a course of feigning—
But, left alone with one another,
I will atone for my disdaining!

Ah, well-beloved,
Mine angry frown
Is but a gown
That serves to dress
My gentleness!

LUIZ. Ah, well-beloved,
Thy cold disdain,
It gives no pain—
'Tis mercy, played
In masquerade!

BOTH. Ah, well-beloved, etc.

CAS. O Luiz, Luiz—what have you said? What have I done? What have I allowed you to do?

LUIZ. Nothing, I trust, that you will ever have reason to repent. (*Offering to embrace her.*)

CAS. (*withdrawing from him*). Nay, Luiz, it may not be. I have embraced you for the last time.

LUIZ (*amazed*). Casilda!

CAS. I have just learnt, to my surprise and indignation, that I was wed in babyhood to the infant son of the King of Barataria!

LUIZ. The son of the King of Barataria? The child who was stolen in infancy by the Inquisition?

CAS. The same. But of course, you know his story.

LUIZ. Know his story? Why, I have often told you that my mother was the nurse to whose charge he was entrusted!

CAS. True. I had forgotten. Well, he has been discovered, and my father has brought me here to claim his hand.

LUIZ. But you will not recognize this marriage? It took place when you were too young to understand its import.

CAS. Nay, Luiz, respect my principles and cease to torture me with vain entreaties. Henceforth my life is another's.

LUIZ. But stay—the present and the future—*they* are another's; but the past—that at least is ours, and none can take it from us. As we may revel in naught else, let us revel in that!

CAS. I don't think I grasp your meaning.

LUIZ. Yet it is logical enough. You say you cease to love me?

CAS. (*demurely*). I say I *may* not love you.

LUIZ. Ah, but you do not say you *did* not love me?

CAS. I loved you with a frenzy that words are powerless to express—and that but ten brief minutes since!

LUIZ. Exactly. My own—that is, until ten minutes since, my own—my lately loved, my recently adored—tell me that until, say a quarter of an hour ago, I was all in all to thee! (*Embracing her.*)

CAS. I see your idea. It's ingenious, but don't do that. (*Releasing herself.*)

LUIZ. There can be no harm in revelling in the past.

CAS. None whatever, but an embrace cannot be taken to act retrospectively.

LUIZ. Perhaps not!

CAS. We may recollect an embrace—I recollect many—but we must not repeat them.

LUIZ. Then let us recollect a few! (*A moment's pause, as they recollect, then both heave a deep sigh.*)

LUIZ. Ah, Casilda, you were to me as the sun is to the earth!

CAS. A quarter of an hour ago?

LUIZ. About that.

CAS. And to think that, but for this miserable discovery, you would have been my own for life!

LUIZ. Through life to death—a quarter of an hour ago!

CAS. How greedily my thirsty ears would have drunk the golden melody of those sweet words a quarter—well, it's now about twenty minutes since. (*Looking at her watch.*)

LUIZ. About that. In such a matter one cannot be too precise.

CAS. And now our love, so full of life, is but a silent, solemn memory!

LUIZ. Must it be so Casilda?

CAS. Luiz, it must be so!

DUET—CASILDA *and* LUIZ

LUIZ. There was a time—
A time for ever gone—ah, woe is me!
It was no crime
To love but thee alone—ah, woe is me!
One heart, one life, one soul,
One aim, one goal—
Each in the other's thrall,
Each all in all, ah, woe is me!

BOTH. Oh, bury, bury—let the grave close o'er
The days that were—that never will be more!
Oh, bury, bury love that all condemn,
And let the whirlwind mourn its requiem!

CAS. Dead as the last year's leaves—
As gathered flowers—ah, woe is me!
Dead as the garnered sheaves,
That love of ours—ah, woe is me!
Born but to fade and die
When hope was high,
Dead and as far away
As yesterday!—ah, woe is me!

BOTH. Oh, bury, bury—let the grave close o'er, etc.

Re-enter from the Ducal Palace the DUKE *and* DUCHESS, *followed by* DON ALHAMBRA DEL BOLERO, *the Grand Inquisitor.*

DUKE. My child, allow me to present to you His Distinction Don Alhambra del Bolero, the Grand Inquisitor of Spain. It was His Distinction who so thoughtfully abstracted your infant husband and brought him to Venice.

DON AL. So this is the little lady who is so unexpectedly called upon to assume the functions of Royalty! And a very nice little lady, too!

DUKE. Jimp, isn't she?

DON AL. Distinctly jimp. Allow me! (*Offers his hand. She turns away scornfully.*) Naughty temper!

DUKE. You must make some allowance. Her Majesty's head is a little turned by her access of dignity.

DON AL. I could have wished that Her Majesty's access of dignity had turned it in this direction.

DUCH. Unfortunately, if I am not mistaken, there appears to be some little doubt as to His Majesty's whereabouts.

CAS. (*aside*). A doubt as to his whereabouts? Then we may yet be saved!

DON AL. A doubt? Oh dear, no—no doubt at all! He is here, in Venice, plying the modest but picturesque calling of a gondolier. I can give you his address—I see him every day! In the entire annals of our history there is absolutely no circumstance so entirely free from all manner of doubt of any kind whatever! Listen, and I'll tell you all about it.

SONG—DON ALHAMBRA
(*with* DUKE, DUCHESS, CASILDA, *and* LUIZ)

I stole the Prince, and brought him here,
And left him gaily prattling
With a highly respectable gondolier,
Who promised the Royal babe to rear,
And teach him the trade of a timoneer
With his own beloved bratling.

Both of the babes were strong and stout,
And, considering all things, clever.
Of that there is no manner of doubt—
No probable, possible shadow of doubt—
No possible doubt whatever.

But owing, I'm much disposed to fear,
To his terrible taste for tippling,
That highly respectable gondolier
Could never declare with a mind sincere
Which of the two was his offspring dear,
And which the Royal stripling!

Which was which he could never make out
Despite his best endeavour.
Of *that* there is no manner of doubt—
No probable, possible shadow of doubt—
No possible doubt whatever.

Time sped, and when at the end of a year
I sought that infant cherished,
That highly respectable gondolier
Was lying a corpse on his humble bier—
I dropped a Grand Inquisitor's tear—
That gondolier had perished.

A taste for drink combined with gout,
Had doubled him up for ever.
Of *that* there is no manner of doubt—
No probable, possible shadow of doubt—
No possible doubt whatever.

The children followed his old career—
(This statement can't be parried)
Of a highly respectable gondolier:
Well, one of the two (who will soon be here)—
But *which* of the two is not quite clear—
Is the Royal Prince you married!

Search in and out and round about,
And you'll discover never
A tale so free from every doubt—
All probable, possible shadow of doubt—
All possible doubt whatever!

CAS. Then do you mean to say that I am married to one of two gondoliers, but it is impossible to say which?

DON AL. Without any doubt of any kind whatever. But be reassured: the nurse to whom your husband was entrusted is the mother of the musical young man who is such a past-master of that delicately modulated instrument (*indicating the drum*). She can, no doubt, establish the King's identity beyond all question.

LUIZ. Heavens, how did he know that?

DON AL. My young friend, a Grand Inquisitor is always up to date. (*To* CAS.) His mother is at present the wife of a highly respectable and old-established brigand, who carries on an extensive practice in the mountains around Cordova. Accompanied by two of my emissaries, he will set off at once for his mother's address. She will return with them, and if she finds any difficulty in making up her mind, the persuasive influence of the torture chamber will jog her memory.

RECIT.—CASILDA *and* DON ALHAMBRA

CAS. But, bless my heart, consider my position!
I am the wife of one, that's very clear;
But who can tell, except by intuition,
Which is the Prince, and which the Gondolier?

DON AL. Submit to Fate without unseemly wrangle:
Such complications frequently occur—
Life is one closely complicated tangle:
Death is the only true unraveller!

QUINTET—DUKE, DUCHESS, CASILDA, LUIZ,
and GRAND INQUISITOR

ALL.
Try we life-long, we can never
Straighten out life's tangled skein,
Why should we, in vain endeavor,
Guess and guess and guess again?

LUIZ. Life's a pudding full of plums,
DUCH. Care's a canker that benumbs.
ALL. Life's a pudding full of plums,
Care's a canker that benumbs.
Wherefore waste our elocution
On impossible solution?
Life's a pleasant institution,
Let us take it as it comes!

Set aside the dull enigma,
We shall guess it all too soon;
Failure brings no kind of stigma—
Dance we to another tune!

LUIZ. String the lyre and fill the cup,
DUCH. Lest on sorrow we should sup.
ALL. String the lyre and fill the cup,
Lest on sorrow we should sup.
Hop and skip to Fancy's fiddle,
Hands across and down the middle—
Life's perhaps the only riddle
That we shrink from giving up!

[*Exeunt all into Ducal Palace except* LUIZ, *who goes off in gondola.*

Enter Gondoliers and Contadine, followed by MARCO, GIANETTA, GIUSEPPE, *and* TESSA

CHORUS

Bridegroom and bride!
  Knot that's insoluble,
  Voices all voluble
Hail it with pride.
Bridegroom and bride!
  We in sincerity
  Wish you prosperity,
Bridegroom and bride!

SONG—TESSA

TESS. When a merry maiden marries,
Sorrow goes and pleasure tarries;
  Every sound becomes a song,
  All is right, and nothing's wrong!
From to-day and ever after
Let our tears be tears of laughter.
  Every sigh that finds a vent
  Be a sigh of sweet content!

When you marry, merry maiden,
Then the air with love is laden;
Every flower is a rose,
Every goose becomes a swan,
Every kind of trouble goes
Where the last year's snows have gone!

CHORUS. Sunlight takes the place of shade
When you marry, merry maid!

TESS. When a merry maiden marries,
Sorrow goes and pleasure tarries;
Every sound becomes a song,
All is right, and nothing's wrong.
Gnawing Care and aching Sorrow,
Get ye gone until to-morrow;
Jealousies in grim array,
Ye are things of yesterday!
When you marry, merry maiden,
Then the air with joy is laden;
All the corners of the earth
Ring with music sweetly played,
Worry is melodious mirth,
Grief is joy in masquerade;

CHORUS. Sullen night is laughing day—
All the year is merry May!

At the end of the song, DON ALHAMBRA *enters at back. The Gondoliers and Contadine shrink from him, and gradually go off, much alarmed.*

GIU. And now our lives are going to begin in real earnest! What's a bachelor? A mere nothing—he's a chrysalis. He can't be said to live—he exists.

MAR. What a delightful institution marriage is! Why have we wasted all this time? Why didn't we marry ten years ago?

TESS. Because you couldn't find anybody nice enough.

GIA. Because you were waiting for *us*.

MAR. I suppose that *was* the reason. We were waiting for you without knowing it. (DON ALHAMBRA *comes forward.*) Hallo!

DON AL. Good morning.

GIU. If this gentleman is an undertaker it's a bad omen.

DON AL. Ceremony of some sort going on?

GIU. (*aside*). He *is* an undertaker! (*Aloud.*) No—a little unimportant family gathering. Nothing in *your* line.

DON AL. Somebody's birthday I suppose?

GIA. Yes, mine!

TESS. And mine!

MAR. And mine!

GIU. And mine!

DON AL. Curious coincidence! And how old may you all be?

TESS. It's a rude question—but about ten minutes.

DON AL. Remarkably fine children! But surely you are jesting?

TESS. In other words, we were married about ten minutes since.

DON AL. Married! You don't mean to say you are married?

MAR. Oh yes, we are married.

DON AL. What, both of you?

ALL. All four of us.

DON AL. (*aside*). Bless my heart, how extremely awkward!

GIA. You don't mind, I suppose?

TESS. You were not thinking of either of us for yourself, I presume? Oh, Giuseppe, look at him—he was. He's heart-broken!

DON AL. No, no, I wasn't! I wasn't!

GIU. Now, my man (*slapping him on the back*), we don't want anything in your line to-day, and if your curiosity's satisfied—you can go!

DON AL. You mustn't call me your man. It's a liberty. I don't think you know who I am.

GIU. Not we, indeed! We are jolly gondoliers, the sons of Baptisto Palmieri, who led the last revolution. Republicans, heart and soul, we hold all men to be equal. As we abhor oppression, we abhor kings: as we detest vain-glory, we detest rank: as we despise effeminacy, we despise wealth. We are Venetian gondoliers—your equals in everything except our calling, and in that at once your masters and your servants.

DON AL. Bless my heart, how unfortunate! One of you may be Baptisto's son, for anything I know to the contrary; but the other is no less a personage than the only son of the late King of Barataria.

ALL. What!

DON AL. And I trust—I *trust* it was that one who slapped me on the shoulder and called me his man!

GIU. One of us a king!
MAR. Not brothers!
TESS. The King of Barataria!
GIA. Well, who'd have thought it!
} *Together.*

MAR. But which is it?

DON AL. What does it matter? As you are both Republicans, and hold kings in detestation, of course you'll abdicate at once. Good morning! (*Going.*)

GIA. *and* TESS. Oh, don't do that! (MARCO *and* GIUSEPPE *stop him.*)

GIU. Well, as to that, of course there are kings and kings. When I say that I detest kings, I mean I detest *bad* kings.

DON AL. I see. It's a delicate distinction.

GIU. Quite so. Now I can conceive a kind of king—an ideal king—the creature of my fancy, you know—who would be absolutely unobjectionable. A king, for instance, who would abolish taxes and make everything cheap, except gondolas——

MAR. And give a great many free entertainments to the gondoliers——

GIU. And let off fireworks on the Grand Canal, and engage all the gondolas for the occasion——

MAR. And scramble money on the Rialto among the gondoliers.

GIU. Such a king would be a blessing to his people, and if I were a king, that is the sort of king I would be.

MAR. And so would I!

DON AL. Come, I'm glad to find your objections are not insuperable.

MAR. *and* GIU. Oh, they're not insuperable.

GIA. *and* TESS. No, they're not insuperable.

GIU. Besides, we are open to conviction.

GIA. Yes; they are open to conviction.

TESS. Oh! they've often been convicted.

GIU. Our views may have been hastily formed on insufficient grounds. They may be crude, ill-digested, erroneous. I've a very poor opinion of the politician who is not open to conviction.

TESS. (*to* GIA.). Oh, he's a fine fellow!

GIA. Yes, that's the sort of politician for *my* money!

DON AL. Then we'll consider it settled. Now, as the country is in a state of insurrection, it is absolutely necessary that you should assume the reins of Government at once; and, until it is ascertained which of you is to be king, I have arranged that you will reign jointly, so that no question can arise hereafter as to the validity of any of your acts.

MAR. As one individual?

DON AL. As one individual.

GIU. (*linking himself with* MARCO). Like this?

DON AL. Something like that.

MAR. And we may take our friends with us, and give them places about the Court?

DON AL. Undoubtedly. That's always done!

MAR. I'm convinced!

GIU. So am I!

TESS. Then the sooner we're off the better.

GIA. We'll just run home and pack up a few things (*going*)——

DON AL. Stop, stop—that won't do at all—ladies are not admitted.

ALL. What!

DON AL. Not admitted. Not at present. Afterwards, perhaps. We'll see.

GIU. Why, you don't mean to say you are going to separate us from our wives!

DON AL. (*aside*). This is very awkward! (*Aloud.*) Only for a time—a few months. After all, what is a few months?

TESS. But we've only been married half an hour! (*Weeps.*)

FINALE—ACT I

SONG—GIANETTA

Kind sir, you cannot have the heart
Our lives to part
From those to whom an hour ago
We were united!
Before our flowing hopes you stem,
Ah, look at them,
And pause before you deal this blow,
All uninvited!
You men can never understand
That heart and hand
Cannot be separated when
We go a-yearning;
You see, you've only women's eyes
To idolize
And only women's hearts, poor men,
To set *you* burning!
Ah me, you men will never understand
That woman's heart is one with woman's hand!

Some kind of charm you seem to find
In womankind—
Some source of unexplained delight
(Unless you're jesting),
But what attracts you, I confess,
I cannot guess,
To me a woman's face is quite
Uninteresting!
If from my sister I were torn
It could be borne—
I should, no doubt, be horrified,
But I could bear it;—
But Marco's quite another thing—
He is my King,
He has my heart and none beside
Shall ever share it!
Ah me, you men will never understand
That woman's heart is one with woman's hand!

RECIT.—DON ALHAMBRA

Do not give way to this uncalled-for grief,
Your separation will be very brief.
To ascertain which is the King
And which the other,
To Barataria's Court I'll bring
His foster-mother;
Her former nurseling to declare
She'll be delighted.
That settled, let each happy pair
Be reunited.

MAR., GIU., GIA., TESS. Viva! His argument is strong!
Viva! We'll not be parted long!
Viva! It will be settled soon!
Viva! Then comes our honeymoon!

[*Exit* DON ALHAMBRA.

QUARTET—MARCO, GIUSEPPE, GIANETTA, TESSA

GIA. Then one of us will be a Queen,
And sit on a golden throne,
With a crown instead,
Of a hat on her head,
And diamonds all her own!
With a beautiful robe of gold and green,
I've always understood;
I wonder whether
She'd wear a feather?
I rather think she should!

ALL. Oh, 'tis a glorious thing, I ween,
To be a regular Royal Queen!
No half-and-half affair, I mean,
But a right-down regular Royal Queen!

MAR. She'll drive about in a carriage and pair,
With the King on her left-hand side,
And a milk-white horse,
As a matter of course,
Whenever she wants to ride!
With beautiful silver shoes to wear
Upon her dainty feet;

With endless stocks
Of beautiful frocks
And as much as she wants to eat!

ALL. Oh, 'tis a glorious thing, I ween, etc.

TESS. Whenever she condescends to walk,
Be sure she'll shine at that,
With her haughty stare
And her nose in the air,
Like a well-born aristocrat!
At elegant high society talk
She'll bear away the bell,
With her "How de do?"
And her "How are you?"
And "I trust I see you well!"

ALL. Oh, 'tis a glorious thing, I ween, etc.

GIU. And noble lords will scrape and bow,
And double themselves in two,
And open their eyes
In blank surprise
At whatever she likes to do.
And everybody will roundly vow
She's fair as flowers in May,
And say, "How clever!"
At whatsoever
She condescends to say!

ALL. Oh, 'tis a glorious thing, I ween,
To be a regular Royal Queen!
No half-and-half affair, I mean,
But a right-down regular Royal Queen!

Enter Chorus of Gondoliers and Contadine

CHORUS

Now, pray, what is the cause of this remarkable hilarity?
This sudden ebullition of unmitigated jollity?
Has anybody blessed you with a sample of his charity?
Or have you been adopted by a gentleman of quality?

MAR. *and* GIU. Replying, we sing
As one individual,

As I find I'm a king,
To my kingdom I bid you all.
I'm aware you object
To pavilions and palaces,
But you'll find I respect
Your Republican fallacies.

CHORUS. As they know we object
To pavilions and palaces,
How can they respect
Our Republican fallacies?

MARCO *and* GIUSEPPE

MAR. For every one who feels inclined,
Some post we undertake to find
Congenial with his frame of mind—
And all shall equal be.

GIU. The Chancellor in his peruke—
The Earl, the Marquis, and the Dook,
The Groom, the Butler, and the Cook—
They all shall equal be.

MAR. The Aristocrat who banks with Coutts—
The Aristocrat who hunts and shoots—
The Aristocrat who cleans our boots—
They all shall equal be!

GIU. The Noble Lord who rules the State—
The Noble Lord who cleans the plate—

MAR. The Noble Lord who scrubs the grate—
They all shall equal be!

GIU. The Lord High Bishop orthodox—
The Lord High Coachman on the box—

MAR. The Lord High Vagabond in the stocks—
They all shall equal be!

BOTH. For every one, etc.

Sing high, sing low,
Wherever they go,
They all shall equal be!

CHORUS. Sing high, sing low,
Wherever they go,
They all shall equal be!

The Earl, the Marquis, and the Dook,
The Groom, the Butler, and the Cook,
The Aristocrat who banks with Coutts,
The Aristocrat who cleans the boots,
The Noble Lord who rules the State,
The Noble Lord who scrubs the grate,
The Lord High Bishop orthodox,
The Lord High Vagabond in the stocks—

For every one, etc.
Sing high, sing low,
Wherever they go,
They all shall equal be!

Then hail! O King,
Whichever you may be,
To you we sing,
But do not bend the knee.
Then hail! O King.

MARCO *and* GIUSEPPE (*together*)

Come, let's away—our island crown awaits me—
Conflicting feelings rend my soul apart!
The thought of Royal dignity elates me,
But leaving thee behind me breaks my heart!
(*Addressing* GIANETTA *and* TESSA.)

GIANETTA *and* TESSA (*together*)

Farewell, my love; on board you must be getting;
But while upon the sea you gaily roam,
Remember that a heart for thee is fretting—
The tender little heart you've left at home!

GIA. Now, Marco dear,
My wishes hear:
While you're away
It's understood
You will be good,
And not too gay.

To every trace
Of maiden grace
  You will be blind,
And will not glance
By any chance
  On womankind!

If you are wise,
You'll shut your eyes
  Till we arrive,
And not address
A lady less
  Than forty-five.
You'll please to frown
On every gown
  That you may see;
And, O my pet,
You won't forget
  You've married me!

And O my darling, O my pet,
Whatever else you may forget
In yonder isle beyond the sea,
Do not forget you've married me!

TESS.

You'll lay your head
Upon your bed
At set of sun.
You will not sing
Of anything
To any one.
You'll sit and mope
All day, I hope,
And shed a tear
Upon the life
Your little wife
Is passing here.

And if so be
You think of me,
Please tell the moon!
I'll read it all
In rays that fall
On the lagoon:
You'll be so kind
As tell the wind
How you may be,
And send me words
By little birds
To comfort me!

And O my darling, O my pet,
Whatever else you may forget,
In yonder isle beyond the sea,
Do not forget you've married me!

QUARTET. Oh, my darling, O my pet, etc.

CHORUS (*during which a "Xebeque" is hauled alongside the quay*)

Then away we go to an island fair
That lies in a Southern sea:
We know not where, and we don't much care,
Wherever that isle may be.

THE MEN (*hauling on boat*).

One, two, three,
Haul!
One, two, three,
Haul!
One, two, three,
Haul!
With a will!

ALL. When the breezes are a-blowing
The ship will be going,
When they don't we shall all stand still!
Then away we go to an island fair,
We know not where, and we don't much care,
Wherever that isle may be.

SOLO—MARCO

Away we go
To a balmy isle,
Where the roses blow
All the winter while.

ALL (*hoisting sail*).

Then away we go to an island fair
That lies in a Southern sea:
Then away we go to an island fair,
Then away, then away, then away!

[*The men embark on the "Xebeque".* MARCO *and* GIUSEPPE *embracing* GIANETTA *and* TESSA. *The girls wave a farewell to the men as the curtain falls.*

END OF ACT I

ACT II

SCENE.—*Pavilion in the Court of Barataria.* MARCO *and* GIUSEPPE, *magnificently dressed, are seated on two thrones, occupied in cleaning the crown and the sceptre. The Gondoliers are discovered, dressed, some as courtiers, officers of rank, etc., and others as private soldiers and servants of various degrees. All are enjoying themselves without reference to social distinctions—some playing cards, others throwing dice, some reading, others playing cup and ball, "morra", etc.*

CHORUS OF MEN *with* MARCO *and* GIUSEPPE

Of happiness the very pith
In Barataria you may see:
A monarchy that's tempered with
Republican Equality.
This form of government we find
The beau-ideal of its kind—
A despotism strict combined
With absolute equality!

MARCO *and* GIUSEPPE

Two kings, of undue pride bereft,
Who act in perfect unity,
Whom you can order right and left
With absolute impunity.
Who put their subjects at their ease
By doing all they can to please!
And thus, to earn their bread-and-cheese,
Seize every opportunity.

CHORUS. Of happiness, the very pith, etc.

MAR. Gentlemen, we are much obliged to you for your expressions of satisfaction and good feeling—I say, we are much obliged to you for your expressions of satisfaction and good feeling.

ALL. We heard you.

MAR. We are delighted, at any time, to fall in with sentiments so charmingly expressed.

ALL. That's all right.

GIU. At the same time there is just one little grievance that we should like to ventilate.

ALL (*angrily*). What?

GIU. Don't be alarmed—it's not serious. It is arranged that, until it is decided which of us two is the actual King, we are to act as one person.

GIORGIO. Exactly.

GIU. Now, although we act as *one* person, we are, in point of fact, *two* persons.

ANNIBALE. Ah, I don't think we can go into that. It is a legal fiction, and legal fictions are solemn things. Situated as we are, we can't recognize two independent responsibilities.

GIU. No; but you can recognize two independent appetites. It's all very well to say we act as one person, but when you supply us with only one ration between us, I should describe it as a legal fiction carried a little too far.

ANNI. It's rather a nice point. I don't like to express an opinion off-hand. Suppose we reserve it for argument before the full Court?

MAR. Yes, but what are we to do in the meantime?

MAR. *and* GIU. We want our tea.

ANNI. I think we may make an interim order for double rations on their Majesties entering into the usual undertaking to indemnify in the event of an adverse decision?

GIOR. That, I think, will meet the case. But you must work hard—stick to it—nothing like work.

GIU. Oh, certainly. We quite understand that a man who holds the magnificent position of King should do something to justify it. We are called "Your Majesty", we are allowed to buy ourselves magnificent clothes, our subjects frequently nod to us in the streets, the sentries always return our salutes, and we enjoy the inestimable privilege of heading the subscription lists to all the principal charities. In return for these advantages the least we can do is to make ourselves useful about the Palace.

SONG—GIUSEPPE *with* CHORUS

Rising early in the morning,
We proceed to light the fire,
Then our Majesty adorning
In its workaday attire,
We embark without delay
On the duties of the day.

First, we polish off some batches
Of political despatches,
And foreign politicians circumvent:
Then, if business isn't heavy,
We may hold a Royal *levée,*
Or ratify some Acts of Parliament.
Then we probably review the household troops—
With the usual "shalloo humps!" and "Shalloo hoops!"
Or receive with ceremonial and state
An interesting Eastern potentate.
After that we generally
Go and dress our private *valet*—
(It's a rather nervous duty—he's a touchy little man)—
Write some letters literary
For our private secretary—
He is shaky in his spelling, so we help him if we can.
Then, in view of cravings inner,
We go down and order dinner;
Then we polish the Regalia and the Coronation Plate—
Spend an hour in titivating
All our Gentlemen-in-Waiting;
Or we run on little errands for the Ministers of State.

Oh, philosophers may sing
Of the troubles of a King;
Yet the duties are delightful, and the privileges great;
But the privilege and pleasure
That we treasure beyond measure
Is to run on little errands for the Ministers of State.

CHORUS. Oh, philosophers may sing, etc.

After luncheon, (making merry
On a bun and glass of sherry),
    If we've nothing in particular to do,
We may make a Proclamation,
Or receive a deputation—
    Then we possibly create a Peer or two.

Then we help a fellow-creature on his path
With the Garter or the Thistle or the Bath
Or we dress and toddle off in semi-state
To a festival, a function, or a *fête*.
    Then we go and stand as sentry
    At the Palace (private entry),
Marching hither, marching thither, up and down and to and fro,
    While the warrior on duty
    Goes in search of beer and beauty
(And it generally happens that he hasn't far to go).
    He relieves us, if he's able,
    Just in time to lay the table,
Then we dine and serve the coffee, and at half-past twelve or one,
    With a pleasure that's emphatic,
    We retire to our attic
With the gratifying feeling that our duty has been done!

Oh, philosophers may sing
Of the troubles of a King,
But of pleasures there are many and of worries there are none;
And the culminating pleasure
That we treasure beyond measure
Is the gratifying feeling that our duty has been done!

CHORUS. Oh, philosophers may sing, etc.

[*Exeunt all but* MARCO *and* GIUSEPPE.

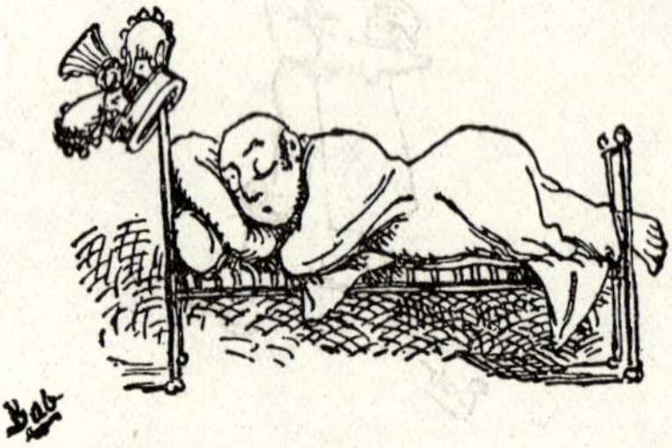

GIU. Yes, it really is a very pleasant existence. They're all so singularly kind and considerate. You don't find them wanting to do this, or wanting to do that, or saying "It's my turn now." No, they let us have all the fun to ourselves, and never seem to grudge it.

MAR. It makes one feel quite selfish. It almost seems like taking advantage of their good nature.

GIU. How nice they were about the double rations.

MAR. Most considerate. Ah! there's only one thing wanting to make us thoroughly comfortable.

GIU. And that is?

MAR. The dear little wives we left behind us three months ago.

GIU. Yes, it *is* dull without female society. We can do without everything else, but we can't do without that.

MAR. And if we have that in perfection, we have everything. There is only one recipe for perfect happiness.

SONG—MARCO

Take a pair of sparkling eyes,
Hidden, ever and anon,
In a merciful eclipse—
Do not heed their mild surprise—
Having passed the Rubicon,
Take a pair of rosy lips;
Take a figure trimly planned—
Such as admiration whets
(Be particular in this);
Take a tender little hand,
Fringed with dainty fingerettes,
Press it—in parenthesis;—
Ah! Take all these, you lucky man—
Take and keep them, if you can!

Take a pretty little cot—
Quite a miniature affair—
Hung about with trellised vine,
Furnish it upon the spot
With the treasures rich and rare
I've endeavoured to define.
Live to love and love to live—
You will ripen at your ease,
Growing on the sunny side—
Fate has nothing more to give.
You're a dainty man to please
If you are not satisfied.
Ah! Take my counsel, happy man;
Act upon it, if you can!

Enter Chorus of Contadine, running in, led by FIAMETTA *and* VITTORIA. *They are met by all the Ex-Gondoliers, who welcome them heartily.*

SCENA—CHORUS OF GIRLS, QUARTET, DUET *and* CHORUS

Here we are, at the risk of our lives,
From ever so far, and we've brought your wives—
And to that end we've crossed the main,
And don't intend to return again!

FIA. Though obedience is strong,
Curiosity's stronger—
We waited for long,
Till we couldn't wait longer.

VIT. It's imprudent, we know,
But without your society
Existence was slow,
And we wanted variety—

ALL. So here we are, at the risk of our lives,
From ever so far, and we've brought your wives—
And to that end we've crossed the main,
And don't intend to return again!

Enter GIANETTA *and* TESSA. *They rush to the arms of* MARCO *and* GIUSEPPE

GIU. Tessa!
TESS. Giuseppe!
GIA. Marco!
MAR. Gianetta!
Embrace.

TESSA *and* GIANETTA

TESS. After sailing to this island—
GIA. Tossing in a manner frightful,
TESS. We are all once more on dry land—
GIA. And we find the change delightful,
TESS. As at home we've been remaining—
We've not seen you both for ages,
GIA. Tell me, are you fond of reigning?—
How's the food, and what's the wages?
TESS. Does your new employment please ye?—
GIA. How does Royalizing strike you?
TESS. Is it difficult or easy?—
GIA. Do you think your subjects like you?
TESS. I am anxious to elicit,
Is it plain and easy steering?
GIA. Take it altogether, is it—
Better fun than gondoliering?
BOTH. We shall both go on requesting
Till you tell us, never doubt it;

Everything is interesting,
Tell us, tell us all about it!

CHORUS. They will both go on requesting, etc.

TESS. Is the populace exacting?
GIA. Do they keep you at a distance?
TESS. All unaided are you acting,
GIA. Or do they provide assistance?
TESS. When you're busy, have you got to
Get up early in the morning?
GIA. If you do what you ought not to,
Do they give the usual warning?
TESS. With a horse do they equip you?
GIA. Lots of trumpeting and drumming?
TESS. Do the Royal tradesmen tip you?
GIA. Ain't the livery becoming!
TESS. Does your human being inner
Feed on everything that nice is?
GIA. Do they give you wine for dinner;
Peaches, sugar-plums, and ices?
BOTH. We shall both go on requesting
Till you tell us, never doubt it;
Everything is interesting,
Tell us, tell us all about it!

CHORUS. They will both go on requesting, etc.

MAR. This is indeed a most delightful surprise!

TESS. Yes, we thought you'd like it. You see, it was like this. After you left we felt very dull and mopey, and the days crawled by, and you never wrote; so at last I said to Gianetta, "I can't stand this any longer; those two poor Monarchs haven't got any one to mend their stockings or sew on their buttons or patch their clothes—at least, I hope they haven't—let us all pack up a change and go and see how they're getting on." And she said, "Done," and they all said, "Done"; and we asked old Giacopo to lend us his boat, and *he* said, "Done"; and we've crossed the sea, and, thank goodness, *that's* done; and here we are, and—and—*I've* done!

GIA. And now—which of you is King?

TESS. And which of us is Queen?

GIU. That we shan't know until Nurse turns up. But never mind that—the question is, how shall we celebrate the commencement of our honeymoon? Gentlemen, will you allow us to offer you a magnificent banquet?

ALL. We will!

GIU. Thanks very much; and, ladies, what do you say to a dance?

TESS. A banquet *and* a dance! O, it's too much happiness!

CHORUS *and* DANCE

Dance a cachucha, fandango, bolero,
Xeres we'll drink—Manzanilla, Montero—
Wine, when it runs in abundance, enhances
The reckless delight of that wildest of dances!
To the pretty pitter-pitter-patter,
And the clitter-clitter-clitter-clatter—
Clitter—clitter—clatter,
Pitter—pitter—patter,
Patter, patter, patter, patter, we'll dance.
Old Xeres we'll drink—Manzanilla, Montero;
For wine, when it runs in abundance, enhances
The reckless delight of that wildest of dances!

(*Cachucha*)

The dance is interrupted by the unexpected appearance of DON ALHAMBRA, *who looks on with astonishment.* MARCO *and* GIUSEPPE *appear embarrassed. The others run off, except Drummer Boy, who is driven off by* DON ALHAMBRA.

DON AL. Good evening. Fancy ball?

GIU. No, not exactly. A little friendly dance. That's all. Sorry you're late.

DON AL. But I saw a groom dancing, and a footman!

MAR. Yes. That's the Lord High Footman.

DON AL. And, dear me, a common little drummer boy!

GIU. Oh no! That's the Lord High Drummer Boy.

DON AL. But surely, surely the servants'-hall is the place for these gentry?

GIU. Oh dear no! *We* have appropriated the servants'-hall. It's the Royal Apartment, and accessible only by tickets obtainable at the Lord Chamberlain's office.

MAR. We really must have some place that we can call our own.

DON AL. (*puzzled*). I'm afraid I'm not quite equal to the intellectual pressure of the conversation.

GIU. You see, the Monarchy has been re-modelled on Republican principles.

DON AL. What!

GIU. All departments rank equally, and everybody is at the head of his department.

DON AL. I see.

MAR. I'm afraid you're annoyed.

DON AL. No. I won't say that. It's not quite what I expected.

GIU. I'm awfully sorry.

MAR. So am I.

GIU. By the by, can I offer you anything after your voyage? A plate of macaroni and a rusk?

DON AL. (*preoccupied*). No, no—nothing—nothing.

GIU. Obliged to be careful?

DON AL. Yes—gout. You see, in every Court there are distinctions that must be observed.

GIU. (*puzzled*). There are, are there?

DON AL. Why, of course. For instance, you wouldn't have a Lord High Chancellor play leapfrog with his own cook.

MAR. Why not?

DON AL. Why not! Because a Lord High Chancellor is a personage of great dignity, who should never, under any circumstances, place himself in the position of being told to tuck in his tuppenny, except by noblemen of his own rank. A Lord High Archbishop, for instance, might tell a Lord High Chancellor to tuck in his tuppenny, but certainly not a cook, gentlemen, certainly not a cook.

GIU. Not even a Lord High Cook?

DON AL. My good friend, that is a rank that is not recognized at the Lord Chamberlain's office. No, no, it won't do. I'll give you an instance in which the experiment was tried.

SONG—DON ALHAMBRA, *with* MARCO *and* GIUSEPPE

DON AL. There lived a King, as I've been told,
In the wonder-working days of old,
When hearts were twice as good as gold,
And twenty times as mellow.
Good-temper triumphed in his face,
And in his heart he found a place
For all the erring human race
And every wretched fellow.
When he had Rhenish wine to drink
It made him very sad to think
That some, at junket or at jink,
Must be content with toddy.

MAR. *and* GIU. With toddy, must be content with toddy.

DON AL. He wished all men as rich as he
(And he was rich as rich could be),
So to the top of every tree
Promoted everybody.

MAR. *and* GIU. Now, that's the kind of King for me—
He wished all men as rich as he,
So to the top of every tree
Promoted everybody!

DON AL. Lord Chancellors were cheap as sprats,
And Bishops in their shovel hats
Were plentiful as tabby cats—
In point of fact, too many.
Ambassadors cropped up like hay,
Prime Ministers and such as they
Grew like asparagus in May,
And Dukes were three a penny.
On every side Field-Marshals gleamed,
Small beer were Lords-Lieutenant deemed,
With Admirals the ocean teemed
All round his wide dominions.

MAR. *and* GIU. With Admirals all round his wide dominions.

DON AL. And Party Leaders you might meet
In twos and threes in every street

Maintaining, with no little heat,
Their various opinions.

MAR. *and* GIU. Now that's a sight you couldn't beat—
Two Party Leaders in each street
Maintaining, with no little heat,
Their various opinions.

DON AL. That King, although no one denies
His heart was of abnormal size,
Yet he'd have acted otherwise
If he had been acuter.
The end is easily foretold,
When every blessed thing you hold
Is made of silver, or of gold,
You long for simple pewter.
When you have nothing else to wear
But cloth of gold and satins rare,
For cloth of gold you cease to care—
Up goes the price of shoddy.

MAR. *and* GIU. Of shoddy, up goes the price of shoddy.

DON AL. In short, whoever you may be,
To this conclusion you'll agree,
When every one is somebodee,
Then no one's anybody!

MAR. *and* GIU. Now that's as plain as plain can be,
To this conclusion we agree—

ALL. When every one is somebodee,
Then no one's anybody!

GIANETTA *and* TESSA *enter unobserved. The two girls, impelled by curiosity, remain listening at the back of the stage.*

DON AL. And now I have some important news to communicate. His Grace the Duke of Plaza-Toro, Her Grace the Duchess, and their beautiful daughter Casilda —I say their beautiful daughter Casilda——

GIU. We heard you.

DON AL. Have arrived at Barataria, and may be here at any moment.

MAR. The Duke and Duchess are nothing to us.

DON AL. But the daughter—the beautiful daughter! Aha! Oh, you're a lucky dog, one of you!

GIU. I think you're a very incomprehensible old gentleman.

DON AL. Not a bit—I'll explain. Many years ago when you (whichever you are) were a baby, you (whichever you are) were married to a little girl who has grown up to be the most beautiful young lady in Spain. That beautiful young lady will be here to claim you (whichever you are) in half an hour, and I congratulate that one (whichever it is) with all my heart.

MAR. Married when a baby!

GIU. But we were married three months ago!

DON AL. One of you—only one. The other (whichever it is) is an unintentional bigamist.

GIA. *and* TESS. (*coming forward*). Well, upon my word!

DON AL. Eh? Who are these young people?

TESS. Who are we? Why their wives, of course. We've just arrived.

DON AL. Their wives! Oh dear, this is very unfortunate! Oh dear, this complicates matters! Dear, dear, what will Her Majesty say?

GIA. And do you mean to say that one of these Monarchs was already married?

TESS. And that neither of us will be a Queen?

DON AL. That is the idea I intended to convey. (TESSA *and* GIANETTA *begin to cry*.)

GIU. (*to* TESSA). Tessa, my dear, dear child——

TESS. Get away! perhaps it's you!

MAR. (*to* GIA.). My poor, poor little woman!

GIA. Don't! Who knows whose husband you are?

TESS. And pray, why didn't you tell us all about it before they left Venice?

DON AL. Because, if I had, no earthly temptation would have induced these gentlemen to leave two such extremely fascinating and utterly irresistible little ladies!

TESS. There's something in that.

DON AL. I may mention that you will not be kept long in suspense, as the old lady who nursed the Royal child is at present in the torture chamber, waiting for me to interview her.

GIU. Poor old girl. Hadn't you better go and put her out of her suspense?

DON AL. Oh no—there's no hurry—she's all right. She has all the illustrated papers. However, I'll go and interrogate her, and, in the meantime, may I suggest the absolute propriety of your regarding yourselves as single young ladies. Good evening!

[*Exit* DON ALHAMBRA.

GIA. Well, here's a pleasant state of things!

MAR. Delightful. One of us is married to two young ladies, and nobody knows which; and the other is married to one young lady whom nobody can identify!

GIA. And one of us is married to one of you, and the other is married to nobody.

TESS. But which of you is married to which of us, and what's to become of the other? (*About to cry.*)

GIU. It's quite simple. Observe. Two husbands have managed to acquire three wives. Three wives—two husbands. (*Reckoning up.*) That's two-thirds of a husband to each wife.

TESS. O Mount Vesuvius, here we are in arithmetic! My good sir, one can't marry a vulgar fraction!

GIU. You've no right to call me a vulgar fraction.

MAR. We are getting rather mixed. The situation entangled. Let's try and comb it out.

QUARTET—MARCO, GIUSEPPE, GIANETTA, TESSA

In a contemplative fashion,
And a tranquil frame of mind,
Free from every kind of passion,
Some solution let us find.
Let us grasp the situation,
Solve the complicated plot—
Quiet, calm deliberation
Disentangles every knot.

TESS. I, no doubt, Giuseppe wedded—
That's, of course, a slice of luck.
He is rather dunder-headed,
Still distinctly, he's a duck.

THE OTHERS. In a contemplative fashion, etc.

GIA. I, a victim, too, of Cupid,
Marco married—that is clear.
He's particularly stupid,
Still distinctly, he's a dear.

THE OTHERS. Let us grasp the situation, etc.

MAR. To Gianetta I was mated;
I can prove it in a trice:
Though her charms are overrated,
Still I own she's rather nice.

THE OTHERS. In a contemplative fashion, etc.

GIU. I to Tessa, willy-nilly,
All at once a victim fell.
She is what is called a silly,
Still she answers pretty well.

THE OTHERS. Let us grasp the situation, etc.

MAR. Now when we were pretty babies
Some one married us, that's clear—

GIA. And if I can catch her
I'll pinch her and scratch her,
And send her away with a flea in her ear.

GIU. He whom that young lady married,
To receive her can't refuse.

TESS. If I overtake her
I'll warrant I'll make her
To shake in her aristocratical shoes!

GIA. (*to* TESS.). If she married your Giuseppe
You and he will have to part—

TESS. (*to* GIA.). If I have to do it
I'll warrant she'll rue it—
I'll teach her to marry the man of my heart!

TESS. (*to* GIA.). If she married Messer Marco
You're a spinster, that is plain—

GIA. (*to* TESS.). No matter—no matter
If I can get at her
I doubt if her mother will know her again!

ALL. Quiet, calm deliberation
Disentangles every knot!

[*Exeunt, pondering.*

MARCH. *Enter procession of Retainers, heralding approach of* DUKE, DUCHESS, *and* CASILDA. *All three are now dressed with the utmost magnificence.*

CHORUS OF MEN, *with* DUKE *and* DUCHESS

With ducal pomp and ducal pride
(Announce these comers,
O ye kettle-drummers!)
Comes Barataria's high-born bride.
(Ye sounding cymbals clang!)
She comes to claim the Royal hand—
(Proclaim their Graces,
O ye double basses!)
Of the King who rules this goodly land.
(Ye brazen brasses bang!)

DUKE *and* DUCH. This polite attention touches
Heart of Duke and heart of Duchess.
Who resign their pet
With profound regret.
She of beauty was a model
When a tiny tiddle-toddle,
And at twenty-one
She's excelled by none!

CHORUS. With ducal pomp and ducal pride, etc.

DUKE (*to his attendants*). Be good enough to inform His Majesty that His Grace the Duke of Plaza-Toro, Limited, has arrived, and begs——

CAS. Desires——

DUCH. Demands——

DUKE. And demands an audience. (*Exeunt attendants.*) And now, my child, prepare to receive the husband to whom you were united under such interesting and romantic circumstances.

CAS. But which is it? There are two of them!

DUKE. It is true that at present His Majesty is a double gentleman; but as soon as the circumstances of his marriage are ascertained, he will, *ipso facto,* boil down to a single gentleman—thus presenting a unique example of an individual who becomes a single man and a married man by the same operation.

DUCH. (*severely*). I have known instances in which the characteristics of both conditions existed concurrently in the same individual.

DUKE. Ah, he couldn't have been a Plaza-Toro.

DUCH. Oh! couldn't he, though!

CAS. Well, whatever happens, I shall, of course, be a dutiful wife, but I can never love my husband.

DUKE. I don't know. It's extraordinary what unprepossessing people one can love if one give's one's mind to it.

DUCH. I loved your father.

DUKE. My love—that remark is a little hard, I think? Rather cruel, perhaps? Somewhat uncalled-for, I venture to believe?

DUCH. It was very difficult, my dear; but I said to myself, "That man is a Duke, and I *will* love him." Several of my relations bet me I couldn't, but I did—desperately!

SONG—DUCHESS

On the day when I was wedded
  To your admirable sire,
I acknowledge that I dreaded
  An explosion of his ire.
I was overcome with panic—
For his temper was volcanic,
  And I didn't dare revolt,
  For I feared a thunderbolt!
I was always very wary,
  For his fury was ecstatic—
His refined vocabulary
  Most unpleasantly emphatic.
    To the thunder
      Of this Tartar
    I knocked under
      Like a martyr;
    When intently
      He was fuming,
    I was gently
      Unassuming—

When reviling
Me completely,
I was smiling
Very sweetly:
Giving him the very best, and getting back the very worst—
That is how I tried to tame your great progenitor—at first!
But I found that a reliance
On my threatening appearance,
And a resolute defiance
Of marital interference,
And a gentle intimation
Of my firm determination
To see what I could do
To be wife and husband too
Was the only thing required
For to make his temper supple,
And you couldn't have desired
A more reciprocating couple.
Ever willing
To be wooing,
We were billing—
We were cooing;
When I merely
From him parted,
We were nearly
Broken-hearted—
When in sequel
Reunited,
We were equal-
Ly delighted.
So with double-shotted guns and colors nailed unto the mast,
I tamed your insignificant progenitor—at last!

CAS. My only hope is that when my husband sees what a shady family he has married into he will repudiate the contract altogether.

DUKE. Shady? A nobleman shady, who is blazing in the lustre of unaccustomed pocket-money? A nobleman shady, who can look back upon ninety-five quarterings?

It is not every nobleman who is ninety-five quarters in arrear—I mean, who can look back upon ninety-five of them! And this, just as I have been floated at a premium! Oh fie!

DUCH. Your Majesty is surely unaware that directly Your Majesty's father came before the public he was applied for over and over again.

DUKE. My dear, Her Majesty's father was in the habit of being applied for over and over again—and very urgently applied for, too—long before he was registered under the Limited Liability Act.

RECIT.—DUKE

To help unhappy commoners, and add to their enjoyment,
Affords a man of noble rank congenial employment;
Of our attempts we offer you examples illustrative:
The work is light, and, I may add, it's most remunerative.

DUET—DUKE *and* DUCHESS

DUKE. Small titles and orders
For Mayors and Recorders
I get—and they're highly delighted—

DUCH. They're highly delighted!

DUKE. M.P.'s baronetted,
Sham Colonels gazetted,
And second-rate Aldermen knighted—

DUCH. Yes, Aldermen knighted.

DUKE. Foundation-stone laying
I find very paying:
It adds a large sum to my makings—

DUCH. Large sums to his makings.

DUKE. At charity dinners
The best of speech-spinners,
I get ten per cent on the takings—

DUCH. One-tenth of the takings.

DUCH. I present my lady
Whose conduct is shady
Or smacking of doubtful propriety—

DUKE. Doubtful propriety.

DUCH. When Virtue would quash her,
I take and whitewash her,
And launch her in first-rate society—

DUKE. First-rate society!

DUCH. I recommend acres
Of clumsy dressmakers—
Their fit and their finishing touches—

DUKE. Their finishing touches.

DUCH. A sum in addition
They pay for permission
To say that they make for the Duchess—

DUKE. They make for the Duchess!

DUKE. Those pressing prevailers,
The ready-made tailors,
Quote me as their great double-barrel—

DUCH. Their great double-barrel.

DUKE. I allow them to do so,
Though Robinson Crusoe
Would jib at their wearing apparel—

DUCH. Such wearing apparel!

DUKE. I sit, by selection,
Upon the direction
Of several Companies bubble—

DUCH. All Companies bubble!

DUKE. As soon as they're floated,
I'm freely bank-noted—
I'm pretty well paid for my trouble—

DUCH. He's paid for his trouble!

DUCH. At middle-class party
I play at *écarté*—
And I'm by no means a beginner—

DUKE (*significantly*). She's not a beginner.

DUCH. To one of my station
The remuneration—
Five guineas a night and my dinner—

DUKE. And wine with her dinner.

DUCH. I write letters blatant
On medicines patent—
And use any other you mustn't—

DUKE. Believe me, you mustn't—

DUCH. And vow my complexion
Derives its perfection
From somebody's soap—which it doesn't—

DUKE (*significantly*). It certainly doesn't!

DUKE. We're ready as witness
To any one's fitness
To fill any place or preferment—

DUCH. A place or preferment.

DUCH. We're often in waiting
At junket or *fêting*,
And sometimes attend an interment—

DUKE. We enjoy an interment.

BOTH. In short, if you'd kindle
The spark of a swindle,
Lure simpletons into your clutches—
Yes; into your clutches.
Or hoodwink a debtor,
You cannot do better

DUCH. Than trot out a Duke or a Duchess—

DUKE. A Duke or a Duchess!

Enter MARCO *and* GIUSEPPE

DUKE. Ah! Their Majesties. Your Majesty! (*Bows with great ceremony.*)

MAR. The Duke of Plaza-Toro, I believe?

DUKE. The same. (MARCO *and* GIUSEPPE *offer to shake hands with him. The* DUKE *bows ceremoniously. They endeavour to imitate him.*) Allow me to present——

GIU. The young lady one of us married?

(MARCO *and* GIUSEPPE *offer to shake hands with her.* CASILDA *curtsies formally. They endeavour to imitate her.*)

CAS. Gentlemen, I am the most obedient servant of one of you. (*Aside.*) Oh, Luiz!

DUKE. I am now about to address myself to the gentleman whom my daughter married; the other may allow his attention to wander if he likes, for what I am about to say does not concern him. Sir, you will find in this young lady a combination of excellences which you would search for in vain in any young lady who had not the good fortune to be my daughter. There is some little doubt as to which of you is the gentleman I am addressing, and which is the gentleman who is allowing his attention to wander; but when that doubt is solved, I shall say (still addressing the attentive gentleman), "Take her, and may she make you happier than her mother has made me."

DUCH. Sir!

DUKE. If possible. And now there is a little matter to which I think I am entitled to take exception. I come here in state with Her Grace the Duchess and Her Majesty my daughter, and what do I find? Do I find, for instance, a guard of honour to receive me? No!

MAR. *and* GIU. No.

DUKE. The town illuminated? No!

MAR. *and* GIU. No.

DUKE. Refreshment provided? No!

MAR. *and* GIU. No.

DUKE. A Royal salute fired? No!

MAR. *and* GIU. No.

DUKE. Triumphal arches erected? No!

MAR. *and* GIU. No.

DUKE. The bells set ringing?

MAR. *and* GIU. No.

DUKE. Yes—one—the Visitors', and I rang it myself. It is not enough! It is not enough!

GIU. Upon my honour, I'm very sorry; but you see, I was brought up in a gondola, and my ideas of politeness are confined to taking off my cap to my passengers when they tip me.

DUCH. That's all very well in its way, but it is not enough.

GIU. I'll take off anything else in reason.

DUKE. But a Royal Salute to my daughter—it costs so little.

CAS. Papa, I don't want a salute.

GIU. My dear sir, as soon as we know which of us is entitled to take that liberty she shall have as many salutes as she likes.

MAR. As for guards of honour and triumphal arches, you don't know our people—they wouldn't stand it.

GIU. They are very off-hand with us—very off-hand indeed.

DUKE. Oh, but you mustn't allow that—you must keep them in proper discipline, you must impress your Court with your importance. You want deportment—carriage——

GIU. We've got a carriage.

DUKE. Manner—dignity. There must be a good deal of this sort of thing—(*business*)—and a little of this sort of thing—(*business*)—and possibly just a *Soupçon* of this sort of thing!—(*business*)—and so on. Oh, it's very useful, and most effective. Just attend to me. You are a King—I am a subject. Very good——

(*Gavotte*)

DUKE, DUCHESS, CASILDA, MARCO, GIUSEPPE

DUKE.
I am a courtier grave and serious
Who is about to kiss your hand:
Try to combine a pose imperious
With a demeanour nobly bland.

MAR. *and* GIU.
Let us combine a pose imperious
With a demeanour nobly bland.

(MARCO *and* GIUSEPPE *endeavour to carry out his instructions.*)

DUKE.
That's, if anything, *too* unbending—
Too aggressively stiff and grand;

(*They suddenly modify their attitudes.*)

Now to the other extreme you're tending—
Don't be so deucedly condescending!

DUCH. *and* CAS.
Now to the other extreme you're tending—
Don't be so dreadfully condescending!

MAR. *and* GIU.
Oh, hard to please some noblemen seem!
At first, if anything, *too* unbending;
Off we go to the other extreme—
Too confoundedly condescending!

DUKE.
Now a gavotte perform sedately—
Offer your hand with conscious pride;
Take an attitude not too stately,
Still sufficiently dignified.

MAR. *and* GIU.
Now for an attitude not too stately,
Still sufficiently dignified.

(*They endeavour to carry out his instructions.*)

DUKE (*beating time*).
Oncely, twicely—oncely, twicely—
Bow impressively ere you glide.
(*They do so.*)
Capital both—you've caught it nicely!
That is the style of thing precisely!

DUCH. *and* CAS.
Capital both—they've caught it nicely!
That is the style of thing precisely!

MAR. *and* GIU.
Oh, sweet to earn a nobleman's praise!
Capital both—we've caught it nicely!
Supposing he's right in what he says,
This is the style of thing precisely!

[GAVOTTE. *At the end exeunt* DUKE *and* DUCHESS, *leaving* CASILDA *with* MARCO *and* GIUSEPPE.

GIU. (*to* MARCO). The old birds have gone away and left the young chickens together. That's called tact.

MAR. It's very awkward. We really ought to tell her how we are situated. It's not fair to the girl.

GIU. Then why don't you do it?

MAR. I'd rather not—you.

GIU. I don't know how to begin. (*To* CASILDA.) A—Madam—I—we, that is, several of us——

CAS. Gentlemen, I am bound to listen to you; but it is right to tell you that, not knowing I was married in infancy, I am over head and ears in love with somebody else.

GIU. Our case exactly! *We* are over head and ears in love with somebody else! (*Enter* GIANETTA *and* TESSA.) In point of fact, with our wives!

CAS. Your wives! Then you are married?

TESS. It's not our fault.

GIA. We knew nothing about it.

BOTH. We are sisters in misfortune.

CAS. My good girls, I don't blame you. Only before we go any further we must really arrive at some satisfactory arrangement, or we shall get hopelessly complicated.

QUINTET AND FINALE

MARCO, GIUSEPPE, CASILDA, GIANETTA, TESSA

ALL. Here is a case unprecedented!
Here are a King and Queen ill-starred!
Ever since marriage was first invented
Never was known a case so hard!

MAR. *and* GIU. I may be said to have been bisected,
By a profound catastrophe!

CAS., GIA., TESS. Through a calamity unexpected
I am divisible into three!

ALL. O moralists all,
How can you call
Marriage a state of unitee,
When excellent husbands are bisected,
And wives divisible into three?
O moralists all,
How can you call
Marriage a state of union true?

CAS., GIA., TESS. One-third of myself is married to half of ye
or you,

MAR. *and* GIU. When half of myself has married one-third
of ye or you?

Enter DON ALHAMBRA, *followed by* DUKE, DUCHESS, *and all the* CHORUS

FINALE

RECIT.—DON ALHAMBRA

Now let the loyal lieges gather round—
The Prince's foster-mother has been found!
She will declare, to silver clarion's sound,
The rightful King—let him forthwith be crowned!

CHORUS. She will declare, etc.

[DON ALHAMBRA *brings forward* INEZ, *the Prince's foster-mother*.

TESS. Speak, woman, speak—
DUKE. We're all attention!
GIA. The news we seek—
DUCH. This moment mention.
CAS. To us they bring—
DON AL. His foster-mother.
MAR. Is he the King?
GIU. Or this my brother?

ALL. Speak, woman, speak, etc.

RECIT.—INEZ

The Royal Prince was by the King entrusted
To my fond care, ere I grew old and crusted;
When traitors came to steal his son reputed,
My own small boy I deftly substituted!
The villains fell into the trap completely—
I hid the Prince away—still sleeping sweetly:
I called him "son" with pardonable slyness—
His name, Luiz! Behold his Royal Highness!

[*Sensation.* LUIZ *ascends the throne, crowned and robed as King.*

CAS. (*rushing to his arms*). Luiz!
LUIZ. Casilda! (*Embrace.*)

ALL. Is this indeed the King?
Oh, wondrous revelation!
Oh, unexpected thing!
Unlooked-for situation!

MAR., GIA., This statement we receive

GIU., TESS.
With sentiments conflicting;
Our hearts rejoice and grieve,
Each other contradicting;
To those whom we adore
We can be reunited—
On one point rather sore,
But, on the whole, delighted!

LUIZ.
When others claimed thy dainty hand,
I waited—waited—waited,

DUKE.
As prudence (so I understand)
Dictated—tated—tated.

CAS.
By virtue of our early vow
Recorded—corded—corded.

DUCH.
Your pure and patient love is now
Rewarded—warded—warded.

ALL.
Then hail, O King of a Golden Land,
And the high-born bride who claims his hand!
The past is dead, and you gain your own,
A royal crown and a golden throne!

[*All kneel:* LUIZ *crowns* CASILDA.

ALL.
Once more *gondolieri,*
Both skilful and wary,
Free from this quandary
Contented are we.
From Royalty flying,
Our gondolas plying,
And merrily crying
Our *"premé," "stalì!"*

So good-bye, cachucha, fandango, bolero—
We'll dance a farewell to that measure—
Old Xeres, adieu—Manzanilla—Montero—
We leave you with feelings of pleasure!

CURTAIN

UTOPIA, LIMITED

OR

THE FLOWERS OF PROGRESS

DRAMATIS PERSONÆ

KING PARAMOUNT THE FIRST (*King of Utopia*)

SCAPHIO, PHANTIS (*Judges of the Utopian Supreme Court*)

TARARA (*the Public Exploder*)

CALYNX (*the Utopian Vice-Chamberlain*)

IMPORTED FLOWERS OF PROGRESS

LORD DRAMALEIGH (*a British Lord Chamberlain*)

CAPTAIN FITZBATTLEAXE (*First Life Guards*)

CAPTAIN SIR EDWARD CORCORAN, K.C.B. (of the Royal Navy)

MR. GOLDBURY (*a Company Promoter; afterwards Comptroller of the Utopian Household*)

SIR BAILEY BARRE, Q.C., M.P.

MR. BLUSHINGTON (*of the County Council*)

THE PRINCESS ZARA (*Eldest Daughter of King Paramount*)

THE PRINCESS NEKAYA, THE PRINCESS KALYBA (*her Younger Sisters*)

THE LADY SOPHY (*their English Gouvernante*)

SALATA, MELENE, PHYLLA (*Utopian Maidens*)

Act I: A UTOPIAN PALM GROVE

Act II: THRONE ROOM IN KING PARAMOUNT'S PALACE

First produced at the Savoy Theatre on October 7, 1893

UTOPIA, LIMITED

OR

THE FLOWERS OF PROGRESS

ACT I

SCENE.—*A Utopian Palm Grove in the gardens of* KING PARAMOUNT'S *Palace, showing a picturesque and luxuriant tropical landscape, with the sea in the distance.* SALATA, MELENE, PHYLLA, *and other Maidens discovered, lying lazily about the stage and thoroughly enjoying themselves in lotus-eating fashion.*

OPENING CHORUS

In lazy languor—motionless,
We lie and dream of nothingness;
For visions come
From Poppydom
Direct at our command:
Or, delicate alternative,
In open idleness we live,
With lyre and lute
And silver flute,
The life of Lazyland!

SOLO—PHYLLA

The song of birds
In ivied towers;
The rippling play
Of waterway;
The lowing herds;
The breath of flowers;
The languid loves
Of turtle doves—
These simple joys are all at hand
Upon thy shores, O Lazyland!

CHORUS

In lazy languor, etc.

Enter CALYNX

CAL. Good news! Great news! His Majesty's eldest daughter, Princess Zara, who left our shores five years since to go to England—the greatest, the most powerful, the wisest country in the world—has taken a high degree at Girton, and is on her way home again, having achieved a complete mastery over all the elements that have tended to raise that glorious country to her present pre-eminent position among civilized nations!

SALATA. Then in a few months Utopia may hope to be completely Anglicized?

CAL. Absolutely and without a doubt.

MELENE (*lazily*). We are very well as we are. Life without a care—every want supplied by a kind and fatherly monarch, who, despot though he be, has no other thought than to make his people happy—what have we to gain by the great change that is in store for us?

SAL. What have we to gain? English institutions, English tastes, and oh, English fashions!

CAL. England has made herself what she is because, in that favoured land, every one has to think for himself. Here we have no need to think, because our monarch anticipates all our wants, and our political opinions are formed for us by the journals to which we subscribe. Oh, think how much more brilliant this dialogue would have been, if we had been accustomed to exercise our reflective powers! They say that in England the conversation of the very meanest is a coruscation of impromptu epigram!

Enter TARARA *in a great rage*

TAR. Lalabalele talala! Callabale lalabalica falahle!

CAL. (*horrified*). Stop—stop, I beg! (*All the ladies close their ears.*)

TAR. Callamalala galalate! Caritalla lalabalee kallalale poo!

LADIES. Oh, stop him! stop him!

CAL. My lord, I'm surprised at you. Are you not aware

that His Majesty, in his despotic acquiescence with the emphatic wish of his people, has ordered that the Utopian language shall be banished from his court, and that all communications shall henceforward be made in the English tongue?

TAR. Yes, I'm perfectly aware of it, although—(*suddenly presenting an explosive "cracker"*). Stop—allow me.

CAL. (*pulls it*). Now, what's that for?

TAR. Why, I've recently been appointed Public Exploder to His Majesty, and as I'm constitutionally nervous, I must accustom myself by degrees to the startling nature of my duties. Thank you. I was about to say that although, as Public Exploder, I am next in succession to the throne, I nevertheless do my best to fall in with the royal decree. But when I am overmastered by an indignant sense of overwhelming wrong, as I am now, I slip into my native tongue without knowing it. I am told that in the language of that great and pure nation, strong expressions do not exist, consequently when I want to let off steam I have no alternative but to say, "Lalabalele molola lililah kallalale poo!"

CAL. But what is your grievance?

TAR. This—by our Constitution we are governed by a Despot who, although in theory absolute—is, in practice, nothing of the kind—being watched day and night by two Wise Men whose duty it is, on his very first lapse from political or social propriety, to denounce him to me, the Public Exploder, and it then becomes my duty to blow up His Majesty with dynamite—allow me. (*Presenting a cracker which* CALYNX *pulls.*) Thank you—and, as some compensation to my wounded feelings, I reign in his stead.

CAL. Yes. After many unhappy experiments in the direction of an ideal Republic, it was found that what may be described as a Despotism tempered by Dynamite provides, on the whole, the most satisfactory description of ruler—an autocrat who dares not abuse his autocratic power.

TAR. That's the theory—but in practice, how does it act? Now, do you ever happen to see the *Palace Peeper?* (*producing a "Society" paper*).

CAL. Never even heard of the journal.

TAR. I'm not surprised, because His Majesty's agents always buy up the whole edition; but I have an aunt in the publishing department, and she has supplied me with a copy. Well, it actually teems with circumstantially convincing details of the King's abominable immoralities! If this high-class journal may be believed, His Majesty is one of the most Heliogabalian profligates that ever disgraced an autocratic throne! And *do* these Wise Men denounce him to me? Not a bit of it! They wink at his immoralities! Under the circumstances I really think I am justified in exclaiming "Lalabalele molola lililah kalabalele poo!" (*All horrified.*) I don't care—the occasion demands it.

[*Exit* TARARA.

March. Enter Guard, escorting SCAPHIO *and* PHANTIS

CHORUS

O make way for the Wise Men!
They are prizemen—
Double-first in the world's university!
For though lovely this island
(Which is *my* land),
She has no one to match them in *her* city.
They're the pride of Utopia—
Cornucopia
Is each in his mental fertility.
O they never make blunder,
And no wonder,
For they're triumphs of infallibility.

DUET—SCAPHIO *and* PHANTIS

In every mental lore
(The statement smacks of vanity)
We claim to rank before
The wisest of humanity.
As gifts of head and heart
We wasted on "utility,"
We're "cast" to play a part
Of great responsibility.

Our duty is to spy
  Upon our King's illicities,
And keep a watchful eye
  On all his eccentricities.
If ever a trick he tries
  That savours of rascality,
At our decree he dies
  Without the least formality.

We fear no rude rebuff,
  Or newspaper publicity;
Our word is quite enough,
  The rest is electricity.
A pound of dynamite
  Explodes in his auriculars;
It's not a pleasant sight—
  We'll spare you the particulars.

Its force all men confess,
  The King needs no admonishing—
We may say its success
  Is something quite astonishing.
Our despot it imbues
  With virtues quite delectable,
He minds his P's and Q's,—
  And keeps himself respectable.

  Of a tyrant polite
  He's a paragon quite.
  He's as modest and mild
  In his ways as a child;
  And no one ever met
  With an autocrat, yet,
  So delightfully bland
  To the least in the land!

So make way for the wise men, etc.

[*Exeunt all but* SCAPHIO *and* PHANTIS.
PHANTIS *is pensive.*

SCA. Phantis, you are not in your customary exuberant spirits. What is wrong?

PHAN. Scaphio, I think you once told me that you have never loved?

SCA. Never! I have often marvelled at the fairy influence which weaves its rosy web about the faculties of the greatest and wisest of our race; but I thank Heaven I have never been subjected to its singular fascination. For, oh, Phantis! there is that within me that tells me that when my time *does* come, the convulsion will be tremendous! When *I* love, it will be with the accumulated fervor of sixty-six years! But I have an ideal—a semi-transparent Being, filled with an inorganic pink jelly—and I have never yet seen the woman who approaches within measurable distance of it. All are opaque—opaque—opaque!

PHAN. Keep that ideal firmly before you, and love not until you find her. Though but fifty-five, I am an old campaigner in the battle-fields of Love; and, believe me, it is better to be as you are, heart-free and happy, than as I am—eternally racked with doubting agonies! Scaphio, the Princess Zara returns from England to-day!

SCA. My poor boy, I see it all.

PHAN. Oh! Scaphio, she is so beautiful. Ah! you smile, for you have never seen her. She sailed for England three months before you took office.

SCA. Now tell me, is your affection requited?

PHAN. I do not know—I am not sure. Sometimes I think it is, and then come these torturing doubts! I feel sure that she does not regard me with absolute indifference, for she could never look at me without having to go to bed with a sick headache.

SCA. That is surely something. Come, take heart, boy! you are young and beautiful. What more could maiden want?

PHAN. Ah! Scaphio, remember she returns from a land where every youth is as a young Greek god, and where such beauty as I can boast is seen at every turn.

SCA. Be of good cheer! Marry her, boy, if so your fancy wills, and be sure that love will come.

PHAN. (*overjoyed*). Then you will assist me in this?

SCA. Why, surely! Silly one, what have you to fear? We have but to say the word, and her father must consent.

Is he not our very slave? Come, take heart. I cannot bear to see you sad.

PHAN. Now I may hope, indeed! Scaphio, you have placed me on the very pinnacle of human joy!

DUET—SCAPHIO *and* PHANTIS

SCA. Let all your doubts take wing—
Our influence is great.
If Paramount our King
Presume to hesitate,
Put on the screw,
And caution him
That he will rue
Disaster grim
That must ensue
To life and limb,
Should he pooh-pooh
This harmless whim.

BOTH. This harmless whim—this harmless whim,
It is, as {I / you} say, a harmless whim.

PHAN. (*dancing*) Observe this dance
Which I employ
When I, by chance,
Go mad with joy.
What sentiment
Does this express?

[PHANTIS *continues his dance while* SCAPHIO *vainly endeavours to discover its meaning.*

Supreme content
And happiness!

BOTH. Of course it does! Of course it does!
Supreme content and happiness!

PHAN. Your friendly aid conferred,
I need no longer pine.
I've but to speak the word,
And lo! the maid is mine!
I do not choose
To be denied.

Or wish to lose
  A lovely bride—
If to refuse
  The King decide,
The Royal shoes
  Then woe betide!

BOTH. Then woe betide—then woe betide!
The Royal shoes then woe betide!

SCA. (*dancing*) This step to use
  I condescend
Whene'er I choose
  To serve a friend.
What it implies
  Now try to guess;

[SCA. *continues his dance while* PHANTIS *is vainly endeavouring to discover its meaning.*

It typifies
  Unselfishness!

BOTH. (*dancing*) Of course it does! Of course it does!
It typifies unselfishness!

[*Exeunt* SCAPHIO *and* PHANTIS.

March. Enter KING PARAMOUNT, *attended by guards and nobles, and preceded by girls dancing before him*

CHORUS

Quaff the nectar—cull the roses—
  Gather fruit and flowers in plenty!
For our King no longer poses—
  Sing the songs of *far niente!*
Wake the lute that sets us lilting,
  Dance a welcome to each comer;
Day by day our year is wilting—
  Sing the sunny songs of summer!
    La, la, la, la!

SONG—KING

A King of autocratic power we—
  A despot whose tyrannic will is law—

Whose rule is paramount o'er land and sea,
    A presence of unutterable awe!
But though the awe that I inspire
Must shrivel with imperial fire
    All foes whom it may chance to touch,
To judge by what I see and hear,
It does not seem to interfere
    With popular enjoyment, much.

CHORUS. No, no—it does not interfere
    With our enjoyment much.

Stupendous when we rouse ourselves to strike,
    Resistless when our tyrant thunder peals,
We often wonder what obstruction's like,
    And how a contradicted monarch feels.
But as it is our Royal whim
Our Royal sails to set and trim
    To suit whatever wind may blow—
What buffets contradiction deals
And how a thwarted monarch feels
    We probably shall never know.

CHORUS. No, no—what thwarted monarch feels
    You'll never, never know.

RECIT.—KING

My subjects all, it is your wish emphatic
That all Utopia shall henceforth be modelled
Upon that glorious country called Great Britain—
To which some add—but others do not—Ireland.

ALL. It is!

KING. That being so, as you insist upon it,
We have arranged that our two younger daughters
Who have been "finished" by an English Lady –
(*tenderly*) A grave and good and gracious English Lady–
Shall daily be exhibited in public,
That all may learn what, from the English standpoint,
Is looked upon as maidenly perfection!
Come hither, daughters!

Enter NEKAYA *and* KALYBA. *They are twins, about fifteen years old; they are very modest and demure in their appearance, dress, and manner. They stand with their hands folded and their eyes cast down.*

CHORUS

How fair! how modest! how discreet!
How bashfully demure!
See how they blush, as they've been taught,
At this publicity unsought!
How English and how pure!

DUET—NEKAYA *and* KALYBA

BOTH. Although of native maids the cream,
We're brought up on the English scheme—
The best of all
For great and small
Who modesty adore.
NEK. For English girls are good as gold,
Extremely modest (so we're told),
Demurely coy—divinely cold—
KAL. And we are that—and more.

To please papa, who argues thus—
All girls should mould themselves on us
Because we are
By furlongs far
The best of all the bunch,
We show ourselves to loud applause
From ten to four without a pause—
NEK. Which is an awkward time because
It cuts into our lunch.

BOTH. Oh, maids of high and low degree,
Whose social code is rather free,
Please look at us and you will see
What good young ladies ought to be!

NEK. And as we stand, like clockwork toys,
A lecturer whom papa employs
Proceeds to praise
Our modest ways
And guileless character—

KAL. Our well-known blush—our downcast eyes—
Our famous look of mild surprise
NEK. (Which competition still defies)—
KAL. Our celebrated "Sir!!!"

Then all the crowd take down our looks
In pocket memorandum books.
To diagnose
Our modest pose
The Kodaks do their best:
NEK. If evidence you would possess
Of what is maiden bashfulness,
You only need a button press—
KAL. And *we* do all the rest.

Enter LADY SOPHY—*an English lady of mature years and extreme gravity of demeanour and dress. She carries a lecturer's wand in her hand. She is led on by the* KING, *who expresses great regard and admiration for her.*

RECIT.—LADY SOPHY

This morning we propose to illustrate
A course of maiden courtship, from the start
To the triumphant matrimonial finish.

[*Through the following song the two Princesses illustrate in gesture the description given by* LADY SOPHY.

SONG—LADY SOPHY

Bold-faced ranger
(Perfect stranger)
Meets two well-behaved young ladies.
He's attractive,
Young and active—
Each a little bit afraid is.
Youth advances,
At his glances
To their danger they awaken;
They repel him
As they tell him
He is very much mistaken.
Though they speak to him politely,
Please observe they're sneering slightly,

Just to show he's acting vainly.
This is Virtue saying plainly,
"Go away, young bachelor,
We are not what you take us for!"
When addressed impertinently,
English ladies answer gently,
"Go away, young bachelor,
We are not what you take us for!"

As he gazes,
Hat he raises,
Enters into conversation.
Makes excuses—
This produces
Interesting agitation.
He, with daring,
Undespairing,
Gives his card—his rank discloses.
Little heeding
This proceeding,
They turn up their little noses.
Pray observe this lesson vital—
When a man of rank and title
His position first discloses,
Always cock your little noses.
When at home, let all the class
Try this in the looking-glass.
English girls of well-bred notions
Shun all unrehearsed emotions.
English girls of highest class
Practise them before the glass.

His intentions
Then he mentions.
Something definite to go on—
Makes recitals
Of his titles,
Hints at settlements, and so on.
Smiling sweetly,
They, discreetly,
Ask for further evidences:

Thus invited,
He, delighted,
Gives the usual references:
This is business. Each is fluttered
When the offer's fairly uttered.
"Which of them has his affection?"
He declines to make selection.
Do they quarrel for his dross?
Not a bit of it—they toss!
Please observe this cogent moral—
English ladies never quarrel.
When a doubt they come across,
English ladies always toss.

RECIT.—LADY SOPHY

The lecture's ended. In ten minutes' space
'Twill be repeated in the market-place!

[*Exit* LADY SOPHY, *followed by* NEKAYA *and* KALYBA.

CHORUS. Quaff the nectar—cull the roses—
Bashful girls will soon be plenty!
Maid who thus at fifteen poses
Ought to be divine at twenty!

[*Exit* CHORUS. *Manet* KING.

KING. I requested Scaphio and Phantis to be so good as to favour me with an audience this morning. (*Enter* SCAPHIO *and* PHANTIS.) Oh, here they are!

SCA. Your Majesty wished to speak with us, I believe. You—you needn't keep your crown on, on our account, you know.

KING. I beg your pardon (*removes it*). I always forget that! Odd, the notion of a King not being allowed to wear one of his own crowns in the presence of two of his own subjects.

PHAN. Yes—bizarre, is it not?

KING. Most quaint. But then it's a quaint world.

PHAN. Teems with quiet fun. I often think what a lucky thing it is that you are blessed with such a keen sense of humour!

KING. Do you know, I find it invaluable. Do what I will, I *cannot* help looking at the humorous side of things—for, properly considered, everything has its humorous side—even the *Palace Peeper* (*producing it*). See here—"Another Royal Scandal," by Junius Junior. "How long is this to last?" by Senex Senior. "Ribald Royalty," by Mercury Major. "Where is the Public Exploder?" by Mephistopheles Minor. When I reflect that all these outrageous attacks on my morality are written by me, at your command—well, it's one of the funniest things that have come within the scope of my experience.

SCA. Besides, apart from that, they have a quiet humour of their own which is simply irresistible.

KING (*gratified*). Not bad, I think. Biting, trenchant sarcasm—the rapier, not the bludgeon—that's my line. But then it's so easy—I'm such a good subject—a bad King but a good Subject—ha! ha!—a capital heading for next week's leading article! (*makes a note*). And then the stinging little paragraphs about our Royal goings-on with our Royal Second Housemaid—delicately sub-acid, are they not?

SCA. My dear King, in that kind of thing no one can hold a candle to you.

PHAN. But the crowning joke is the Comic Opera you've written for us—"King Tuppence, or A Good Deal Less than Half a Sovereign"—in which the celebrated English tenor, Mr. Wilkinson, burlesques your personal appearance and gives grotesque imitations of your Royal peculiarities. It's immense!

KING. Ye—es—That's what I wanted to speak to you about. Now I've not the least doubt but that even *that* has its humorous side, too—if one could only see it. As a rule I'm pretty quick at detecting latent humour—but I confess I do *not* quite see where it comes in, in this particular instance. It's so horribly personal!

SCA. Personal? Yes, of course it's personal—but consider the antithetical humour of the situation.

KING. Yes. I—I don't think I've quite grasped that.

SCA. No? You surprise me. Why, consider. During the day thousands tremble at your frown, during the night (from 8 to 11) thousands roar at it. During the day your most arbitrary pronouncements are received by your subjects with abject submission—during the night, they shout with joy at your most terrible decrees. It's not every monarch who enjoys the privilege of undoing by night all the despotic absurdities he's committed during the day.

KING. Of course! Now I see it! Thank you very much. I was sure it had its humorous side, and it was very dull of me not to have seen it before. But, as I said just now, it's a quaint world.

PHAN. Teems with quiet fun.

KING. Yes. Properly considered, what a farce life is, to be sure!

SONG—KING

First you're born—and I'll be bound you
Find a dozen strangers round you.
"Hallo," cries the new-born baby,
"Where's my parents? which may they be?"
    Awkward silence—no reply—
    Puzzled baby wonders why!
Father rises, bows politely—
Mother smiles (but not too brightly)—
Doctor mumbles like a dumb thing—

Nurse is busy mixing something.—
Every symptom tends to show
You're decidedly *de trop*—

ALL. Ho! ho! ho! ho! ho! ho! ho! ho!
Time's teetotum,
If you spin it,
Gives its quotum
Once a minute.
I'll go bail
You hit the nail,
And if you fail
The deuce is in it!

You grow up and you discover
What it is to be a lover.
Some young lady is selected—
Poor, perhaps, but well-connected,
Whom you hail (for Love is blind)
As the Queen of fairy kind.
Though she's plain—perhaps unsightly,
Makes her face up—laces tightly,
In her form your fancy traces
All the gifts of all the graces.
Rivals none the maiden woo,
So you take her and she takes you!

ALL. Ho! ho! ho! ho! ho! ho! ho! ho!
Joke beginning,
Never ceases,
Till your inning
Time releases,
On your way
You blindly stray,
And day by day
The joke increases!

Ten years later—Time progresses—
Sours your temper—thins your tresses;
Fancy, then, her chain relaxes;
Rates are facts and so are taxes.
Fairy Queen's no longer young—
Fairy Queen has got a tongue.

Twins have probably intruded—
Quite unbidden—just as you did—
They're a source of care and trouble—
Just as you were—only double.
Comes at last the final stroke—
Time has had his little joke!

ALL. Ho! ho! ho! ho! ho! ho! ho! ho!
Daily driven
(Wife as drover)
Ill you've thriven—
Ne'er in clover;
Lastly, when
Three-score and ten
(And not till then),
The joke is over!
Ho! ho! ho! ho! ho! ho! ho! ho!
Then—and then
The joke is over!

[*Exeunt* SCAPHIO *and* PHANTIS. *Manet* KING.

KING (*putting on his crown again*). It's all very well. I always like to look on the humorous side of things; but I do *not* think I ought to be required to write libels on my own moral character. Naturally, I see the joke of it—anybody would—but Zara's coming home to-day; she's no longer a child, and I confess I should *not* like her to see my Opera—though it's uncommonly well written; and I should be sorry if the *Palace Peeper* got into her hands—though it's certainly smart—very smart indeed. It is almost a pity that I have to buy up the whole edition, because it's really too good to be lost. And Lady Sophy—that blameless type of perfect womanhood! Great Heavens, what would *she* say if the Second Housemaid business happened to meet *her* pure blue eye!

Enter LADY SOPHY

LADY S. My monarch is soliloquizing. I will withdraw (*going*).

KING. No—pray don't go. Now I'll give you fifty chances, and you won't guess whom I was thinking of.

LADY S. Alas, sir, I know too well. Ah! King, it's an old, old story, and I'm wellnigh weary of it! Be warned in time—from my heart I pity you, but I am not for you! (*going*).

KING. But hear what I have to say.

LADY S. It is useless. Listen. In the course of a long and adventurous career in the principal European Courts, it has been revealed to me that I unconsciously exercise a weird and supernatural fascination over all Crowned Heads. So irresistible is this singular property, that there is not a European Monarch who has not implored me, with tears in his eyes, to quit his kingdom, and take my fatal charms elsewhere. As time was getting on it occurred to me that by descending several pegs in the scale of Respectability I might qualify your Majesty for my hand. Actuated by this humane motive and happening to possess Respectability enough for Six, I consented to confer Respectability enough for Four upon your two younger daughters—but although I have, alas, only Respectability enough for Two left, there is still, as I gather from the public press of this country (*producing the "Palace Peeper"*), a considerable balance in my favour.

KING (*aside*). Da—! (*Aloud.*) May I ask how you came by this?

LADY S. It was handed to me by the officer who holds the position of Public Exploder to your Imperial Majesty.

KING. And surely, Lady Sophy, surely you are not so unjust as to place any faith in the irresponsible gabble of the Society press!

LADY S. (*referring to paper*). I read on the authority of Senex Senior that your Majesty was seen dancing with your Second Housemaid on the Oriental Platform of the Tivoli Gardens. That is untrue?

KING. Absolutely. Our Second Housemaid has only one leg.

LADY S. (*suspiciously*). How do you know that?

KING. Common report, I give you my honour.

LADY S. It may be so. I further read—and the statement is vouched for by no less an authority than Mephistopheles Minor—that your Majesty indulges in a bath of hot rum-punch every morning. I trust I do not lay myself open to the charge of displaying an indelicate curiosity as to the mysteries of the royal dressing-room when I ask if there is any foundation for this statement?

KING. None whatever. When our medical adviser exhibits rum-punch it is as a draught, not as a fomentation. As to our bath, our valet plays the garden hose upon us every morning.

LADY S. (*shocked*). Oh, pray—pray spare me these unseemly details. Well, you are a Despot—have you taken steps to slay this scribbler?

KING. Well, no—I have *not* gone so far as that. After all, it's the poor devil's living, you know.

LADY S. It is the poor devil's living that surprises me. If this man lies, there is no recognized punishment that is sufficiently terrible for him.

KING. That's precisely it. I—I am waiting until a punishment is discovered that will exactly meet the enormity of the case. I am in constant communication with the Mikado of Japan, who is a leading authority on such points; and, moreover, I have the ground plans and sectional elevations of several capital punishments in my desk at this moment. Oh, Lady Sophy, as you are powerful, be merciful!

DUET—KING *and* LADY SOPHY

KING. Subjected to your heavenly gaze
(Poetical phrase),
My brain is turned completely.
Observe me now,
No Monarch, I vow,
Was ever so far afflicted!

LADY S. I'm pleased with that poetical phrase,
"A heavenly gaze,"
But though you put it neatly,
Say what you will,
These paragraphs still
Remain uncontradicted.

Come, crush me this contemptible worm
(A forcible term),

If he's assailed you wrongly.
The rage display,
Which, as you say,
Has moved your Majesty lately.

KING. Though I admit that forcible term,
"Contemptible worm,"
Appeals to me most strongly,
To treat this pest
As you suggest
Would pain my Majesty greatly.

LADY S. This writer lies!
KING. Yes, bother his eyes!
LADY S. He lives, you say?
KING. In a sort of a way.
LADY S. Then have him shot.
KING. Decidedly not.
LADY S. Or crush him flat.
KING. I cannot do that.

BOTH. O royal Rex,
My / Her } blameless sex
Abhors such conduct shady.
You / I } plead in vain,
You / I } never will gain
Respectable English lady!

[*Dance of repudiation by* LADY SOPHY. *Exit, followed by* KING.

March. Enter all the Court, heralding the arrival of the PRINCESS ZARA, *who enters, escorted by* CAPTAIN FITZBATTLEAXE *and four Troopers, all in the full uniform of the First Life Guards.*

CHORUS

Oh, maiden, rich
In Girton lore,
That wisdom which
We prized before,

We do confess
Is nothingness,
And rather less,
Perhaps, than more.
On each of us
Thy learning shed.
On calculus
May we be fed.
And teach us, please,
To speak with ease
All languages,
Alive and dead!

SOLO—PRINCESS *and* CHORUS

ZARA. Five years have flown since I took wing—
Time flies, and his footstep ne'er retards—
I'm the eldest daughter of your king.

TROOPERS. And we are her escort—First Life Guards!
On the royal yacht,
When the waves were white,
In a helmet hot
And a tunic tight,
And our great big boots,
We defied the storm:
For we're not recruits,
And his uniform
A well-drilled trooper ne'er discards—
And we are her escort—First Life Guards!

ZARA. These gentlemen I present to you,
The pride and boast of their barrack-yards;
They've taken, O! such care of me!

TROOPERS. For we are her escort—First Life Guards!
When the tempest rose,
And the ship went *so*—
Do you suppose
We were ill? No, no!
Though a qualmish lot
In a tunic tight,
And a helmet hot,
And a breastplate bright

(Which a well-drilled trooper ne'er discards),
We stood as her escort—First Life Guards!

FULL CHORUS

Knightsbridge nursemaids—serving fairies—
Stars of proud Belgravian airies;
At stern duty's call you leave them,
Though you know how that must grieve them!

ZARA. Tantantarara-rara-rara!

CAPT. FITZ. Trumpet-call of Princess Zara!

CHORUS. That's trump-call, and they're all trump cards—
They are her escort—First Life Guards!

ENSEMBLE

CHORUS

LADIES

Knightsbridge nursemaids, etc.

MEN

When the tempest rose, etc.

PRINCESS ZARA *and* FITZBATTLEAXE (*aside*)

Oh! the hours are gold,
And the joys untold,
When my eyes behold
My beloved Princess;
And the years will seem
But a brief day-dream,
In the joy extreme
Of our happiness!

FULL CHORUS. Knightsbridge nursemaids, serving fairies, etc.

Enter KING, PRINCESSES NEKAYA *and* KALYBA, *and* LADY SOPHY. *As the* KING *enters the escort present arms.*

KING. Zara! my beloved daughter! Why, how well you look and how lovely you have grown! (*embraces her*).

ZARA. My dear father! (*embracing him*). And my two beautiful little sisters! (*embracing them*).

NEK. Not beautiful.

KAL. Nice-looking.

ZARA. But first let me present to you the English warrior who commands my escort, and who has taken, O! such care of me during the voyage—Captain Fitzbattleaxe!

TROOPERS. The First Life Guards.
When the tempest rose,
And the ship went *so*—

[CAPT. FITZBATTLEAXE *motions them to be silent. The Troopers place themselves in the four corners of the stage, standing at ease, immovably, as if on sentry. Each is surrounded by an admiring group of young ladies, of whom they take no notice.*

KING (*to* CAPT. FITZ.). Sir, you come from a country where every virtue flourishes. We trust that you will not criticize too severely such shortcomings as you may detect in our semi-barbarous society.

FITZ. (*looking at* ZARA). Sir, I have eyes for nothing but the blameless and the beautiful.

KING. We thank you—he is really very polite! (LADY SOPHY, *who has been greatly scandalized by the attentions paid to the Lifeguardsmen by the young ladies, marches the* PRINCESSES NEKAYA *and* KALYBA *towards an exit.*) Lady Sophy, do not leave us.

LADY S. Sir, your children are young, and, so far, innocent. If they are to remain so, it is necessary that they be at once removed from the contamination of their present disgraceful surroundings. (*She marches them off.*)

KING (*whose attention has thus been called to the proceedings of the young ladies—aside*). Dear, dear! They really shouldn't. (*Aloud.*) Captain Fitzbattleaxe——

FITZ. Sir.

KING. Your Troopers appear to be receiving a troublesome amount of attention from those young ladies. I know how strict you English soldiers are, and I should be extremely distressed if anything occurred to shock their puritanical British sensitiveness.

FITZ. Oh, I don't think there's any chance of that.

KING. You think not? They won't be offended?

FITZ. Oh no! They are quite hardened to it. They get a good deal of that sort of thing, standing sentry at the Horse Guards.

KING. It's English, is it?

FITZ. It's particularly English.

KING. Then, of course, it's all right. Pray proceed, ladies, it's particularly English. Come, my daughter, for we have much to say to each other.

ZARA. Farewell, Captain Fitzbattleaxe! I cannot thank you too emphatically for the devoted care with which you have watched over me during our long and eventful voyage.

DUET—ZARA *and* CAPTAIN FITZBATTLEAXE

ZARA. Ah! gallant soldier, brave and true
In tented field and tourney,
I grieve to have occasioned you
So very long a journey.
A British warrior gives up all—
His home and island beauty—
When summoned by the trumpet-call
Of Regimental Duty!

ALL. Tantantarara-rara-rara!
Trumpet-call of Princess Zara!

ENSEMBLE

MEN

A British warrior gives up all, etc.

LADIES

Knightsbridge nursemaids, etc.

FITZBATTLEAXE *and* ZARA (*aside*)

Oh, my joy, my pride,
My delight to hide,
Let us sing, aside,
What in truth we feel.
Let us whisper low
Of our love's glad glow,
Lest the truth we show
We would fain conceal.

FITZ. Such escort duty, as his due,
To young Lifeguardsman falling
Completely reconciles him to
His uneventful calling.
When soldier seeks Utopian glades
In charge of Youth and Beauty,
Then pleasure merely masquerades
As Regimental Duty!

ALL. Tantantarara-rara-rara!
Trumpet-call of Princess Zara!

ENSEMBLE

CHORUS

MEN

A British warrior, etc.

WOMEN

Knightsbridge nursemaids, etc.

FITZBATTLEAXE *and* ZARA (*aside*)

Oh! the hours are gold,
And the joys untold,
When my eyes behold
My beloved Princess;
And the years will seem
But a brief day-dream,
In the joy extreme
Of our happiness!

[*Exeunt* KING *and* PRINCESS *in one direction, Lifeguardsmen and crowd in opposite direction. Enter, at back,* SCAPHIO *and* PHANTIS, *who watch the* PRINCESS *as she goes off.* SCAPHIO *is seated, shaking violently, and obviously under the influence of some strong emotion.*

PHAN. There—tell me, Scaphio, is she not beautiful? Can you wonder that I love her so passionately?

SCA. No. She is extraordinarily—miraculously lovely! Good heavens, what a singularly beautiful girl!

PHAN. I knew you would say so!

SCA. What exquisite charm of manner! What surprising delicacy of gesture! Why, she's a goddess! a very goddess!

PHAN. (*rather taken aback*). Yes—she's—she's an attractive girl.

SCA. Attractive? Why, you must be blind!—She's entrancing—enthralling!—intoxicating! (*Aside.*) God bless my heart, what's the matter with me?

PHAN. (*alarmed*). Yes. You—you promised to help me to get her father's consent, you know.

SCA. Promised! Yes, but the convulsion has come, my good boy! It is she—my ideal! Why, what's this? (*staggering*). Phantis! Stop me—I'm going mad—mad with the love of her!

PHAN. Scaphio, compose yourself, I beg. The girl is perfectly opaque! Besides, remember—each of us is helpless without the other. You can't succeed without my consent, you know.

SCA. And you dare to threaten? Oh, ungrateful! When you came to me, palsied with love for this girl, and implored my assistance, did I not unhesitatingly promise it? And this is the return you make? Out of my sight, ingrate! (*Aside.*) Dear! dear! what is the matter with me?

Enter CAPT. FITZBATTLEAXE *and* ZARA

ZARA. Dear me. I'm afraid we are interrupting a *tête-à-tête*.

SCA. (*breathlessly*). No, no. You come very appropriately. To be brief, we—we love you—this man and I—madly—passionately!

ZARA. Sir!

SCA. And we don't know how we are to settle which of us is to marry you.

FITZ. Zara, this is very awkward.

SCA. (*very much overcome*). I—I am paralysed by the singular radiance of your extraordinary loveliness. I know I am incoherent. I never was like this before—it shall not occur again. I—shall be fluent, presently.

ZARA (*aside*). Oh, dear, Captain Fitzbattleaxe, what *is* to be done?

FITZ. (*aside*). Leave it to me—I'll manage it. (*Aloud.*) It's a common situation. Why not settle it in the English fashion?

BOTH. The English fashion? What is that?

FITZ. It's very simple. In England, when two gentlemen are in love with the same lady, and until it is settled which gentleman is to blow out the brains of the other, it is provided, by the Rival Admirers' Clauses Consolidation Act, that the lady shall be entrusted to an officer of Household Cavalry as stakeholder, who is bound to hand her over to the survivor (on the Tontine principle) in a good condition of substantial and decorative repair.

SCA. Reasonable wear and tear and damages by fire excepted?

FITZ. Exactly.

PHAN. Well, that seems very reasonable. (*To* SCAPHIO.) What do you say—Shall we entrust her to this officer of Household Cavalry? It will give us time.

SCA. (*trembling violently*). I—I am not at present in a condition to think it out coolly—but if he *is* an officer of Household Cavalry, and if the Princess consents——

ZARA. Alas, dear sirs, I have no alternative—under the Rival Admirers' Clauses Consolidation Act!

FITZ. Good—then that's settled.

QUARTET

FITZBATTLEAXE, ZARA, SCAPHIO, *and* PHANTIS

FITZ. It's understood, I think, all round
That, by the English custom bound

I hold the lady safe and sound
  In trust for either rival,
Until you clearly testify
By sword or pistol, by and by,
Which gentleman prefers to die,
  And which prefers survival.

ENSEMBLE

SCA. *and* PHAN.	ZARA *and* FITZ. (*aside*)
It's clearly understood, all round,	We stand, I think, on safish ground,
That, by your English custom bound,	Our senses weak it will astound
He holds the lady safe and sound	If either gentleman is found
In trust for either rival,	Prepared to meet his rival.
Until we clearly testify	Their machinations we defy;
By sword or pistol, by and by,	We won't be parted, you and I—
Which gentleman prefers to die,	Of bloodshed each is rather shy—
And which prefers survival.	They both prefer survival.

PHAN. (*aside to* FITZ.). If I should die and he should live,
To you, without reserve, I give
Her heart so young and sensitive,
  And all her predilections.

SCA. (*aside to* FITZ.). If he should live and I should die,
I see no kind of reason why
You should not, if you wish it, try
  To gain her young affections.

ENSEMBLE

SCA. *and* PHAN. (*angrily to each other*)	FITZ. *and* ZARA (*aside*)
If I should die and you should live,	As both of us are positive
To this young officer I give	That both of them intend to live,
Her heart so soft and sensitive,	There's nothing in the case to give
And all her predilections.	Us cause for grave reflections.
If you should live and I should die,	As both will live and neither die
I see no kind of reason why	I see no kind of reason why
He should not, if he chooses, try	I should not, if I wish it, try
To win her young affections.	To gain your young affections!

[*Exeunt* SCAPHIO *and* PHANTIS *together*

DUET—ZARA *and* FITZBATTLEAXE

ENSEMBLE. Oh, admirable art!
  Oh, neatly-planned intention!

Oh, happy intervention—
Oh, well-constructed plot!

When sages try to part
Two loving hearts in fusion,
Their wisdom's a delusion,
And learning serves them not!

FITZ. Until quite plain
Is their intent,
These sages twain
I represent.
Now please infer
That, nothing loth,
You're henceforth, as it were,
Engaged to marry both—
Then take it that I represent the two—
On that hypothesis, what would you do?

ZARA (*aside*). What would I do? what would I do?
(*To* FITZ.) In such a case,
Upon your breast,
My blushing face
I think I'd rest—(*doing so*).
Then perhaps I might
Demurely say—
"I find this breastplate bright
Is sorely in the way!"

FITZ. Our mortal race
Is never blest—
There's no such case
As perfect rest;
Some petty blight
Asserts its sway—
Some crumpled roseleaf light
Is always in the way!

[*Exit* FITZBATTLEAXE. *Manet* ZARA.

Enter KING

KING. My daughter! At last we are alone together.

ZARA. Yes, and I'm glad we are, for I want to speak to you very seriously. Do you know this paper?

KING (*aside*). Da—! (*Aloud.*) Oh yes—I've—I've seen it. Where in the world did you get this from?

ZARA. It was given to me by Lady Sophy—my sisters' governess.

KING (*aside*). Lady Sophy's an angel, but I do sometimes wish she'd mind her own business! (*Aloud.*) It's —ha! ha!—it's rather humorous.

ZARA. I see nothing humorous in it. I only see that you, the despotic King of this country, are made the subject of the most scandalous insinuations. Why do you permit these things?

KING. Well, they appeal to my sense of humour. It's the only really comic paper in Utopia, and I wouldn't be without it for the world.

ZARA. If it had any literary merit I could understand it.

KING. Oh, it *has* literary merit. Oh, distinctly, it has literary merit.

ZARA. My dear father, it's mere ungrammatical twaddle.

KING. Oh, it's not ungrammatical. I can't allow that. Unpleasantly personal, perhaps, but written with an epigrammatical point that is very rare nowadays—very rare indeed.

ZARA (*looking at cartoon*). Why do they represent you with such a big nose?

KING (*looking at cartoon*). Eh? Yes, it *is* a big one! Why, the fact is that, in the cartoons of a comic paper, the size of your nose always varies inversely as the square of your popularity. It's the rule.

ZARA. Then you must be at a tremendous discount just now! I see a notice of a new piece called "King Tuppence," in which an English tenor has the audacity to personate you on a public stage. I can only say that I am surprised that any English tenor should lend himself to such degrading personalities.

KING. Oh, he's not really English. As it happens he's a Utopian, but he calls himself English.

ZARA. Calls himself English?

KING. Yes. Bless you, they wouldn't listen to any tenor who didn't call himself English.

ZARA. And you permit this insolent buffoon to caricature you in a pointless burlesque! My dear father—if you were a free agent, you would never permit these outrages.

KING (*almost in tears*). Zara—I—I admit I am not altogether a free agent. I—I am controlled. I try to make the best of it, but sometimes I find it very difficult—very difficult indeed. Nominally a Despot, I am, between ourselves, the helpless tool of two unscrupulous Wise Men, who insist on my falling in with all their wishes and threaten to denounce me for immediate explosion if I remonstrate! (*Breaks down completely.*)

ZARA. My poor father! Now listen to me. With a view to remodelling the political and social institutions of Utopia, I have brought with me six Representatives of the principal causes that have tended to make England the powerful, happy, and blameless country which the consensus of European civilization has declared it to be. Place yourself unreservedly in the hands of these gentlemen, and they will reorganize your country on a footing that will enable you to defy your persecutors. They are all now washing their hands after their journey. Shall I introduce them?

KING. My dear Zara, how can I thank you? I will consent to anything that will release me from the abominable tyranny of these two men. (*Calling.*) What ho! Without there! (*Enter* CALYNX.) Summon my Court without an instant's delay!

[*Exit* CALYNX.

FINALE

Enter every one, except the Flowers of Progress

CHORUS

Although your Royal summons to appear
From courtesy was singularly free,
Obedient to that summons we are here—
What would your Majesty?

RECIT.—KING

My worthy people, my beloved daughter
Most thoughtfully has brought with her from England
The types of all the causes that have made
That great and glorious country what it is.

CHORUS. Oh, joy unbounded!

SCA., TAR., *and* PHAN. (*aside*). Why, what *does* this mean?

RECIT.—ZARA

Attend to me, Utopian populace,
Ye South Pacific Island viviparians;
All, in the abstract, types of courtly grace,
Yet, when compared with Britain's glorious race,
But little better than half-clothed barbarians!

CHORUS

Yes! Contrasted when
With Englishmen,
Are little better than half-clothed barbarians!

Enter all the Flowers of Progress, led by FITZBATTLEAXE

SOLO—ZARA

(*Presenting* CAPT. FITZBATTLEAXE.)

When Britain sounds the trump of war
(And Europe trembles),
The army of that conqueror
In serried ranks assembles;
'Tis then this warrior's eyes and sabre gleam
For our protection—
He represents a military scheme
In all its proud perfection!

CHORUS. Yes—yes—
He represents a military scheme
In all its proud perfection!
Ulahlica! Ulahlica! Ulahlica!

SOLO—ZARA

(*Presenting* SIR BAILEY BARRE, Q.C., M.P.)

A complicated gentleman allow me to present,
Of all the arts and faculties the terse embodiment,
He's a great Arithmetician who can demonstrate with ease
That two and two are three, or five, or anything you please;
An eminent Logician who can make it clear to you

That black is white—when looked at from the proper
point of view;
A marvellous Philologist who'll undertake to show
That "yes" is but another and a neater form of "no."

SIR BAILEY. Yes—yes—yes—
"Yes" is but another and a neater form of "no."
All preconceived ideas on any subject I can scout,
And demonstrate beyond all possibility of doubt,
That whether you're an honest man or whether you're
a thief
Depends on whose solicitor has given me my brief.

CHORUS. Yes—yes—yes—
That whether you're an honest man, etc.
Ulahlica! Ulahlica! Ulahlica!

SOLO—ZARA

(*Presenting* LORD DRAMALEIGH *and County Councillor.*)

What these may be, Utopians all,
Perhaps you'll hardly guess—
They're types of England's physical
And moral cleanliness.
This is a Lord High Chamberlain,
Of purity the gauge—
He'll cleanse our Court from moral stain
And purify our Stage.

LORD D. Yes—yes—yes—
Court reputations I revise,
And presentations scrutinize,
New plays I read with jealous eyes,
And purify the Stage.

CHORUS. Court reputations, etc.

ZARA. This County Councillor acclaim,
Great Britain's latest toy—
On anything you like to name
His talents he'll employ—

All streets and squares he'll purify
Within your city walls,
And keep meanwhile a modest eye
On wicked music halls.

C. C. Yes—yes—yes—
In towns I make improvements great,
Which go to swell the County Rate—
I dwelling-houses sanitate,
And purify the Halls!

CHORUS. In towns he makes improvements great, etc.
Ulahlica! Ulahlica! Ulahlica!

SOLO—ZARA

(*Presenting* MR. GOLDBURY.)

A Company Promoter this, with special education,
Which teaches what Contango means and also Backwardation—
To speculators he supplies a grand financial leaven,
Time was when *two* were company—but now it must be seven.

MR. GOLD. Yes—yes—yes—
Stupendous loans to foreign thrones
I've largely advocated;
In ginger-pops and peppermint-drops
I've freely speculated;
Then mines of gold, of wealth untold,
Successfully I've floated,
And sudden falls in apple-stalls
Occasionally quoted:
And soon or late I always call
For Stock Exchange quotation—
No schemes too great and none too small
For Companification!

CHORUS. Yes! Yes! Yes! No schemes too great, etc.
Ulahlica! Ulahlica! Ulahlica!

ZARA. (*Presenting* CAPT. SIR EDWARD CORCORAN, R.N.)

And lastly I present
Great Britain's proudest boast,
Who from the blows
Of foreign foes
Protects her sea-girt coast—

And if you ask him in respectful tone,
He'll show you how you may protect your own!

SOLO—CAPTAIN CORCORAN

I'm Captain Corcoran, K.C.B.,
I'll teach you how we rule the sea,
And terrify the simple Gauls;
And how the Saxon and the Celt
Their Europe-shaking blows have dealt
With Maxim gun and Nordenfelt
(Or will, when the occasion calls).
If sailor-like you'd play your cards,
Unbend your sails and lower your yards,
Unstep your masts—you'll never want 'em more.
Though we're no longer hearts of oak,
Yet we can steer and we can stoke,
And, thanks to coal, and thanks to coke,
We never run a ship ashore!

ALL. What never?

CAPT. No, never!

ALL. What *never*?

CAPT. Hardly ever!

ALL. Hardly ever run a ship ashore!
Then give three cheers, and three cheers more,
For the tar who never runs his ship ashore;
Then give three cheers, and three cheers more,
For he never runs his ship ashore!

CHORUS

All hail, ye types of England's power—
Ye heaven-enlightened band!
We bless the day, and bless the hour
That brought you to our land.

QUARTET

Ye wanderers from a mighty State,
Oh, teach us how to legislate—
Your lightest word will carry weight
In our attentive ears.
Oh, teach the natives of this land

(Who are not quick to understand)
How to work off their social and
Political arrears!

CAPT. FITZ. Increase your army!

LORD D. Purify your Court!

CAPT. COR. Get up your steam and cut your canvas short!

SIR B. BAR. To speak on both sides teach your sluggish brains!

MR. B., C.C. Widen your thoroughfares, and flush your drains!

MR. GOLD. Utopia's much too big for one small head—
I'll float it as a Company Limited!

KING. A Company Limited? What may that be?
The term, I rather think, is new to me.

CHORUS. A Company Limited? etc.

SCA., PHAN., *and* TAR. (*aside*).
What does he mean? What does he mean?
Give us a kind of clue!
What does he mean? What does he mean?
What is he going to do?

SONG—MR. GOLDBURY

Some seven men form an Association
(If possible, all Peers and Baronets),
They start off with a public declaration
To what extent they mean to pay their debts.
That's called their Capital: if they are wary
They will not quote it at a sum immense.
The figure's immaterial—it may vary
From eighteen million down to eighteenpence.
I should put it rather low;
The good sense of doing so
Will be evident at once to any debtor.
When it's left to you to say
What amount you mean to pay,
Why, the lower you can put it at, the better.

CHORUS. When it's left to you to say, etc.

They then proceed to trade with all who'll trust 'em,
    Quite irrespective of their capital
(It's shady, but it's sanctified by custom);
    Bank, Railway, Loan, or Panama Canal.
You can't embark on trading too tremendous—
    It's strictly fair, and based on common sense—
If you succeed, your profits are stupendous—
    And if you fail, pop goes your eighteenpence.

Make the money-spinner spin!
For you only stand to win,
And you'll never with dishonesty be twitted,
For nobody can know,
To a million or so,
To what extent your capital's committed!

CHORUS. No, nobody can know, etc.

If you come to grief, and creditors are craving
(For nothing that is planned by mortal head
Is certain in this Vale of Sorrow—saving
That one's Liability is Limited),—
Do you suppose that signifies perdition?
If so you're but a monetary dunce—
You merely file a Winding-Up Petition,
And start another Company at once!
Though a Rothschild you may be
In your own capacity,
As a Company you've come to utter sorrow—
But the Liquidators say,
"Never mind—you needn't pay,"
So you start another Company to-morrow!

CHORUS. But the Liquidators say, etc.

RECIT.

KING. Well, at first sight it strikes us as dishonest,
But if it's good enough for virtuous England—
The first commercial country in the world—
It's good enough for us.

SCA., PHAN., *and* TAR. (*aside to* KING).
You'd best take care—
Please recollect *we* have not been consulted.

KING (*not heeding them*).
And do I understand you that Great Britain
Upon this Joint Stock principle is governed?

MR. GOLD. We haven't come to that, exactly—but
We're tending rapidly in that direction.
The date's not distant.

KING (*enthusiastically*). We will be before you!
We'll go down to Posterity renowned
As the First Sovereign in Christendom
Who registered his Crown and Country under
The Joint Stock Company's Act of Sixty-Two.

ALL. Ulahlica!

SOLO—KING

Henceforward, of a verity,
With Fame ourselves we link—
We'll go down to Posterity
Of sovereigns all the pink!

SCA., PHAN., *and* TAR. (*aside to* KING).
If you've the mad temerity
Our wishes thus to blink,
You'll go down to Posterity
Much earlier than you think!

TAR. (*correcting them*).
He'll go *up* to Posterity,
If *I* inflict the blow!

SCA. *and* PHAN. (*angrily*).
He'll go *down* to Posterity—
We think we ought to know!

TAR. (*explaining*).
He'll go *up* to Posterity,
Blown up with dynamite!

SCA. *and* PHAN. (*apologetically*),
He'll go *up* to Posterity,
Of course he will, you're right!

ENSEMBLE

KING, LADY SOPHY, NEK., KAL, CALYNX, *and* CHORUS	SCA., PHAN., *and* TAR (*aside*)	FITZBATTLEAXE *and* ZARA (*aside*)
Henceforward, of a verity, With fame ourselves we link— And go down to Posterity, Of sovereigns all the pink!	If he has the temerity Our wishes thus to blink, He'll go up to Posterity Much earlier than they think!	Who love with all sincerity, Their lives may safely link; And as for our Posterity— We don't care what they think!

CHORUS

Let's seal this mercantile pact—
The step we ne'er shall rue—
It gives whatever we lacked —
The statement's strictly true.

All hail, astonishing Fact!
All hail, Invention new—
The Joint Stock Company's Act—
The Act of Sixty-Two!

END OF ACT I

ACT II

SCENE.—*Throne Room in the Palace. Night.* FITZBATTLEAXE *discovered, singing to* ZARA.

RECIT.—FITZ.

Oh, Zara, my beloved one, bear with me!
Ah, do not laugh at my attempted C!
Repent not, mocking maid, thy girlhood's choice—
The fervour of my love affects my voice!

SONG—FITZ.

A tenor, all singers above
(This doesn't admit of a question),
Should keep himself quiet,
Attend to his diet
And carefully nurse his digestion;
But when he is madly in love
It's certain to tell on his singing—
You can't do chromatics
With proper emphatics
When anguish your bosom is wringing!
When distracted with worries in plenty,
And his pulse is a hundred and twenty,
And his fluttering bosom the slave of mistrust is,
A tenor can't do himself justice.
Now observe—(*sings a high note*),
You see, I can't do myself justice!
I could sing if my fervour were mock,
It's easy enough if you're acting—
But when one's emotion

Is born of devotion
You mustn't be over-exacting.
One ought to be firm as a rock
To venture a shake in *vibrato,*
When fervour's expected
Keep cool and collected
Or never attempt *agitato.*
But, of course, when his tongue is of leather,
And his lips appear pasted together,
And his sensitive palate as dry as a crust is,
A tenor can't do himself justice
Now observe—(*sings a cadence*),
It's no use—I can't do myself justice!

ZARA. Why, Arthur, what *does* it matter? When the higher qualities of the heart are all that can be desired, the higher notes of the voice are matters of comparative insignificance. Who thinks slightingly of the cocoanut because it is husky? Besides (*demurely*), you are not singing for an engagement (*putting her hand in his*), you have that already!

FITZ. How good and wise you are! How unerringly your practised brain winnows the wheat from the chaff—the material from the merely incidental!

ZARA. My Girton training, Arthur. At Girton all is wheat, and idle chaff is never heard within its walls! But tell me, is not all working marvellously well? Have not our Flowers of Progress more than justified their name?

FITZ. We have indeed done our best. Captain Corcoran and I have, in concert, thoroughly remodelled the sister-services—and upon so sound a basis that the South Pacific trembles at the name of Utopia!

ZARA. How clever of you!

FITZ. Clever? Not a bit. It's as easy as possible when the Admiralty and Horse Guards are not there to interfere. And so with the others. Freed from the trammels imposed upon them by idle Acts of Parliament, all have given their natural talents full play and introduced reforms which, even in England, were never dreamt of!

ZARA. But perhaps the most beneficent change of all has been effected by Mr. Goldbury, who, discarding the exploded theory that some strange magic lies hidden in the number Seven, has applied the Limited Liability principle to individuals, and every man, woman, and child is now a Company Limited with liability restricted to the amount of his declared Capital! There is not a christened baby in Utopia who has not already issued his little Prospectus!

FITZ. Marvellous is the power of a Civilization which can transmute, by a word, a Limited Income into an Income Limited.

ZARA. Reform has not stopped here—it has been applied even to the costume of our people. Discarding their own barbaric dress, the natives of our land have unanimously adopted the tasteful fashions of England in all their rich entirety. Scaphio and Phantis have undertaken a contract to supply the whole of Utopia with clothing designed upon the most approved English models—and the first Drawing-Room under the new state of things is to be held here this evening.

FITZ. But Drawing-Rooms are always held in the afternoon.

ZARA. Ah, we've improved upon that. We all look so much better by candle-light! And when I tell you, dearest, that my Court train has just arrived, you will understand that I am longing to go and try it on.

FITZ. Then we must part?

ZARA. Necessarily, for a time.

FITZ. Just as I wanted to tell you, with all the passionate enthusiasm of my nature, how deeply, how devotedly I love you!

ZARA. Hush! Are these the accents of a heart that really feels? True love does not indulge in declamation—its voice is sweet, and soft, and low. The west wind whispers when he woos the poplars!

DUET—ZARA *and* FITZBATTLEAXE

ZARA. Words of love too loudly spoken
Ring their own untimely knell;
Noisy vows are rudely broken,
Soft the song of Philomel.
Whisper sweetly, whisper slowly,
Hour by hour and day by day;
Sweet and low as accents holy
Are the notes of lover's lay!

BOTH. Sweet and low, etc.

FITZ. Let the conqueror, flushed with glory,
Bid his noisy clarions bray;
Lovers tell their artless story
In a whispered virelay.
False is he whose vows alluring
Make the listening echoes ring;
Sweet and low when all-enduring
Are the songs that lovers sing!

BOTH. Sweet and low, etc.

[*Exit* ZARA.

Enter KING, *dressed as Field-Marshal*

KING. To a Monarch who has been accustomed to the uncontrolled use of his limbs, the costume of a British Field-Marshal is, perhaps, at first, a little cramping. Are you sure that this is all right? It's not a practical joke, is it? No one has a keener sense of humour than I have, but the First Statutory Cabinet Council of Utopia Limited must be conducted with dignity and impressiveness. Now, where are the other five who signed the Articles of Association?

FITZ. Sir, they are here.

Enter LORD DRAMALEIGH, CAPTAIN CORCORAN, SIR BAILEY BARRE, MR. BLUSHINGTON, *and* MR. GOLDBURY *from different entrances.*

KING. Oh! (*Addressing them.*) Gentlemen, our daughter holds her first Drawing-Room in half an hour, and we shall have time to make our half-yearly report in the interval. I am necessarily unfamiliar with the forms of an English Cabinet Council—perhaps the Lord Chamberlain will kindly put us in the way of doing the thing properly, and with due regard to the solemnity of the occasion.

LORD D. Certainly—nothing simpler. Kindly bring your chairs forward—His Majesty will, of course, preside.

[*They range their chairs across stage like Christy Minstrels.* KING *sits* C., LORD DRAMALEIGH *on his* L., MR. GOLDBURY *on his* R., CAPT. CORCORAN L. *of* LORD DRAMALEIGH, CAPT. FITZBATTLEAXE R. *of* MR. GOLDBURY, MR. BLUSHINGTON *extreme* R., SIR BAILEY BARRE *extreme* L.

KING. Like this?

LORD D. Like this.

KING. We take your word for it that this is all right. You are not making fun of us? This is in accordance with the practice at the Court of St. James's?

LORD D. Well, it is in accordance with the practice at the Court of St. James's Hall.

KING. Oh! it seems odd, but never mind.

SONG—KING

Society has quite forsaken all her wicked courses,
Which empties our police courts, and abolishes divorces.

CHORUS. Divorce is nearly obsolete in England.

KING. No tolerance we show to undeserving rank and splendour;
For the higher his position is, the greater the offender.

CHORUS. That's a maxim that is prevalent in England.

KING. No peeress at our Drawing-Room before the Presence passes
Who wouldn't be accepted by the lower-middle classes.
Each shady dame, whatever be her rank, is bowed out neatly.

CHORUS. In short, this happy country has been Anglicized completely!
It really is surprising
What a thorough Anglicizing
We have brought about—Utopia's quite another land;
In her enterprising movements,
She is England—with improvements,
Which we dutifully offer to our mother-land!

KING. Our city we have beautified—we've done it willy-nilly—
And all that isn't Belgrave Square is Strand and Piccadilly.

CHORUS. We haven't any slummeries in England!

KING. We have solved the labour question with discrimination polished,
So poverty is obsolete and hunger is abolished—

CHORUS. We are going to abolish it in England.

KING. The Chamberlain our native stage has purged, beyond a question,
Of "risky" situation and indelicate suggestion;
No piece is tolerated if it's costumed indiscreetly—

CHORUS. In short, this happy country has been Anglicized completely!
It really is surprising, etc.

KING. Our Peerage we've remodelled on an intellectual basis,
Which certainly is rough on our hereditary races—

CHORUS. We are going to remodel it in England.

KING. The Brewers and the Cotton Lords no longer seek admission,
And Literary Merit meets with proper recognition—

CHORUS. As Literary Merit does in England!

KING. Who knows but we may count among our intellectual chickens,
Like you, an Earl of Thackeray and p'r'aps a Duke of Dickens—
Lord Fildes and Viscount Millais (when they come) we'll welcome sweetly—

CHORUS. In short, this happy country has been Anglicized completely!
It really is surprising, etc.

[*At the end all rise and replace their chairs.*

KING. Now, then, for our first Drawing-Room. Where are the Princesses? What an extraordinary thing it is that since European looking-glasses have been supplied to the Royal bedrooms my daughters are invariably late!

LORD D. Sir, their Royal Highnesses await your pleasure in the Ante-room.

KING. Oh. Then request them to do us the favour to enter at once.

MARCH. *Enter all the Royal Household, including (besides the Lord Chamberlain) the Vice-Chamberlain, the Master of the Horse, the Master of the Buckhounds, the Lord High Treasurer, the Lord Steward, the Comptroller of the Household, the Lord-in-Waiting, the Groom-in-Waiting, the Field Officer in Brigade Waiting, the Gold and Silver Stick, and the Gentlemen Ushers. Then enter the three Princesses (their trains carried by Pages of Honour),* LADY SOPHY, *and the Ladies-in-Waiting.*

KING. My daughters, we are about to attempt a very solemn ceremonial, so no giggling, if you please. Now, my Lord Chamberlain, we are ready.

LORD D. Then, ladies and gentlemen, places, if you

please. His Majesty will take his place in front of the throne, and will be so obliging as to embrace all the *débutantes.* (LADY SOPHY *much shocked.*)

KING. What—must I really?

LORD D. Absolutely indispensable.

KING. More jam for the *Palace Peeper*!

[*The* KING *takes his place in front of the throne, the* PRINCESS ZARA *on his left, the two younger Princesses on the left of* ZARA.

KING. Now, is every one in his place?

LORD D. Every one is in his place.

KING. Then let the revels commence.

Enter the ladies attending the Drawing-Room. They give their cards to the Groom-in-Waiting, who passes them to the Lord-in-Waiting, who passes them to the Vice-Chamberlain, who passes them to the Lord Chamberlain, who reads the names to the KING *as each lady approaches. The ladies curtsey in succession to the* KING *and the three Princesses, and pass out. When all the presentations have been accomplished, the* KING, *Princesses, and* LADY SOPHY *come forward, and all the ladies re-enter.*

RECIT.—KING

This ceremonial our wish displays
To copy all Great Britain's courtly ways.
Though lofty aims catastrophe entail,
We'll gloriously succeed or nobly fail!

UNACCOMPANIED CHORUS

Eagle high in cloudland soaring—
Sparrow twittering on a reed—
Tiger in the jungle roaring—
Frightened fawn in grassy mead—
Let the eagle, not the sparrow,
Be the object of your arrow—
Fix the tiger with your eye—
Pass the fawn in pity by.
Glory then will crown the day—
Glory, glory, anyway!

[*Then exeunt all.*

Enter SCAPHIO *and* PHANTIS, *now dressed as judges in red and ermine robes and undress wigs. They come down stage melodramatically—working together.*

DUET—SCAPHIO *and* PHANTIS

SCA. With fury deep we burn—
PHAN. We do—
SCA. We fume with smothered rage—
PHAN. We do—
SCA. These Englishmen who rule supreme,
Their undertaking they redeem
By stifling every harmless scheme
In which we both engage—
PHAN. They do—
SCA. In which we both engage.
PHAN. We think it is our turn—
SCA. We do—
PHAN. We think our turn has come—
SCA. We do.
PHAN. These Englishmen, they must prepare
To seek at once their native air.
The King as heretofore, we swear,
Shall be beneath our thumb—
SCA. He shall—
PHAN. Shall be beneath our thumb—
SCA. He shall.
BOTH (*with great energy*).
For this mustn't be, and this won't do,
If you'll back me, then I'll back you,
No, this won't do,
No, this mustn't be.

Enter the KING

KING. Gentlemen, gentlemen—really! This unseemly display of energy within the Royal Precincts is altogether unpardonable. Pray, what do you complain of?

SCA. (*furiously*). What do we complain of? Why, through the innovations introduced by the Flowers of Progress all our harmless schemes for making a provision for our old age are ruined. Our Matrimonial Agency is at a standstill, our Cheap Sherry business is in bankruptcy, our Army Clothing contracts are paralysed, and even our Society paper, the *Palace Peeper,* is practically defunct!

KING. Defunct? Is that so? Dear, dear, I am truly sorry.

SCA. Are you aware that Sir Bailey Barre has introduced a law of libel by which all editors of scurrilous newspapers are publicly flogged—as in England? And six of our editors have resigned in succession! Now, the editor of a scurrilous paper can stand a good deal—he takes a private thrashing as a matter of course—it's considered in his salary—but no gentleman likes to be publicly flogged.

KING. Naturally. I shouldn't like it myself.

PHAN. Then our Burlesque Theatre is absolutely ruined!

KING. Dear me. Well, theatrical property is not what it was.

PHAN. Are you aware that the Lord Chamberlain, who has his own views as to the best means of elevating the national drama, has declined to license any play that is not in blank verse and three hundred years old—as in England?

SCA. And as if that wasn't enough, the County Councillor has ordered a four-foot wall to be built up right across the proscenium, in case of fire—as in England.

PHAN. It's so hard on the company—who are liable to be roasted alive—and this has to be met by enormously increased salaries—as in England.

SCA. You probably know that we've contracted to supply the entire nation with a complete English outfit. But perhaps you do *not* know that, when we send in our bills, our customers plead liability limited to a declared capital of eighteenpence, and apply to be dealt with under the Winding-up Act—as in England?

KING. Really, gentlemen, this is very irregular. If you will be so good as to formulate a detailed list of your grievances in writing, addressed to the Secretary of Utopia Limited, they will be laid before the Board, in due course, at their next monthly meeting.

SCA. Are we to understand that we are defied?

KING. That is the idea I intended to convey.

PHAN. Defied! We are defied!

SCA. (*furiously*). Take care—you know our powers. Trifle with us, and you die!

TRIO—SCA., PHAN., *and* KING

SCA. If you think that, when banded in unity,
We may both be defied with impunity,
You are sadly misled of a verity!

PHAN. If you value repose and tranquillity,
You'll revert to a state of docility,
Or prepare to regret your temerity!

KING. If my speech is unduly refractory
You will find it a course satisfactory
At an early Board meeting to show it up.
Though if proper excuse you can trump any,
You may *wind* up a Limited Company,
You cannot conveniently *blow* it up!

(SCAPHIO *and* PHANTIS *thoroughly baffled.*)

KING (*dancing quietly*).
Whene'er I chance to baffle you
I, also, dance a step or two—
Of this now guess the hidden sense:

(SCAPHIO *and* PHANTIS *consider the question as* KING *continues dancing quietly—then give it up.*)

It means—complete indifference.

SCA. *and* PHAN. Of course it does—indifference!
It means complete indifference!

(KING *dancing quietly.* SCA. *and* PHAN. *dancing furiously.*)

SCA. *and* PHAN. As we've a dance for every mood
With *pas de trois* we will conclude.
What this may mean you all may guess—
It typifies remorselessness!

KING. It means unruffled cheerfulness!

[KING *dances off placidly as* SCAPHIO *and* PHANTIS *dance furiously.*

PHAN. (*breathless*). He's right—we are helpless! He's no longer a human being—he's a Corporation, and so long as he confines himself to his Articles of Association we can't touch him! What are we to do?

SCA. Do? Raise a Revolution, repeal the Act of Sixty-Two, reconvert him into an individual, and insist on his immediate explosion! (TARARA *enters.*) Tarara, come here; you're the very man we want.

TAR. Certainly, allow me. (*Offers a cracker to each; they snatch them away impatiently.*) That's rude.

SCA. We have no time for idle forms. You wish to succeed to the throne?

TAR. Naturally.

SCA. Then you won't unless you join us. The King has defied us, and, as matters stand, we are helpless. So are you. We must devise some plot at once to bring the people about his ears.

TAR. A plot?

PHAN. Yes, a plot of superhuman subtlety. Have you such a thing about you?

TAR. (*feeling*). No, I think not. No. There's one on my dressing-table.

SCA. We can't wait—we must concoct one at once, and put it into execution without delay. There is not a moment to spare!

TRIO—SCAPHIO, PHANTIS, *and* TARARA

ENSEMBLE

With wily brain upon the spot
A private plot we'll plan,
The most ingenious private plot
Since private plots began.
That's understood. So far we've got
And, striking while the iron's hot,
We'll now determine like a shot
The details of this private plot.

SCA. I think we ought—(*whispers*).
PHAN. *and* TAR. Such bosh I never heard!
PHAN. Ah! happy thought!—(*whispers*).
SCA. *and* TAR. How utterly dashed absurd!
TAR. *I'll* tell you how—(*whispers*).

SCA. *and* PHAN. Why, what put that in your head?
SCA. I've got it now—(*whispers*).
PHAN. *and* TAR. Oh, take him away to bed!
PHAN. Oh, put him to bed!
TAR. Oh, put him to bed!
SCA. What! put *me* to bed?
PHAN. *and* TAR. Yes, certainly put him to bed!
SCA. But, bless me, don't you see—
PHAN. Do listen to me, I pray—
TAR. It certainly seems to me—
SCA. Bah—this is the only way!
PHAN. It's rubbish absurd you growl!
TAR. You talk ridiculous stuff!
SCA. You're a drivelling barndoor owl!
PHAN. You're a vapid and vain old muff!

(*All, coming down to audience.*)

So far we haven't quite solved the plot—
They're not a very ingenious lot—
But don't be unhappy,
It's still on the *tapis,*
We'll presently hit on a capital plot!

SCA. Suppose we all—(*whispers*).
PHAN. Now *there* I think you're right.
Then we might all—(*whispers*).
TAR. That's true—we certainly might.
I'll tell you what—(*whispers*).
SCA. We will if we possibly can.
Then on the spot—(*whispers*).
PHAN. *and* TAR. Bravo! a capital plan!
SCA. That's exceedingly neat and new!
PHAN. Exceedingly new and neat.
TAR. I fancy that that will do.
SCA. It's certainly very complete.
PHAN. Well done, you sly old sap!
TAR. Bravo, you cunning old mole!
SCA. You very ingenious chap!
PHAN. You intellectual soul!

(*All, coming down and addressing audience.*)

At last a capital plan we've got
We won't say how and we won't say what:
It's safe in my noddle—
Now off we will toddle,
And slyly develop this capital plot!

[*Business. Exeunt* SCAPHIO *and* PHANTIS *in one direction, and* TARARA *in the other.*

Enter LORD DRAMALEIGH *and* MR. GOLDBURY

LORD D. Well, what do you think of our first South Pacific Drawing-Room? Allowing for a slight difficulty with the trains, and a little want of familiarity with the use of the rouge-pot, it was, on the whole, a meritorious affair?

GOLD. My dear Dramaleigh, it redounds infinitely to your credit.

LORD D. One or two judicious innovations, I think?

GOLD. Admirable. The cup of tea and the plate of mixed biscuits were a cheap and effective inspiration.

LORD D. Yes—my idea entirely. Never been done before.

GOLD. Pretty little maids, the King's youngest daughters, but timid.

LORD D. That'll wear off. Young.

GOLD. *That'll* wear off. Ha! here they come, by George! And without the Dragon! What can they have done with her?

Enter NEKAYA *and* KALYBA, *timidly*

NEK. Oh, if you please, Lady Sophy has sent us in here, because Zara and Captain Fitzbattleaxe are going on, in the garden, in a manner which no well-conducted young ladies ought to witness.

LORD D. Indeed, we are very much obliged to her Ladyship.

KAL. Are you? I wonder why.

NEK. Don't tell us if it's rude.

LORD D. Rude? Not at all. We are obliged to Lady Sophy because she has afforded us the pleasure of seeing you.

NEK. I don't think you ought to talk to us like that.

KAL. It's calculated to turn our heads.

NEK. Attractive girls cannot be too particular.

KAL. Oh pray, pray do not take advantage of our unprotected innocence.

GOLD. Pray be reassured—you are in no danger whatever.

LORD D. But may I ask—is this extreme delicacy—this shrinking sensitiveness—a general characteristic of Utopian young ladies?

NEK. Oh no; we are crack specimens.

KAL. We are the pick of the basket. *Would* you mind not coming quite so near? Thank you.

NEK. And please don't look at us like that; it unsettles us.

KAL. And we don't like it. At least, we *do* like it; but it's wrong.

NEK. *We* have enjoyed the inestimable privilege of being educated by a most refined and easily shocked English lady, on the very strictest English principles.

GOLD. But, my dear young ladies——

KAL. Oh, don't! You mustn't. It's too affectionate.

NEK. It really does unsettle us.

GOLD. Are you really under the impression that English girls are so ridiculously demure? Why, an English girl of the highest type is the best, the most beautiful, the bravest, and the brightest creature that Heaven has conferred upon this world of ours. She is frank, openhearted, and fearless, and never shows in so favourable a light as when she gives her own blameless impulses full play!

NEK. *and* KAL. Oh, you shocking story!

GOLD. Not at all. I'm speaking the strict truth. I'll tell you all about her.

SONG—MR. GOLDBURY

A wonderful joy our eyes to bless,
In her magnificent comeliness,
Is an English girl of eleven stone two,
And five foot ten in her dancing shoe!
She follows the hounds, and on she pounds—
The "field" tails off and the muffs diminish—

Over the hedges and brooks she bounds
    Straight as a crow, from find to finish.
At cricket, her kin will lose or win—
    She and her maids, on grass and clover,
Eleven maids out—eleven maids in—
    And perhaps an occasional "maiden over!"

Go search the world and search the sea,
Then come you home and sing with me
There's no such gold and no such pearl
As a bright and beautiful English girl!

With a ten-mile spin she stretches her limbs,
She golfs, she punts, she rows, she swims—
She plays, she sings, she dances, too,
From ten or eleven till all is blue!
    At ball or drum, till small hours come
        (Chaperon's fan conceals her yawning)

She'll waltz away like a teetotum,
And never go home till daylight's dawning.
Lawn-tennis may share her favours fair—
Her eyes a-dance and her cheeks a-glowing—
Down comes her hair, but what does she care?
It's all her own and it's worth the showing!
Go search the world, etc.

Her soul is sweet as the ocean air,
For prudery knows no haven there;
To find mock-modesty, please apply
To the conscious blush and the downcast eye.
Rich in the things contentment brings,
In every pure enjoyment wealthy,
Blithe as a beautiful bird she sings,
For body and mind are hale and healthy.
Her eyes they thrill with right goodwill—
Her heart is light as a floating feather—
As pure and bright as the mountain rill
That leaps and laughs in the Highland heather!
Go search the world, etc.

QUARTET

NEK. Then I may sing and play?
LORD D. You may!
KAL. And I may laugh and shout?
GOLD. No doubt!
NEK. These maxims you endorse?
LORD D. Of course!
KAL. You won't exclaim "Oh fie!"
GOLD. Not I!

GOLD. Whatever you are—be that:
Whatever you say—be true:
Straightforwardly act—
Be honest—in fact,
Be nobody else but *you*.

LORD D. Give every answer pat—
Your character true unfurl;
And when it is ripe,
You'll then be a type
Of a capital English girl.

ALL Oh, sweet surprise—oh, dear delight,
To find it undisputed quite,
All musty, fusty rules despite,
That Art is wrong and Nature right!

NEK. When happy I,
With laughter glad
I'll wake the echoes fairly,
And only sigh
When I am sad—
And that will be but rarely!

KAL. I'll row and fish,
And gallop, soon—
No longer be a prim one—
And when I wish
To hum a tune,
It needn't be a hymn one?

GOLD. *and* LORD D. No, no!
It needn't be a hymn one!

ALL (*dancing*). Oh, sweet surprise and dear delight
To find it undisputed quite—
All musty, fusty rules despite—
That Art is wrong and Nature right!

[*Dance, and off*

Enter LADY SOPHY

RECIT.—LADY SOPHY

Oh, would some demon power the gift impart
To quell my over-conscientious heart—
Unspeak the oaths that never had been spoken,
And break the vows that never should be broken!

SONG—LADY SOPHY

When but a maid of fifteen year,
Unsought—unplighted—
Short-petticoated—and, I fear,
Still shorter-sighted—
I made a vow, one early spring,
That only to some spotless King
Who proof of blameless life could bring
I'd be united.

For I had read, not long before,
Of blameless kings in fairy lore,
And thought the race still flourished here—
Well, well—
I was a maid of fifteen year!

The KING *enters and overhears this verse*

Each morning I pursued my game
(An early riser);
For spotless monarchs I became
An advertiser:
But all in vain I searched each land,
So, kingless, to my native strand
Returned, a little older, and
A good deal wiser!

I learnt that spotless King and Prince
Have disappeared some ages since—
Even Paramount's angelic grace—
Ah, me!—
Is but a mask on Nature's face!

[KING *comes forward.*

RECIT.

KING. Ah, Lady Sophy—then you love me!
For so you sing—

LADY S. (*indignant and surprised. Producing "Palace Peeper"*).
No, by the stars that shine above me,
Degraded King!
For while these rumours, through the city bruited,
Remain uncontradicted, unrefuted,
The object thou of my aversion rooted,
Repulsive thing!

KING. Be just—the time is now at hand
When truth may published be.
These paragraphs were written and
Contributed by me!

LADY S. By you? No, no!

KING. Yes, yes, I swear, by me!
I, caught in Scaphio's ruthless toil,
Contributed the lot!

LADY S. And *that* is why you did not boil
The author on the spot!

KING. And *that* is why I did not boil
The author on the spot!

LADY S. I *couldn't* think why you did not boil!

KING. But *I* know why I did not boil
The author on the spot!

DUET—LADY SOPHY *and* KING

LADY S. Oh, the rapture unrestrained
Of a candid retractation!
For my sovereign has deigned
A convincing explanation—
And the clouds that gathered o'er
All have vanished in the distance,
And of Kings of fairy lore
One, at least, is in existence!

KING. Oh, the skies are blue above,
And the earth is red and rosal,
Now the lady of my love
Has accepted my proposal!
For that *asinorum pons*
I have crossed without assistance,
And of prudish paragons
One, at least, is in existence!

[KING *and* LADY SOPHY *dance gracefully. While this is going on* LORD DRAMALEIGH *enters unobserved with* NEKAYA *and* MR. GOLDBURY *with* KALYBA. *Then enter* ZARA *and* CAPT. FITZBATTLEAXE. *The two girls direct* ZARA'S *attention to the* KING *and* LADY SOPHY, *who are still dancing affectionately together. At this point the* KING *kisses* LADY SOPHY, *which causes the Princesses to make an exclamation. The* KING *and* LADY SOPHY *are at first much confused at being detected, but eventually throw off all reserve, and the four couples break into a wild Tarantella, and at the end exeunt severally.*

Enter all the male Chorus, in great excitement, from various entrances, led by SCAPHIO, PHANTIS, *and* TARARA, *and followed by the female Chorus.*

CHORUS

Upon our sea-girt land
At our enforced command
Reform has laid her hand
    Like some remorseless ogress—
And made us darkly rue
The deeds she dared to do—
And all is owing to
    Those hated Flowers of Progress!

    So down with them!
    So down with them!
Reform's a hated ogress.
    So down with them!
    So down with them!
Down with the Flowers of Progress!

Flourish. Enter KING, *his three daughters,* LADY SOPHY, *and the Flowers of Progress*

KING. What means this most unmannerly irruption?
Is this your gratitude for boons conferred?

SCA. Boons? Bah! A fico for such boons, say we!
These boons have brought Utopia to a standstill!
Our pride and boast—the Army and the Navy—
Have both been reconstructed and remodelled
Upon so irresistible a basis
That all the neighbouring nations have disarmed—
And War's impossible! Your County Councillor
Has passed such drastic Sanitary laws
That all the doctors dwindle, starve, and die!
The laws, remodelled by Sir Bailey Barre,
Have quite extinguished crime and litigation:
The lawyers starve, and all the jails are let
As model lodgings for the working-classes!
In short—
Utopia, swamped by dull Prosperity,
Demands that these detested Flowers of Progress
Be sent about their business, and affairs
Restored to their original complexion!

KING (*to* ZARA). My daughter, this is a very unpleasant state of things. What is to be done?

ZARA. I don't know—I don't understand it. We must have omitted something.

KING. Omitted something? Yes, that's all very well, but——

[SIR BAILEY BARRE *whispers to* ZARA

ZARA (*suddenly*). Of course! Now I remember! Why, I had forgotten the most essential element of all!

KING. And that is?—

ZARA. Government by Party! Introduce that great and glorious element—at once the bulwark and foundation of England's greatness—and all will be well! No political measures will endure, because one Party will assuredly undo all that the other Party has done; and while grouse is to be shot, and foxes worried to death, the legislative action of the country will be at a standstill. Then there will be sickness in plenty, endless lawsuits, crowded jails, interminable confusion in the Army and Navy, and, in short, general and unexampled prosperity!

ALL. Ulahlica! Ulahlica!

PHAN. (*aside*). Baffled!

SCA. But an hour *will* come!

KING. Your hour has come already—away with them, and let them wait my will! (SCAPHIO *and* PHANTIS *are led off in custody*.) From this moment Government by Party is adopted, with all its attendant blessings; and henceforward Utopia will no longer be a Monarchy Limited, but, what is a great deal better, a Limited Monarchy!

FINALE

ZARA. There's a little group of isles beyond the wave—
  So tiny, you might almost wonder where it is—
That nation is the bravest of the brave,
  And cowards are the rarest of all rarities.
The proudest nations kneel at her command;
  She terrifies all foreign-born rapscallions;
And holds the peace of Europe in her hand
  With half a score invincible battalions!

Such, at least, is the tale
Which is borne on the gale,
From the island which dwells in the sea.
Let us hope, for her sake,
That she makes no mistake—
That she's all she professes to be!

KING. Oh, may we copy all her maxims wise,
And imitate her virtues and her charities;
And may we, by degrees, acclimatize
Her Parliamentary peculiarities!
By doing so, we shall, in course of time,
Regenerate completely our entire land—
Great Britain is that monarchy sublime,
To which some add (but others do not) Ireland.
Such, at least, is the tale, etc.

CURTAIN

THE GRAND DUKE

OR

THE STATUTORY DUEL

DRAMATIS PERSONÆ

RUDOLPH (*Grand Duke of Pfennig Halbpfennig*)

ERNEST DUMMKOPF (*a Theatrical Manager*)

LUDWIG (*his Leading Comedian*)

DR. TANNHÄUSER (*a Notary*)

THE PRINCE OF MONTE CARLO

VISCOUNT MENTONE

BEN HASHBAZ (*a Costumier*)

HERALD

THE PRINCESS OF MONTE CARLO (*betrothed to* RUDOLPH)

THE BARONESS VON KRAKENFELDT (*betrothed to* RUDOLPH)

JULIA JELLICOE (*an English Comédienne*)

LISA (*a Soubrette*)

OLGA
GRETCHEN
BERTHA
ELSA
MARTHA
(*Members of Ernest Dummkopf's Company*)

Chamberlains, Nobles, Actors, Actresses, etc.

Act I: SCENE. PUBLIC SQUARE OF SPEISESAAL

Act II: SCENE. HALL IN THE GRAND DUCAL PALACE

Date 1750

First produced at the Savoy Theatre on March 7, 1896

THE GRAND DUKE

OR

THE STATUTORY DUEL

ACT I

SCENE.—*Market-place of Speisesaal, in the Grand Duchy of Pfennig Halbpfennig. A well, with decorated ironwork, up* L.C. GRETCHEN, BERTHA, OLGA, MARTHA, *and other members of* ERNEST DUMMKOPF'S *theatrical company are discovered, seated at several small tables, enjoying a repast in honour of the nuptials of* LUDWIG, *his leading comedian, and* LISA, *his soubrette.*

CHORUS

Won't it be a pretty wedding?
Will not Lisa look delightful?
Smiles and tears in plenty shedding—
Which in brides of course is rightful.
One could say, if one were spiteful,
Contradiction little dreading,
Her bouquet is simply frightful—
Still, 'twill be a pretty wedding!
Oh, it is a pretty wedding!
Such a pretty, pretty wedding!

ELSA. If her dress *is* badly fitting,
Theirs the fault who made her *trousseau.*

BERTHA. If her gloves *are* always splitting,
Cheap kid gloves, we know, will do so.

OLGA. If upon her train she stumbled,
On one's train one's always treading.

GRET. If her hair *is* rather tumbled,
Still, 'twill be a pretty wedding!

CHORUS. Such a pretty, pretty wedding!

CHORUS

Here they come, the couple plighted—
    On life's journey gaily start them.
Soon to be for aye united,
    Till divorce or death shall part them.

[LUDWIG *and* LISA *come forward*

DUET—LUDWIG *and* LISA

LUD. Pretty Lisa, fair and tasty,
    Tell me now, and tell me truly,
Haven't you been rather hasty?
    Haven't you been rash unduly?
Am I quite the dashing *sposo*
    That your fancy could depict you?
Perhaps you think I'm only so-so?
(*She expresses admiration.*)
    Well, I will not contradict you!
CHORUS. No, he will not contradict you!
LISA. Who am I to raise objection?
    I'm a child, untaught and homely—
When you tell me you're perfection,
    Tender, truthful, true, and comely—
That in quarrel no one's bolder,
    Though dissensions always grieve you—
Why, my love, you're so much older
    That, of course, I must believe you!

CHORUS. Yes, of course, she must believe you!

CHORUS

If he ever acts unkindly,
Shut your eyes and love him blindly—
Should he call you names uncomely,
Shut your mouth and love him dumbly—
Should he rate you, rightly—leftly—
Shut your ears and love him deafly.
  Ha! ha! ha! ha! ha! ha! ha!
    Thus and thus and thus alone
    Ludwig's wife may hold her own!

[LUDWIG *and* LISA *sit at table*

Enter NOTARY TANNHÄUSER

NOT. Hallo! Surely I'm not late? (*All chatter unintelligibly in reply.*)

NOT. But, dear me, you're all at breakfast! Has the wedding taken place? (*All chatter unintelligibly in reply.*)

NOT. My good girls, one at a time, I beg. Let me understand the situation. As solicitor to the conspiracy to dethrone the Grand Duke—a conspiracy in which the members of this company are deeply involved—I am invited to the marriage of two of its members. I present myself in due course, and I find, not only that the ceremony has taken place—which is not of the least consequence—but the wedding breakfast is half eaten—which is a consideration of the most serious importance.

[LUDWIG *and* LISA *come down.*

LUD. But the ceremony has *not* taken place. We can't get a parson!

NOT. Can't get a parson! Why, how's that? They're three a penny!

LUD. Oh, it's the old story—the Grand Duke!

ALL. Ugh!

LUD. It seems that the little imp has selected this, our wedding day, for a convocation of all the clergy in the town to settle the details of his approaching marriage with the enormously wealthy Baroness von Krakenfeldt, and there won't be a parson to be had for love or money until six o'clock this evening!

LISA. And as we produce our magnificent classical revival of *Troilus and Cressida* to-night at seven, we have no alternative but to eat our wedding breakfast before we've earned it. So sit down, and make the best of it.

GRET. Oh, I should like to pull his Grand Ducal ears for him, that I should! He's the meanest, the cruellest, the most spiteful little ape in Christendom!

OLGA. Well, we shall soon be freed from his tyranny. To-morrow the Despot is to be dethroned.

LUD. Hush, rash girl! You know not what you say.

OLGA. Don't be absurd! We're all in it—we're all tiled, here.

LUD. That has nothing to do with it. Know ye not that in alluding to our conspiracy without having first given and received the secret sign, you are violating a fundamental principle of our Association?

SONG—LUDWIG

By the mystic regulation
Of our dark Association,
Ere you open conversation
With another kindred soul,
You must eat a sausage-roll!
(*Producing one.*)

ALL. You must eat a sausage-roll!

LUD. If, in turn, he eats another,
That's a sign that he's a brother—
Each may fully trust the other.
It is quaint and it is droll,
But it's bilious on the whole.

ALL. Very bilious on the whole.

LUD. It's a greasy kind of pasty,
Which, perhaps, a judgment hasty
Might consider rather tasty:
Once (to speak without disguise)
It found favour in our eyes.

ALL. It found favour in our eyes.

LUD. But when you've been six months feeding
(As we have) on this exceeding
Bilious food, it's no ill-breeding
If at these repulsive pies
Our offended gorges rise!

ALL. Our offended gorges rise!

MARTHA. Oh, bother the secret sign! I've eaten it until I'm quite uncomfortable! I've given it six times already to-day—and (*whimpering*) I can't eat any breakfast!

BERTHA. And it's so unwholesome. Why, we should be as yellow as frogs if it wasn't for the make-up!

LUD. All this is rank treason to the cause. I suffer as much as any of you. I loathe the repulsive thing—I can't contemplate it without a shudder—but I'm a conscientious conspirator, and if you won't give the sign I will. (*Eats sausage-roll with an effort.*)

LISA. Poor martyr! He's always at it, and it's a wonder where he puts it!

NOT. Well now, about *Troilus and Cressida*. What do *you* play?

LUD. (*struggling with his feelings*). If you'll be so obliging as to wait until I've got rid of this feeling of warm oil at the bottom of my throat, I'll tell you all about it. (LISA *gives him some brandy.*) Thank you, my love; it's gone. Well, the piece will be produced upon a scale of unexampled magnificence. It is confidently predicted that my appearance as King Agamemnon, in a Louis Quatorze wig, will mark an epoch in the theatrical annals of Pfennig Halbpfennig. I endeavoured to persuade Ernest Dummkopf, our manager, to lend us the classical dresses for our marriage. Think of the effect of a real Athenian wedding procession cavorting through the streets of Speisesaal; Torches burning—cymbals banging—flutes tootling—citharæ twanging—and a throng of fifty lovely Spartan virgins capering before us, all down the High Street, singing "Eloia! Eloia! Opoponax, Eloia!" It would have been tremendous!

NOT. And he declined?

LUD. He did, on the prosaic ground that it might rain, and the ancient Greeks didn't carry umbrellas! If, as is confidently expected, Ernest Dummkopf is elected to succeed the dethroned one, mark my words, he will make a mess of it. [*Exit* LUDWIG *with* LISA.

OLGA. He's sure to be elected. His entire company has promised to plump for him on the understanding that all the places about the Court are filled by members of his troupe, according to professional precedence.

ERNEST *enters in great excitement*

BERTHA (*looking off*). Here comes Ernest Dummkopf. Now we shall know all about it!

ALL. Well—what's the news? How is the election going?

ERN. Oh, it's a certainty—a practical certainty! Two of the candidates have been arrested for debt, and the third is a baby in arms—so, if you keep your promises, and vote solid, I'm cocksure of election!

OLGA. Trust to us. But you remember the conditions?

ERN. Yes—all of you shall be provided for, for life. Every man shall be ennobled—every lady shall have unlimited credit at the Court Milliner's, and all salaries shall be paid weekly in advance!

GRET. Oh, it's quite clear he knows how to rule a Grand Duchy!

ERN. Rule a Grand Duchy? Why, my good girl, for ten years past I've ruled a theatrical company! A man who can do that can rule anything!

SONG—ERNEST

Were I a king in very truth,
And had a son—a guileless youth—
In probable succession;
To teach him patience, teach him tact,
How promptly in a fix to act,
He should adopt, in point of fact,
A manager's profession.
To that condition he should stoop
(Despite a too fond mother),
With eight or ten "stars" in his troupe,
All jealous of each other!
Oh, the man who can rule a theatrical crew,
Each member a genius (and some of them two),
And manage to humour them, little and great,
Can govern this tuppenny State!

ALL. Oh, the man, etc.

Both A and B rehearsal slight
They say they'll be "all right at night"
(They've both to go to school yet);

C in each act *must* change her dress,
D *will* attempt to "square the press";
E won't play Romeo unless
    His grandmother plays Juliet;
F claims all hoydens as her rights
    (She's played them thirty seasons);
And G must show herself in tights
    For two convincing reasons—
    Two very well-shaped reasons!

Oh, the man who can drive a theatrical team,
With wheelers and leaders in order supreme,
Can govern and rule, with a wave of his fin,
    All Europe with Ireland thrown in!

ALL. Oh, the man, etc.

[*Exeunt all but* ERNEST.

ERN. Elected by my fellow-conspirators to be Grand Duke of Pfennig Halbpfennig as soon as the contemptible little occupant of the historical throne is deposed—here is promotion indeed! Why, instead of playing Troilus of

Troy for a month, I shall play Grand Duke of Pfennig Halbpfennig for a lifetime! Yet, am I happy? No—far from happy! The lovely English *comédienne*—the beautiful Julia, whose dramatic ability is so overwhelming that our audiences forgive even her strong English accent—that rare and radiant being treats my respectful advances with disdain unutterable! And yet, who knows? She is haughty and ambitious, and it may be that the splendid change in my fortunes may work a corresponding change in her feelings towards me!

Enter JULIA JELLICOE

JULIA. Herr Dummkopf, a word with you, if you please.

ERN. Beautiful English maiden——

JULIA. No compliments, I beg. I desire to speak with you on a purely professional matter, so we will, if you please, dispense with allusions to my personal appearance, which can only tend to widen the breach which already exists between us.

ERN. (*aside*). My only hope shattered! The haughty Londoner still despises me! (*Aloud.*) It shall be as you will.

JULIA. I understand that the conspiracy in which we are all concerned is to develop to-morrow, and that the company is likely to elect you to the throne on the understanding that the posts about the Court are to be filled by members of your theatrical troupe, according to their professional importance.

ERN. That is so.

JULIA. Then all I can say is that it places me in an extremely awkward position.

ERN. (*very depressed*). I don't see how it concerns you.

JULIA. Why, bless my heart, don't you see that, as your leading lady, I am bound under a serious penalty to play the leading part in all your productions?

ERN. Well?

JULIA. Why, of course, the leading part in this production will be the Grand Duchess!

ERN. My wife?

JULIA. That is another way of expressing the same idea.

ERN. (*aside—delighted*). I scarcely dared even to hope for this!

JULIA. Of course, as your leading lady, you'll be mean enough to hold me to the terms of my agreement. Oh, that's so like a man! Well, I suppose there's no help for it—I shall have to do it!

ERN. (*aside*). She's mine! (*Aloud.*) But—do you really think you would care to play that part? (*Taking her hand.*)

JULIA (*withdrawing it*). Care to play it? Certainly not—but what am I to do? Business is business, and I am bound by the terms of my agreement.

ERN. It's for a long run, mind—a run that may last many, many years—no understudy—and once embarked upon there's no throwing it up.

JULIA. Oh, we're used to these long runs in England: they are the curse of the stage—but, you see, I've no option.

ERN. You think the part of Grand Duchess will be good enough for you?

JULIA. Oh, I think so. It's a very good part in Gerolstein, and oughtn't to be a bad one in Pfennig Halbpfennig. Why, what did you suppose I was going to play?

ERN. (*keeping up a show of reluctance*). But, considering your strong personal dislike to me and your persistent rejection of my repeated offers, won't you find it difficult to throw yourself into the part with all the impassioned enthusiasm that the character seems to demand? Remember, it's a strongly emotional part, involving long and repeated scenes of rapture, tenderness, adoration, devotion—all in luxuriant excess, and all of the most demonstrative description.

JULIA. My good sir, throughout my career I have made it a rule never to allow private feeling to interfere with my professional duties. You may be quite sure that (however distasteful the part may be) if I undertake it, I shall consider myself professionally bound to throw myself into it with all the ardour at my command.

ERN. (*aside—with effusion*). I'm the happiest fellow alive! (*Aloud.*) Now—would you have any objection—to—to give me some idea—if it's only a mere sketch—as to how you would play it? It would be really interesting—to me—to know your conception of—of—the part of my wife.

JULIA. How would I play it? Now, let me see—let me see. (*Considering.*) Ah, I have it!

BALLAD—JULIA

How would I play this part—
The Grand Duke's Bride?
All rancour in my heart
I'd duly hide—
I'd drive it from my recollection
And 'whelm you with a mock affection,
Well calculated to defy detection—
That's how I'd play this part—
The Grand Duke's Bride.

With many a winsome smile
I'd witch and woo;
With gay and girlish guile
I'd frenzy you—
I'd madden you with my caressing,
Like turtle, her first love confessing—
That it was "mock", no mortal would be guessing,
With so much winsome wile
I'd witch and woo!

Did any other maid
With you succeed,
I'd pinch the forward jade—
I would indeed!
With jealous frenzy agitated
(Which would, of course, be simulated),
I'd make her wish she'd never been created—
Did any other maid
With you succeed!

And should there come to me,
Some summers hence,
In all the childish glee
Of innocence,
Fair babes, aglow with beauty vernal,
My heart would bound with joy diurnal!
This sweet display of sympathy maternal,
Well, that would also be
A mere pretence!

My histrionic art
Though you deride,
That's how I'd play that part—
The Grand Duke's Bride!

ENSEMBLE

ERNEST	JULIA
Oh joy! when two glowing young hearts,	My boy, when two glowing young hearts,
From the rise of the curtain,	From the rise of the curtain,
Thus throw themselves into their parts,	Thus throw themselves into their parts,
Success is most certain!	Success is most certain!
If the *rôle* you're prepared to endow	The *rôle* I'm prepared to endow
With such delicate touches,	With most delicate touches,
By the heaven above us, I vow	By the heaven above us, I vow
You shall be my Grand Duchess!	I will be your Grand Duchess!

[*Dance.*

Enter all the Chorus with LUDWIG, NOTARY, *and* LISA—*all greatly agitated*

EXCITED CHORUS

My goodness me! what shall we do? Why, what
A dreadful situation!
(*To* LUD.) It's all your fault, you booby you—you lump of indiscrimination!
I'm sure I don't know where to go—it's put me into such a tetter—
But this at all events I know—the sooner we are off, the better!

ERN. What means this *agitato?* What d'ye seek?
As your Grand Duke elect I bid you speak!

SONG—LUDWIG

Ten minutes since I met a chap
Who bowed an easy salutation—
Thinks I, "This gentleman, mayhap,
Belongs to our Association."
But, on the whole,
Uncertain yet,
A sausage-roll
I took and eat—
That chap replied (I don't embellish)
By eating *three* with obvious relish.

CHORUS (*angrily*). Why, gracious powers,
No chum of ours
Could eat three sausage-rolls with relish!

LUD. Quite reassured, I let him know
Our plot—each incident explaining;
That stranger chuckled much, as though
He thought me highly entertaining.
I told him all,
Both bad and good;
I bade him call—
He said he would:
I added much—the more I muckled,
The more that chuckling chummy chuckled!

ALL (*angrily*). A bat could see
He couldn't be
A chum of ours if he chuckled!

LUD. Well, as I bowed to his applause,
Down dropped he with hysteric bellow—
And *that* seemed right enough, because
I *am* a devilish funny fellow.
Then suddenly,
As still he squealed,
It flashed on me
That I'd revealed
Our plot, with all details effective,
To Grand Duke Rudolph's own detective!

ALL. What folly fell,
To go and tell
Our plot to any one's detective!

CHORUS

(*Attacking* LUDWIG). You booby dense—
You oaf immense,
With no pretence
To common sense!
A stupid muff
Who's made of stuff
Not worth a puff
Of candle-snuff!

Pack up at once and off we go, unless we're anxious to exhibit
Our fairy forms all in a row, strung up upon the Castle gibbet!

[*Exeunt Chorus. Manent* LUDWIG, LISA, ERNEST, JULIA, *and* NOTARY.

JULIA. Well, a nice mess you've got us into! There's an end of our precious plot! All up—pop—fizzle—bang —done for!

LUD. Yes, but—ha! ha!—fancy my choosing the Grand Duke's private detective, of all men, to make a confidant of! When you come to think of it, it's really devilish funny!

ERN. (*angrily*). When you come to think of it, it's extremely injudicious to admit into a conspiracy every pudding-headed baboon who presents himself!

LUD. Yes—I should never do that. If I were chairman of this gang, I should hesitate to enrol *any* baboon who couldn't produce satisfactory credentials from his last Zoological Gardens.

LISA. Ludwig is far from being a baboon. Poor boy, he could not help giving us away—it's his trusting nature—he was deceived.

JULIA (*furiously*). His trusting nature! (*To* LUDWIG.) Oh, I should like to talk to you in my own language for five minutes—only five minutes! I know some good, strong, energetic English remarks that would shrivel your trusting nature into raisins—only you wouldn't understand them!

LUD. Here we perceive one of the disadvantages of a neglected education!

ERN. (*to* JULIA). And I suppose you'll never be my Grand Duchess now!

JULIA. Grand Duchess? My good friend, if you don't produce the piece how can I play the part?

ERN. True. (*To* LUDWIG). You see what you've done.

LUD. But, my dear sir, you don't seem to understand that the man ate three sausage-rolls. Keep that fact steadily before you. Three large sausage-rolls.

JULIA. Bah!—Lots of people eat sausage-rolls who are not conspirators.

LUD. Then they shouldn't. It's bad form. It's not the game. When one of the Human Family proposes to eat a sausage-roll, it is his duty to ask himself, "Am I a conspirator?" And if, on examination, he finds that he is *not* a conspirator, he is bound in honour to select some other form of refreshment.

LISA. Of course he is. One should always play the game. (*To* NOTARY, *who has been smiling placidly through this.*) What are you grinning at, you greedy old man?

NOT. Nothing—don't mind me. It is always amusing to the legal mind to see a parcel of laymen bothering themselves about a matter which to a trained lawyer presents no difficulty whatever.

ALL. No difficulty!

NOT. None whatever! The way out of it is quite simple.

ALL. Simple?

NOT. Certainly! Now attend. In the first place, you two men fight a Statutory Duel.

ERN. A Statutory Duel?

JULIA. A Stat-tat-tatutory Duel! Ach! what a crack-jaw language this German is!

LUD. Never heard of such a thing.

NOT. It is true that the practice has fallen into abeyance through disuse. But all the laws of Pfennig Halbpfennig run for a hundred years, when they die a natural death, unless, in the meantime, they have been revived for another century. The Act that institutes the Statutory Duel was passed a hundred years ago, and as it has never been revived, it expires to-morrow. So you're just in time.

JULIA. But what is the use of talking to us about Statutory Duels when we none of us know what a Statutory Duel is?

NOT. Don't you? Then I'll explain.

SONG—NOTARY

About a century since,
The code of the duello
To sudden death
For want of breath
Sent many a strapping fellow.
The then presiding Prince
(Who useless bloodshed hated),
He passed an Act,
Short and compact,
Which may be briefly stated.
Unlike the complicated laws
A Parliamentary draftsman draws,
It may be briefly stated.

ALL. We know that complicated laws,
Such as a legal draftsman draws,
Cannot be briefly stated.

NOT. By this ingenious law,
If any two shall quarrel,
They may not fight
With falchions bright
(Which seemed to him immoral);
But each a card shall draw,
And he who draws the lowest
Shall (so 'twas said)
Be thenceforth dead—
In fact, a legal "ghoest"
(When exigence of rhyme compels,
Orthography forgoes her spells,
And "ghost" is written "ghoest").

ALL (*aside*). With what an emphasis he dwells
Upon "orthography" and "spells"!
That kind of fun's the lowest.

NOT. When off the loser's popped
(By pleasing legal fiction),
And friend and foe
Have wept their woe
In counterfeit affliction,
The winner must adopt
The loser's poor relations—
Discharge his debts,
Pay all his bets,
And take his obligations.
In short, to briefly sum the case,
The winner takes the loser's place,
With all its obligations.

ALL. How neatly lawyers state a case!
The winner takes the loser's place,
With all its obligations!

LUD. I see. The man who draws the lowest card——

NOT. Dies, *ipso facto,* a social death. He loses all his civil rights—his identity disappears—the Revising Barrister expunges his name from the list of voters, and the winner takes his place, whatever it may be, discharges all his functions, and adopts all his responsibilities.

ERN. This is all very well, as far as it goes, but it only protects one of us. What's to become of the survivor?

LUD. Yes, that's an interesting point, because *I* might be the survivor.

NOT. The survivor goes at once to the Grand Duke, and, in a burst of remorse, denounces the dead man as the moving spirit of the plot. He is accepted as King's evidence, and, as a matter of course, receives a free pardon. To-morrow, when the law expires, the dead man will, *ipso facto,* come to life again—the Revising Barrister will restore his name to the list of voters, and he will resume all his obligations as though nothing unusual had happened.

JULIA. When he will be at once arrested, tried, and executed on the evidence of the informer! Candidly, my friend, I don't think much of your plot!

NOT. Dear, dear, dear, the ignorance of the laity!

My good young lady, it is a beautiful maxim of our glorious Constitution that a man can only die once. Death expunges crime, and when he comes to life again, it will be with a clean slate.

ERN. It's really very ingenious.

LUD. (*to* NOTARY). My dear sir, we owe you our lives!

LISA (*aside to* LUDWIG). May I kiss him?

LUD. Certainly not: you're a big girl now. (*To* ERNEST). Well, miscreant, are you prepared to meet me on the field of honour?

ERN. At once. By Jove, what a couple of fire-eaters we are!

LISA. Ludwig doesn't know what fear is.

LUD. Oh, I don't mind this sort of duel!

ERN. It's not like a duel with swords. I hate a duel with swords. It's not the blade I mind—it's the blood.

LUD. And I hate a duel with pistols. It's not the ball I mind—it's the bang.

NOT. Altogether it's a great improvement on the old method of giving satisfaction.

QUINTET

LUDWIG, LISA, NOTARY, ERNEST, JULIA

Strange the views some people hold!
Two young fellows quarrel—
Then they fight, for both are bold—
Rage of both is uncontrolled—
Both are stretched out, stark and cold!
Prithee, where's the moral?
Ding dong! Ding dong!
There's an end to further action,
And this barbarous transaction
Is described as "satisfaction"!
Ha! ha! ha! ha! satisfaction!
Ding dong! Ding dong!
Each is laid in churchyard mould—
Strange the views some people hold!

Better than the method old,
Which was coarse and cruel,
Is the plan that we've extolled.

Sing thy virtues manifold
(Better than refinèd gold),
Statutory Duel!
Sing song! Sing song!
Sword or pistol neither uses—
Playing card he lightly chooses,
And the loser simply loses!
Ha! ha! ha! ha! simply loses.
Sing song! Sing song!
Some prefer the churchyard mould!
Strange the views some people hold!

NOT. (*offering a card to* ERNEST).
Now take a card and gaily sing
How little you care for Fortune's rubs—

ERN. (*drawing a card*).
Hurrah, hurrah!—I've drawn a King!

ALL. He's drawn a King!
He's drawn a King!
Sing Hearts and Diamonds, Spades and Clubs!

ALL (*dancing*). He's drawn a King!
How strange a thing!
An excellent card—his chance it aids—
Sing Hearts and Diamonds, Spades and Clubs—
Sing Diamonds, Hearts and Clubs and Spades!

NOT. (*to* LUDWIG).
Now take a card with heart of grace—
(Whatever our fate, let's play our parts).

LUD. (*drawing a card*).
Hurrah, hurrah!—I've drawn an Ace!

ALL. He's drawn an Ace!
He's drawn an Ace!
Sing Clubs and Diamonds, Spades and Hearts!

ALL (*dancing*). He's drawn an Ace!
Observe his face—
Such very good fortune falls to few—
Sing Clubs and Diamonds, Spades and Hearts—
Sing Clubs, Spades, Hearts and Diamonds, too!

NOT. That both these maids may keep their troth,
And never misfortune them befall,
I'll hold 'em as trustee for both—

ALL. He'll hold 'em both!
He'll hold 'em both!
Sing Hearts, Clubs, Diamonds, Spades and all!

ALL (*dancing*). By joint decree
As {our / your} trustee
This Notary {we / you} will now instal—
In custody let him keep {their / our} hearts,
Sing Hearts, Clubs, Diamonds, Spades and all!

[*Dance and exeunt* LUDWIG, ERNEST, *and* NOTARY *with the two Girls.*

March. Enter the seven Chamberlains of the GRAND DUKE RUDOLPH

CHORUS OF CHAMBERLAINS

The good Grand Duke of Pfennig Halbpfennig,
Though, in his own opinion, very, very big,
In point of fact he's nothing but a miserable prig
Is the good Grand Duke of Pfennig Halbpfennig!

Though quite contemptible, as every one agrees,
We must dissemble if we want our bread and cheese,
So hail him in a chorus, with enthusiasm big,
The good Grand Duke of Pfennig Halbpfennig!

Enter the GRAND DUKE RUDOLPH. *He is meanly and miserably dressed in old and patched clothes, but blazes with a profusion of orders and decorations. He is very weak and ill, from low living.*

SONG—RUDOLPH

A pattern to professors of monarchical autonomy,
I don't indulge in levity or compromising *bonhomie,*
But dignified formality, consistent with economy,
Above all other virtues I particularly prize.

I never join in merriment—I don't see joke or jape any—
I never tolerate familiarity in shape any—
This, joined with an extravagant respect for tuppence-ha'penny,
A keynote to my character sufficiently supplies.

(*Speaking.*) Observe. (*To Chamberlains.*) My snuff-box!

[*The snuff-box is passed with much ceremony from the Junior Chamberlain, through all the others, until it is presented by the Senior Chamberlain to* RUDOLPH, *who uses it.*

That incident a keynote to my character supplies.

RUD. I weigh out tea and sugar with precision mathematical—
Instead of beer, a penny each—my orders are emphatical—
(Extravagance unpardonable, any more than that I call),
But, on the other hand, my Ducal dignity to keep—
All Courtly ceremonial—to put it comprehensively—
I rigidly insist upon (but not, I hope, offensively)
Whenever ceremonial can be practised inexpensively—
And, when you come to think of it, it's really very cheap!

(*Speaking.*) Observe. (*To Chamberlains.*) My handkerchief!

[*Handkerchief is handed by Junior Chamberlain to the next in order, and so on until it reaches* RUDOLPH, *who is much inconvenienced by the delay.*

It's sometimes inconvenient, but it's always very cheap!

RUD. My Lord Chamberlain, as you are aware, my marriage with the wealthy Baroness von Krakenfeldt will take place to-morrow, and you will be good enough to see that the rejoicings are on a scale of unusual liberality.

Pass that on. (*Chamberlain whispers to Vice-Chamberlain, who whispers to the next, and so on.*) The sports will begin with a Wedding Breakfast Bee. The leading pastry-cooks of the town will be invited to compete, and the winner will not only enjoy the satisfaction of seeing his breakfast devoured by the Grand Ducal pair, but he will also be entitled to have the Arms of Pfennig Halbpfennig tattoo'd between his shoulder-blades. The Vice-Chamberlain will see to this. All the public fountains of Speisesaal will run with Gingerbierheim and Currantweinmilch at the public expense. The Assistant Vice-Chamberlain will see to this. At night, everybody will illuminate; and as I have no desire to tax the public funds unduly, this will be done at the inhabitants' private expense. The Deputy Assistant Vice-Chamberlain will see to this. All my Grand Ducal subjects will wear new clothes, and the Sub-Deputy Assistant Vice-Chamberlain will collect the usual commission on all sales. Wedding presents (which, on this occasion, should be on a scale of extraordinary magnificence) will be received at the Palace at any hour of the twenty-four, and the Temporary Sub-Deputy Assistant Vice-Chamberlain will sit up all night for this purpose. The entire population will be commanded to enjoy themselves, and with this view the Acting Temporary Sub-Deputy Assistant Vice-Chamberlain will sing comic songs in the Market-place from noon to nightfall. Finally, we have composed a Wedding Anthem, with which the entire population are required to provide themselves. It can be obtained from our Grand Ducal publishers at the usual discount price, and all the Chamberlains will be expected to push the sale. (*Chamberlains bow and exeunt.*) I don't feel at all comfortable. I hope I'm not doing a foolish thing in getting married. After all, it's a poor heart that never rejoices, and this wedding of mine is the first little treat I've allowed myself since my christening. Besides, Caroline's income is very considerable, and as her ideas of economy are quite on a par with mine, it ought to turn out well. Bless her tough old heart, she's a mean little darling! Oh, here she is, punctual to her appointment!

Enter BARONESS VON KRAKENFELDT

BAR. Rudolph! Why, what's the matter?

RUD. Why, I'm not quite myself, my pet. I'm a little worried and upset. I want a tonic. It's the low diet, I think. I am afraid, after all, I shall have to take the bull by the horns and have an egg with my breakfast.

BAR. I shouldn't do anything rash, dear. Begin with a jujube. (*Gives him one.*)

RUD. (*about to eat it, but changes his mind*). I'll keep it for supper. (*He sits by her and tries to put his arm round her waist.*)

BAR. Rudolph, don't! What in the world are you thinking of?

RUD. I was thinking of embracing you, my sugar-plum. Just as a little cheap treat.

BAR. What, here? In public? Really, you appear to have no sense of delicacy.

RUD. No sense of delicacy, Bon-bon!

BAR. No. I can't make you out. When you courted me, all your courting was done publicly in the Market-place. When you proposed to me, you proposed in the Market-place. And now that we're engaged you seem to desire that our first *tête-à-tête* shall occur in the Market-place! Surely you've a room in your Palace—with blinds—that would do?

RUD. But, my own, I can't help myself. I'm bound by my own decree.

BAR. Your own decree?

RUD. Yes. You see, all the houses that give on the Market-place belong to me, but the drains (which date back to the reign of Charlemagne) want attending to, and the houses wouldn't let—so, with a view to increasing the value of the property, I decreed that all love-episodes between affectionate couples should take place, in public, on this spot, every Monday, Wednesday, and Friday, when the band doesn't play.

BAR. Bless me, what a happy idea! So moral too! And have you found it answer?

RUD. Answer? The rents have gone up fifty per cent, and the sale of opera-glasses (which is a Grand Ducal monopoly) has received an extraordinary stimulus! So, under the circumstances, *would* you allow me to put my arm round your waist? As a source of income! Just once!

BAR. But it's so very embarrassing. Think of the opera-glasses!

RUD. My good girl, that's just what I *am* thinking of. Hang it all, we must give them *something* for their money! What's that?

BAR. (*unfolding paper, which contains a large letter, which she hands to him*). It's a letter which your detective asked me to hand to you. I wrapped it up in yesterday's paper to keep it clean.

RUD. Oh, it's only his report! That'll keep. But, I say, you've never been and bought a newspaper?

BAR. My dear Rudolph, do you think I'm mad? It came wrapped round my breakfast.

RUD. (*relieved*). I thought you were not the sort of girl to go and buy a newspaper! Well, as we've got it, we may as well read it. What does it say?

BAR. Why—dear me—here's your biography! "Our Detested Despot!"

RUD. Yes—I fancy that refers to me.

BAR. And it says—Oh, it can't be!

RUD. What can't be?

BAR. Why, it says that although you're going to marry me to-morrow, you were betrothed in infancy to the Princess of Monte Carlo!

RUD. Oh yes—that's quite right. Didn't I mention it?

BAR. Mention it! You never said a word about it!

RUD. Well, it doesn't matter, because, you see, it's practically off.

BAR. Practically off?

RUD. Yes. By the terms of the contract the betrothal is void unless the Princess marries before she is of age. Now, her father, the Prince, is stony-broke, and hasn't left his house for years for fear of arrest. Over and over again he has implored me to come to him to be married—but in vain. Over and over again he has implored me to advance him the money to enable the Princess to come to me—but in vain. I am very young, but not as young as that; and as the Princess comes of age at two to-morrow, why at two to-morrow I'm a free man, so I appointed that hour for our wedding, as I shall like to have as much marriage as I can get for my money.

BAR. I see. Of course, if the married state is a happy state, it's a pity to waste any of it.

RUD. Why, every hour we delayed I should lose a lot of you and you'd lose a lot of me!

BAR. My thoughtful darling! Oh, Rudolph, we ought to be very happy!

RUD. If I'm not, it will be my first bad investment. Still, there *is* such a thing as a slump even in Matrimonials.

BAR. I often picture us in the long, cold, dark December evenings, sitting close to each other and singing impassioned duets to keep us warm, and thinking of all the lovely things we could afford to buy if we chose, and, at the same time, planning out our lives in a spirit of the most rigid and exacting economy!

RUD. It's a most beautiful and touching picture of connubial bliss in its highest and most rarefied development!

DUET—BARONESS *and* RUDOLPH

BAR. As o'er our penny roll we sing,
It is not reprehensive,
To think what joys our wealth would bring
Were we disposed to do the thing
Upon a scale extensive.
There's rich mock-turtle—thick and clear—

RUD. (*confidentially*). Perhaps we'll have it once a year!
BAR. (*delighted*). You *are* an open-handed dear!

RUD. Though, mind you, it's expensive.

BAR. No doubt it *is* expensive.

BOTH. How fleeting are the glutton's joys!
With fish and fowl he lightly toys,

RUD. And pays for such expensive tricks
Sometimes as much as two-and-six!

BAR. As two-and-six?

RUD. As two-and-six.

BOTH. Sometimes as much as two-and-six!

BAR. It gives him no advantage, mind—
For you and he have only dined,
And you remain when once it's down
A better man by half-a-crown.

RUD. By half-a-crown?

BAR. By half-a-crown.

BOTH. Yes, two-and-six is half-a-crown.
Then let us be modestly merry,
And rejoice with a derry down derry
For to laugh and to sing
No extravagance bring—
It's a joy economical, very!

BAR. Although as you're of course aware
(I never tried to hide it)
I moisten my insipid fare
With water—which I can't abear—

RUD. Nor I—I can't abide it.

BAR. This pleasing fact our souls will cheer,
With fifty thousand pounds a year
We *could* indulge in table beer!

RUD. Get out!

BAR. We could—I've tried it!

RUD. Yes, yes, of course you've tried it!

BOTH. Oh, he who has an income clear
Of fifty thousand pounds a year—

BAR. Can purchase all his fancy loves
Conspicuous hats—

RUD. Two-shilling gloves—

BAR. (*doubtfully*). Two-shilling gloves?

RUD. (*positively*). Two-shilling gloves—

BOTH. Yes, think of that, two-shilling gloves!

BAR. Cheap shoes and ties of gaudy hue,
And Waterbury watches, too—
And think that he could buy the lot
Were he a donkey—

RUD. Which he's *not!*

BAR. Oh, no, he's *not!*

RUD. Oh, no, he's *not!*

BOTH (*dancing*).
That kind of donkey he is *not!*
Then let us be modestly merry,
And rejoice with a derry down derry.
For to laugh and to sing
Is a rational thing—
It's a joy economical, very!

[*Exit* BARONESS.

RUD. Oh, now for my detective's report. (*Opens letter.*) What's this! Another conspiracy! A conspiracy to depose *me!* And my private detective was so convulsed with laughter at the notion of a conspirator selecting him for a confidant that he was physically unable to arrest the malefactor! Why, it'll come off! This comes of engaging a detective with a keen sense of the ridiculous! For the future I'll employ none but Scotchmen. And the plot is to explode to-morrow! My wedding day! Oh, Caroline, Caroline! (*Weeps.*) This is perfectly frightful! What's to be done? I don't know! I ought to keep cool and think, but you *can't* think when your veins are full of hot soda-water, and your brain's fizzing like a firework, and all your faculties are jumbled in a perfect whirlpool of tumblication! And I'm going to be ill! I know I am! I've been living too low, and I'm going to be very ill indeed!

SONG—RUDOLPH

When you find you're a broken-down critter,
Who is all of a trimmle and twitter,
With your palate unpleasantly bitter,
As if you'd just eaten a pill—

When your legs are as thin as dividers,
And you're plagued with unruly insiders,
And your spine is all creepy with spiders,
And you're highly gamboge in the gill—
When you've got a beehive in your head,
And a sewing machine in each ear,
And you feel that you've eaten your bed,
And you've got a bad headache *down here*—
When such facts are about,
And these symptoms you find
In your body or crown—
Well, you'd better look out,
You may make up your mind
You had better lie down!

When your lips are all smeary—like tallow,
And your tongue is decidedly yallow,
With a pint of warm oil in your sw*a*llow,
And a pound of tin-tacks in your chest—
When you're down in the mouth with the vapours,
And all over your Morris wall-papers,
Black-beetles are cutting their capers,
And crawly things never at rest—

When you doubt if your head is your own,
And you jump when an open door slams—
Then you've got to a state which is known
To the medical world as "jim-jams".
If such symptoms you find
In your body or head,
They're not easy to quell—
You may make up your mind
You are better in bed,
For you're not at all well!

[*Sinks exhausted and weeping at foot of well.*

Enter LUDWIG

LUD. Now for my confession and full pardon. They told me the Grand Duke was dancing duets in the Market-place, but I don't see him. (*Sees* RUDOLPH.) Hallo! Who's this? (*Aside.*) Why, it *is* the Grand Duke!

RUD. (*sobbing*). Who are you, sir, who presume to address me in person? If you've anything to communicate, you must fling yourself at the feet of my Acting Temporary Sub-Deputy Assistant Vice-Chamberlain, who will fling himself at the feet of his immediate superior, and so on, with successive foot-flingings through the various grades—your communication will, in course of time, come to my august knowledge.

LUD. But when I inform your Highness that in me you see the most unhappy, the most unfortunate, the most completely miserable man in your whole dominion——

RUD. (*still sobbing*). *You* the most miserable man in my whole dominion? How can you have the face to stand there and say such a thing? Why, look at me! Look at me! (*Bursts into tears.*)

LUD. Well, I wouldn't be a cry-baby.

RUD. A cry-baby? If you had just been told that you were going to be deposed to-morrow, and perhaps blown up with dynamite for all I know, wouldn't *you* be a cry-baby? I do declare if I could only hit upon some cheap and painless method of putting an end to an existence which has become insupportable, I would unhesitatingly adopt it!

LUD. You would? (*Aside.*) I see a magnificent way out of this! By Jupiter, I'll try it! (*Aloud.*) Are you, by any chance, in earnest?

RUD. In earnest? Why, look at me!

LUD. If you are really in earnest—if you really desire to escape scot-free from this impending—this unspeakably horrible catastrophe—without trouble, danger, pain, or expense—why not resort to a Statutory Duel?

RUD. A Statutory Duel?

LUD. Yes. The Act is still in force, but it will expire to-morrow afternoon. You fight—you lose—you are dead for a day. To-morrow, when the Act expires, you will come to life again and resume your Grand Duchy as though nothing had happened. In the meantime, the explosion will have taken place and the survivor will have had to bear the brunt of it.

RUD. Yes, that's all very well, but who'll be fool enough to *be* the survivor?

LUD. (*kneeling*). Actuated by an overwhelming sense of attachment to your Grand Ducal person, I unhesitatingly offer myself as the victim of your subjects' fury.

RUD. You do? Well, really that's very handsome. I daresay being blown up is not nearly as unpleasant as one would think.

LUD. Oh, yes it is. It mixes one up, awfully!

RUD. But suppose I were to lose?

LUD. Oh, that's easily arranged. (*Producing cards.*) I'll put an Ace up my sleeve—you'll put a King up yours. When the drawing takes place, I shall seem to draw the higher card and you the lower. And there you are!

RUD. Oh, but that's cheating.

LUD. So it is. I never thought of that. (*Going.*)

RUD. (*hastily*). Not that I mind. But I say—you won't take an unfair advantage of your day of office? You won't go tipping people, or squandering my little savings in fireworks, or any nonsense of that sort?

LUD. I am hurt—really hurt—by the suggestion.

RUD. You—you wouldn't like to put down a deposit, perhaps?

LUD. No. I don't think I should like to put down a deposit.

RUD. Or give a guarantee?

LUD. A guarantee would be equally open to objection.

RUD. It would be more regular. Very well, I suppose you must have your own way.

LUD. Good. I say—we must have a devil of a quarrel!

RUD. Oh, a devil of a quarrel!

LUD. Just to give colour to the thing. Shall I give you a sound thrashing before all the people? Say the word —it's no trouble.

RUD. No, I think not, though it would be very convincing, and it's extremely good and thoughtful of you to suggest it. Still, a devil of a quarrel!

LUD. Oh, a devil of a quarrel!

RUD. No half measures. Big words—strong language —rude remarks. Oh, a devil of a quarrel!

LUD. Now the question is, how shall we summon the people?

RUD. Oh, there's no difficulty about that. Bless your heart, they've been staring at us through those windows for the last half-hour!

FINALE

RUD. Come hither, all you people—
When you hear the fearful news,
All the pretty women weep'll,
Men will shiver in their shoes.

LUD. And they'll all cry "Lord, defend us!"
When they learn the fact tremendous
That to give this man his gruel
In a Statutory Duel—

BOTH. This plebeian man of shoddy—
This contemptible nobody—
Your Grand Duke does not refuse!

[*During this, Chorus of men and women have entered, all trembling with apprehension under the impression that they are to be arrested for their complicity in the conspiracy.*

CHORUS

With faltering feet,
And our muscles in a quiver,
Our fate we meet
With our feelings all unstrung!
If our plot complete
He has managed to diskiver,
There is no retreat—
We shall certainly be hung!

RUD. (*aside to* LUDWIG).
Now *you* begin and pitch it strong—walk into me abusively—

LUD. (*aside to* RUDOLPH).
I've several epithets that I've reserved for you exclusively.
A choice selection I have here when you are ready *to* begin.

RUD. Now *you* begin——
LUD. No, *you* begin——
RUD. No, *you* begin——
LUD. No, *you* begin!

CHORUS (*trembling*).
Has it happed as we expected?
Is our little plot detected?

DUET—RUDOLPH *and* LUDWIG

RUD. (*furiously*).
Big bombs, small bombs, great guns and little ones!
Put him in a pillory!
Rack him with artillery!

LUD. (*furiously*).
Long swords, short swords, tough swords and brittle ones!
Fright him into fits!
Blow him into bits!

RUD. You muff, sir!
LUD. You lout, sir!
RUD. Enough, sir!
LUD. Get out, sir! (*Pushes him.*)
RUD. A hit, sir?

LUD. Take that, sir! (*Slaps him.*)
RUD. It's tit, sir,
LUD. For tat, sir!
CHORUS (*appalled*).
When two doughty heroes thunder,
All the world is lost in wonder;
When such men their temper lose,
Awful are the words they use!
LUD. Tall snobs, small snobs, rich snobs and needy ones!
RUD. (*jostling him*). Whom are you alluding to?
LUD. (*jostling him*). Where are you intruding to?
RUD. Fat snobs, thin snobs, swell snobs and seedy ones!
LUD. I rather think you err.
To whom do you refer?
RUD. To you, sir!
LUD. To me, sir?
RUD. I do, sir!
LUD. We'll see, sir!
RUD. I jeer, sir!
(*Makes a face at* LUDWIG.) Grimace, sir!
LUD. Look here, sir——
(*Makes a face at* RUDOLPH.) A face, sir!
CHORUS (*appalled*).
When two heroes, once pacific,
Quarrel, the effect's terrific!
What a horrible grimace!
What a paralysing face!
ALL. Big bombs, small bombs, etc.
LUD. *and* RUD. (*recit.*).
He has insulted me, and, in a breath,
This day we fight a duel to the death!
NOT. (*checking them*).
You mean, of course, by duel (*verbum sat.*),
A Statutory Duel.
ALL. Why, what's that?
NOT. According to established legal uses,
A card apiece each bold disputant chooses—
Dead as a doornail is the dog who loses—
The winner steps into the dead man's shoeses!
ALL. The winner steps into the dead man's shoeses!
RUD. *and* LUD. Agreed! Agreed!

RUD. Come, come—the pack!
LUD. (*producing one*). Behold it here!
RUD. I'm on the rack!
LUD. I quake with fear!

(NOTARY *offers card to* LUDWIG.)

LUD. First draw to you!
RUD. If that's the case,
Behold the King! (*Drawing card from his sleeve.*)
LUD. (*same business*). Behold the Ace!
CHORUS. Hurrah, hurrah! Our Ludwig's won.
And wicked Rudolph's course is run—
So Ludwig will as Grand Duke reign
Till Rudolph comes to life again—
RUD. Which will occur to-morrow!
I come to life to-morrow!
GRET. (*with mocking curtsey*).
My Lord Grand Duke, farewell!
A pleasant journey, very,
To your convenient cell
In yonder cemetery!
LISA (*curtseying*).
Though malcontents abuse you,
We're much distressed to lose you!
You were, when you were living,
So liberal, so forgiving!
BERTHA. So merciful, so gentle!
So highly ornamental!
OLGA. And now that you've departed,
You leave us broken-hearted!
ALL (*pretending to weep*). Yes, truly, truly, truly, truly—
Truly broken-hearted!
Ha! ha! ha! ha! ha! ha! (*Mocking him.*)
RUD. (*furious*). Rapscallions, in penitential fires,
You'll rue the ribaldry that from you falls!
To-morrow afternoon the law expires.
And then—look out for squalls!
[*Exit* RUDOLPH, *amid general ridicule.*
CHORUS. Give thanks, give thanks to wayward fate—
By mystic fortune's sway,

Our Ludwig guides the helm of State
For one delightful day!
(*To* LUDWIG.) We hail you, sir!
We greet you, sir!
Regale you, sir!
We treat you, sir!
Our ruler be
By fate's decree
For one delightful day!

NOT. You've done it neatly! Pity that your powers
Are limited to four-and-twenty hours!

LUD. No matter, though the time will quickly run,
In hours twenty-four much may be done!

SONG—LUDWIG

Oh, a Monarch who boasts intellectual graces
Can do, if he likes, a good deal in a day—
He can put all his friends in conspicuous places,
With plenty to eat and with nothing to pay!
You'll tell me, no doubt, with unpleasant grimaces,
To-morrow, deprived of your ribbons and laces,
You'll get your dismissal—with very long faces—
But wait! on that topic I've something to say!
(*Dancing.*) I've something to say—I've something to say
—I've something to say!
Oh, our rule shall be merry—I'm not an ascetic—
And while the sun shines we will get up our hay—
By a pushing young Monarch, of turn energetic,
A very great deal may be done in a day!

CHORUS. Oh, his rule will be merry, etc.

(*During this,* LUDWIG *whispers to* NOTARY, *who writes.*)

For instance, this measure (his ancestor drew it),
(*alluding to* NOTARY)
This law against duels—to-morrow will die—
The Duke will revive, and you'll certainly rue it—
He'll give you "what for" and he'll let you know why!
But in twenty-four hours there's time to renew it—
With a century's life I've the right to imbue it—
It's easy to do—and, by Jingo, I'll do it!

(*Signing paper, which* NOTARY *presents.*)

It's done! Till I perish your Monarch am I!
Your Monarch am I—your Monarch am I—your Monarch am I!
Though I do not pretend to be very prophetic,
I fancy I know what you're going to say—
By a pushing young Monarch, of turn energetic,
A very great deal may be done in a day!

ALL (*astonished*).
Oh, it's simply uncanny, his power prophetic—
It's perfectly right—we *were* going to say,
By a pushing, etc.

Enter JULIA, *at back*

LUD. (*recit.*). This very afternoon—at two (about)—
The Court appointments will be given out.
To each and all (for that was the condition)
According to professional position!

ALL. Hurrah!

JULIA (*coming forward*).
According to professional position?

LUD. According to professional position!

JULIA. Then, horror!

ALL. Why, what's the matter? What's the matter?
What's the matter?

SONG—JULIA. (LISA *clinging to her*)

Ah, pity me, my comrades true,
Who love, as well I know you do,
This gentle child,
To me so fondly dear!

ALL. Why, what's the matter?

JULIA. Our sister love so true and deep
From many an eye unused to weep
Hath oft beguiled
The coy reluctant tear!

ALL. Why, what's the matter?

JULIA. Each sympathetic heart 'twill bruise
When you have heard the frightful news
(O will it not?)
That I must now impart!

ALL. Why, what's the matter?
JULIA. Her love for him is all in all!
Ah, cursed fate! that it should fall
Unto *my* lot
To break my darling's heart!
ALL. Why, what's the matter?
LUD. What means our Julia by those fateful looks?
Please do not keep us all on tenter-hooks—
Now, what's the matter?
JULIA. Our duty, if we're wise,
We never shun.
This Spartan rule applies
To every one.
In theatres, as in life,
Each has her line—
This part—the Grand Duke's wife
(Oh agony!) is mine!
A maxim new I do not start—
The canons of dramatic art
Decree that this repulsive part
(The Grand Duke's wife)
Is mine!
ALL. Oh, *that's* the matter!
LISA (*appalled, to* LUDWIG). Can that be so?
LUD. I do not know—
But time will show
If that be so.
CHORUS. Can that be so? etc.
LISA (*recit.*). Be merciful!

DUET—LISA *and* JULIA

LISA. Oh, listen to me, dear—
I love him only, darling!
Remember, oh, my pet,
On him my heart is set!
This kindness do me, dear—
Nor leave me lonely, darling!
Be merciful, my pet,
Our love do not forget!
JULIA. Now don't be foolish, dear—
You couldn't play it, darling!
It's "leading business," pet.

And you're but a soubrette.
So don't be mulish, dear—
Although I say it, darling,
It's not your line, my pet—
I play that part, you bet!
I play that part—
I play that part, you bet!

[LISA *overwhelmed with grief.*

NOT. The lady's right. Though Julia's engagement
Was for the stage meant—
It certainly frees Ludwig from his
Connubial promise.
Though marriage contracts—or whate'er you call 'em—
Are very solemn,
Dramatic contracts (which you all adore so)
Are even more so!

ALL. That's very true!
Though marriage contracts, etc.

SONG—LISA

The die is cast,
My hope has perished!
Farewell, O Past,
Too bright to last,
Yet fondly cherished!
My light has fled,
My hope is dead,
Its doom is spoken—
My day is night,
My wrong is right
In all men's sight—
My heart is broken!

[*Exit weeping.*

LUD. (*recit.*). Poor child, where will she go? What will she do?

JULIA. *That* isn't in your part, you know.

LUD. (*sighing*). Quite true!
(*With an effort.*) Depressing topics we'll not touch upon—
Let us begin as we are going on!
For this will be a jolly Court, for little and for big!

ALL. Sing hey, the jolly jinks of Pfennig Halbpfennig!
LUD. From morn to night our lives shall be as merry as a grig!
ALL. Sing hey, the jolly jinks of Pfennig Halbpfennig!
LUD. All state and ceremony we'll eternally abolish—
We don't mean to insist upon unnecessary polish—
And, on the whole, I rather think you'll find our rule tollolish!
ALL. Sing hey, the jolly jinks of Pfennig Halbpfennig!

JULIA. But stay—your new-made Court
Without a courtly coat is—
We shall require
Some Court attire,
And at a moment's notice.
In clothes of common sort
Your courtiers must not grovel—
Your new *noblesse*
Must have a dress
Original and novel!

LUD. Old Athens we'll exhume!
The necessary dresses,
Correct and true
And all brand-new,
The company possesses:
Henceforth our Court costume
Shall live in song and story,
For we'll upraise
The dead old days
Of Athens in her glory!

ALL. Yes, let's upraise
The dead old days
Of Athens in her glory!

ALL. Agreed! Agreed!
For this will be a jolly Court for little and for big! etc.

[*They carry* LUDWIG *round stage and deposit him on the ironwork of well.* JULIA *stands by him, and the rest group round them.*

END OF ACT I

ACT II

(THE NEXT MORNING)

SCENE.—*Entrance Hall of the Grand Ducal Palace.*

Enter a procession of the members of the theatrical company (now dressed in the costumes of Troilus and Cressida), *carrying garlands, playing on pipes, citharæ, and cymbals, and heralding the return of* LUDWIG *and* JULIA *from the marriage ceremony, which has just taken place.*

CHORUS

As before you we defile,
Eloia! Eloia!
Pray you, gentles, do not smile
If we shout, in classic style,
Eloia!
Ludwig and his Julia true
Wedded are each other to—
So we sing, till all is blue,
Eloia! Eloia!
Opoponax! Eloia!

Wreaths of bay and ivy twine,
Eloia! Eloia!
Fill the bowl with Lesbian wine,
And to revelry incline—
Eloia!
For as gaily we pass on
Probably we shall, anon,
Sing a Diergeticon—
Eloia! Eloia!
Opoponax! Eloia!

RECIT—LUDWIG

Your loyalty our Ducal heartstrings touches:
Allow me to present your new Grand Duchess.

Should she offend, you'll graciously excuse her—
And kindly recollect *I* didn't choose her!

SONG—LUDWIG

At the outset I may mention it's my sovereign intention
To revive the classic memories of Athens at its best,
For the company possesses all the necessary dresses
And a course of quiet cramming will supply us with the rest.
We've a choir hyporchematic (that is, ballet-operatic)
Who respond to the *choreutæ* of that cultivated age,
And our clever chorus-master, all but captious criticaster
Would accept as the *choregus* of the early Attic stage.
This return to classic ages is considered in their wages,
Which are always calculated by the day or by the week—
And I'll pay 'em (if they'll back me) all in *oboloi* and *drachmæ,*
Which they'll get (if they prefer it) at the Kalends that are Greek!

(*Confidentially to audience.*)

At this juncture I may mention
That this erudition sham
Is but classical pretension,
The result of steady "cram.":
Periphrastic methods spurning,
To this audience discerning
I admit this show of learning
Is the fruit of steady "cram."!

CHORUS. Periphrastic methods, etc.

In the period Socratic every dining-room was Attic
(Which suggests an architecture of a topsy-turvy kind),
There they'd satisfy their thirst on a *recherché* cold *ἄριστον,*
Which is what they called their lunch—and so may you, if you're inclined.
As they gradually got on, they'd *τρέπεσθαι πρὸς τὸν πότον*
(Which is Attic for a steady and a conscientious drink).

But they mixed their wine with water—which I'm sure they didn't oughter—
And we modern Saxons know a trick worth two of that, I think!

Then came rather risky dances (under certain circumstances)
Which would shock that worthy gentleman, the Licenser of Plays,
Corybantian mani*ac* kick—Dionysiac or Bacchic—
And the Dithyrambic revels of those undecorous days.

(*Confidentially to audience.*)

And perhaps I'd better mention,
Lest alarming you I am,
That it isn't our intention
To perform a Dithyramb—
It displays a lot of stocking,
Which is always very shocking,
And of course I'm only mocking
At the prevalence of "cram"!

CHORUS. It displays a lot, etc.

Yes, on reconsideration, there are customs of that nation
Which are not in strict accordance with the habits of our day,
And when I come to codify, their rules I mean to modify,
Or Mrs. Grundy, p'r'aps, may have a word or two to say.
For they hadn't mackintoshes or umbrellas or galoshes—
And a shower with their dresses must have played the very deuce,
And it must have been unpleasing when they caught a fit of sneezing,
For, it seems, of pocket-handkerchiefs they didn't know the use.
They wore little underclothing—scarcely anything—or nothing—
And their dress of Coan silk was quite transparent in design—
Well, in fact, in summer weather, something like the "altogether."
And it's *there,* I rather fancy, I shall have to draw the line!

(*Confidentially to audience.*)

And again I wish to mention
That this erudition sham
Is but classical pretension,
The result of steady "cram."
Yet my classic lore aggressive
(If you'll pardon the possessive)
Is exceedingly impressive
When you're passing an exam.

CHORUS. Yet his classic lore, etc.

[*Exeunt Chorus. Manent* LUDWIG, JULIA, *and* LISA.

LUD. (*recit.*).
Yes, Ludwig and his Julia are mated!
For when an obscure comedian, whom the law backs,
To sovereign rank is promptly elevated,
He takes it with its incidental drawbacks!
So Julia and I are duly mated!

[LISA, *through this, has expressed intense distress at having to surrender* LUDWIG.

SONG—LISA

Take care of him—he's much too good to live,
With him you must be very gentle:
Poor fellow, he's so highly sensitive,
And O, so sentimental!
Be sure you never let him sit up late
In chilly open air conversing—
Poor darling, he's extremely delicate,
And wants a deal of nursing!

LUD. I want a deal of nursing!

LISA. And O, remember this—
When he is cross with pain,
A flower and a kiss—
A simple flower—a tender kiss
Will bring him round again!

His moods you must assiduously watch:
When he succumbs to sorrow tragic,
Some hardbake or a bit of butter-scotch
Will work on him like magic.
To contradict a character so rich
In trusting love were simple blindness—
He's one of those exalted natures which
Will only yield to kindness!

LUD. I only yield to kindness!

LISA. And O, the bygone bliss!
And O, the present pain!
That flower and that kiss—
That simple flower—that tender kiss
I ne'er shall give again! [*Exit, weeping.*

JULIA. And now that everybody has gone, and we're happily and comfortably married, I want to have a few words with my new-born husband.

LUD. (*aside*). Yes, I expect you'll often have a few words with your new-born husband! (*Aloud.*) Well, what is it?

JULIA. Why, I've been thinking that as you and I have to play our parts for life, it is most essential that we should come to a definite understanding as to how they shall be rendered. Now, I've been considering how I can make the most of the Grand Duchess.

LUD. Have you? Well, if you'll take my advice, you'll make a very fine part of it.

JULIA. Why, that's quite *my* idea.

LUD. I shouldn't make it one of your hoity-toity vixenish viragoes.

JULIA. You think not?

LUD. Oh, I'm quite clear about that. I should make her a tender, gentle, submissive, affectionate (but not too affectionate) child-wife—timidly anxious to coil herself into her husband's heart, but kept in check by an awe-struck reverence for his exalted intellectual qualities and his majestic personal appearance.

JULIA. Oh, that is your idea of a good part?

LUD. Yes—a wife who regards her husband's slightest wish as an inflexible law, and who ventures but rarely into his august presence, unless (which would happen seldom) he should summon her to appear before him. A crushed, despairing violet, whose blighted existence would culminate (all too soon) in a lonely and pathetic death-scene! A fine part, my dear.

JULIA. Yes. There's a good deal to be said for your view of it. Now there are some actresses whom it would fit like a glove.

LUD. (*aside*). I wish I'd married one of 'em!

JULIA. But, you see, I *must* consider my temperament. For instance, my temperament would demand some strong scenes of justifiable jealousy.

LUD. Oh, there's no difficulty about that. You shall have *them*.

JULIA. With a lovely but detested rival——

LUD. Oh, *I'll* provide the rival.

JULIA. Whom I should stab—stab—stab!

LUD. Oh, I wouldn't stab her. It's been done to death. I should treat her with a silent and contemptuous disdain, and delicately withdraw from a position which, to one of your sensitive nature, would be absolutely untenable. Dear me, I can see you delicately withdrawing, up centre and off!

JULIA. *Can* you?

LUD. Yes. It's a fine situation—and in your hands, full of quiet pathos!

DUET—LUDWIG *and* JULIA

LUD. Now Julia, come,
Consider it from
This dainty point of view—
A timid tender
Feminine gender,
Prompt to coyly coo—
Yet silence seeking,
Seldom speaking
Till she's spoken to—
A comfy, cosy,
Rosy-posy
Innocent *ingenoo*!
The part you're suited to—
To give the deuce her due)
A sweet (O, jiminy!)
Miminy-piminy,
Innocent inge*noo*!

ENSEMBLE

LUD.	JULIA
The part you're suited to—	I'm much obliged to you,
(To give the deuce her due)	I don't think that would do—
A sweet (O, jiminy!)	To play (O, jiminy!)
Miminy-piminy,	Miminy-piminy,
Innocent inge*noo*!	Innocent inge*noo*!

JULIA. You forget my special magic
(In a high dramatic sense)
Lies in situations tragic—
Undeniably intense.
As I've justified promotion
In the histrionic art,
I'll submit to you my notion
Of a first-rate part.

LUD. Well, let us see your notion
Of a first-rate part.

JULIA (*dramatically*).
I have a rival! Frenzy-thrilled,
I find you both together!
My heart stands still—with horror chilled—
Hard as the millstone nether!
Then softly, slyly, snaily, snaky—
Crawly, creepy, quaily, quaky—
I track her on her homeward way,
As panther tracks her fated prey!
(*Furiously.*) I fly at her soft white throat—
The lily-white laughing leman!
On her agonized gaze I gloat
With the glee of a dancing demon!
My rival she—I have no doubt of her—
So I hold on—till the breath is out of her!
—till the breath is out of her!

And then—Remorse! Remorse!
O cold unpleasant corse,
Avaunt! Avaunt!
That lifeless form
I gaze upon—
That face, still warm
But weirdly wan—
Those eyes of glass
I contemplate—
And then, alas,
Too late—too late!
I find she is—your Aunt!
(*Shuddering.*) Remorse! Remorse!

Then, mad—mad—mad!
With fancies wild—chimerical—
Now sorrowful—silent—sad—
Now hullaballoo hysterical!
Ha! ha! ha! ha!
But whether I'm sad or whether I'm glad,
Mad! mad! mad! mad!

This calls for the resources of a high-class art,
And satisfies my notion of a first-rate part!
[*Exit* JULIA.

Enter all the Chorus, hurriedly, and in great excitement

CHORUS

Your Highness, there's a party at the door—
Your Highness, at the door there is a party—
She says that we expect her,
But we do not recollect her,
For we never saw her countenance before!

With rage and indignation she is rife,
Because our welcome wasn't very hearty—
She's as sulky as a super,
And she's swearing like a trooper,
O, you never heard such language in your life!

Enter BARONESS VON KRAKENFELDT, *in a fury*

BAR. With fury indescribable I burn!
With rage I'm nearly ready to explode!
There'll be grief and tribulation when I learn
To whom this slight unbearable is owed!
For whatever may be due I'll pay it double—
There'll be terror indescribable and trouble!
With a hurly-burly and a hubble-bubble
I'll pay you for this pretty episode!

ALL. Oh, whatever may be due she'll pay it double!—
It's very good of her to take the trouble—
But we don't know what she means by "hubble-bubble"—
No doubt it's an expression *à la mode.*

BAR. (*to* LUDWIG).
Do you know who I am?

LUD. (*examining her*). I don't;
Your countenance I can't fix, my dear.

BAR. This proves I'm not a sham.
(*Showing pocket-handkerchief.*)

LUD. (*examining it*). It won't;
It only says "Krakenfeldt, Six," my dear.

BAR. Express your grief profound!

LUD. I shan't!
This tone I never allow, my love.

BAR. Rudolph at once produce!

LUD. I can't;
He isn't at home just now, my love.

BAR. (*astonished*). He isn't at home just now!

ALL. He isn't at home just now,
(*Dancing derisively.*) He has an appointment particular, very—
You'll find him, I think, in the town cemetery;
And that's how we come to be making so merry,
For he isn't at home just now!

BAR. But bless my heart and soul alive, it's impudence personified!
I've come here to be matrimonially matrimonified!

LUD. For any disappointment I am sorry unaffectedly,
But yesterday that nobleman expired quite unexpectedly—

ALL (*sobbing*). Tol the riddle lol!
Tol the riddle lol!
Tol the riddle, lol the riddle, lol lol lay!
(*Then laughing wildly.*) Tol the riddle, lol the riddle, lol lol lay!

BAR. But this is most unexpected. He was well enough at a quarter to twelve yesterday.

LUD. Yes. He died at half-past eleven.

BAR. Bless me, how very sudden!

LUD. It *was* sudden.

BAR. But what in the world am I to do? I was to have been married to him to-day!

ALL (*singing and dancing*).
For any disappointment we are sorry unaffectedly,
But yesterday that nobleman expired quite unexpectedly—
Tol the riddle lol!

BAR. Is this Court Mourning or a Fancy Ball?

LUD. Well, it's a delicate combination of both effects. It is intended to express inconsolable grief for the decease of the late Duke and ebullient joy at the accession of his successor. *I* am his successor. Permit me to present you to my Grand Duchess. (*Indicating* JULIA.)

BAR. Your Grand Duchess? Oh, your Highness! (*Curtseying profoundly.*)

JULIA (*sneering at her*). Old frump!

BAR. Humph! A recent creation, probably?

LUD. We were married only half an hour ago.

BAR. Exactly. I thought she seemed new to the position.

JULIA. Ma'am, I don't know who you are, but I flatter myself I can do justice to *any* part on the very shortest notice.

BAR. My dear, under the circumstances you are doing admirably—and you'll improve with practice. It's so difficult to be a lady when one isn't born to it.

JULIA (*in a rage, to* LUDWIG). Am I to stand this? Am I not to be allowed to pull her to pieces?

LUD. (*aside to* JULIA). No, no—it isn't Greek. Be a violet, I beg.

BAR. And now tell me all about this distressing circumstance. How did the Grand Duke die?

LUD. He perished nobly—in a Statutory Duel.

BAR. In a Statutory Duel? But that's only a civil death! —and the Act expires to-night, and then he will come to life again!

LUD. Well, no. Anxious to inaugurate my reign by conferring some inestimable boon on my people, I signalized this occasion by reviving the law for another hundred years.

BAR. For another hundred years? Then set the merry joybells ringing! Let festive epithalamia resound through these ancient halls! Cut the satisfying sandwich—broach the exhilarating Marsala—and let us rejoice to-day, if we never rejoice again!

LUD. But I don't think I quite understand. We have already rejoiced a good deal.

BAR. Happy man, you little reck of the extent of the good things you are in for. When you killed Rudolph you adopted all his overwhelming responsibilities. Know then that I, Caroline von Krakenfeldt, am the most overwhelming of them all!

LUD. But stop, stop—I've just been married to somebody else!

JULIA. Yes, ma'am, to somebody else, ma'am! Do you understand, ma'am? To somebody else!

BAR. Do keep this young woman quiet; she fidgets me!

JULIA. Fidgets you!

LUD. (*aside to* JULIA). Be a violet—a crushed, despairing violet.

JULIA. Do you suppose I intend to give up a magnificent part without a struggle?

LUD. My good girl, she has the law on her side. Let us both bear this calamity with resignation. If you must struggle, go away and struggle in the seclusion of your chamber.

SONG—BARONESS *and* CHORUS

Now away to the wedding we go,
So summon the charioteers—
No kind of reluctance they show
To embark on their married careers.
Though Julia's emotion may flow
For the rest of her maidenly years,
ALL. To the wedding we eagerly go,
So summon the charioteers!

Now away, etc.

[*All dance off to wedding except* JULIA.

RECIT.—JULIA

So ends my dream—so fades my vision fair!
Of hope no gleam—distraction and despair!
My cherished dream, the Ducal throne to share.
That aim supreme has vanished into air!

SONG—JULIA

Broken every promise plighted—
All is darksome—all is dreary.
Every new-born hope is blighted!
Sad and sorry—weak and weary!
Death the Friend or Death the Foe,
Shall I call upon thee? No!

I will go on living, though
Sad and sorry—weak and weary!

No, no! Let the bygone go by!
No good ever came of repining:
If to-day there are clouds o'er the sky,
To-morrow the sun may be shining!
To-morrow, be kind,
To-morrow, to me!
With loyalty blind
I curtsey to thee!
To-day is a day of illusion and sorrow,
So *viva* To-morrow, To-morrow, To-morrow!
God save you, To-morrow!
Your servant, To-morrow!
God save you, To-morrow, To-morrow, To-morrow!
[*Exit* JULIA.

Enter ERNEST

ERN. It's of no use—I can't wait any longer. At any risk I must gratify my urgent desire to know what is going on. (*Looking off.*) Why, what's that? Surely I see a wedding procession winding down the hill, dressed in my *Troilus and Cressida* costumes! That's Ludwig's doing! I see how it is—he found the time hang heavy on his hands, and is amusing himself by getting married to Lisa. No—it can't be to Lisa, for here she is!

Enter LISA

LISA (*not seeing him*). I really cannot stand seeing my Ludwig married twice in one day to somebody else!

ERN. Lisa!

(LISA *sees him, and stands as if transfixed with horror.*)

ERN. Come here—don't be a little fool—I want you.

(LISA *suddenly turns and bolts off.*)

ERN. Why, what's the matter with the little donkey? One would think she saw a ghost! But if he's not marrying Lisa, whom *is* he marrying? (*Suddenly.*) Julia! (*Much overcome.*) I see it all! The scoundrel! He had to adopt all my responsibilities, and he's shabbily taken advantage of the situation to marry the girl I'm engaged to! But no, it can't be Julia, for here *she* is!

Enter JULIA

JULIA (*not seeing him*). I've made up my mind. I won't stand it! I'll send in my notice at once!

ERN. Julia! Oh, what a relief!

(JULIA *gazes at him as if transfixed.*)

ERN. Then you've not married Ludwig? You are still true to me?

(JULIA *turns and bolts in grotesque horror.* ERNEST *follows and stops her.*)

ERN. Don't run away! Listen to me. Are you all crazy?

JULIA (*in affected terror*). What would you with me, spectre? Oh, ain't his eyes sepulchral! And ain't his voice hollow! What are you doing out of your tomb at this time of day—apparition?

ERN. I do wish I could make you girls understand that I'm only technically dead, and that physically I'm as much alive as ever I was in my life!

JULIA. Oh, but it's an awful thing to be haunted by a technical bogy!

ERN. You won't be haunted much longer. The law must be on its last legs, and in a few hours I shall come to life again—resume all my social and civil functions, and claim my darling as my blushing bride!

JULIA. Oh—then you haven't heard?

ERN. My love, I've heard nothing. How could I? There are no daily papers where I come from.

JULIA. Why, Ludwig challenged Rudolph and won, and now *he's* Grand Duke, and he's revived the law for another century!

ERN. What! But you're not serious—you're only joking!

JULIA. My good sir, I'm a light-hearted girl, but I don't chaff bogies.

ERN. Well, that's the meanest dodge I ever heard of!

JULIA. Shabby trick, *I* call it.

ERN. But you don't mean to say that you're going to cry off!

JULIA. I really can't afford to wait until your time is up. You know, I've always set my face against long engagements.

ERN. Then defy the law and marry me now. We will fly to your native country, and I'll play broken-English in London as you play broken-German here!

JULIA. No. These legal technicalities cannot be defied. Situated as you are, you have no power to make me your wife. At best you could only make me your widow.

ERN. Then be my widow—my little dainty, winning, winsome widow!

JULIA. Now what would be the good of that? Why, you goose, I should marry again within a month!

DUET—ERNEST *and* JULIA

ERN. If the light of love's lingering ember
Has faded in gloom,
You cannot neglect, O remember,
A voice from the tomb!
That stern supernatural diction
Should act as a solemn restriction,
Although by a mere legal fiction
A voice from the tomb!

JULIA (*in affected terror*).
I own that that utterance chills me—
It withers my bloom!
With awful emotion it thrills me—
That voice from the tomb!
Oh, spectre, won't anything lay thee?
Though pained to deny or gainsay thee,
In this case I cannot obey thee,
Thou voice from the tomb!

(*Dancing.*) So, spectre appalling,
I bid you good-day—
Perhaps you'll be calling
When passing this way.
Your bogydom scorning,
And all your love-lorning,
I bid you good-morning,
I bid you good-day.

ERN. (*furious*). My offer recalling,
Your words I obey—
Your fate is appalling
And full of dismay.
To pay for this scorning
I give you fair warning
I'll haunt you each morning,
Each night, and each day!

[*Repeat Ensemble, and exeunt in opposite directions.*

Re-enter the Wedding Procession dancing

CHORUS

Now bridegroom and bride let us toast
In a magnum of merry champagne—
Let us make of this moment the most,
We may not be so lucky again.
So drink to our sovereign host
And his highly intelligent reign—
His health and his bride's let us toast
In a magnum of merry champagne!

SONG—BARONESS *with* CHORUS

I once gave an evening party
(A sandwich and cut-orange ball),
But my guests had such appetites hearty
That I couldn't enjoy it, enjoy it at all!
I made a heroic endeavour
To look unconcerned, but in vain,
And I vow'd that I never—oh never—
Would ask anybody again!
But there's a distinction decided—
A difference truly immense—
When the wine that you drink is provided, provided,
At somebody else's expense.
So bumpers—aye, ever so many—
The cost we may safely ignore!
For the wine doesn't cost us a penny,
Tho' it's Pomméry seventy-four!

CHORUS. So bumpers—aye, ever so many—etc.

Come, bumpers—aye, ever so many—
  And then, if you will, many more!
This wine doesn't cost us a penny,
  Tho' it's Pomméry, Pomméry seventy-four!
Old wine is a true panacea
  For ev'ry conceivable ill,
When you cherish the soothing idea
  That somebody else pays the bill!
Old wine is a pleasure that's hollow
  When at your own table you sit,
For you're thinking each mouthful you swallow
  Hast cost you, has cost you a threepenny-bit!
So bumpers—aye, ever so many—
  And then, if you will, many more!
This wine doesn't cost us a penny,
  Tho' it's Pomméry seventy-four!

CHORUS. So, bumpers—aye, ever so many—etc.

(*March heard*)

LUD. (*recit.*). Why, who is this approaching,
    Upon our joy encroaching?
    Some rascal come a-poaching
    Who's heard that wine we're broaching?

ALL. Who may this be?
    Who may this be?
    Who is he? Who is he? Who is he?

Enter HERALD

HER. The Prince of Monte Car*lo,*
      From Mediterranean water,
    Has come here to bestow
      On you his beautiful daughter.
    They've paid off all they owe,
      As every statesman oughter—
    That Prince of Monte Car*lo*
      And his be-eautiful daughter!

CHORUS. The Prince of Monte Car*lo,* etc.

HER. The Prince of Monte Car*lo,*
      Who is so very partickler,

Has heard that you're also
For ceremony a stickler—
Therefore he lets you know
By word of mouth auric'lar—
(That Prince of Monte Car*lo*
Who is so very particklar)--

CHORUS. The Prince of Monte Car*lo,* etc.

HER. That Prince of Monte Car*lo,*
From Mediterranean water,
Has come here to bestow
On you his be-eautiful daughter!

LUD. (*recit.*). His Highness we know not—nor the locality
In which is situate his Principality;
But, as he guesses by some odd fatality,
This *is* the shop for cut and dried formality!
Let him appear—
He'll find that we're
Remarkable for cut and dried formality.

(*Reprise of March. Exit* HERALD.
LUDWIG *beckons his Court.*)

LUD. I have a plan—I'll tell you all the plot of it—
He wants formality—he shall have a lot of it!

(*Whispers to them, through symphony.*)

Conceal yourselves, and when I give the cue,
Spring out on him—you all know what to do!

(*All conceal themselves behind the draperies that enclose the stage.*)

Pompous March. Enter the PRINCE *and* PRINCESS OF MONTE CARLO, *attended by six theatrical-looking nobles and the Court Costumier.*

DUET—PRINCE *and* PRINCESS.

PRINCE. We're rigged out in magnificent array
(Our own clothes are much gloomier)
In costumes which we've hired by the day
From a very well-known costumier.

COST. (*bowing*). *I* am the well-known costumier.

PRINCESS. With a brilliant staff a Prince should make a show
(It's a rule that never varies),
So we've engaged from the Theatre Monaco
Six supernumeraries.

NOBLES. We're the supernumeraries.

ALL. At a salary immense,
Quite regardless of expense,
Six supernumeraries!

PRINCE. They do not speak, for they break our grammar's laws,
And their language is lamentable—
And they never take off their gloves, because
Their nails are not presentable.

NOBLES. Our nails are not presentable!

PRINCESS. To account for their shortcomings manifest
We explain, in a whisper bated,
They are wealthy members of the brewing interest
To the Peerage elevated.

NOBLES. To the Peerage elevated.

ALL. They're / We're } very, very rich,
And accordingly, as sich,
To the Peerage elevated.

PRINCE. Well, my dear, here we are at last—just in time to compel Duke Rudolph to fulfil the terms of his marriage contract. Another hour and we should have been too late.

PRINCESS. Yes, papa, and if you hadn't fortunately discovered a means of making an income by honest industry, we should never have got here at all.

PRINCE. Very true. Confined for the last two years within the precincts of my palace by an obdurate bootmaker who held a warrant for my arrest, I devoted my enforced leisure to a study of the doctrine of chances—mainly with the view of ascertaining whether there was the remotest chance of my ever going out for a walk again—and this led to the discovery of a singularly fascinating little round game which I have called Roulette, and by which, in one sitting, I won no less than five thousand francs! My first act was to pay my bootmaker—my second, to engage a good useful working set of second-hand nobles—and my third, to hurry you off to Pfennig Halbpfennig as fast as a *train de luxe* could carry us!

PRINCESS. Yes, and a pretty job-lot of second-hand nobles you've scraped together!

PRINCE (*doubtfully*). Pretty, you think? Humph! I don't know. I should say tol-lol, my love—only tol-lol. They are not wholly satisfactory. There is a certain air of unreality about them—they are not convincing.

COST. But, my goot friend, vhat can you expect for eighteenpence a day!

PRINCE. Now take this Peer, for instance. What the deuce do you call *him?*

COST. Him? Oh, he's a swell—he's the Duke of Riviera.

PRINCE. Oh, he's a Duke, is he? Well, that's no reason why he should look so confoundedly haughty. (*To* NOBLE.) Be affable, sir! (NOBLE *takes attitude of affability.*) That's better. (*Passing to another.*) Now, who's this with his moustache coming off?

COST. Vhy, you're Viscount Mentone, ain't you?

NOBLE. Blest if I know. (*Turning up sword-belt.*) It's wrote here—yes, Viscount Mentone.

COST. Then vhy don't you say so? 'Old yerself up—you ain't carryin' sandwich boards now. (*Adjusts his moustache.*)

PRINCE. Now, once for all, you Peers—when His Highness arrives, don't stand like sticks, but appear to take an intelligent and sympathetic interest in what is going on. You needn't say anything, but let your gestures be in accordance with the spirit of the conversation. Now take the word from me. Affability! (*attitude*). Submission! (*attitude*). Surprise! (*attitude*). Shame! (*attitude*). Grief! (*attitude*). Joy! (*attitude*). That's better! You can do it if you like!

PRINCESS. But, papa, where in the world is the Court? There is positively no one here to receive us! I can't help feeling that Rudolph wants to get out of it because I'm poor. He's a miserly little wretch—that's what he is.

PRINCE. Well, I shouldn't go so far as to say that. I should rather describe him as an enthusiastic collector of coins—of the realm—and we must not be too hard upon a numismatist if he feels a certain disinclination to part with some of his really very valuable specimens. It's a pretty hobby: I've often thought I should like to collect some coins myself.

PRINCESS. Papa, I'm sure there's some one behind that curtain. I saw it move!

PRINCE. Then no doubt they are coming. Now mind, you Peers—haughty affability combined with a sense of what is due to your exalted ranks, or I'll fine you half a franc each—upon my soul I will!

[*Gong. The curtains fly back and the Court are discovered. They give a wild yell and rush on to the stage dancing wildly, with* PRINCE, PRINCESS, *and* NOBLES, *who are taken by surprise at first, but eventually join in a reckless dance. At the end all fall down exhausted.*

LUD. There, what do you think of that? That's our official ceremonial for the reception of visitors of the very highest distinction.

PRINCE (*puzzled*). It's very quaint—very curious indeed. Prettily footed, too. Prettily footed.

LUD. Would you like to see how we say "good-bye" to visitors of distinction? That ceremony is also performed with the foot.

PRINCE. Really, this tone—ah, but perhaps you have not completely grasped the situation?

LUD. Not altogether.

PRINCE. Ah, then I'll give you a lead over. (*Significantly.*) I am the father of the Princess of Monte Carlo. Doesn't that convey any idea to the Grand Ducal mind?

LUD. (*stolidly*). Nothing definite.

PRINCE (*aside*). H'm—very odd! Never mind—try again! (*Aloud.*) This is the daughter of the Prince of Monte Carlo. Do you take?

LUD. (*still puzzled*). No—not yet. Go on—don't give it up—I daresay it will come presently.

PRINCE. Very odd—never mind—try again. (*With sly significance.*) Twenty years ago! Little doddle doddle! *Two* little doddle doddles! Happy father—hers and yours. Proud mother—yours and hers! Hah! *Now* you take? I see you do! I see you do!

LUD. Nothing is more annoying than to feel that you're not equal to the intellectual pressure of the conversation. I wish he'd say something intelligible.

PRINCE. You didn't expect me?

LUD. (*jumping at it*). No, no. I grasp that—thank you very much. (*Shaking hands with him.*) No, I did *not* expect you!

PRINCE. I thought not. But ha! ha! at last I have escaped from my enforced restraint. (*General movement of alarm.*) (*To crowd who are stealing off.*) No, no—you misunderstand me. I mean I've paid my debts!

ALL. Oh! (*They return.*)

PRINCESS (*affectionately*). But, my darling, I'm afraid that even now you don't quite realize who I am! (*Embracing him.*)

BARONESS. Why, you forward little hussy, how dare you? (*Takes her away from* LUDWIG.)

LUD. You mustn't do that, my dear—never in the presence of the Grand Duchess, I beg!

PRINCESS (*weeping*). Oh, papa, he's got a Grand Duchess!

LUD. *A* Grand Duchess! My good girl, I've got three Grand Duchesses!

PRINCESS. Well, I'm sure! Papa, let's go away—this is not a respectable Court.

PRINCE. All these Grand Dukes have their little fancies, my love. This potentate appears to be collecting wives. It's a pretty hobby—I should like to collect a few myself. This (*admiring* BARONESS) is a charming specimen—an antique, I should say—of the early Merovingian period, if I'm not mistaken; and here's another—a Scotch lady, I think (*alluding to* JULIA), and (*alluding to* LISA) a little one thrown in. Two half-quarterns and a makeweight! (*To* LUDWIG.) Have you such a thing as a catalogue of the Museum?

PRINCESS. But I cannot permit Rudolph to keep a museum——

LUD. Rudolph? Get along with you, I'm not Rudolph! Rudolph died yesterday!

PRINCE *and* PRINCESS. What!

LUD. Quite suddenly—of—of—a cardiac affection.

PRINCE *and* PRINCESS. Of a cardiac affection?

LUD. Yes, a pack-of-cardiac affection. He fought a Statutory Duel with me and lost, and I took over all his engagements—including this imperfectly preserved old lady, to whom he has been engaged for the last three weeks.

PRINCESS. Three weeks! But I've been engaged to him for the last twenty years!

BARONESS, LISA, *and* JULIA. Twenty years!

PRINCE (*aside*). It's all right, my love—they can't get over that. (*Aloud.*) He's yours—take him, and hold him as tight as you can!

PRINCESS. My own! (*Embracing* LUDWIG.)

LUD. Here's another!—the fourth in four-and-twenty hours! Would anybody else like to marry me? You ma'am—or you—anybody! I'm getting used to it!

BARONESS. But let me tell you, ma'am——

JULIA. Why, you impudent little hussy——

LISA. Oh, here's another—here's another! (*Weeping.*)

PRINCESS. Poor ladies, I'm very sorry for you all; but, you see, I've a prior claim. Come, away we go—there's not a moment to be lost!

CHORUS (*as they dance towards exit*)

Away to the wedding we'll go
  To summon the charioteers,
No kind of reluctance we show
  To embark on our married careers—

[*At this moment* RUDOLPH, ERNEST, *and* NOTARY *appear. All kneel in astonishment.*

RECITATIVE

RUD., ERN., *and* NOT.

Forbear! This may not be!
  Frustrated are your plans!
With paramount decree
  The Law forbids the banns!

ALL. The Law forbids the banns!

LUD. Not a bit of it! I've revived the law for another century!

RUD. You didn't revive it! You couldn't revive it! You—you are an impostor, sir—a tuppenny rogue, sir! You—you never were, and in all human probability never will be—Grand Duke of Pfennig Anything!

ALL. What!!!

RUD. Never—never, never! (*Aside.*) Oh, my internal economy!

LUD. That's absurd, you know. I fought the Grand Duke. He drew a King, and I drew an Ace. He perished in inconceivable agonies on the spot. Now, as that's settled, we'll go on with the wedding.

RUD. It—it isn't settled. You—you can't. I—I— (*to* NOTARY). Oh, tell him—tell him! I can't!

NOT. Well, the fact is, there's been a little mistake here. On reference to the Act that regulates Statutory Duels, I find it is expressly laid down that the Ace shall count invariably as lowest!

ALL. As lowest!

RUD. (*breathlessly*). As—lowest—lowest—lowest! So *you're* the ghoest—ghoest—ghoest! (*Aside.*) Oh, what *is* the matter with me inside here!

ERN. Well, Julia, as it seems that the law hasn't been revived—and as, consequently, I shall come to life in about three minutes—(*consulting his watch*)——

JULIA. My objection falls to the ground. (*Resignedly.*) Very well!

PRINCESS. And am I to understand that I was on the point of marrying a dead man without knowing it? (*To* RUDOLPH, *who revives.*) Oh, my love, what a narrow escape I've had!

RUD. Oh—you are the Princess of Monte Carlo, and

you've turned up just in time! Well, you're an attractive little girl, you know, but you're as poor as a rat! (*They retire up together.*)

LISA. That's all very well, but what is to become of *me?* (*To* LUDWIG.) If you're a dead man——(*Clock strikes three.*)

LUD. But I'm not. Time's up—the Act has expired—I've come to life—the parson is still in attendance, and we'll all be married directly.

ALL. Hurrah!

FINALE

Happy couples, lightly treading,
    Castle chapel will be quite full!
Each shall have a pretty wedding,
    As, of course, is only rightful,
    Though the brides be fair or frightful
Contradiction little dreading,
    This will be a day delightful—
Each shall have a pretty wedding!
    Such a pretty, pretty wedding!
        Such a pretty wedding!

[*All dance off to get married as the curtain falls.*

THE END

THE PALACE OF TRUTH

DRAMATIS PERSONÆ

KING PHANOR

PRINCE PHILAMIR

CHRYSAL

ZORAM

ARISTÆUS

GÉLANOR

QUEEN ALTEMIRE

PRINCESS ZEOLIDE

MIRZA

PALMIS

AZÈMA

ACT I

GARDENS OF KING PHANOR'S COUNTRY HOUSE

Morning

ACT II

INTERIOR OF THE PALACE OF TRUTH

Noon

ACT III

THE AVENUE OF PALMS

Night

[*The action of the piece takes place within the space of twenty-four hours.*

THE PALACE OF TRUTH

ACT I

SCENE.—*Garden of* KING PHANOR'S *Country House.* KING PHANOR *discovered with* CHRYSAL, ZORAM, ARISTÆUS, *and* PALMIS. ARISTÆUS *is standing sulkily apart.*

As the curtain rises, KING PHANOR *is finishing a recitation which he is accompanying on a mandolin, in a very affected manner.*

PHANOR. "Oh, I would not—no, I would *not* be there!"

(ZORAM *and* CHRYSAL *applaud vigorously.*)

CHRYSAL. My lord, I pray you read it once again,
My ears are greedy for the golden sound.

PHAN. Chrysal, you make me blush!

CHRYS. My lord, a blush
Is modesty's sole herald—and true worth
Is ever modest. Pray you, sir, again!

PHAN. It's a poor thing—a string of platitudes—
Stale metaphors—time-honoured similes.
I'm a poor poet, gentlemen!

CHRYS. I swear
There never lived a poet till now!

ZORAM. And then
The music you have wedded to the words
(I speak of this with some authority)
Shames, in its flow of rhythmic melody,
The counterpoint of Adam de la Halle!

PHAN. (*bashfully*). The merit is not altogether mine.
I wrote the music—but I did not make
This dainty instrument. Why, who could fail
To charm, with such a mandolin as this?

ZOR. Believe me, the result would be the same,
Whether your lordship chose to play upon
The simple tetrachord of Mercury
That knew no diatonic intervals,
Or the elaborate dis-diapason
(Four tetrachords and one redundant note),
Embracing in its perfect consonance
All simple, double and inverted chords!

PHAN. (*to* CHRYSAL). A wonderful musician—and a man
Of infinite good taste!

ZOR. Why, from my birth
I have made melope and counterpoint
My favorite study.

PHAN. And you really care
To hear my work again, O melodist?

ZOR. Again, my lord, and even then again!

PHAN. (*recites*). "When pitch-encrusted night aloft prevails;
"When no still goddess through the mid-air sails;
"When scorpions vomit forth their poisonous scum;
"When to the demon tryst gaunt witches come;
"When noisome pestilence stalks through the glen,
"Bellowing forth its enmity to men;
"When ghastly toads scream loudly through the air;
"Oh, I would not—no, I would *not* be there!"

CHRYS. (*in raptures*). Why, where's the cunning of the sorcerer
Placed by the magic of such words as these?
"When pitch-encrusted night aloft prevails";
Why, there's an epithet might make day night,
And shame the swallows to their couching place!
"When no still goddess through the mid-air sails!"
Why, here's a blackness, Zoram, so intense
It scares the very deities away!

PHAN. (*explaining*). "Still goddess" means the moon.

CHRYS. The moon—my lord?
Of course—the moon! See how, in ignorance,
We seek upon the surface of the wave
For pearls that lie uncounted fathoms deep.
The darkness frightens e'en the moon away!
The metaphor is perfect!

PHAN. (*annoyed*). No, no, no!
The moon has not yet risen, sir! The moon
Frightens the darkness—darkness don't fright *her!*
Why sits the genial Aristæus there
All solitary? How d'you like my work?
(*Aside to* CHRYSAL.) We'll have some fun with him.
(*Aloud*.) Your verdict, come!

ARIST. I'm blunt and honest. I can't teach my tongue
To lie, as Zoram here, and Chrysal do.
I tell the truth, sir. If you want to know
My estimate of what you've given us,
I think your poetry contemptible—
Your melody, my lord, beneath contempt.

PHAN. That's rather strong.

ARIST. It's strong, my lord, but true.
I'm blunt—outspoken. If I've angered you,
So much the worse; I always speak the truth.

CHRYS. Heed not the yelping of this surly cur;
Nought satisfies him, Phanor!

ARIST. There you're wrong,
For I was satisfied to hear it once;
'Twas you that wanted it a second time!

CHRYS. Back to your kennel, sham Diogenes!

ARIST. I'm no Diogenes. *He* spent his life
Seeking an honest man. *I* live in courts.

ZOR. My lord, I pray you send the fellow hence,
For he and we are always out of tune.
An inharmonious bracketing of notes,
Whose musical extremes don't coalesce:
He's sharp and we are flat.

ARIST. Extremely flat!

CHRYS. He's vinegar, my lord, and we are oil.

ARIST. Oil is a sickening insipid food
Unless it's qualified with vinegar.

I'm rough and honest. If I've angered you,
I'll go.

PHAN. No, no, you have not angered us.
(*Aside to* ZORAM.) I like the fellow's humour—he may rave!
I'm tired of hearing truths, so let him lie!
But where's Queen Altemire?

CHRYS. My lord, she comes—
A perfect type of perfect womanhood.
The dew of forty summers on her head
Has but matured her beauty, by my life!
For five and thirty years, a bud—and now
A rose full blown!

ARIST. Say over-blown.

PHAN. What's that?

ARIST. My lord, the Queen's too fat.

PHAN. Well, that may be.
But don't you tell her so. Your insolence
Amuses me—it won't amuse the Queen;
She has no sense of humour. So take care.

ARIST. My lord, I'm rough, but honest. I've a tongue
That cannot frame a lie.

PHAN. But bear in mind
Besides that very rough and honest tongue,
You have a palate, and a set of teeth,
And several delicate contrivances
That aid digestion. Tell her she's too fat,
And she may take offence; and, if she does,
She'll throw that apparatus out of work:
That's all.

Enter the QUEEN *and* MIRZA

Good morning, Altemire, my queen.
Why, you seem sad.

ALTEM. My lord, I'm very sad.

PALMIS. The Queen is sad! Zoram, attune your lyre
And soothe her melancholy.

ALTEM. No, no, no—
I'm not in cue for music—leave us, pray—
I would take counsel with my lord—look, sirs,
I am not well.

[*The three* COURTIERS *exeunt into house.*

PHAN. (*aside to* PALMIS). Palmis, what's here amiss?
What causes this? Have *I* done anything?
PALMIS. I know not, but I think it bears upon
Your daughter's troth to brave Prince Philamir.
Whenever we have spoken on the point
She has commanded silence.
PHAN. Well, we'll see.
Chrysal awaits you—you may go to him;
Talk to him of your pledge to marry *him,*
And he'll not silence you. There, you may go.

[*Exit* PALMIS *into house.*

Now what's the matter?
ALTEM. Oh, I'm sick at heart
With apprehension! Our dear Zeolide
To-morrow is betrothed to Philamir,
The bravest and the most accomplished Prince
In Christendom. Phanor, she loves him not!
PHAN. What makes you think so?
ALTEM. Phanor, you are blind!
Why, see how coldly Zeolide receives
His songs of love—his bursts of metaphor:
"I love you, Philamir," and there's an end.
She will vouchsafe her spouse-elect no more—
No tenderness—no reciprocity;
A cold, half-sullen and half-wayward smile,
And that is all. The maiden lavishes
More love upon her horse!
PHAN. Perhaps she thinks
Her horse will bear such tokens of regard
With more discretion than her lover would!
ALTEM. Phanor, I tell you she loves him not.
I am a woman, with a woman's tact.
PHAN. She *says* she loves him.
ALTEM. So indeed she says,
And says no more. Phanor, had I been woo'd
With ardent songs of overwhelming love,
Framed by so fair a poet as Philamir,
It would have turned my giddy woman's brain,
And thrilled my reason to its very core!

PHAN. I never thought my wooing poetry,
Now I begin to think it may have been.

MIRZA. Oh, sir, *I* love the Princess. Pause before
You sacrifice her earthly happiness
For sordid ends of selfish policy.
The Prince is rich. What then? The girl is poor.
But what is wealth of gold to wealth of love?
What famine's so deplorable as his
Who hungers for a love he cannot find?
What luxury so wearisome as hers
Who's surfeited with love she values not?
King Phanor, let the Princess be released!

ALTEM. My lady Mirza, you forget yourself!

MIRZA. I do forget myself, rememb'ring her;
I have her happiness at heart. The maid
Is more than life to me. Forgive me, Queen.
I could not help but speak.

PHAN. Well, say no more.
I'll question her, and if it then appears
She loves not Philamir, she shall be free.
I also love the girl—but, here she comes.
I'll find some test which shall decide the point.

[*Exit* PHANOR *into house.*

Enter ZEOLIDE

ALTEM. My daughter, where's the Prince?

ZEO. I cannot say;
I saw his highness yesterday, but since
Have not set eyes on him.

ALTEM. Has he returned
From hunting?

ZEO. Yes, I heard the Prince's voice
Not half an hour ago.

ALTEM. And, in return.
You made no sign to him?

ZEO. No sign, indeed.
I heard his song—'twas very sweetly sung;
It told of love—it called for no reply.

ALTEM. A song of love that called for no reply?

ZEO. It asked no question, mother.

ALTEM. Surely, girl,
There may be questions that are not expressed.
ZEO. And answers, mother—mine was one of them!
ALTEM. Come, Zeolide, I've much to say to you.
Renounce Prince Philamir ere 'tis too late!
He will release you; he is proud and brave,
And would not force a hated life on you.
Come, Zeolide, throw off this weary bond,
And marry whom you love, or marry none!
ZEO. As I am bound, dear mother, I'll remain,
So let me stay with Mirza.
ALTEM. (*annoyed*). You can stay!

[*Exit* QUEEN ALTEMIRE *into house, glancing angrily at* MIRZA; ZEOLIDE *notices this with some surprise.*

ZEO. Why, Mirza, how my mother frowns at you!
How have you angered her?
MIRZA. I love you well;
And when I told her of my sister-love,
In words more passionate than politic,
The Queen rebuked me sternly.
ZEO. Oh, for shame!
MIRZA. She is your mother, and she claims your love,
And cannot brook that I should share that love.
I can forgive the noble jealousy
That comes of woman's love for woman.
ZEO. Yes;
For you are Mirza—queen of womankind—
The best, the noblest woman in the world!
MIRZA. Why, here is warmth! and people call you cold,
Because you are so cold to Philamir.
ZEO. Why, Mirza, he's a man!

Enter PHILAMIR *from house—he overhears* MIRZA

MIRZA. A man indeed!
The bravest warrior that wields a sword;
The rarest poet that ever penned a lay;
An admirable knight—gay, handsome, young,
Brave, wealthy, and accomplished—with a tongue
Might shame a siren's!

ZEO. Hush! a siren's tongue
Is not renowned for much sincerity.
MIRZA. *He* is sincere.
ZEO. Indeed, I hope he is!
PHIL. (*coming forward*). I thank you, Lady Mirza, for those words.
MIRZA (*coldly*). I little thought that they were overheard.
This is ungenerous, Prince Philamir.

[*Bows coldly and exit;* PHILAMIR *rushes to* ZEOLIDE, *who receives him very quietly.*

PHIL. Dear Zeolide, at last we are alone!
Oh, I have longed for this!
ZEO. Indeed! And why?
PHIL. And why? We can converse without reserve.
ZEO. What should I say when we are quite alone
That I should leave unsaid were others here?
I can but say, "I love you," Philamir.
PHIL. And is that all?
ZEO. And is not that enough?
PHIL. All the world knows you love me!
ZEO. That is why
I do not blush to own it in the world.
PHIL. But give me more—*I* love *you,* Zeolide,
As the earth loves the sun!
ZEO. The earth is glad
To see the sun, and asks no more than that.
You would do well to imitate the earth.
PHIL. I am content to imitate the earth—
I am content to sit and gaze at you,
Tranced in a lazy glow of happiness;
But if you speak and wake me from that trance,
Wake me, dear Zeolide, with warmer words.
"I love you!" Why, I know you love me well!
Say nothing, Zeolide, and I'm content.
If you say anything, say more than that!
ZEO. What words could I employ which, tested in
The crucible of unimpassioned truth,
Would not resolve themselves into those three?
Now I must go—your sun's about to set—
So farewell earth!

PHIL. And when the sun is down
The earth is inconsolable!
ZEO. Until
The moon appears! Perhaps there is a moon
That fills my place until I rise again?
PHIL. No more, dear Zeolide; or, if there be,
She floats in one perpetual eclipse!
ZEO. The moon is not the less a moon because
The earth thinks fit to hide her from the sun!
PHIL. Nay; you pursue the metaphor too far.
If I, the earth, conceal a nightly moon,
Why, you, the sun, have many worlds to warm,
And some are nearer to you than this earth!
ZEO. Hush, Philamir! I'm ready to believe
That you're an earth that knows no moon at all,
If you'll allow that I, although a sun,
Consent to warm no other world than this!

(*Kissing his forehead, and going.*)

PHIL. Oh, do not leave me thus, dear Zeolide.
I am a beggar, begging charity;
Throw me more coin that bears the stamp of love!
ZEO. I have one coin that bears that holy stamp—
I give you that—I have no more to give.
PHIL. Tell me its value, then, in words of love!
ZEO. What! would you have me advertise my alms,
And trumpet forth my largess to the world?
PHIL. Not to the world, dear Zeolide—to me!
ZEO. Ah, you would have me say, "*You* are my world!"
You see, I have the trick of ardent speech,
And I could use it, were I so disposed.
But surely, Philamir, the mendicant
Who is not satisfied to take my alms
Until he knows how much that alms be worth,
Can scarcely stand in need of alms at all!
I love you, Philamir—be satisfied.
Whose vows are made so earnestly as hers
Who would deceive you by her earnestness?
Why, if I sought to trick you, Philamir,

I should select such phrases for my end—
So passionate—and yet so delicate,
So fierce—from overflow of gentle love,
So furious—from excess of tenderness,
That even your expressions of regard,
Unbounded in their hot extravagance,
Would pale before the fury of *my* words,
And you, from very shame, would call them back,
And beg my pardon for their want of warmth!
I love you, Philamir—I'll say no more! [*Exit.*

PHIL. Gone! But I'll follow her——(*going*).

Enter PHANOR *from house.*

PHAN. Stop, Philamir,
If, as she says, she loves you, well and good;
She'll give you proof of it in her good time;
But if she don't, why, take an old boy's word
(Who speaks of love with some authority),
She'll love you none the better for the warmth
That prompts you to perpetual persecution.
The girl has taken this road—take you that.

[PHILAMIR *stands irresolute, then goes off slowly in the direction indicated.*

That's good advice!

Enter QUEEN ALTEMIRE *from house*

ALTEM. My lord, old Gélanor,
The steward of your palace, has arrived
And waits without.

PHAN. We'll see him presently.

ALTEM. (*with some hesitation*). Now, do you know, I often wonder why,
Possessing such a palace, furnished with
The rarest luxuries that wealth can buy
You hold your Court in this secluded place?
I have been married to you eighteen years,
Yet I have never seen this palace, which
Stands barely twenty miles away, and which
You visit regularly once a month.

PHAN. (*rather confused*). There are good reasons, Altemire.

ALTEM. (*angrily*). No doubt!
Exceedingly good reasons! When a man
Maintains a bachelor establishment,
He has the best of reasons to decline
To take his wife there!

PHAN. You're a jealous fool.

ALTEM. Jealous I am, and possibly a fool,
But not a fool for being jealous.

PHAN. Peace,
And I will tell you why I take you not.
That palace is enchanted. Every one
Who enters there is bound to speak the truth—
The simple, unadulterated truth.
To every question that is put to him
He must return the unaffected truth.
And, strange to say, while publishing the truth
He's no idea that he is doing so;
And while he lets innumerable cats
Out of unnumbered bags, he quite believes
That all the while he's tightening the strings
That keep them from a too censorious world.
What do you say to that?

ALTEM. (*amazed*). Say? Would the world
Were one such palace, Phanor!

PHAN. If it were,
At least we all should meet on equal terms;
But to be taken from a world in which
That influence don't exist, and to be placed
Inside a fairy palace where it does
(Accompanied, moreover, by one's wife),
Might take one at a disadvantage!

ALTEM. Well,
I am prepared to undergo the test
If you'll accompany me.

PHAN. No, no, no!
You are a worthy woman, Altemire,
But, Altemire, you have your faults!

ALTEM. My lord,
I am a woman!

PHAN. Yes, exactly so!
If you were *not* a woman, Altemire,
Or, being one, were some one else's wife,
I'd take you there to-morrow!

ALTEM. But, my lord,
Why won't you take me, being what I am?

PHAN. Because, my wife, I don't know what you are.

ALTEM. You know, at least, that I'm a faithful wife.

PHAN. I think you're more than faithful. I believe
You are a perfect woman, Altemire,
A pattern as a mother and a wife—
And, so believing, why, I do not care
To run the risk of being undeceived!

ALTEM. (*annoyed*). My lord, you are unjust! Can you believe
I should expose myself to such a test
Had I been guilty of unfaithfulness?
I am no perfect woman, Phanor. I have faults
That advertise themselves. No need to say
That I'm quick-tempered, jealous, over-prone
To underrate the worth of womankind—
Impetuous—unreasonable—vain—
I am a woman, with a woman's faults.
But, being woman, Phanor, I'm a wife;
And, in that I am one, I need not blush.
You have some better reason. Possibly
You dread the palace on your own account?

PHAN. *I* dread the palace, Altemire? No, no.
I am a child of impulse. All my faults
Lie on the surface. I have nought to hide.
Such little faults as sully me you know.

ALTEM. Or guess.

PHAN. Ha! Am I then to understand
My Queen suspects her husband?

ALTEM. Yes, you are!

PHAN. Then this decides me. You *shall* go with me.

ALTEM. But——

PHAN. Not a word—King Phanor cannot brook
The breath of jealousy. With all his faults,
His married life has been as pure as snow.
We two will go this morning.

ALTEM. Stay! A thought
Let us take Zeolide and Philamir,
They shall not know the fairy influence
To which they are subjected. If the maid
Does not love Philamir, she'll show it then,
And the betrothal can be cancelled. If
She loves him, why, she'll show it all the more!
Then the betrothal shall be ratified.

PHAN. We *will* take Zeolide and Philamir,
Chrysal and Zoram—Aristæus too,
And Palmis—yes, and blameless Lady Mirza—
Mirza, the good, the beautiful, the pure!

ALTEM. Mirza! Eternal Mirza! Everywhere
I hear her irritating virtues praised!
I'm weary of the woman!

PHAN. Stop a bit,
Till we are in the palace. Then we'll learn
Not only your opinion of her worth,
But also why you hold it.

ALTEM. Well, well, well!
The maid is young and beautiful, and I
Am envious of that youth and beauty. See,
I can anticipate the influence
To which I'm going to subject myself.
There I was wrong. Mirza *shall* go with us,
And by her conduct under such a test,
Prove the injustice of my estimate.
I'll go and warn the court.

[*Exit* QUEEN ALTEMIRE *into house.*

PHAN. The course I take
Is rather rash, but the experiment
Will not be destitute of interest.

Enter GÉLANOR *from house*

Well, Gélanor, what tidings do you bring?
About our palace?

GÉLAN. Sir, the old, old tale.
Men come and go—and women come and go.
Although the palace gates are opened wide
To rich and poor alike—and rich and poor

Alike receive full hospitality
For any length of time they care to stay,
Few care to stay above a day or two.
Free entertainment in a princely home
Is little valued when it's coupled with
The disadvantage of a dwelling-place
Where every one is bound to speak the truth.
When does my lord propose to start?

PHAN. To-day.
But this time not alone, good Gélanor.

GÉLAN. And who is to accompany you, sir?

PHAN. My wife.

GÉLAN. Your wife?

PHAN. My wife.

GÉLAN. Great heavens, my lord,
Have you reflected?

PHAN. Yes.

GÉLAN. To any place
Where one is bound to speak the baldest truth
Concerning all the actions of one's life,
It's hardly politic to take one's wife!

PHAN. Oh, I've the fullest confidence in her.
She's a good woman, Gélanor.

GÉLAN. Ah, sir.
I have seen married couples, by the score,
Who, when they passed within our crystal walls,
Have boldly advertised themselves prepared
To stake their souls upon each other's faith—
But who, before they've spent an hour at most
Under the castle's mystic influence,
Have separated ne'er to meet again!
Oh, have a care!

PHAN. Queen Altemire knows all,
And knowing all, she fears not for herself,
So I've no fear for her!

GÉLAN. But *you,* my liege—
How will *you* bear yourself 'neath such a test?
You have been married nearly eighteen years:
That's a long time!

Enter MIRZA, *unobserved*

PHAN. Well, yes—I've thought of that.
I'm a good husband—as good husbands go.
I love my wife—but still—you understand—
Boys will be boys! There *is* a point or two—
Say two, as being nearer to the mark—
On which I do not altogether care
To stand examination by my wife.
Perhaps I may have given out that I've
Been dining *here*—when I've been dining *there*—
I may have said "with A"—when 'twas with B——
I may have said "with *him*"—when 'twas with *her*—
Distinctions such as these, good Gélanor,
Though strangely unimportant in themselves,
Still have a value, which the female mind's
Particularly quick to apprehend.
Now here's a talisman—a crystal box—(*producing it*).
Whoever carries this within those walls
May overcome the castle's influence,
And utter truth or falsehood as he wills.
I should do well, I think, to take this box?

GÉLAN. From all accounts, my lord, I think you would!
(*Sees* MIRZA.) Ahem! We are observed!

MIRZA. My lord, I trust
My presence here is not inopportune?
I will withdraw.

PHAN. No, Lady Mirza, no!
I was exhibiting to Gélanor
A curious specimen of crystal work—
He understands such things.

MIRZA (*taking box.*) And so do I.
How marvellously pure! No single flaw
Affects its exquisite transparency!
A perfect emblem of a spotless life!

GÉLAN. But, Lady Mirza, perfect spotlessness
Is apt to smack of insipidity.

MIRZA. No—hold it to the light, and see the change!
See how its exquisite prismatic hues,

Under the influence of searching light,
Are instantly made clear and manifest.
As shines this crystal in the sun, so shines
A perfect woman in the light of truth.
The modest beauties of a spotless life
Remain unknown and unsuspected, till
A ray of truth-light starts them into life,
And shows them—all unwilling—to the world!

GÉLAN. But there are hidden qualities of soul
That even truth cannot detect. Suppose
This crystal, peerless in its spotlessness,
Turned out to be a potent talisman,
With power to work all kinds of devilry?
There are such things!

PHAN. (*aside*). Why, there are women, too
(I have known many such), to whom the box
Might still be very properly compared!

MIRZA. Impossible, my lord. I'll not believe
That aught so beautiful could be so base.
(*Returning it.*) I thank you sir. I've read a lesson here
That I shall take good heed to profit by.

Enter the QUEEN ALTEMIRE, *with* ZEOLIDE, PHANOR, ARISTÆUS, ZORAM, *and* PALMIS, *from house*

ALTEM. Here comes your Court, my lord.

PHAN. That's well. My friends,
I have a palace, twenty miles away—
A lovely place, engirt with crystal walls;
Its grounds will show fair flowers and shady groves,
Huge forest trees, rare fountains, hill and dale.
There's hunting, fishing—eighteen years preserved!
There the sun shines unclouded all day long.
What say you—will you go?

CHRYS. Go? What care I
Whether it rain or shine so that I may
Bask in the sunshine of my King and Queen!

PHAN. In half an hour we start. Once there, our life
Shall be a song, and Aristæus here,

The jolly, genial, laughing Aristæus,
Shall strike the key-note!

ARIST. Well, I'll do my best.

ZOR. But pray consider. If the intervals
Throughout the diatonic series, sir,
Were mathematically equal, why,
It would not greatly matter, as you know,
Upon what note your melody commenced.
But as it is not so, we must respect
The intervals the melody demands.
No key-note struck by Aristæus could
Be correspondent with those intervals!

PHIL. *I'll* give the key-note. We will pass the day
By quivering willows at the waterside,
Lapped in a lazy luxury of love!
There we'll forget the world of work-a-day,
And crown our happiness with songs of love
What say you, dearest Zeolide?

ZEO. I've said
As much as it is maidenly to say—
I love you, Philamir—be satisfied!

ACT II

SCENE.—*Interior of the Palace of Truth.*

Enter GÉLANOR, *meeting* KING PHANOR *and* QUEEN ALTEMIRE *and* ZEOLIDE

GÉLAN. Welcome, my lord! Madam, I humbly trust
The palace realizes all the hopes
That you had entertained concerning it.

ALTEM. Indeed, it far exceeds them, Gélanor.
There is no lovelier abode on earth!
And so says Zeolide.

ZEO. Indeed she does!
Why, father, I have lived near eighteen years,
And never knew until three hours ago
That you possessed so lovely a domain!

Why have I wasted eighteen years on earth,
When such a heaven as this awaited me?

CÉLAN. (*aside to* PHANOR). You have not told the Princess or your Court
The palace's peculiarity?

PHAN. Not I. The secret is our own, as yet—
The Queen's, and yours, and mine.

GÉLAN. With you and me
The secret's safe. But then—Queen Altemire—
If you have told *her* all——

PHAN. No, no—not all!
Here is a secret which is yours and mine;
(*producing crystal box*)
And yours and mine the secret shall remain.
Protected by this talisman, I stand,
A sturdy rock amid the shifting sands—
A salamander in a world of fire—
Achilles in a crowd of myrmidons—
Achilles, with an iron-plated heel!
Go, send my courtiers—I anticipate
No ordinary sport from watching them.

[*Exeunt* GÉLANOR *and* PHANOR.

ALTEM. What are you reading, Zeolide?

ZEO. (*with scroll*). A song
Written by Chrysal set to Zoram's notes;
They gave it me before we left our home,
But in the hurry of the journey here,
I managed to mislay it—here it is.

Enter ZORAM, CHRYSAL, *and* ARISTÆUS

ALTEM. And here are author and composer, too—
And Critic, teeming with humanity.
Come let us hear it.

[ZEOLIDE *sings a song. At its conclusion* CHRYSAL *and* ZORAM *applaud.*

CHRYS. (*coming forward with all the action of a man who is expressing extreme approval*). Oh, I protest, my ears have never heard
A goodly song more miserably sung.

(*Clapping hands.*) Oh, very poor indeed—oh, very weak;
No voice—no execution—out of tune—
Pretentious too—oh, very, very poor! (*Applauding as if in ecstasies.*)

ALTEM. (*amused*). Indeed! I think I've often heard you say
No voice could rival Princess Zeolide's?

CHRYS. (*enthusiastically*). I've often said so—I have praised her voice,
Because I am a courtier—paid to praise.
I never meant one word of what I said;
I have the worst opinion of her voice,.
And so has Zoram.

ZOR. I? Oh, dear me, no!
I can form no opinion on the point,
I am no judge of music.

CHRYS. Eh?

ZOR. Not I!
I hardly know the treble from the bass,
And as to harmony—I know the word,
But hang me if I guess at what it means!

ZEO. Oh, Zoram, you are jesting—why, you wrote
The air I sung!

ZOR. *I* wrote the air? Not, I,
I paid a poor musician for his work,
And palmed it off upon you as my own.
A common trick with melodists who stand
Far higher in the world's esteem than I!

ALTEM. Well, Aristæus there has still to speak.
What says that rollicking philosopher?
Come, growl it out!

ARIST. (*gruffly, as if finding fault*). It's sweetly pretty, ma'am,
And very nicely sung. I like it much.

ZEO. What! Aristæus pleased?

ARIST. (*very savagely*). Of course I am;
I'm always pleased with everything.

ALTEM. Indeed!
Men look on Aristæus as a man
Whom nothing satisfies.

ARIST. (*with outrageous bluntness*). Then men are wrong,
No child's more easily amused than I.
But, here at Court, where every one is pleased
With everything, my amiability
Would go for nought; so I have coined myself
A disposition foreign to my own,
In hopes my clumsy boorish insolence
Might please you by its very novelty;
And prove, perchance, a not unwelcome foil
To Zoram's mockery of cultured taste,
And Chrysal's chronic insincerity!
I'm rough and honest, frank—outspoken—blunt.

CHRYS. Boor! when you dare to say I'm insincere
You tell the truth—there, make the most of that!

ZEO. Chrysal, your hand; I'm glad to find at last
Your eyes are opened to your many faults.

CHRYS. How, sir, is this intentional affront?

ZOR. No, not intentional. I tried to frame
A pleasant speech, but, by some awkward slip,
The truth escaped me quite against my will.
(*With great admiration.*) You systematic liar!

CHRYS. Insolent!

ZOR. Sir!

CHRYS. This shall cost or you or me his life,
In half an hour you shall hear from me!

[*Exit* CHRYSAL.

ZOR. (*in terror*). What *have* I said?

ALTEM. (*aside*). These boobies must not fight,
But how to stop them? Here comes Philamir!
Now he and Zeolide can meet. But first
I must get rid of Zoram. (*To* ZORAM.) Get you hence,
I will contrive to pacify your foe.

ZOR. But——

ALTEM. Go!

ZOR. (*piteously*). I'm sure I don't know what I've done!

[*Exeunt* ZORAM *and* QUEEN ALTEMIRE.

Enter PHILAMIR,—ZEOLIDE *runs to him and embraces him—he turns away*

ZEO. My love, is Philamir unhappy?
PHIL. Yes.
I have heard people talking of our troth,
And prophesying that it will soon cease.
ZOR. Indeed! They think you do not love me, then?
PHIL. They doubt not that—they doubt your love for me
Some say it sleeps; some say that it is dead;
Some that it never lived. Oh, Zeolide,
If love for Philamir is yet unborn,
Why bring it now to light! Where will you find
A fitter nursery for love than this?
If that love lives, but sleeps, why, wake it now
And let it revel in these golden groves.
If it is dead, why, here's a paradise
That well might summon it to second life!
ZEO. It sleeps not, Philamir, nor is it dead;
It lives and cannot die.
PHIL. But people say
That love should advertise itself in words
More fervid than the weary formula,
"I love you, Philamir." You love your friends.
Why, Zeolide, I think I've heard you say
You love your horse!
ZEO. Unjust! You ask me, then,
To limit my illimitable love,
And circle, with a boundary of words,
A wealth of love that knows no bounds at all!
There is a love that words may typify—
A mere material love—that one may weigh
As jewellers weigh gold. Such love is worth
The gold one pays for it—it's worth no more.
Why, Philamir, I might as well attempt
To set a price upon the universe—
Or measure space—or time eternity,
As tell my love in words!
PHIL. (*astonished*). Why, Zeolide,
At last you speak! Why, this, indeed, is love.
ZEO. (*aside*). What have I said? (*Aloud and coldly.*)
Indeed, I'm glad to think
My words have pleased you!

PHIL. (*with enthusiasm.*) Pleased me? They've done more—
They've gratified my vanity, and made
Me feel that I am irresistible!

ZEO. Indeed!

PHIL. Indeed, dear Zeolide, they have.
Why, how you frown!

ZEO. (*coldly*). If such a love as mine
Serves but to feed your sense of vanity,
I think it is misplaced.

PHIL. My vanity
Must needs be fed, and with such love as yours.
I have worked hard to gain it, Zeolide!
You are not nearly as attractive as
Five hundred other ladies I could name,
Who, when I said I loved them, stopped my lips——

ZEO. (*astonished*). I'm glad they did!

PHIL. With kisses, ere I could
Repeat the sentence; and it hurt me much
That you, who are comparatively plain,
Should give me so much trouble, Zeolide.

ZEO. (*aside*). What can he mean? (*Aloud.*) Oh, you are mocking me——

PHIL. Mocking you, Zeolide? You do me wrong!
(*With enthusiasm.*) Oh, place the fullest value on my words,
And you'll not overvalue them! I swear,
As I'm a Christian knight, I speak the truth!

ZEO. Why, Philamir, you've often told me that
You never loved a woman till we met!

PHIL. (*with all the appearance of rapture*). I always say that. I have said the same
To all the women that I ever woo'd!

ZEO. And they believ'd you?

PHIL. Certainly they did.
They always do! Whatever else they doubt,
They don't doubt that! (*He tries to embrace her.*)

ZEO. (*horror-struck*). Away, and touch me not!

PHIL. What? Has my earnestness offended you,
Or do you fear that my impassioned speech
Is over-coloured? Trust me, Zeolide.
If it be over-charged with clumsy love,
Or teem with ill-selected metaphor,
It is because my soul is not content
To waste its time in seeking precious stones,
When paste will answer every end as well!

ZEO. Why, Philamir, dare you say this to me?

PHIL. All this, and more than this, I dare to say.
I dare to tell you that I like you much,
For you are amiable, refined, and good—
Saving a little girlish diffidence
I have no serious fault to find with you!

ZEO. You're very good!

PHIL. Indeed, I think I am,
But let that pass. In truth I like you much.
At first I loved you in an off-hand way!

ZEO. At first?

PHIL. Until the novelty wore off,
And then, receiving but a cold response
To all the seeming fury of my love,
My pride was nettled, and I persevered
Until I made you tell me of your love,
In words that bore comparison with mine.
I've done that, and I'm amply satisfied.

ZEO. (*in blank astonishment*). And this is Philamir, who used to breathe
Such words of passion and such songs of love!
Those words that fiercely burnt with such false fire,
Those songs that sung so lovingly of lies,
Bore unsuspected fruit—I gathered it
And garnered it away. Oh, Philamir,
As misers store up gold, I stored my love
In all the inmost corners of my heart,
Dreading to speak or look at Philamir,
Lest some unguarded word or tell-tale glance
Should give a clue to all the wealth within!
I laughed within myself, as misers laugh,
To find my hoard increasing day by day,

And now—the coin I hoarded up is base—
The flowers that decked my life are worthless weeds—
The fruit I plucked is withered at the core—
And all my wealth has faded into air!

PHIL. Faded? Why, Zeolide, what do you mean?
I do not love you as a lover should,
Yet you reproach me! Oh, you are unjust.

ZEO. Indeed, I'll not reproach you! Let me go.
My grief shall be as silent as my love.
Farewell! [*Exit.*

PHIL. That woman's mad! Unquestionably mad!
My show of love has sent her brain adrift.
Poor girl! I really like her very much.
I tell her that I love her—and in words
Which never yet were known to miss their mark
When uttered by Prince Philamir—in words
So charged with passion that they well might charm
The very proudest maid in Christendom;
And off she bounces as indignantly
As if I'd told the very plainest truth!

Enter CHRYSAL

CHRYS. Your Royal Highness seems disturbed.

PHIL. I am!
I'm much annoyed with Princess Zeolide.
You know how coldly she has hitherto
Received the protestations of my love?

CHRYS. (*politely*). I do indeed. You've been the laughing-stock
Of all the Court for months on that account.

PHIL. (*amazed*). Oh, have I so?

CHRYS. Upon my soul, you have.

PHIL. You're candid, sir.

CHRYS. (*still as if paying a compliment*). I can afford to be
Extremely candid with Prince Philamir.
But let that pass. You were reminding me
How coldly Princess Zeolide received
Your vows. What then?

PHIL. Why, not ten minutes since
Her manner changed, and all her pent-up love
Burst from her lips in frenzied eloquence.
I was astounded!—I, of course, began
To echo all her sentiments tenfold.
I picked the very fairest flowers that grow
Upon the dreamy plains of metaphor,
And showered them upon her. White with rage
She started from me—telling me, with tears,
Her dream of love had melted into air!
I see you don't believe me, Chrysal——

CHRYS. Well,
I half believe you. I can scarcely think
The Princess spoke with rapture of your love;
But I can quite believe that when you spoke
In what you're pleased to think is metaphor,
The well-bred Princess shrank instinctively
From such a florid prince as Philamir
(*with a respectful bow*).

PHIL. (*haughtily*). This form of compliment is new to me!

CHRYS. My lord, my speciality consists
In framing novel forms of compliment.
But who comes here?—a modest little maid—

Enter AZÈMA—*she starts on seeing* PHILAMIR *and* CHRYSAL

And rather pretty, too.

PHIL. (*angrily*). She hears you, sir!
(*Politely to* AZÈMA.) I fear we've frightened you?

AZÈMA. Oh no, indeed,
I am not frightened, though I seem to be.

[AZÈMA's *manner is characterized by the extremest modesty and timidity throughout this scene.*

CHRYS. But why affect a fear you do not feel?

AZÈMA (*with extreme timidity*). Because, although I entered here to seek
Prince Philamir, I'm anxious he should think
This meeting is a simple accident.
Do not suppose that this is modesty;
'Tis but an artifice to make you think
That I am timid as a startled fawn!

CHRYS. (*aside to* PHILAMIR). This is a character. I'll open fire,
And storm her weakest point—her vanity.
Now, my artillery of compliments,
A salvo, if you please. (*Aloud, with the air of one who is paying an elaborate compliment*). I have remarked
That you've a certain girlish prettiness,
Although your nose is sadly underbred.
(*Aside.*) That's rather neat!

AZÈMA. Are you Prince Philamir?

CHRYS. Not I, indeed, fair lady. This is he—
The most conceited coxcomb in the world (*with an elaborate bow to* PHILAMIR, *who starts angrily*).
No thanks—indeed 'tis true.

AZÈMA (*to* CHRYSAL). Then go your way—
I don't want you! I only want the prince.
'Twas Philamir I came to captivate.

CHRYS. Here's candour if you like!

AZÈMA. Oh, leave us, sir!
Find some excuse to go, that he and I
May be alone together.

PHIL. Leave me, sir.
I'll give your tongue a lesson ere the night!

CHRYS. How has my tongue offended?—Oh, I see—
Exactly—don't explain! (Aside.) Poor Zeolide!
[*Exit.*

PHIL. Insolent scoundrel! (*following him*).

AZÈMA. Oh, don't follow him.
I want you here alone. You can begin—
I am not shy, though I appear to be.
Indeed, I entered here ten minutes since,
Because I heard from those outside the gates,
That you, Prince Philamir, had just arrived.

PHIL. Then you're a stranger here?

AZÈMA. I am, indeed!
The people told me any one was free
To enter.

PHIL. Yes, quite right. Did they say more?

AZÈMA. Oh, yes, much more. They told me then that you
Received but sorry treatment at the hands
Of Princess Zeolide. They told me, too,
That your betrothal might ere long collapse;
(*With extreme modesty.*) So, thought I, as I am beyond dispute
The fairest maid for many a mile around—
And as, moreover, I possess the gift
Of feigning an enchanting innocence
I possibly may captivate the prince,
And fill the place once filled by Zeolide.

(*Sits; her ankle is exposed.*)

PHIL. The Princess has a candid enemy!
I beg your pardon, but the furniture
Has caught your dress.

AZÈMA (*re-arranging her dress hastily*). Oh, I arranged it so,
That you might see how truly beautiful
My foot and ankle are (*as if much shocked at the exposé*).

PHIL. I saw them well;
They're very neat.

AZÈMA. I now remove my glove
That you may note the whiteness of my hand.
I place it there in order that you may
Be tempted to enclose it in your own.

PHIL. To that temptation I at once succumb.

(*Taking her hand—she affects to withdraw it angrily.*)

AZÈMA (*with affected indignation*). Go on! If you had any enterprise,
You'd gently place your arm around my waist
And kiss me. (*Struggling to release herself.*)

PHIL. It might anger you!

AZÈMA. Oh no!
It's true that I should start with every show
Of indignation, just in order to
Maintain my character for innocence—
But that is all.

PHIL. (*puts his arm round her and kisses her*). There, then—'tis done!

AZÈMA (*starting, with a great show of rage*). How, sir? I think it's time that I should take my leave.
(*Very indignantly.*) I shall be in the Avenue of Palms.
At ten o'clock to-night. I mention this
That you may take the hint and be there, too! (*going.*)

PHIL. One moment, pray. Let me assure you now,
That such an unmistakable coquette,
And one who shows her cards so candidly,
Will not supplant the Princess Zeolide!

AZÈMA (*surprised*). Supplant the Princess Zeolide? Why, sir,
By what authority do you imply
That I have cherished any such design?

PHIL. Your own admission.

AZÈMA. Oh, impossible!
(*Indignantly.*) But as it seems that I've no chance with you,
I'll try the gentleman who left us here.
He comes!

Enter CHRYSAL

Oh, sir, I crave a word with you!
Are you a wealthy man? (*with extreme delicacy of manner.*)

CHRYS. I am, indeed.

AZÈMA. And you've a title?

CHRYS. Yes, of highest rank.

AZÈMA. A bachelor.

CHRYS. A bachelor as yet,
Betrothed to Palmis.

AZÈMA (*shrinking*). Oh! (*Hopefully.*) But possibly
You do not love her much?

CHRYS. (*with enthusiasm*). Oh, not at all!

AZÈMA. You'll do—give me your arm. (*He does so—she shrinks.*) Oh, sir, indeed——
(*Impatiently to* CHRYSAL, *who hesitates*). Do take my hand and put it through your arm.
(*He does so.*) That's it! Oh, sir, indeed I know you not!

[*Exeunt* CHRYSAL *and* AZÈMA,—AZÈMA *affecting to try and release herself*. PHILAMIR *stands astounded for a moment.*

PHIL. I've found a clue that solves these mysteries!
This palace is enchanted ground! It's plain
That there's some subtle influence at work,
Affecting everybody here—but me!
Chrysal, the honey-tongued, turns out to be
A blunt and scurrilous outspoken boor;
Zoram, the musical enthusiast,
Can hardly tell the treble from the bass;
Then Aristæus, surly, blunt, and gruff,
Turns out to be the gentlest soul alive;
And, most inexplicable change of all,
The amiable but prudish Zeolide
Becomes a foolish vixen, blind with love,
Maddened with jealous and unreasoning rage!
Then comes a girl—a commonplace coquette—
Who, while she lays her plans with practised skill,
Explains their aim, and holds them to the light
That all may see their arrant hollowness!
It's evident there's some enchantment here
That shows up human nature as it is,
And I alone resist its influence!
Ah, here is Mirza—lovely paragon—
I'll notice how it operates on her.

Enter MIRZA

MIRZA (*starts*). I beg your pardon. I was looking for
My diary; I've dropped it hereabouts.

PHIL. Allow me to assist you in your search?

MIRZA (*hastily*). No, no; that must not be. My diary
Must ne'er be seen by other eyes than mine!

PHIL. Indeed! and why?

MIRZA. My very inmost thoughts—
The secret utterances of my heart—
Are there inscribed. I would not for my life
That any eyes but mine should rest on it.

PHIL. Can Lady Mirza harbour any thought
That all the world may not participate?
I'll not believe it.

MIRZA (*eagerly*). Hush—I charge you, sir!
Ask me no questions here—for I have learnt
That this is fairy ground, where every one
Is bound, against his will, to speak the truth.
If you interrogate me, I am bound
To answer truly. I need say no more
To such a courteous knight as Philamir.

PHIL. (*aside*). It is then as I thought! (*Aloud.*) I guessed the truth—
This palace doubtless *is* enchanted ground,
And I alone resist its influence!

MIRZA. Indeed!

PHIL. I had occasion some time since
To feign unbounded love for Zeolide
(For whom I don't particularly care):
Well, notwithstanding my indifference,
I spoke with all my usual gush of love,
From which I venture to conclude that I
Am unaffected by this magic power.

MIRZA. You do not love the Princess Zeolide?
You who professed unutterable love?

PHIL. I liked her well enough at first, but now
I'm weary of my liking. She displays
So much unreasonable petulance,
Such causeless anger—such unbridled wrath,
That I'm resolved to break the weary link
That binds us. I'll be free to love again.
[*Taking* MIRZA's *hand.*

MIRZA. (*releasing herself*). Oh, Philamir! Oh, shame upon you, sir.
She loves you! You are loved by Zeolide!
Why, there's a heaven opened to your eyes,
And you'll not enter, Philamir! Oh, shame
To blight so true a heart as hers! Oh, fool,
To throw aside in wrath so fair a prize!

PHIL. But listen—I've a fairer prize in view.
Mirza—I love *you!*

MIRZA. (*shuddering with terror*). Spare me, sir, I pray!

PHIL. Now by this castle's mystic influence,
I challenge you to answer truthfully—
Do you love me?

MIRZA (*shrinking from him*). Have pity, Philamir!
Withdraw your question, I beseech you, sir!
If you insist, I must perforce reply—
I charge you, on your knighthood, press me not!

(PHILAMIR *pauses, struggling with his feelings.*)

PHIL. (*releasing her*). My Lady Mirza, you are free to go.

[*Exit* MIRZA *hastily.*

How subtly works the mystic influence,
That all seem subject to,—excepting me!
And from the fearful ordeal only one
Of all the women here comes out unscathed.
The peerless Mirza—good, and wise, and pure,
Most excellent and unapproachable!
To know that Mirza loves me is to know
That she is mortal—that I knew before.
To know that Mirza's worthy of my love,
And that, despite the searching influence
That I alone resist—oh, this indeed
Is happiness!—I'm sure she loves me well!

Enter ZEOLIDE

ZEO. Indeed she does! If half an hour ago
She spoke abruptly to her Philamir,
She bitterly repents it. Oh, my love,
Forgive me, for in truth I love you well!

PHIL. (*embracing her fondly*). But my remark did not apply to you;
I spoke of Lady Mirza.

ZEO. (*recoiling*). Mirza?

PHIL. Yes,
I'm quite convinced she loves me!

ZEO. Philamir,
You should not jest with such a sacred word.
You've played your joke upon me, and you've seen
How readily I fell into the trap;
Let that content you. There—I'm not annoyed—
I'll not be caught again!

PHIL. (*earnestly*). Dear Zeolide,
Indeed I do not jest—nor did I when
You left me in unwarrantable rage.
I love the Lady Mirza—she loves me.

ZEO. (*horrified*). She told you so?

PHIL. Well, no. I'm bound to say
She did not tell me so in open words;
Her love for you restrained her. She's too good—
Too pure—too honourable—to allow
A passion for her dearest friend's betrothed
To master her. You should have heard her plead
Your hopeless cause. She struggles with her love,
And tries to keep it down—but still she loves.

ZEO. (*astounded*). And you return this love?

PHIL. Most heartily.
(*With affectionate gesture.*) I'm getting weary of you, and I wish
That I could find sufficient argument
To justify me in releasing you. (*She shrinks from him.*)
Why, now you frown again! Oh, Zeolide,
This wilfulness is insupportable!

ZEO. (*enraged*). Support it then no longer, Philamir!
There—you are free—our bond is at an end;
Choose your path, I'll choose mine. Our roads diverge.
We part and may not meet again. Farewell!
(*Changing her manner.*) Oh Philamir, heed not my words; I spoke
In reckless haste—I spoke my death-warrant!
Philamir, do not leave me, let me live;
See how I love you! I am at your feet—
I, Zeolide, whom once you thought so cold—
I, Zeolide, who am not wont to kneel!
Oh, give me till to-night, and pass the hours
That intervene in marshalling the past,
And let that plead my cause! You loved me once,
You asked me for my love—I gave my life,
For I must die if you abandon me!

Have mercy on me! Give me till to-night!
There's some enchantment in this fearful place.
This is not Philamir—it is his shape,
But does not hold his soul. Before the night
I'll seek my father, and I'll gain from him
The key that solves this fearful mystery.
Go now—nay, do not speak—no—not a word—
I'll not believe that this is Philamir.
Go, leave me now—and we will meet to-night!
[*He hesitates; then exit.*

Oh, Philamir, my love, my love, my love! (*She falls sobbing on couch.*)

Enter PALMIS

PALMIS. What? Zeolide in tears? Has Philamir
Been too emphatic in his vows of love?
Have pity on him!

ZEO. Palmis, pity *me*—
He loves me not!

PALMIS. Indeed!

ZEO. He told me so.

PALMIS (*relieved*). Oho! He told you so?

ZEO. Most openly.

PALMIS. Then there is hope for you. Come, dry your eyes;
When men are over head and ears in love,
They cannot tell the truth—they must deceive,
Though the deception tell against themselves!
Here Chrysal comes—(*astonished*) a lady on his arm!

Enter CHRYSAL *and* AZÈMA—*he leaves* AZÈMA *abruptly on seeing* PALMIS

PALMIS. Why, Chrysal, who is this? Where have you been?

CHRYS. (*affectionately*). I have been wandering through shady groves
With that exceedingly attractive girl.

PALMIS. You have been flirting, sir?

CHRYS. (*putting his arm round her waist*). Exceedingly!
I always do when I'm away from you.

PALMIS (*to* AZÈMA). Oh, you're a brazen woman!

AZÈMA (*with great modesty*). That I am!
An ordinary every-day coquette
Who lives on admiration, and resolves
To gain it by whatever means she can.

ZEO. (*aside to* PALMIS). Palmis, there's some enchantment in this place—
I know not what—it influences all.
Do not dismiss him yet, until we learn
Its nature!

CHRYS. (*with affection*). Yes, my Palmis, wait awhile,
Do not dismiss me yet; although it's true
I never loved you, yet I want your love
Because you have much influence at Court,
And have it in your power to help me on
To further favour.

PALMIS (*astounded*). Chrysal, are you mad?
You never loved me?

CHRYS. (*enthusiastically*). Never, on my soul!
In point of fact, I always hated you,
And mean to tell you so when I have won
The highest rank your mistress can confer.
In the mean time, however, I am fain
To make you think that I adore you still.
Observe the heaving of my swelling heart;
My fervid manner—my ecstatic gaze—
It's all assumed!

PALMIS. Oh, miserable man!
Go—get you hence, sir.

CHRYS. (*astonished*). Palmis, what on earth
Possesses you?

PALMIS. Don't speak to me again;
I can't endure you!

Re-enter ZORAM

ZOR. I am glad of this.
Dear Palmis, I for many a weary day
Have sought to win your love from Chrysal here,
By every mean, contemptible device
That my unequalled cunning could suggest.

CHRYS. (*amazed*). And you admit this to my very face?
ZOR. (*cordially*). With pleasure, Chrysal. I have sought in vain,
By daily blackening your character,
To sicken pretty Palmis of her love.
I've told her you're an unexampled rake,
A gambler and a spendthrift, mean, poor, base,
Selfish and sordid; cruel, tyrannical;
But all in vain, she loves you all the more.
(*Taking his hand.*) Forget the angry words you spoke to-day;
In the glad glow of hope that I shall gain
Your Palmis' love, I freely pardon you.
CHRYS. (*in furious rage*). This evening, in the Avenue of Palms,
I shall await you, sir.
ZOR. (*in blank astonishment*). Oh dear, oh dear,
What *have* I said?

Enter GÉLANOR

GÉLAN. Hush, gentlemen—the Queen.

Re-enter QUEEN ALTEMIRE *hastily*

ALTEM. (*in a rage*). Where is the King? Go, send him here to me,
Oh, Zeolide, go, get you hence away,
For I have words for Phanor that 'twere best
His daughter did not hear.
ZEO. My father comes.

Re-enter PHANOR *and* MIRZA

ALTEM. Now, sir, I've every reason to believe,
From what I've heard, that you're deceiving me!
I'll question you—oh, infamous old man!
PHAN. (*aside*). The Queen is jealous. Where's my talisman? (*Finds it.*)
All right—it's well I have it with me now.
(*Aloud.*) Interrogate me. Conscious innocence
Has little fear of palaces of Truth!
ALTEM. You have been walking in the shrubbery;
What were you doing there?

PHAN. (*with great show of love for* ALTEMIRE). Why, making love
To Mirza. I invariably do
Whenever I've a chance; but all in vain.
She's a good woman, and despises me.
(*To* MIRZA.) Haven't I offered love to you?

MIRZA. You have.

PHAN. And you despise me, don't you?

MIRZA. Heartily.

PHAN. (*to* ALTEMIRE). I told you so, and she endorses it
Believe me, I am bound to speak the truth!

ALTEM. (*bitterly*). I do believe you.

PHAN. (*taking her by the hand*). Thank you, Altemire.

ALTEM. Stand off, don't touch me, horrible old man!
You tell me you've made love to Mirza?

PHAN. (*astonished*). No!
Did I say that?

ALTEM. Most unmistakably.

PHAN. Oh, come, I say!

ZOR. You did indeed, my lord!

PHAN. I said that I made love to Mirza?

CHRYS. Yes,
Those were the very words!

PHAN. Oh, Mirza, come,
You can deny this!

MIRZA. Would, my lord, I could.
To spare the Queen I would be silent, but
Some unknown power masters me, and makes
Me own, against my will, that it was so!

ALTEM. There, sir—you hear her words!

PHAN. (*aside to* GÉLANOR). Why, Gélanor,
How's this? The talisman is out of gear!

(*Showing box to* GÉLANOR.)

GÉLAN. Let me examine it. (*Takes it and returns it.*)
A forgery!
A clever imitation; virtueless!
It lacks the small inscription on the hinge!

(PHANOR *falls breathless into a chair.*

PHAN. To-morrow morning we go home again!

ACT III

SCENE.—*The Avenue of Palms—night.* CHRYSAL *discovered with a drawn sword in his hand.*

Enter GÉLANOR

GÉLAN. Chrysal, alone! And with a naked sword!
CHRYS. I'm waiting Zoram. I have challenged him.
He meets me here—the Avenue of Palms.
GÉLAN. Has he offended you?
CHRYS. Most grievously.
You heard the words he used to me to-day?
GÉLAN. I did.
CHRYS. Then blood must flow. I am a knight,
My knightly honour claims this sacrifice.
I've been insulted—one of us must die!
GÉLAN. You are a valiant man, if one may judge
By your demeanour.
CHRYS. (*very valiantly*). My demeanour? Bounce!
Mere idle empty froth and nothing more.
Why, notwithstanding that I look so brave,
I'd give the riches of a universe
To find some decent means of backing out;
But, no, my honour must be satisfied!
If I endured with patience Zoram's taunts,
I should deserve to have my knightly spurs
Struck from my heels! 'Sdeath, sir, I'm bound to fight!
GÉLAN. Is Zoram a good swordsman?
CHRYS. Not at all.
I'm far more skilled—but still I can't repress
A certain sense of terror. Accident
May give him victory.
GÉLAN. Apologize!
CHRYS. (*indignantly*). To Zoram? Never! Would you have me stain
My hitherto untarnished 'scutcheon? Shame!
Stand back—he comes!

Enter ZORAM, *with drawn sword*

Well, sir, you've kept your word.

ZOR. Of course I have!

CHRYS. (*very sternly*). I'm very much surprised—
I may say disappointed—to remark
That you're prepared to fight and do not show
The signs of terror that I hoped to see.

ZOR. (*very bravely*). Oh, sir, I pray you don't deceive yourself!
My valiant manner hides an inward fear
That almost robs me of the power of thought!
Chrysal, you've grievously insulted me;
My sense of honour forces me to fight!
But I would rather have my hand cut off
(Could that be done without inflicting pain)
Than measure swords with you!

CHRYS. You craven hound!

ZOR. Craven yourself!

CHRYS. (*furiously*). I am, but you don't know it,
You musical impostor!

ZOR. Ha, what's that?
I can stand much abuse and never flinch,
But when you twit me with my ignorance
Of musical expressions, blood alone
(Unless we're interrupted) can extract
The venom of the insult! Come! On guard!

(*They fight.*)

GÉLAN. (*aside*). These donkeys must not fight! (*Aloud.*) Come—let me try
To reconcile you.

CHRYS. Reconcile us? No!
But you can interfere to stop the fight! (*They desist.*)

ZOR. (*looking reproachfully at* GÉLANOR). I little thought when I called Chrysal on,
That such a venerable gentleman
Would suffer two impetuous headstrong youths
To cut each other's throats.

GÉLAN. Come, come—desist.

CHRYS. This hound abused me!
ZOR. He insulted me;
BOTH. Our honour *must* be satisfied!
(*They cross swords.*)
GÉLAN. No, no—
Attend to me. Within these crystal walls
A strange mysterious influence prevails:
All men are bound to speak the plainest truth!
And this they do, without suspecting it.
(*To* ZORAM.) When Chrysal spoke the words that angered you
He did not mean to speak them. He believed
That he was paying you a compliment.
(*To* CHRYSAL.) When Zoram said that he considered you
A systematic liar, mean, poor, base,
Selfish, and sordid, cruel, tyrannical,
'Twas what he *thought*—not what he would have *said!*
CHRYS. I see—if that was only what he *thought,*
It makes a difference.
GÉLAN. What *could* he say?
He was compelled, you know, to speak the truth.
CHRYS. Of course, I understand. Zoram, your hand!
ZOR. With pleasure. (*Shaking hands with* CHRYSAL.)
Chrysal, I should like to say
That I esteem you—but indeed I can't.
My detestation of you knows no bounds.
CHRYS. How, sir? A fresh affront?
ZOR. What can I do?
I try my best to say agreeable things,
But you're so utterly contemptible!
I'd put it more politely, but I can't!
I'm bound against my will to speak the truth!
I'd not insult you openly, for worlds—
Indeed, it's only what I *think* of you!
CHRYS. If it is only what you *think* of me,
Why, say no more; give me your hand again—
My knightly honour's amply satisfied!
[*They sheathe their swords, then exeunt arm in arm.*

GÉLAN. So dies that breeze away! Oh, honour, honour!
Let no one take you at the estimate
Your self-elected champions price you at!
More harm is worked in that one virtue's name,
Than springs from half the vices of the earth!

Enter QUEEN ALTEMIRE, *in violent rage*

ALTEM. Why, Gélanor, this is no spot for you,
You'd better go—the King will wish you gone.
GÉLAN. Indeed! And why?
ALTEM. I'll tell you, Gélanor,
His majesty has an appointment here.
Oh, Gélanor, I've been alone with him
This afternoon, and I have learnt such things!
Why, even here—despite the castle's charm,
Despite the sacred influence of the place,
He prosecutes his infidelities!
At first he persecuted Mirza, but
Failing to find much favour in her eyes,
He looked for other game. Why, Gélanor,
He meets some woman called Azèma here,
At ten o'clock to-night!
GÉLAN. The deuce he does!
ALTEM. Then I resolved to know the very worst.
I locked him in my room and questioned him
For full three hours about his married life.
Oh, I elicited such fearful things!
Why, Gélanor, there's not a woman's name
In all the long baptismal catalogue
That's not identified with his intrigues!
Tall, short, stout, slender, fair, dark, old and young,
High, low, rich, poor, good, bad, maid, widow, wife,
Of every country and of every clime!
All's fish that his nets catch!
GÉLAN. And a king's net
Is very comprehensive. Here she comes!

Enter AZÈMA

ALTEM. Is this the woman? Tell me, who are you?

AZÈMA. I am Azèma.
ALTEM. And *I* am the Queen!
AZÈMA (*bowing*). Then, madam, you're extremely in the way.
ALTEM. How so?
AZÈMA. I've an appointment with the King,
Of which you are entirely unaware;
But though I'm much annoyed to find you here,
I'm glad to find you here with Gélanor.
ALTEM. And why?
AZÈMA. If our intrigue should come to light,
We can retaliate by giving out
That you and Gélanor are just as bad.
ALTEM. Upon my word!
GÉLAN. Oh, this is past belief!
ALTEM. Infamous hussy, you shall pay for this!
AZÈMA. Why, madam, how have *I* offended you?
ALTEM. How?—you are here to meet the King, alone;
At night—by pre-arrangement—in the dark!
AZÈMA. Oh, madam, this indeed is terrible!
That poor Azèma should be charged with this!
It's true I've an appointment with the King,
But as you're not aware of it, your words
Are utterly unjustifiable.
These flashing eyeballs and this angry blush
(At least I hope I'm blushing) represent
The noble rage of outraged innocence.
I'll to the King, and let him know at once
How, as I wandered through the grove, alone,
I found you here with wicked Gélanor,
At night—by pre-arrangement—in the dark.
Oh, shame upon you—shame upon you, Queen!

[*Exit* AZÈMA—ALTEMIRE *and* GÉLANOR *stand confounded.*

GÉLAN. Your majesty, I think I'd better go.
ALTEM. Absurd! the notion is preposterous!
You're old enough to be my father.
GÉLAN. Quite!
And wise enough to know that proper folk
Will only say "that makes the matter worse!"

ALTEM. But surely here, in this enchanted home,
Where all are bound to speak the truth, our word
Will guarantee our perfect innocence!

GÉLAN. Yes, if the King is pleased to take our word;
But, as you've brought a charge against the King,
Analogous to that which will be brought
Against ourselves, he may ignore the fact
That truth is truth. No, no, upon the whole,
I think, your majesty, I'd better go!
[*Exit* GÉLANOR.

Enter PALMIS *and* ZEOLIDE, ZEOLIDE *weeping*

PALMIS. Nay, do not weep, dear mistress.

ZEO. Ah, my friend,
What comfort can *you* offer me?

PALMIS. I've heard
That when one is oppressed with weight of woe,
Some solace may be found in dwelling on
The grief of one more sorely laden still.

ZEO. More sorely laden? Where will Zeolide
Find one whose misery outweighs her own?

PALMIS. Your misery, though great, is but a grain
When balanced in the scales with mine!

ZEO. With yours?

PALMIS. Yes; Philamir respects you. He esteems
Your moral excellence, although no doubt
He does not love you as a lover should;
But Chrysal always hated me, and sought
To gain that love I gave so willingly
To hasten his promotion at the Court.
Your case and mine are different. Besides,
You angered Philamir. I never gave
My Chrysal any reason for his hate.

ZEO. How did I anger him?

PALMIS. Your petulance
Annoyed him.

ZEO. Petulance! He told me that
He only liked me!

ALTEM. (*coming forward*). True, but you forget
He was compelled to speak the plainest truth,
And knew not that he spoke it. He believed
(While he was telling you he loved you not)
That he was breathing ardent words of love;
Believing this, your reasonable rage
Seemed in his eyes irrational caprice,
And changed his waning love to sheer dislike.

ZEO. Is this the truth, then?

ALTEM. Yes, I think it is.
The test has been exceedingly severe.

ZEO. I'll wed no man who cannot stand this test.

PALMIS. Then Zeolide, you'll surely die a maid!

ALTEM. Come, come, be reasonable. Philamir
Is but a man—a vain and idle one,
But under this veneer of coxcombry
There's sterling stuff. The man is honest gold
And vanity has silver-plated him.

PALMIS. At all events, you know he *likes* you well.
How many maidens when they wed a man
Have reason to be sure of half as much!

ZEO. But then his love for Mirza!

ALTEM. Idle pique!
No doubt he hoped—as other lovers hope—
In the fierce whirlpool of a new-born love
To drown remembrance of the love just dead.
Here comes the Lady Mirza! We will go,
And leave you with her. Tell her everything;
She is a noble lady—wise and pure!
She will not rob you of your Philamir.
There—tell her all!

ZEO. Forgive me, mother dear,
My heart is softened. I have been unjust.

[*Exeunt* ALTEMIRE *and* PALMIS.

Enter MIRZA

MIRZA. Oh, Zeolide, I know what you would say.
Say on, dear Zeolide, and have no fear.

ZEO. Mirza, for three long years we two have been
As sisters are, and I would speak to you
As younger sister speaks to elder-born.

Give me your counsel, Mirza; it will be
As pure, as true, as honest as those eyes.

MIRZA. If counsel such as mine can serve you aught,
'Tis thine, dear Zeolide. My sister, speak.

ZEO. With all my soul I love Prince Philamir.
A lady—good and beautiful and wise—
Unwittingly hath robbed me of my love;
She is too pure, too gentle, too divine,
To seek a love that rightly is not hers.
No, no, this lady hath not sought his love—
Of that I'm certain, yet she hath his love!
Oh, Mirza, when my Philamir declared
His love for me, I cast away the world
To enter Paradise. Now, Philamir
Has led this lady (all unwillingly)
Within its gates, and I am left without—
A lonely wanderer 'twixt earth and heaven.
Mirza, dear sister, say—what shall I do?
Give me thy counsel—I'll abide by it.

MIRZA. No need to speak to me in parable.
I am that lady whom you over-praise—
That most unhappy woman, Zeolide!
Despite myself, I must admit the truth,
I do love Philamir—shrink not from me.
Mine is no idle love. Four years ago,
Ere you had ever seen Prince Philamir,
I was a lady of his father's Court.
He loved me even then, and I loved him—
No need to tell you, dearest Zeolide,
The nature of that love; you know too well
How women love who love Prince Philamir!
We were betrothed, but secretly. Alas!
I was a humble waiting lady, he
A mighty Prince—so we concealed our love.
Then it was rumoured that he sought your hand,
That policy, the curse of kings, required
That he should marry you. Then I fell ill—
(*Struggling with her emotion.*) Pass over that.
Let it suffice that I
Released him—for I loved him passing well!

ZEO. (*amazed*). I never knew of this!

MIRZA. No, Zeolide,
I've learnt to bear my sorrow silently.
But for the sacred genius of this spot,
Whose influence no mortal can resist,
My secret would have passed away with me.
But I was true to you; for though I saw
How coldly you received his vows of love——

ZEO. (*rising, astonished*). Coldly! Why, every word he spoke to me
Rang through my brain, and would have waked up love
Had love been dead!

MIRZA. I thought you loved him not.
But though I grieved for him, yet when he spake
(As he at times would speak) of our old love,
I checked him with a simulated scorn,
For then, dear Zeolide, I loved you both!

ZEO. You love me still?

MIRZA. Most heartily!

ZEO. Why, then,
Have mercy on me, give me Philamir—
He is the soul and essence of my life!
Dear sister Mirza, give him back to me.
Oh, rather take my life than take my love,
And leave me here to linger on, alone!

MIRZA. Fear not, dear Zeolide, I love him well,
But I will never see his face again!

ZEO. Promise me this—swear to renounce his love!

MIRZA. As there's a shining sun in heaven I swear!
See, I am brave, and I will fight my love
As I have fought ere this. Take courage, dear;
I'll leave this place to-night, and Philamir
Shall ne'er set eyes upon my face again.
There, go—I'll tell him this. He's coming now—
Go, dry your eyes—he should not see them so.
Come back again when they are at their best.

[*Exit* ZEOLIDE.

Enter PHILAMIR

PHIL. Mirza—I have some words to say to you—
The diary you lost to-day?

MIRZA (*eagerly*). Well, sir,
And have you found it?

PHIL. Mirza, I have found
A portion of it—one loose leaf—behold! (*Producing page.*)

MIRZA. And you have read it, Philamir?

PHIL. (*guilty*). I have!

MIRZA. Oh, shame upon you—shame upon you, sir!
You gave your knightly word—you are forsworn!

PHIL. But, Mirza, hear me out, ere you condemn.
I saw a paper tossed before the wind
And little dreaming 'twas your diary,
I picked it up. I knew not what it was
Till I began to read it. Then I knew,
And knowing so much, burnt to know still more!

MIRZA. But when you knew it held my secret thoughts
You read no further?

PHIL. (*abashed*). Mirza, I read on!

MIRZA. Lost! lost! Give me that leaf, Prince Philamir;
You have deceived me, sir—I trusted you.

PHIL. But, Mirza, where's the knight who would have stopped
When of himself he read such words as these?—
(*Reads*) "I still love Philamir, but I must strive
To battle with my love. Oh, give me grace
To fight this fight."

MIRZA. I charge you read no more!

PHIL. "By day his every look—his every word—
Renews some mem'ry that should be long dead;
By night the phantom of my loved one's face
Burns in my eyes and robs me of my rest!"

MIRZA. My secret has gone forth. I strove to keep
That love as silent as my silent heart;
But it was not to be. You now know all!
Yet no—not all!

PHIL. Then, Mirza, tell me all.
Speak openly—hide nothing from me now.

MIRZA. I will speak openly. I love you, sir,
And, loving you, I leave the Court to-night,
That I may never see your face again.

PHIL. Recall those words!—we will not—must not part!
(*He detains her.*)

Enter ZEOLIDE, *unobserved*

MIRZA. Release me, Philamir, and let me go!
I love you! Let me hide myself away.
I love you! Leave me with myself alone.
I love you! Show me gratitude for this,
And leave me free to sanctify my vow,
For I have sworn to see your face no more!

PHIL. To whom have you sworn this?

MIRZA. To Zeolide,
Whom you once loved so well—who still loves you.

PHIL. I never loved her, Mirza—who is she,
That she should come between me and my love?
She loves me not, and I have done with her.

MIRZA. Oh, this will kill her, sir!

ZEO. No—Mirza—no!
It will not kill me. I can bear this blow.
(*Coming forward.*)
Prince Philamir, we two have been betrothed—
Your word is plighted—well, I set you free.
Mirza, you swore to leave Prince Philamir—
Your word is plighted—well, I set you free.

(*She takes* MIRZA'S *hand and places it in* PHILAMIR'S.)

Oh, Philamir—this is indeed the end!
Be true to her—such sacred love as hers
Should purify its object—oh, be true!
I'm but a chapter in your book of life,
I who had thought to be the book itself!
The chapter's ended, and to Zeolide
The book is closed for ever! Philamir,
When you are tempted to do Mirza wrong,
Turn to that chapter—read it through and through—

And let the tale of all that I have borne
Warn you from fresh inconstancy; my grief
May thus be Mirza's safeguard to the end.
Mirza—my sister—he will love you well—
Here, in the home of truth, he tells you so.
May you be happy in his new-born love,
May he be worthy of such love as yours—

(*To* PHILAMIR.) Speak not, but let me go.
(*Kisses* MIRZA'S *forehead.*)
Farewell—farewell!

[*Exit* ZEOLIDE, *weeping*—PHILAMIR *and* MIRZA *stand for a moment gazing at each other—then they fall into each other's arms.*

PHIL. Mirza, my own! At last—at last my own!
MIRZA. Oh, Philamir! I am so cruelly racked.
By sentiments I cannot reconcile;
I know not whether this is joy or grief!
True, when I think of Philamir, the air
Seems charged with music, and the earth I tread
All flowers. When I remember Zeolide
I could go mad with sorrow!
PHIL. Then, my love,
Think not of Zeolide!
MIRZA. Ah, Philamir,
You speak as men speak of a worn-out love.
You only know one kind of love, you men!
My love for Zeolide is otherwise,
Unselfish, generous, a sister's love.
Yet have I stolen from her gentle heart
That which in all the world she loved the best!
PHIL. You are too sensitive. Say rather, she
Hath freely given that she prizes least.
MIRZA. Oh, Philamir, indeed you do her wrong,
And may perchance wrong me, as you wronged her.
PHIL. (*rising*). Impossible! For if the words I breathe
Were dashed with any mockery of love,
I should, against my will, confess it now.
Mirza, I love you! These are idle words
When spoken in the unenchanted world,

But, spoken here, they bear significance
That rivals in its worth a life-long test!
Let us exchange some trinket which shall serve
As evidence of this our solemn troth.
Here is my pledge. (*Giving a ring.*)

MIRZA. My love, what can I give?
I have no trinkets—I am very poor!

PHIL. A handkerchief—a glove—no matter what!

(*She feels in pocket and takes out handkerchief—the crystal box falls out with it—he picks it up and retains it.*)

This crystal box—nay, give it me, 'twill serve
To chronicle——

MIRZA (*hastily*). No, no, Prince Philamir!
Not that—not that! it is a talisman!

PHIL. Then I will steal it as I stole your heart,
And I will keep it while I keep that heart.

MIRZA. Give me that box, or I must own the truth—
That I am miserably false in all!
(*Throwing herself at his feet.*)
That my morality is all assumed!
That I am mean, and base, and treacherous!
A shameless schemer! heartless—impudent!
Give me that box, or I must own that I
Abstracted it from Phanor's cabinet,
And substituted one that I possessed
Exactly like it. I must own to you
That I'm unutterably infamous—
A hypocrite—a traitress to my friend—
All this, and more, I must admit, if you
Retain that talisman! Oh, give it me,
And let this locket testify our love!
The King! The King! The King! I am undone!
[*Exit* MIRZA *hastily.*

PHIL. Gone, gone!—and Philamir, who thought he knew
The ways of women well, had still to learn
That in one woman's body there is place
For such a goodly show of purity,
And such unequalled treachery of heart!

Oh, Zeolide, for how much infamy
Have I rejected thine unequalled love?

Enter PHANOR *with* CHRYSAL *and* ZORAM

PHAN. Congratulate me, I'm half mad with joy;
Azèma comes to tell me that she found
The Queen and Gélanor together here—
Alone—at night!
PHIL. Well, sir, and what of that?
PHAN. Nothing at all, my boy! Why, that's the joke.
Old Gélanor has dandled Altemire
Upon his aged knee five hundred times!
PHIL. What—lately?
PHAN. No! I won't commit myself
By telling you how many years ago,
But long before her majesty was weaned.
PHIL. (*shrugging his shoulders*). I see no reason to condole with you,
Because her majesty and Gélanor
Were here together—neither do I see
Why you should be congratulated, sir!
PHAN. You're very dull! The Queen has just found out
That I had an appointment in this grove
To meet Azèma—don't you understand?
I can retort and take indignant ground.
What was she doing here with Gélanor?
You'll see! (*Sees box.*) Hallo! what's that?
PHIL. A talisman.
It fell from Mirza's pocket as you came.
PHAN. The deuce it did! Allow me; this is mine!
(*Taking it.*)
PHIL. I know: she stole it from your cabinet;
She owned as much!
PHAN. Confound her impudence!
PHIL. Oh, I have been deceived!
PHAN. And so have I!
Most seriously deceived! Hush, here's the Queen,
And with that gay deceiver, Gélanor!
The talisman has turned up just in time.

Enter ALTEMIRE *and* GÉLANOR, *with* AZÈMA *and* MIRZA

So, madam, I've detected you!

ALTEM. (*Indignantly*). How, sir?

PHAN. Never mind how—and you too, Gélanor.
Oh, I'm ashamed of you! (*Crossing to* GÉLANOR.)

GÉLAN. Your majesty,
I don't know what you mean.

PHAN. You bad old man!
(*Affecting to weep*) You whom I trusted so! (*Aside.*)
Don't be alarmed,
I'm not in earnest. (*Aloud.*) Oh, it's infamous!
Why, let me see—how old are you?

GÉLAN. My lord,
If you imply——

PHAN. Imply! (*Aside.*) Don't be a fool,
I'm not in earnest; I have found the box!
(*Aloud.*) Explain this conduct!

ALTEM. Sir, is this a joke?

PHAN. Well, not exactly, madam; you've been found
Philandering at night with Gélanor.
Being within the influence of these walls,
You're bound to speak the truth. If you can say
Your meeting's innocent, I'm satisfied.

ALTEM. As innocent as truth itself, I swear.

PHAN. I'm satisfied! Your hand——

ALTEM. Nay, hear me first.
I charge you with appointing here to meet
Azèma; you are bound to tell the truth,
Being within the influence of these walls.
If you can unreservedly deny
This charge, I also shall be satisfied.

PHAN. Emphatically I deny the charge!

ALTEM. (*astounded*). You do?

PHAN. I do! (*Piously.*) This is the Home of Truth,
And all are subject to its influence.

ALTEM. (*puzzled*). But you admitted it when you confessed
Your gallantries to me this afternoon!

PHAN. Oh, you've been dreaming!

ALTEM. Do I understand
That you deny that you confessed all this?

PHAN. Distinctly! (*Piously.*) This is the Abode of Truth.

ALTEM. I *have* been dreaming! Phanor, there's my hand.
I've deeply wronged you.

PHAN. Altemire, you have!
But say no more—we are good friends again.

ALTEM. Then you forgive me?

PHAN. Heartily I do!

ALTEM. I'll never be a jealous fool again.

PHAN. I'm very glad indeed to hear you say so.

Enter ZEOLIDE—ALTEMIRE *retires with* GÉLANOR *and converses with* ZEOLIDE—PHILAMIR, *seeing* ZEOLIDE, *comes down abashed.*

PHAN. (*to* PHILAMIR). Well, and what's wrong with you?

PHIL. I've been a fool,
A madman, and a true-born idiot!

PHAN. By the mysterious influence of this place,
I can believe it!

PHIL. I have given up
The noblest woman that I ever knew,
For that abominable cockatrice
Who quitted me as you arrived.

PHAN. Well! well!
You may regain her yet.

PHIL. Impossible!

PHAN. Oh, not at all! there—take this talisman.
(ZEOLIDE *overhears this speech.*)
With this you're proof against the influence
That rules this place; you can declare to her
That you adore the very ground she walks,
And wallow in the foolish flummery
That used to make you so ridiculous.
She will believe it all—there, take it, boy,
And make good use of it to win her back.

PHIL. I'll use it, Phanor, and I'll use it well!

ZEO. (*aside*). He takes the box. And thus he thinks to win
The hand of his forsaken Zeolide!
Oh, Philamir, this is contemptible.

I think I could have loved you, but for this!

PHIL. Dear Zeolide, I hold a talisman,
Enabling me to counteract the charm
That reigns within these walls. With this in hand
I can tell truth or falsehood as I please,
And you must needs believe me. Zeolide,
I've learned to set a value on your love
Transcending all the riches of the earth;.
Yet would I rather live without that love—
A life of self-reproach without that love—
Repentant and alone without that love—
Than stoop to gain it by such treachery.
Here is the talisman. (ZEOLIDE *takes it.*) No longer armed
Against the sacred influence of Truth,
I tell you of my sorrow and my love
With all the warmth of a repentant heart!
(*He presses* ZEOLIDE *to his heart and kisses her.*)

ALTEM. (*indignantly*). Give me that talisman! (*Takes it.*) I have a clue
To much that was a mystery: Behold!
[*She breaks it—a loud crash—all come forward.*

Enter ARISTÆUS

GÉLAN. You know not what you've done! The castle's charm
Is bound up with that mystic talisman!
Now that the box is broken, these fair walls
Are disenchanted!

PHAN. P'raps it's quite as well.
Now that the place has lost its influence
We shall get on much better. We have learnt
A lesson that should last us till we die—
We've learnt how matrimonial constancy
By causeless jealousy is sometimes tried—
(*Looking reproachfully at* ALTEMIRE.)

ALTEM. How jealousy is sometimes justified—
(*Looking reproachfully at* PHANOR.)

CHRYS. How Zoram—music's vaunted pioneer—
Don't even know his notes—and has no ear!

Even his cant expressions are the wrong ones!

ZOR. I *have* an ear!

PHAN. (*shaking his hand*). You have—two very long ones!

PALMIS. You've learnt to doubt the love that those profess,
Who by such love gain temporal success—
(*Looking angrily at* CHRYSAL.)

ZOR. That surly misanthropes, with venom tainted—

ARIST. Are often not as black as they are painted!

AZÈMA. To doubt all maids who of their virtue boast:
That they're the worst who moralize the most!
(*Looking at* MIRZA.)

MIRZA. That blushes, though they're most becoming, yet
Proclaim, too oft, the commonplace coquette!
(*Looking at* AZÈMA.)
I can declare, with pardonable pride,
I never blush!

AZÈMA. You couldn't if you tried!

PHIL. Under the influence that lately reigned
Within these walls I breathed my love unfeigned;
Now that that power no longer reigns above,
I ratify the accents of my love.
Forgive me, Zeolide, my life, my bride!

ZEO. (*very demurely*). I love you, Philamir—be satisfied!

CURTAIN

THE MOUNTEBANKS

DRAMATIS PERSONÆ

ARROSTINO ANNEGATO, *Captain of the Tamorras—a Secret Society*

GIORGIO RAVIOLI } *Members of his Band*
LUIGI SPAGHETTI }

ALFREDO, *a Young Peasant, loved by* ULTRICE, *but in love with* TERESA

PIETRO, *Proprietor of a Troupe of Mountebanks*

BARTOLO, *his Clown*

ELVINO DI PASTA, *an Innkeeper*

RISOTTO, *one of the Tamorras—just married to* MINESTRA

BEPPO

TERESA, *a Village Beauty, loved by* ALFREDO, *and in love with herself*

ULTRICE, *in love with, and detested by,* ALFREDO

NITA, *a Dancing Girl*

MINESTRA, *Risotto's Bride*

Tamorras, Monks, Village Girls, etc.

ACT I

EXTERIOR OF ELVINO'S INN, ON A PICTURESQUE SICILIAN PASS

Morning

ACT II

EXTERIOR OF A DOMINICAN MONASTERY

Moonlight

Date—Early in the 19th Century

Produced at the Lyric Theatre, London, under the management of Mr. Horace Sedger, on Monday, January 4, 1890

THE MOUNTEBANKS

ACT I

SCENE.—*A mountain Inn on a picturesque Sicilian pass. A range of mountains, with Etna in the distance. In the middle distance, a Monastery on a steep rocky elevation.*

As the curtain rises, a procession of DOMINICAN MONKS *winds down the set pieces on to the stage*

CHAUNT

Miserere!
Umbra fere,
Pauper sum diabolus.
Semper dolens—
Nolens, volens,
Monachus moestissimus!
Quum oramus
Jejunamus—
Eheu, otiose dens!
Sitiens sumque,
Ac, plerumque,
Acriter esuriens!

[*The procession of* MONKS *exit. As they are going off,* GIORGIO, *a member of the Tamorra Secret Society, appears on the set, and watches them off. As soon as the coast is clear, he comes down, and beckons to the rest of the band, who, headed by* LUIGI, *appear from various entrances, and come down mysteriously.*

CHORUS OF TAMORRAS

We are members of a Secret Society,
Working by the moon's uncertain disc;
Our motto is "Revenge without Anxiety"—
That is, without unnecessary risk.

We pass our nights on damp straw and squalid hay
When trade is not particularly brisk;
But now and then we take a little holiday,
And spend our honest earnings in a frisk.

SOLO—GIORGIO

Five hundred years ago,
Our ancestor's next door neighbour
Had a mother whose brother,
By some means or other,
Incurred three months' hard labour.

This wrongful sentence, though,
On his head he contrived to do it,
As it tarnished our scutcheon,
Which ne'er had a touch on,
We swore mankind should rue it!

ALL. Yes—yes—yes!
We swore mankind should rue it!

So we're members of a Secret Society,
Working by the moon's uncertain disc;
Our motto is "Revenge without Anxiety"—
That is, without unnecessary risk.

Enter from Inn, ELVINO DI PASTA

EL. Bless my heart, what are you all doing here? How comes it that you have ventured in so large a body so near to the confines of civilization? And by daylight, too! It seems rash.

GIO. Elvino, we are here under circumstances of a romantic and sentimental description. We are all going to be married!

EL. What, all of you?

LUI. One each day during the next three weeks. What do you say to that?

EL. Why, that it strikes at the root of your existence as a Secret Society, that's all. And who is to be the first?

GIO. The first is Risotto, who went down to the village this morning, disguised as a stockbroker, to be married to Minestra, and we expect the happy couple back every minute. The next is Giuseppe, he's to be married to-morrow, Luigi on Thursday, and so on until we are all worked off. As we are twenty-four in number, that will occupy twenty-four days, which are to be passed in unceasing revelry—and our captain, Arrostino, intends to confer upon you the benefit of our custom.

EL. There I think he is right. I am out of wine just now, but I have a family prescription for fine old crusted Chianti, which I will send to the nearest chemist to be compounded at once. There's only one thing for which I must stipulate; let these revels be as joyous, as reckless, as rollicking as you please—only, let them be conducted in a whisper.

LUI. What, because we are a Secret Society? We are not as secret as all that.

EL. No; but because there is a considerable portion of a poor old Alchemist on the second floor who is extremely unwell. You wouldn't go for to disturb the dying moments of a considerable portion of a poor old Alchemist?

GIO. You are unusually considerate. What's the matter with him?

EL. Why, the poor old boy is continually blowing himself up with dynamite in his researches after the Philosopher's Stone. Well, that's nothing—it's all in the day's work, and he's used to it. But this time he has blown himself up worse than usual, and several of the bits are missing; if you come across anything of the kind they are his, and I'm sure you'll behave honourably, and give them up at once.

GIO. We swear.

EL. Bless you! Now, the Alchemist has hitherto paid for his board and lodging in halfpence, with a written undertaking to turn them all into gold as soon as his discovery is completed; consequently the dictates of common humanity prompt us to give him every chance. (*Noise of explosion within.*) Up he goes again! Excuse me one minute, while I go and collect him.

[*Exit* ELVINO.

Enter Chorus of Village Girls, dancing, and heralding the approach of RISOTTO *and* MINESTRA

CHORUS OF GIRLS

Come all the maidens in merry community
Gay and jocose,
Hither we wend.
Risotto, Minestra, are knitted in unity;
Nobody knows
How it will end.
Risotto is handsome and really delectable—
Stalwart and tall;
Second to none.
Minestra, nice-looking and very respectable.
So we are all—
Every one.

ALL. So {you / we} are all—
Every one.

Enter RISOTTO *and* MINESTRA

DUET—RISOTTO *and* MINESTRA

MIN. If you please, I'm now a member of your band—
RIS. If you please, she's—
MIN. Now allow me, pray, to speak
I am married—
RIS. She's my wife, you understand.
MIN. If you interrupt, I'll leave you in a week.
RIS. I really think I might—
MIN. You are very impolite!
RIS. But I wanted to explain—
MIN. Well, now, there you go again!
If you kindly will permit me,
I can perfectly acquit me:
I'm a lady!
RIS. She's a lady!
MIN. Very good, then I refrain!
RIS. Allow me to present to you—my wife!
MIN. I think you'd better keep her to yourself.
RIS. She's the treasure and the pleasure of my life—
MIN. I dare say—until she's laid upon the shelf!
RIS. She's a poem, she's a song—
MIN. (*relenting*). You don't mean it—go along!

RIS. I shall love her when she's grey!
MIN. Will you really?—I dare say;
With your snapping and your snarling!
RIS. You're a dear, and you're a darling!
MIN. Do you mean it?
RIS. Yes, I mean it!
BOTH. Oh, my darling! Oh, my dear!

Enter ARROSTINO

GIO. Three secret cheers for the Captain!

ALL (*pianissimo*). Hurrah! hurrah! hurrah!

ARR. How do? How do? Ah! the bride and bridegroom. Allow me. (*Kisses her.*) Charming—at least I think so—another. (*Kisses her again.*) Yes, charming. Risotto, my poor fellow, accept my condolences.

RIS. Condolences! You don't see anything wrong with her?

ARR. With her? Oh, no—not with *her*. My dear friend, she's bewitching. (*To* MINESTRA.) You *are* bewitching, aren't you?

MIN. I believe I'm nice.

ARR. You do? I'm delighted to hear it on such good authority.

RIS. Still, I don't see why you should condole with me.

ARR. Don't you? Never mind—you will. Now tell me, Minestra, candidly—what was it you saw in him to admire? It's not his face, of course; nor his figure—we'll put them out of the question. It can't be his conversation, because he hasn't any.

MIN. I don't know. He's got a way with him.

ARR. Has he got it with him now?

MIN. I don't know. I suppose so.

ARR. (*imperatively*). Risotto, give us an example of the way you have with you.

RIS. It's something like this—(*business of ogling*).

ARR. Oh, but my dear girl—really—dear, dear, dear!

MIN. (*apologetically*). You've got to be nearer to him for it to tell.

ARR. Well, but even then! Now, look at it in cold blood. Think of it ten years hence—when the novelty's worn off.

MIN. It does look foolish from here. Oh, I almost wish I hadn't!

RIS. My dear! (*Consoling her.*)

MIN. Don't—I'm so inexperienced!

ARR. I suppose so. Pity—pity! Never mind—next time you'll be older. Now, girls, I have some news for you: the Duke and Duchess of Pallavicini are to pass through the village this evening on their way to Palermo. You don't see a real Duke and Duchess every day, so the best thing you can do is to run down and prepare to receive them.

1ST GIRL. A real Duke and Duchess! Oh, that will be delightful.

CHORUS OF GIRLS

Only think, a Duke and Duchess!
Oh, but we are lucky lasses!
Hie we to our looking-glasses
For a few artistic touches.
Let us decorate our tresses
Ere the grand procession passes,
And receive the upper classes
In our most becoming dresses!

SOLO—MINESTRA

Go and wash your pretty faces,
Dress in ribbons and in laces,
Or expect from both their Graces
A well-merited rebuke;
And your hair I pray you frizz it—
For it isn't often—is it?—
That you're favoured with a visit
From a Duchess and a Duke!

CHORUS

Yes, we'll wash our pretty faces,
Dress in ribbons and in laces,
For it isn't often—is it?—
That we're favoured with a visit
From a Duke and from a Duchess,
From a Duchess and a Duke!

[*Exeunt* GIRLS—*all but* MINESTRA.

ARR. Now then, to business. Anything to report?

GIO. Yes. A travelling Englishman passed our encampment this morning.

ARR. Good. We have a vendetta against all travelling Englishmen. The relation of our ancestor's neighbour was arrested by a travelling Englishman. Well?

GIO. No—very bad. The cowardly ruffian was armed.

ARR. What a lily-livered hound! That's so like these Englishmen. This growing habit of carrying revolvers is the curse of our profession. Anything else?

LUI. Only an old market-woman on a mule.

ARR. Well, we have a vendetta against all old market-women on a mule. The principal evidence against the relation of our ancestor's neighbour was an old market-woman on a mule. Did you arrest her?

LUI. We were about to do so, but she passed us in silent contempt.

ARR. Humph! This growing habit of passing us in silent contempt strikes at the very root of our little earnings. Of course you could do nothing?

GIO. Nothing whatever. You see, as we are all to be married in the course of the next three weeks, we are bound, as men of honour, to hand over our personal charms in the same condition of substantial and decorative repair that they were in when we captivated these confiding creatures.

ARR. Naturally. It is plain that a man who offers a girl his hand, and comes to claim her with his arm amputated at the shoulder, is no longer in a position to fulfil his contract. A man who proposes with a Roman nose and turns up at the altar with a snub is guilty of flat dishonesty, on the face of it. At the same time, that's no reason why you shouldn't pick off the bits of cotton wool in which you are in the habit of putting yourselves away at night. (*Picking scraps of wool from the coats of* PIETRO *and* GIORGIO.) To people who are unacquainted with the circumstances it might look a little unmanly. I don't know—perhaps not. (*Replacing the scraps of wool on their coats.*) However, take heart. I have an enterprise in hand which promises the very maximum of profit with the very minimum of risk. The Duke and

Duchess—I believe we have a vendetta against all Dukes and Duchesses?

GIO. The judge who sentenced the relation of our ancestor's neighbour would have been a duke if they had created him one.

ARR. The scoundrel! Then I intend to secure this Duke and Duchess.

GIO. Ah! But how? Remember the motto of our band—"Heroism without risk."

ARR. We shall do it diplomatically, of course. In the first place, we shall seize on yonder monastery——

LUI. When the monks are asleep?

ARR. Why, of course—and dress ourselves in their robes. In the mean time, Minestra, disguised as an old woman, will lure the Duke away from his escort and into our power.

MIN. *I* think I could do it better as a *young* woman.

ARR. Nonsense, you little goose—you know nothing at all about it! Listen!

SONG—ARROSTINO

The Duke and the Duchess as they travel through the lands
With the clips of their whips and their high jerry ho!
Will pass by the rock where that monastery stands,
In a first-class fine-folk fashion,
With their high jerry ho!
Their postilion in vermilion
And the rattle of their cattle,
And their high jerry ho!

CHORUS. With their high jerry ho! etc.

Minestra they'll find as a tottering old crone,
With her moans and her groans and her high jerry ho!
Who has tumbled down the rock, and is lying all alone,
And her cries will excite their compassion—
With her high jerry ho!
And her cropper so improper,
And her fussy, "Lawk ha' mussy,"
And her high jerry ho!

CHORUS. With her high jerry ho! etc.

She'll beg that the Duke will convey her to the friars,
  With their splint and their lint and their high jerry ho!
Then he'll take her up at once through the brambles and
    the briars;
  And her woes to the monks she'll explain them.
      With their high jerry ho!
    With their wrappings and their strappings,
    With their cackle on diachylon—
      Their high jerry ho!

CHORUS. With their high jerry ho! etc.

By this time the monks will have fallen in our clutches,
  With their cries of surprise and their high jerry ho!
And, disguised in their robes, we'll receive the Duke and
    Duchess;
  And in custody close we'll detain them,
      With their high jerry ho!
    And the pusses of those cusses,
    And a ransom very handsome
      And a high jerry ho!

CHORUS. With their high jerry ho! etc.

[*Exeunt all.*

Enter ALFREDO

RECITATIVE—ALFREDO

Teresa! little word so glibly spoken!
Take pity on a heart that's all but broken!
Teresa! one-word poem trisyllabic;
An Eastern ode in sensuous *Arabic*—
Would that thou wert as tender in thy nature
As in thy soft and tender nomenclature!

BALLAD—ALFREDO

Bedecked in fashion trim,
  With every curl a-quiver;
Or leaping, light of limb,
  O'er rivulet and river;
Or skipping o'er the lea
  On daffodil and daisy;
Or stretched beneath a tree,

All languishing and lazy—
Whatever be her mood;
Be she demurely prude,
Or languishingly lazy;
My lady drives me crazy
In vain her heart is wooed,
Whatever be her mood!

What profit should I gain
Suppose she loved me dearly?
Her coldness turns my brain
To *verge* of madness merely.
Her kiss—though, Heaven knows,
To dream of it were treason—
Would tend, as I suppose,
To utter loss of reason!
My state is not amiss;
I would not have a kiss

Which, in or out of season,
Might tend to loss of reason:
What profit in such bliss?
A fig for such a kiss!

ALF. What shabby things a man will do when he's eaten up with jealousy! But what a comfort those shabby things are to him! To prevent Teresa joining the Tamorras with the other girls, I was mean enough to bribe a farm girl to lock her in her room! I'm disgusted with myself for having stooped to such a contemptible act. Still, I'm very glad I did it.

Enter TERESA

ALF. Teresa! *You* here?

TER. Didn't expect me, I fancy?

ALF. No—I——

TER. Locked me in my room, didn't you? Well, I escaped through the window.

ALF. Never thought of the window! However, you are too late—the Tamorras have gone. Ah! forgive me; I couldn't bear the thought of your spending the day with them.

TER. My dear Alfredo, now do you really think I am the sort of girl who would throw herself away upon a contemptible outlaw? Why, I'd much sooner marry *you!*

ALF. (*delighted*). You would? My darling! (*Putting his arm round her.*)

TER. Infinitely. Don't!

ALF. Why not?

TER. It's a liberty.

ALF. But after the tender avowal you have just made, surely I may be permitted——

TER. My dear Alfredo, you jump at conclusions. I said I would rather throw myself away on a respectable young farmer than on a contemptible outlaw. But I haven't the smallest intention of throwing myself away on either.

ALF. Teresa, have some pity on me; I am so desperately in love with you. I have founded my hopes of happiness upon you, for you are the very air I breathe, the very sunlight of my life!

TER. You are, of course, quite at liberty to profit by any light I may happen to emit; but without wishing to say a word that would hurt your feelings, it is only right to tell you that I look a great deal higher than a mere clod-hopper. For you do hop clods, you know.

ALF. I have certainly hopped some in my time.

TER. It's not my own idea. To be quite candid with you, I have often wondered what people can see in me to admire. Personally, I have a poor opinion of my attractions. They are not at all what I would have chosen if I had had a voice in the matter. But the conviction that I am a remarkably attractive girl is so generally entertained that, in common modesty, I feel bound to yield to the pressure of popular sentiment, and to look upon myself as an ineffective working minority.

ALF. But you used to like me.

TER. Decidedly. Personally, I entertain a great admiration for you. *I* think you extremely good-looking.

ALF. (*delighted*). Teresa!

TER. But the general opinion on the subject of your good looks is so entirely against me that (again regarding myself as an ineffective working minority) I feel bound to yield to the pressure of popular prejudice, and admit that you cannot be as good-looking as I feel sure you are.

ALF. (*despondingly*). Perhaps not.

BALLAD—TERESA

It's my opinion—though I own
In thinking so I'm quite alone—
In some respects I'm but a fright.
You like my features, I suppose?
I'm disappointed with my nose:
Some rave about it—perhaps they're right.
My figure just sets off a fit;
But when they say it's exquisite
(And they *do* say so), that's too strong.
I hope I'm not what people call
Opinionated! After all,
I'm but a goose, and may be wrong!

When charms enthral
    There's some excuse
        For measures strong;
And, after all,
    I'm but a goose,
        And may be wrong!

My teeth are very neat, no doubt;
But, after all, they *may* fall out:
    I think they will—some think they won't.
My hands are small, as you may see,
But not as small as they might be,
    At least, *I* think so—others don't.
But there, a girl may preach and prate
From morning six to evening eight,
    And never stop to dine,
When all the world, although misled,
Is quite agreed on any head—
    And it is quite agreed on mine!

All said and done,
It's little I
Against a throng
I'm only one,
And possibly
I may be wrong!

TER. Now, come and talk it over, like a sensible boy. (*They sit—he at her feet.*) Come, tell me all about it. You know you used always to confide your little troubles to me.

ALF. I've nothing to say, except that I'm over head and ears in love with you.

TER. Now, first of all, you mustn't say "you"; it's too personal. Say, "I'm over head and ears in love with Teresa!"

ALF. Well, so I am.

TER. Poor boy! Well, I can quite understand it, for, with all her faults, she's far and away the nicest girl hereabouts. Now, look at it sensibly. If you, a plain young man, married a conspicuous beauty (for, after all's said and done, that's what it comes to), you would be under a perpetual disadvantage from sheer force of contrast; and as for jealousy—well, I've known Teresa since she was quite a little girl, and, take my word for it, she would keep you on chronic tenterhooks. Now, if you married a thoroughly plain girl—like Elvino's niece Ultrice, for instance—

ULTRICE *enters, and overhears what follows*

who couldn't possibly, under any circumstances, give you the least uneasiness on the score of her personal attractions—you might count on being as happy as two thoroughly unattractive little birds could reasonably expect to be.

ALF. Ultrice! What do I want with Ultrice? She follows me everywhere. She worries my life out.

TER. Ultrice is quite a good sort of girl; and as to her personal appearance, why, you'd get used even to that in a couple of years!

ULTRICE *comes forward*

QUARTETTE—ULTRICE, TERESA, ALFREDO, *And Afterwards* ELVINO

ULT. Upon my word, miss!
TER. Oh, it's you, miss!
How d'ye do, miss?
Didn't know you
Overheard, miss!
ULT. Oh, you spiteful—
TER. (*curtseying*). How politeful!
ULT. One I owe you,
You tittling, tattling, reckless, rattling, twopenny-ha'penny parcel of vanity!
TER. High gentility, amiability, both combined with true humility!
ULT. You mischief-making, character-taking, clicking clacking bit of inanity!
TER. Play propriety, or society may suppose it's inebriety.
ALF. Now, ladies, pray you, listen to me.
Dicky-birds in their nests agree.
If they can do so, do so too.
TER. *and* ULT. What has it, pray, to do with you?
ULT. Dicky-birds don't, to gain their ends,
Depreciate their absent friends.
TER. Dicky-birds don't, whate'er they hear,
Forget that they are *ladies,* dear!
ALL THREE. Dicky-birds tweetle, tweetle tweek,
Which may be silly, and does sound weak;
But dicky-birds don't whate'er they hear,
Forget that they are *ladies,* dear!

Enter ELVINO

EL. Now, pray you, attention! I've something to mention
That ought your approval to win—
ULT. (*interrupting*). And dicky-birds never, or rarely, endeavour—
EL. Now, ladies, a truce to this din!
TER. (*interrupting*). And dicky-birds don't—
EL. Be quiet!
TER. I won't!—

EL. My fortune's about to begin—
The Duke and Duchess (their quality such is)—
Themselves, and their kith and kin—
ULT. (*interrupting*). And dicky-birds try to—
TER. (*interrupting*). And you too—and I too—
EL. Are going to stop at the inn!
ALL THREE. What!
EL. They're going to stop at the inn!
ALL THREE. What!
EL. They're going to stop at the inn!
ULT. The Duke and Duchess fall into our clutches?
A penance, no doubt, for some sin!
TER. Perhaps it's his figure, too portly for vigour,
He's stout, and he wants to be thin!
ALF. At least their intention shows great condescension,
For comfort they can't care a pin:
Indifferent eating—
ULT. Hard beds and damp sheeting—
TER. (I hope they've some Keating)—
ALL THREE. Afford a poor greeting
To people who stop at this inn!

ELVINO	THE OTHERS
For excellent eating,	Indifferent eating,
Good beds and warm sheeting,	Hard beds and damp sheeting
That never want Keating,	(I hope they've some Keating),
Afford a good greeting	Afford a poor greeting
To people who stop at my inn!	To people who stop at this inn!

EL. I don't know how I shall accommodate them. My only bedroom is occupied by the exploded Alchemist, who is much too incomplete to be moved. There's the scullery. Do you think they'd put up with a shakedown in the scullery?

ALF. I don't know. The Duke is an awful stickler for etiquette.

ULT. He gave an innkeeper at Palermo six months because he used his pocket-handkerchief in his presence.

TER. And he fined the Mayor of Syracuse a hundred crowns because he didn't.

EL. This is terrible. I know I shall make some fearful mistake with these people! I've never in my life addressed anybody of higher rank than an Oil and Italian Warehouseman!

ALF. My good sir, they're not people—they're Personages.

EL. Of course they are! There I go—putting my foot into it at the first go off! If I could only practise a little! Now, if you'd be so kind—so very kind—as to impersonate the Duke, just for a dress rehearsal of the reception (I've got a lot of beautiful clothes left behind by some strolling players in pawn for their bill), you shall be treated with all the consideration due to your exalted rank, and have the entire run of the bar, except rum-shrub!

ALF. It's a tempting offer. But I must have a Duchess.

EL. Of course you must. (*Aside.*) How many Duchesses go to a Duke?

ALF. Only one at a time.

EL. You don't say so?

ALF. Yes—Dukes are very particular about that.

EL. Dear me! (*Aloud.*) Well, here are two to choose from—my cousin Teresa and my niece Ultrice—both charming.

ULT. *and* TER. What's that?

EL. Well, one charming and one—umph! Will that do?

ULT. *and* TER. That will do.

EL. Now, come; we've no time to lose. Choose your Duchess and begin.

QUARTETTE—ALFREDO, ULTRICE, TERESA, *and* ELVINO

ALF. (*to* TERESA). Fair maid, take pity on my state!
Look down with eyes compassionate
On my condition lonely;
Nor think me too impertinent,
If I implore you to relent,
And my sweet Duchess represent
On this occasion only!

TER. I thank you, sir, but it would be
Presumptuous, indeed, in me
To personate a Duchess.
But I know one who'd have the face
To jump at mimicking her Grace

No compliment seems out of place
Her vanity that touches.

ULT. D'you mean me, miss?
ALF. I mean you, miss,
All above.
ULT. You're too free, miss.
TER. Try it, do, miss—
There's a love!
ULT. I agree, miss!
TER. That's explicit:
Take your ground!
ULT. You shall see, miss.
TER. Wouldn't miss it
For a pound!

ULT. Though your spite all bounds surpasses,
Pay attention, I beseech you.
Manners of the upper classes
I shall be most pleased to teach you.

TER. Thank you, dear—pray, take your station—
Malice soon will spread the rumour.
It will be a personation
Teeming with unconscious humour!

ENSEMBLE

ULTRICE	ALFREDO, TERESA, AND ELVINO
Watch me as I take my station,	Watch her as she takes her station.
Spread abroad the welcome rumour.	Malice soon will spread the rumour.
No attempt at provocation	It will be a personation
Touches my extreme good humour.	Teeming with unconscious humour.

ULT. Now, look at me,
And you will see
How ladies grand
Present their hand;
It's copied from the highest ladies in the land.

TER. I always thought
A lady ought
To walk with grace
And not grimace;
But that, it's very evident, is not the case.

ULT. Then as they walk,
They blandly talk,
And look at us
With eye-glass—thus—
And what they'll have for dinner they, perhaps discuss.

TER. It would appear
They flout and fleer,
Stick up their nose,
Turn in their toes—
You're teaching me gratuitously, I suppose?

ULT. Then as she takes her place upon the throne that is prepared,
The people bow them to the ground, and every head is bared.
They keep their proper places as she looks them through and through—

TER. And I suppose they try to keep their countenances too?
If that is what is called Court etiquette, it's very plain
The ways of high society I never shall attain;
It seems you must be ill-bred, and as awkward as can be,
Which is A B C to you, my love, but difficult for me.

[*Exeunt* ELVINO, *bowing before* ALFREDO *and* ULTRICE, TERESA *following and mimicking* ULTRICE'S *walk and gestures.*

Charivari without. Enter CHORUS OF GIRLS, *running and heralding the approach of* PIETRO, BARTOLO, *and* NITA. PIETRO *is driving a Palermo donkey-cart.* BARTOLO *is dressed as a clown,* NITA *as a rope-dancer.* BARTOLO *carries a big drum and Pandean pipes.*

CHORUS OF GIRLS

Tabor and drum!
Mummers have come!

Hey for their mummery,
Frolic and flummery!
For to my dull
Countrified skull
Nothing sublunary
Equals buffoonery!
Folk of our kind
Frequently find
Jokes that are sensible
Incomprehensible.
Here, I admit,
Genuine wit,
As a commodity,
Ranks below oddity.

SOLO (PIETRO) *and* CHORUS

Come, strike up, Mr. Merriman, while I inform the universe,
In metrical and tuny verse—
BAR. In metrical and tuny verse—
PIE. That here's an exhibition that's highly intellectual—
To see it we expect you all—
BAR. To see it we expect you all.
PIE. Come, empty all your pockets, for I'm not a common mountebank,
I've money in the County Bank—
BAR. He's money in the County Bank.
PIE. And I can give you value for your coppers insignificant—
And I'll return 'em *if* I can't—
BAR. And he'll return 'em *if* he can't.

SONG—BARTOLO

Though I'm a buffoon, recollect
I command your respect!
I cannot for money
Be vulgarly funny,
My object's to make you reflect!

True humour's a matter in which
I'm exceedingly rich.

It ought to delight you,
Although, at first sight, you
May not recognize it as sich.

Other clowns make you laugh till you sink,
When they tip you a wink;
With attitude antic,
They render you frantic—
I don't. I compel you *to think!*

For, oh, this is a world of insincerity and trouble,
And joy is imbecility, and happiness a bubble,
And you're a lot of butterflies who flutter through a summer,
And he's a mountebank, and I'm a miserable mummer!

ALL. It's possible the world is insincerity and trouble,
And happiness, for all I know, is nothing but a bubble;
Perhaps we may be butterflies who flutter through a summer,
But you're, without a doubt, a *very* miserable mummer!

NITA (*dancing*).

I've a dance
That came from France
Not long ago—
It's worthy of your silver and your copper.
It's my own,
And I alone
Its mazes know—
It's graceful and particularly proper.
I assist
As soloist,
Upon a squeeze,
On the trumpet and the kettledrum sonorous,
I've a song
That's just as long
As you may please—
Twenty verses, and each verse has got a chorus!

ALL. Now that's the kind of merriment you ought to set before us;
Only fancy—twenty verses, and each verse has got a chorus.
To such an entertainment we could listen for a summer;
But save us from the humour of this melancholy mummer!

PIE. Oh, you lucky people! Oh, you fortunate villagers! A perfectly remote and altogether obscure corner of Europe favoured with the presence of a company of artists whom all the crowned heads of Europe are quarrelling to possess! (*To* BARTOLO.) Solo, if you please, expressive of a general withdrawal of ambassadors from all the European Courts. (*Flourish.*) The Czar of Russia is no longer on terms with the Empress of New York because I visited her first. A lady, you know! As a man of gallantry I couldn't refuse. But, mum! I must be discreet. (*To* BARTOLO.) Solo, if you please, expressive of the honourable silence of a self-respecting man of gallantry. (BARTOLO *flourishes his drumsticks and pretends to play Pandean pipes, but without eliciting any sound.*) Now, what do you think we come for?

ALL. Gold!

PIE. Gold? Bah! Try again.

ALL. Silver!

PIE. Silver? Why, we're sick of gold and silver!

BAR. Could you oblige me with my last week's salary?

PIE. Gold! (*Taking a handful from his pocket and looking at it in disgust.*) Ugh! (*Shuddering.*) Here—catch! (*About to throw it to them.*) Stop! On second thoughts it will only give you ideas above your station. But, come—I will be frank with you. The greatest men have their weaknesses, and I have mine. I have been cursed through life with a morbid craving for copper! I was cradled in a copper. I have frequently been taken up by a copper. A bull once tossed me for a copper. "Heads!" I cried. I came down tails, and he won. I was hurt. I felt it very much. (*To* BARTOLO.) Solo, if you please, expressive of feelings that may be more easily imagined than described. (*Flourish.*) Now to business. At half-past three will be presented a dress rehearsal of the performance to be given before the Duke and Duchess of Pallavicini, comprising an exhibition of conjuring, necromancy, spirit manifestations, thought-reading, hypnotism, mesmeric psychology, psychography, sensory hallucination, dancing on the slack wire and ground, and lofty tumbling. Also will be exhibited the two world-renowned life-size clock-work automata, representing Hamlet and Ophelia (*unrolling two posters representing the figures*) as they appeared in the bosoms of their families before they disgraced their friends by taking to the stage for a livelihood. The price of admission will be one penny for the aristocracy, members of the upper middle classes half price. At half-past five. Be in time—be in time—be in time!

[*During this speech* PIETRO *has frequently refreshed himself from a large wine-skin, which is also referred to by* BARTOLO *when* PIETRO *is not looking.*

CHORUS. Now that's the sort of merriment you ought to set before us;
To mark our approbation we'll extemporize a chorus.
To such an entertainment we could listen for a summer;
But save us from the humour of that melancholy mummer!

[*Exeunt Village Girls.*

PIE. Humph! Not a remunerative lot, I fancy. But if the Duke, who is a mad enthusiast in the matter of automata, should take a fancy to our Hamlet and Ophelia, he'll buy them, and our fortune's made! By-the-by, where's Beppo with the figures?

NI. Bless you, he couldn't be here yet—all uphill.

PIE. True. Nita!

NI. Well. (*She is talking to* BARTOLO.)

PIE. Not quite so near Bartolo, please.

NI. Oh, I forgot—force of habit.

PIE. You must recollect that you are no longer engaged to be married to him. That's over. You are engaged to be married to *me,* now. Try and remember it—*were* to him, *are* to me. It's quite easy, if you put it like that. Thank you. (*Leads donkey off.*)

NI. Yes, but it's *not* so easy. A girl who's been deeply in love with a gentleman for the last six months may be forgiven if she forgets, now and then, that she doesn't care a bit for him any more.

BAR. (*gloomily*). We were happy!

NI. Very. (*Sighing.*)

BAR. How we carried on!

NI. Didn't we!

BAR. Do you remember when I used to go like *that* to you?

NI. Don't I! (*Sighing.*)

BAR. Does *he* ever go like that to you?

NI. Not he—he doesn't know how.

BAR. And yet we have a School Board! How you loved me!

NI. Yes; but when I loved you you told me you were a leading tragedian. But a clown—I really don't see how I *could* love a clown.

BAR. I didn't deceive you. I've played the first acts—and the first alone—of all our tragedies. No human eye has seen me in the second act of anything! My last appearance was three months ago. I played the moody Dane. As no one else had ever played him, so I played that Dane. Gods! how they laughed! I see them now—I hear their ribald roars. The whole house rocked with laughter! I've a soul that cannot brook contempt. "Laugh on!" I said; "laugh on, and laugh your fill—you laugh your last! No man shall ever laugh at me again—I'll be a clown!" I kept my word—they laugh at me no more.

Enter BEPPO, *running and meeting* PIETRO

BEP. (*breathless*). Oh, master! here's a misfortune—here's a calamity!

PIE. Eh? What's the matter? Where are the figures?

BEP. They're at Palermo!

PIE., BAR., *and* NI. What!

BEP. It's no fault of mine. They've been detained by the police because they hadn't any passports.

NI. That's because they're so life-like. After all, it's a compliment.

PIE. A compliment! Yes; but we can't dine on cold compliments. (*To* BEPPO.) Didn't you open the figures and show their clockwork insides?

BEP. Yes; but the police said that was no rule, they might be foreigners.

PIE. Very true—so they might.

BAR. Chock-full of eccentric wheels—might almost be English. What's to be done?

Enter ELVINO *and* ULTRICE

EL. Here's a misfortune!

ULT. Here's a calamity!

PIE. What, another?

EL. We're ruined—ruined!

BAR. What is the matter with the licensed victualler?

ULT. The Alchemist—it's all over—he's gone! The last explosion did it!

EL. And this (*producing halfpence*) is all I've been paid for six weeks' board, lodging, and medical attendance!

PIE. It seems cheap. But you can seize his effects.

EL. I've seized 'em! Here they are (*producing medicine phial with label*)—all he possessed in the world—a bottle of medicine with a label on it!

PIE. What's this?

EL. Read it—our education's not what it was.

PIE. (*pretending to read label*). "Two tablespoonfuls, at bed-time."

EL. Is that all?

PIE. Here's a greedy fellow!

EL. But I say—it takes a lot of writing to say that.

PIE. Well, it's a very strong medicine.

EL. Oh, I see.

ULT. (*aside*). *I* don't.

PIE. (*returning it*). Take it.

EL. Thankye; take it yourself—it will do you good.

[*Exit* ELVINO, ULTRICE *remains listening unobserved.*

PIE. (*changing his manners*). Has he gone? Come here; there's more in this than meets the eye!

NI. What, more than two tablespoons?

PIE. More than two fiddlesticks! Listen to this. (*Reads.*) *"Man is a hypocrite, and invariably affects to be better and wiser than he really is. This liquid, which should be freely diluted, has the effect of making every one who drinks it exactly what he pretends to be. The hypocrite becomes a man of piety; the swindler, a man of honour; the quack, a man of learning; and the braggart, a man of war."*

ULT. (*aside*). I thought as much—this may be useful.

[*Exit* ULTRICE.

PIE. Now the question is—what's to be done with it?

NI. Give some to Bartolo, and make him funny!

BAR. Naughty sly-boots!

PIE. Give some to Bartolo? Yes, and give some to Nita, too. Don't you understand?

NI. Candidly, no.

PIE. Why, the Duke and Duchess want to buy the figures, and the figures are missing. What's to be done? Why, it's obvious. You and Bartolo dress and make up as the two figures—when dressed, you drink a few drops of the potion, diluted with wine. (*Tasting the cork and shuddering.*) It's—it's not at all nasty—and you will not only look like the two figures, but you'll actually *be* the two figures—clockwork and all!

NI. Whew! (*Whistles.*)

BAR. What! I become a doll—a dandled doll? A mere conglomerate of whizzing wheels, salad of springs and hotch-potch of escapements! Exchange all the beautiful things I've got inside here for a handful of common clockwork? It's a large order. Perish the thought and he who uttered it!

PIE. Come, come! The figures are our joint property, and we are all equally interested in selling them.

NI. That's true. Well, I've no objection. Besides, it will be fun.

PIE. Good girl! The potion must be diluted, so I'll pour

it into this wine-skin and we can draw it off as we want it. (*Does so.*)

NI. But stop a bit. I don't want to be clockwork all my life! How are we to get back again?

PIE. I never thought of that!

NI. It wouldn't do at all.

PIE. Oh, not at all. Perhaps it says. (*Refers to label.*) Yes! (*Reads.*) *"If the charm has been misapplied, matters can be restored to their original condition by burning this label."* There you are—nothing could be simpler.

NI. I say—don't lose that.

PIE. Not if I know it. (*Puts it in his pocket-book, which he places in his pocket.*) I shall be back in a minute, and, in the mean time, try and wheedle him into joining us.

[*Exit* PIETRO.

BAR. (*who has been fuming in silence*). I protest! It is an indignity! I have a soul that cannot brook an indignity!

NI. An indignity? Nonsense—just think—you'll appear as Hamlet, your favourite character, before the Duke—complete dress—scene from the second act, too—

BAR. Ha!

NI. I shall be desperately in love with you—and you with me—we shall bill, and we shall coo, and we shall be as happy as two little birds.

BAR. Can clockwork coo? A nice point.

NI. Ah! There *was* a time when you wouldn't refuse me anything.

BAR. Yes, but then you used to coax me. I have a soul that can do nothing unless it's coaxed.

NI. Then sit down, and I'll coax you.

BAR. Coax me hard.

NI. Oh, very hard! (*Business.*)

BAR. Oh, coax me harder than that!

NI. Will *that* do? (*Business.*)

BAR. That sort of thing, prolonged indefinitely, will do.

[*During this* PIETRO *has been occupied in hanging up the posters on each side of the Inn door. Exit* PIETRO *into Inn.*

SONG—NITA

Those days of old
How mad were we
To banish!
Thy love was told,
Querido mi,
In Spanish—
And timid I,
A-flush with shame
Elysian,
Could only sigh,
Dieu, comme je t'aime?
(Parisian.)
No matter, e'en
Hadst thou been coined
A Merman,
Thou wouldst have been
Mein lieber freund—
(That's German.)
Thy face, a-blaze
With loving pats,
Felt tinglish,
For in those days
I loved thee—that's
Plain English!

[*During this* BARTOLO *has gradually yielded to* NITA's *blandishments, and at the end expresses, in gesture, his acquiescence with her wishes.* PIETRO *re-enters from Inn.*

DANCING TRIO—PIETRO, NITA, *and* BARTOLO

PIE. (*enters, dancing*). Allow that the plan I devise
Is new and sufficiently clever
To testify joy and surprise,
Perhaps you will kindly endeavour?

BAR. *and* NITA (*dancing*). With anything clever or wise,
I never should credit you—never.
To testify joy and surprise,
Observe our united endeavour.

[*Dance*—NITA *stops suddenly.*

NITA. But what a catastrophe! Stop!

[BARTOLO *and* PIETRO *stop dancing.*

I see of objections a crop.
Suppose, by some horrible fluke,
I should chance to be bought by the Duke!

PIE. (*resuming his dance*). Be easy, I'll certainly see
You'll never get into his clutches.

BAR. (*dancing*). But don't be alarmed about me—
I should like to be bought by the Duchess!
I have certain society touches
That ought to appeal to a Duchess.
Though pride I abhor,
I've a "jenny say quor"
That is sure to appeal to a Duchess!

ALL. But don't be alarmed about {me, / he,} etc.

[*Dance, and dance off.*

Enter TERESA

TER. There's absolutely no limit to the vanity of some people. Ultrice actually believes that she has captivated Alfredo! Ha! ha! ha! Well, I'll let her remain under that fond delusion a little longer—it amuses me. When I'm tired of it, I have only to hold up my little finger and he'll fling himself at my feet in a moment!

BALLAD—TERESA

When man in love-sick passion lingers,
A maid can twist him round her fingers:
A word from me
Of eloquent,
Yet maidenly
Encouragement—
A faint recall—
A dainty hint
That, after all,
I'm not a flint—

And such permissible pretences
Will put to flight his seven senses.
Then, as he cries, "My own, for ever!
No power on earth our lives shall sever!"
I'll answer him with laugh provoking,
"Upon my word,
You're too absurd!
Why, bless my heart, I'm only joking!
Ha! ha! ha! ha!
I'm only joking!"

Enter ALFREDO *unperceived. He overhears the following verse.*

And should that fail—it doesn't often—
His heart by other means I'll soften:
With eyes that stream,
And tears that sob,
In joy supreme,
I'll make it throb—
I'll vow his scorn
My heart will break,
And all forlorn
For his sweet sake—
Which more than life itself I cherish—
I'll constant live and constant perish!
Then, as he cries, "My dearest treasure,
Adored beyond all earthly measure!"
I'll answer him (my triumph cloaking),
"Upon my word,
You're too absurd—
Get up, you goose, I'm only joking!
Ha! ha! ha! ha!
I'm only joking!"

ALF. (*coming forward—recitative*). Ah, cruel one!
TER. Alfredo!
ALF. Madam, good morning! (*Going.*)

DUET—TERESA *and* ALFREDO

TER. Oh, whither, whither, whither, do you speed you?
Oh, hither, hither, hither, hither hie?

ALF. Another—nother—nother time I'll heed you,
I've other, other, other fish to fry.

ENSEMBLE

ALFREDO (*aside*)

To punish her I'll try,
I'll soften by-and-by.
(*Aloud.*) My lady, I am sorry, but
I've other fish to fry!

TERESA (*aside*)

There's a twinkle in his eye,
He'll soften by-and-by.
(*Aloud.*) I'm very, very sorry that
you've other fish to fry.

TER. A merry, merry, merry maid invites you,
Who's very, very, very short of sense.
ALF. It's flirti-flirti-flirtiness incites you,
Imperti-perti-perti-pertinence!

ENSEMBLE

ALFREDO (*aside*)

Of taking some offence,
I'm making a pretence,
I'll punish her imperti-perti-perti-
pertinence!

TERESA (*aside*)

He thinks me very dense,
I see through his pretence,
(*Aloud.*) Oh, pardon my imperti-
perti-perti-pertinence!

TER. Now, listen to me, dear,
'Twas waywardness wilful
(In which, as you see, dear,
I'm not very skilful)
That makes you so tearful;
Take heart, and be cheerful,
No mischief is done, dear—
I was only in fun, dear!
ALF. Now, listen to me, love—
My sentiments store them;
When maidens like thee, love,
On hearts that adore them
Unfeelingly trample,
They always give ample
Occasion for scorning—
I bid you good morning!
TER. I was only in fun, dear!
ALF. I pray you take warning.
TER. No mischief is done, dear!
ALF. I bid you good morning!

ENSEMBLE

ALF. (*aside*)

She was only in fun—
No mischief is done;
Of taking offence
I am making pretence.
(*Aloud.*) I bid you good morning!

TER. (*furiously*)

I was only in fun,
But the mischief is done;
Of taking offence
It is not a pretence.
For he bids me good morning!

[*Exit* ALFREDO.

RECIT—TERESA

Despised! Rejected! Do I wake or dream?
By him rejected? Oh, the shame of it!
Rather than this I'll overwhelm him with
The torrent of my passion—make him think
My brain is tottering for the love of him;
And when at last he yields to my protesting,
I'll say, "Ha! ha! poor fool—I was but jesting!"

[*Exit.*

Flourish. Enter CHORUS OF GIRLS, *running*

CHORUS

Come, and take your places all,
The show is just beginning;
Don't you hear the trumpet's call,
And the drummer's dinning?
Frolic, fun, and flummery—
Magic, mirth, and mummery—
(That's the showman's summary)
Set us all a-grinning!

[*During this* ALFREDO *has returned, followed by* TERESA, *who expresses heart-broken passion in gesture.*

Enter ULTRICE *and* ELVINO, *who carries a theatrical cloak, sword, hat, and lady's train*

ULT. (*recit.*). Allow me, madam, if you have quite done with him.

ALF. (*leaving* TERESA). Good morning, miss!

TER. (*enraged—aside*). Oh, some day I'll be one with him!

[*Exit* TERESA.

EL. (*to* ALF.). Allow me. 'Twill assist your Grace
If on your noble brow I place
This hat and feather.
[ALFREDO *puts them on.*

(*To* ULT.). The Duchess, perhaps, will kindly deign
To wear these jewels and this train—
They go together. [ULTRICE *puts them on.*

[ALFREDO *and* ULTRICE *walk pompously to seats that are placed for them in front of the Inn door, the* CHORUS *curtsying with mock humility.*

CHORUS. Your Graces, as you wend,
We humbly bow and bend.
You look, we're quite aware,
A most imposing pair!
Ha! ha! ha! ha!

Enter procession of TAMORRAS, *disguised as Dominican monks:* ARROSTINO *as Prior*

CHAUNT

[*The* GIRLS, *believing the Monks to be genuine, all kneel.*

MOCK MONKS. **Attamen er cunctis supra reliquisque notandum—**

ARR. **Omne quod erit in um (hoec verba, I don't understand 'em).**

MOCK MONKS. **Esse genus neutrium—sic invariabile nomen—**

ARR. **Which is Greek to most of us here, and perhaps Double-Dutch to the showmen.**

[*The* TAMORRAS *throw off their hoods and reveal themselves.*

TAMORRAS. Ha! ha! ha! ha!

CHORUS OF GIRLS

Oh, you wicked,
Base—deceiving—
It's distressing!
It's degrading!
We are trickèd
Through believing,

Never guessing
Masquerading!
Friars mocking!
Goodness gracious;
What a wrong, sir!
Why, how dare you?
It is shocking!
It's audacious!
Go along, sir!
I can't bear you!

MEN. It is wicked—ha! ha! ha!
They are trickèd—ha! ha! ha!

ALL. This disguising
Is surprising,
Friars mocking,
It is shocking—
It is blameful—
It is shameful—
It is shameful—
Ha! ha! ha!

Enter MINESTRA, *disguised as a very old woman*

MIN. Come and listen, pretty ladies—
Cross my hand with maravedis—
For to prophesy my trade is,
And my prophecies are sound.

Fear no trick of double-dealing
I am clever at revealing,
Neither good nor ill concealing.
So, my pretties, gather round.

[*The Girls gather round her to have their fortunes told.* MINESTRA *throws off her hood and reveals herself.*

ALL. They / We } are trickèd—ha! ha! ha!
It is wicked—ha! ha! ha!
This disguising
Is surprising:
Ladies mocking!
Conduct shocking!

It is blameful—
It is shameful—
It is blameful—ha! ha! ha!

[*During the above* PIETRO *has brought on* BARTOLO *and* NITA *made up as wax-work figures of Hamlet and Ophelia.*

SOLO—PIETRO

Now, all you pretty villagers who haven't paid, stand *you* aside,
And listen to a tragic tale of love, despair, and suicide.
The gentleman's a noble prince—a marvel of ventriloquy—
Unhappily afflicted with a mania for soliloquy.
The lady is the victim of the God of Love tyrannical—
You see it in her gestures, which are morbidly mechanical;
He's backed himself at heavy odds, in proof of his ability
That he'll soliloquize her into utter imbecility.
She wildly begs him to desist—appeals to his humanity,
But all in vain—observe her eyes a-goggling with insanity.
He perseveres, improving the occasion opportunatic—
She sticks straws in her hair—he's won his wager—she's a lunatic!

[*During this,* BARTOLO *and* NITA *have gone through the movements described in a ridiculously jerky and mechanical fashion.*

ENSEMBLE

CHORUS—TERESA AND ULTRICE

CHORUS

Astonishing,
What science can contrive!
In everything
You'd think they were alive.
Her lovely face—
Her eloquent despair!
His princely grace,
His beautiful back hair.

TER. (*to* ALF.)

To thee I cling
To gain thy love I strive;
My heart you wring,
I shall not long survive!

ULT.

From his embrace
Thyself directly tear,
Or I'll deface
Thy beautiful back hair!

ALF. Appreciation of such skill
Should not be shown by stealth.
In bumpers round (I'll pay the bill),
We'll drink the showman's health.

[*Taking up wine-skin which* PIETRO *left at entrance to Inn.*

This wine-skin I devote to you,
We'll drink it till it's dry.
I'm sure that's what the Duke would do,
Were he as pleased as I!

ALL. Hurrah!
I'm sure that's what the Duke would do,
Were he as pleased as I!

PIE. (*horrified*). Beware!
That wine is mine,
You must not drink it.

ALF. Forbear!
I pay my way!
You may not think it!

[*Gives money to* PIETRO.

PIE. Take care!
The wine is poisoned, on my word rely,
And he who drinks in agony will die!
Commencing with a gentle pain
Scarce worth a question,
It grows apace, till you complain
Of indigestion.
Then follows an internal fire
That scorns emulsions,
Until, ere nightfall, you expire
In fierce convulsions!

ALL. Ha! ha!
An idle tale we think it!
Ho! ho!
We saw you freely drink it.

[*During this* ALFREDO *has filled a number of goblets with wine from the wine-skin, and handed them round to* ARROSTINO *and the* MALE CHORUS.

ALF. It can't be worse than 'Vino's wine accurst—
If we're to die of it, be thou the first!

[*Draws sword and offers cup to* PIETRO. *During this the two figures express galvanic agitation.*

PIE. I can't obey you!
ALL. Drink!
ALF. Come, why delay you?
ALL. Drink!
PIE. I beg—I pray you!
ALL. Drink!
ALF. Quick, or I'll slay you!
ALL. Drink!

[*During this* ELVINO *has poured the wine down* PIETRO'S *throat.* PIETRO *immediately begins to feel the effect of the wine, which he described as poison, and which has become poison to him.*

ALF. Oh, ye who are weary of life,
Don't trifle with pistol and knife—
This potion is far from amiss;
If you've ducats of gold in your purse,
Why, then, you may surely do worse
Than die of such poison as this!

CHORUS. Oh, ye who are weary of life, etc.

[*During this,* TERESA *has pretended to fall insensible at* ALFREDO'S *feet. He supports her, and supposing that she has fainted, pours some of the wine down her throat. All the others* (*except the* CHORUS OF GIRLS) *raise the cups to their lips, and drink as the Act Drop falls.*

ACT II

SCENE.—*Exterior of Monastery by moonlight. Mountain range and river in distance.*

RISOTTO *discovered*

RIS. (*looking at watch*). Now, Minestra, where are you? This is the appointed spot, and you are not here. Dear, dear, dear! She never kept me waiting before. (*Looking off.*) Ah, I see her! Here she comes, toddling along like an old lady of eighty! What a thorough little artist it is! She keeps up the character even when she thinks no one is looking!

Enter MINESTRA, *now really transformed into an old crone*

My darling, you're late. Why—what a wonderful disguise! I never saw anything more perfect in my life! I can hardly believe that this is my pretty, dainty, delicate, little bride!

MIN. Oh, Risotto, don't be angry with your little wifey, but something terrible has happened—I—I can't get it off!

RIS. Can't get what off, my pet?

MIN. The make-up! I lined my face, just as you told me—and—and now they're real wrinkles!

RIS. (*examining her face*). What!

MIN. Then you told me to cover my teeth with cobbler's wax. They've all come out! Then you told me to pretend I had gout and rheumatism—and I've got 'em! Ugh! (*Groaning.*)

RIS. But, my dearest girl——

MIN. Then my hair! Oh, my poor hair!

RIS. It's a capital wig.

MIN. That's it—it's not a wig! It's my own, and it won't come off—and I hate it!

RIS. This is a most remarkable circumstance. How did it happen?

MIN. After I had dressed myself as an old woman we all drank some wine out of the conjuror's wine-skin, and I gradually became an old lady of seventy-four!

RIS. This is most embarrassing. I may say, most disappointing. On one's wedding-day, too!

MIN. My poor husband, I'm so sorry for you! But I'm an old woman, and you won't be troubled with me long; that's one comfort for you.

RIS. Yes—I mean, no. I—I trust that, notwithstanding this—this modification of the implied terms of our agreement—there are many years of—of—yes, bliss—in store for us. (*Aside.*) If it had only happened yesterday, it wouldn't have mattered so much!

MIN. Of course, you won't love your little woman now!

RIS. Oh, I beg your pardon. I shall have much pleasure in—in showing you every attention compatible with the —the respect due to a lady of your advanced years, my —my pet!

DUET—RISOTTO *and* MINESTRA

MIN. I'd be a young girl if I could!
RIS. You're very good—you're very good;
But that unlikely I'm afraid is!
MIN. I'd be as lovely as a rose!
RIS. So I suppose—so I suppose.
And so, no doubt, would most old ladies!
MIN. I'll rouge my face, make up my eyes,
With cunning dyes—with cunning dyes—
My venerable looks anointing.
I'll try my best your heart to thrill.
RIS. I'm sure you will, my love, but still
It *is* a little disappointing!
It *is* a little—
MIN. Just a little—
RIS. Yes, a little—
BOTH. Little—little disappointing!
RIS. You're certain that you're wide awake?
There's no mistake—there's no mistake?
Your rugged wrinkles you can't thin off?

MIN. I've scrubbed, and scrubbed, and scrubbed away
For half a day, for half a day,
Until I've almost scrubbed the skin off!
So gouty and rheumatic I,
That though I try, that though I try,
I scarce can fasten my shoe-buckles.

RIS. (*looking at her fingers*). My bride could write (so gouty she)
"No Popery! No Popery!"
On all the walls with all her knuckles!
It is a little—

MIN. Just a little—

RIS. Yes, a little—

BOTH. Little—little disappointing!

[*Exit* RISOTTO, *slowly and despondingly*.

MIN. It's a sad thing to be transformed into an old woman in the very flower of one's life! Ah, deary me! this is but a dismal wedding-day! Why, who comes here? Teresa, as I live—and crying too! What has *she* to cry for? She's young enough, *I'm* sure!

Enter TERESA. (*Her manner suggests that she is crazed*)

RECITATIVE AND SONG—TERESA

All alone to my eerie I wander aweary,
A desolate maid of her lover bereft;
What matter? 'tis only a heart that is lonely—
A-many the maids that a lover has left!

BALLAD

Whispering breeze,
Bring me my dear!
Wind-shaken trees,
Beckon him here!
Rivulet, hie—
Prithee go see—
Birds, as ye fly,
Call him to me!
Tell him the tale of the tears that I shed—
Tell him I die for the love that is dead!

Heart that in jest
Laughed him to scorn,
Now in my breast
Lying forlorn—
Idle to plead!
Cherish thy chain—
Thou shall be freed
Never again!
My heart it is sad and a-weary my head,
For I weep and I die for the love that is dead!

[*She sinks, weeping, on a seat.*

MIN. Why, take heart, little one! What ails thee? Come, tell me thy sorrow. I'm an old body now, but time was when I was as young as thou art—and not so long since, either!

TER. Oh, mother, mother, I think I am bewitched!

MIN. (*aside*). Here's another!

TER. I am as though in a dream! Shall I tell thee? Yes, for thou hast a kindly old face. To serve an unworthy end I must needs feign to be going mad for the love of Alfredo, and so feigning, I fell at his feet. He, thinking I had swooned, in good sooth, placed a wine-cup to my lips, and I drank, and oh, mother, it must have been some love-philtre, for, behold, a wondrous change came over me, and he who was naught to me before became as the very breath of my life!

MIN. Well, the potion has done thee good service, for he's a good lad, and will make thee a strapping husband.

TER. Nay, herein is the mischief of it—it was too late, for he had already given his heart to another, and would none of me, and I, whose very soul is possessed by my love of him, have retained the village fiddler to compose crazy love-songs for me to sing when occasion ariseth, for I am going mad—mad—mad—and be a girl never so crazy, her songs should be in accordance with the rules of thorough-bass.

MIN. Ha! Now, mark me—that mountebanking fellow is at the bottom of this. Why, he hath also bewitched *me?*

TER. Thou? *Thou* lovest not Alfredo?

MIN. A fig for Alfredo; Why, look at me, child; I am Minestra!

TER. (*looking at her*). Thou Minestra, who was married this morning? Nay, I am mad; but not so mad as that! Minestra is young and rather pretty—not so pretty as I, but still pretty—whereas thou art—oh! I ask pardon—my brain wanders—wanders—wanders!

MIN. I am Minestra, I tell thee. For a purpose—also an unworthy one—I feigned to be an old dame, and so feigning, I drank—and, hang the knave, I am seventy!

TER. Thou Minestra? Why, let me look! As I live, it is true! Oh, poor, poor Risotto!

MIN. Even so; thy pity is for him—not for me. No matter. But if I can find this Jack-pudding, trust me, I'll make him set matters straight again. Oh, I have as much to regain as thou!

DUET—MINESTRA *and* TERESA

MIN. If I can catch this jolly Jack-Patch—
TER. Ah, me! my heart is weary, oh!
MIN. He'll go for a year with a flea in his ear!
TER. And my days are dark and dreary, oh!
MIN. He'll find his joke is a pig in a poke—
TER. For love my soul is aching, oh!
MIN. Though scarce a score, I'm seventy-four!—
TER. And my heart, my heart is breaking, oh!
MIN. When a woman has come to seventy year
It's well to be withered and old and blear;
But when she is only a score like me,
It's better a fair young girl to be!
TER. 'Tis well to be young when all is well,
And lovers are true to the tales they tell;
But ah! when love is a upas tree,
'Tis better an aged dame to be!

[*Exeunt together.*

Symphony. Enter BARTOLO *and* NITA *(still as waxwork Hamlet and Ophelia). They walk down the stage mechanically, as though controlled by clockwork. Their keys are fitted with keyholes in the small of their backs. Each wears a placard inscribed "Put a penny in the slot."*

DUET—BARTOLO *and* NITA

BAR. If our action's stiff and crude,
Do not laugh because it's rude.
NI. If our gestures promise larks,
Do not make unkind remarks.
BAR. Clockwork figures may be found
Everywhere and all around.
NI. Ten to one, if we but knew,
You are clockwork figures too.
BAR. And the motto of the lot,
NI. "Put a penny in the slot!"

NI. Usurer, for money lent,
Making out his cent. per cent.—
BAR. Widow plump or maiden rare,
Deaf and dumb to suitor's prayer—

NI. Tax collectors, whom in vain
You implore to "call again"—
BAR. Cautious voter, whom you find
Slow in making up his mind.
NI. If you'd move them on the spot,
BAR. Put a penny in the slot!

BAR. Bland reporters in the courts,
Who suppress police reports—
NI. Sheriff's yeoman, pen in fist,
Making out a jury list—
BAR. Stern policemen, tall and spare,
Acting all "upon the square"—
NI. (Which in words that plainer fall
Means that you can square them all)—
BAR. If you want to move the lot,
NI. Put a penny in the slot!

BAR. Nita.

NI. Well?

BAR. This is a very uncomfortable state of things.

NI. Very. How do you find your clockwork this evening?

BAR. Ticking, ticking, thank you. And you?

NI. I fancy I want regulating.

BAR. Eh?

NI. I think I'm rather fast.

BAR. Nita, you surprise and shock me.

NI. Mechanically speaking, I mean.

BAR. Oh, I take you. This condition of existence is rather degrading. We are quite common clockwork, I believe?

NI. Mere Geneva. The cheapest thing in the trade.

BAR. So I was given to understand.

NI. It might have been worse. We might have been Waterbury, with interchangeable insides.

BAR. That's true. But when I remember the delicately-beautiful apparatus with which I was filled from head to foot—and which never, never ticked—when I contemplate the exquisite adjustment of means to end—which never, never wanted oiling—I am shocked to think that I am reduced to a mere mechanical complication of arbors, pallets, wheels, mainsprings, and escapements!

NI. Still you were always complaining. You never were quite well.

BAR. Because I eat too much.

NI. That's true.

BAR. Never weary of putting into operation the exquisitely-beautiful apparatus of digestion, I over-taxed its powers. I was a scientific enthusiast and I over-did it. Still, it is something to have an apparatus that never, never aches. I—I—hallo!

NI. What's the matter?

BAR. (*very slowly*). I—beg your pardon. I—think—I—must be running down. May—I—trouble you? They've thoughtlessly—put the key-hole—in—the—small of my back—and—I—can't get at it. (NITA *winds him up.*) Thank you. That's very nice, indeed. Now I can go on again. Hallo! c'ck! c'ck! c'ck!

NI. What's wrong now?

BAR. I—c'ck—c'ck—I am not conversant with clock-work; but do you feel, from time to time, a kind of jerkiness that catches you just *here?*

NI. No; I work as smooth as butter. The continued ticking is tiresome; but it's only for an hour.

BAR. The ticking is simply maddening. C'ck! c'ck! There it is again!

NI. Something wrong with your works, I'm afraid. Stop a bit—I'll see. (*Opens door in chest, revealing a quantity of clockwork.*) No; all right there. Turn round. (*He does so; she opens door in the back of his head.*) No; the head appears to be empty. (*Opens door in his side.*) I see what it is; a halfpenny has got into your escapement. Stop a bit. (*Takes out halfpenny.*)

BAR. Bless my heart, how dangerous! What a relief! Thank you very much. You may keep it for your trouble; but do not—oh, do not spend it in foolishness.

NI. While I'm about it, I'll just oil you, and then—— (*Proceeds to oil his works with a feather.*)

BAR. (*squirming*). Don't! You tickle!

Enter PIETRO, *looking very ill*

PIE. (*not seeing them*). The Duke and Duchess will be here in half an hour—their escort is already in sight.

Dying by slow poison is a very painful process, and I couldn't have held out much longer. (*Sees them.*) Nita! what are you doing?

NI. I'm oiling Bartolo.

BAR. I am being oiled by Nita, and she *does* tickle! I don't like it. At least I do like it, but it's wrong.

PIE. How dare you take such a liberty? Shut the gentleman up at once. Nice occupation for a young lady!

NI. But there's something wrong with his works.

PIE. That's no affair of yours. If Bartolo's works are out of order, that is a matter for Bartolo's medical attendant —I mean his clockmaker. Don't let me catch you oiling him again.

NI. Ha! ha! ha!

PIE. If this occurs again, I'll take both your keys away —upon my word I will!

TRIO—BARTOLO, NITA, *and* PIETRO

BAR. When gentlemen are eaten up with jealousy,
They make themselves exceedingly ridiculous,
For everything around they tinted yellow see—
Their antics and extravagances tickle us.
Their antics and extravagances
Tic-tic, tic-tic, tic-tic, tic-tic—
They tic-tic, tic-tic, tickle us!

ALL. They tic-tic, etc.

NI. Here's a gentleman, as fierce as a Mahometan,
So carried off by jealousy vehicular,
He's down on an unfortunate Automaton;
Some people are so terribly particular!
Some people are too terribly
Partic-tic, tic-tic, tic-tic, tic-tic—
Partic-tic, tic-tic, ticular!

ALL. Partic-tic, tic-tic, etc.

PIE. When a lady is disposed to be tyrannical,
She's equal to unlimited iniquity:
And flirting may be flirting, though mechanical—
A fact that has the sanction of antiquity—

Antic-tic, tic-tic, tic-tic, tic-tic—
Antic-tic, tic-tic, tiquity!

ALL. Antic-tic, etc.

[*Exeunt* NITA *and* BARTOLO *at opposite entrances, walking mechanically to symphony.* PIETRO *accompanying* NITA.

Enter from monastery a procession of TAMORRAS (*now transformed into Dominican Monks*) *chaunting from black-letter volumes;* ARROSTINO *as the Prior.*

CHAUNT

Time there was when earthly joy
Gave our senses full employ;
In those days for ever gone,
Bless us, how we carried on!
Clinking glasses—
Lovely lasses—
Revel hearty—
Pic-nic party—
Gay donzella—
Tarantella!
In those days, for ever gone,
Bless us, how we carried on!

(*Confidentially to audience*)

It's a most unaccountable thing—
An hour ago, as banditti,
We played like young lovers in spring,
The mischief in village and city;
But since we got merry and mellow
On the wine of that conjuring fellow,
Transmogrified we're
Into friars austere,
Unwashed and unpleasantly yellow!
Whatever you say or you sing,
It's a most unaccountable thing!

Enter CHORUS OF GIRLS, *from various directions*

CHORUS OF GIRLS

After a weary search
Hiding, at last, we find you;

Leaving us in the lurch
Isn't good breeding, mind you.
Offer apologee—
We shall want some persuading;
When do you think you'll be
Tired of masquerading?

[*During this chorus, the* GIRLS *have been endeavouring to induce the* MONKS *to pay them attentions. The* MONKS, *however, have kept their eyes studiously on their books.*

ARR. These blandishments I pray you curb,
Nor think us churls—nor think us churls;
Our pious calm do not disturb,
Now there's good girls—now there's good girls!
Though our emotions, as you see,
We try to freeze—we try to freeze!
We don't, as yet, pretend to be
St. Anthonies—St. Anthonies;
So go along—nor think us churls.
Now there's good girls—now there's good girls!

THE GIRLS. Ah, cruel ones!
Time was, your love was stronger!
Ah, cruel ones!
You love us then no longer!

MONKS. (*confidingly to* GIRLS). It's a most unaccountable thing—
An hour ago, as banditti,
We played like young lovers in spring,
The mischief in village and city.
But since we got merry and mellow
On the wine of that conjuring fellow,
Transmogrified we're
Into friars austere,
Unwashed and unpleasantly yellow!

ALL. Whatever you say or sing,
It's a most unaccountable thing!

Enter PIETRO, *still very ill*

ALL (*seeing him*). Ah!
What does this mean—what have you done?
Do not attempt away to run
Nor questions try to parry.
The men to whom {we / they} were betrothed,
{We / They} find as holy friars clothed,
Who mustn't ever marry!
Who mustn't ever marry!

PIE. Now I'll explain,
(If calm you'll be)
As well as I can
Though I'm in pain
And ought to see
A medical man.

RECITATIVE—PIETRO

My worthy friends, the wine you chose to drink
Makes every one what he pretends to be;
You personated monks, and monks you are,
And will be monks until the spell's removed.

ALL. Oh, horror!
Oh, horror and despair unprecedented!

GIRLS. But how long must they wait—to dreary cell,
To life-long celibacy sternly vowed?

MEN. Yes, say—how long?

PIE. Have patience, for I hold the antidote,
[*Producing pocket-book*.
And in an hour or two, or thereabouts,
The spell shall be removed, and you may wed
As quickly and as often as you please!

ALL. Oh, rapture!
Oh, rapture, joy, and bliss unprecedented!

CHORUS OF GIRLS (*dancing*). An hour! 'twill rapidly pass,
Our freedom we then shall recover;
Each lover will welcome his lass—
Each lass will return to her lover!
The bells for our wedding will chime,

Delight in each bosom implanting,
So, gentlemen, in the mean time,
Proceed, if you please, with your chaunting!

ENSEMBLE

MEN	GIRLS
Earthly pleasures that allure, For an hour we abjure, etc.	An hour! 'twill rapidly pass, Our freedom we then shall recover, etc.

[*Exeunt* GIRLS. *Manent* ARROSTINO, GIORGIO, LUIGI, *and* MONKS.

ARR. This is a remarkable change, my son. A great improvement on our recent condition. Devoted as we now are to a life of contemplation—restricted by the rules of our order to a diet of bread and herbs—and not much of that—indigestion and its attendant inconveniences will be matters of tradition.

LUI. Still, it must be admitted that the old life was a pleasant one!

ARR. Yes, we had a jolly time of it while it lasted. (*Correcting himself.*) I should say that worldly allurements have the faculty of enlivening their devotees for the moment, but the evening's enjoyment seldom bears the morning's reflection, and the choicest banquet is but a feast of Dead Sea apples which turn to ashes in the mouth!

GIO. Under the circumstances, we might have spared ourselves the trouble of luring the Duke and Duchess to the monastery.

ARR. No—no, I think not. It is true that, having regard to our present condition, we are bound to receive our distinguished guests with scrupulous hospitality, but an hour will soon pass, and we shall then, unhappily, lapse once more into the deplorable condition of being able to avail ourselves of any small change their Highnesses may happen to have about them. It is dreadful to think of, but that's what we shall be in about an hour.

[LUIGI *ascends to balcony of monastery.*

RECITATIVE

LUI. The Duke and Duchess hither wend their ways,
Shall we receive them with a song of praise?
ARR. With glad acclaim we'll make the welkin ring,
The only question is—what shall we sing?

CHORUS

We know no song
That fits a throng
Of friars snug and greasy:
Our worldly lays
Of bygone days
Are much too free and easy;
Though suited to
A bandit crew,
They're not at all monastic,
And can't be sung
By sober tongue
Of mild ecclesiastic.

ARR. Stout-hearted be!
So many here
We need not fear
The ordeal before us;
No single word
Is ever heard
When singers sing in chorus.
So sing with me—

Enter ALFREDO, *dressed magnificently as the Duke, supporting* MINESTRA, *who is apparently insensible*

ALL. La la la la la,
La la la, etc.

DUKE (*very impressively*). La la la la la,
La la la, etc.

[*The* MONKS *are much impressed with* ALFREDO'S *reply and express in gestures their satisfaction with the sentiments he has expressed.*

ALL. La la la la, etc.

[*Exeunt all the* MONKS *except* ARROSTINO, GIORGIO, *and* LUIGI.

ALF. (*to* ARROSTINO). May I ask if you are the Prior of this monastery?

ARR. Well, I am and I am not. That is, I am now, but I wasn't an hour ago.

ALF. I see—a recent appointment.

ARR. Yes, for an hour. Present tense, I am a Prior. Imperfect tense, I was a rollicking young rantipole. Future tense, I shall be a rollicking young rantipole—in an hour. I hope I make myself clear?

ALF. Perfectly. (*Aside.*) Very like my own case. (*Aloud.*) I found this poor old lady almost insensible at the foot of the mountain. She had just strength enough to beg me to bring her here to you.

ARR. Exactly. You call her an old lady. Well, she *is* an old lady, and she isn't an old lady. Present tense, she *is* an old lady. Imperfect tense, she *was* a young lady.

ALF. Of course she was.

ARR. Ah! but, Future tense, she will be a young lady again—in an hour. That's the curious part of it. (*To* MINESTRA.) Go in, my dear—I should say my aged sister —and we will take every care of you.

[LUIGI *carries* MINESTRA *into monastery.*

ALF. You are very good.

ARR. Well, I am, and I am not. Present tense, I *am* very good. Imperfect tense, I was confoundedly bad. Future tense, I shall be confoundedly bad again—in an hour.

ALF. We are fortunate in having dropped in upon you during your virtuous phase.

LUIGI *re-enters*

ARR. Particularly so. It's altogether a curious state of things. I'm such a creature of habit that I find it difficult to remember that I am no longer a rantipole. For instance, I see you have a watch. Perhaps it is a valuable watch. Don't tell me it is; I would rather not know. Now, you can't imagine how difficult I find it not to take that watch. Oh, I know it's wrong; but then I always knew that. (*Adopting a clerical manner.*) By the way, I am collecting a few gold watches to send out to the poor naked savages of—— (*Aside.*) No, hang it all, let the man alone; you ought to be ashamed of yourself! (*Aloud.*) Pardon me, your handkerchief's hanging out. Will you oblige me by putting it out of sight? (ALFREDO *does so.*) Thank you, thank you so much! Temptation, you know, temptation! We are all weak, and it is sometimes difficult to resist.

ALF. (*aside*). Singular character, this Prior. (*Aloud.*) Of course I am prepared to give a donation to this monastery in consideration of your taking charge of the old lady. (*Feeling for his purse.*) By-the-by, where's my purse?

ARR., GIO., *and* LUI. (*falling on their knees*). Not guilty, your worship!

ALF. Of course not. Ha! ha! (*Finds it.*) Oh, here it is!

ALL. Ha! ha! ha!

ARR. Yes, but you frightened us!

ALF. Allow me to present this sum to the funds of the monastery.

ARR. No, thank ye; I'd rather not. Here, give it to Father Luigi.

[*Exit* ARROSTINO *into monastery.*

LUI. No, thank ye; not for me. Father Giorgio will take it.

[*Exit into monastery.*

GIO. Oh no; Father Giorgio won't. Father Giorgio's a good little boy now—for an hour.

[*Exit into monastery.*

ALF. This is an unaccountable state of things! To please Elvino I pretended to be a Duke, and I selected Ultrice as my Duchess. We drank the wine and we became a Duke and Duchess in real earnest, and, what is odder still, that unpleasant young person exercises an extraordinary fascination over me; while Teresa, whom I used to love so passionately, has completely faded out of my recollection.

Enter TERESA, *crazed*

SONG—TERESA

Willow, willow, where's my love?
Lovers ways are mazy;
All who hear me,
Much I fear me,
Think I'm going crazy.
Willow, willow, where's my love?
Waiting I, and weary—
Willow, willow, where's my love?
Where's my duck-a-deary?

TER. 'Tis but a silly song, and passing dear at the ducat I paid for it. They think anything is good enough for a mad maiden to sing; but though the maid be mad, her ducats are sound, and good gold should buy good wares, and there are none so mad but that they want value for cash!

ALF. Teresa!

TER. (*not recognizing him*). My lord Duke, is it not? My service to your Grace and to your Grace's bravery. (*Kissing his cloak.*) In good sooth, these are fine trappings, but they'll not trap *me,* for I love a lad who will none of me! My song says he's my duck-a-deary, which is true, in fact; but the expression is weak, and I am not yet mad enough for it. But I shall be, soon—I shall be, soon!

ALF. Teresa!—do you not know Alfredo, who used to love you so dearly?

TER. Alfredo! Alfredo! It is—it is—ha! ha! ha! (*About to embrace him.*)

ALF. Don't. That I cannot permit. Under the circumstances, it would be in the last degree unbecoming.

TER. Oh, I had forgotten! Thou lovest another now—a plain girl, compared with me. Methinks thou too must be mad to take up with such a one! But we are all mad—all—all mad.

ALF. I sometimes think so too. But take heart, little one; it is true I love thee not, for I have a bride, and no married man ever loves anybody but his wife.

TER. I am not so mad but that I know *that.* Why, I learnt it at school! But thou art like the rest—thou thinkest that any truism is good enough for a mad girl!

ALF. As I was saying, take heart, for although you are nothing to me now, yet I have ascertained that this spell under which we all labour will be removed in an hour, and I shall then love you as dearly, as passionately as heretofore!

TER. Is this indeed so? In one brief hour? No, no; I dare not believe it!

DUET—ALFREDO *and* TERESA

ALF. In days gone by,
But soon to come again,
With ardour pure
I used to pine,
And strove to lure
That heart of thine
With all my might and main.

I know not why,
But now, for thee, I find
I do not care:
To be exact,
Thy beauty rare
Does not attract—
To all thy charms I'm blind!
But take good heart—an hour will pass amain,
And all my love will then come back again!

TER. In days gone by
I played an idle part:
With scornful smile,
And heartless jest
And worldly guile,
Made manifest,
I grieved thy faithful heart.

How changed am I!
The love I dared decline,
Is now the breath
Of life to me.
And till kind death
Shall set me free
My love shall live for thine!
Be brave, poor heart—an hour will pass amain,
And all his love will then come back again!

Enter ULTRICE

RECITATIVE

ULT. So, I have found you!

ALF. (*leaving* TERESA, *and rushing to* ULTRICE, *as though under the influence of a spell*).

Passionately loved one!
Thy dainty hand I kiss—I mean the gloved one!
Oh, thou adored with passion most romantic!
Worshipped with all the fire of frenzy frantic!
For one short hour my love consent to share it—
It won't last longer than an hour—I swear it!

ENSEMBLE

ULT. (*aside*)	ALF. (*aside*)	TER.
The days of scorn are past—	The scorn I felt is past—	An hour will soon have passed—
With passion he's demented!	With passion I'm demented!	With passion I'm demented!
Triumphant I, at last!	But still, it will not last—	It won't much longer last—
My heart is now contented.	With that I'll be contented.	With that I'll be contented.
A suppliant at my feet,	A suppliant at her feet,	Though he is at her feet,
Thanks to the wizard's potion—	Thanks to the wizard's potion—	Thanks to the wizard's potion—
With insolence I'll treat	An hour—and obsolete	An hour—and obsolete
His newly-born devotion!	My newly-born devotion!	His newly-born devotion!

[*Exit* ALFREDO *into monastery.* TERESA *attempts to follow him; she is stopped by* ULTRICE, *who sends her off in the opposite direction.* ULTRICE *remains.*

RECITATIVE—ULTRICE

An hour? Nay, nay—
A lifetime rather—that is as I will.
His love is mine—yes, mine alone, until
His dying day!
Go, cheat yourselves with promises, poor fools!
I hold the talisman that overrules
The potion's power! (*Producing the pocket-book.*)

I found the conjuror sleeping and alone—
I stole it! It's mine! my very own!
Alfredo, till he dies, shall wear my gyves!
An hour? Poor fools, that hour shall last your lives!
Ha! ha! an hour!

[*Exit.*

Enter all the CHORUS OF GIRLS, *running.* ALFREDO *comes out of monastery and joins* ULTRICE. *He is followed by all the* MONKS. *Enter, also,* PIETRO, BARTOLO, *and* NITA, *the two last still as clockwork figures.*

CHORUS OF GIRLS. Oh, please you not to go away
Until you've seen the clockwork play.
Two figures carry on the plot,
And one's a man—the other's not.
They're full of complicated springs,
And weights, and wheels, and catgut strings—
You wind 'em up, just in the back,
With cracky, cracky, cracky, crack—
Then all the wheels, revolving quick,
Go ticky, ticky, ticky, tick—
And then the figures eat and drink,
And walk and talk, and wink and think,
And quarrel, just like lovers twain,
And kiss and make it up again.

ALL. It's very true, and very quaint—
The one's a man, the other ain't.
You wind 'em up, just in the back,
With cracky, cracky, cracky, crack—
And all the wheels, revolving quick,
Go ticky, ticky, ticky, tick.
It's very true—it's very quaint—
The one's a man—the other ain't!

[*During this,* PIETRO *has been dusting and arranging the figures, who have entered, jerkily, into the spirit of the chorus.*

PIE. (*coming forward*). May it please your Graces—
These are figures two,
Who, in port and paces,
Show you something new,

Note their human faces,
And the things they do;
We've reserved front places—
(*Recognizing them.*) Hallo! Why, it's you!
(*To the others.*) Alfredo and Ultrice! Peasants two!

ALL. Oh!
What do you mean by this sheer audacity?
What do you mean by this ill-timed joke?
How do you dare defy veracity?

ULT. Spare your unrestrained loquacity,
Listen while we the truth uncloke
At 'Vino's base design—
The Duke and Duchess aping—
We drank the cursed wine,
For which we all were gaping.
Then all at once we fell
Into the wizard's clutches,
Who changed us, strange to tell,
To genuine Duke and Duchess.

ALL. But——

ULT. Don't ask for further details—cease your chatter;
We've told you all we know about the matter.

[*Exeunt* ALFREDO *and* ULTRICE.

CHORUS. We may as well restrain our useless chatter;
They've told us all they know about the matter!

PIE. (*despondingly*). There's only one thing to be done,
Destroy the antidote by fierce ignition,
And thereby bring back every one
To his (or her) original condition!

ALL. Hurrah!

THE MEN. Sandal and robe we gladly lose,
Here is an end to our calling clerical.

THE GIRLS. Now they may marry whenever they choose,
All of us are with joy hysterical.

BAR. *and* NITA. We shall be human, body and limb,
Happy to think our state is curable.

PIE. I shall be free from these tortures grim;

They're getting exceedingly unendurable!

ALL. Hurrah!

[PIETRO *feels for pocket-book. He can't find it.*

Quick, quick—the antidote!
How horrified you look!

PIE. I had it in this coat—
Safe in my pocket-book.

[*Feeling for it.*

The truth I must admit,
Some thief has stolen it!

ALL. Oh, horror!
Accursed sorcerer!

[*Threateningly to* PIETRO.

Thou demon-leagued traitor!
Ill-omened harbinger!
Low-born equivocator!
This is a hideous plot
To rob us of our senses—
Restore us on the spot,
Or dread the consequences!

[*Exeunt all but* PIETRO, BARTOLO, *and* NITA. PIETRO *sits in great pain and distress.* BARTOLO *and* NITA *make ineffective attempts to move and speak, but they have "run down."*

PIE. (*observing their efforts*). Now, then, what's wrong with *you?* Oh, I see. (*Winds them up.*)

Spoken together very rapidly.

BAR. Upon my honour, this is a pretty state of things. Clockwork for life, I suppose! It's monstrous—outrageous! What's to become of Nita, and, above all, what's to become of me?

NI. Well, a nice mess you've made of this; to go and lose the only thing that could bring us back to life again. What do you mean by it, you ridiculous old donkey?

PIE. What do you want?

NI. Why, if I'm to be Ophelia for the rest of my life, it would be convenient to know what Ophelia did.

BAR. She coaxed Hamlet, a good deal.

PIE. Nothing of the kind; she committed suicide because Hamlet wouldn't marry her.

NI. What—lately?

PIE. Lately! Several hundred years ago. (NITA *and* BARTOLO *turn and walk rapidly up stage.*) Where are you going?

NI. We're going back several hundred years.

PIE. It's not necessary. You can do it here. (NITA *begins to cry.*)

BAR. I have it. If Hamlet had married Ophelia she wouldn't have committed suicide.

PIE. Well? What then?

BAR. What then? Why; if I marry her at once the motive for the act will be removed!

PIE. Nonsense! Hamlet and Ophelia never married. It would be trifling with the text.

BAR. Anyhow, it's a new reading. What! am I to be the only Hamlet who is not permitted to discover new readings? Bah!

TRIO—PIETRO, NITA, AND BARTOLO

PIE. Ophelia was a daintly little maid,
Who loved a very melancholy Dane;
Whose affection of the heart, so it is said,
Preceded his affection of the brain.
Heir-apparent to the Crown,
He thought lightly of her passion.
Having wandered up and down,
In an incoherent fashion,
When she found he wouldn't wed her
In a river, in a meadder,
Took a header, and a deader
Was Ophelia!

NITA. Ophelia to her sex was a disgrace,
Whom nobody could feel compassion for.
Ophelia should have gone to Ely Place
To consult an eminent solicitor.

When such promises as these
Breaks a suitor, rich and regal,
Why, substantial damages
Is the panacea legal—
From a jury—sons of Adam,
Though as stony as Macadam,
Maid or madam, she'd have had 'em,
Would Ophelia!

BAR. There's a venerable proverb in my mind,
Which applies to this catastrophe, I think,
To a horse who is unfortunately blind
Any nod is just as good as any wink.
Opportunity I'll seize
Of avoiding any error:
Of substantial damages
I have always had a terror.
That calamity to parry
Not a moment will I tarry,
Off I'll carry and I'll marry
Poor Ophelia!

[*Exeunt* BARTOLO *and* NITA. *As they go off,* PIETRO *slyly steals their respective keys, and goes off triumphantly in the opposite direction.*

Enter ULTRICE *and* TERESA

ULT. She comes! Ah, Madame Jilt!
Oh, crazy insolent! Ah, wonder as thou wilt,
Thy scornful head is bent!
TER. Ultrice! Ultrice!
ULT. Ah, cruel one!
Thou knowest now
The torture of a love that's gone astray!
TER. Ah! spare me!
ULT. Thou knowest now
The fate of those who will not when they may
TER. Ah! spare me!
ULT. Thou knowest now
The sting of jealousy's envenomed dart.

TER. Ah! spare me!

ULT. Thou knowest now
The deadly famine of a hungry heart.

TER. Ah! spare me!
Farewell, Alfredo! [*Turning to* ULTRICE.
Ere deathly cold
I lie on yonder strand
Ah, let me hold
The hand that is his hand;
[*Taking her hand.*
Ere lost I be
In yonder cold eclipse,
Vouchsafe to me
The lips that are his lips!

[*Kissing* ULTRICE, *who remains motionless.*

May he forget
His love of old—
Her sun has set
Her tale is told!

[*Goes up stage and mounts parapet overhanging the river. She is about to throw herself off, when* ULTRICE, *who has been struggling with her better feelings, relents.*

ULT. Hold! Stay thy hand! Teresa, come to me;
My soul is softened and my heart is stirred!
Come to me quickly—I have wrongèd thee.
Pardon, Teresa, I have greatly erred!

TER. Ultrice! [*She rushes to her arms.*

ULT. Take heart, take heart, for thou shalt righted be;
Live—for thy love shall be restored to thee!
Come hither, all!

Enter all the characters from different entrances—PIETRO *in great agony*

CHORUS. Now, what is this, and what is that?
We wish to go to yonder valley.
What do you want? what are you at?
Explain your conduct generally!

ULT. Proud of my new-born rank
Which raised me from my clan,
From yonder mountebank
I stole the talisman!

[*She produces it.* PIETRO *clutches at it.*

ALL. Ah, false one!
From yonder mountebank
She stole the talisman!

[*Exit* ULTRICE.

PIE. Another minute and my fate were sealed!
A light—quick—quick!—my fortune for a light!

[*A light is given to him—he burns the parchment.*

The parchment burns—my tortures slowly yield—
'Tis gone and with it our distorted plight!

[*Gong—all change to their original characters: the* MONKS *becoming brigands,* MINESTRA *becoming a young woman,* ALFREDO *and* ULTRICE *becoming peasants,* BARTOLO *and* NITA *are restored to humanity, and* PIETRO *recovers his health.* ALFREDO *embraces* TERESA.

CHORUS

Hurrah!
The spell's removed,
Hurrah!
The {men we / girls they} loved,
Hurrah!
Are {ours / theirs} again,
Hurrah!
With might and main,
Hurrah!

ARR. The Duke and the Duchess, when they travel through the land,
How the pair they will stare, with their high jerry ho!

They will yet fall a prey to the valour of our band,
For we shall not be happy till we get them;
With our high jerry ho!
And our canticle pedantical,
And our mystic, though artistic,
Jerry high, jerry ho!

ALL. With their high jerry ho! etc.

PIE., BAR., NI. The Duke and the Duchess, had they travelled through our land,
With their cries of surprise and their high jerry ho!
They'd have seen many things that they wouldn't understand;
Not the least is our show, you may bet them—
With our high jerry ho!
And our clickings and our tickings—
Our emphatic automatic
Jerry high, jerry ho!

ALL. With their high jerry ho! etc.

ALF. *and* TER. The Duke and the Duchess, if they travel through our land,
As they may, any day, with their high jerry ho!
They will find that we're linked, heart in heart, hand in hand,
And a loving example we'll set them,
With our high jerry ho!
And our notion of devotion,
And our gentle sentimental
Jerry high, jerry ho!

ALL. With their high jerry ho!

CURTAIN

HIS EXCELLENCY

DRAMATIS PERSONÆ

THE PRINCE REGENT, *disguised as Nils Egilsson, a Strolling Player*

GEORGE GRIFFENFELD, *Governor of Elsinore*

ERLING SYKKE, *a Young Sculptor*

DR. TORTENSSEN, *a Young Physician*

MATS MUNCK, *Syndic of Elsinore*

CORPORAL HAROLD, *of the King's Hussars*

A SENTRY

FIRST OFFICER

SECOND OFFICER

CHRISTINA, *a Ballad Singer*

NANNA }
THORA } *Griffenfeld's Daughters*

DAME HECLA CORTLANDT, *a Lady of Property*

BLANCA, *a Vivandière*

ELSA, *a Peasant Girl*

ACT I

MARKET PLACE OF ELSINORE

ACT II

COURTYARD OF THE CASTLE

DATE—1801

HIS EXCELLENCY

ACT I

SCENE.—*Market place of Elsinore. The townspeople (led by* MATS MUNCK, *the Syndic) are assembled to congratulate* ERLING SYKKE *on the completion of the statue of the Prince Regent of Denmark, which occupies the centre of the stage. Colours flying, bells ringing, cannon firing, and general symptoms of rejoicing.*

OPENING CHORUS

Set the merry bunting flying,
Fire the cannon—ring the bells—
Our great townsman glorifying,
Who with sculptor's skill undying,
All competitors excels.
He, with his artistic spells,
So the stubborn marble quells,
That, to all intents elastic,
It assumes, in manner plastic,
Shapes heroic—shapes fantastic,
As his mighty will compels!

MATS MUNCK. Chosen from his fellow creatures
By our King—'twas wisely done—
To perpetuate the features
Of the Regent Prince, his son—
Then created, by a penmark,
At our gracious King's decree,
Sculptor to the Court of Denmark
And the Royal Familee!

ALL. Sculptor to the Court of Denmark
And the Royal Familee!
Leisure take—*festina lentè*—
You have time before you, plenty,

When at only two-and-twenty,
(*Nemine dissentientè*)
You're created with a penmark,
Sculptor to the Court of Denmark—
Sculptor to the Court of Denmark
And the Royal Familee!

RECIT.—ERLING

Most worthy Syndic and all friends assembled,
I thank you for your kind and cordial greeting—
But when you sing my praises, oh remember
How many worthier brethren pine and perish
For lack of that sunbeam of Royal favour,
Which by sheer April chance, has fallen on me
And warmed my budding powers into blossom!

CHORUS. No, no!
No April chance is here—
Thine art hath no compeer—
It triumphs all completely:
And, sooth to say, 'twere well
If Royal sunbeams always fell
So wisely, so discreetly!
So scatter flowers at his feet,
Sing him songs of jubilation,
And the king of sculptors greet
With a rosy coronation!
[*Crowning him with flowers.*

MEN. Raise him on our brawny shoulders,
Cynosure of all beholders. (*They do so.*)

WOMEN. Hail him, scholar—hail him, gownsman—
As your worthiest fellow townsman!

ALL. Hail him, dunce and ignoramus,
For his fame will make you famous—
Hail him great, and hail him small,
Hail him one, and hail him all!

[*They carry him round stage, then place him on his feet; then exeunt all except* ERLING *and* CHRISTINA, *who is then discovered seated at the foot of the pedestal.*

RECIT.—ERLING

My pretty one, why silent and alone?
Why sit you thus in pensive meditation?
Has melancholy marked you for her own,
Or sad disaster checked your heart's elation?
I pray reply!

RECIT.—CHRISTINA

Good sir, although I sit apart all day,
I am no prey to grief or sad disaster,
Truth is, I cannot tear myself away
From this fair form—thy work, oh, mighty master!
I'll tell you why!

BALLAD—CHRISTINA

I see with a silent awe,
In this faultless form allied
The exquisite grace
Of a royal race,
And the glory of knightly pride:
No blemish, or fault, or flaw,
But perfect in all is he,
I've learnt, in fine,
What a god divine
A chivalrous knight may be.
As gentle as lover's lay,
Or the dawn of a bright May-day,
Yet cast in the knightly mould
Of the glorious days of old—
My eyes are opened; at last I see
What he who would win my heart must be.

Why look at the men we've known—
Their mouths will open and close—
They've ears likewise,
And a couple of eyes,
And the usual nubbly nose;
Each has a head of his own,
They've bodies, and legs, and feet—
I'm bound to admit

That in every whit
The catalogue's quite complete:—
But where is the godlike grace
That lights that marvellous face?
Where is the brow serene?
Where is the lordly mien?
Ah, dullards and dolts are all I've known,
Compared with that marvellous, matchless stone!

[*Exit* CHRISTINA.

ERL. That's a typical instance of feminine perversity—doesn't fall in love with me, which would be rational enough, but with the senseless inanimate work of my hands! My dear fellow (*addressing statue*), I little thought, when I cut you out, that in course of time you'd return the compliment!

Enter TORTENSSEN

TOR. Erling, congratulate me! I've just received my patent of appointment as Personal Physician to His Majesty King Christian. I have let my house, sold my practice, and I start for Copenhagen this day week!

ERL. My dear friend, I'm overjoyed. I'm in daily expectation of a Royal command to take up my office as Sculptor Extraordinary to the Royal Family—and we'll travel together. Of course, you've heard that I've been promised a Countship?

TOR. And I am to be created a Baron!

ERL. You don't say so! To think that we two, who have toiled in obscurity from boyhood for a bare subsistence, should both be raised at the same moment to such social and professional distinction!

TOR. It seems incredible! It can't be—but, no—that's out of the question.

ERL. What can't be?

TOR. It can't be one of Governor Griffenfeld's practical jokes?

ERL. My dear fellow, don't suggest such a thing. It would be too cruel—why, it would be our ruin!

TOR. But he is cruel. When a scheme for a practical joke enters his head he sticks at nothing in its accomplishment. Why, he has caused the very soldiers of the garrison—war-worn veterans as they are—to be drilled as ballet-girls, and to perform all their evolutions to dance steps, simply in order to make them ridiculous in the eyes of the girls they're engaged to!

ERL. He's a malicious devil enough, but he would hardly venture to play pranks in the name of his Sovereign. Besides, there's the statue—a commission from the King.

TOR. True. By the way, I suppose it *is* a commission from the King? *That's* not one of his Excellency's practical jokes?

ERL. Nonsense! Now, does that look like a practical joke? Why, I'm to get ten thousand rix-dollars for it! Now, as you know, I love his daughter Nanna devotedly, and she has hitherto treated me with contempt, because, as she says, I'm a mere tuppenny-halfpenny stone-cutter. Of course, that's only her humorous way of putting it.

TOR. And I adore Thora, who has always treated my pretensions with derision, because, as she says, I'm only a pitiful pill-roller. That's her epigrammatic way of expressing it.

ERL. But now that our positions are so immensely improved, surely we might renew our proposals with every prospect of success!

TOR. The very idea that occurred to me! My incomparable Thora——

ERL. Your what!

TOR. My incomparable Thora——

ERL. Ah—exactly! But—don't think me inquisitive—why don't you think Nanna incomparable?

TOR. Why, my dear fellow, if for no other reason, because you do.

ERL. What an obstinate dog you must be to refuse to consider her the divinest creature in the world, because I do! And you call yourself my friend!

TOR. Well, but really——

ERL. It's most unjust to the poor girl.

TOR. But if I loved Nanna you'd call me out.

ERL. What, you—call *you* out? Call out my old friend

because he was of the same way of thinking as myself? —no!

TOR. But suppose I were successful?

ERL. Ah, but you wouldn't be. That is a contingency that we need not consider. Now do give up Thora and love Nanna—do, to oblige me.

TOR. Do you want everybody to love Nanna?

ERL. Of course I do. What I want is that all the world shall go mad over her, and that I shall be triumphant. Surely that's an intelligible position! Now mark:—

SONG—ERLING

When I bestow my bosom's store,
No room for doubt
Must I descry:
All men must love whom I adore,
Or we fall out,
All men and I.
Though poor their chance and slight their hope
Who with my suit presume to cope,
Yet must all men to gain her try,
Or we fall out, all men and I.

When I am wed I'll hold them cheap
Who sing and shout
With joyous cry.
At such a time all men must weep,
Or we fall out,
All men and I.
As all men must my rivals be,
When Nanna gives her hand to me
All men must broken-hearted, sigh,
Or we fall out, all men and I.

If I my lady vainly woo,
And, her without,
I pine and die,
Mankind at large must perish, too,
Or we fall out,
Mankind and I.
Who lives when I find life too long
Would seem to say that I am wrong.

When I expire all men must die,
Or we fall out, all men and I!

Enter NANNA *and* THORA

NANNA (*pretending not to see* ERLING *and* TORTENSSEN). And they're so clever, said I—such talented young men—so extraordinarily good-looking, too—and so kind to their poor old mothers!

THORA. And now that they're going to be raised to the peerage they'll have nothing to say to a couple of middle-class nobodies like us! (*Suddenly.*) Oh my goodness, here they are! Oh what have I said!

DUET—NANNA *and* THORA

THORA. Oh my goodness, here's the nobility!
NANNA. Gracious me, how very embarrassing!
THORA. We're such every day gentility—
Bless me, how exceedingly harassing!
NANNA. Pray, you pardon us!
Don't be hard on us!
THORA. Most confusing your regard on us!
BOTH. Never was I so dazed, I think!
Into the ground I'd like to sink!
THORA. Can't you see they're high society?
NANNA. Don't they sneer like people of quality?
THORA. If we seem to lack propriety,
Pray forgive our silly frivolity!
NANNA. Treat with charity
Our vulgarity—
THORA. 'Twixt us there's so much disparity
BOTH. Very superior persons, you!
Gracious goodness, what shall we do?

ERL. Then, Miss Nanna, you've heard of our good fortune?

NANNA. Indeed I have! I'm quite uncomfortable in the presence of such grandees!

THORA. We're so unaccustomed to aristocratic circles that really we hardly know how we ought to address you!

TOR. Oh, we haven't been ennobled yet.

THORA. Haven't you really? Come, that makes conversation easier. Still, a Personal Physician to the King——

NANNA. And a Sculptor Extraordinary to the Royal Family—

THORA. And we're only the daughters of an obscure provincial Governor! Oh, really I think we'd better go. It's so much wiser to keep to one's own rank in life!

ERL. Miss Nanna, pray be reassured; we have no desire to presume on our promotion. Indeed, you overrate our importance.

THORA. It seems impossible. I really think we'd better go.

TOR. No, don't do that. Be quite unembarrassed—entirely at your ease, and try to imagine that we are nobody in particular.

THORA. Oh, but that demands a tremendous effort of the imagination. Still, I'll try (*tries*).

TOR. Have you got it?

THORA. Not yet, but I won't be beaten. I'll try again (*tries again*).

NANNA (*trying*). Oh, I shall never do it! Did you say nobody in particular?

ERL. Just a couple of mere everyday, commonplace professional men.

NANNA. Well, it can't be done—that's all! It's ridiculous to expect it.

ERL (*aside*). Now's my time, I think! (*Aloud.*) Miss Nanna, as you know, we have both loved you and your sister—and we've often told you so, and you snubbed us, and we deserved it. But now that we are well off, and Court personages, and going to be ennobled, we venture to—to——

NANNA. Not to offer us your hands. No—don't say that—don't turn our heads and give us ideas above our station!

THORA. Oh! (*crying out*). Oh, I've got an idea above my station! Oh, it's all the way up there, ever so high!

[*Pointing up.*

THE OTHERS (*looking up*). Where? Where?

THORA. Bal-loon! Ha! ha! ha!

ERL. I do believe you are laughing at us!

THORA (*to* NANNA). Oh, aren't the nobility shrewd?

NANNA. And isn't the aristocracy quick at grasping a situation?

THORA. But come, we'll be serious. Are you really in earnest when you make us this intoxicating offer?

TOR. Absolutely.

ERL. More serious than we ever were in our lives.

NANNA. Very good, that's business, and I'll tell you what we'll do.

QUARTETTE—NANNA, THORA, ERLING, *and* TORTENSSEN

NANNA. If all is as you say—
If honour and wealth and glory
Of every sort
Are your's—

THORA. In short,
If you're not telling a story—

NANNA. If you are a Count some day—

THORA. A Baron if you're created—
And all turns out
Beyond all doubt
Precisely as you've stated—

NANNA. Court sculptor and a peer,
With eversomuch a year,
Precisely as you've stated—

THORA. Physician to the King
With honours and everything,
Precisely as you've stated—

NANNA *and* THORA. Then I will be your bride—

ERL. *and* TOR. Oh joy!

NANNA *and* THORA. And I your bride will be!

ERL. *and* TOR. Then let us make merry.
It's evident, very,
That day we soon shall see—

NANNA *and* THORA. When you are qualified—

ERL. *and* TOR. Oh joy!

NANNA *and* THORA. To marry you we agree!

ERL. *and* TOR. Oh happy decision!
Oh vision Elysian!
That day we soon shall see!

ERL. Compared with our own
All others are inkiness!

TOR. They are, alone,
Two visions of pinkiness!

ERL. Pinkiness, veiled
With ivory pellicle—

TOR. Everywhere hailed
As simply angelical!

NANNA. That isn't true,
Ridiculous chatterer!

THORA. Go along, do,
Unscrupulous flatterer!

NANNA. Only a sweet
In*divi*duality!

THORA. Dainty and neat,
But merely mortality!

ERL. *and* TOR. Merely mortality? Merely mortality?
With such a bewitching in*divi*duality?

NANNA *and* THORA. Merely two pretty young ladies of quality,
Piquante and pleasant—but merely mortality!

ALL. Then { I / you } will be my bride—oh joy!
And { I your / you my } bride will be! &c.

[*Dance and exeunt* ERLING *and* TORTENSSEN.

NANNA. Oh, Thora! (*laughing.*)

THORA. Oh, Nanna! (*laughing.*)

NANNA. They believe it all!

THORA. Every word!

NANNA. What geese!

THORA. Personal Physician to the King!

NANNA. Sculptor Extraordinary to the Royal Family!

THORA. It serves them right for presuming to aspire to our affections. It was papa's idea! Oh, it's a grand thing to have a father who will condescend to play practical jokes on the very meanest rather than allow the family dignity to be insulted.

NANNA. Dear papa! He has such humour!

THORA. So much invention!

NANNA. Such an uncontrollable flow of animal spirits!

THORA. Such a gentle, harmless, refined, and utterly inoffensive notion of fun! Here he comes, attended by his guard—all drilled as ballet-girls. Now there's a happy idea!

NANNA. Delightful! Dear papa is never so happy as when he is making dignified people ridiculous!

Enter Chorus of Girls, led by ELSA

CHORUS

Here are warriors all ablaze,
  Sabre and epaulettes, ha! ha!
All of them ordered to spend their days
  Practising minuets, ha! ha!
Never was seen such tawdry trickery,
Soldiers, tough as oak or hickory,
Turned to votaries of Terpsichore,
  Mincing marionettes, ha! ha!
Never was seen in soldier's training
Spectacle half so entertaining!
Never was seen such tuppenny trickery—
Soldiers, tough as the oak or hickory,
Turned to votaries of Terpsichore,
  Mincing marionettes, ha! ha!

Enter Soldiers dancing, led by HAROLD *and followed by* BLANCA

HAR. Though I'm a soldier, all pugnacity,
  Into your presence I'm made to come
In the contemptible capacity
  Of a confounded teetotum!

CHORUS OF SOLDIERS. In the contemptible capacity
  Of a confounded teetotum.

HAR. Although the Governor's jokes are numerous,
  This is a joke we fail to see—
If this is the Governor's fun so humorous,
  Bother the Governor's fun, say we!

CHORUS OF SOLDIERS. If this is the Governor's fun so humorous,
  Bother the Governor's fun, say we!

HAR. Oh you may laugh at our dancing-schoolery—

It's all very well, it amuses *you*,
But how would *you* like this dashed tomfoolery
Every day from ten to two?

CHORUS OF SOLDIERS. How would *you* like this dashed tomfoolery
Every day from ten to two?

HAR. (*to Soldiers*). You can halt for a moment. The Governor's stopped to make a butter slide on the Syndic's doorstep. (*Soldiers halt—to* BLANCA.) It's a little unkind to laugh at us, Blanca, for you know *we* can't help it—from 10 to 2.

BLAN. It's a little unkind to complain of our laughing at you, for you know *we* can't help it—from 10 to 2.

ELSA. We can none of us help it—you're all so ridiculous!

HAR. I think my betrothed wife might sympathize with the absurdity of my position. I think *all* our betrothed wives might sympathize with the absurdity of *all* our positions.

ELSA. We sympathize with you as hard as we can, *after* 2. We can't do it *before* 2, because we're laughing all the time.

BLAN. From 2 to 10 you're men, and we're engaged to you. From 10 to 2 you're hoppedegigs, and it's off.

ELSA. That exactly describes it.

HAR. Yes, but at that rate we shall never get any forrarder. Besides, who knows what may happen from 10 to 2? You might get engaged to somebody else—to the Sergeant-Major, for instance—he's always fooling around you.

BLAN. Well, of course we don't want to waste our mornings; but even if I were engaged to him from 10 to 2, I should always be true to you from 2 to 10.

HAR. It's not enough. It's incomplete.

ELSA. Take care, the Governor's coming.

HAR. Oh, confound it—off we go again!

[*Soldiers resume dancing.*

Enter GOVERNOR GRIFFENFELD. *He has a pound of butter in his hand*

GRIF. (*to Soldiers*). Ah, my fine fellows, still at it? Got your second wind? That's right—capital exercise! Nothing like it. Here, you can eat this—I've done with it. (*Giving butter to* HAROLD.) The Syndic went down like a shot!

HAR. (*dancing*). I beg your Excellency's pardon, but—may we halt for a moment? We've danced for nearly three miles up-hill, and it's a hot day, and we're feeling a little faint.

GRIF. Always craving for some unreasonable indulgence! Selfish dogs, all of you! Well, you may halt for five minutes.

HAR. Thank you very much. (*To Soldiers.*) Selfish dogs—Halt! (*They halt.*)

GRIF. Anything else?

HAR. Well, I *have* a request to make. The fact is, the troops do feel the humiliation of being drilled like ballet-girls.

GRIF. Bless my heart, you surprise me! Don't they like ballet-girls?

HAR. Oh, they're very fond of ballet-girls, but they don't want to *be* ballet-girls, because when you *are* a ballet-girl, you don't seem to care so much about ballet-girls as you do when—when you're something quite different.

GRIF. But don't your men see how much amusement they create? Can't they see that all the girls are laughing at them? Have they *no* sense of humour?

HAR. Oh, they've a distinct sense of humour; but to enjoy this sort of thing completely you want to see it from a distance. *You* see it from a distance, and it ought to be devilish funny; but *we* are close to it—in fact, we *are* it—and when you *are* it, you don't seem to care so much about it, as you do when—when you are something quite different. The fact is, the point of a joke is like the point of a needle—hold the needle sideways and it's plain enough, but when it is directed straight at you—well, it's not always very easy to see the point of it.

GRIF. Nonsense! I can see a joke plain enough even when I'm its victim. Take my unfortunate love affair——

HAR. Ah, ridiculous business that! [*Soldiers laugh.*

GRIF. No comments, sir!

HAR. (*to Soldiers*). No comments, gentlemen!

GRIF. Take my unfortunate love affair. The late Governor, when I was only his deputy, was about to be married to an elderly lady of a singularly explosive disposition. They simply doted on each other. Now when you see two old donkeys simply doting on each other, your course is obvious—you set to work——

HAR. To wheedle the old lady——

GRIF. Away from the old gentleman.

HAR. Ha! ha! you little rogue!

[HAROLD *digs* GRIFFENFELD *in the ribs.*

GRIF. Don't do that, sir!

HAR. (*to Soldiers*). Don't do that, gentlemen!

GRIF. Well, after some respectful attention, she accepted me in this letter (*producing a letter*) in which she stipulated that the matter should be kept a profound secret until an excuse could be found for sending the old gentleman about his business. But, as luck would have it, the Governor died suddenly and I succeeded him, before I had time to explain that it was only my fun——

HAR. *and* SOLDIERS. Ha! ha! (*Suddenly serious*)—I beg your pardon—I don't know what they're laughing at.

GRIF. And so there I was—regularly trapped into a ridiculous engagement, which I can't for the life of me see my way out of. The situation is most unpleasant—*most* unpleasant. But do you suppose I don't see the fun of it? Why, I can't think of it without going into convulsions! Ha! ha!

HAR. *and* SOLDIERS. Ha! ha! ha!

GRIF. She's sixty!

HAR. *and* SOLDIERS. Ha! ha! ha!

GRIF. Wears a wig!

HAR. *and* SOLDIERS. Ha! ha! ha!

GRIF. Don't overdo it, sir!

HAR. Don't overdo it, gentlemen!

GRIF. That's quite enough. It's a very good joke, but not as good a joke as all that. Impudent puppies!—be off with you.

HAR. (*to* SOLDIERS). Impudent puppies!—inwards turn—Chassez!

[HAROLD *and* SOLDIERS *dance off, followed by girls laughing and chattering.*

GRIF. Upon my word, there's no such thing as gratitude. I do all I can to make my soldiers amusing—I place them in all kinds of ridiculous situations—I make them a source of entertainment to a whole township of attractive girls, and instead of being pleased and grateful for the attention, they growl like so many sore-eared bears!

Enter Dame CORTLANDT *skittishly, with a folded note in her hand*

DAME. Why, here's my little man after all! I've been looking for him everywhere. Why does he hide himself away from his loving Hecla?

GRIF. Eh? Oh, it's you, is it? (*She puts her arm round his neck.*) Don't do that—you rumple me. What have you got there?

DAME. It's a note, you jealous boy! Not for you—oh dear no! It's a pretty little pink and white *billet doux* addressed to a pretty little pink and white gentleman, begging him to make an appointment to meet a pretty little pink and white lady, all alone! That's me! Now what do you think of *that*?

GRIF. Well, if you ask me, I don't think he'll come.

DAME. Oh yes, he will! He'll come fast enough. But there—it's cruel to keep my pet in suspense——

GRIF. God bless me, you don't suppose *I* care whom you meet!

DAME (*suddenly furious*). What's that? Say that again! Once more! Come, out with it!

GRIF. (*alarmed*). I say that I've such perfect confidence in your moral character that I don't trouble myself to enquire whom you make appointments with.

DAME (*relieved*). Oh, was that all? But you shouldn't upset me, George. Within this fragile body two tremendous powers are in perpetual antagonism—a Diabolical Temper and an Iron Will. At first it didn't seem to be any affair of mine, and I determined to let them fight it out among themselves; but this internal conflict of irresistible forces is very wearing, George, and I begin to wish they'd settle it one way or the other.

GRIF. Oh, what's the odds?

DAME (*temper rising*). About seven to two on the Temper just now, George. (*Struggling to repress it.*) No, the Will triumphs! (*Playfully.*) Now, shall I tell my little man who it is? [*Placing her arm round his neck.*

GRIF. Oh, bother! Don't go on like that! You're too old!

DAME (*suddenly furious*). Eh? What was that? Too old! I'm too old! Oh, hold me down—hold me down! Bottle me up, and tie down the cork, or I shall go mad! mad! mad!

GRIF. Don't go on like that—it's so jumpy!

DAME (*struggling with herself*). You—you said I was too old!

GRIF. Well, *I'm* too old. You're not, but I am. Can't *you* take a joke? Can't anybody take a joke?

DAME. You were not in earnest?

GRIF. Earnest! Am I ever in earnest?

DAME (*with an effort*). All right, dear—don't be afraid—it's down again! Well, then, this is a letter requesting Master Mats Munck, the Syndic, to take my instructions for drawing up the settlements with a view to my forthcoming marriage. But I shan't tell *you* how I'm going to deal with my property. That will be a little surprise for you during the honeymoon.

GRIF. (*aside*). A letter to the Syndic? The very thing! It may help me to carry out my plot for compromising her with him. (*Aloud.*) Give it to me. I shall see him presently, and I'll hand it to him.

DAME. To be sure I will. (*Giving it to him.*) And now about the date.

GRIF. What date?

DAME. Why, the date of our marriage, you ardent creature!

GRIF. Oh, yes!—come and sit down, and we'll talk it over. (*She sits at his feet.*) There—like that. Cosy, isn't it?

DAME (*shyly*). Oh, George!

GRIF. Now suppose—I only say suppose, you know——

DAME. Yes—like a fairy tale.

GRIF. Exactly—like a fairy tale. Now suppose that one fine morning you discovered that all this lovemaking of mine was only one of my practical jokes! Ha! ha! ha!

DAME. Ha! ha! ha! (*working herself up into a rage*). Stop a bit! stop a bit! They're fighting it out.

GRIF. (*earnestly*). Two to one on the Will! Two to one on the Will!

DAME. Wins easy, George! It's all right again. Go on, dear.

GRIF. No, but really now, what would you say if you found out, quite unexpectedly, that I wasn't in earnest, and that I only proposed to you because—because somebody bet me I wouldn't?

DAME (*working herself up*). Bet you you wouldn't—bet you you wouldn't! What would I do—what would I do—what would I do?

GRIF. Now don't go on like that! It's most unpleasant. I don't think you know how creepy you are when you do that. Oh, Lord, she's off again!

DUET—GOVERNOR *and* DAME CORTLANDT

DAME. Now what would I do if you proved untrue, and the suit you pressed were an idle jest, and the conjugal joke a brainless joke, and if marry your darling you couldn't?

GRIF. Yes, what would you do if I proved untrue,
And if marry my darling I couldn't?

DAME. What would I say if you owned some day that, a wager to win, you had taken me in, and the fact disclosed that you just proposed because somebody bet you you wouldn't?

GRIF. If I owned some day that I sung that lay,
Because somebody bet me I wouldn't?

DAME. Why, the trembling rock from an earthquake's shock, and the ocean's roar on the rock-bound shore, and the hell-babe's scream were a peaceful dream, to the terrible broth of my brewing;
The tiger's gnash, and the cut-throat's gash, and the foe-

man's clash, and the thunder-crash of eternal smash were unmeaning trash, compared with my hullabalooing!

ENSEMBLE

GOVERNOR (*aside*)	DAME
It might, perhaps, be rather rash	Take care, you'll find it rather rash
The truth upon her mind to flash	My matrimonial hopes to dash,
If an earthquake's shock were idle trash	For an earthquake's shock were idle trash
Compared with her hullaballooing!	Compared with my hullaballooing!

DAME. Like grey screech-owl (that hideous fowl) in a midnight cowl I'd slink and prowl till a horrible howl and a tiger's growl had told the world I'd found you!
With object fell and a yelp and yell, on Vengeance's wing at my foe I'd spring, and face to face in a close embrace I'd wind my arms around you!
Your heart I'd tear from its loathsome lair—I'd pluck out your eyes, and your tongue likewise—and limb from limb, with a growling grim, I'd rend him who pooh poohs me!
(*Recovering herself.*) Excuse me, please—when people tease, by slow degrees I kick up a breeze which you can't appease—it's quite a disease—I'll go and lie down—excuse me!

[*Exit* DAME CORTLANDT.

GRIF. This is getting a little too hot to be pleasant. But this letter to the Syndic is simply providential. It's exactly what I wanted to make my innocent little plot complete (*tears it up*). Now where are those two girls of mine? They ought to be back by this time. (*Enter* NANNA *and* THORA.) Oh, here you are! Well, have you seen the Syndic?

NANNA. Yes, and we've carried out all your instructions.

GRIF. Good girls.

NANNA. We told him that we had the best possible reason to know that the wealthy old lady was particularly well disposed towards him, and that a declaration from him would receive polite and immediate attention.

THORA. So the silly old gentleman went off his head with joy—did extraordinary things with the office-stool, and at once wrote his declaration, and gave to us to deliver (*produces it*). Here it is.

GRIF. Thank you (*giving her the letter which he formerly received from* DAME CORTLANDT). The old lady's reply.

THORA. What, already?

NANNA. Wonderful invention, steam!

GRIF. Hush! (*Aside to them.*) It's the very letter in which she accepted me under seal of secrecy, when I was only Deputy Governor!

NANNA. Oh, you sly old papa!

GRIF. Ha! ha! ha! It will do for him just as well as it did for me. And it will make him so happy!

TRIO—GRIFFENFELD, NANNA, *and* THORA

ALL. Oh what a fund of joy jocund lies hid in harmless hoaxes!
What keen enjoyment springs
From cheap and simple things!

What deep delight from sources trite inventive humour coaxes,
That pain and trouble brew
For every one but you!

GRIF. Gunpowder placed inside its waist improves a mild Havanah,
Its unexpected flash
Burns eyebrows and moustache.

NANNA. When people dine no kind of wine beats ipecacuanha,
But common-sense suggests
You keep it for your guests—

THORA. Then naught annoys the organ boys like throwing red-hot coppers,

NANNA. And much amusement bides
In common butter-slides:

GRIF. And stringy snares across the stairs cause unexpected croppers.

THORA. Coal scuttles, recollect,
Produce the same effect.

GRIF. A man possessed
Of common-sense
Need not invest
At great expense—

NANNA. It does not call
For pocket deep,

THORA. These jokes are all
Extremely cheap.

ALL. If you commence with eighteenpence—it's all you'll have to pay;
You may command a pleasant and a most instructive day.

GRIF. A good spring gun breeds endless fun, and makes men jump like rockets—

THORA. And turnip-heads on posts
Make very decent ghosts.

GRIF. Then hornets sting like anything, when placed in waistcoat pockets—

NANNA Burnt cork and walnut juice
Are not without their use.

GRIF. No fun compares with easy chairs whose seats are stuffed with needles—

THORA. Live shrimps their patience tax
When put down people's backs—

GRIF. Surprising, too, what one can do with a pint of fat black-beetles—

NANNA. And treacle on a chair
Will make a Quaker swear!

THORA. Then sharp tin tacks
And pocket squirts—

GRIF. And cobbler's wax
For ladies' skirts—

NANNA. And slimy slugs
On bedroom floors—

GRIF. And water jugs
On open doors—

ALL. Prepared with these cheap properties, amusing tricks to play,
Upon a friend a man may spend a most delightful day! [*Exeunt.*

Enter two Officers, who look cautiously round

1ST OFF. Is the coast clear?

2ND OFF. Quite—there's no one in sight.

[FIRST OFFICER *beckons off. Enter the* REGENT *dressed picturesquely as a tattered vagabond. Both Officers bow deferentially.*

REG. Who were those who left as you arrived?

1ST OFF. The Governor Griffenfeld, your Royal Highness, and his two daughters.

REG. The fellow whose disgraceful practical jokes are the subject of such general complaint?

2ND OFF. The same, sir.

REG. Well, the expostulations of the townspeople have reached us in shoals, and we are resolved to judge for ourselves as to their truth or falsehood. For the purpose of our present disguise, we are Nils Egilsson—a strolling player—a vagabond—and as such you may describe me if any question as to my identity should arise. You can leave me now, but hold yourselves in readiness in case of emergency.

1ST OFF. As your Royal Highness pleases.

[*Officers bow and exeunt.*

REG. Whom have we here? (*looking at statue*). Oho! my princely self, eh? Upon my word, fairly good for a provincial town. In truth, a very public-spirited thing to have done. Governor Griffenfeld must have inspired this—upon my word, my heart softens towards the little scoundrel. But no—on second thoughts, *he* would have commissioned a caricature. (*Enter* CHRISTINA *with her guitar.*) Who is this? A dainty maiden indeed!

CHRIS. (*not seeing him*). It is a strange fascination that draws me hither! I have yet three principal streets, two squares, and the Castle Green to sing to—and they are all sure pay.—(*Puts down her guitar.*) Then how comes it that I find myself, every half hour, instinctively drifting towards the Market-place. It is not market-day, and there's nobody here except—(*looking at statue*) and if I sing to him he does not hear me, and if I talk to him I must needs talk for two. As thus: Good-morrow, my Lord. "Ah, Christina—hast thou done well to-day?" But indifferent well, my lord Prince, for I have taken naught and given all! "That were idly done, Christina. What hast thou given, and to whom?" My heart, my lord Prince, and to your Highness, for look you, I love you passing well—even I, who never loved a living man!

"Somewhat unmaidenly, this avowal—is it not, Christina?" It may seem so, my lord. "Thou shouldst have waited until I gave some sign." I might have waited long, my lord, for your Highness is strangely reticent; and I might have peaked, pined, dwindled, drooped, and died in the waiting. "That were pitiful indeed, Christina." I thank your lordship. Will you hear a poor ballad, my lord? "If it be fairly sung, Christina, and not too long." It is not long, my lord, and I will sing it with all my poor skill, so it shall please you. "Well, tune up, Christina—but I have no small change." I thank your Highness; I sing to you, not for your money, but for your love. The song runneth thus;—(*sees* REGENT, *who comes forward, offering her the guitar*) Oh, sir!

CHRIS. Ah!

[*Looks at statue, then at* REGENT, *and shows signs of terror.*

REG. Why, what is amiss with thee?

CHRIS. Sir, I am frightened! I thought at first—but I am a silly fool! I ask your pardon; but—you are so strangely like the Regent's statue, that, for the moment, I —oh, *who* are you?

REG. I am Nils Egilsson—a strolling player—a flotsam and jetsam on the world's tide—tossed hither and thither as the wild waves will; but come good, come ill, always at the service of all pretty maids who need my offices.

CHRIS. Then—you are not a prince?

REG. Not a prince? Oh, but I *am* a prince—very often! Every prince in turn from Nebuchadnezzar down to Louis the Sixteenth, when an engagement offers. A trifle out of repair just now, but even your theatrical princes have their vicissitudes, and Elsinore is not stage struck. But times may mend, and who knows but that I shall yet play Hamlet on his native battlements?

CHRIS. Still, a real Prince——

REG. Is not to be envied, take my word for it. Why, the very fact that he can't show his nose out of doors without an everlasting accompaniment of National Anthem is enough to make him turn Revolutionist, and cry aloud for his own downfall!

SONG—REGENT

A King, though he's pestered with cares,
Though, no doubt, he can often trepan them;
But one comes in a shape he can never escape—
The implacable National Anthem!
Though for quiet and rest he may yearn,
It pursues him at every turn—
No chance of forsaking
Its *rococo* numbers;
They haunt him when waking—
They poison his slumbers!
Like the Banbury Lady, whom every one knows,
He's cursed with its music wherever he goes!
Though its words but imperfectly rhyme,
And the devil himself couldn't scan them,
With composure polite he endures day and night,
That illiterate National Anthem!
It serves a good purpose I own:
Its strains are devout and impressive—
Its heartstirring notes raise a lump in our throats
As we burn with devotion excessive;

But the King, who's been bored by that song
From his cradle—each day—all day long—
Who's heard it loud-shouted
By throats operatic,
And loyally spouted
By courtiers emphatic—
By soldier—by sailor—by drum and by fife—
Small blame if he thinks it the plague of his life!
While his subjects sing loudly and long,
Their King—who would willingly ban them—
Sits, worry disguising, anathematizing
That Bogie, the National Anthem!

CHRIS. It is pleasant to know that we are of kindred lot, for if you are a strolling player, why I am but a poor ballad-singer, and our callings have much in common. I am at my ease now, but at first—you will laugh at me, I know—I almost thought I was speaking to the Regent himself!

REG. I have been given to understand that there is a certain resemblance.

CHRIS. It is marvellous! Do you know his Highness, sir? [*Anxiously.*

REG. Well, I can scarcely say. We have never met, face to face.

CHRIS. (*disappointed*). Then you do *not* know him.

REG. Very good—then I do *not* know him: but—I know his tailor.

CHRIS. His tailor?

REG. Yes. I frequently see his tailor, and his tailor tells me, in strictest confidence, that (*impressively*) his Highness is *at least three inches more round the waist* than he is here represented to be! So be prepared for a disappointment!

CHRIS. (*laughing*). Why, sir, I believe there is nothing in this wide world that concerns me less than the measure of his Highness's waist! Such a trifle weighs but little with me.

REG. (*aside*). It weighs a good deal with *me!* (*Aloud.*) And do you pass much time in the society of his Highness's effigy?

CHRIS. Why, in truth, much more than is prudent.

REG. Oh, *he* won't hurt you—I should say that you were quite safe with *him*. But beware of the Regent himself, for men say that he is a terrible Turk!

CHRIS. The Regent, sir, is nought to me. Yet, to speak truly, I am loth to believe that there can be aught but good in one whom that statue so strongly resembles!

REG. Then—I may take it that you do not believe there is much of evil in me?

CHRIS. (*confused*). Why, sir—in truth—nay, this is scarcely fair dealing. I spake not of yourself, but of the Regent.

REG. And I so strongly resemble him!

CHRIS. I think, sir, I will go.

REG. Nay, be not angry with me for drawing so pleasant a conclusion from premises of your own making! (*Tenderly.*) I would fain hope that you are not angry with me.

CHRIS. Nay, sir, I am not angry. I spake foolishly, and I am well served. But I have tarried too long; I have to go to the Castle Green—I am to sing there.

REG. Why, I am likewise bound thither, for I have to see the Governor. (*Tenderly.*) Who knows but that we may meet again!

CHRIS. (*moved*). It is very like. (*Recovering herself.*) But the day is speeding, and I have to sing for my supper. So fare you well, Master ——!

REG. Nils Egilsson. (*Kissing her hand.*)

CHRIS. (*dreamily*). Nils Egilsson: I shall not forget that name, be very sure! [*Exit* CHRISTINA.

REG. Well, as a bachelor heir-apparent, I've had a tolerably comprehensive experience of young ladies; but of all the maids I ever met, this is the fairest, the most winning, and the most original! What a refreshing experience! It's like the breath of the hay-field after a season of hot ball-rooms! We shall meet again, my pretty ballad-singer, unless I greatly err. And now to encounter this precious Governor.

Enter GOVERNOR GRIFFENFELD

GRIF. The Syndic has received his charmer's letter, and

he's on the tip-toe of expectation and delight. I shall get rid of her—I shall get rid of her!

REG. Not knowing the lady, but speaking on general principles, I should say that you couldn't do better.

GRIF. Hallo, sir, who are you to presume to convert into a duologue that which was intended for a soliloquy?

REG. I'm Nils Egilsson—strolling player—sadly out of repair, and greatly in need of a handsome salary, paid weekly in advance.

GRIF. A professional rogue, eh?

REG. Well—a technical rogue—much as a lawyer is a technical gentleman—that is to say, by Act of Parliament.

GRIF. You pipe to a sharp note, sir. We keep a cage for such gaol-birds as you. (*Aside.*) Where have I seen this fellow's face?

REG. Well, I think I sing best behind bars.

GRIF. (*aside*). Where have I seen this fellow's face?

REG. Surely you're not the Governor?

GRIF. Yes, sir, I am the Governor of this Province.

REG. A thousand pardons! I took you for the borough constable. A hasty conclusion based upon a commendable absence of that superficial polish which the vulgar are but too apt to associate with the conception of a gentleman. The Governor! (*Bowing.*) A worshipful gentleman, I'll be sworn, appearances notwithstanding. A thousand pardons!

GRIF. (*who, during this speech, has been studying the* REGENT's *face*). I have it! It's the statue! Why, he's marvellously like it! (*Aloud.*) Hark ye, sirrah! you are an actor, you say?

REG. A poor actor.

GRIF. Ready at a moment's notice to play any part that may be entrusted to you? Kings, princes, and so forth?

REG. Why, I'm famous for my kings. There's an air of aristocratic impudence about me—you may have remarked it—which is eminently suited to your monarchs of genteel comedy. My tyrants, too, are much admired. "What, bearded to our face, and by a very boy? The moat is dry—load him with chains, and stifle him in its reeking mud! Ha! ha! I *will* be obeyed!"

GRIF. Yes—that's not good, you know. Rather amateurish, I should say. Played a long engagement in the Theatre Royal Back Drawing Room, I should imagine. By the way, have you ever heard it remarked that you bear a close resemblance to a very dignified personage?

REG. Eh? Oh, you mean the man who mends boots on the quay. That's very likely—he's my aunt.

GRIF. The man who mends fiddlesticks!

REG. I don't think I know him.

GRIF. No, sir—not to the man who mends boots—to no less a person than the Prince Regent of Denmark.

REG. The Prince Regent?

GRIF. There he is. He's a common-looking fellow, and you are singularly like him. [*Pointing to statue.*

REG. You flatter me, I'm sure (*looking at statue*). Well, some fellows have the deuce's own luck. Here is a man—the heir to a throne—caressed, courted, and flattered by the highest in the land—pampered with every luxury that the ingenuity of the devil or man can devise—and, hang me! if, in addition to all this, he isn't exactly like me! It's enough to turn the fellow's head!

GRIF. He's an ugly fellow, sir, and so are you. Therein lies the chief resemblance. Now attend to me. If you will consent to personate His Highness for twenty-four hours, acting exactly as I shall prescribe to you, you shall have—well, you shall have five golden Friedrichs!

REG. Five golden Friedrichs!

GRIF. Then you consent?

REG. Consent? What is there that I wouldn't consent to for five golden Friedrichs? But my dress—it's a convenient outfit for summer weather; but not, I should say, what the Regent of Denmark would wear—except, perhaps, in the bosom of his family after the cares of State are over for the day.

GRIF. I've provided for that. The sculptor of that statue borrowed a left-off suit of the Regent's from His Highness's valet—for artistic purposes. It's now at the Castle, packed up, ready to be returned. I should say it would fit you to a nicety.

REG. (*aside*). I've not the least doubt of it. When am I to begin?

GRIF. To-morrow morning. It'll be great fun!

REG. It will be a tremendous joke.

GRIF. So original! With such possibilities! Fancy—a sham Regent dispensing sham wealth and sham honours untold on all my sham friends—and then their disappointment when they discover that it's only my fun!

REG. Ha! ha! I'm longing to begin!

[*During the last few lines,* CHRISTINA *has entered. She listens, concealed behind statue.*

DUET—REGENT *and* GRIFFENFELD

REG. I've grasped your scheme, if I may say as much without intrusion:
As Regent-Prince I must ennoble all without exclusion,
And scatter honours all around in liberal profusion—
Then you'll step in and, with a word, dispel the fond illusion!

GRIF. Then I'll step in—
REG. Then you'll step in—
GRIF. And with a word—
REG. And with a word—
Then you'll step in and, with a word, dispel the fond illusion!

GRIF. (*excitedly*). Exactly so! exactly so! exactly so! exactly so!
For understand what I require—
Give every man his heart's desire,
Then I'll explain the ins and out—
In half an hour or thereabouts!

BOTH. Then {I'll / you'll} explain the ins and outs—
In half an hour or thereabouts!

ENSEMBLE

Oh, human joy at best is brief—
Alas, too soon it's turned to grief!
So it's our duty, you'll allow,
Our fellow creatures to endow
With happiness complete and vast—

REG. Although that happiness may last—
GRIF. Although that happiness may last—
BOTH. But half an hour or thereabouts!
But half an hour—
But half an hour—
But half an hour or thereabouts!
[*Exit* GRIFFENFELD.

CHRIS. (*coming forward from behind statue*).
I overheard!
REG. You did? Confusion!
But not a word
Of this delusion—
No single phrase—
No faint suggestion—
To haply raise
A doubt or question!

If fault or blunder visible
I make in this experiment—
Control your muscles risible,
And check untimely merriment.
Address me most respectfully—
Regard with silent shyness me—
With eyes cast down subjectively;—
And mind you "Royal Highness" me!
Now don't forget—now don't forget,
Be sure you "Royal Highness" me!

CHRIS. With all devotion beautiful,
I'll favour your expedient—
I'll be your very dutiful—
I'll be your most obedient—
You'll find me all docility,
You miracle of slyness, you!
I'll curtsey with humility,
And always "Royal Highness" you!
I won't forget—I won't forget—
I'll always "Royal Highness" you!

ENSEMBLE

Oh, never was seen
Such a pearl of a Prince,

With {his / my} dignified mien
He is / I am } sure to convince:
In {his / my} gracious address
There is Royalty shown—
And a baby could guess
He's / I'm } the heir to a throne!
Ha! ha! ha! ha!—Ha! ha! ha! ha!
Oh a baby could guess he's the heir to a throne!
[*Exit in opposite directions.*

Enter the SYNDIC, *with* DAME CORTLANDT'S *letter in his hand*

SYN. It's a singular thing, but I never yet proposed to a very unattractive old lady without being immediately accepted. Now here is an unattractive old lady—about to be married to no less a personage than the Governor of this Province, and I have only to beckon to her, and down comes the confiding, old dove with no further thought about the governor, except to stipulate that her change of intention shall be kept a secret from him for the present! Here comes the old dear, true to the appointment of her own making. How—how rich she looks, to be sure!

Enter DAME CORTLANDT

DAME (*bashfully*). Master Munck—I—I ventured to send you a letter this morning.

SYN. A most delightful letter, and one that, believe me, I shall prize while I live!

DAME (*surprised*). You are vastly obliging! (*Aside.*) Collecting autographs, I suppose. (*Aloud.*) Now, you will understand that, for the reasons explained in my letter, I am most anxious that the subject of our conversation shall be kept a profound secret.

SYN. Madam, I will be most careful. You—you are the discreetest little gipsy in Denmark!

DAME. Sir!

SYN. Quite right—can't be too cautious, even between ourselves. I quite grasp the idea.

DAME (*aside*). He is singularly effusive for a confidential family lawyer! (*Aloud.*) I daresay that you are aware that I am well to do.

SYN. Well, I certainly have heard that Dame Cortlandt is a lady of some means—but oh, she does her lover a grave injustice if she imagines that he allowed a mercenary consideration to influence him.

DAME (*surprised*). Why, of course I know that!

SYN. Such a dainty, tight, trim, bewitching little rogue requires no——

DAME (*suddenly furious*). Eh? What's that? I'm a little rogue! This man presumes to tell *me* that I am a little rogue!

SYN. But, my dear lady—

DAME. Don't speak—they're fighting it out—they're fighting it out!

SYN. Bless my heart, how very interesting!

DAME (*having swallowed her anger—severely*). It's all right, Master Munck, and, for the moment, the Tempter is floored, but don't try that again. Perhaps—perhaps we had better discuss my affairs at another time—when you have slept it off, whatever it is.

SYN. No, don't go—let me gaze a little longer on—(DAME *about to break out.*) I didn't say it! I didn't say it! I stopped in time!

DAME (*aside*). He's very eccentric for a confidential family lawyer! (*Aloud.*) I wish you to take instructions about the settlements on the occasion of—(*bashfully*) my forthcoming marriage.

SYN. My dear lady! [*Takes out notebook.*

DAME. There are my two freehold farms, the three houses in Dentheim, and twelve thousand rix-dollars in Government securities. I wish to settle all this, absolutely, on my dear husband.

SYN. What, all!!!

DAME. Every penny.

SYN. Dearest! (DAME *about to break out again.* SYNDIC *checks himself.*) I didn't say it! I didn't say it! I thought it, but I didn't say it!

DUET—DAME *and* SYNDIC

DAME. Now all that we've agreed upon, O—
And all that's passed between us—
No human soul must know,
Be he a friend or foe.

SYN. You lean no broken reed upon, O—
In Courts of Law and Venus
(I've practised much in both)
I'm always on my oath!

DAME. What always?

SYN. Always!

DAME. Always?

SYN. Always!
Always on my oath!
You'll find I am
Discreetly dumb,
So trust me, ma'am—

DAME. The word is mum—

SYN. Of all I know
I'll give no clue,
You little ro—
guey poguey, you!
You little roguey poguey!

DAME (*indignantly*). Sir!

SYN. You little roguey poguey!

DAME. Sir!!

SYN. You roguey poguey, roguey poguey, roguey poguey!

DAME. Sir!!!

ENSEMBLE

DAME (*aside*)

Although of men's vulgarity, O—
I'm no unfair inquisitor,
I hate familiarity, O—
In a family solicitor!

SYNDIC (*aside*)

If called upon in charity, O—
To justify my visitor,
I'll quote my popularity, O—
As a family solicitor.

BOTH. As a family, family, family, family—
A family solicitor!

DAME. Your tone is not professional, O—
It's neither grave nor courtly:
Such lack of common-sense
Inspires no confidence.

SYN. By gradual steps progressional, O—
I'll reach the haven shortly;
But till that moment sweet
I'll never be indiscreet.

DAME. What never?
SYN. Never!
DAME. Never?
SYN. Never!
Never be indiscreet!

(*Dancing.*)
Those lips command,
And I obey,
Though close at hand,
The joyous day
When I may sip
Their honey dew—
You little pip—
sy wipsy you!
You little pipsy wipsy!
DAME. Sir!
SYN. You little pipsy wipsy!
DAME. Sir!!
SYN. You pipsy wipsy, pipsy wipsy, pipsy wipsy!
DAME. Sir!!!

ENSEMBLE

DAME (*aside*)
What sentiments transgressional! O—
It's bad, I've understood, for them,
When gentlemen professional, O—
Take more than is quite good for them!

SYNDIC (*aside*)
These gradual steps progressional, O—
Wait any time I would for them—
When gentlemen professional, O—
Gain widows rich, it's good for them!

BOTH. When gentlemen, gentlemen, gentlemen, gentlemen—
{Take more than is good for them!
{Widows gain, it's good for them!

[*Exeunt separately*

Enter ERLING SYKKE, *with large unopened official letter in his hand*

ERL. At last—the reply to my letter announcing to His Majesty the completion of the statue! Every hope and every fear of my life lies within the four corners of this document. What may it not contain? Perhaps an order on the King's Treasurer for my ten thousand rix-dollars! Perhaps my appointment as Court Sculptor! Perhaps even my patent of Countship! I tremble so that I can scarcely open it!

[NANNA *has entered at the back. She creeps up to him with suppressed fun in her face.*

NANNA. Oh, what a big letter! Whom is it from, and what's it all about?

ERL. Nanna, this letter is to seal your destiny and mine—so, as you are as much concerned with it as I am, I think we ought to open it together. It's—it's from the King's private secretary!

NANNA. Oh, do be quick and let's see what's in it!

ERL. You open it—I can't! (*Giving her the letter.*)

NANNA. *I* can. Now then—one! two! three!

[NANNA *opens it.*

ERL. Read—read!

NANNA (*looking at it*). Oh! I don't think you'll like it. Oh! I'm sure you won't like it! (*Reads.*) "Sir—In reply to a letter in which you announce the completion of a statue of His Royal Highness Prince Frederick, alleged by you to have been commissioned by His Majesty, I have to inform you that His Majesty knows nothing about it."

ERL. (*stunned*). Knows nothing about it!

NANNA. There seems to be some mistake.

ERL. Some mistake! Why, what do you mean?

NANNA. Why that, at the first blush, it bears the appearance of being one of dear papa's practical jokes.

ERL. But it's ruin! Absolute ruin! Why, I spent every penny I possessed on the marble alone!

NANNA. I'm so sorry!

ERL. Sorry! I can't realize it! It stuns me! It's too cruel—too cruel! And the promise you made me——

NANNA. Oh, the promise! Yes—es—the *conditional* promise.

ERL. Don't tell me that was a hoax too! Give me some hope to cling to! I can bear it all if you'll only tell me that *you* won't discard me!

NANNA. Really, it's extremely awkward; but one must be a little prudent. I'm a very expensive young lady, and as it seems that you have no immediate prospect of being able to maintain an establishment, it would be really criminal on my part to involve you in further embarrassments.

[ERLING *sinks helplessly on pedestal of statue, and buries his head in his hands.*

SONG—NANNA

My wedded life
Must every pleasure bring
On scale extensive!—
If I'm your wife
I must have everything
That's most expensive—
A lady's maid—
(My hair alone to do
I am not able)—
And I'm afraid
I've been accustomed to
A first-rate table.
These things one must consider when one marries—
And everything I wear must come from Paris!
Oh, think of that!
Oh, think of that!
I can't wear anything that's not from Paris!
From top to toes
Quite Frenchified I am,
If you examine.
And then—who knows?—
Perhaps some day a fam—
Perhaps a famine!
My argument's correct, if you examine,
What should we do, if there should come a f-famine!
Though in green pea
Yourself you needn't stint

In July sunny,
In Januaree
It really costs a mint—
A mint of money!
No lamb for us—
House lamb at Christmas sells
At prices handsome:
Asparagus,
In winter, parallels
A Monarch's ransom.
When purse to bread and butter barely reaches,
What is your wife to do for hot-house peaches?
Ah! tell me that!
Ah! tell me that!
What is your wife to do for hot-house peaches?
Your heart and hand
Though at my feet you lay,
All others scorning!
As matters stand,
There's nothing else to say
Except—good morning!
Though virtue be a husband's best adorning,
That won't pay rates and taxes—so, good morning!
[*Exit* NANNA.

ERL. Cruel, cold calculating girl! What on earth am I to do? Ruin and desolation stare me in the face!

Enter TORTENSSEN *in great excitement, with an open letter in his hand*

TOR. Erling! I am tricked, swindled, undone! I have just received a letter from the King's secretary to say that my appointment is a hoax! I've sold my local practice, let my house, and Thora repudiates me with indignation and contempt!

ERL. Again the Governor's doing! I, also, have just learnt that the commission for the Regent's statue is a heartless fabrication, and I, too, am ruined—utterly and completely ruined!

TOR. My poor Erling!

ERL. But this is no time for idle regrets. A term must be put to this scoundrel's practices. We will call the people together, tell them of the infamous trick that has been played upon us, and then away to Copenhagen to lay the whole matter before the Regent himself!

TOR. We will, we will!

FINALE

ERL. *and* TOR.

Come hither, every one,
Come hither, all!
Let every mother's son
Obey our call!
Come hither in your might,
In stern parade,
And learn the deadly slight
Upon you played!

During this the Chorus, CHRISTINA, HAROLD, *and* BLANCA *have entered*

ALL.
Why, who the deuce has dared to play
A trick, at Elsinore, to-day?
Come, tell us quick,
This scurvy trick,
Why, who the deuce has dared to play?

ERL. (*passionately*). That statue—who commissioned it?

ALL. The King!
ERL. And on that spot positioned it?
ALL. The King!
Court sculptor who created me,
And told me rank awaited me,
Which pleased you and elated me?
ALL. The King!
TOR. (*furiously*). Who raised me from obscurity?
ALL. The King!
TOR. And gilded my futurity?
ALL. The King!
TOR. Physician who appointed me?
With baron's rank anointed me,
Till foolish pride disjointed me?
ALL. The King!
The King he did and said it all,
He did this noble thing!
Give him the fame and credit all,
His Majesty the King!
God save the King!
Hurrah!
ERL. A lie! No monarch honoured you by honouring us,
Or for that cursed statue gave commission;
No monarch with perception generous,
Appointed Tortenssen his Court Physician!
No royal sunlight on our labours shone—
You have been cheated, tricked, and played upon!
ALL. We have been cheated, tricked, and played upon?
Oh, shame!
Who is the culprit? We've no time for trifling!
With choking indignation we are stifling!

Enter DAME CORTLANDT *in a towering rage, followed by* SYNDIC, *who tries in vain to appease her*

DAME. The truth's revealed, the mystery dispelled—
The culprit is—the Governor Griffenfeld!
He doesn't confine to lowly folks
His base barbarian dealings,

But dares to play his practical jokes
  Upon *my* tenderest feelings!
Assuming that for you I glowed (*to* SYNDIC),
  You Syndical mountebank, you!
He—(*symptoms of an approaching outbreak*).

ALL. Pray be careful or you'll explode!

DAME (*with an effort*). I'm keeping it under, thank you!

ALL. Hurrah! Hurrah! Hurrah! Hurrah!
  She's keeping it under! thank you!

DAME. Henceforth I vow, with hate intense,
  To crush that Governor pagan!
Whatever the cost, at my expense,
  We'll go to Copenhagen.
There to the Regent we'll complain,
  In volleys of vocal thunder—

[*Further symptoms of an outbreak.*

ALL. Now steady, or you'll be off again!

DAME (*with an effort*). All right, I'm keeping it under!

ALL. Brava! Brava! Brava! Brava!
  Dame Cortlandt's keeping it under!

Enter GRIFFENFELD, NANNA, *and* THORA

ALL. Ah!
Here's the monkey undiscerning,
Who, all thought of mercy spurning,
Dares with men of light and learning
  Thus to play the pranksome fool!
Launch at him our loudest thunder—
Tear him limb from limb asunder!
Long enough we've suffered under
  His detested monkey-rule!

GRIF. What means this uproar which my comfort
  shatters!
Explain, I beg! Are ye March hares, or hatters?

DAME. No madmen we—but matters not to mince,
  To Copenhagen we depart,
  With rage and fury in each heart,
To interview our sovereign Regent-Prince!

GRIF. The Regent?

ALL. Aye, the Regent!

GRIF. Not so loud.
Be pacified, I beg, excited crowd!
This state of indignation do not foment—
The Regent's here, in Elsinore, at this moment!
ALL. The Regent here!
GRIF., NANNA, *and* THORA. In Elsinore at this moment!

TRIO—GOVERNOR, NANNA, *and* THORA

After a travelling troublesome,
Quit of the Court and the quality—
Weary of bobbery bubblesome,
Weary of party and polity,
Full of jolly jocosity,
Out of the pale of propriety—
Hating the pride of pomposity—
Sick of that sort of society,
Regent is resting his brain
Here is our little domain! (*repeat*)
Seeking a time of tranquillity,
Free from all fear of formality,
Finds it in jolly gentility
Here in this lovely locality—
Doffing all duty and dignity
(Follies that fidget him fearfully),
Vows that our merry malignity
Favours his chirrupping cheerfully—
Vows he'll again and again
Visit our little domain! (*repeat*)
ALL. Seeking a time of tranquillity, etc.

[GRIFFENFELD, NANNA, *and* THORA *dancing through this.*

CHORUS. This is our chance to explain—
Tell of our sorrow and pain!

SEXTET

ERLING, TORTENSSEN, SYNDIC, HAROLD, CHRISTINA, *and* DAME CORTLANDT

HAR. This is our opportunity—
It may not come again.
GRIF., NANNA, *and* THORA (*in affected terror*). No, no!
ER. To lay bare with impunity
Our misery and pain.

GRIF., NANNA, *and* THORA (*in affected terror*). No, no!
TORT. We'll beg, with due severity,
His speedy punishment.
GRIF., NANNA, *and* THORA (*in affected terror*). No, no!
THE SIX. And that with all celerity
To gaol he might be sent!
GRIF., NANNA, *and* THORA (*in affected terror*). No, no!
No, no! not that; avert our doom!
Why it would be our ruin!
Can you resist when we assume
This attitude to sue in. (*Kneeling—repeat.*)
ALL. Yes, yes!
Ha! ha!
Yes, yes!
Ha! ha!
We can resist though you assume
That attitude to sue in!

[*Laughing derisively at* GRIFFENFELD *and* DAUGHTERS.

Ha, ha! ha, ha! ha, ha! ha, ha!
GRIF. *and* DAUGHTERS (*as if crying*). Ho, ho! ho, ho! &c.
GRIF. Oh, pray have mercy! Do not pour
Upon a hapless Governor,
Who treads a rather devious path,
The vials of your mighty wrath!
NANNA *and* THORA. Oh, pray you be magnanimous,
'Twill ruin him and ruin us—
In sheer good humour it was done—
Oh, haven't you any sense of fun?
ALL THREE. Oh, haven't you any sense of fun?
Oh, haven't you any sense of fun?
(*pretending to cry.*)

THORA. Ah, don't be hard on one whose passion ruling
Was, from his birth, a taste for April fooling!
ALL THREE. Ah, don't be hard, &c.
ERL. *and* TOR. Go, traitress, go!
Of such a foe
I scorn the vain appeal.
With rage I fume!
Your father's doom
This day the Prince shall seal.

In vain you cry,
And sob and sigh,
In vain you kneel, I say!

GRIF., NANNA, and THORA. Oh, pity me, pity me, pity me, pity me,
Pity me, pity me, pray!

CHORUS. Of all that's mean
And vile, I ween,
In an underhand way,
Epitome-pitome-pitome-pitome-pitome-pitome-they!

ENSEMBLE

ALL (*except* GRIFFENFELD, NANNA, *and* THORA)

Shall we endure this outrage, say?
Are we but toys to serve his whim?
Is he on heartstrings thus to play,
As may, perchance, seem good to him?

GRIFFENFELD, NANNA, *and* THORA (*aside*)

When a Governor triumphs through quibble and quiddity,
He may employ with a cheerful avidity,
Any amount of tol-lol-the-rol liddity,
Tol-the-rol, lol-the-rol, lol-the-rol-lay.

ALL. To the Regent, away!

GRIF., NANNA, *and* THORA. Tol-the-rol-the-rol-lay!

ALL. To the Regent, away!

GRIF., NANNA, *and* THORA. Tol-the-rol-the-rol-lay!

ALL. To the Regent—the Regent—the Regent, away!

GRIF., NANNA, *and* THORA. Tol-the-rol-the-rol, lol-the-rol, lol-the-rol-lay.

[*All rush up furiously, except* CHRISTINA, *who remains laughing up stage, and* GRIFFENFELD, NANNA, *and* THORA, *who sink, exhausted with laughter, on seat at foot of statue.*

END OF ACT I

ACT II

SCENE.—*The Castle Court-yard.* ERLING, TORTENSSEN, SYNDIC, DAME CORTLANDT, CHRISTINA, *and Chorus of men and girls discovered. A sentry is mounting guard on the Castle gate.*

OPENING CHORUS

With anger stern
And fierce determination,
We wait to learn
The fate of our appeal.
To Regent just
We've given information,
And this, we trust,
The tyrant's doom will seal.

ERL. This mite of a man who'll plot and plan
To ruin us all for his delight—
TOR. The mannikin ape in human shape—
DAME. This tuppenny ha'penny lump of spite!
ALL. This tuppenny ha'penny, tuppenny ha'-penny,
Tuppenny ha'penny lump of spite!

[CHRISTINA *comes forward.*

RECIT—CHRISTINA

Be comforted—his downfall I foresee,
All who exceed the bounds of strict simplicity,
And, yielding to a taste for eccentricity,
Fly in the face of orthodox morality,
Must dearly pay for their originality—
You know the story of the wilful bee?

ALL. (*furiously*). We don't! We never heard it!

ERL. Who was he?

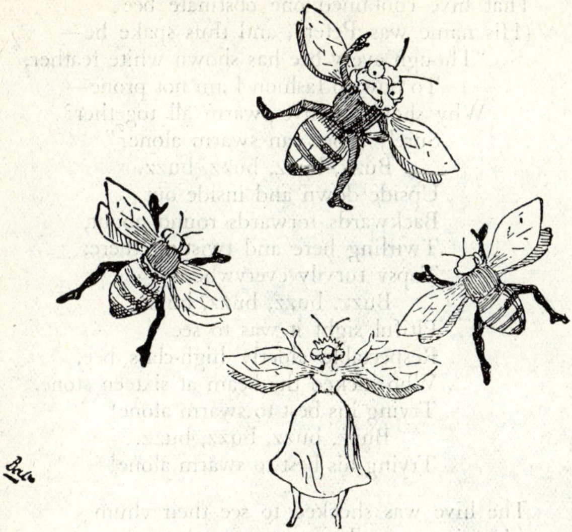

SONG—CHRISTINA. (*Guitar accompaniment*)

A hive of bees, as I've heard say,
Said to their Queen one sultry day—
"Please, your Majesty's high position,
The hive is full and the weather is warm.
We rather think, with a due submission,
The time has come when we ought to swarm?"
Buzz, buzz, buzz, buzz.
Outspake their Queen, and thus spake she—
"This is a matter that rests with me,
Who dares opinions thus to form?
I'll tell you when it is time to swarm!"
Buzz, buzz, buzz, buzz.
Her Majesty wore an angry frown,
In fact Her Majesty's foot was down—
Her Majesty sulked—declined to sup—
In short Her Majesty's back was up.
Buzz, buzz, buzz, buzz.
Her foot was down and her back was up!

That hive contained one obstinate bee
(His name was Peter), and thus spake he—
"Though every bee has shown white feather,
To bow to fashion I am not prone—
Why should a hive swarm all together?
Surely a bee can swarm alone?"
Buzz, buzz, buzz, buzz.
Upside down and inside out,
Backwards forwards round about,
Twirling here and twisting there,
Topsy turvily everywhere—
Buzz, buzz, buzz, buzz.
Pitiful sight it was to see
Respectable elderly high-class bee,
Who kicked the beam at sixteen stone,
Trying his best to swarm alone!
Buzz, buzz, buzz, buzz.
Trying his best to swarm alone!

The hive was shocked to see their chum
(A strict teetotaller) teetotum—
The Queen exclaimed, "How terrible, very!
It's perfectly clear to all the throng
Peter's been at the old brown sherry.
Old brown sherry is much too strong—
Buzz, buzz, buzz, buzz.
Of all who thus themselves degrade
A stern example must be made,
To Coventry go, you tipsy bee!"
So off to Coventry town went he.
Buzz, buzz, buzz, buzz.

There, classed with all who misbehave,
Both plausible rogue and noisome knave,
In dismal dumps he lived to own
The folly of trying to swarm alone!
Buzz, buzz, buzz, buzz.
All came of trying to swarm alone.

CHORUS. All came of trying to, &c.

Enter MATS MUNCK *from Castle*

ALL. Well, well—what news?
Does he refuse
Our rightful dues?
What news—what news?

MATS. Good news! the Regent, whom we all revere,
Will read your neatly drawn appeal—
(I drew it!)
Without an hour's delay he'll meet you here,
And if we prove our case the Governor'll rue it!

ALL. Hurrah!

MATS. If these our charges home we bring,
He swears the Governor's neck he'll wring;
And when he says he'll do a thing,
He'll do it!

ALL. Hurrah!
The sorrows that damped our lives are past,
And happily all will end at last.
As soon as the audience has been held,
Good-bye to the Governor Griffenfeld!
MEN. Good-bye!
GIRLS. Good-bye!
MEN. Good-bye!
GIRLS. Good-bye!
ALL. Good-bye to the Governor Griffenfeld!

Enter NANNA *and* THORA. *They come forward humbly*

ERL. *and* TORT. (*recit.*). Ah, false one!
THORA. With humbled head—in desperation dire—
I tidings bring from my repentant sire.
He much regrets his foolish whim—
NANNA. And hopes you'll intercede for him;
For, though his gore at retractation rises,
He's very sorry—and apologizes,
THORA. He can't say more—
BOTH. He's very sorry—and apologizes!
ERL *and* TOR. Be comforted—I can't resist that tear!
At once I'll seek our Sovereign Prince's ear,
And tell him—though our future you destroy it—
I don't mind ruination—I enjoy it!

Enter GRIFFENFELD *from Castle*

GRIF. (*humbly*). Complying with the popular request,
So prettily expressed—
SYN. (*aside*). I drew it!
GRIF. The Regent comes—forgive our little plot—
Our penitence, do not
Pooh pooh it!
NANNA. If still to press your grievance you agree,
Then I feel certain we
Shall rue it!
THORA. So please withdraw, as we are penitent,
That well-worn document!
SYN. (*aside*). I drew it!
ALL. No, no; no mercy will we show—
Away with you! you plead in vain!
No word of ours shall stop the blow;
Your prayer we will not entertain!

Flourish. Enter REGENT

PRINCIPALS *and* CHORUS. Hail, O Regent Prince,
Coming to requite us!
Matters not to mince,
You will nobly right us.
Your disgust evince—
Make the tyrant wince—
Hail, O Sovereign Prince,
Whose decrees delight us!

RECIT—REGENT

I've read your dutiful memorial:
If any other for reprisals call,
Or, suffering grievance, wish me to abate it.
This is your opportunity to state it.
HAR. (*recit.*). May it please your Highness!

AIR

HAR. Though we're eager for to sally
To the doughty field of Mars—
SOLDIERS. May it please your Royal Highness!
HAR. And encounter, generally,
Any quantity of scars—

SOLDIERS. May it please your Royal Highness!
HAR. Yet for mischief, principally,
He has turned us into ballet,
And we feel it personally—
It is rough on brave Hussars!
REG. Yes, it's rough on brave Hussars!
ALL. Yes, you're right, your Royal Highness, it is rough on brave Hussars!
HAR. If we urge, in accents courtly,
That it wounds our proper pride—
SOLDIERS. May it please your Royal Highness!
HAR. Why, he answers as retortly,
And for mutiny we're tried—
SOLDIERS. May it please your Royal Highness!
HAR. We are soldiers grave and portly,
And it aggravates us mort'lly,
For, to put the matter shortly,
Well, it is not dignified!
ALL. No, it isn't dignified!
REG. No, it isn't dignified!
ALL. Look at this, your Royal Highness—it is far from dignified!

BALLET OF HUSSARS

SONG—REGENT.

My people, who've submitted to the Governor's absurdities,
I sympathize most heartily with every word you say;
His Excellency's conduct is too bad—upon my word it is—
But all his wrong I'll rectify without undue delay.
On Erling, who has suffered from his mischievous malignity,
We shed the sunny summer of our Sovereign benignity,
And ratify all promises of dollars and of dignity.
So consequently Nanna will be his this very day.
ALL. So consequently Nanna will be his this very day.

ENSEMBLE

REGENT (*aside to* GRIF.)

Your orders I am trying to obey,
I hope I don't exceed in any way;
For so nobly you array me,
So magnificently pay me,
That your orders I am anxious to obey.

GRIF. (*aside to* REGENT)

My orders you implicitly obey,
Proceed with perfect certainty you may;
Now unmercifully flay me,
And with punishment dismay me.
Or my orders you will surely disobey.

ERLING (*aside*)

Oh, Nanna will be mine this very day,
And all my sorrows hide themselves away;
For the trick he dared to play me,
It will handsomely repay me,
If Miss Nanna will be mine this very day.

NANNA (*aside*)

It's fortunate that this is all in play.
I shouldn't like to marry him today;
It would terrible dismay be,
If he really came to claim me,
It is lucky that it's only said in play.

THORA, *Other Principals and Chorus*

Oh, Nanna will be his this very day,
And all his sorrows hide themselves away;
I will handsomely array me
In my very best to play me,
For Miss Nanna will be his this very day!

REGENT

You, Tortenssen,—whom Griffenfeld with impudent audacity
Appointed our Physician—why, that gift is ratified
With promised rank of Baron—in that dignified capacity
He's warranted in claiming pretty Thora as his bride.
And Harold, gallant Corporal, whom with a spite oppressional,
Was made to twist and turn about like ballet-girl professional,
Dispensing with the many intermediate steps progressional,
A Colonel he's created at one mighty giant stride!

ALL. A Colonel he's created at one mighty giant stride!

ENSEMBLE

REGENT (*aside to* GRIF.)

I trust your Excellency's satisfied,
To carry out your wishes I have tried—
If I haven't acted rightly
You will mention it politely,
But I trust your Excellency's satisfied.

GRIF. (*aside to* REGENT)

So far, my Excellency's satisfied,
To carry out my wishes you have tried;
When you fail to do it rightly
I will mention it politely,
But, so far, my Excellency's satisfied.

HAROLD *and* TORTENSSEN

Upon my word, I'm truly gratified,
To justify your choice will be my pride;
For I think you've chosen rightly,
And I thank you most politely,
For, upon my word, I'm truly gratified.

THORA (*aside*)

If he thinks that I intend to be his bride,
He'll find it a mistake unqualified,
If I know my feelings rightly,
I will thank him most politely,
And decline, on any terms, to be his bride.

Other Principals and Chorus

Upon my word, we're truly gratified,
To justify your choice will be their pride;
For we think you've chosen rightly,
And we thank you most politely,
For, upon my word, we're truly gratified.

REGENT

And now for Governor Griffenfeld—we highly to extol you meant,
But finding you're addicted to discreditable pranks,
We strip you of your dignity, position, and emolument,
And name Mats Munck as Governor—we don't want any thanks.
And, as in these proceedings we are banded all in unity,
I think we couldn't find a more convenient opportunity
Of proving that imposture can't be practised with impunity.

(*To* GRIFFENFELD.)

For all your impositions you're degraded to the ranks!

ALL. For all his impositions he's degraded to the ranks!

ENSEMBLE

REG. (*aside to* GRIF.)

I think I have done exactly as you said,
I am sure I hope I haven't been misled;
When I receive my payment,
I'll surrender all this raiment,
And resume my old habiliments instead.

GRIF. (*aside to* REG.)

You've done it pretty nearly as I've said,
If you hadn't you'd have sacrificed your head.
You shall now receive your payment,
So take off that handsome raiment,
And resume your old habiliments instead.

SYNDIC

Now really this is like to turn my head,
For I'm to rule as Governor instead!
When I get my quarter's payment,
I'll buy all his left-off raiment,
And it's possible Dame Cortlandt I may wed.

NANNA *and* THORA (*aside to each other*)

Did you hear what that audacious fellow said?
My goodness, how exceedingly ill-bred!
Let us give the man his payment,
Then he'll doff his splendid raiment,
And resume his own habiliments instead.

CHORUS, *and other Principals*

Assuredly there's nothing to be said,
He's lucky in escaping with his head!
He loses all his payment,
And his most expensive raiment,
And he'll take his turn at sentry-go instead!

REG. Now all you men and maidens true,
Who troth have duly plighted—
(I understand you're not a few)
Your wrongs shall all be righted
At his expense a banquet to
You're cordially invited.
And in the Castle Chapel you
This day shall be united!

ALL. Hurrah!
(*all dancing*) Oh, bright delight—go, find a priest!
The wedding and the wedding feast,
At your expense, will soon be held—
So thank you, Private Griffenfeld!
Ha, ha, ha, ha, etc.
At your expense they will be held,
Three cheers for Private Griffenfeld!

ALL. So thank you—
GRIF. Thank you—
ALL. Thank you—
GRIF. Thank you—
ALL. Thank you, Private Griffenfeld!

[*All dance off in couples, except* GRIFFENFELD *and* REGENT.

REG. (*changing his manner—very humbly*). I trust I've fairly carried out your Excellency's instructions?

GRIF. You've done pretty well, sir—only pretty well!

REG. May I ask in what respect I have failed?

GRIF. Your manner is not sufficiently dignified for a Royal Prince—you want a great deal more of this sort of thing—(*business*)—you are not at all Royal, sir!

REG. I see what you mean. (*Imitating him.*) Thank you, I'm sure—it will be most useful to me in my profession, and I'll take care to remember it. But pray bear in mind that, as a poor stroller, I have not enjoyed your Excellency's many opportunities of making myself acquainted with the deportment of the very highest classes.

GRIF. True, but I told you this afternoon that you must endeavour to assume an air of—of this sort of thing—(*business*). Then again, your instructions were to order me to be shot in twenty-four hours. Why didn't you do that?

REG. Well, I was about to give the order, but when I saw the temper of the people and how cordially you are detested—most unjustly, I'm sure—I was afraid to do so lest, in their fury, they should execute the order on the spot.

GRIF. I see what you mean.

REG. I might not have had time to stop them.

GRIF. Very true.

REG. But it's not too late—they can be sent for directly and the order given, without delay. (*About to go off.*)

GRIF. No—on second thoughts it's not necessary. It will do as it is.

REG. I trust you think I exercised a wise discretion?

GRIF. Well, on the whole, perhaps yes. I say—it's—it's a good joke, isn't it?

REG. It's a perfect monument of practical humour. Only—forgive the suggestion—isn't it a little risky?

GRIF. Risky? What do you mean?

REG. Somehow these practical jokes have such a tendency to recoil on the heads of their perpetrators. Now, mere verbal humour is so much safer—a quip, a crank, a jibe, jape or jest——

GRIF. Nonsense, sir, don't talk to me about japes and jests! Return to the Castle, and when you've resumed your rags, I will pay you the golden Friedrichs I promised you. Be off!

REG. As your Excellency pleases.

[*Exit* REGENT *into Castle.*

GRIF. What does he mean about practical jokes recoiling on their perpetrator? I ought to know. I've played them with impunity for five-and-forty years! It's all very well to talk about verbal humour, but where is it to come from? Why, everything of the kind has been said—there's absolutely nothing left!

SONG—GRIFFENFELD

Quixotic is his enterprise, and hopeless his adventure is,
  Who seeks for jocularities that haven't yet been said.
The world has joked incessantly for over fifty centuries,
  And every joke that's possible has long ago been made.
I started as a humourist with lots of mental fizziness,
  But humour is a drug which it's the fashion to abuse;
For my stock in trade, my fixtures, and the goodwill of
    the business
  No reasonable offer I am likely to refuse.
      And if anybody choose
      He may circulate the news
  That no reasonable offer I am likely to refuse.

Oh happy was that humourist—the first that made a
    pun at all—
  Who when a joke occurred to him, however poor and
    mean,
Was absolutely certain that it never had been done at
    all—
  How popular at dinners must that humourist have
    been!

Oh the days when some stepfather for the query held a
handle out,
The door-mat from the scraper, is it distant very far?
And when no one knew where Moses was when Aaron
put the candle out,
And no one had discovered that a door could be a-jar!

But your modern hearers are
In their tastes particular,
And they sneer if you inform them that a door can
be a-jar!

In search of quip and quiddity I've sat all day, alone,
apart—
And all that I could hit on as a problem was—to find
Analogy between a scrag of mutton and a Bony-part,
Which offers slight employment to the speculative
mind:
For you cannot call it very good, however great your
charity—
It's not the sort of humour that is greeted with a
shout—

And I've come to the conclusion that the mine of jocularity,
In present Anno Domini, is worked completely out!
Though the notion you may scout,
I can prove beyond a doubt
That the mine of jocularity is utterly worked out!
[*Exit into Castle.*

Enter HAROLD (*now dressed as Colonel*) *followed by* BLANCA

HAR. Now, don't worry me—I can't attend to you now. I've the responsibility of a Regiment on my shoulders, and I've no time to listen to chatterboxes. If you've anything to say, mention it to the Sergeant-Major.

BLAN. The Sergeant-Major? Oh, very good—only if I tell the Sergeant-Major what I was going to tell *you,* the Sergeant-Major'll do something affectionate, that's all. [*Going.*

HAR. Stop! Now you are not going to say anything to the Sergeant-Major that will unsettle him and make him neglect his duties?

BLAN. Only his Regimental duties. Not the others.

HAR. Oh! It would be a pity to unsettle the Sergeant-Major. Well, what was it you were going to say?

BLAN. (*nestling up against him*). Only this, dear—that this sudden rise—dear—from corporal to colonel at one step—dear—is more like fiction than fact, isn't it, dear?

HAR. Is that all? Cut out the "dears," and I don't think it'll hurt him. But, as you say, it *is* remarkable.

BLAN. What a novel it would make!

HAR. A three-volume novel! So it would. Let's write it together.

BLAN. Very well—you begin.

HAR. Now, let me see—

DUET—HAROLD *and* BLANCA

HAR. There once was a corporal bold—
BLAN. Yes—gawky, round-shouldered and lean—
HAR. No, very good-looking with plenty of dash,
In battle courageous, hot-headed and rash,
With a small but extremely becoming moustache—

BLAN. Ah! it isn't the one that I mean.

HAR. (*speaks*). Now it's your turn.

BLAN. There was once a Vivandière—

HAR. Old,
Short, stumpy, red-headed and vain—

BLAN. Not at all—very young with no sort of defect,
Exceedingly lovely and highly correct.

HAR. Oh, don't make her pretty—these girls, recollect,
Are always remarkably plain!

BLAN. (*speaking*). Rather rude, isn't it?

HAR. Not a bit. True to life—that's all. Now we must have an incident.

BLAN. Suppose we make her— (*Whispers.*)

HAR. No—Mudie wouldn't take it. No, I don't think that would do. Stop, I have an idea for a sensational incident of a striking and dramatic character.

The Regent one morning, by chance,
Observing the Corporal, said—
"It would be nothing short of public disgrace
To keep such a trump in a Corporal's place—
So we'll make him a Colonel, all covered with lace."

BLAN. (*confidentially to audience*). The Regent was weak in the head!

HAR. She, taking the facts at a glance,
To his bosom unblushingly flew—

BLAN. And he was so deeply in love, I declare.
That he married her then, and he married her there—

BOTH. So it ends with a wedding at Hanover Square,
As a three volume novel should do!

[*Exeunt together.*

Enter MATS MUNCK, *now dressed in* GRIFFENFELD'S *uniform*

MATS. When a man is promoted unexpectedly to a position of the highest official distinction, it is always a satisfactory circumstance when his figure is calculated to set off his uniform to advantage. (*Sentry presents arms to him.*) Eh? Oh, thank you very much. You're extremely polite, I'm sure!

SENT. Please to remember the sentry.

MATS. Eh? Oh, certainly.

[*Gives him money.*

Enter DAME CORTLANDT *unobserved. She comes forward*

DAME C. (*putting her arm round him*). Mats! Little man!

MATS. Eh? Oh, it's you. Don't. I'm busy now. (*Aside.*) It was all very well when I was only a Syndic, but as a Governor I can look a good deal higher than this sort of person. (*Aloud, to sentry.*) Will you kindly do that again?

SENT. Certainly. [*Presents arms.*

MATS. Most gratifying, I'm sure! (*Tips him again.* DAME *again embraces* MATS.) Now, don't worry—can't you see that I have business with a gentleman?

[*Reverts to sentry.*

DAME C. (*suppressing her rage with difficulty*). Mats! Take care! This is strange treatment—at the very outset of our engagement!

MATS. But, my good soul, you speak of our engagement as if——

DAME C. Don't deny it, Mats. I have your letter of proposal in my pocket—you have my letter of acceptance in yours! I'm trying to keep it down, Mats.

MATS. But as you very properly observed, that wasn't addressed to me but to the ex-Governor.

DAME C. It does just as well for you, Mats. I accepted the Governor, and you *are* the Governor.

MATS. If it comes to that, you were proposed to by the Syndic, and I'm not the Syndic. Go find the Syndic—go seek, go find—there's a good girl! (*Reverts to sentry.*) Will you oblige me once more?

[*Giving him money.*

DAME C. (*heaving with suppressed rage*). I'm doing my best to subdue it, Mats, but it's a tremendous effort.

MATS. Hold your breath and count six, my dear.

DAME C. (*does so*). It's all right, dear—it's down again!

MATS. (*occupied with sentry*). So glad!

DAME C. We must settle this at once, Mats. It's a very nice point. Shall we refer it to arbitration?

MATS. By all means. I find this gentleman (*indicating sentry*) full of delicate appreciation—suppose we leave it to him?

DAME C. You will undertake to abide by the result, Mats?

MATS. With pleasure. (*Aside.*) I've tipped him till he doesn't know whether he stands on his head or his heels!

QUARTET

MATS MUNCK, DAME CORTLANDT, SENTRY, *and afterwards* GRIFFENFELD

MATS (*to* SENTRY). One day, the Syndic of this town
(Whose time of life is shady)
Affectionately kneeling down,
Proposed to this old lady.
Now your opinion give politely
And riddle me this and riddle me rightly—
Who claims her hand? (*Aside.*) Here's half-a-crown!
[*Tipping him.*

SENT. No doubt the Syndic of this town.

MATS (*dancing*). Exactly so—the truth you speak—
(*To* DAME). Away—your love-sick Syndic seek—
You have no claim upon me, for
Unhappily I'm the Governor!

SENT. Oh yes, he is the Governor!

MATS (*delighted*). There!

SENT. No doubt he is the Governor!

MATS. There!

SENT. Against you, ma'am, I must declare—
This gentleman is the Governor!

MATS. There!

DAME. But bless my soul—

MATS. The man is right!

DAME. That's not the whole—

MATS. It's settled quite!

ENSEMBLE

DAME	MATS
It's now *my* turn my wrongs to air,	I've taken steps the Court to square,
So Governor Munck for squalls prepare!	So fire away, ma'am—*I* don't care!

[*During the Ensemble a corporal's guard enters—the sentry is relieved, and* GRIFFENFELD, *now dressed as a private Hussar, is left in his place. The change is not noticed by the* DAME *or* MATS.

DAME. One moment, pray—your words retrace,
Oh, sentinel, shortsighted!
I to the Governor of this place,
My troth securely plighted—
Now pray don't treat this question lightly,
But riddle me this and riddle me rightly—
Who claims my conjugal embrace?
GRIF. Of course, the Governor of this place!
DAME. (*dancing*). Exactly so! you well decide!
I am, ha! ha! the Governor's bride—
The Governor you, you can't deny—
Argal, the Governor's lady, I!
GRIF. She *is* the Governor's lady!
MATS, What!
GRIF. Of course, the Governor's lady!
MATS. What!
GRIF. You *are* the Governor, are you not?
Then she's the Governor's lady!
MATS. What!
But bless my heart—
DAME. (*still dancing*). That man is right!
That's but a part—
DAME. It's settled quite!

ENSEMBLE

DAME	MATS	GRIF. (*aside*)
Though basely you may plan and plot,	If I consent, may I be shot,	How capitally I plan and plot
With me you'll share your Governor's lot!	With her to share my Governor's lot!	To cleverly cut the Gordian knot!

[DAME *dances off in front of* MATS, *who tries in vain to escape*.

GRIF. (*alone*). It's alright! they're both committed to it, and *that* little difficulty is off my hands at last! Hallo! what's wrong now?

Enter NANNA *and* THORA *tidying their caps and much out of temper*

THORA. Papa, a joke's a joke,—but I don't think it fair to make us plot against ourselves!

NANNA. I'm sure I enjoy a bit of fun as much as anybody, but when it comes to our being coupled, if only for an afternoon, with a brace of penniless admirers, who are disposed to take every advantage of the position in which they temporarily find themselves, why, it's going a little too far—that's all!

GRIF. Why, what have they been doing?

THORA. Why, they've been unnecessarily realistic in their attentions.

GRIF. Unpleasantly so?

THORA. I said unnecessarily so. Goodness knows, I don't mind realism when there's any prospect of its coming to anything definite, but as neither of these young men has a penny, the sooner it's put a stop to the better!

GRIF. Hasn't a penny! What are you talking about? Why, they're magnificent matches!—Court Physician with the rank of Baron!—Sculptor Extraordinary to the Royal Family with the title of Count! Why, you grasping girls, what more do you want?

NANNA. Oh, papa! that's all nonsense! If these persons were really what they believe themselves to be, we wouldn't mind, but as they're both penniless young men, and we are penniless young ladies, the sooner we tell them the truth, the better.

GRIF. But, my good girls, consider! Don't go and spoil it all! Think of the fun of it when they discover how they've been cheated! Oh, my dear girls, there's a rich and rare treat in store for us all!

[*The girls, who have been chuckling through his speech, burst into hearty laughter.*

THORA. Upon my word, it ought to be extremely amusing!

PATTER TRIO

GOVERNOR, NANNA, *and* THORA

GRIF. When a gentleman supposes that he comfortably dozes on a pleasant bed of roses (which are singularly rare)—

NANNA. And discovers that it bristles with uncomfortable thistles, in intemperate epistles his annoyance he'll declare—

THORA. When a man his temper loses his remarks he never choses, but expressive language uses, with a tendency to swear—

GRIF. And when lovers are discarded their upbraiding will be larded with some epithets unguarded—you had better not be there!

NANNA (*disappointed*). We had better not be there?

THORA (*disappointed*). We had better not be there?

GRIF. (*decidedly*). You had better not be there!

ALL. {We / You} had better not be there!

NANNA *and* THORA. When these gentlemen conceited both discover they've been cheated, all our fun will be defeated—that's a thing we couldn't bear—

So, however they may rave it, we'll unquestionably brave it; you may take your affidavit we will certainly be there!

{We / They} will certainly be there—

{We / They} will certainly be there—

Though {you / I} flout it, never doubt it,

{we / they} will certainly be there!

GRIF. Their despair and their distraction and their keen dissatisfaction—their exaggerated action, and the tearing of their hair—

NANNA. Their disgust and desperation when they see the situation some congenial occupation for the lawyers will prepare—

THORA. We shall find their loud abusing both instructive

and amusing, and of violent accusing there'll be symptoms in the air—

GRIF. And their libellous expressions and their angry indiscretions will be tried at Quarter Sessions, when I occupy the chair!

NANNA (*gleefully*). When you occupy the chair—

THORA (*gleefully*). When you occupy the chair—

GRIF. When I occupy the chair!

ALL THREE. When {you / I} occupy the chair.

GRIF. When the case is quite completed, then the prisoner defeated with severity is treated as you're probably aware—

For it's awfully provided that the jury shall be guided by my summary one-sided—which distresses Labouchere.

ALL THREE. It is rough on Labouchere—
It is hard on Labouchere—
Oh, the dickens, how it sickens tender-hearted Labouchere!

[*Exit* GRIFFENFELD.

NANNA. Really, Thora, I can't help feeling rather conscience-stricken. Poor boys! I'm really afraid we've broken their hearts.

THORA. It's a pity they're such nobodies. I sometimes think between ourselves——

NANNA. Hush! So do I—but here they come.

Enter ERLING *and* TORTENSSEN. *The girls retire up stage and listen*

TORT. Do you know, I don't care to be repulsed by a girl I'm engaged to, Count.

ERL. They certainly treated us very coldly, Baron. Mere innocent attentions—such as every girl expects from the man she's going to marry——

TORT. Remember, Count, we are no longer a couple of adventurers, we are great men, and we are entitled to expect that attentions shall be paid to *us*, now. (*Girls indulge in suppressed chuckles.*) I think a little condescension on our part, a little stand-offishness, an air of doing them a considerable favour, would not be misplaced.

ERL. I see what you mean, Baron. A little of this sort of thing—"Good-day to you, my dear; good-day to you. Pleased to see you, pleased to see you——"

TORT. "A little further off, please. We'll tell you when we want the mixture as before." Don't you think so, Count?

ERL. I really think it's only what is due to us, Baron, I do indeed.

[*The Girls come forward pretending to weep bitterly.*

NANNA (*in affected tears*). Oh, please, we've been thinking it over, and we're very sorry we were so un-kuk-kuk-kuk-kind to you just now.

ERL. (*condescendingly*). Thank you, thank you. Pray don't name it.

TORT. We thought you'd like a little attention—but it's not of the smallest consequence. There—go away—there's good girls.

THORA (*pretending to sob*). Oh, but we *did* like it—only—

[*Bursts into tears.*

NANNA (*sobbing*). We thought it more mai-mai-maid-enly to be cuc-cuc-cuc-coy!

[*Tears.*

NANNA. By such a par-par-particular pa-pa-papa!

THORA. And we're *so* afraid of Mrs. Gug-gug-gug-Grundy! (*Violent burst of tears.*)

[*Both burst into floods of tears.*

Together.

ERL. Now, my darling child—Nanna—dearest—don't cry like that! I can't bear it! See, on my knees I swear to you that I will always—always love you as I love you now! Oh, don't cry like that—you'll break my heart—indeed you will!

TORT. My dearest Thora—you mustn't—really you mustn't! It's dreadful to see those pretty eyes so red with weeping—Oh, I was a brute to be unkind to you, there—don't be a little goose! I didn't mean it—upon my word I didn't!

[*Both men are on their knees trying to console the two girls. The girls, who have been pretending to weep hysterically through this, suddenly burst into peals of hearty laughter.*

ERL. (*springing up*). Tortenssen, I do believe they're laughing at us!

THORA. Oh, aren't the nobility shrewd!

NANNA. And isn't the aristocracy quick at grasping a situation!

DANCING QUARTET

ERLING, TORTENSSEN, NANNA, *and* THORA

NANNA. So this is how you'd have us sue you—
Bowing, bending—turning to you—
But you don't exact it, do you?
That's so kind (ERLING *kisses her*). Impertinence! (*aside*).

THORA. Pleading party pray you pity!
You are wise and wondrous witty—
Don't despise our doleful ditty!
Thanks so much (TORTENSSEN *kisses her*).
What impudence! (*aside*).

ERL. *and* TORT. Ha, ha! ha, ha! Ha! ha! ha! ha!

NANNA *and* THORA. Ha, ha! ha, ha! Ha! ha! ha! ha!

ALL. Topsy turvy turn the tables!
Tit for tat and tat for tit—
As in fusty fairy fables,
Badly is the biter bit!
Takes a time to tame a Tartar!
Dad's delightful darling darter,
Mostly makes a man a martyr—
Here's a hero hardly hit!

ERL. As you sue for pardon sweetly
Though you've acted indiscreetly,
We forgive you both completely,
Thus I'll prove it—(*tries to kiss her*).

NANNA. That you won't!

TORT. Though you've ridiculed us sadly—
Cheated and deceived us badly,
As we love you fondly—madly—
We forgive you—(*trying to kiss her*).

THORA. No, you don't!
Topsy turvy turn the tables, &c.

[ERLING *and* TORTENSSEN *dance off—waving an adieu to the two girls, who remain on the stage.*

THORA (*sighing*). Oh, Nanna, they're good fellows! I wish it was all real!

NANNA. No use wishing, dear. We'd better try and forget all about them. (*Looking off.*) Oh—look! All the people coming to get married!

THORA. Poor people! We—we must go and find our bridegrooms.

NANNA. Poor bridegrooms? It's—it's a capital joke! (*About to cry.*)

THORA. Capital! (*Looking at* NANNA'S *face*). Why, a real tear, I do believe!

NANNA (*holding it on her finger*). Yes, it's real this time.

THORA (*examining it*). Funny, isn't it?

NANNA. Very amusing.

THORA. Put it back. (NANNA *does so.*) All right now?

NANNA (*brightly*). All right now!

[*Exeunt in opposite directions.*

MARCH

Enter men and girls in couples for wedding. They come two and two down stage

CHORUS. (*To bell accompaniment*)

Ring the bells and bang the brasses!
Cut the cake and fill the glasses!
Lovers and their blushing lasses
Will be duly coupled soon.
When, in Castle chapel plighted,
Man and maid are once united,
Off they'll go in mood delighted
On a happy honeymoon!

Enter GRIFFENFELD, *also* NANNA *with* ERLING, THORA *with* TORTENSSEN, DAME CORTLANDT *with* SYNDIC, *and* CHRISTINA *alone*

GRIF. Stop! You can all go home. There will be no weddings to-day.

ERL. What do you mean?

GRIF. I mean that you've all been imposed upon—deluded—cheated. The Regent is no Regent, but a common vagabond personating him. Ha! ha! ha! Here comes His Royal Highness in his true colours!

Enter REGENT *in his vagabond dress.* CHRISTINA *runs to his arms*

ERL. (*to* REGENT). Now, sir, the truth. Are you a prince to be worshipped or a swindler to be whipped?

REG. Really it's a point upon which I'm not quite satisfied myself! I'll think it over and let you know.

Enter the two OFFICERS

1ST OFFICER (*kneeling*). Sir, the enemy's fleet has entered the Baltic, and your immediate presence at Copenhagen is indispensable.

[*Giving a dispatch to* REGENT.

GRIF. Why, what's all this? Who are these jack-a-dandies?

REG. (*reading dispatch*). Merely two of my trusted officers. They bring me weighty news indeed!

GRIF. Why, you don't mean to tell me that you are the Regent, after all?

REG. The very Regent, at your service.

[*All kneel.*

GRIF. I've made an ass of myself!

REG. Don't say that. We are indebted to you for some invaluable hints for promotions, appointments, and marriage arrangements, all of which will take effect to-day—as indeed will the best and wisest of your suggestions—your permanent degradation to the ranks. (REGENT *sees* CHRISTINA *weeping.*) Why, Christina in tears!

CHRIS. I weep, sir, because my heart is broken, and, alas, it is your Highness's doing, for your Highness gave me Nils Egilsson, and he has gone from me for ever!

REG. Nay, Christina, be not so sure of that. I have found the very love I have sought this many a year, and if my being heir to a crown is to stand in my way, why I'll e'en be Nils Egilsson to the end!

CHRIS. (*amazed*). Sir!

REG. Come, Christina, what say you?

CHRIS. Sir, I am your Highness's handmaid!

[*They retire up stage together.*

FINALE

ERL. *and* TORT. Now all that we've agreed upon, O,
And all that's passed between us;
Ere half an hour go by
We'll surely ratify.

NANNA *and* THORA. As life's career we speed upon, O,
So fondly we'll demean us;
Thy love shall never say
That he repents this day.

ERL. *and* TORT. What, never?
NANNA *and* THORA. Never!
ERL. *and* TORT. Never?
NANNA *and* THORA. Never!
ALL FOUR. Never repent this day!
ERL. *and* TORT. Resentment sink,
My own {Nan*na*. / Tho*ra*.}
NANNA *and* THORA. But only think
Of poor papa,
Position low
Degraded to!

[*Pointing to* GRIFFENFELD, *who is standing sentry.*

ERL. *and* TORT. (*to* GRIFFENFELD). You little roguey
poguey, you—
SYN. You little roguey poguey—
GRIF. (*hurt.*) Sir!
HAR. You little roguey poguey—
GRIF. Sir!!
ALL. You roguey poguey, roguey poguey, roguey poguey!
GRIF. Sir!!!
ALL. We love with all sincerity, O.
And pleasure is elating us—
Away with all celerity, O,

The priest is there awaiting us!
In verity, verity, verity, verity,
Priest is there awaiting us!

[*All except* REGENT *and* CHRISTINA *dance off in couples into Castle, waving an adieu to* GRIFFENFELD, *who stands as sentry, presenting arms to them as the curtain falls.*

THE BAB BALLADS

CAPTAIN REECE

Of all the ships upon the blue
No ship contained a better crew
Than that of Worthy CAPTAIN REECE,
Commanding of *The Mantelpiece*.

He was adored by all his men,
For worthy CAPTAIN REECE, R.N.,
Did all that lay within him to
Promote the comfort of his crew.

If ever they were dull or sad,
Their captain danced to them like mad,
Or told, to make the time pass by,
Droll legends of his infancy.

A feather bed had every man,
Warm slippers and hot-water can,
Brown windsor from the captain's store,
A valet, too, to every four.

Did they with thirst in summer burn?
Lo, seltzogenes at every turn,
And on all very sultry days
Cream ices handed round on trays.

Then currant wine and ginger pops
Stood handily on all the "tops";
And, also, with amusement rife,
A "Zoetrope, or Wheel of Life."

New volumes came across the sea
From MISTER MUDIE's libraree;
The Times and *Saturday Review*
Beguiled the leisure of the crew.

Kind-hearted CAPTAIN REECE, R.N.,
Was quite devoted to his men;
In point of fact, good CAPTAIN REECE
Beatified *The Mantelpiece*.

One summer eve, at half past ten,
He said (addressing all his men):
"Come, tell me, please, what I can do
To please and gratify my crew?

"By any reasonable plan
I'll make you happy, if I can;
My own convenience count as *nil;*
It is my duty, and I will."

Then up and answered WILLIAM LEE
(The kindly captain's coxswain he,
A nervous, shy, low-spoken man),
He cleared his throat and thus began:

"You have a daughter, CAPTAIN REECE,
Ten female cousins and a niece,
A ma, if what I'm told is true,
Six sisters, and an aunt or two.

"Now, somehow, sir, it seems to me,
More friendly-like we all should be
If you united of 'em to
Unmarried members of the crew.

"If you'd ameliorate our life,
Let each select from them a wife;
And as for nervous me, old pal,
Give me your own enchanting gal!"

Good CAPTAIN REECE, that worthy man,
Debated on his coxswain's plan:
"I quite agree," he said, "O BILL;
It is my duty, and I will.

"My daughter, that enchanting gurl,
Has just been promised to an earl,
And all my other familee,
To peers of various degree.

"But what are dukes and viscounts to
The happiness of all my crew?
The word I gave you I'll fulfil;
It is my duty, and I will.

"As you desire it shall befall,
I'll settle thousands on you all,
And I shall be, despite my hoard,
The only bachelor on board."

The boatswain of *The Mantelpiece,*
He blushed and spoke to CAPTAIN REECE,
"I beg your honour's leave," he said,
"If you would wish to go and wed,

"I have a widowed mother who
Would be the very thing for you—
She long has loved you from afar,
She washes for you, CAPTAIN R."

The captain saw the dame that day—
Addressed her in his playful way—
"And did it want a wedding ring?
It was a tempting ickle sing!

"Well, well, the chaplain I will seek,
We'll all be married this day week—
At yonder church upon the hill;
It is my duty, and I will!"

The sisters, cousins, aunts, and niece,
And widowed ma of CAPTAIN REECE,
Attended there as they were bid;
It was their duty, and they did.

THE RIVAL CURATES

List while the poet trolls
  Of MR. CLAYTON HOOPER,
Who had a cure of souls
  At Spiffton-extra-Sooper.

He lived on curds and whey,
  And daily sang their praises,
And then he'd go and play
  With buttercups and daisies.

Wild crôquet HOOPER banned,
  And all the sports of Mammon,
He warred with cribbage, and
  He exorcised backgammon.

His helmet was a glance
  That spoke of holy gladness;
A saintly smile his lance,
  His shield a tear of sadness.

His Vicar smiled to see
  This armour on him buckled;
With pardonable glee
  He blessed himself and chuckled:

"In mildness to abound
  My curate's sole design is,
In all the country round
  There's none so mild as mine is!"

And Hooper, disinclined
  His trumpet to be blowing,
Yet didn't think you'd find
  A milder curate going.

A friend arrived one day
  At Spiffton-extra-Sooper,
And in this shameful way
  He spoke to Mr. Hooper:

"You think your famous name
For mildness can't be shaken,
That none can blot your fame—
But, HOOPER, you're mistaken!

"Your mind is not as blank
As that of HOPLEY PORTER,
Who holds a curate's rank
At Assesmilk-cum-Worter.

"*He* plays the airy flute,
And looks depressed and blighted,
Doves round about him 'toot,'
And lambkins dance delighted.

"*He* labours more than you
At worsted work, and frames it;
In old maids' albums, too,
Sticks seaweed—yes, and names it!"

The tempter said his say,
Which pierced him like a needle—
He summoned straight away
His sexton and his beadle.

These men were men who could
Hold liberal opinions:
On Sundays they were good—
On week-days they were minions.

"To Hopley Porter go,
Your fare I will afford you—
Deal him a deadly blow,
And blessings shall reward you.

"But stay—I do not like
Undue assassination,
And so, before you strike,
Make this communication:

"I'll give him this one chance—
If he'll more gaily bear him,
Play crôquet, smoke, and dance,
I willingly will spare him."

They went, those minions true,
To Assesmilk-cum-Worter,
And told their errand to
The Reverend Hopley Porter.

"What?" said that reverend gent,
"Dance through my hours of leisure?
Smoke?—bathe myself with scent?—
Play crôquet? Oh, with pleasure!

"Wear all my hair in curl?
  Stand at my door, and wink—so—
At every passing girl?
  My brothers, I should think so!

"For years I've longed for some
  Excuse for this revulsion:
Now that excuse has come—
  I do it on compulsion!!!"

He smoked and winked away—
  This REVEREND HOPLEY PORTER—
The deuce there was to pay
  At Assesmilk-cum-Worter.

And HOOPER holds his ground,
  In mildness daily growing—
They think him, all around,
  The mildest curate going.

ONLY A DANCING GIRL

Only a dancing girl,
  With an unromantic style,
With borrowed colour and curl,
  With fixed mechanical smile,
  With many a hackneyed wile,
With ungrammatical lips,
And corns that mar her trips!

Hung from the "flies" in air,
  She acts a palpable lie;
She's as little a fairy there
  As unpoetical I!
  I hear you asking, Why—
Why in the world I sing
This tawdry, tinselled thing?

No airy fairy she,
  As she hangs in arsenic green,
From a highly impossible tree,
  In a highly impossible scene
  (Herself not over clean).
For fays don't suffer, I'm told,
From bunions, coughs, or cold.

And stately dames that bring
  Their daughters there to see,
Pronounce the "dancing thing"
  No better than she should be.
  With her skirt at her shameful knee,
And her painted, tainted phiz:
Ah, matron, which of us is?

(And, in sooth, it oft occurs
  That while these matrons sigh,
Their dresses are lower than hers,
  And sometimes half as high;
  And their hair is hair they buy.
And they use their glasses, too,
In a way she'd blush to do.)

But change her gold and green
  For a coarse merino gown,

And see her upon the scene
  Of her home, when coaxing down
  Her drunken father's frown,
In his squalid cheerless den:
She's a fairy truly, then!

GENERAL JOHN

The bravest names for fire and flames
  And all that mortal durst,
Were General John and Private James,
  Of the Sixty-seventy-first.

General John was a soldier tried,
  A chief of warlike dons;
A haughty stride and a withering pride
  Were Major-General John's.

A sneer would play on his martial phiz,
  Superior birth to show;
"Pish!" was a favourite word of his,
  And he often said "Ho! ho!"

FULL-PRIVATE JAMES described might be,
As a man of a mournful mind;
No characteristic trait had he
Of any distinctive kind.

From the ranks, one day, cried PRIVATE JAMES,
"Oh! MAJOR-GENERAL JOHN,
I've doubts of our respective names,
My mournful mind upon.

"A glimmering thought occurs to me
(Its source I can't unearth),
But I've a kind of a notion we
Were cruelly changed at birth.

"I've a strange idea that each other's names
We've each of us here got on.
Such things have been," said PRIVATE JAMES.
"They have!" sneered GENERAL JOHN.

"My GENERAL JOHN, I swear upon
My oath I think 'tis so——"
"Pish!" proudly sneered his GENERAL JOHN,
And he also said "Ho! ho!"

"My GENERAL JOHN! my GENERAL JOHN!
My GENERAL JOHN!" quoth he,
"This aristocratical sneer upon
Your face I blush to see!

"No truly great or generous cove
Deserving of them names,
Would sneer at a fixed idea that's drove
In the mind of a PRIVATE JAMES!"

Said GENERAL JOHN, "Upon your claims
No need your breath to waste;
If this is a joke, FULL-PRIVATE JAMES,
It's a joke of doubtful taste.

"But, being a man of doubtless worth,
If you feel certain quite
That we were probably changed at birth,
I'll venture to say you're right."

So GENERAL JOHN as PRIVATE JAMES
Fell in, parade upon;
And PRIVATE JAMES, by change of names,
Was MAJOR-GENERAL JOHN.

TO A LITTLE MAID

BY A POLICEMAN

Come with me, little maid!
Nay, shrink not, thus afraid—
I'll harm thee not!
Fly not, my love, from me—
I have a home for thee—
A fairy grot,
Where mortal eye
Can rarely pry,
There shall thy dwelling be!

List to me, while I tell
The pleasures of that cell,
Oh, little maid!

What though its couch be rude—
Homely the only food
  Within its shade?
    No thought of care
    Can enter there,
No vulgar swain intrude!

Come with me, little maid,
Come to the rocky shade
  I love to sing;
Live with us, maiden rare—
Come, for we "want" thee there,
  Thou elfin thing,
    To work thy spell,
    In some cool cell
In stately Pentonville!

JOHN AND FREDDY

JOHN courted lovely MARY ANN,
  So likewise did his brother, FREDDY.
FRED was a very soft young man,
  While JOHN, though quick, was most unsteady.

FRED was a graceful kind of youth,
But JOHN was very much the strongest.
"Oh, dance away," said she, "in truth,
I'll marry him who dances longest."

JOHN tries the maiden's taste to strike
With gay, grotesque, outrageous dresses,
And dances comically, like
CLODOCHE AND Co., at the Princess's.

But FREDDY tries another style,
He knows some graceful steps and does 'em—
A breathing Poem—Woman's smile—
A man all poesy and buzzem.

Now FREDDY's operatic *pas*—
Now JOHNNY's hornpipe seems entrapping:
Now FREDDY's graceful *entrechats*—
Now JOHNNY's skilful "cellar-flapping."

For many hours—for many days—
For many weeks performed each brother,
For each was active in his ways,
And neither would give in to t'other.

After a month of this, they say
  (The maid was getting bored and moody)
A wandering curate passed that way
  And talked a lot of goody-goody.

"Oh my," said he, with solemn frown,
  "I tremble for each dancing *frater*,
Like unregenerated clown
  And harlequin at some the-ayter."

He showed that men, in dancing, do
  Both impiously and absurdly,
And proved his proposition true,
  With Firstly, Secondly, and Thirdly.

For months both JOHN and FREDDY danced,
  The curate's protests little heeding;
For months the curate's words enhanced
  The sinfulness of their proceeding.

At length they bowed to Nature's rule—
  Their steps grew feeble and unsteady,
Till FREDDY fainted on a stool,
  And JOHNNY on the top of FREDDY.

"Decide!" quoth they, "let him be named,
Who henceforth as his wife may rank you."
"I've changed my views," the maiden said,
"I only marry curates, thank you!"

Says FREDDY, "Here is goings on!
To bust myself with rage I'm ready."
"I'll be a curate!" whispers JOHN—
"And I," exclaimed poetic FREDDY.

But while they read for it, these chaps,
The curate booked the maiden bonny—
And when she's buried him, perhaps,
She'll marry FREDERICK or JOHNNY.

SIR GUY THE CRUSADER

SIR GUY was a doughty crusader,
A muscular knight,
Ever ready to fight,
A very determined invader,
And DICKEY DE LION's delight.

LENORE was a Saracen maiden,
Brunette, statuesque,
The reverse of grotesque,
Her pa was a bagman from Aden,
Her mother she played in burlesque.

A *coryphée,* pretty and loyal,
In amber and red
The ballet she led;
Her mother performed at the Royal,
LENORE at the Saracen's Head.

Of face and of figure majestic,
She dazzled the cits—
Ecstaticised pits;—
Her troubles were only domestic,
But drove her half out of her wits.

Her father incessantly lashed her,
On water and bread
She was grudgingly fed;
Whenever her father he thrashed her
Her mother sat down on her head.

Guy saw her, and loved her, with reason,
For beauty so bright
Sent him mad with delight;
He purchased a stall for the season,
And sat in it every night.

His views were exceedingly proper,
He wanted to wed,
So he called at her shed
And saw her progenitor whop her—
Her mother sit down on her head.

"So pretty," said he, "and so trusting!
You brute of a dad,
You unprincipled cad,
Your conduct is really disgusting,
Come, come, now admit it's too bad!

"You're a turbaned old Turk, and malignant—
Your daughter Lenore
I intensely adore,
And I cannot help feeling indignant,
A fact that I hinted before;

"To see a fond father employing
A deuce of a knout
For to bang her about,
To a sensitive lover's annoying."
Said the bagman, "Crusader, get out."

Says Guy, "Shall a warrior laden
With a big spiky knob,
Sit in peace on his cob
While a beautiful Saracen maiden
Is whipped by a Saracen snob?

"To London I'll go from my charmer."
Which he did, with his loot
(Seven hats and a flute),
And was nabbed for his Sydenham armour
At Mr. Ben-Samuel's suit.

Sir Guy he was lodged in the Compter,
Her pa, in a rage,
Died (don't know his age),
His daughter, she married the prompter,
Grew bulky and quitted the stage.

HAUNTED

Haunted? Ay, in a social way,
By a body of ghosts in a dread array:
But no conventional spectres they—
Appalling, grim, and tricky:
I quail at mine as I'd never quail
At a fine traditional spectre pale,
With a turnip head and a ghostly wail,
And a splash of blood on the dicky!

Mine are horrible social ghosts,
Speeches and women and guests and hosts,
Weddings and morning calls and toasts,
In every bad variety:
Ghosts that hover about the grave
Of all that's manly, free, and brave:
You'll find their names on the architrave
Of that charnel-house, Society.

Black Monday—black as its schoolroom ink—
With its dismal boys that snivel and think
Of nauseous messes to eat and drink,
And a frozen tank to wash in.
That was the first that brought me grief
And made me weep, till I sought relief
In an emblematical handkerchief
To choke such baby bosh in.

First and worst in the grim array—
Ghosts of ghosts that have gone their way,
Which I wouldn't revive for a single day
    For all the wealth of PLUTUS—
Are the horrible ghosts that schooldays scared:
If the classical ghost that BRUTUS dared
Was the ghost of his "Cæsar" unprepared,
    I'm sure I pity BRUTUS.

I pass to critical seventeen:
The ghost of that terrible wedding scene,
When an elderly colonel stole my queen,
    And woke my dream of heaven:
No school-girl decked in her nursery curls
Was my gushing innocent queen of pearls;
If she wasn't a girl of a thousand girls,
    She was one of forty-seven!

I see the ghost of my first cigar—
Of the thence-arising family jar—
Of my maiden brief (I was at the bar),
    When I called the judge "Your wushup"!
Of reckless days and reckless nights,
With wrenched-off knockers, extinguished lights,
Unholy songs, and tipsy fights,
    Which I strove in vain to hush up.

Ghosts of fraudulent joint-stock banks,
Ghosts of copy, "declined with thanks,"
Of novels returned in endless ranks,
    And thousands more, I suffer.
The only line to fitly grace
My humble tomb, when I've run my race,
Is "Reader, this is the resting-place
    Of an unsuccessful duffer."

I've fought them all, these ghosts of mine,
But the weapons I've used are sighs and brine,
And now that I'm nearly forty-nine,
    Old age is my only bogy;
For my hair is thinning away at the crown,
And the silver fights with the worn-out brown;
And a general verdict sets me down
    As an irreclaimable fogy.

THE BISHOP AND THE 'BUSMAN

It was a Bishop bold,
  And London was his see,
He was short and stout and round about
  And zealous as could be.

It also was a Jew,
  Who drove a Putney 'bus—
For flesh of swine however fine
  He did not care a cuss.

His name was Hash Baz Ben,
  And Jedediah too,
And Solomon and Zabulon—
  This 'bus-directing Jew.

The Bishop said, said he,
  "I'll see what I can do
To Christianise and make you wise,
  You poor benighted Jew."

So every blessed day
  That 'bus he rode outside,
From Fulham town, both up and down
  And loudly thus he cried:

"His name is Hash Baz Ben,
  And Jedediah too,
And Solomon and Zabulon—
  This 'bus-directing Jew."

At first the 'busman smiled,
  And rather liked the fun—
He merely smiled, that Hebrew child,
  And said "Eccentric one!"

And gay young dogs would wait
  To see the 'bus go by
(These gay young dogs, in striking togs),
  To hear the Bishop cry:

"Observe his grisly beard,
  His race it clearly shows,
He sticks no fork in ham or pork—
  Observe, my friends, his nose.

"His name is Hash Baz Ben,
  And Jedediah too,
And Solomon and Zabulon—
  This 'bus-directing Jew."

But though at first amused,
  Yet after seven years,
This Hebrew child got rather riled,
  And melted into tears.

He really almost feared
  To leave his poor abode,
His nose, and name, and beard became
  A byword on that road.

At length he swore an oath,
  The reason he would know—
"I'll call and see why ever he
  Does persecute me so!"

The good old Bishop sat
  On his ancestral chair,
The 'busman came, sent up his name,
  And laid his grievance bare.

"Benighted Jew," he said
  (The good old Bishop did),
"Be Christian, you, instead of Jew—
  Become a Christian kid!

"I'll ne'er annoy you more."
  "Indeed?" replied the Jew;
"Shall I be freed?" "You will, indeed!"
  Then "Done!" said he, "with you!"

The organ which, in man,
  Between the eyebrows grows,
Fell from his face, and in its place
  He found a Christian nose.

His tangled Hebrew beard,
  Which to his waist came down,
Was now a pair of whiskers fair—
  His name ADOLPHUS BROWN!

He wedded in a year
  That prelate's daughter JANE,
He's grown quite fair—has auburn hair—
  His wife is far from plain.

THE TROUBADOUR

A Troubadour he played
  Without a castle wall,
Within, a hapless maid
  Responded to his call.

"Oh, willow, woe is me!
  Alack and well-a-day!
If I were only free
  I'd hie me far away!"

Unknown her face and name,
  But this he knew right well,
The maiden's wailing came
  From out a dungeon cell.

A hapless woman lay
Within that prison grim—
That fact, I've heard him say,
Was quite enough for him.

"I will not sit or lie,
Or eat or drink, I vow,
Till thou art free as I,
Or I as pent as thou!"

Her tears then ceased to flow,
Her wails no longer rang,
And tuneful in her woe
The prisoned maiden sang:

"Oh, stranger, as you play
I recognise your touch;
And all that I can say,
Is thank you very much!"

He seized his clarion straight,
  And blew thereat, until
A warder oped the gate,
  "Oh, what might be your will?"

"I've come, sir knave, to see
  The master of these halls:
A maid unwillingly
  Lies prisoned in their walls."

With barely stifled sigh
  That porter drooped his head,
With teardrops in his eye,
  "A many, sir," he said.

He stayed to hear no more,
  But pushed that porter by,
And shortly stood before
  SIR HUGH DE PECKHAM RYE.

SIR HUGH he darkly frowned,
  "What would you, sir, with me?"
The troubadour he downed
  Upon his bended knee.

"I've come, DE PECKHAM RYE,
  To do a Christian task,
You ask me what would I?
  It is not much I ask.

"Release these maidens, sir,
  Whom you dominion o'er—
Particularly her
  Upon the second floor!

"And if you don't, my lord"—
  He here stood bolt upright.
And tapped a tailor's sword—
  "Come out at once and fight!"

SIR HUGH he called—and ran
  The warden from the gate,
"Go, show this gentleman
  The maid in forty-eight."

By many a cell they passed
  And stopped at length before
A portal, bolted fast:
  The man unlocked the door.

He called inside the gate
  With coarse and brutal shout,
"Come, step it, forty-eight!"
  And forty-eight stepped out.

"They gets it pretty hot,
  The maidens wot we cotch—
Two years this lady's got
  For collaring a wotch."

"Oh, ah!—indeed—I see,"
  The troubadour exclaimed—
"If I may make so free,
  How is this castle named?"

The warden's eyelids fill,
  And, sighing, he replied,
"Of gloomy Pentonville
  This is the Female Side!"

The minstrel did not wait
  The warden stout to thank,
But recollected straight
  He'd business at the Bank.

FERDINANDO AND ELVIRA

OR, THE GENTLE PIEMAN

PART I

At a pleasant evening party I had taken down to supper
One whom I will call Elvira, and we talked of love and
Tupper,

Mr. Tupper and the poets, very lightly with them deal-
ing,
For I've always been distinguished for a strong poetic
feeling.

Then we let off paper crackers, each of which contained
a motto,
And she listened while I read them, till her mother told
her not to.

Then she whispered, "To the ball-room we had better,
dear, be walking;
If we stop down here much longer, really people will be
talking."

There were noblemen in coronets, and military cousins,
There were captains by the hundred, there were baronets
by dozens.

Yet she heeded not their offers, but dismissed them with
a blessing;
Then she let down all her back hair which had taken
long in dressing.

Then she had convulsive sobbings in her agitated throttle,
Then she wiped her pretty eyes and smelt her pretty
smelling-bottle.

So I whispered, "Dear ELVIRA, say—what can the matter
be with you?
Does anything you've eaten, darling POPSY, disagree with
you?"

But spite of all I said, her sobs grew more and more dis-
tressing,
And she tore her pretty back hair, which had taken long
in dressing.

Then she gazed upon the carpet, at the ceiling then
above me,
And she whispered, "FERDINANDO, do you really, *really*
love me?"

"Love you?" said I, then I sighed, and then I gazed
upon her sweetly—
For I think I do this sort of thing particularly neatly—

"Send me to the Arctic regions, or illimitable azure,
On a scientific goose-chase, with my COXWELL or my
GLAISHER.

"Tell me whither I may hie me, tell me, dear one, that
I *may* know—
Is it up the highest Andes? down a horrible volcano?"

But she said, "It isn't polar bears, or hot volcanic grottoes,
Only find out who it is that writes those lovely cracker
mottoes!"

PART II

"Tell me, HENRY WADSWORTH, ALFRED, POET CLOSE, or
MISTER TUPPER,
Do you write the bonbon mottoes my ELVIRA pulls at
supper?"

But HENRY WADSWORTH smiled, and said he had not
had that honour;
And ALFRED, too, disclaimed the words that told so much
upon her.
"MISTER MARTIN TUPPER, POET CLOSE, I beg of you
inform us";
But my question seemed to throw them both into a rage
enormous.

MISTER CLOSE expressed a wish that he could only get
anigh to me.
And MISTER MARTIN TUPPER sent the following reply to
me:—
"A fool is bent upon a twig, but wise men dread a
bandit."
Which I think must have been clever, for I didn't under-
stand it.
Seven weary years I wandered—Patagonia, China, Nor-
way,
Till at last I sank exhausted at a pastrycook his doorway.

There were fuchsias and geraniums, and daffodils and
myrtle,
So I entered, and I ordered half a basin of mock turtle.

He was plump and he was chubby, he was smooth and
he was rosy,
And his little wife was pretty, and particularly cosy.

And he chirped and sang, and skipped about, and
laughed with laughter hearty—
He was wonderfully active for so very stout a party.

And I said, "Oh, gentle pieman, who so very, very
merry?
Is it purity of conscience, or your one-and-seven sherry?"

But he answered, "I'm so happy—no profession could be
dearer—
If I am not humming 'Tra! la! la!' I'm singing, 'Tirer,
lirer!'

"First I go and make the patties, and the puddings and
the jellies,
Then I make a sugar birdcage, which upon a table swell
is;

"Then I polish all the silver, which a supper-table
lacquers;
Then I write the pretty mottoes which you find inside
the crackers"—

"Found at last!" I madly shouted, "Gentle pieman, you
astound me!"
Then I waved the turtle soup enthusiastically round me.

And I shouted and I danced until he'd quite a crowd
around him—
And I rushed away, exclaiming, "I have found him! I
have found him!"

And I heard the gentle pieman in the road behind me
trilling,
" 'Tira! lira!' stop him, stop him! 'Tra! la! la!' the soup's
a shilling!"

But until I reached ELVIRA's home, I never, never waited,
And ELVIRA to her FERDINANDO's irrevocably mated!

LORENZO DE LARDY

Dalilah de Dardy adored
  The very correctest of cards,
Lorenzo de Lardy, a lord—
  He was one of Her Majesty's Guards.

Dalilah de Dardy was fat,
  Dalilah de Dardy was old—
(No doubt in the world about that)
  But Dalilah de Dardy had gold.

Lorenzo de Lardy was tall,
  The flower of maidenly pets,
Young ladies would love at his call,
  But Lorenzo de Lardy had debts.

His money-position was queer,
  And one of his favourite freaks
Was to hide himself three times a year,
  In Paris, for several weeks.

Many days didn't pass him before
  He fanned himself into a flame,
For a beautiful "Dam du Comptwore,"
  And this was her singular name:

Alice Eulalie Coraline
  Euphrosine Colombina Thérèse
Juliette Stephanie Celestine
  Charlotte Russe de la Sauce Mayonnaise.

She booked all the orders and tin,
  Accoutred in showy fal-lal,
At a two-fifty Restaurant, in
  The glittering Palais Royal.

He'd gaze in her orbit of blue,
  Her hand he would tenderly squeeze,
But the words of her tongue that he knew
  Were limited strictly to these:

"Coraline Celestine Eulalie,
  Houp là! Je vous aime, oui, mossoo,
Combien donnez moi aujourd'hui
  Bonjour, Mademoiselle, parlez voo."

MADEMOISELLE DE LA SAUCE MAYONNAISE
Was a witty and beautiful miss,
Extremely correct in her ways,
But her English consisted of this:

"Oh my! pretty man, if you please,
Blom boodin, biſtek, currie lamb,
Bouldogue, two franc half, quite ze cheese,
Rosbif, me spik Angleesh, godam."

A waiter, for seasons before,
Had basked in her beautiful gaze,
And burnt to dismember MILOR,
He loved DE LA SAUCE MAYONNAISE.

He said to her, "Méchante THÉRÈSE,
Avec désespoir tu m'accables.
Penses-tu, DE LA SAUCE MAYONNAISE,
Ses intentions sont honorables?

"Flirtez toujours, ma belle, si tu ôses—
Je me vengerai ainsi, ma chère,
Je lui dirai de quoi l'on compose
Vol au vent à la Financière!"

LORD LARDY knew nothing of this—
The waiter's devotion ignored,
But he gazed on the beautiful miss,
And never seemed weary or bored.

The waiter would screw up his nerve,
His fingers he'd snap and he'd dance—
And LORD LARDY would smile and observe,
"How strange are the customs of France!"

Well, after delaying a space,
His tradesmen no longer would wait:
Returning to England apace,
He yielded himself to his fate.

LORD LARDY espoused, with a groan,
MISS DARDY's developing charms,
And agreed to tag on to his own,
Her name and her newly-found arms.

The waiter he knelt at the toes
  Of an ugly and thin coryphée,
Who danced in the hindermost rows
  At the Théatre des Variétés.

Mademoiselle de la Sauce Mayonnaise
  Didn't yield to a gnawing despair
But married a soldier, and plays
  As a pretty and pert Vivandière.

DISILLUSIONED

BY AN EX-ENTHUSIAST

Oh, that my soul its gods could see
As years ago they seemed to me
  When first I painted them;
Invested with the circumstance
Of old conventional romance:
  Exploded theorem!

The bard who could, all men above,
Inflame my soul with songs of love,
And, with his verse, inspire
The craven soul who feared to die
With all the glow of chivalry
And old heroic fire;

I found him in a beerhouse tap
Awaking from a gin-born nap,
With pipe and sloven dress;
Amusing chums, who fooled his bent,
With muddy, maudlin sentiment,
And tipsy foolishness!

The novelist, whose painting pen
To legions of fictitious men
A real existence lends,
Brain-people whom we rarely fail,
Whene'er we hear their names, to hail
As old and welcome friends;

I found in clumsy snuffy suit,
In seedy glove, and blucher boot,
Uncomfortably big.
Particularly commonplace,
With vulgar, coarse, stockbroking face,
And spectacles and wig.

My favourite actor who, at will,
With mimic woe my eyes could fill
With unaccustomed brine:
A being who appeared to me
(Before I knew him well) to be
A song incarnadine;

I found a coarse unpleasant man
With speckled chin—unhealthy, wan—
Of self-importance full:
Existing in an atmosphere
That reeked of gin and pipes and beer—
Conceited, fractious, dull.

The warrior whose ennobled name
Is woven with his country's fame,
Triumphant over all,
I found weak, palsied, bloated, blear;
His province seemed to be, to leer
At bonnets in Pall Mall.

Would that ye always shone, who write,
Bathed in your own innate limelight,
And ye who battles wage,
Or that in darkness I had died
Before my soul had ever sighed
To see you off the stage!

BABETTE'S LOVE

Babette she was a fisher gal,
With jupon striped and cap in crimps.
She passed her days inside the Halle,
Or catching little nimble shrimps.
Yet she was sweet as flowers in May,
With no professional bouquet.

JACOT was, of the Customs bold,
  An officer, at gay Boulogne,
He loved BABETTE—his love he told,
  And sighed, "Oh, soyez vous my own!"
But "Non!" said she, "JACOT, my pet,
Vous êtes trop scraggy pour BABETTE.

Of one alone I nightly dream,
  An able mariner is he,
And gaily serves the Gen'ral Steam-
  Boat Navigation Companee.
I'll marry him, if he but will—
His name, I rather think, is BILL.

"I see him when he's not aware,
  Upon our hospitable coast,
Reclining with an easy air
  Upon the *Port* against a post,
A-thinking of, I'll dare to say,
His native Chelsea far away!"

"Oh, mon!" exclaimed the Customs bold,
  "Mes yeux!" he said (which means "my eye").
"Oh, chère!" he also cried, I'm told,
  "Par Jove," he added, with a sigh.
"Oh, mon! oh, chère! mes yeux! par Jove!
Je n'aime pas cet enticing cove!"

The *Panther's* captain stood hard by,
  He was a man of morals strict;
If e'er a sailor winked his eye,
  Straightway he had that sailor licked,
Mast-headed all (such was his code)
Who dashed or jiggered, blessed or blowed.

He wept to think a tar of his
  Should lean so gracefully on posts,
He sighed and sobbed to think of this,
  On foreign, French, and friendly coasts.
"It's human natur', p'raps—if so,
Oh, isn't human natur' low!"

He called his Bill, who pulled his curl,
  He said, "My Bill, I understand
You've captivated some young gurl
  On this here French and foreign land.
Her tender heart your beauties jog—
They do, you know they do, you dog.

"You have a graceful way, I learn,
  Of leaning airily on posts,
By which you've been and caused to burn
  A tender flame on these here coasts.
A fisher gurl, I much regret,—
Her age, sixteen—her name, Babette.

"You'll marry her, you gentle tar—
  Your union I myself will bless,
And when you matrimonied are,
  I will appoint her stewardess."
But William hitched himself and sighed,
And cleared his throat, and thus replied:

"Not so: unless you're fond of strife,
  You'd better mind your own affairs,
I have an able-bodied wife

Awaiting me at Wapping Stairs;
If all this here to her I tell,
She'll larrup you and me as well.

"Skin-deep, and valued at a pin,
Is beauty such as VENUS *owns*—
Her beauty is beneath her skin,
And lies in layers on her bones.
The other sailors of the crew
They always calls her 'Whopping Sue!' "

"Oho!" the Captain said, "I see!
And is she then so very strong?"
"She'd take your honour's scruff," said he,
"And pitch you over to Bolong!"
"I pardon you," the Captain said,
"The fair BABETTE you needn't wed."

Perhaps the Customs had his will,
And coaxed the scornful girl to wed,
Perhaps the Captain and his BILL,
And WILLIAM's little wife are dead;
Or p'raps they're all alive and well:
I cannot, cannot, cannot tell.

TO MY BRIDE

(WHOEVER SHE MAY BE)

Oh! little maid!—(I do not know your name,
Or who you are, so, as a safe precaution
I'll add)—Oh, buxom widow! married dame!
(As one of these must be your present portion)
Listen, while I unveil prophetic lore for you,
And sing the fate that Fortune has in store for you.

You'll marry soon—within a year or twain—
A bachelor of *circa* two-and-thirty,
Tall, gentlemanly, but extremely plain,
And, when you're intimate, you call him "BERTIE."
Neat—dresses well; his temper has been classified
As hasty; but he's very quickly pacified.

You'll find him working mildly at the Bar,
After a touch at two or three professions,
From easy affluence extremely far,
A brief or two on Circuit—"soup" at Sessions;
A pound or two from whist and backing horses,
And, say, three hundred from his own resources.

Quiet in harness; free from serious vice,
His faults are not particularly shady;
You'll never find him *"shy"*—for, once or twice
Already, he's been driven by a lady,
Who parts with him—perhaps a poor excuse for him—
Because she hasn't any further use for him.

Oh! bride of mine—tall, dumpy, dark, or fair!
Oh! widow—wife, maybe, or blushing maiden,
I've told *your* fortune: solved the gravest care
With which *your* mind has hitherto been laden.
I've prophesied correctly, never doubt it;
Now tell me mine—and please be quick about it!

You—only you—can tell me, and you will,
To whom I'm destined shortly to be mated,
Will she run up a heavy *modiste's* bill?

If so, I want to hear her income stated.
(This is a point which interests me greatly),
To quote the bard, "Oh! have I seen her lately?"

Say, must I wait till husband number one
Is comfortably stowed away at Woking?
How is her hair most usually done?
And tell me, please, will she object to smoking?
The colour of her eyes, too, you may mention:
Come, Sibyl, prophesy—I'm all attention.

THE FOLLY OF BROWN

BY A GENERAL AGENT

I knew a boor—a clownish card
(His only friends were pigs and cows and
The poultry of a small farmyard),
Who came into two hundred thousand.

Good fortune worked no change in Brown,
  Though she's a mighty social chymist;
He was a clown—and by a clown
  I do not mean a pantomimist.

It left him quiet, calm, and cool,
  Though hardly knowing what a crown was—
You can't imagine what a fool
  Poor rich uneducated Brown was!

He scouted all who wished to come
  And give him monetary schooling;
And I propose to give you some
  Idea of his insensate fooling.

I formed a company or two—
  (Of course I don't know what the rest meant,
I formed them solely with a view
  To help him to a sound investment).

Their objects were—their only cares—
  To justify their Boards in showing
A handsome dividend on shares
  And keep their good promoter going.

But no—the lout sticks to his brass,
  Though shares at par I freely proffer:
Yet—will it be believed?—the ass
  Declines, with thanks, my well-meant offer!

He adds, with bumpkin's stolid grin
  (A weakly intellect denoting),
He'd rather not invest it in
  A company of my promoting!

"You have two hundred 'thou' or more,"
  Said I. "You'll waste it, lose it, lend it;
Come, take my furnished second floor,
  I'll gladly show you how to spend it."

But will it be believed that he,
  With grin upon his face of poppy,
Declined my aid, while thanking me
  For what he called my "philanthroppy"?

Some blind, suspicious fools rejoice
  In doubting friends who wouldn't harm them;
They will not hear the charmer's voice,
  However wisely he may charm them!

I showed him that his coat, all dust,
  Top boots and cords provoked compassion,
And proved that men of station must
  Conform to the decrees of fashion.

I showed him where to buy his hat
  To coat him, trouser him, and boot him;
But no—he wouldn't hear of that—
  "He didn't think the style would suit him!"

I offered him a county seat,
  And made no end of an oration;
I made it certainty complete,
  And introduced the deputation.

But no—the clown my prospect blights—
  (The worth of birth it surely teaches!)
"Why should I want to spend my nights
  In Parliament, a-making speeches?

"I haven't never been to school—
  I ain't had not no eddication—
And I should surely be a fool
  To publish that to all the nation!"

I offered him a trotting horse—
  No hack had ever trotted faster—
I also offered him, of course,
  A rare and curious "old master."

I offered to procure him weeds—
  Wines fit for one in his position—
But, though an ass in all his deeds,
  He'd learnt the meaning of "commission."

He called me "thief" the other day,
  And daily from his door he thrusts me;
Much more of this, and soon I may
  Begin to think that Brown mistrusts me.

So deaf to all sound Reason's rule
  This poor uneducated clown is,
You can*not* fancy what a fool
  Poor rich uneducated Brown is.

SIR MACKLIN

Of all the youths I ever saw
  None were so wicked, vain, or silly,
So lost to shame and Sabbath law
  As worldly Tom, and Bob, and Billy.

For every Sabbath day they walked
  (Such was their gay and thoughtless natur')
In parks or gardens, where they talked
  From three to six, or even later.

Sir Macklin was a priest severe
  In conduct and in conversation,

It did a sinner good to hear
  Him deal in ratiocination.

He could in every action show
  Some sin, and nobody could doubt him.
He argued high, he argued low,
  He also argued round about him.

He wept to think each thoughtless youth
  Contained of wickedness a skinful,
And burnt to teach the awful truth,
  That walking out on Sunday's sinful.

"Oh, youths," said he, "I grieve to find
  The course of life you've been and hit on—
Sit down," said he, "and never mind
  The pennies for the chairs you sit on.

"My opening head is 'Kensington,'
  How walking there the sinner hardens;
Which when I have enlarged upon,
  I go to 'Secondly'—its Gardens.

"My 'Thirdly' comprehendeth 'Hyde,'
  Of Secrecy the guilts and shameses;
My 'Fourthly'—'Park'—its verdure wide—
  My 'Fifthly' comprehends 'St. James's.'

"That matter settled I shall reach
  The 'Sixthly' in my solemn tether,
And show that what is true of each,
  Is also true of all, together.

"Then I shall demonstrate to you,
According to the rules of Whately,
That what is true of all, is true
Of each, considered separately."

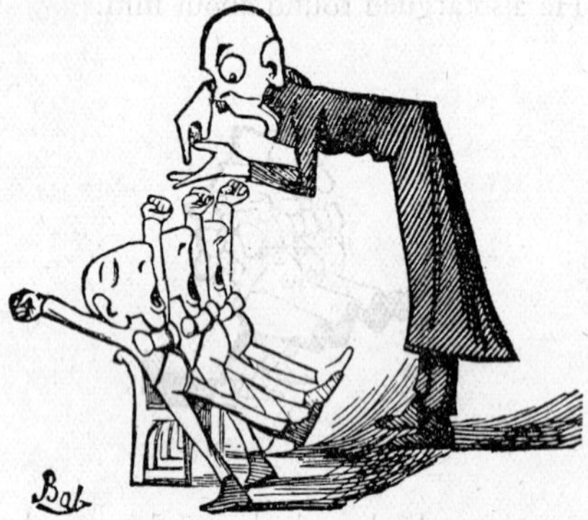

In lavish stream his accents flow,
TOM, BOB, and BILLY dare not flout him;
He argued high, he argued low,
He also argued round about him.

"Ha, ha!" he said, "you loathe your ways,
Repentance on your souls is dawning,
In agony your hands you raise."
(And so they did, for they were yawning.)

To "Twenty-firstly" on they go,
The lads do not attempt to scout him;
He argued high, he argued low,
He also argued round about him.

"Ho, ho!" he cries, "you bow your crests—
My eloquence has set you weeping;
In shame you bend upon your breasts!"
(They bent their heads, for they were sleeping.)

He proved them this—he proved them that
This good but wearisome ascetic;

He jumped and thumped upon his hat,
He was so very energetic.

His bishop at this moment chanced
To pass, and found the road encumbered;
He noticed how the Churchman danced,
And how his congregation slumbered.

The hundred and eleventh head
The priest completed of his stricture;
"Oh, bosh!" the worthy bishop said,
And walked him off, as in the picture.

THE YARN OF THE "NANCY BELL"

'Twas on the shores that round our coast
From Deal to Ramsgate span,
That I found alone on a piece of stone
An elderly naval man.

His hair was weedy, his beard was long,
And weedy and long was he,
And I heard this wight on the shore recite,
In a singular minor key:

"Oh, I am a cook and a captain bold,
And the mate of the *Nancy* brig,
And a bo'sun tight, and a midshipmite,
And the crew of the captain's gig."

And he shook his fists and he tore his hair,
Till I really felt afraid,
For I couldn't help thinking the man had been drinking,
And so I simply said:

"Oh, elderly man, it's little I know
Of the duties of men of the sea,
But I'll eat my hand if I understand
How you can possible be

"At once a cook, and a captain bold,
And the mate of the *Nancy* brig,
And a bo'sun tight, and a midshipmite,
And the crew of the captain's gig."

Then he gave a hitch to his trousers, which
Is a trick all seamen larn,
And having got rid of a thumping quid,
He spun this painful yarn:

" 'Twas in the good ship *Nancy Bell*
That we sailed to the Indian sea,
And there on a reef we come to grief,
Which has often occurred to me.

"And pretty nigh all o' the crew was drowned
(There was seventy-seven o' soul),
And only ten of the *Nancy's* men
Said 'Here' to the muster-roll.

"There was me and the cook and the captain bold,
And the mate of the *Nancy* brig,
And the bo'sun tight, and a midshipmite,
And the crew of the captain's gig."

"For a month we'd neither wittles nor drink,
Till a-hungry we did feel,
So we drawed a lot, and accordin' shot
The captain for our meal.

"The next lot fell to the *Nancy's* mate,
And a delicate dish he made;
Then our appetite with the midshipmite
We seven survivors stayed.

"And then we murdered the bo'sun tight,
And he much resembled pig;
Then we wittled free, did the cook and me,
On the crew of the captain's gig.

"Then only the cook and me was left,
And the delicate question, 'Which
Of us two goes to the kettle?' arose
And we argued it out as sich.

"For I loved that cook as a brother, I did,
And the cook he worshipped me;
But we'd both be blowed if we'd either be stowed
In the other chap's hold, you see.

" 'I'll be eat if you dines off me,' says Tom,
'Yes, that,' says I, 'you'll be,'—
'I'm boiled if I die, my friend,' quoth I,
And 'Exactly so,' quoth he.

"Says he, 'Dear JAMES, to murder me
  Were a foolish thing to do,
For don't you see that you can't cook *me,*
  While I can—and will—cook *you!'*

"So he boils the water, and takes the salt
  And the pepper in portions true
(Which he never forgot), and some chopped shalot,
  And some sage and parsley too.

" 'Come here,' says he, with a proper pride,
  Which his smiling features tell,
' 'Twill soothing be if I let you see,
  How extremely nice you'll smell.'

"And he stirred it round and round and round,
  And he sniffed at the foaming froth;
When I ups with his heels, and smothers his squeals
  In the scum of the boiling broth.

"And I eat that cook in a week or less,
  And—as I eating be
The last of his chops, why, I almost drops,
  For a wessel in sight I see!

* * * * *

"And I never grin, and I never smile,
  And I never larf nor play,
But I sit and croak, and a single joke
  I have—which is to say:

"Oh, I am a cook and a captain bold,
  And the mate of the *Nancy* brig,
And a bo'sun tight, *and* a midshipmite,
  And the crew of the captain's gig!"

THE BISHOP OF RUM-TI-FOO

From east and south the holy clan
Of Bishops gathered, to a man;
To Synod, called Pan-Anglican,
  In flocking crowds they came.

Among them was a Bishop, who
Had lately been appointed to
The balmy isle of Rum-ti-Foo,
    And PETER was his name.

His people—twenty-three in sum—
They played the eloquent tum-tum,
And lived on scalps served up in rum—
    The only sauce they knew.
When first good Bishop PETER came
(For PETER was that Bishop's name),
To humour them, he did the same
    As they of Rum-ti-Foo.

His flock, I've often heard him tell,
(His name was PETER) loved him well,
And summoned by the sound of bell,
    In crowds together came.
"Oh, massa, why you go away?
Oh, Massa PETER, please to stay."
(They called him PETER, people say,
    Because it was his name.)

He told them all good boys to be,
And sailed away across the sea,
At London Bridge that Bishop he
    Arrived one Tuesday night—
And as forthwith he homeward strode
To his Pan-Anglican abode,
He passed along the Borough Road
    And saw a gruesome sight.

He saw a crowd assembled round
A person dancing on the ground,
Who straight began to leap and bound
With all his might and main.
To see that dancing man he stopped,
Who twirled and wriggled, skipped and hopped,
Then down incontinently dropped,
And then sprang up again.

The Bishop chuckled at the sight,
"This style of dancing would delight
A simple Rum-ti-Foozleite,
I'll learn it if I can,
To please the tribe when I get back."
He begged the man to teach his knack.
"Right Reverend Sir, in half a crack,"
Replied that dancing man.

The dancing man he worked away—
And taught the Bishop every day—
The dancer skipped like any fay—
Good Peter did the same.
The Bishop buckled to his task
With *battements,* cuts, and *pas de basque*
(I'll tell you, if you care to ask,
That Peter was his name).

"Come, walk like this," the dancer said,
"Stick out your toes—stick in your head,
Stalk on with quick, galvanic tread—
Your fingers thus extend;
The attitude's considered quaint."
The weary Bishop, feeling faint,
Replied, "I do not say it ain't,
But Time, my Christian friend."

"We now proceed to something new—
Dance as the Paynes and Lauris do,
Like this—one, two—one, two—one, two."
The Bishop, never proud,
But in an overwhelming heat
(His name was Peter, I repeat)
Performed the Payne and Lauri feat,
And puffed his thanks aloud.

Another game the dancer planned—
"Just take your ankle in your hand,
And try, my lord, if you can stand—
Your body stiff and stark.
If, when revisiting your see,
You learnt to hop on shore—like me—
The novelty would striking be,
And must attract remark."

"No," said the worthy Bishop, "No;
That is a length to which, I trow,
Colonial Bishops cannot go.
You may express surprise
At finding Bishops deal in pride—
But, if that trick I ever tried,
I should appear undignified
In Rum-ti-Foozle's eyes.

"The islanders of Rum-ti-Foo
Are well-conducted persons, who
Approve a joke as much as you,
And laugh at it as such;
But if they saw their Bishop land,
His leg supported in his hand,
The joke they wouldn't understand—
'Twould pain them very much!"

THE PRECOCIOUS BABY

A VERY TRUE TALE

(*To be sung to the Air of the "Whistling Oyster"*)

An elderly person—a prophet by trade—
With his quips and tips
On withered old lips,
He married a young and a beautiful maid;
The cunning old blade,
Though rather decayed,
He married a beautiful, beautiful maid.

She was only eighteen, and as fair as could be,
With her tempting smiles
And maidenly wiles,
And he was a trifle of seventy-three:
Now what she could see
Is a puzzle to me,
In a prophet of seventy—seventy-three!

Of all their acquaintances bidden (or bade)
With their loud high jinks
And underbred winks
None thought they'd a family have—but they had;
A singular lad
Who drove 'em half mad,
He proved such a horribly fast little cad.

For when he was born he astonished all by,
With their "Law, dear me!"
"Did ever you see."
He'd a weed in his mouth and a glass in his eye,
A hat all awry—
An octagon tie,
And a miniature—miniature glass in his eye.

He grumbled at wearing a frock and a cap,
With his "Oh dear, no!"
And his "Hang it! 'oo know!"
And he turned up his nose at his excellent pap—
"My friends, it's a tap
Dat is not worf a rap."
(Now this was remarkably excellent pap.)

He'd chuck his nurse under the chin, and he'd say,
With his "Fal, lal, lal"—
" 'Oo doosed fine gal!"
This shocking precocity drove 'em away:
"A month from to-day
Is as long as I'll stay—
Then I'd wish, if you please, for to go, if I may."

His father, a simple old gentleman, he
With nursery rhyme
And "Once on a time,"
Would tell him the story of "Little Bo-P,"
"So pretty was she,
So pretty and wee,
As pretty, as pretty, as pretty could be."

But the babe, with a dig that would startle an ox,
With his "C'ck! Oh my!—
Go along wiz 'oo, fie!"
Would exclaim, "I'm afraid 'oo a socking ole fox."

Now a father it shocks,
And it whitens his locks
When his little babe calls him a shocking old fox.

The name of his father he'd couple and pair
(With his ill-bred laugh,
And insolent chaff)
With those of the nursery heroines rare;
Virginia the fair,
Or Good Goldenhair,
Till the nuisance was more than a prophet could bear.

"There's Jill and White Cat" (said the bold little brat,
With his loud, "Ha, ha!")
" 'Oo sly ickle pa!
Wiz 'oo Beauty, Bo-Peep, and 'oo Mrs. Jack Sprat!
I've noticed 'oo pat
My pretty White Cat—
I sink dear mamma ought to know about dat!"

He early determined to marry and wive,
For better or worse
With his elderly nurse—
Which the poor little boy didn't live to contrive:
His health didn't thrive—
No longer alive,
He died an enfeebled old dotard at five!

MORAL

Now elderly men of the bachelor crew,
With wrinkled hose
And spectacled nose,
Don't marry at all—you may take it as true
If ever you do
The step you will rue,
For your babes will be elderly—elderly too.

TO PHŒBE

"Gentle, modest, little flower,
Sweet epitome of May,
Love me but for half-an-hour,
Love me, love me, little fay."
Sentences so fiercely flaming
In your tiny shell-like ear,
I should always be exclaiming
If I loved you, PHŒBE, dear.

"Smiles that thrill from any distance
Shed upon me while I sing!
Please ecstaticise existence,
Love me, oh thou fairy thing!"
Words like these, outpouring sadly,
You'd perpetually hear,
If I loved you, fondly, madly;—
But I do not, PHŒBE, dear.

BAINES CAREW, GENTLEMAN

Of all the good attorneys who
Have placed their names upon the roll,
But few could equal BAINES CAREW
For tender-heartedness and soul.

Whene'er he heard a tale of woe
From client A or client B,
His grief would overcome him so,
He'd scarce have strength to take his fee.

It laid him up for many days,
  When duty led him to distrain;
And serving writs, although it pays,
  Gave him excruciating pain.

He made out costs, distrained for rent,
  Foreclosed and sued, with moistened eye—
No bill of costs could represent
  The value of such sympathy.

No charges can approximate
  The worth of sympathy with woe;—
Although I think I ought to state
  He did his best to make them so.

Of all the many clients who
  Had mustered round his legal flag,
No single client of the crew
  Was half so dear as CAPTAIN BAGG.

Now CAPTAIN BAGG had bowed him to
  A heavy matrimonial yoke:
His wifey had of faults a few—
  She never could resist a joke.

Her chaff at first he meekly bore,
  Till unendurable it grew.
"To stop this persecution sore
  I will consult my friend CAREW.

"And when CAREW's advice I've got,
  Divorce *a mensâ* I shall try."
(A legal separation—not
  A *vinculo conjugii.*)

"O BAINES CAREW, my woe I've kept
  A secret hitherto, you know!"—
(And BAINES CAREW, ESQUIRE, he wept
  To hear that BAGG had any woe).

"My case, indeed, is passing sad,
  My wife—whom I considered true—
With brutal conduct drives me mad."
  "I am appalled," said BAINES CAREW.

"What! sound the matrimonial knell
  Of worthy people such as these!
Why was I an attorney? Well—
  Go on to the *sævitia,* please."

"Domestic bliss has proved my bane,
  A harder case you never heard,
My wife (in other matters sane)
  Pretends that I'm a Dicky Bird!

"She makes me sing, 'Too-whit, too-wee!'
  And stand upon a rounded stick,
And always introduces me
  To every one as 'Pretty Dick'!"

"Oh dear," said weeping BAINES CAREW,
  "This is the direst case I know"—
"I'm grieved," said BAGG, "at paining you
  To COBB and POLTERTHWAITE I'll go.

"To COBB's cold calculating ear
  My gruesome sorrows I'll impart"—
"No; stop," said BAINES, "I'll dry my tear
  And steel my sympathetic heart!"

"She makes me perch upon a tree,
  Rewarding me with, 'Sweety—nice!'
And threatens to exhibit me
  With four or five performing mice."

"Restrain my tears I wish I could"
  (Said BAINES), "I don't know what to do."
Said CAPTAIN BAGG, "You're very good."
  "Oh, not at all," said BAINES CAREW.

"She makes me fire a gun," said BAGG;
  "And at a preconcerted word
Climb up a ladder with a flag,
  Like any street-performing bird.

"She places sugar in my way—
  In public places calls me 'Sweet!'—
She gives me groundsel every day,
  And hard canary seed to eat."

"Oh, woe! oh, sad! oh, dire to tell!"
  (Said BAINES), "Be good enough to stop."
And senseless on the floor he fell
  With unpremeditated flop.

Said CAPTAIN BAGG, "Well, really I
  Am grieved to think it pains you so.
I thank you for your sympathy;
  But, hang it—come—I say, you know!"

But BAINES lay flat upon the floor,
  Convulsed with sympathetic sob—
The Captain toddled off next door,
  And gave the case to MR. COBB.

THOMAS WINTERBOTTOM HANCE

In all the towns and cities fair
  On Merry England's broad expanse,
No swordsman ever could compare
  With THOMAS WINTERBOTTOM HANCE.

The dauntless lad could fairly hew
  A silken handkerchief in twain,
Divide a leg of mutton, too—
  And this without unwholesome strain.

On whole half-sheep, with cunning trick,
  His sabre sometimes he'd employ—
No bar of lead, however thick,
  Had terrors for the stalwart boy.

At Dover daily he'd prepare
  To hew and slash, behind, before—
Which aggravated Monsieur Pierre,
  Who watched him from the Calais shore.

It caused good Pierre to swear and dance,
  The sight annoyed and vexed him so;
He was the bravest man in France—
  He said so, and he ought to know.

"Regardez, donc, ce cochon gros—
  Ce polisson; Oh, sacré bleu!
Son sabre, son plomb, et ses gigots!
  Comme cela m'ennuye, enfin, mon Dieu!

"Il sait que les foulards de soie
  Give no retaliating whack—
Les gigots morts n'ont pas de quoi—
  Le plomb don't ever hit you back."

But every day the zealous lad
  Cut lead and mutton more and more;
And every day, poor PIERRE, half mad,
  Shrieked loud defiance from his shore.

HANCE had a mother, poor and old,
  A simple, harmless village dame,
Who crowed and clapped as people told
  Of WINTERBOTTOM's rising fame.

She said, "I'll be upon the spot
  To see my TOMMY's sabre-play";
And so she left her leafy cot,
  And walked to Dover in a day.

PIERRE had a doting mother, who
  Had heard of his defiant rage:
His ma was nearly eighty-two,
  And rather dressy for her age.

At HANCE's doings every morn,
With sheer delight *his* mother cried;
And MONSIEUR PIERRE's contemptuous scorn
Filled *his* mamma with proper pride.

But HANCE's powers began to fail—
His constitution was not strong—
And PIERRE, who once was stout and hale,
Grew thin from shouting all day long.

Their mothers saw them pale and wan,
Maternal anguish tore each breast,
And so they met to find a plan
To set their offsprings' minds at rest.

Said MRS. HANCE, "Of course I shrinks
From bloodshed, ma'am, as you're aware,
But still they'd better meet, I thinks."
"Assurément!" said MADAME PIERRE.

A sunny spot in sunny France
Was hit upon for this affair;
The ground was picked by MRS. HANCE,
The stakes were pitched by MADAME PIERRE.

Said MRS. H., "Your work you see—
Go in, my noble boy, and win."

"En garde, mon fils!" said Madame P.
"Allons!" "Go on!" "En garde!" "Begin!"

Loud sneered the doughty man of France,
"Ho! ho! Ho! ho! Ha! ha! Ha! ha!"
"The French for 'Pish!' " said Thomas Hance.
Said Pierre, "L'Anglais, Monsieur, pour 'bah!' "

Said Mrs. H., "Come, one! two! three!—
We're sittin' here to see all fair";
"C'est magnifique!" said Madame P.,
"Mais, parbleu! ce n'est pas la guerre!"

"Je scorn un foe si lâche que vous,"
Said Pierre, the doughty son of France.
"I fight not coward foe like you!"
Said our undaunted Tommy Hance.

"The French for 'Pooh!' " our Tommy cried.
"L'Anglais pour 'Va!' " the Frenchman crowed.
And so, with undiminished pride,
Each went on his respective road.

A DISCONTENTED SUGAR BROKER

A gentleman of City fame
  Now claims your kind attention;
West India broking was his game,
  His name I shall not mention;
    No one of finely pointed sense
    Would violate a confidence,
      And shall *I* go
      And do it? No.
  His name I shall not mention.

He had a trusty wife and true,
  And very cosy quarters,
A manager, a boy or two,
  Six clerks, and seven porters.
    A broker must be doing well
    (As any lunatic can tell)
      Who can employ
      An active boy,
  Six clerks, and seven porters.

His knocker advertised no dun,
  No losses made him sulky,
He had one sorrow—only one—
  He was extremely bulky.

A man must be, I beg to state,
Exceptionally fortunate
Who owns his chief
And only grief
Is being very bulky.

"This load," he'd say, "I cannot bear,
I'm nineteen stone or twenty!
Henceforward I'll go in for air
And exercise in plenty."
Most people think that, should it come,
They can reduce a bulging tum
To measures fair
By taking air
And exercise in plenty.

In every weather, every day,
Dry, muddy, wet, or gritty,
He took to dancing all the way
From Brompton to the City.

You do not often get the chance
Of seeing sugar-brokers dance
From their abode
In Fulham Road
Through Brompton to the City.

He braved the gay and guileless laugh
Of children with their nusses,
The loud uneducated chaff
Of clerks on omnibuses.
Against all minor things that rack
A nicely balanced mind, I'll back
The noisy chaff
And ill-bred laugh
Of clerks on omnibuses.

His friends, who heard his money chink,
And saw the house he rented,
And knew his wife, could never think
What made him discontented.
It never struck their simple minds
That fads are of eccentric kinds,
Nor would they own
That fat alone
Could make one discontented.

"Your riches know no kind of pause,
Your trade is fast advancing,
You dance—but not for joy, because
You weep as you are dancing.
To dance implies that man is glad,
To weep implies that man is sad.
But here are you
Who do the two—
You weep as you are dancing!"

His mania soon got noised about
And into all the papers—
His size increased beyond a doubt
For all his reckless capers:

It may seem singular to you,
But all his friends admit it true—
The more he found
His figure round,
The more he cut his capers.

His bulk increased—no matter that—
He tried the more to toss it—
He never spoke of it as "fat"
But "adipose deposit."
Upon my word, it seems to me
Unpardonable vanity
(And worse than that)
To call your fat
An "adipose deposit."

At length his brawny knees gave way,
And on the carpet sinking,
Upon his shapeless back he lay
And kicked away like winking.
Instead of seeing in his state
The finger of unswerving Fate,
He laboured still
To work his will,
And kicked away like winking.

His friends, disgusted with him now,
Away in silence wended—
I hardly like to tell you how
This dreadful story ended.

The shocking sequel to impart,
I must employ the limner's art—
If you would know,
This sketch will show
How his exertions ended.

MORAL

I hate to preach—I hate to prate—
I'm no fanatic croaker,
But learn contentment from the fate
Of this West India broker.
He'd everything a man of taste
Could ever want, except a waist:
And discontent
His size anent,
And bootless perseverance blind,
Completely wrecked the peace of mind
Of this West India broker.

THE PANTOMIME "SUPER" TO HIS MASK

Vast, empty shell!
Impertinent, preposterous abortion:
With vacant stare,
And ragged hair,
And every feature out of all proportion!
Embodiment of echoing inanity,
Excellent type of simpering insanity,
Unwieldy, clumsy nightmare of humanity,
I ring thy knell!

To-night thou diest,
Beast that destroy'st my heaven-born identity!
Twelve weeks of nights
Before the lights,
Swamped in thine own preposterous nonentity,
I've been ill-treated, cursed, and thrashed diurnally,
Credited for the smile you wear externally—
I feel disposed to smash thy face, infernally,
As there thou liest!

I've been thy brain:
I've been the brain that lit thy dull concavity!
The human race
Invest *my* face
With thine expression of unchecked depravity:

Invested with a ghastly reciprocity,
I've been responsible for thy monstrosity,
I, for thy wanton, blundering ferocity—
But not again!

'Tis time to toll
Thy knell, and that of follies pantomimical:
A twelve weeks' run,
And thou hast done
All thou canst do to make thyself inimical.
Adieu, embodiment of all inanity!
Excellent type of simpering insanity!
Unwieldy, clumsy nightmare of humanity!
Freed is thy soul!

(*The Mask respondeth*)

Oh! master mine,
Look thou within thee, ere again ill-using me.
Art thou aware
Of nothing there
Which might abuse thee, as thou art abusing me?
A brain that mourns *thine* unredeemed rascality?
A soul that weeps at *thy* threadbare morality?
Both grieving that *their* individuality
Is merged in thine?

THE GHOST, THE GALLANT, THE GAEL, AND THE GOBLIN

O'er unreclaimed suburban clay
Some years ago were hobblin',
An elderly ghost of easy ways,
And an influential goblin.
The ghost was a sombre spectral shape,
A fine old five-act fogy,
The goblin imp, a lithe young ape,
A fine low-comedy bogy.

And as they exercised their joints,
Promoting quick digestion,
They talked on several curious points,
And raised this pregnant question:
"Which of us two is Number One—
The ghostie, or the goblin?"

And o'er the point they raised in fun
  They fairly fell a-squabblin'.

They'd barely speak, and each, in fine,
  Grew more and more reflective,
Each thought his own particular line
  By far the more effective.
At length they settled some one should
  By each of them be haunted,
And so arranged that either could
  Exert his prowess vaunted.

"The Quaint against the Statuesque"—
  By competition lawful—
The goblin backed the Quaint Grotesque,
  The ghost the Grandly Awful.
"Now," said the goblin, "here's my plan—
  In attitude commanding,
I see a stalwart Englishman
  By yonder tailor's standing.

"The very fittest man on earth
  My influence to try on—
Of gentle, p'raps of noble birth,
  And dauntless as a lion!

Now wrap yourself within your shroud—
  Remain in easy hearing—
Observe—you'll hear him scream aloud
  When I begin appearing!"

The imp with yell unearthly—wild—
  Threw off his dark enclosure:
His dauntless victim looked and smiled
  With singular composure.
For hours he tried to daunt the youth,
  For days, indeed, but vainly—
The stripling smiled!—to tell the truth,
  The stripling smiled inanely.

For weeks the goblin weird and wild,
  That noble stripling haunted;
For weeks the stripling stood and smiled
  Unmoved and all undaunted.
The sombre ghost exclaimed, "Your plan
  Has failed you, goblin, plainly:
Now watch yon hardy Hieland man,
  So stalwart and ungainly.

"These are the men who chase the roe,
  Whose footsteps never falter,
Who bring with them where'er they go,
  A smack of old SIR WALTER.
Of such as he, the men sublime
  Who lead their troops victorious,
Whose deeds go down to after-time,
  Enshrined in annals glorious!

"Of such as he the bard has said
  'Hech thrawfu' raltie rawkie!
Wi' thecht ta' croonie clapperhead
  And fash' wi' unco pawkie!'
He'll faint away when I appear
  Upon his native heather;
Or p'raps he'll only scream with fear,
  Or p'raps the two together."

The spectre showed himself, alone,
  To do his ghostly battling,
With curdling groan and dismal moan
  And lots of chains a-rattling!
But no—the chiel's stout Gaelic stuff
  Withstood all ghostly harrying.
His fingers closed upon the snuff
  Which upwards he was carrying.

For days that ghost declined to stir,
  A foggy, shapeless giant—
For weeks that splendid officer
  Stared back again defiant!
Just as the Englishman returned
  The goblin's vulgar staring,
Just so the Scotchman boldly spurned
  The ghost's unmannered scaring.

For several years the ghostly twain
  These Britons bold have haunted,
But all their efforts are in vain—
  Their victims stand undaunted.
Unto this day the imp and ghost
  (Whose powers the imp derided)
Stand each at his allotted post—
  The bet is undecided.

KING BORRIA BUNGALEE BOO

King Borria Bungalee Boo
  Was a man-eating African swell;
His sigh was a hullaballoo,
  His whisper a horrible yell—
  A horrible, horrible yell!

Four subjects, and all of them male,
  To Borria doubled the knee,
They were once on a far larger scale,
  But he'd eaten the balance, you see
  ("Scale" and "balance" is punning, you see).

There was haughty Pish-Tush-Pooh-Bah,
  There was lumbering Doodle-Dum-Deh,
Despairing Alack-a-Dey-Ah,
  And good little Tootle-Tum-Teh—
  Exemplary Tootle-Tum-Teh.

One day there was grief in the crew,
  For they hadn't a morsel of meat,
And Borria Bungalee Boo
  Was dying for something to eat—
  "Come, provide me with something to eat!

"Alack-a-Dey, famished I feel;
  Oh, good little Tootle-Tum-Teh,
Where on earth shall I look for a meal?
  For I haven't had dinner to-day!—
Not a morsel of dinner to-day!

"Dear Tootle-Tum, what shall we do?
  Come, get us a meal, or in truth,
If you don't we shall have to eat you,
  Oh, adorable friend of our youth!
Thou beloved little friend of our youth!"

And he answered, "Oh, Bungalee Boo,
  For a moment I hope you will wait,—
Tippy-Wippity Tol-the-Rol-Loo
  Is the Queen of a neighbouring state—
  A remarkably neighbouring state.

"TIPPY-WIPPITY TOL-THE-ROL-LOO,
She would pickle deliciously cold—
And her four pretty Amazons, too,
Are enticing, and not very old—
Twenty-seven is not very old.

"There is neat little TITTY-FOL-LEH,
There is rollicking TRAL-THE-RAL-LAH,
There is jocular WAGGETY-WEH,
There is musical DOH-REH-MI-FAH—
There's the nightingale DOH-REH-MI-FAH!"

So the forces of BUNGALEE BOO
Marched forth in a terrible row,
And the ladies who fought for QUEEN LOO
Prepared to encounter the foe—
This dreadful insatiate foe!

But they sharpened no weapons at all,
And they poisoned no arrows—not they:
They made ready to conquer or fall
In a totally different way—
A perfectly different way.

With a crimson and pearly-white dye
  They endeavoured to make themselves fair;
With black they encircled each eye,
  And with yellow they painted their hair,
  (It was wool, but they thought it was hair).

The warriors met in the field:
  And the men of King Borria said,
"Amazonians, immediately yield!"
  And their arrows they drew to the head—
  Yes, drew them right up to the head.

But jocular Waggety-Weh
  Ogled Doodle-Dum-Deh (which was wrong),
And neat little Titty-Fol-Leh
  Said, "Tootle-Tum, you go along!
  You naughty old dear, go along!"

And rollicking Tral-the-Ral-Lah
  Tapped Alack-a-Dey-Ah with her fan;
And musical Doh-Reh-Mi-Fah
  Said, "Pish, go away, you bad man!
  Go away, you delightful young man!"

And the Amazons simpered and sighed,
  And they ogled, and giggled, and flushed,
And they opened their pretty eyes wide,
  And they chuckled, and flirted, and blushed
  (At least, if they could, they'd have blushed).

But haughty Pish-Tush-Pooh-Bah
  Said, "Alack-a-Dey, what does this mean?"
And despairing Alack-a-Dey-Ah
  Said, "They think us uncommonly green!"
  Ha! ha! most uncommonly green!"

Even blundering Doodle-Dum-Deh
  Was insensible quite to their leers,
And said good little Tootle-Tum-Teh,
  "It's your blood that we're wanting, my dears—
  We have come for our dinners, my dears!"

And the Queen of the Amazons fell
To Borria Bungalee Boo,—
In a mouthful he gulped, with a yell,
Tippy-Wippity Tol-the-Rol-Loo—
The pretty Queen Tol-the-Rol-Loo.

And neat little Titty-Fol-Leh
Was eaten by Pish-Pooh-Bah,
And light-hearted Waggety-Weh
By dismal Alack-a-Dey-Ah—
Despairing Alack-a-Dey-Ah.

And rollicking Tral-the-Ral-Lah
Was eaten by Doodle-Dum-Deh,
And musical Doh-Reh-Mi-Fah
By good little Tootle-Tum-Teh—
Exemplary Tootle-Tum-Teh.

THE PERIWINKLE GIRL

I've often thought that headstrong youths
  Of decent education,
Determine all-important truths,
  With strange precipitation.

The ever-ready victims they,
  Of logical illusions,
And in a self-assertive way
  They jump at strange conclusions.

Now take my case: Ere sorrow could
  My ample forehead wrinkle,
I had determined that I should
  Not care to be a winkle.

"A winkle," I would oft advance
  With readiness provoking,
"Can seldom flirt, and never dance,
  Or soothe his mind by smoking."

In short, I spurned the shelly joy,
  And spoke with strange decision—
Men pointed to me as a boy
  Who held them in derision.

But I was young—too young, by far—
Or I had been more wary,
I knew not then that winkles are
The stock-in-trade of Mary.

I had not watched her sunlight blithe
As o'er their shells it dances—
I've seen those winkles almost writhe
Beneath her beaming glances.

Of slighting all the winkly brood
I surely had been chary,
If I had known they formed the food
And stock-in-trade of Mary.

Both high and low and great and small
Fell prostrate at her tootsies,
They all were noblemen, and all
Had balances at Coutts's.

Dukes with the lovely maiden dealt,
Duke Bailey and Duke Humphy,
Who ate her winkles till they felt
Exceedingly uncomfy.

Duke Bailey greatest wealth computes,
And sticks, they say, at no-thing,
He wears a pair of golden boots
And silver underclothing.

Duke Humphy, as I understand,
Though mentally acuter,
His boots are only silver, and
His underclothing pewter.

A third adorer had the girl,
A man of lowly station—
A miserable grov'ling Earl
Besought her approbation.

This humble cad she did refuse
With much contempt and loathing,
He wore a pair of leather shoes
And cambric underclothing!

"Ha! ha!" she cried. "Upon my word!
Well, really—come, I never!
Oh, go along, it's too absurd!
My goodness! Did you ever?

"Two Dukes would Mary make a bride,
And from her foes defend her"—
"Well, not exactly that," they cried,
"We offer guilty splendour.

"We do not offer marriage rite,
So please dismiss the notion!"
"Oh dear," said she, "that alters quite
The state of my emotion."

The Earl he up and says, says he,
"Dismiss them to their orgies,
For I am game to marry thee
Quite reg'lar at St. George's."

(He'd had, it happily befell,
A decent education,
His views would have befitted well
A far superior station.)

His sterling worth had worked a cure,
She never heard him grumble;
She saw his soul was good and pure,
Although his rank was humble.

Her views of earldoms and their lot,
All underwent expansion—
Come, Virtue in an earldom's cot!
Go, Vice in ducal mansion!

THOMSON GREEN AND HARRIET HALE

(*To be sung to the Air of "An 'Orrible Tale"*)

Oh, list to this incredible tale
Of Thomson Green and Harriet Hale;
Its truth in one remark you'll sum—

"Twaddle twaddle twaddle twaddle twaddle twaddle
twum!"

Oh, THOMSON GREEN was an auctioneer,
And made three hundred pounds a year;
And HARRIET HALE, most strange to say,
Gave pianoforte lessons at a sovereign a day.

Oh, THOMSON GREEN, I may remark,
Met HARRIET HALE in Regent's Park,
Where he, in a casual kind of way,
Spoke of the extraordinary beauty of the day.

They met again, and strange, though true,
He courted her for a month or two,
Then to her pa he said, says he,
"Old man, I love your daughter and your daughter
worships me!"

Their names were regularly banned,
The wedding day was settled, and
I've ascertained by dint of search
They were married on the quiet at St. Mary Abbot's
Church.

Oh, list to this incredible tale
Of THOMSON GREEN and HARRIET HALE;
Its truth in one remark you'll sum—
"Twaddle twaddle twaddle twaddle twaddle twaddle
twum!"

That very self-same afternoon
They started on their honeymoon,
And (oh, astonishment!) took flight
To a pretty little cottage close to Shanklin, Isle of Wight.

But now—you'll doubt my word, I know—
In a month they both returned, and lo!
Astounding fact! this happy pair
Took a gentlemanly residence in Canonbury Square!

They led a weird and reckless life,
They dined each day, this man and wife
(Pray disbelieve it, if you please),
On a joint of meat, a pudding, and a little bit of cheese.

In time came those maternal joys
Which take the form of girls or boys,
And strange to say of each they'd one—
A tiddy-iddy daughter, and a tiddy-iddy son!

Oh, list to this incredible tale
Of THOMSON GREEN and HARRIET HALE;
Its truth in one remark you'll sum—
"Twaddle twaddle twaddle twaddle twaddle twaddle twum!"

My name for truth is gone, I fear,
But, monstrous as it may appear,
They let their drawing-room one day
To an eligible person in the cotton-broking way.

Whenever THOMSON GREEN fell sick
His wife called in a doctor, quick,
From whom some words like these would come—
Fiat mist. sumendum haustus, in a *cochleyareum.*

For thirty years this curious pair
Hung out in Canonbury Square,
And somehow, wonderful to say,
They loved each other dearly in a quiet sort of way.

Well, THOMSON GREEN fell ill and died;
For just a year his widow cried,
And then her heart she gave away
To the eligible lodger in the cotton-broking way.

Oh, list to this incredible tale
Of THOMSON GREEN and HARRIET HALE;
Its truth in one remark you'll sum—
"Twaddle twaddle twaddle twaddle twaddle twaddle twum!"

BOB POLTER

BOB POLTER was a navvy, and
His hands were coarse, and dirty too,
His homely face was rough and tanned,
His time of life was thirty-two.

He lived among a working clan
  (A wife he hadn't got at all),
A decent, steady, sober man—
  No saint, however—not at all.

He smoked, but in a modest way,
  Because he thought he needed it:
He drank a pot of beer a day,
  And sometimes he exceeded it.

At times he'd pass with other men
  A loud convivial night or two,
With, very likely, now and then,
  On Saturdays, a fight or two.

But still he was a sober soul,
  A labour-never-shirking man,
Who paid his way—upon the whole,
  A decent English working-man.

One day, when at the Nelson's Head
  (For which he may be blamed of you),
A holy man appeared and said,
  "Oh, Robert, I'm ashamed of you."

He laid his hand on Robert's beer
  Before he could drink up any,
And on the floor, with sigh and tear,
  He poured the pot of "thruppenny."

"Oh, Robert, at this very bar,
  A truth you'll be discovering,
A good and evil genius are
  Around your noddle hovering.

"They both are here to bid you shun
  The other one's society,
For Total Abstinence is one,
  The other, Inebriety."

He waved his hand—a vapour came—
  A wizard, Polter reckoned him:
A bogy rose and called his name,
  And with his finger beckoned him.

The monster's salient points to sum,
His breath was hot as cautery;
His glowing nose suggested rum;
His eyes were gin-and-watery.

His dress was torn—for dregs of ale
And slops of gin had rusted it;
His pimpled face was wan and pale,
Where filth had not encrusted it.

"Come, POLTER," said the fiend, "begin
And keep the bowl a-flowing on—
A working-man needs pints of gin
To keep his clockwork going on."

BOB shuddered: "Ah, you've made a miss,
If you take me for one of you—

You filthy brute, get out of this—
  Bob Polter don't want none of you."

The demon gave a drunken shriek,
  And crept away in stealthiness,
And lo, instead, a person sleek
  Who seemed to burst with healthiness.

"In me, as your adviser hints,
  Of Abstinence you've got a type—
Of Mr. Tweedie's pretty prints
  I am the happy prototype.

"If you abjure the social toast,
  And pipes, and such frivolities,
You possibly some day may boast
  My prepossessing qualities!"

Bob rubbed his eyes, and made 'em blink,
  "You almost make me tremble, you!
If I abjure fermented drink,
  Shall I, indeed, resemble you?

"And will my whiskers curl so tight?
My cheeks grow smug and muttony?
My face become so pink and white?
My coat so blue and buttony?

"Will trousers, such as yours, array
Extremities inferior?
Will chubbiness assert its sway
All over my exterior?

"In this, my unenlightened state,
To work in heavy boots I comes—
Will pumps henceforward decorate
My tiddle toddle tootsicums?

"And shall I get so plump and fresh,
And look no longer seedily?
My skin will henceforth fit my flesh
So tightly and so TWEEDIE-ly?"

The phantom said, "You'll have all this,
You'll have no kind of huffiness,
Your life will be one chubby bliss,
One long unruffled puffiness!"

"Be off," said irritated BOB,
"Why come you here to bother one?
You pharisaical old snob,
You're wuss, almost, than t'other one!

"I takes my pipe—I takes my pot,
And drunk I'm never seen to be
I'm no teetotaller or sot,
And as I am I mean to be!"

ELLEN M'JONES ABERDEEN

MACPHAIRSON CLONGLOCKETTY ANGUS M'CLAN
Was the son of an elderly labouring man,
You've guessed him a Scotchman, shrewd reader, at sight,
And p'raps altogether, shrewd reader, you're right.

From the bonnie blue Forth to the hills of Deeside,
Round by Dingwall and Wrath to the mouth of the Clyde,
There wasn't a child or a woman or man
Who could pipe with CLONGLOCKETTY ANGUS M'CLAN.

No other could wake such detestable groans,
With reed and with chaunter—with bag and with drones:
All day and all night he delighted the chiels
With sniggering pibrochs and jiggety reels.

He'd clamber a mountain and squat on the ground,
And the neighbouring maidens would gather around
To list to his pipes and to gaze in his e'en,
Especially ELLEN M'JONES ABERDEEN.

All loved their M'CLAN, save a Sassenach brute,
Who came to the Highlands to fish and to shoot;
He dressed himself up in a Highlander way,
Though his name it was PATTISON CORBY TORBAY.

TORBAY had incurred a good deal of expense
To make him a Scotchman in every sense;
But this is a matter, you'll readily own,
That isn't a question of tailors alone.

A Sassenach chief may be bonily built,
He may purchase a sporran, a bonnet, and kilt;
Stick a skean in his hose—wear an acre of stripes—
But he cannot assume an affection for pipes.

CLONGLOCKETTY's pipings all night and all day
Quite frenzied poor PATTISON CORBY TORBAY;
The girls were amused at his singular spleen,
Especially ELLEN M'JONES ABERDEEN.

"MACPHAIRSON CLONGLOCKETTY ANGUS, my lad,
With pibrochs and reels you are driving me mad;
If you really must play on that cursed affair,
My goodness! play something resembling an air."

Boiled over the blood of MACPHAIRSON M'CLAN—
The clan of Clonglocketty rose as one man;
For all were enraged at the insult, I ween—
Especially ELLEN M'JONES ABERDEEN.

"Let's show," said M'CLAN, "to this Sassenach loon
That the bagpipes can play him a regular tune.
Let's see," said M'CLAN, as he thoughtfully sat,
"*'In My Cottage'* is easy—I'll practise at that."

He blew at his "Cottage," and blew with a will,
For a year, seven months, and a fortnight, until
(You'll hardly believe it) M'CLAN, I declare,
Elicited something resembling an air.

It was wild—it was fitful—as wild as the breeze—
It wandered about into several keys;
It was jerky, spasmodic, and harsh, I'm aware,
But still it distinctly suggested an air.

The Sassenach screamed, and the Sassenach danced,
He shrieked in his agony—bellowed and pranced;
And the maidens who gathered rejoiced at the scene,
Especially ELLEN M'JONES ABERDEEN.

"Hech gather, hech gather, hech gather around;
And fill a' yer lugs wi' the exquisite sound.
An air frae the bagpipes—beat that if ye can!
Hurrah for CLONGLOCKETTY ANGUS M'CLAN!"

The fame of his piping spread over the land:
Respectable widows proposed for his hand,
And maidens came flocking to sit on the green—
Especially ELLEN M'JONES ABERDEEN.

One morning the fidgety Sassenach swore
He'd stand it no longer—he drew his claymore,
And (this was, I think, in extremely bad taste),
Divided CLONGLOCKETTY close to the waist.

Oh! loud were the wailings for ANGUS M'CLAN—
Oh! deep was the grief for that excellent man—
The maids stood aghast at the horrible scene,
Especially ELLEN M'JONES ABERDEEN.

It sorrowed poor Pattison Corby Torbay
To find them "take on" in this serious way,
He pitied the poor little fluttering birds,
And solaced their souls with the following words:—

"Oh, maidens," said Pattison, touching his hat,
"Don't snivel, my dears, for a fellow like that;
Observe, I'm a very superior man,
A much better fellow than Angus M'Clan."

They smiled when he winked and addressed them as "dears,"
And they all of them vowed, as they dried up their tears,
A pleasanter gentleman never was seen—
Especially Ellen M'Jones Aberdeen.

PETER THE WAG

Policeman Peter Forth I drag
From his obscure retreat:
He was a merry, genial wag,
Who loved a mad conceit.
If he were asked the time of day
By country bumpkins green,
He not infrequently would say,
"A quarter past thirteen."

If ever you by word of mouth
Enquired of Mister Forth
The way to somewhere in the South,
He always sent you North.
With little boys his beat along
He loved to stop and play;
He loved to send old ladies wrong,
And teach their feet to stray.

He would in frolic moments, when
Such mischief bent upon,
Take Bishops up as betting men—
Bid Ministers move on.

Then all the worthy boys he knew
He regularly licked,
And always collared people who
Had had their pockets picked.

He was not naturally bad,
Or viciously inclined,
But from his early youth he had
A waggish turn of mind.
The Men of London grimly scowled
With indignation wild;
The Men of London gruffly growled
But PETER calmly smiled.

Against this minion of the Crown
The swelling murmurs grew—
From Camberwell to Kentish Town—
From Rotherhithe to Kew.
Still humoured he his wagsome turn,
And fed in various ways
The coward rage that dared to burn
But did not dare to blaze.

Still, Retribution has her day
  Although her flight is slow:
One day that Crusher lost his way
  Near Poland Street, Soho.
The haughty youth, too proud to ask,
  To find his way resolved,
And in the tangle of his task
  Got more and more involved.

The Men of London, overjoyed,
  Came there to jeer their foe—
And flocking crowds completely cloyed
  The mazes of Soho.
The news, on telegraphic wires,
  Sped swiftly o'er the lea—
Excursion trains from distant shires
  Brought myriads to see.

For weeks he trod his self-made beats
  Through Newport, Gerrard, Bear,
Greek, Rupert, Frith, Dean, Poland Streets,
  And into Golden Square:
But all, alas, in vain, for when
  He tried to learn the way
Of little boys or grown-up men
  They none of them would say.

Their eyes would flash—their teeth would grind—
  Their lips would tightly curl—
They'd say, "Thy way thyself must find,
  Thou misdirecting churl!"
And, similarly, also, when
  He tried a foreign friend;
Italians answered, "Il balen"—
  The French, "No comprehend."

The Russ would say with gleaming eye
  "Sevastopol!" and groan.
The Greek said, "*Τυπτω, τυπτομαι,*
  Τυπτω, τυπτειν, τυπτων."
To wander thus for many a year
  That Crusher never ceased—
The Men of London dropped a tear,
  Their anger was appeased.

At length exploring gangs were sent
  To find poor FORTH's remains—
A handsome grant by Parliament
  Was voted for their pains.
To seek the poor policeman out
  Bold spirits volunteered,
And when at length they solved the doubt
  The Men of London cheered.

And in a yard, dark, dank, and drear,
  They found him, on the floor—
(It leads from Richmond Buildings—near
  The Royalty stage-door.)
With brandy cold and brandy hot
  They plied him, starved and wet,
And made him sergeant on the spot—
  The Men of London's pet!

THE THREE KINGS OF CHICKERABOO

There were three niggers of Chickeraboo—
Pacifico, Bang-bang, Popchop—who
Exclaimed, one terribly sultry day,
"Oh, let's be kings in a humble way."

The first was a highly-accomplished "bones,"
The next elicited banjo tones,
The third was a quiet, retiring chap,
Who danced an excellent break-down "flap."

"We niggers," said they, "have formed a plan
By which, whenever we like, we can
Extemporise kingdoms near the beach,
And then we'll collar a kingdom each.

"Three casks, from somebody else's stores,
Shall represent our island shores,
Their sides the ocean wide shall lave,
Their heads just topping the briny wave.

"Great Britain's navy scours the sea,
And everywhere her ships they be;
She'll recognise our rank, perhaps,
When she discovers we're Royal Chaps.

"If to her skirts you want to cling,
It's quite sufficient that you're a king;
She does not push inquiry far
To learn what sort of king you are."

A ship of several thousand tons,
And mounting seventy-something guns,
Ploughed, every year, the ocean blue,
Discovering kings and countries new.

The brave Rear-Admiral Bailey Pip,
Commanding that magnificent ship,

Perceived one day, his glasses through,
The kings that came from Chickeraboo.

"Dear eyes!" said ADMIRAL PIP, "I see
Three flourishing islands on our lee.
And, bless me! most remarkable thing!
On every island stands a king!

"Come, lower the Admiral's gig," he cried,
"And over the dancing waves I'll glide;
That low obeisance I may do
To those three kings of Chickeraboo!"

The Admiral pulled to the islands three;
The kings saluted him gracious*lee*.
The Admiral, pleased at his welcome warm,
Unrolled a printed Alliance form.

"Your majesty, sign me this, I pray—
I come in a friendly kind of way—
I come, if you please, with the best intents,
And QUEEN VICTORIA's compliments."

The kings were pleased as they well could be;
The most retiring of the three,
In a "cellar-flap" to his joy gave vent
With a banjo-bones accompaniment.

The great Rear-Admiral Bailey Pip
Embarked on board his jolly big ship,
Blue Peter flew from his lofty fore,
And off he sailed to his native shore.

Admiral Pip directly went
To the Lord at the head of the Government,
Who made him, by a stroke of the quill,
Baron de Pippe, of Pippetonneville.

The College of Heralds permission yield
That he should quarter upon his shield
Three islands, *vert,* on a field of blue,
With the pregnant motto "Chickeraboo."

Ambassadors, yes, and attachés, too,
Are going to sail for Chickeraboo.
And, see, on the good ship's crowded deck,
A bishop, who's going out there on spec.

And let us all hope that blissful things
May come of alliance with darky kings,
And, may we never, whatever we do,
Declare a war with Chickeraboo!

GENTLE ALICE BROWN

It was a robber's daughter, and her name was Alice Brown,
Her father was the terror of a small Italian town;
Her mother was a foolish, weak, but amiable old thing;
But it isn't of her parents that I'm going for to sing.

As Alice was a-sitting at her window-sill one day
A beautiful young gentleman he chanced to pass that way;

She cast her eyes upon him, and he looked so good and true,
That she thought, "I could be happy with a gentleman like you!"

And every morning passed her house that cream of gentlemen,
She knew she might expect him at a quarter unto ten,
A sorter in the Custom-house, it was his daily road
(The Custom-house was fifteen minutes' walk from her abode).

But Alice was a pious girl, who knew it wasn't wise
To look at strange young sorters with expressive purple eyes;
So she sought the village priest to whom her family confessed—
The priest by whom their little sins were carefully assessed.

"Oh, holy father," Alice said, "'twould grieve you, would it not?
To discover that I was a most disreputable lot!
Of all unhappy sinners I'm the most unhappy one!"
The padre said, "Whatever have you been and gone and done?"

"I have helped mamma to steal a little kiddy from its dad,
I've assisted dear papa in cutting up a little lad.
I've planned a little burglary and forged a little cheque,
And slain a little baby for the coral on its neck!"

The worthy pastor heaved a sigh, and dropped a silent tear—
And said, "You mustn't judge yourself too heavily, my dear—
It's wrong to murder babies, little corals for to fleece;
But sins like these one expiates at half-a-crown apiece.

"Girls will be girls—you're very young, and flighty in your mind;
Old heads upon young shoulders we must not expect to find:
We mustn't be too hard upon these little girlish tricks—
Let's see—five crimes at half-a-crown—exactly twelve-and-six."

"Oh, father," little ALICE cried, "your kindness makes
me weep,
You do these little things for me so singularly cheap—
Your thoughtful liberality I never can forget;
But oh, there is another crime I haven't mentioned yet!

"A pleasant-looking gentleman, with pretty purple eyes,—
I've noticed at my window, as I've sat a-catching flies;
He passes by it every day as certain as can be—
I blush to say I've winked at him, and he has winked at
me!"

"For shame," said FATHER PAUL, "my erring daughter!
On my word
This is the most distressing news that I have ever heard.
Why, naughty girl, your excellent papa has pledged your
hand
To a promising young robber, the lieutenant of his band!

"This dreadful piece of news will pain your worthy
parents so!
They are the most remunerative customers I know;
For many, many years they've kept starvation from my
doors,
I never knew so criminal a family as yours!

"The common country folk in this insipid neighbourhood
Have nothing to confess, they're so ridiculously good;
And if you marry any one respectable at all,
Why, you'll reform, and what will then become of
FATHER PAUL?"

The worthy priest, he up and drew his cowl upon his
crown,
And started off in haste to tell the news to ROBBER
BROWN;
To tell him how his daughter, who was now for marriage
fit,
Had winked upon a sorter, who reciprocated it.

Good ROBBER BROWN he muffled up his anger pretty well,
He said, "I have a notion, and that notion I will tell;
I will nab this gay young sorter, terrify him into fits,
And get my gentle wife to chop him into little bits.

"I've studied human nature, and I know a thing or two;
Though a girl may fondly love a living gent, as many do,
A feeling of disgust upon her senses there will fall
When she looks upon his body chopped particularly
small."

He traced that gallant sorter to a still suburban square;
He watched his opportunity and seized him unaware;
He took a life-preserver and he hit him on the head,
And MRS. BROWN dissected him before she went to bed.

And pretty little Alice grew more settled in her mind,
She never more was guilty of a weakness of the kind,
Until at length good Robber Brown bestowed her pretty hand
On the promising young robber, the lieutenant of his band.

THE BUMBOAT WOMAN'S STORY

I'm old, my dears, and shrivelled with age, and work, and grief,
My eyes are gone, and my teeth have been drawn by Time, the Thief!
For terrible sights I've seen, and dangers great I've run—
I'm nearly seventy now, and my work is almost done!

Ah! I've been young in my time, and I've played the deuce with men!

I'm speaking of ten years past—I was barely sixty then:
My cheeks were mellow and soft, and my eyes were large and sweet,
Poll Pineapple's eyes were the standing toast of the Royal Fleet!

A bumboat woman was I, and I faithfully served the ships
With apples and cakes, and fowls and beer, and halfpenny dips,
And beef for the generous mess, where the officers dine at nights,
And fine fresh peppermint drops for the rollicking midshipmites.

Of all the kind commanders who anchored in Portsmouth Bay,
By far the sweetest of all was kind Lieutenant Belaye.
Lieutenant Belaye commanded the gunboat *Hot Cross Bun,*
She was seven and seventy feet in length, and she carried a gun.

With the laudable view of enhancing his country's naval pride,
When people inquired her size, Lieutenant Belaye replied,
"Oh, my ship, my ship is the first of the Hundred and Twenty-ones!"
Which meant her tonnage, but people imagined it meant her guns.

Whenever I went on board he would beckon me down below,
"Come down, Little Buttercup, come" (for he loved to call me so),
And he'd tell of the fights at sea in which he'd taken a part,
And so Lieutenant Belaye won poor Poll Pineapple's heart!

But at length his orders came, and he said one day, said he,
"I'm ordered to sail with the *Hot Cross Bun* to the German Sea."
And the Portsmouth maidens wept when they learnt the evil day,
For every Portsmouth maid loved good LIEUTENANT BELAYE.

And I went to a back back street, with plenty of cheap cheap shops,
And I bought an oilskin hat, and a second-hand suit of slops,
And I went to LIEUTENANT BELAYE (and he never suspected *me!*)
And I entered myself as a chap as wanted to go to sea.

We sailed that afternoon at the mystic hour of one,—
Remarkably nice young men were the crew of the *Hot Cross Bun*.
I'm sorry to say that I've heard that sailors sometimes swear,
But I never yet heard a *Bun* say anything wrong, I declare.

When Jack Tars meet, they meet with a "Messmate, ho!
What cheer?"
But here, on the *Hot Cross Bun,* it was "How do you do,
my dear?"
When Jack Tars growl, I believe they growl with a big
big D—
But the strongest oath of the *Hot Cross Buns* was a mild
"Dear me!"

Yet, though they were all well bred, you could scarcely
call them slick:
Whenever a sea was on, they were all extremely sick;
And whenever the weather was calm, and the wind was
light and fair,
They spent more time than a sailor should on his back
back hair.

They certainly shivered and shook when ordered aloft
to run,
And they screamed when LIEUTENANT BELAYE discharged
his only gun.
And as he was proud of his gun—such pride is hardly
wrong—
The Lieutenant was blazing away at intervals all day
long.

They all agreed very well, though at times you heard it
said
That BILL had a way of his own of making his lips look
red—
That JOE looked quite his age—or somebody might
declare
That BARNACLE's long pig-tail was never his own own
hair.

BELAYE would admit that his men were of no great use
to him,
"But then," he would say, "there is little to do on a gun-
boat trim.
I can hand, and reef, and steer, and fire my big gun too—
And it *is* such a treat to sail with a gentle well-bred
crew."

I saw him every day! How the happy moments sped!
Reef topsails! Make all taut! There's dirty weather ahead!
(I do not mean that tempests threatened the *Hot Cross Bun:*
In *that* case, I don't know whatever we *should* have done!)

After a fortnight's cruise we put into port one day,
And off on leave for a week went kind LIEUTENANT BELAYE,
And after a long long week had passed (and it seemed like a life),
LIEUTENANT BELAYE returned to his ship with a fair young wife!

He up, and he says, says he, "Oh, crew of the *Hot Cross Bun,*
Here is the wife of my heart, for the Church has made us one!"
And as he uttered the word, the crew went out of their wits,
And all fell down in so many separate fainting fits.

And then their hair came down, or off, as the case might
    be,
And lo! the rest of the crew were simple girls, like me,
Who all had fled from their homes in a sailor's blue
    array,
To follow the shifting fate of kind LIEUTENANT BELAYE!

It's strange to think that *I* should ever have loved young
    men,
But I'm speaking of ten years past—I was barely sixty
    then;
And now my cheeks are furrowed with grief and age, I
    trow!
And poor POLL PINEAPPLE's eyes have lost their lustre
    now!

THE TWO OGRES

Good children, list, if you're inclined,
  And wicked children too—
This pretty ballad is designed
  Especially for you.

Two ogres dwelt in Wickham Wold—
  Each *traits* distinctive had:
The younger was as good as gold,
  The elder was as bad.

A wicked, disobedient son
  Was JAMES M'ALPINE, and
A contrast to the elder one,
  Good APPLEBODY BLAND.

M'ALPINE—brutes like him are few—
  In greediness delights,
A melancholy victim to
  Unchastened appetites.

Good, well-bred children every day
  He ravenously ate,—
All boys were fish who found their way
  Into M'ALPINE's net:

Boys whose good breeding is innate,
  Whose sums are always right;
And boys who don't expostulate
  When sent to bed at night;

And kindly boys who never search
  The nests of birds of song;
And serious boys for whom, in church,
  No sermon is too long.

Contrast with JAMES's greedy haste
  And comprehensive hand,
The nice discriminating taste
  Of APPLEBODY BLAND.

BLAND only eats bad boys, who swear—
  Who *can* behave, but *don't*—
Disgraceful lads who say "don't care,"
  And "shan't," and "can't," and "won't."

Who wet their shoes and learn to box,
And say what isn't true,
Who bite their nails and jam their frocks,
And make long noses too;

Who kick a nurse's aged shin,
And sit in sulky mopes;
And boys who twirl poor kittens in
Distracting zoëtropes.

But JAMES, when he was quite a youth,
Had often been to school,
And though so bad, to tell the truth,
He wasn't quite a fool.

At logic few with him could vie,
To his peculiar sect
He could propose a fallacy
With singular effect.

So, when his Mentors said, "Expound—
Why eat good children—why?"
Upon his Mentors he would round
With this absurd reply:

"I have been taught to love the good—
The pure—the unalloyed—
And wicked boys, I've understood,
I always should avoid.

"Why do I eat good children—why?
Because I love them so!"
(But this was empty sophistry,
As your Papa can show.)

Now, though the learning of his friends
Was truly not immense,
They had a way of fitting ends
By rule of common sense.

"Away, away!" his Mentors cried,
"Thou uncongenial pest!
A quirk's a thing we can't abide,
A quibble we detest!

"A fallacy in your reply
Our intellect descries,
Although we don't pretend to spy
Exactly where it lies.

"In misery and penal woes
Must end a glutton's joys;
And learn how ogres punish those
Who dare to eat good boys.

"Secured by fetter, cramp, and chain,
And gagged securely—so—
You shall be placed in Drury Lane,
Where only good lads go.

"Surrounded there by virtuous boys,
You'll suffer torture wus
Than that which constantly annoys
Disgraceful TANTALUS.

("If you would learn the woes that vex
Poor TANTALUS, down there,
Pray borrow of Papa an ex-
Purgated LEMPRIÈRE).

"But as for BLAND who, as it seems,
Eats only naughty boys,
We've planned a recompense that teems
With gastronomic joys.

"Where wicked youths in crowds are stowed
He shall unquestioned rule,
And have the run of Hackney Road
Reformatory School!"

LITTLE OLIVER

EARL JOYCE he was a kind old party
Whom nothing ever could put out,
Though eighty-two, he still was hearty,
Excepting as regarded gout.

He had one unexampled daughter,
The LADY MINNIE-HAHA JOYCE,
Fair MINNIE-HAHA, "Laughing Water,"
So called from her melodious voice.

By Nature planned for lover-capture,
Her beauty every heart assailed;
The good old nobleman with rapture
Observed how widely she prevailed.

Aloof from all the lordly flockings
Of titled swells who worshipped her,
There stood, in pumps and cotton stockings,
One humble lover—OLIVER.

He was no peer by Fortune petted,
His name recalled no bygone age;
He was no lordling coronetted—
Alas! he was a simple page!

With vain appeals he never bored her,
But stood in silent sorrow by—
He knew how fondly he adored her,
And knew, alas; how hopelessly!

Well grounded by a village tutor
In languages alive and past,
He'd say unto himself, "Knee-suitor,
Oh, do not go beyond your last!"

But though his name could boast no handle,
He could not every hope resign;
As moths will hover round a candle,
So hovered he about her shrine.

The brilliant candle dazed the moth well:
One day she sang to her Papa
The air that MARIE sings with BOTHWELL
In NEIDERMEYER's opera.

(Therein a stable boy, it's stated,
Devoutly loved a noble dame,
Who ardently reciprocated
His rather injudicious flame.)

And then, before the piano closing
(He listened coyly at the door),
She sang a song of her composing—
I give one verse from half a score:

BALLAD

Why, pretty page, art ever sighing?
Is sorrow in thy heartlet lying?
Come, set a-ringing
Thy laugh entrancing,
And ever singing
And ever dancing.
Ever singing, Tra! la! la!
Ever dancing, Tra! la! la!
Ever singing, ever dancing,
Ever singing, Tra! la! la!

He skipped for joy like little muttons,
He danced like Esmeralda's kid.
(She did not mean a boy in buttons,
Although he fancied that she did.)

Poor lad! convinced he thus would win her,
He wore out many pairs of soles;
He danced when taking down the dinner—
He danced when bringing up the coals.

He danced and sang (however laden)
With his incessant "Tra! la! la!"
Which much surprised the noble maiden,
And puzzled even her Papa.

He nourished now his flame and fanned it,
He even danced at work below.
The upper servants wouldn't stand it,
And Bowles the butler told him so.

At length on impulse acting blindly,
His love he laid completely bare;
The gentle Earl received him kindly
And told the lad to take a chair.

"Oh, sir," the suitor uttered sadly,
"Don't give your indignation vent;

I fear you think I'm acting madly,
Perhaps you think me insolent?"

The kindly Earl repelled the notion;
His noble bosom heaved a sigh,
His fingers trembled with emotion,
A tear stood in his mild blue eye:

For, oh! the scene recalled too plainly
The half-forgotten time when he,
A boy of nine, had worshipped vainly
A governess of forty-three!

"My boy," he said, in tone consoling,
"Give up this idle fancy—do—
The song you heard my daughter trolling
Did not, indeed, refer to you.

"I feel for you, poor boy, acutely;
I would not wish to give you pain;
Your pangs I estimate minutely,—
I, too, have loved, and loved in vain.

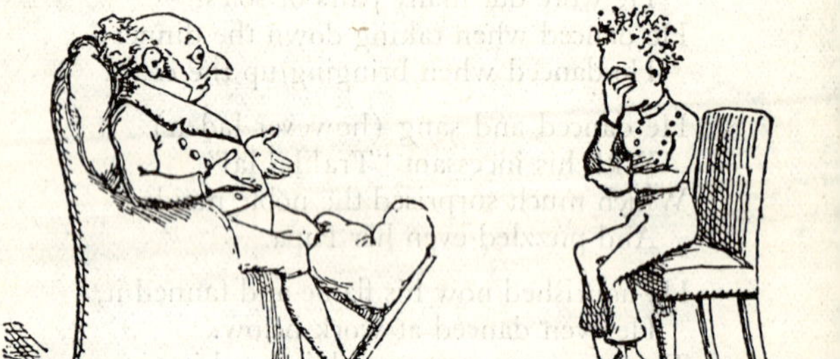

"But still your humble rank and station
For MINNIE surely are not meet"—
He said much more in conversation
Which it were needless to repeat.

Now I'm prepared to bet a guinea,
  Were this a mere dramatic case,
The page would have eloped with MINNIE,
  But, no—he only left his place.

The simple Truth is my detective,
  With me Sensation can't abide;
The Likely beats the mere Effective,
  And Nature is my only guide.

MISTER WILLIAM

Oh, listen to the tale of MISTER WILLIAM, if you please,
Whom naughty, naughty judges sent away beyond the
    seas.
He forged a party's will, which caused anxiety and strife,
Resulting in his getting penal servitude for life.

He was a kindly goodly man, and naturally prone,
Instead of taking others' gold, to give away his own.
But he had heard of Vice, and longed for only once to
    strike—
To plan *one* little wickedness—to see what it was like.

He argued with himself, and said, "A spotless man am I;
I can't be more respectable, however hard I try;
For six and thirty years I've always been as good as gold,
And now for half-an-hour I'll deal in infamy untold!

"A baby who is wicked at the early age of one,
And then reforms—and dies at thirty-six a spotless son,
Is never, never saddled with his babyhood's defect,
But earns from worthy men consideration and respect.

"So one who never revelled in discreditable tricks
Until he reached the comfortable age of thirty-six,
Is free for half-an-hour to perpetrate a deed of shame,
Without incurring permanent disgrace, or even blame.

"That babies don't commit such crimes as forgery is true,
But little sins develop, if you leave 'em to accrue;
And he who shuns all vices as successive seasons roll,
Should reap at length the benefit of so much self-control.

"The common sin of babyhood—objecting to be drest—
If you leave it to accumulate at compound interest,
For anything you know, may represent, if you're alive,
A burglary or murder at the age of thirty-five.

"Still, I wouldn't take advantage of this fact, but be content
With some pardonable folly—it's a mere experiment.
The greater the temptation to go wrong, the less the sin;
So with something that's particularly tempting I'll begin.

"I would not steal a penny, for my income's very fair—
I do not want a penny—I have pennies and to spare—
And if I stole a penny from a money-bag or till,
The sin would be enormous—the temptation being *nil*.

"But if I broke asunder all such pettifogging bounds,
And forged a party's Will for (say) Five Hundred Thousand Pounds,
With such an irresistible temptation to a haul,
Of course the sin must be infinitesimally small.

"There's Wilson who is dying—he has wealth from Stock and rent—
If I divert his riches from their natural descent,
I'm placed in a position to indulge each little whim."
So he diverted them—and they, in turn, diverted him.

Unfortunately, though, by some unpardonable flaw,
Temptation isn't recognised by Britain's Common Law;
Men found him out by some peculiarity of touch,
And William got a "lifer," which annoyed him very much.

For ah! he never reconciled himself to life in gaol,
He fretted and he pined, and grew dispirited and pale;
He was numbered like a cabman, too, which told upon
him so,
That his spirits, once so buoyant, grew uncomfortably
low.

And sympathetic gaolers would remark, "It's very true,
He ain't been brought up common, like the likes of me
and you."
So they took him into hospital, and gave him mutton
chops,
And chocolate, and arrowroot, and buns, and malt and
hops.

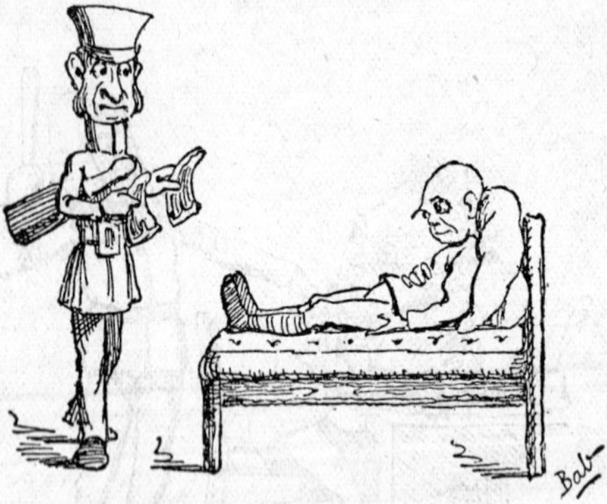

Kind clergymen, besides, grew interested in his fate,
Affected by the details of his pitiable state.
They waited on the Secretary, somewhere in Whitehall,
Who said he would receive them any day they liked to
call.

"Consider, sir, the hardship of this interesting case:
A prison life brings with it something very like disgrace;
It's telling on young WILLIAM, who's reduced to skin and
bone—
Remember he's a gentleman, with money of his own.

"He had an ample income, and of course he stands in need
Of sherry with his dinner, and his customary weed;
No delicacies now can pass his gentlemanly lips—
He misses his sea-bathing and his continental trips.

"He says the other prisoners are commonplace and rude;
He says he cannot relish the disgusting prison food,
For when a boy they taught him to distinguish Good from Bad,
And other educational advantages he's had.

"A burglar or garrotter, or, indeed, a common thief
Is very glad to batten on potatoes and on beef,
Or anything, in short, that prison kitchens can afford,—
A cut above the diet in a common workhouse ward.

"But beef and mutton-broth don't seem to suit our William's whim,
A boon to other prisoners—a punishment to him:
It never was intended that the discipline of gaol
Should dash a convict's spirits, sir, or make him thin or pale."

"Good Gracious Me!" that sympathetic Secretary cried,
"Suppose in prison fetters MISTER WILLIAM should have died!
Dear me, of course! Imprisonment for *Life* his sentence saith:
I'm very glad you mentioned it—it might have been For Death!

"Release him with a ticket—he'll be better then, no doubt,
And tell him I apologise." So MISTER WILLIAM's out.
I hope he will be careful in his manuscripts, I'm sure,
And not begin experimentalising any more.

PASHA BAILEY BEN

A proud Pasha was BAILEY BEN,
His wives were three, his tails were ten;
His form was dignified, but stout,
Men called him "Little Roundabout."

His Importance

Pale pilgrims came from o'er the sea
To wait on PASHA BAILEY B.,
All bearing presents in a crowd,
For B. was poor as well as proud.

His Presents

They brought him onions strung on ropes,
And cold boiled beef, and telescopes,
And balls of string, and shrimps, and guns,
And chops, and tacks, and hats, and buns.

More of them

They brought him white kid gloves, and pails,
And candlesticks, and potted quails,
And capstan-bars, and scales and weights,
And ornaments for empty grates.

Why I mention these

My tale is not of these—oh no!
I only mention them to show
The divers gifts that divers men
Brought o'er the sea to BAILEY BEN.

His Confidant

A confidant had BAILEY B.,
A gay Mongolian dog was he;
I am not good at Turkish names,
And so I call him SIMPLE JAMES.

His Confidant's Countenance

A dreadful legend you might trace
In SIMPLE JAMES's honest face,
For there you read, in Nature's print,
"A Scoundrel of the Deepest Tint."

His Character

A deed of blood, or fire, or flames,
Was meat and drink to SIMPLE JAMES:
To hide his guilt he did not plan,
But owned himself a bad young man.

The Author to his Reader

And why on earth good Bailey Ben
(The wisest, noblest, best of men)
Made Simple James his right-hand man
Is quite beyond my mental span.

The same, continued

But there—enough of gruesome deeds!
My heart, in thinking of them, bleeds;
And so let Simple James take wing,—
'Tis not of him I'm going to sing.

The Pasha's Clerk

Good Pasha Bailey kept a clerk
(For Bailey only made his mark),
His name was Matthew Wycombe Coo,
A man of nearly forty-two.

His Accomplishments

No person that I ever knew
Could "yödel" half as well as Coo,
And Highlanders exclaimed, "Eh, weel!"
When Coo began to dance a reel.

His Kindness to the Pasha's Wives

He used to dance and sing and play
In such an unaffected way,
He cheered the unexciting lives
Of Pasha Bailey's lovely wives.

The Author to his Reader

But why should I encumber you
With histories of Matthew Coo?
Let Matthew Coo at once take wing,—
'Tis not of Coo I'm going to sing.

The Author's Muse

Let me recall my wandering Muse;
She *shall* be steady if I choose—
She roves, instead of helping me
To tell the deeds of Bailey B.

The Pasha's Visitor

One morning knocked, at half-past eight,
A tall Red Indian at his gate.
In Turkey, as you're p'raps aware,
Red Indians are extremely rare.

The Visitor's Outfit

Moccasins decked his graceful legs,
His eyes were black, and round as eggs,
And on his neck, instead of beads,
Hung several Catawampous seeds.

What the Visitor said

"Ho, ho!" he said, "thou pale-faced one,
Poor offspring of an Eastern sun,
You've *never* seen the Red Man skip
Upon the banks of the Mississip!"

The Author's Moderation

To say that Bailey oped his eyes

Would feebly paint his great surprise—
To say it almost made him die
Would be to paint it much too high.

The Author to his Reader

But why should I ransack my head
To tell you all that Indian said;
We'll let the Indian man take wing,—
'Tis not of him I'm going to sing.

The Reader to the Author

Come, come, I say, that's quite enough
Of this absurd disjointed stuff;
Now let's get on to that affair
About Lieutenant-Colonel Flare.

LIEUTENANT-COLONEL FLARE

The earth has armies plenty,
And semi-warlike bands,
I dare say there are twenty
In European lands;
But, oh! in no direction
You'd find one to compare
In brotherly affection
With that of Colonel Flare.

His soldiers might be rated
As military Pearls:
As unsophisticated
As pretty little girls!
They never smoked or ratted,
Or talked of Sues or Polls;
The Sergeant-Major tatted,
The others nursed their dolls.

He spent his days in teaching
These truly solemn facts;
There's little use in preaching,
Or circulating tracts.

(The vainest plan invented
  For stifling other creeds,
Unless it's supplemented
  With charitable *deeds.*)

He taught his soldiers kindly
  To give at Hunger's call:
"Oh, better far give blindly,
  Than never give at all!
Though sympathy be kindled
  By Imposition's game,
Oh, better far be swindled
  Than smother up its flame!"

His means were far from ample
  For pleasure or for dress,
Yet note this bright example
  Of single-heartedness:

Though ranking as a Colonel,
His pay was but a groat,
While their reward diurnal
Was—each a five-pound note.

Moreover,—this evinces
His kindness, you'll allow,—
He fed them all like princes,
And lived himself on cow.
He set them all regaling
On curious wines, and dear,
While he would sit pale-ale-ing,
Or quaffing ginger-beer.

Then at his instigation
(A pretty fancy this)
Their daily pay and ration
He'd take in change for his;

They brought it to him weekly,
And he without a groan,
Would take it from them meekly
And give them all his own!

Though not exactly knighted
As knights, of course, should be,
Yet no one so delighted
In harmless chivalry.
If peasant girl or ladye
Beneath misfortunes sank,
Whate'er distinctions made he,
They were not those of rank.

No maiden young and comely
Who wanted good advice
(However poor or homely)
Need ask him for it twice.
He'd wipe away the blindness
That comes of teary dew;
His sympathetic kindness
No sort of limit knew.

He always hated dealing
With men who schemed or planned;
A person harsh—unfeeling—
The Colonel could not stand.
He hated cold, suspecting,
Official men in blue,
Who pass their lives detecting
The crimes that others do.

For men who'd shoot a sparrow,
Or immolate a worm
Beneath a farmer's harrow,
He could not find a term.
Humanely, ay, and knightly
He dealt with such an one;
He took and tied him tightly,
And blew him from a gun.

The earth has armies plenty,
And semi-warlike bands,

I'm certain there are twenty
  In European lands.
But, oh! in no direction
  You'd find one to compare
In brotherly affection
  With that of COLONEL FLARE.

LOST MR. BLAKE

MR. BLAKE was a regular out-and-out hardened sinner,
  Who was quite out of the pale of Christianity, so to speak:
He was in the habit of smoking a long pipe and drinking a glass of grog on Sunday after dinner,
  And seldom thought of going to church more than twice (or if Good Friday or Christmas Day happened to come in it) three times a week.

He was quite indifferent as to the particular kinds of dresses
  That the clergyman wore at the church where he used to go to pray,
And whatever he did in the way of relieving a chap's distresses,
  He always did in a nasty, sneaking, underhanded, hole-and-corner sort of way.

I have known him indulge in profane, ungentlemanly emphatics,
When the Protestant Church has been divided on the subject of the width of a chasuble's hem;
I have even known him to sneer at albs—and as for dalmatics,
Words can't convey an idea of the contempt he expressed for *them*.

He didn't believe in persons who, not being well off themselves, are obliged to confine their charitable exertions to collecting money from wealthier people,
And looked upon individuals of the former class as ecclesiastical hawks;
He used to say that he would no more think of interfering with his priest's robes than with his church or his steeple,
And that he did not consider his soul imperilled because somebody over whom he had no influence whatever, chose to dress himself up like an ecclesiastical GUY FAWKES.

This shocking old vagabond was so unutterably shameless
That he actually went a-courting a very respectable and pious middle-aged sister, by the name of BIGGS:
She was a rather attractive widow whose life, as such, had always been particularly blameless;
Her first husband had left her a secure but moderate competence owing to some fortunate speculations in the matter of figs.

She was an excellent person in every way—and won the respect even of MRS. GRUNDY,
She was a good housewife, too, and wouldn't have wasted a penny if she had owned the Koh-i-noor;
She was just as strict as he was lax in her observance of Sunday,
And being a good economist, and charitable besides, she took all the bones and cold potatoes and broken pie-crusts and candle-ends (when she had quite done with them), and made them into an excellent soup for the deserving poor.

I am sorry to say that she rather took to Blake—that outcast of society;
  And when respectable brothers who were fond of her began to look dubious and to cough,
She would say, "Oh, my friends, it's because I hope to bring this poor benighted soul back to virtue and propriety"
  (And besides, the poor benighted soul, with all his faults, was uncommonly well off).

And when Mr. Blake's dissipated friends called his attention to the frown or the pout of her,
  Whenever he did anything which appeared to her to savour of an unmentionable place,
He would say she would be a very decent old girl when all that nonsense was knocked out of her—
  And his method of knocking it out of her is one that covered him with disgrace.

She was fond of going to church services four times every Sunday, and four or five times in the week, and never seemed to pall of them,
  So he hunted out all the churches within a convenient distance that had services at different hours, so to speak;

And when he had married her he positively insisted upon their going to all of them,
So they contrived to do about twelve churches every Sunday, and, if they had luck, from twenty-two to twenty-three in the course of the week.

She was fond of dropping his sovereigns ostentatiously into the plate, and she liked to see them stand out rather conspicuously against the commonplace half-crowns and shillings,
So he took her to all the charity sermons, and if by any extraordinary chance there wasn't a charity sermon anywhere, he would drop a couple of sovereigns (one for him and one for her) into the poor-box at the door;
And as he always deducted the sums thus given in charity from the housekeeping money, and the money he allowed her for her bonnets and frillings,
She soon began to find that even charity, if you allow it to interfere with your personal luxuries, becomes an intolerable bore.

On Sundays she was always melancholy and anything but good society,
For that day in her household was a day of sighings and sobbings and wringing of hands and shaking of heads:
She wouldn't hear of a button being sewn on a glove, because it was a work neither of necessity nor of piety,
And strictly prohibited her servants from amusing themselves, or indeed doing anything at all except dusting the drawing-rooms, cleaning the boots and shoes, cooking the dinner, waiting generally on the family, and making the beds.

But Blake even went farther than that, and said that, on Sundays, people should do their own works of necessity, and not delegate them to persons in a menial situation,
So he wouldn't allow his servants to do so much as even answer a bell.

Here he is making his wife carry up the water for her bath to the second floor, much against her inclination,—
And why in the world the gentleman who illustrates these ballads has put him into a cocked hat is more than I can tell.

After about three months of this sort of thing, taking the smooth with the rough of it
(Blacking her own boots and peeling her own potatoes was not her notion of connubial bliss),
MRS. BLAKE began to find that she had pretty nearly had enough of it,
And came, in course of time, to think that BLAKE's own original line of conduct wasn't so much amiss.

And now that wicked person—that detestable sinner ("BELIAL BLAKE" his friends and well-wishers call him for his atrocities),
And his poor deluded victim whom all her Christian brothers dislike and pity so,
Go to the parish church only on Sunday morning and afternoon and occasionally on a week-day, and spend their evenings in connubial fondlings and affectionate reciprocities,
And I should like to know where in the world (or rather, out of it) they expect to go.

THE BABY'S VENGEANCE

Weary at heart and extremely ill
Was PALEY VOLLAIRE of Bromptonville,
In a dirty lodging, with fever down,
Close to the Polygon, Somers Town.

PALEY VOLLAIRE was an only son
(For why? His mother had had but one),
And PALEY inherited gold and grounds
Worth several hundred thousand pounds.

But he, like many a rich young man,
Through this magnificent fortune ran,
And nothing was left for his daily needs
But duplicate copies of mortgage-deeds.

Shabby and sorry and sorely sick,
He slept, and dreamt that the clock's "tick, tick,"
Was one of the Fates, with a long sharp knife,
Snicking off bits of his shortened life.

He woke and counted the pips on the walls,
The outdoor passengers' loud footfalls,
And reckoned all over, and reckoned again,
The little white tufts on his counterpane.

A medical man to his bedside came
(I can't remember that doctor's name),
And said, "You'll die in a very short while
If you don't set sail for Madeira's isle."

"Go to Madeira? goodness me!
I haven't the money to pay your fee!"
"Then, PALEY VOLLAIRE," said the leech, "good-bye;
I'll come no more, for you're sure to die."

He sighed and he groaned and smote his breast;
"Oh, send," said he, "for FREDERICK WEST,
Ere senses fade or my eyes grow dim:
I've a terrible tale to whisper him!"

Poor was FREDERICK's lot in life,—
A dustman he with a fair young wife,
A worthy man with a hard-earned store,
A hundred and seventy pounds—or more.

FREDERICK came, and he said, "Maybe
You'll say what you happen to want with me?"
"Wronged boy," said PALEY VOLLAIRE, "I will,
But don't you fidget yourself—sit still.

* * * * *

" 'Tis now some thirty-seven years ago
Since first began the plot that I'm revealing,
A fine young woman, wed ten years or so,

Lived with her husband down in Drum Lane, Ealing,
Herself by means of mangling reimbursing,
And now and then (at intervals) wet-nursing.

"Two little babes dwelt in her humble cot:
One was her own—the other only lent to her:
Her own she slighted. Tempted by a lot
Of gold and silver regularly sent to her,
She ministered unto the little other
In the capacity of foster-mother.

"I was her own. Oh! how I lay and sobbed
In my poor cradle—deeply, deeply cursing
The rich man's pampered bantling, who had robbed
My only birthright—an attentive nursing!
Sometimes, in hatred of my foster-brother
I gnashed my gums—which terrified my mother.

"One darksome day (I should have mentioned that
We were alike in dress and baby feature)
I *in* MY cradle having placed the brat,
Crept into his—the pampered little creature!
It was imprudent—well, disgraceful maybe,
For, oh! I was a bad, black-hearted baby!

"So rare a luxury was food, I think
  There was no wickedness I wouldn't try for it.
Now if I wanted anything to drink
  At any time, I only had to cry for it!
Once, if I dared to weep, the bottle lacking,
My blubbering involved a serious smacking!

"We grew up in the usual way—my friend,
  My foster-brother, daily growing thinner,
While gradually I began to mend,
  And thrived amazingly on double dinner.
And every one, besides my foster-mother,
Believed that either of us was the other.

"I came into his wealth—I bore his name,
  I bear it still—his property I squandered—
I mortgaged everything—and now (oh, shame!)
  Into a Somers Town shake-down I've wandered!
I am no PALEY—no VOLLAIRE—it's true, my boy!
The only rightful PALEY V. is *you,* my boy!

"And all I have is yours—and yours is mine.
  I still may place you in your true position:
Give me the pounds you've saved, and I'll resign
  My noble name, my rank, and my condition.
So for my sin in fraudulently owning
Your vasty wealth, I am at last atoning!"

* * * * *

FREDERICK he was a simple soul,
He pulled from his pocket a bulky roll,
And gave to PALEY his hard-earned store,
A hundred and seventy pounds or more.

PALEY VOLLAIRE, with many a groan,
Gave FREDERICK all that he'd called his own,—
Two shirts and a sock, and a vest of jean,
A Wellington boot and a bamboo cane.

And FRED (entitled to all things there)
He took the fever from MR. VOLLAIRE,
Which killed poor FREDERICK WEST. Meanwhile
VOLLAIRE sailed off to Madeira's isle.

THE CAPTAIN AND THE MERMAIDS

I sing a legend of the sea,
So hard-a-port upon your lee!
A ship on starboard tack!
She's bound upon a private cruise—
(This is the kind of spice I use
To give a salt-sea smack).

Behold, on every afternoon
(Save in a gale or strong monsoon)
Great Captain Capel Cleggs
(Great morally, though rather short)
Sat at an open weather-port
And aired his shapely legs.

And Mermaids hung around in flocks,
On cable chains and distant rocks,
To gaze upon those limbs;
For legs like his, of flesh and bone,
Are things "not generally known"
To any Merman Timbs.

But Mermen didn't seem to care
Much time (as far as I'm aware)
With Cleggs's legs to spend;
Though Mermaids swam around all day
And gazed, exclaiming, "That's the way
A gentleman should end!

"A pair of legs with well-cut knees
And calves and ankles such as these
Which we in rapture hail,
Are far more eloquent, it's clear,
When clothed in silk and kerseymere,
Than any nasty tail."

And Cleggs—a worthy kind old boy—
Rejoiced to add to others' joy,
And, though he scarce knew why
(Perhaps to please the lookers-on),
He sat there every day—though con-
Stitutionally shy.

At first the Mermen sneered pooh-pooh,
But finally they jealous grew,
And sounded loud recalls;
But vainly. So these fishy males
Declared they too would clothe their tails
In silken hose and smalls.

They set to work, these water-men,
And made their nether robes—but when
They drew with dainty touch
The kerseymere upon their tails,
They found it scraped against their scales,
And hurt them very much.

The silk, besides, with which they chose
To deck their tails, by way of hose
(They never thought of shoon),
For such a use was much too thin,—
It tore against the caudal fin
And "went in ladders" soon.

So they designed another plan:
They sent their most seductive man
This note to CLEGGS to show—
"Our Monarch sends to CAPTAIN CLEGGS
His humble compliments, and begs
He'll join him down below;

"We've pleasant homes below the sea—
Besides, if CAPTAIN CLEGGS should be
(As our advices say)
A judge of Mermaids, he will find
Our lady-fish of every kind
Inspection will repay."

Good CAPEL sent a kind reply,
For CAPEL thought he could descry
An admirable plan
To study all their ways and laws—
(But not their lady-fish, because
He was a married man).

The Mermen sank—the Captain too
Jumped overboard, and dropped from view
Like stone from catapult;
And when he reached the Merman's lair
He certainly was welcomed there,
But, ah! with what result?

They didn't let him learn their law,
Or make a note of what he saw,
Or interesting mem.:
The lady-fish he couldn't find,
But that, of course, he didn't mind—
He didn't come for them.

For though when CAPTAIN CAPEL sank,
The Mermen drawn in double rank
Gave him a hearty hail;
Yet when secure of CAPTAIN CLEGGS,
They cut off both his lovely legs,
And gave him *such* a tail!

When CAPTAIN CLEGGS returned aboard,
His blithesome crew convulsive roar'd,
To see him altered so.

The Admiralty did insist
That he upon the Half-pay list
Immediately should go.

In vain declared the poor old salt,
"It's my misfortune—not my fault,"
With tear and trembling lip—
In vain poor Capel begged and begged—
"A man must be completely legged
Who rules a British ship."

So spake the stern First Lord aloud—
He was a wag, though very proud,
And much rejoiced to say,
"You're only half a captain now—
And so, my worthy friend, I vow
You'll only get half pay."

ANNIE PROTHEROE

A LEGEND OF STRATFORD-LE-BOW

Oh! listen to the tale of little Annie Protheroe,
She kept a small post-office in the neighbourhood of Bow,
She loved a skilled mechanic, who was famous in his day—
A gentle executioner whose name was Gilbert Clay.

I think I hear you say, "A dreadful subject for your
rhymes!"
O reader, do not shrink—he didn't live in modern times!
He lived so long ago (the sketch will show it at a
glance)
That all his actions glitter with the limelight of Romance.

In busy times he laboured at his gentle craft all day—
"No doubt you mean his Cal-craft" you amusingly will
say—
But, no—he didn't operate with common bits of string,
He was a Public Headsman, which is quite another thing.

And when his work was over, they would ramble o'er
the lea,
And sit beneath the frondage of an elderberry tree;
And ANNIE's simple prattle entertained him on his walk,
For public executions formed the subject of her talk.

And sometimes he'd explain to her, which charmed her very much,
How famous operators vary very much in touch,
And then, perhaps, he'd show how he himself performed the trick,
And illustrate his meaning with a poppy and a stick.

Or, if it rained, the little maid would stop at home, and look
At his favourable notices, all pasted in a book,
And then her cheek would flush—her swimming eyes would dance with joy
In a glow of admiration at the prowess of her boy.

One summer eve, at supper-time, the gentle GILBERT said
(As he helped his pretty ANNIE to a slice of collared head),
"This collared head reminds me that to-morrow is the day
When I decapitate your former lover, PETER GRAY."

He saw his ANNIE tremble and he saw his ANNIE start,
Her changing colour trumpeted the flutter at her heart;
Young GILBERT's manly bosom rose and sank with jealous fear,
And he said, "O gentle ANNIE, what's the meaning of this here?"

And ANNIE answered, blushing in an interesting way,
"You think, no doubt, I'm sighing for that felon PETER GRAY:
That I was his young woman is unquestionably true,
But not since I began a-keeping company with you."

Then GILBERT, who was irritable, rose and loudly swore
He'd know the reason why if she refused to tell him more;
And she answered (all the woman in her flashing from her eyes),
"You mustn't ask no questions, and you won't be told no lies!

"Few lovers have the privilege enjoyed, my dear, by you,
Of chopping off a rival's head and quartering him, too!
Of vengeance, dear, to-morrow you will surely take your fill!"
And GILBERT ground his molars as he answered her, "I will!"

Young GILBERT rose from table with a stern determined look,
And, frowning, took an inexpensive hatchet from its hook;
And ANNIE watched his movements with an interested air—
For the morrow—for the morrow he was going to prepare!

He chipped it with a hammer and he chopped it with a bill,
He poured sulphuric acid on the edge of it, until
This terrible Avenger of the Majesty of Law
Was far less like a hatchet than a dissipated saw.

And ANNIE said, "O GILBERT, dear, I do not understand
Why ever you are injuring that hatchet in your hand?"
He said, "It is intended for to lacerate and flay
The neck of that unmitigated villain PETER GRAY!"

"Now, GILBERT," ANNIE answered, "wicked headsman, just beware—
I won't have PETER tortured with that horrible affair;
If you attempt to flay him, you will surely rue the day."
But GILBERT said, "Oh, shall I?" which was just his nasty way.

He saw a look of anger from her eyes distinctly dart,
For ANNIE was a *woman,* and had pity in her heart!
She wished him a good evening—he answered with a glare;
She only said, "Remember, for your ANNIE will be there!"

* * * * *

The morrow GILBERT boldly on the scaffold took his stand,
With a vizor on his face and with a hatchet in his hand,
And all the people noticed that the Engine of the Law
Was far less like a hatchet than a dissipated saw.

The felon very coolly loosed his collar and his stock,
And placed his wicked head upon the handy little block—
The hatchet was uplifted for to settle PETER GRAY,
When GILBERT plainly heard a woman's voice exclaiming, "Stay!"

'Twas ANNIE, gentle ANNIE, as you'll easily believe—
"O GILBERT, you must spare him, for I bring him a reprieve,
It came from our Home Secretary many weeks ago,
And passed through that post-office which I used to keep at Bow.

"I loved you, loved you madly, and you know it, GILBERT CLAY,
And having quite surrendered all idea of PETER GRAY,
I quietly suppressed it, as you'll clearly understand,
For I thought it might be awkward if he came and claimed my hand.

"In anger at my secret (which I could not tell before)
To lacerate poor PETER GRAY vindictively you swore;
I told you if you used that blunted axe you'd rue the day,
And so you will, you monster, for I'll marry PETER GRAY!"

[*And so she did.*

AN UNFORTUNATE LIKENESS

I've painted SHAKESPEARE all my life—
"An infant" (even then at play),
"A boy," with stage-ambition rife,
Then "Married to ANN HATHAWAY."

"The bard's first ticket night" (or "ben."),
His "First appearance on the stage,"
His "Call before the curtain"—then
"Rejoicings when he came of age."

The bard play-writing in his room,
  The bard a humble lawyer's clerk,
The bard a lawyer [1]—parson [2]—groom [3]—
  The bard deer-stealing, after dark.

The bard a tradesman [4]—and a Jew [5]—
  The bard a botanist [6]—a beak [7]—
The bard a skilled musician [8] too—
  A sheriff [9] and a surgeon [10] eke!

1 "Go with me to a notary—seal me there
Your single bond."—*Merchant of Venice,* Act I., sc. 3.

2 "And there she shall, at Friar Lawrence' cell,
Be shrived and married."—*Romeo and Juliet,* Act II., sc. 4.

3 "And give their fasting horses provender."
—*Henry the Fifth,* Act IV., sc. 2.

4 "Let us, like merchants, show our foulest wares."
—*Troilus and Cressida,* Act I., sc. 3.

5 "Then must the Jew be merciful."
—*Merchant of Venice,* Act IV., sc. 1.

6 "The spring, the summer,
The childing autumn, angry winter, change
Their wonted liveries."—*Midsummer Night's Dream,* Act II., sc. 2.

7 "In the county of Glo'ster, justice of the peace and *coram.*"
—*Merry Wives of Windsor,* Act I., sc. 1.

8 "What lusty trumpet thus doth summon us?"
—*King John,* Act V., sc. 2.

9 "And I'll provide his executioner."
—*Henry the Sixth* (Second Part), Act III., sc. 1.

10 "The lioness had torn some flesh away,
Which all this while had bled."—*As You Like It,"* Act IV., sc. 3.

Yet critics say (a friendly stock)
That, though with all my skill I try,
Yet even I can barely mock
The glimmer of his wondrous eye!

One morning as a work I framed,
There passed a person, walking hard:
"My gracious goodness," I exclaimed,
"How very like my dear old bard!

"Oh, what a model he would make!"
I rushed outside—impulsive me!—
"Forgive the liberty I take,
But you're so very"—"Stop!" said he.

"You needn't waste your breath or time,—
I know what you are going to say,—
That you're an artist, and that I'm
Remarkably like SHAKESPEARE. Eh?

"You wish that I would sit to you?"
I clasped him madly round the waist,
And breathlessly replied, "I do!"
"All right," said he, "but please make haste."

I led him by his hallowed sleeve,
And worked away at him apace,
I painted him till dewy eve,—
There never was a nobler face!

"Oh, sir," I said, "a fortune grand
Is yours, by dint of merest chance,—
To sport *his* brow at second-hand,
To wear *his* cast-off countenance!

"To rub *his* eyes whene'er they ache—
To wear *his* baldness ere you're old—
To clean *his* teeth when you awake—
To blow *his* nose when you've a cold!"

His eyeballs glistened in his eyes—
I sat and watched and smoked my pipe;
"Bravo!" I said, "I recognise
The phrensy of your prototype!"

His scanty hair he wildly tore:
  "That's right," said I, "it shows your breed."
He danced—he stamped—he wildly swore—
  "Bless me, that's very fine indeed!"

"Sir," said the grand Shakespearian boy
  (Continuing to blaze away),
"You think my face a source of joy;
  That shows you know not what you say.

"Forgive these yells and cellar-flaps,
  I'm always thrown in some such state
When on his face well-meaning chaps
  This wretched man congratulate.

"For, oh! this face—this pointed chin—
  This nose—this brow—these eyeballs too,
Have always been the origin
  Of all the woes I ever knew!

"If to the play my way I find,
  To see a grand Shakespearian piece,
I have no rest, no ease of mind
  Until the author's puppets cease!

"Men nudge each other—thus—and say,
  'This certainly is SHAKESPEARE's son,'
And merry wags (of course in play)
  Cry 'Author!' when the piece is done.

"In church the people stare at me,
  Their soul the sermon never binds;
I catch them looking round to see,
  And thoughts of SHAKESPEARE fill their minds.

"And sculptors, fraught with cunning wile,
  Who find it difficult to crown
A bust with BROWN's insipid smile,
  Or TOMKINS's unmannered frown,

"Yet boldly make my face their own,
  When (oh, presumption!) they require
To animate a paving-stone
  With SHAKESPEARE's intellectual fire.

"At parties where young ladies gaze,
  And I attempt to speak my joy,
'Hush, pray,' some lovely creature says,
  'The fond illusion don't destroy!'

"Whene'er I speak my soul is wrung
  With these or some such whisperings;
' 'Tis pity that a SHAKESPEARE's tongue
  Should say such un-Shakespearian things!'

"I should not thus be criticised
  Had I face of common wont:
Don't envy me—now, be advised!"
  And, now I think of it, I don't!

GREGORY PARABLE, LL.D.

A leafy cot, where no dry rot
Had ever been by tenant seen,
Where ivy clung and wopses stung,
Where beeses hummed and drummed and strummed,
Where treeses grew and breezes blew—
A thatchy roof, quite waterproof,
Where countless herds of dicky-birds
Built twiggy beds to lay their heads
(My mother begs I'll make it "eggs,"
But though it's true that dickies do
Construct a nest with chirpy noise,
With view to rest their eggy joys,
'Neath eavy sheds, yet eggs and beds,
As I explain to her in vain
Five hundred times, are faulty rhymes)
'Neath such a cot, built on a plot
Of freehold land, dwelt MARY and
Her worthy father, named by me
GREGORY PARABLE, LL.D.

He knew no guile, this simple man,
No worldly wile, or plot, or plan,
Except that plot of freehold land
That held the cot, and MARY, and
Her worthy father, named by me
GREGORY PARABLE, LL.D.

A grave and learned scholar he,
Yet simple as a child could be.
He'd shirk his meal to sit and cram
A goodish deal of Eton Gram.
No man alive could him nonplus
With vocative of *filius;*
No man alive more fully knew
The passive of a verb or two;
None better knew the worth than he
Of words that end in *b, d, t.*
Upon his green in early spring
He might be seen endeavouring
To understand the hooks and crooks
Of HENRY and his Latin books;
Or calling for his "Cæsar on
The Gallic War," like any don;
Or, p'raps, expounding unto all
How mythic BALBUS built a wall.
So lived a sage who's named by me
GREGORY PARABLE, LL.D.

To him one autumn day there came
A lovely youth of mystic name:
He took a lodging in the house,
And fell a-dodging snipe and grouse,
For, oh! that mild scholastic one
Let shooting for a single gun.

By three or four, when sport was o'er,
The Mystic One laid by his gun,
And made sheep's eyes of giant size,
Till after tea, at MARY P.
And MARY P. (so kind was she),
She, too, made eyes of giant size,
Whose every dart right through the heart

Appeared to run that Mystic One.
The Doctor's whim engrossing him,
He did not know they flirted so.

For, save at tea, *"musa musæ,"*
As I'm advised, monopolised
And rendered blind his giant mind.
But looking up above his cup
One afternoon, he saw them spoon.
"Aha!" quoth he, "you naughty lass.
As quaint old OVID says, 'Amas!'"

The Mystic Youth avowed the truth,
And, claiming ruth, he said, "In sooth
I love your daughter, aged man:
Refuse to join us if you can.
Treat not my offer, sir, with scorn,
I'm wealthy though I'm lowly born."
"Young sir," the aged scholar said,
"I never thought you meant to wed:
Engrossed completely with my books,
I little noticed lovers' looks.
I've lived so long away from man,
I do not know of any plan

By which to test a lover's worth,
Except, perhaps, the test of birth.
I've half forgotten in this wild
A father's duty to his child.
It is his place, I think it's said,
To see his daughters richly wed
To dignitaries of the earth—
If possible, of noble birth.
If noble birth is not at hand,
A father may, I understand
(And this affords a chance for you),
Be satisfied to wed her to
A Boucicault or Baring—which
Means any one who's very rich.
Now, there's an Earl who lives hard by,—
My child and I will go and try
If he will make the maid his bride—
If not, to you she shall be tied."

They sought the Earl that very day;
The Sage began to say his say.
The Earl (a very wicked man,
Whose face bore Vice's blackest ban),
Cut short the scholar's simple tale,
And said in voice to make them quail,
"Pooh! go along! you're drunk, no doubt—
Here, Peters, turn these people out!"

The Sage, rebuffed in mode uncouth,
Returning, met the Mystic Youth.
"My darling boy," the Scholar said,
"Take MARY—blessings on your head!"

The Mystic Boy undid his vest,
And took a parchment from his breast,
And said, "Now, by that noble brow,
I ne'er knew father such as thou!
The sterling rule of common sense
Now reaps its proper recompense.
Rejoice, my soul's unequalled Queen,
For I am DUKE OF GRETNA GREEN!"

THE KING OF CANOODLE-DUM

The story of FREDERICK GOWLER,
  A mariner of the sea,
Who quitted his ship, the *Howler,*
  A-sailing in Caribbee.
For many a day he wandered,
  Till he met, in a state of rum,
CALAMITY POP VON PEPPERMINT DROP,
  The King of Canoodle-Dum.

That monarch addressed him gaily,
"Hum! Golly de do to-day?
Hum! Lily-white Buckra Sailee"—
(You notice his playful way?)—
"What dickens you doin' here, sar?
Why debbil you want to come?
Hum! Picaninnee, dere isn't no sea
In City Canoodle-Dum!"

And Gowler he answered sadly,
"Oh, mine is a doleful tale!
They've treated me werry badly
In Lunnon, from where I hail.
I'm one of the Family Royal—
No common Jack Tar you see;
I'm William the Fourth, far up in the North,
A King in my own countree!"

Bang-bang! How the tom-toms thundered!
Bang-bang! How they thumped the gongs!
Bang-bang! How the people wondered!
Bang-bang! At it, hammer and tongs!
Alliance with Kings of Europe
Is an honour Canoodlers seek;
Her monarchs don't stop with Peppermint Drop
Every day in the week!

Fred told them that he was *un*done,
For his people all went insane,
And fired the Tower of London,
And Grinnidge's Naval Fane.
And some of them racked St. James's,
And vented their rage upon
The Church of St. Paul, the Fishmongers' Hall,
And the "Angel" at Islington.

Calamity Pop implored him
At Canoodle-Dum to remain
Till those people of his restored him
To power and rank again.
Calamity Pop he made him
A Prince of Canoodle-Dum,
With a couple of caves, some beautiful slaves,
And the run of the royal rum.

Pop gave him his only daughter,
  Hum Pickety Wimple Tip:
Fred vowed that if over the water
  He went, in an English ship,
He'd make her his Queen,—though truly,
  It is an unusual thing
For a Caribbee brat who's as black as your hat
  To be wife of an English King.

And all the Canoodle-Dummers
  They copied his rolling walk,
His method of draining rummers,
  His emblematical talk.
For his dress and his graceful breeding,
  His delicate taste in rum,
And his nautical way, were the talk of the day
  In the Court of Canoodle-Dum.

Calamity Pop most wisely
  Determined in everything
To model his Court precisely
  On that of the English King;
And ordered that every lady
  And every lady's lord
Should masticate jacky (a kind of tobaccy)
  And scatter its juice abroad.

They signified wonder roundly
  At any astounding yarn,
By darning their dear eyes roundly
  ('Twas all that they had to darn).
They "hoisted their slacks," adjusting
  Garments of plantain-leaves
With nautical twitches (as if they wore—stitches,
  Instead of a dress like Eve's!)

They shivered their timbers proudly,
  At a phantom fore-lock dragged,
And called for a hornpipe loudly
  Whenever amusement flagged.
"Hum! Golly! him Pop resemble,
  Him Britisher sov'reign, hum!
Calamity Pop Von Peppermint Drop,
  De King of Canoodle-Dum!"

The mariner's lively "Hollo!"
  Enlivened Canoodle's plain
(For blessings unnumbered follow
  In Civilisation's train).
But fortune, who loves a bathos,
  A terrible ending planned,
For Admiral D. Chickabiddy, C.B.,
  Placed foot on Canoodle land!

That officer seized King Gowler;
He threatened his royal brains,
And put him aboard the *Howler,*
And fastened him down with chains.
The *Howler* she weighed her anchor,
With Frederick nicely nailed,
And off to the North with William the Fourth
That Admiral slowly sailed.

Calamity said (with folly)
"Hum! nebber want him again—
Him civilise all of us, golly!
Calamity suck him brain!"
The people, however, were pained when
They saw him aboard the ship,
But none of them wept for their Freddy, except
Hum Pickity Wimple Tip.

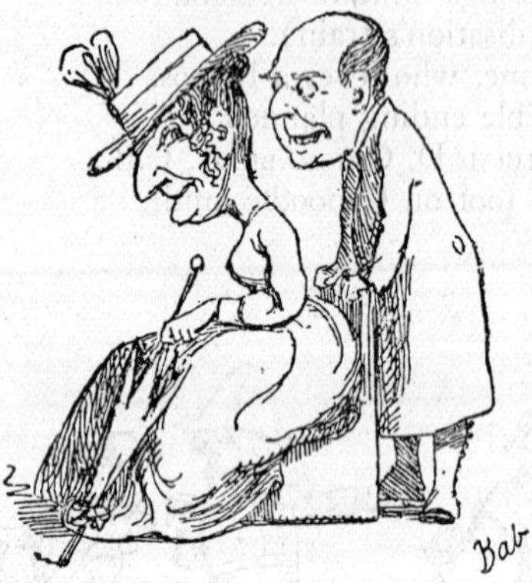

FIRST LOVE

A clergyman in Berkshire dwelt,
The Reverend Bernard Powles,
And in his church there weekly knelt
At least a hundred souls.

There little ELLEN you might see,
 The modest rustic belle;
In maidenly simplicity,
 She loved her BERNARD well.

Though ELLEN wore a plain silk gown
 Untrimmed with lace or fur,
Yet not a husband in the town
 But wished his wife like her.

Though sterner memories might fade,
 You never could forget
The child-form of that baby-maid,
 The Village Violet!

A simple frightened loveliness,
 Whose sacred spirit-part
Shrank timidly from worldly stress,
 And nestled in your heart.

POWLES woo'd with every well-worn plan
 And all the usual wiles
With which a well-schooled gentleman
 A simple heart beguiles.

The hackneyed compliments that bore
 World-folks like you and me,
Appeared to her as if they wore
 The crown of Poesy.

His winking eyelid sang a song
 Her heart could understand,
Eternity seemed scarce too long
 When BERNARD squeezed her hand.

He ordered down the martial crew
 Of GODFREY'S Grenadiers,
And COOTE conspired with TINNEY to
 Ecstaticise her ears.

Beneath her window, veiled from eye,
 They nightly took their stand;
On birthdays supplemented by
 The Covent Garden band.

And little Ellen, all alone,
  Enraptured sat above,
And thought how blest she was to own
  The wealth of Powles's love.

I often, often wonder what
  Poor Ellen saw in him;
For calculated he was *not*
  To please a woman's whim.

He wasn't good, despite the air
  An M.B. waistcoat gives;
Indeed, his dearest friends declare
  No greater humbug lives.

No kind of virtue decked this priest,
  He'd nothing to allure;
He wasn't handsome in the least,—
  He wasn't even poor.

No—he was cursed with acres fat
  (A Christian's direst ban),
And gold—yet, notwithstanding that
  Poor Ellen loved the man.

As unlike BERNARD as could be
  Was poor old AARON WOOD
(Disgraceful BERNARD's curate he):
  He was extremely good.

A BAYARD in his moral pluck
  Without reproach or fear,
A quiet venerable duck
  With fifty pounds a year.

No fault had he—no fad, except
  A tendency to strum,
In mode at which you would have wept,
  A dull harmonium.

He had no gold with which to hire
  The minstrels who could best
Convey a notion of the fire
  That raged within his breast.

And so, when COOTE and TINNEY's Own
  Had tootled all they knew,
And when the Guards, completely blown,
  Exhaustedly withdrew,

And NELL began to sleepy feel,
  Poor AARON then would come,
And underneath her window wheel
  His plain harmonium.

He woke her every morn at two,
And having gained her ear,
In vivid colours AARON drew
The sluggard's grim career.

He warbled Apiarian praise,
And taught her in his chant
To shun the dog's pugnacious ways,
And imitate the ant.

Still NELL seemed not, how much he played,
To love him out and out,
Although the admirable maid
Respected him, no doubt.

She told him of her early vow,
And said as BERNARD's wife
It might be hers to show him how
To rectify his life.

"You are so pure, so kind, so true,
Your goodness shines so bright,
What use would ELLEN be to you?
Believe me, you're all right."

She wished him happiness and health,
And flew on lightning wings
To BERNARD with his dangerous wealth
And all the woes it brings.

BRAVE ALUM BEY

Oh, big was the bosom of brave ALUM BEY,
And also the region that under it lay,
In safety and peril remarkably cool,
And he dwelt on the banks of the river Stamboul.

Each morning he went to his garden, to cull
A bunch of zenana or sprig of bul-bul,
And offered the bouquet, in exquisite bloom,
To BACKSHEESH, the daughter of RAHAT LAKOUM.

No maiden like BACKSHEESH could tastily cook
A kettle of kismet or joint of tchibouk,
As ALUM, brave fellow! sat pensively by,
With a bright sympathetic ka-bob in his eye.

Stern duty compelled him to leave her one day—
(A ship's supercargo was brave ALUM BEY)—
To pretty young BACKSHEESH he made a salaam,
And sailed to the isle of Seringapatam.

"O ALUM," said she, "think again, ere you go—
Hareems may arise and Moguls they may blow;
You may strike on a fez, or be drowned, which is wuss!'
But ALUM embraced her and spoke to her thus:

"Cease weeping, fair BACKSHEESH! I willingly swear
Cork jackets and trousers I always will wear,
And I also throw in a large number of oaths
That I never—no, *never*—will take off my clothes!"

* * * * *

They left Madagascar away on their right,
And made Clapham Common the following night,
Then lay on their oars for a fortnight or two,
Becalmed in the ocean of Honolulu.

One day Alum saw, with alarm in his breast,
A cloud on the nor-sow-sow-nor-sow-nor-west;
The wind it arose, and the crew gave a scream,
For they knew it—they knew it!—the dreaded Hareem!!

The mast it went over, and so did the sails,
Brave Alum threw over his casks and his bales;
The billows arose as the weather grew thick,
And all except Alum were terribly sick.

The crew were but three, but they holloa'd for nine,
They howled and they blubbered with wail and with
whine:
The skipper he fainted away in the fore,
For he hadn't the heart for to skip any more.

"Ho, coward!" said Alum, "with heart of a child!
Thou son of a party whose grave is defiled!
Is Alum in terror? is Alum afeard?
Ho! ho! If you had one I'd laugh at your beard."

His eyeball it gleamed like a furnace of coke;
He boldly inflated his clothes as he spoke;
He daringly felt for the corks on his chest,
And he recklessly tightened the belt at his breast.

For he knew, the brave Alum, that, happen what might,
With belts and cork-jacketing, *he* was all right;
Though others might sink, he was certain to swim,—
No Hareem whatever had terrors for him!

They begged him to spare from his personal store
A single cork garment—they asked for no more;
But he couldn't, because of the number of oaths
That he never—no, never!—would take off his clothes.

The billows dash o'er them and topple around,
They see they are pretty near sure to be drowned.
A terrible wave o'er the quarter-deck breaks,
And the vessel it sinks in a couple of shakes!

The dreadful Hareem, though it knows how to blow,
Expends all its strength in a minute or so;
When the vessel had foundered, as I have detailed,
The tempest subsided, and quiet prevailed.

One seized on a cork with a yelling "Ha! ha!"
(Its bottle had 'prisoned a pint of Pacha)—

Another a toothpick—another a tray—
"Alas! it is useless!" said brave ALUM BEY.

"To holloa and kick is a very bad plan:
Get it over, my tulips, as soon as you can;
You'd better lay hold of a good lump of lead,
And cling to it tightly until you are dead.

"Just raise your hands over your pretty heads—so—
Right down to the bottom you're certain to go.
Ta! ta! I'm afraid we shall not meet again"—
For the truly courageous are truly humane.

Brave ALUM was picked up the very next day—
A man-o'-war sighted him smoking away;
With hunger and cold he was ready to drop,
So they sent him below and they gave him a chop.

O reader, or readress, whichever you be,
You weep for the crew who have sunk in the sea?
O reader, or readress, read farther, and dry
The bright sympathetic ka-bob in your eye.

That ship had a grapple with three iron spikes,—
It's lowered, and, ha! on a something it strikes!
They haul it aboard with a British "heave-ho!"
And what it has fished the drawing will show.

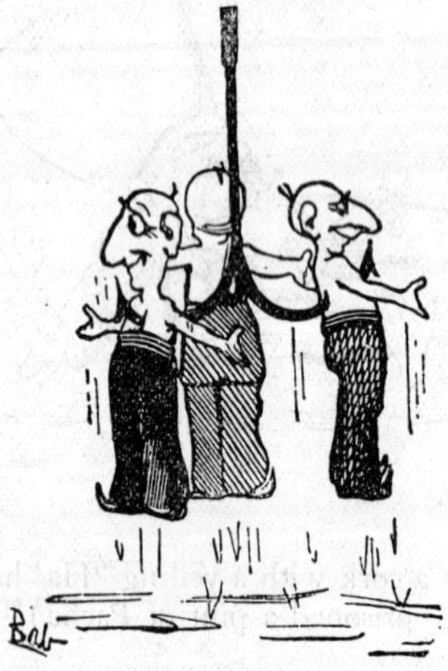

There was WILSON, and PARKER, and TOMLINSON, too—
(The first was the captain, the others the crew)—
As lively and spry as a Malabar ape,
Quite pleased and surprised at their happy escape.

And ALUM, brave fellow, who stood in the fore,
And never expected to look on them more,
Was really delighted to see them again,
For the truly courageous are truly humane.

SIR BARNABY BAMPTON BOO

This is SIR BARNABY BAMPTON BOO,
  Last of a noble race,
BARNABY BAMPTON, coming to woo,
  All at a deuce of a pace.
    BARNABY BAMPTON BOO,
    Here is a health to you:
  Here is wishing you luck, you elderly buck—
    BARNABY BAMPTON BOO!

The excellent women of Tuptonvee
  Knew SIR BARNABY BOO;
One of them surely his bride would be,
  But dickens a soul knew who.

Women of Tuptonvee,
Here is a health to ye:
For a Baronet, dears, you would cut off your ears,
Women of Tuptonvee!

Here are old Mr. and Mrs. de Plow
(Peter his Christian name),
They kept seven oxen, a pig, and a cow—
Farming it was their game.
Worthy old Peter de Plow,
Here is a health to thou:
Your race isn't run, though you're seventy-one,
Worthy old Peter de Plow!

To excellent Mr. and Mrs. de Plow
Came Sir Barnaby Boo,
He asked for their daughter, and told 'em as how
He was as rich as a Jew.
Barnaby Bampton's wealth,
Here is your jolly good health:
I'd never repine if you came to be mine,
Barnaby Bampton's wealth!

"O great SIR BARNABY BAMPTON BOO"
  (Said PLOW to that titled swell),
"My missus has given me daughters two—
  AMELIA and VOLATILE NELL!"
      AMELIA and VOLATILE NELL,
      I hope you're uncommonly well:
  You two pretty pearls—you extremely nice girls—
      AMELIA and VOLATILE NELL!

"AMELIA is passable only, in face,
  But, oh! she's a worthy girl;
Superior morals like hers would grace
  The home of a belted Earl."
      Morality, heavenly link!
      To you I'll eternally drink:
  I'm awfully fond of that heavenly bond,
      Morality, heavenly link!

"Now NELLY's the prettier, p'raps, of my gals,
But, oh! she's a wayward chit;
She dresses herself in her showy fal-lals,
And doesn't read TUPPER a bit!"
O TUPPER, philosopher true,
How do you happen to do?
A publisher looks with respect on your books,
For they *do* sell, philosopher true!

The Bart. (I'll be hanged if I drink him again,
Or care if he's ill or well),
He sneered at the goodness of MILLY THE PLAIN,
And cottoned to VOLATILE NELL!
O VOLATILE NELLY DE P.!
Be hanged if I'll empty to thee:
I like worthy maids, not mere frivolous jades,
VOLATILE NELLY DE P.!

They bolted, the Bart. and his frivolous dear,
And MILLY was left to pout;
For years they've got on very well, as I hear,
But soon he will rue it, no doubt.
O excellent MILLY DE PLOW,
I really can't drink to you now;
My head isn't strong, and the song has been long,
Excellent MILLY DE PLOW!

THE MODEST COUPLE

When man and maiden meet, I like to see a drooping eye,
I always droop my own—I am the shyest of the shy.
I'm also fond of bashfulness, and sitting down on thorns,
For modesty's a quality that womankind adorns.

Whenever I am introduced to any pretty maid,
My knees they knock together, just as if I were afraid;
I flutter, and I stammer, and I turn a pleasing red,
For to laugh, and flirt, and ogle I consider most ill-bred.

But still in all these matters, as in other things below,
There is a proper medium, as I'm about to show.
I do not recommend a newly-married pair to try
To carry on as PETER carried on with SARAH BLIGH.

Betrothed they were when very young—before they'd
learnt to speak
(For SARAH was but six days old, and PETER was a
week);
Though little more than babies at those early ages, yet
They bashfully would faint when they occasionally met.

They blushed, and flushed, and fainted, till they reached
the age of nine,
When PETER's good papa (he was a Baron of the Rhine)
Determined to endeavour some sound argument to find
To bring these shy young people to a proper frame of
mind.

He told them that as SARAH was to be his PETER's bride,
They might at least consent to sit at table side by side;

He begged that they would now and then shake hands,
till he was hoarse,
Which SARAH thought indelicate, and PETER very coarse.

And PETER in a tremble to the blushing maid would say,
"You must excuse papa, MISS BLIGH,—it is his mountain
way."
Says SARAH, "His behaviour I'll endeavour to forget,
But your papa's the coarsest person that I ever met.

"He plighted us without our leave, when we were very
young,
Before we had begun articulating with the tongue.
His underbred suggestions fill your SARAH with alarm;
Why, gracious me! he'll ask us next to walk out arm-in-
arm!"

At length when SARAH reached the legal age of twenty-
one,
The Baron he determined to unite her to his son;
And SARAH in a fainting-fit for weeks unconscious lay,
And PETER blushed so hard you might have heard him
miles away.

And when the time arrived for taking SARAH to his heart,
They were married in two churches half-a-dozen miles
apart

(Intending to escape all public ridicule and chaff),
And the service was conducted by electric telegraph.

And when it was concluded, and the priest had said his say,
Until the time arrived when they were both to drive away,
They never spoke or offered for to fondle or to fawn,
For *he* waited in the attic, and *she* waited on the lawn.

At length, when four o'clock arrived, and it was time to go,
The carriage was announced, but decent SARAH answered "No!
Upon my word, I'd rather sleep my everlasting nap,
Than go and ride alone with MR. PETER in a trap."

And PETER's over-sensitive and highly-polished mind
Wouldn't suffer him to sanction a proceeding of the kind;
And further, he declared he suffered overwhelming shocks
At the bare idea of having any coachman on the box.

So PETER into one turn-out incontinently rushed,
While SARAH in a second trap sat modestly and blushed;
And MR. NEWMAN's coachman, on authority I've heard,
Drove away in gallant style upon the coach-box of a third.

Now, though this modest couple in the matter of the car
Were very likely carrying a principle too far,
I hold their shy behaviour was more laudable in them
Than that of PETER's brother with MISS SARAH's sister EM.

ALPHONSO, who in cool assurance all creation licks,
He up and said to EMMIE (who had impudence for six),
"MISS EMILY, I love you—will you marry? Say the word!"
And EMILY said, "Certainly, ALPHONSO, like a bird!"

I do not recommend a newly-married pair to try
To carry on as PETER carried on with SARAH BLIGH,
But still their shy behaviour was more laudable in them
Than that of PETER's brother with MISS SARAH's sister EM.

THE MARTINET

Some time ago, in simple verse,
I sang the story true
Of CAPTAIN REECE, *The Mantelpiece,*
And all her happy crew.

I showed how any captain may
Attach his men to him,
If he but heeds their smallest needs,
And studies every whim.

Now mark how, by Draconic rule
And *hauteur* ill-advised,
The noblest crew upon the blue
May be demoralised.

When his ungrateful country placed
Kind REECE upon half-pay,
Without much claim SIR BERKELY came,
And took command one day.

Sir Berkely was a martinet—
  A stern unyielding soul—
Who ruled his ship by dint of whip
  And horrible black-hole.

A sailor who was overcome
  From having freely dined,
And chanced to reel when at the wheel,
  He instantly confined!

And tars who, when an action raged,
  Appeared alarmed or scared,
And those below who wished to go,
  He very seldom spared.

E'en he who smote his officer
  For punishment was booked,
And mutinies upon the seas
  He rarely overlooked.

In short, the happy *Mantelpiece*
  Where all had gone so well,
Beneath that fool SIR BERKELY's rule
  Became a floating hell.

When first SIR BERKELY came aboard
  He read a speech to all,
And told them how he'd made a vow
  To act on duty's call.

Then WILLIAM LEE, he up and said
  (The captain's coxswain he):
"We've heard the speech your honour's made,
  And werry pleased we be.

"We won't pretend, my lad, as how
  We're glad to lose our REECE;
Urbane, polite, he suited quite
  The saucy *Mantelpiece*.

"But if your honour gives your mind
  To study all our ways,
With dance and song we'll jog along
  As in those happy days.

"I like your honour's looks, and feel
  You're worthy of your sword.
Your hand, my lad—I'm doosid glad
  To welcome you aboard!"

Sir Berkely looked amazed, as though
  He did not understand.
"Don't shake your head," good William said,
  "It is an honest hand.

"It's grasped a better hand than yourn—
  Come, gov'nor, I insist!"
The Captain stared—the coxswain glared—
  The hand became a fist!

"Down, upstart!" said the hardy salt;
  But Berkely dodged his aim,
And made him go in chains below:
  The seamen murmured "Shame!"

He stopped all songs at 12 p.m.,
  Stopped hornpipes when at sea,
And swore his cot (or bunk) should not
  Be used by aught than he.

He never joined their daily mess,
  Nor asked them to his own,
But chaffed in gay and social way
  The officers alone.

His First Lieutenant, Peter, was
  As useless as could be,
A helpless stick, and always sick
  When there was any sea.

This First Lieutenant proved to be
  His foster-sister May,
Who went to sea for love of he,
  In masculine array.

And when he learnt the curious fact,
  Did he emotion show,
Or dry her tears, or end her fears
  By marrying her? No!

Or did he even try to soothe
  This maiden in her teens?
Oh no!—instead he made her wed
  The Sergeant of Marines!

Of course such Spartan discipline
  Would make an angel fret.
They drew a lot, and straightway shot
  This fearful martinet.

The Admiralty saw how ill
  They'd treated Captain Reece;
He was restored once more aboard
  The saucy *Mantelpiece.*

THE SAILOR BOY TO HIS LASS

I go away, this blessed day,
  To sail across the sea, Matilda!
My vessel sails for various parts
  At twenty after three, Matilda;
I hardly know where we may go,

Or if it's near or far, Matilda,
For Captain Hyde does not confide
In any 'fore-mast tar, Matilda!

Beneath my ban that mystic man
Shall suffer, *coûte que coûte*, Matilda!
What right has he to keep from me
The Admiralty route, Matilda?
Because, forsooth! I am a youth
Of common sailors' lot, Matilda!
Am I a man on human plan
Designed, or am I not, Matilda?

But there, my lass, we'll let that pass!
With anxious love I burn, Matilda.
I want to know if we shall go
To church when I return, Matilda?
Your eyes are red, you bow your head;
It's pretty clear you thirst, Matilda,
To name the day—What's that you say?—
"You'll see me further first," Matilda?

I can't mistake the signs you make,
  Although you barely speak, MATILDA;
Though pure and young, you thrust your tongue
  Right in your pretty cheek, MATILDA!
My dear, I fear I hear you sneer—
  I do—I'm sure I do, MATILDA—
With simple grace you make a face,
  Ejaculating, "Ugh!" MATILDA.

Oh, pause to think before you drink
  The dregs of Lethe's cup, MATILDA!
Remember, do, what I've gone through,
  Before you give me up, MATILDA!
Recall again the mental pain
  Of what I've had to do, MATILDA!
And be assured that I've endured
  It, all along of you, MATILDA!

Do you forget, my blithesome pet,
  How once with jealous rage, MATILDA,
I watched you walk and gaily talk
  With some one thrice your age, MATILDA?
You squatted free upon his knee,
  A sight that made me sad, MATILDA?
You pinched his cheek with friendly tweak,
  Which almost drove me mad, MATILDA!

I knew him not, but thought to spot
  Some man you wished to wed, MATILDA!
I took a gun, my darling one,
  And shot him through the head, MATILDA!
I'm made of stuff that's rough and gruff
  Enough, I own; but, ah, MATILDA!
It *did* annoy your poor old boy
  To find it was your pa, MATILDA!

I've passed a life of toil and strife,
  And disappointments deep, MATILDA;
I've lain awake with dental ache
  Until I fell asleep, MATILDA;
At times again I've missed a train,
  Or p'raps run short of tin, MATILDA,
And worn a boot on corns that shoot,
  Or, shaving, cut my chin, MATILDA!

But, oh! no trains—no dental pains—
  Believe me when I say, MATILDA,
No corns that shoot—no pinching boot
  Upon a summer day, MATILDA—
It's my belief, could cause such grief
  As that I've suffered for, MATILDA,
My having shot in vital spot
  Your old progenitor, MATILDA!

Bethink you how I've kept the vow
  I made one winter day, MATILDA—
That, come what could, I never would
  Remain too long away, MATILDA.
And, oh! the crimes with which, at times,
  I've charged my gentle mind, MATILDA,
To keep the vow I made—and now
  You treat me so unkind, MATILDA!

For when at sea off Caribbee,
  I felt my passion burn, MATILDA;
By impulse egged, I went and begged
  The captain to return, MATILDA;
And when, my pet, I couldn't get
  That captain to agree, MATILDA,
Right through a sort of open port
  I pitched him in the sea, MATILDA!

Remember, too, how all the crew,
  With indignation blind, Matilda,
Distinctly swore they ne'er before
  Had thought me so unkind, Matilda;
And how they'd shun me one by one—
  An unforgiving group, Matilda—
I stopped their howls and sulky scowls
  By pizening their soup, Matilda!

So pause to think, before you drink
  The dregs of Lethe's cup, Matilda;
Remember, do, what I've gone through,
  Before you give me up, Matilda.
Recall again the mental pain
  Of what I've had to do, Matilda,
And be assured that I've endured
  It, all along of you, Matilda!

THE REVEREND SIMON MAGUS

A rich advowson, highly prized,
For private sale was advertised;
And many a parson made a bid;
The Reverend Simon Magus did.

He sought the agent's: "Agent, I
Have come prepared at once to buy
(If your demand is not too big)
The Cure of Otium-cum-Digge."

"Ah!" said the agent, *"there's* a berth—
The snuggest vicarage on earth;
No sort of duty (so I hear),
And fifteen hundred pounds a year!

"If on the price we should agree,
The living soon will vacant be:
The good incumbent's ninety-five,
And cannot very long survive.

"See—here's his photograph—you see,
He's in his dotage." "Ah, dear me!
Poor soul!" said Simon. "His decease
Would be a merciful release!"

The agent laughed—the agent blinked—
The agent blew his nose and winked
And poked the parson's ribs in play—
It was that agent's vulgar way.

The Reverend Simon frowned: "I grieve
This light demeanour to perceive;
It's scarcely *comme il faut,* I think:
Now—pray oblige me—do not wink.

"Don't dig my waistcoat into holes—
Your mission is to sell the souls
Of human sheep and human kids
To that divine who highest bids.

"Do well in this, and on your head
Unnumbered honours will be shed."
The agent said, "Well, truth to tell,
I *have* been doing pretty well."

"You should," said Simon, "at your age;
But now about the parsonage.
How many rooms does it contain?
Show me the photograph again.

"A poor apostle's humble house
Must not be too luxurious;
No stately halls with oaken floor—
It should be decent and no more.

"No billiard-rooms—no stately trees—
No croquêt-grounds or pineries."
"Ah!" sighed the agent, "very true:
This property won't do for you.

"All these about the house you'll find"—
"Well," said the parson, "never mind;
I'll manage to submit to these
Luxurious superfluities.

"A clergyman who does not shirk
The various calls of Christian work,
Will have no leisure to employ
These 'common forms' of worldly joy.

"To preach three times on Sabbath days—
To wean the lost from wicked ways—
The sick to soothe—the sane to wed—
The poor to feed with meat and bread;

"These are the various wholesome ways
In which I'll spend my nights and days:
My zeal will have no time to cool
At croquêt, archery, or pool."

The agent said, "From what I hear,
This living will not suit, I fear—
There are no poor, no sick at all;
For services there is no call."

The reverend gent looked grave. "Dear me!
Then there is *no* 'society'?—
I mean, of course, no sinners there
Whose souls will be my special care?"

The cunning agent shook his head,
"No, none—except"—(the agent said)—
"The DUKE OF A., the EARL OF B.,
The MARQUIS C., and VISCOUNT D.

"But you will not be quite alone,
For, though they've chaplains of their own,
Of course this noble well-bred clan
Receive the parish clergyman."

"Oh, silence, sir!" said SIMON M.,
"Dukes—earls! What should I care for them?
These worldly ranks I scorn and flout!"
"Of course," the agent said, "no doubt."

"Yet I might show these men of birth
The hollowness of rank on earth."
The agent answered, "Very true—
But I should not, if I were you."

"Who sells this rich advowson, pray?"
The agent winked—it was his way—
"His name is HART; 'twixt me and you,
He is, I'm griev'd to say, a Jew!"

"A Jew?" said SIMON, "happy find!
I purchase this advowson, mind.
My life shall be devoted to
Converting that unhappy Jew!"

DAMON *v.* PYTHIAS

Two better friends you wouldn't pass
Throughout a summer's day,
Than DAMON and his PYTHIAS,—
Two merchant princes they.

At school together they contrived
  All sorts of boyish larks;
And, later on, together thrived
  As merry merchants' clerks.

And then, when many years had flown,
  They rose together till
They bought a business of their own—
  And they conduct it still.

They loved each other all their lives,
  Dissent they never knew,
And, stranger still, their very wives
  Were rather friendly too.

Perhaps you think, to serve my ends,
  These statements I refute,
When I admit that these dear friends
  Were parties to a suit?

But 'twas a friendly action, for
  Good PYTHIAS, as you see,
Fought merely as executor,
  And DAMON as trustee.

They laughed to think, as through the throng
  Of suitors sad they passed,
That they, who'd lived and loved so long,
  Should go to law at last.

The junior briefs they kindly let
  Two sucking counsel hold;
These learned persons never yet
  Had fingered suitors' gold.

But though the happy suitors two
  Were friendly as could be,
Not so the junior counsel who
  Were earning maiden fee.

They too, till then, were friends. At school
  They'd done each other's sums,
And under Oxford's gentle rule
  Had been the closest chums.

But now they met with scowl and grin
  In every public place,
And often snapped their fingers in
  Each other's learned face.

It almost ended in a fight
  When they on path or stair
Met face to face. They made it quite
  A personal affair.

And when at length the case was called
  (It came on rather late),
Spectators really were appalled
  To see their deadly hate.

One junior rose—with eyeballs tense,
  And swollen frontal veins:
To all his powers of eloquence
  He gave the fullest reins.

His argument was novel—for
  A verdict he relied
On blackening the junior
  Upon the other side.

"Oh," said the Judge, in robe and fur,
  "The matter in dispute
To arbitration pray refer—
  This is a friendly suit."

And PYTHIAS, in merry mood,
  Digged DAMON in the side;
And DAMON, tickled with the feud,
  With other digs replied.

But oh! those deadly counsel twain,
  Who were such friends before,
Were never reconciled again—
  They quarrelled more and more.

At length it happened that they met
  On Alpine heights one day,
And thus they paid each one his debt,
  Their fury had its way—

They seized each other in a trice,
  With scorn and hatred filled,
And, falling from a precipice,
  They, both of them, were killed.

MY DREAM

The other night, from cares exempt,
I slept—and what d'you think I dreamt?
I dreamt that somehow I had come
To dwell in Topsy-Turveydom!—

Where vice is virtue—virtue, vice:
Where nice is nasty—nasty, nice:
Where right is wrong and wrong is right—
Where white is black and black is white.

Where babies, much to their surprise,
Are born astonishingly wise;
With every Science on their lips,
And Art at all their finger-tips.

For, as their nurses dandle them,
They crow binomial theorem,
With views (it seems absurd to us)
On differential calculus.

But though a babe, as I have said,
Is born with learning in his head,
He must forget it, if he can,
Before he calls himself a man.

For that which we call folly here,
Is wisdom in that favoured sphere;
The wisdom we so highly prize
Is blatant folly in their eyes.

A boy, if he would push his way,
Must learn some nonsense every day;
And cut, to carry out this view,
His wisdom teeth and wisdom too.

Historians burn their midnight oils,
Intent on giant-killers' toils;
And sages close their aged eyes
To other sages' lullabies.

Our magistrates, in duty bound,
Commit all robbers who are found;
But there the beaks (so people said)
Commit all robberies instead.

Our judges, pure and wise in tone,
Know crime from theory alone,
And glean the motives of a thief
From books and popular belief.

But there, a judge who wants to prime
His mind with true ideas of crime,
Derives them from the common sense
Of practical experience.

Policemen march all folks away
Who practise virtue every day—
Of course, I mean to say, you know,
What we call virtue here below.

For only scoundrels dare to do
What we consider just and true,
And only good men do, in fact,
What we should think a dirty act.

But strangest of these social twirls,
The girls are boys—the boys are girls!
The men are women, too—but then
Per contra, women all are men.

To one who to tradition clings
This seems an awkward state of things,
But if to think it out you try,
It doesn't really signify.

With them, as surely as can be,
A sailor should be sick at sea,
And not a passenger may sail
Who cannot smoke right through a gale.

A soldier (save by rarest luck)
Is always shot for showing pluck—
That is, if others can be found
With pluck enough to fire a round.

"How strange," I said to one I saw,
"You quite upset our every law.
However can you get along
So systematically wrong?"

"Dear me," my mad informant said,
"Have you no eyes within your head?
You sneer when you your hat should doff:
Why, we begin where you leave off!

"Your wisest men are very far
Less learned than our babies are!"
I mused awhile—and then, oh me!
I framed this brilliant repartee:

"Although your babes are wiser far
Than our most valued sages are,
Your sages, with their toys and cots,
Are duller than our idiots!"

But this remark, I grieve to state,
Came just a little bit too late;
For as I framed it in my head,
I woke and found myself in bed.

Still I could wish that, 'stead of here,
My lot were in that favoured sphere!—
Where greatest fools bear off the bell
I ought to do extremely well.

THE BISHOP OF RUM-TI-FOO AGAIN

I often wonder whether you
Think sometimes of that Bishop, who
From black but Balmy Rum-ti-foo
Last summer twelvemonth came.

Unto your mind I p'raps may bring
Remembrance of the man I sing
To-day, by simply mentioning
That PETER was his name.

Remember how that holy man
Came with the great Colonial clan
To Synod, called Pan-Anglican;
And kindly recollect
How, having crossed the ocean wide,
To please his flock all means he tried
Consistent with a proper pride
And manly self-respect.

He only, of the reverend pack
Who minister to Christians black,
Brought any useful knowledge back
To his Colonial fold.
In consequence a place I claim
For "PETER" on the scroll of Fame
(For PETER was that Bishop's name,
As I've already told).

He carried Art, he often said,
To places where that timid maid
(Save by Colonial Bishops' aid)
Could never hope to roam.
The Payne-cum-Lauri feat he taught
As he had learnt it; for he thought
The choicest fruits of Progress ought
To bless the Negro's home.

And he had other work to do,
For, while he tossed upon the blue,
The islanders of Rum-ti-foo
Forgot their kindly friend.
Their decent clothes they learnt to tear—
They learnt to say, "I do not care,"
Though they, of course, were well aware
How folks, who say so, end.

Some sailors whom he did not know,
Had landed there not long ago,
And taught them "Bother!" also "Blow!"
(Of wickedness the germs.)
No need to use a casuist's pen
To prove that they were merchantmen;
No sailor of the Royal N.
Would use such awful terms.

And so, when Bishop PETER came
(That was the kindly Bishop's name),
He heard these dreadful oaths with shame,
And chid their want of dress.
(Except a shell—a bangle rare—
A feather here—a feather there—
The South Pacific negroes wear
Their native nothingness.)

He taught them that a Bishop loathes
To listen to unseemly oaths,
He gave them all his left-off clothes—
They bent them to his will.
The Bishop's gift spreads quickly round;
In PETER's left-off clothes they bound
(His three-and-twenty suits they found
In fair condition still).

The Bishop's eyes with water fill,
Quite overjoyed to find them still
Obedient to his sovereign will,
 And said, "Good Rum-ti-foo!
Half-way to meet you I'll prepare:
I'll dress myself in cowries rare,
And fasten feathers in my hair,
 And dance the 'Cutch-chi-boo'!"

And to conciliate his see
He married PICCADILLILLEE,
The youngest of his twenty-three,
 Tall—neither fat nor thin.
(And though the dress he made her don
Looks awkwardly a girl upon,
It was a great improvement on
 The one he found her in.)

The Bishop in his gay canoe
(His wife, of course, went with him too),
To some adjacent island flew,
 To spend his honeymoon.
Some day in sunny Rum-ti-foo
A little PETER 'll be on view;
And that (if people tell me true)
 Is like to happen soon.

A WORM WILL TURN

I love a man who'll smile and joke
    When with misfortune crowned;
Who'll pun beneath a pauper's yoke,
And as he breaks his daily toke,
    Conundrums gay propound.

Just such a man was BERNARD JUPP,
    He scoffed at Fortune's frown;
He gaily drained his bitter cup—
Though Fortune often threw him up,
    It never cast him down.

Though years their share of sorrow bring,
    We know that far above
All other griefs, are griefs that spring
From some misfortune happening
    To those we really love.

E'en sorrow for another's woe
    Our BERNARD failed to quell;
Though by this special form of blow

No person ever suffered so,
Or bore his grief so well.

His father, wealthy and well clad,
And owning house and park,
Lost every halfpenny he had,
And then became (extremely sad!)
A poor attorney's clerk.

All sons it surely would appal,
Except the passing meek,
To see a father lose his all,
And from an independence fall
To one pound ten a week!

But JUPP shook off his sorrow's weight,
And, like a Christian son,
Proved Poverty a happy fate—
Proved Wealth to be a devil's bait.
To lure poor sinners on.

With other sorrows BERNARD coped,
For sorrows came in packs;
His cousins with their housemaids sloped—
His uncles forged—his aunts eloped—
His sisters married blacks.

But BERNARD, far from murmuring
(Exemplar, friends, to us),
Determined to his faith to cling,—
He made the best of everything.
And argued softly thus:

" 'Twere harsh my uncles' forging knack
Too rudely to condemn—
My aunts, repentant, may come back,
And blacks are nothing like as black
As people colour them!"

Still Fate, with many a sorrow rife,
Maintained relentless fight:
His grandmamma next lost her life,
Then died the mother of his wife,
But still he seemed all right.

His brother fond (the only link
To life that bound him now)
One morning, overcome by drink,
He broke his leg (the right, I think)
In some disgraceful row.

But did my BERNARD swear and curse?
Oh no—to murmur loth,
He only said, "Go, get a nurse:
Be thankful that it isn't worse;
You might have broken both!"

But worms who watch without concern
The cockchafer on thorns,
Or beetles smashed, themselves will turn
If, walking through the slippery fern,
You tread upon their corns.

One night as BERNARD made his track
Through Brompton home to bed,
A footpad, with a vizor black,
Took watch and purse, and dealt a crack
On BERNARD'S saint-like head.

It was too much—his spirit rose,
He looked extremely cross.
Men thought him steeled to mortal foes,
But no—he bowed to countless blows,
But kicked against this loss.

He finally made up his mind
Upon his friends to call;
Subscription lists were largely signed,
For men were really glad to find
Him mortal, after all!

THE HAUGHTY ACTOR

An actor—GIBBS, of Drury Lane—
Of very decent station,
Once happened in a part to gain
Excessive approbation;

It sometimes turns a fellow's brain
And makes him singularly vain
When he believes that he receives
Tremendous approbation.

His great success half drove him mad,
But no one seemed to mind him;
Well, in another piece he had
Another part assigned him.
This part was smaller, by a bit,
Than that in which he made a hit.
So, much ill-used, he straight refused
To play the part assigned him.

* * * * *

That night that actor slept, and I'll attempt
To tell you of the vivid dream he dreamt:

THE DREAM

In fighting with a robber band
(A thing he loved sincerely)
A sword struck GIBBS upon the hand
And wounded it severely.
At first he didn't heed it much,
He thought it was a simple touch,
But soon he found the weapon's bound
Had wounded him severely.

To Surgeon COBB he made a trip,
Who'd just effected featly
An amputation at the hip
Particularly neatly.
A rising man was Surgeon COBB,
But this extremely ticklish job
He had achieved (as he believed)
Particularly neatly.

The actor rang the surgeon's bell.
"Observe my wounded finger;
Be good enough to strap it well,
And prithee do not linger,

That I, dear sir, may fill again
The Theatre Royal, Drury Lane:
This very night I have to fight—
So prithee do not linger."

"I don't strap fingers up for doles,"
Replied the haughty surgeon;
"To use your can't, I don't play *rôles*
'Utility' that verge on.
'First amputation'—nothing less—
That is my line of business:
We surgeon nobs despise all jobs
Utility that verge on.

"When in your hip there lurks disease"
(So dreamt this lively dreamer),
"Or devastating *caries*
In *humerus* or *femur*,

If you can pay a handsome fee,
Oh, then you may remember me,
With joy elate I'll amputate
Your *humerus* or *femur*."

The disconcerted actor ceased
The haughty leech to pester,
But when the wound in size increased,
And then began to fester,
He sought a learned Counsel's lair,
And told that Counsel, then and there,
How Cobb's neglect of his defect
Had made his finger fester.

"Oh, bring my action, if you please,
The case I pray you urge on,
And win me thumping damages
From Cobb, that haughty surgeon.
He culpably neglected me
Although I proffered him his fee,
So pray come down, in wig and gown,
On Cobb, that haughty surgeon!"

That Counsel, learned in the laws,
With passion almost trembled,
He just had gained a mighty cause
Before the Peers assembled!
Said he, "How dare you have the face
To come with Common Jury case
To one who wings rhetoric flings
Before the Peers assembled?"

Dispirited became our friend—
Depressed his moral pecker—
"But stay! a thought! I'll gain my end,
And save my poor exchequer.
I won't be placed upon the shelf,
I'll take it into Court myself,
And legal lore display before
The Court of the Exchequer."

He found a Baron—one of those
Who with our laws supply us—
In wig and silken gown and hose,
As if at *Nisi Prius*.

But he'd just given, off the reel,
A famous judgment on Appeal:
It scarce became his heightened fame
To sit at *Nisi Prius*.

Our friend began, with easy wit,
That half concealed his terror:
"Pooh!" said the Judge, "I only sit
In *Banco* or in Error.
Can you suppose, my man, that I'd
O'er *Nisi Prius* Courts preside,
Or condescend my time to spend
On anything but Error?"

"Too bad," said GIBBS, "my case to shirk!
You must be bad innately,
To save your skill for mighty work
Because it's valued greatly!"
But here he woke, with sudden start.

* * * * *

He wrote to say he'd play the part.
I've but to tell he played it well —
The author's words—his native wit
Combined, achieved a perfect "hit"—
The papers praised him greatly.

THE TWO MAJORS

An excellent soldier who's worthy the name,
Loves officers dashing and strict:
When good, he's content with escaping all blame,
When naughty, he likes to be licked.

He likes for a fault to be bullied and stormed,
Or imprisoned for several days;
And hates, for a duty correctly performed,
To be slavered with sickening praise.

No officer sickened with praises his *corps*
So little as MAJOR LA GUERRE—
No officers swore at his warriors more
Than MAJOR MAKREDI PREPERE.

Their soldiers adored them, and every grade
Delighted to hear them abuse;
Though whenever these officers came on parade,
They shivered and shook in their shoes.

"No doubt we deserve it—no mercy we crave—
Go on—you're conferring a boon;
We would rather be slanged by a warrior brave
Than praised by a wretched poltroon!"

MAKREDI would say that in battle's fierce rage
  True happiness only was met:
Poor MAJOR MAKREDI, though fifty his age,
  Had never known happiness yet!

LA GUERRE would declare, "With the blood of a foe
  No tipple is worthy to clink."
Poor fellow! he hadn't, though sixty or so,
  Yet tasted his favourite drink!

They agreed at their mess—they agreed in the glass—
  They agreed in the choice of their "set,"
And they also agreed in adoring, alas!
  The Vivandière, pretty FILLETTE.

Agreement, we know, may be carried too far,
  And after agreeing all round
For years—in this soldierly "maid of the bar,"
  A bone of contention they found.

"On the day that you marry her," muttered PREPERE
  (With a pistol he quietly played),
"I'll scatter the brains in your noddle, I swear,
  All over the stony parade!"

"I cannot do *that* to you," answered LA GUERRE,
"Whatever events may befall;
But this *I can* do—if you wed her, *mon cher!*
I'll eat you, moustachios and all!

The rivals, although they would never engage,
Yet quarrelled whenever they met;
They met in a fury and left in a rage,
But neither took pretty FILLETTE.

"I am not afraid," thought MAKREDI PREPERE:
"For my country I'm ready to fall;
But nobody wants, for a mere Vivandière,
To be eaten, moustachios and all!

"Besides, though LA GUERRE has his faults, I'll allow
He's one of the bravest of men:
My goodness; if I disagree with him now,
I might disagree with him then!"

"No coward am I," said LA GUERRE, "as you guess—
I sneer at an enemy's blade;
But I don't want PREPERE to get into a mess
For splashing the stony parade!"

One day on parade to PREPERE and LA GUERRE
Came CORPORAL JACOT DEBETTE,
And, trembling all over, he prayed of them there
To give him the pretty FILLETTE.

"You see, I am willing to marry my bride
  Until you've arranged this affair;
I will blow out my brains when your honours decide
  Which marries the sweet Vivandière!"

"Well, take her," said both of them in a duet
  (A favourite form of reply),
"But when I am ready to marry FILLETTE,
  Remember you've promised to die!"

He married her then: from the flowery plains
  Of existence the roses they cull:
He lived and he died with his wife; and his brains
  Are reposing in peace in his skull.

EMILY, JOHN, JAMES, AND I

A DERBY LEGEND

EMILY JANE was a nursery maid—
  JAMES was a bold Life Guard,
And JOHN was a constable, poorly paid
  (And I am a doggerel bard).

A very good girl was Emily Jane,
Jimmy was good and true,
And John was a very good man in the main
(And I am a good man, too).

Rivals for Emmie were Johnny and James,
Though Emily liked them both;
She couldn't tell which had the strongest claims
(And *I* couldn't take my oath).

But sooner or later you're certain to find
Your sentiments can't lie hid—
Jane thought it was time that she made up her mind
(And I think it was time she did).

Said Jane, with a smirk, and a blush on her face,
"I'll promise to wed the boy
Who takes me to-morrow to Epsom Race!"
(Which *I* would have done, with joy.)

From Johnny escaped an expression of pain,
But Jimmy said, "Done with you!
I'll take you with pleasure, my Emily Jane"
(And I would have said so too).

John lay on the ground, and he roared like mad
(For Johnny was sore perplexed),
And he kicked very hard at a very small lad
(Which *I* often do, when vexed).

For JOHN was on duty next day with the Force,
To punish all Epsom crimes;
Some people *will* cross, when they're clearing the course
(I do it myself, sometimes).

* * * * *

The Derby Day sun glittered gaily on cads,
On maidens with gamboge hair,
On sharpers and pickpockets, swindlers and pads
(For I, with my harp, was there).

And JIMMY went down with his JANE that day,
And JOHN by the collar or nape
Seized everybody who came in his way
(And *I* had a narrow escape).

He noticed his EMILY JANE with JIM,
And envied the well-made elf;
And people remarked that he muttered "Oh, dim!"
(I often say "dim!" myself).

JOHN dogged them all day, without asking their leaves:
For his sergeant he told, aside,
That JIMMY and JANE were notorious thieves
(And I think he was justified).

But James wouldn't dream of abstracting a fork,
And Jenny would blush with shame
At stealing so much as a bottle or cork
(A bottle I think fair game).

But, ah! there's another more serious crime!
They wickedly strayed upon
The course, at a critical moment of time
(I pointed them out to John).

The crusher came down on the pair in a crack—
And then, with a demon smile,
Let JENNY cross over, but sent JIMMY back
(I played on my harp the while).

Stern Johnny their agony loud derides
With a very triumphant sneer—
They weep and they wail from the opposite sides
(And *I* shed a silent tear).

And Jenny is crying away like mad,
And Jimmy is swearing hard;
And Johnny is looking uncommonly glad
(And I am a doggerel bard).

But Jimmy he ventured on crossing again
The scenes of our Isthmian Games—
John caught him, and collared him, giving him pain
(I felt very much for James).

John led him away with a victor's hand,
And Jimmy was shortly seen
In the station-house under the grand Grand Stand
(As many a time *I've* been).

And Jimmy, bad boy, was imprisoned for life,
Though Emily pleaded hard;
And Johnny had Emily Jane to wife
(And I am a doggerel bard).

THE PERILS OF INVISIBILITY

Old Peter led a wretched life—
Old Peter had a furious wife;
Old Peter, too, was truly stout,
He measured several yards about.

The little fairy Picklekin
One summer afternoon looked in,
And said, "Old Peter, how-de-do?
Can I do anything for you?

"I have three gifts—the first will give
Unbounded riches while you live;
The second, health where'er you be;
The third, invisibility."

"O, little fairy Picklekin,"
Old Peter answered, with a grin,
"To hesitate would be absurd,—
Undoubtedly I choose the third."

" 'Tis yours," the fairy said; "be quite
Invisible to mortal sight
Whene'er you please. Remember me
Most kindly, pray, to Mrs. P."

Old Mrs. Peter overheard
Wee Picklekin's concluding word,
And, jealous of her girlhood's choice,
Said, "That was some young woman's voice!"

Old Peter let her scold and swear—
Old Peter, bless him, didn't care.
"My dear, your rage is wasted quite—
Observe, I disappear from sight!"

A well-bred fairy (so I've heard)
Is always faithful to her word:
Old Peter vanished like a shot,
But then—*his suit of clothes did not.*

For when conferred the fairy slim
Invisibility on him,
She popped away on fairy wings,
Without referring to his "things."

So there remained a coat of blue,
A vest and double eyeglass too,
His tail, his shoes, his socks as well,
His pair of—no, I must not tell.

Old Mrs. Peter soon began
To see the failure of his plan,
And then resolved (I quote the bard)
To "hoist him with his own petard."

Old Peter woke next day and dressed,
Put on his coat and shoes and vest,
His shirt and stock—*but could not find*
His only pair of—never mind!

Old Peter was a decent man,
And though he twigged his lady's plan,
Yet, hearing her approaching, he
Resumed invisibility.

"Dear Mrs. P., my only joy,"
Exclaimed the horrified old boy;
"Now give them up, I beg of you—
You know what I'm referring to!"

But no; the cross old lady swore
She'd keep his—what I said before—
To make him publicly absurd;
And Mrs. Peter kept her word.

The poor old fellow had no rest;
His coat, his stock, his shoes, his vest,
Were all that now met mortal eye—
The rest, invisibility!

"Now, madam, give them up, I beg—
I've bad rheumatics in my leg;
Besides, until you do, it's plain
I cannot come to sight again!

"For though some mirth it might afford
To see my clothes without their lord,
Yet there would rise indignant oaths
If he were seen without his clothes!"

But no; resolved to have her quiz,
The lady held her own—and his—
And PETER left his humble cot
To find a pair of—you know what.

But—here's the worst of this affair—
Whene'er he came across a pair
Already placed for him to don,
He was too stout to get them on!

So he resolved at once to train,
And walked and walked with all his main;
For years he paced this mortal earth,
To bring himself to decent girth.

At night, when all around is still,
You'll find him pounding up a hill;
And shrieking peasants whom he meets,
Fall down in terror on the peats!

Old PETER walks through wind and rain
Resolved to train, and train, and train,
Until he weighs twelve stone or so—
And when he does, I'll let you know.

OLD PAUL AND OLD TIM.

When rival adorers come courting a maid,
There's something or other may often be said,
Why *he* should be pitched upon rather than *him*.
This wasn't the case with Old PAUL and Old TIM.

No soul could discover a reason at all
For marrying TIMOTHY rather than PAUL;
Though all could have offered good reasons, on oath,
Against marrying either—or marrying both.

They were equally wealthy and equally old,
They were equally timid and equally bold;
They were equally tall as they stood in their shoes—
Between them, in fact, there was nothing to choose.

Had I been young EMILY, I should have said,
"You're both much too old for a pretty young maid,
Threescore at the least you are verging upon";
But I wasn't young EMILY. Let us get on.

No coward's blood ran in young EMILY's veins,
Her martial old father loved bloody campaigns;
At the rumours of battles all over the globe
He pricked up his ears like the war-horse in "Job."

He chuckled to hear of a sudden surprise—
Of soldiers, compelled, through an enemy's spies,
Without any knapsacks or shakos to flee—
For an eminent army-contractor was he.

So when her two lovers, whose patience was tried,
Implored her between them at once to decide,
She told them she'd marry whichever might bring
Good proofs of his doing the pluckiest thing.

They both went away with a qualified joy:
That coward, Old PAUL, chose a very small boy,
And when no one was looking, in spite of his fears,
He set to work boxing that little boy's ears.

The little boy struggled and tugged at his hair,
But the lion was roused, and Old PAUL didn't care;
He smacked him, and whacked him, and boxed him, and
kicked
Till the poor little beggar was royally licked.

Old TIM knew a trick worth a dozen of that,
So he called for his stick and he called for his hat.
"I'll cover myself with cheap glory—I'll go
And wallop the Frenchmen who live in Soho!

"The German invader is ravaging France
With infantry rifle and cavalry lance,
And beautiful Paris is fighting her best
To shake herself free from her terrible guest.

"The Frenchmen in London, in craven alarms,
Have all run away from the summons to arms;
They haven't the pluck of a pigeon—I'll go
And wallop the Frenchmen who skulk in Soho!"

Old TIMOTHY tried it and found it succeed:
That day he caused many French noses to bleed;
Through foggy Soho he spread fear and dismay,
And Frenchmen all round him in agony lay.

He took care to abstain from employing his fist
On the old and the crippled, for they might resist;
A crippled old man may have pluck in his breast,
But the young and the strong ones are cowards confest.

Old Tim and Old Paul, with the list of their foes,
Prostrated themselves at their Emily's toes:
"Oh, which of us two is the pluckier blade?"
And Emily answered and Emily said:

"Old Tim has thrashed runaway Frenchmen in scores
Who ought to be guarding their cities and shores;
Old Paul has made little chaps' noses to bleed—
Old Paul has accomplished the pluckier deed!"

THE MYSTIC SELVAGEE

Perhaps already you may know
Sir Blennerhasset Portico?
A Captain in the Navy, he—
A Baronet and K.C.B.
You do? I thought so!
It was that captain's favourite whim
(A notion not confined to him)
That Rodney was the greatest tar
Who ever wielded capstan-bar.
He had been taught so.

"Benbow? Cornwallis? Hood?—Belay!
Compared with Rodney"—he would say—
"No other tar is worth a rap;
The great Lord Rodney was the chap
The French to polish!

"Though, mind you, I respect Lord Hood;
Cornwallis, too, was rather good;
Benbow could enemies repel;
Lord Nelson, too, was pretty well—
That is, tol-lol-ish!"

Sir Blennerhasset spent his days
In learning Rodney's little ways,
And closely imitated, too,
His mode of talking to his crew—
His port and paces.
An ancient tar he tried to catch
Who'd served in Rodney's famous batch;
But since his time long years have fled,
And Rodney's tars are mostly dead:
Eheu fugaces!

But after searching near and far,
At last he found an ancient tar
Who served with Rodney and his crew
Against the French in 'eighty-two
(That gained the peerage).

He gave him fifty pounds a year,
His rum, his baccy, and his beer;
And had a comfortable den
Rigged up in what, by merchantmen,
Is called the steerage.

"Now, JASPER"—'twas that sailor's name—
"Don't fear that you'll incur my blame
By saying, when it seems to you,
That there is anything I do
That RODNEY wouldn't."
The ancient sailor turned his quid,
Prepared to do as he was bid:
"Ay, ay, yer honour; to begin,
You've done away with 'swifting in'—
Well, sir, you shouldn't!

"Upon your spars I see you've clapped
Peak-halliard blocks, all iron-capped;
I would not christen that a crime,
But 'twas not done in RODNEY's time.
It looks half-witted!
Upon your maintop-stay, I see,
You always clap a selvagee;
Your stays, I see, are equalised—
No vessel, such as RODNEY prized,
Would thus be fitted.

"And RODNEY, honoured sir, would grin
To see you turning deadeyes in,
Not *up,* as in the ancient way,
But downwards, like a cutter's stay—
You didn't oughter!
Besides, in seizing shrouds on board,
Breast backstays you have quite ignored;
Great RODNEY kept unto the last
Breast backstays on topgallant mast—
They make it tauter."

SIR BLENNERHASSET "swifted in,"
Turned deadeyes up, and lent a fin
To strip (as told by JASPER KNOX)
The iron capping from his blocks,
Where there was any.

Sir Blennerhasset does away
With selvagees from maintop-stay;
And though it makes his sailors stare,
He rigs breast backstays everywhere—
In fact, too many.

One morning, when the saucy craft
Lay calmed, old Jasper toddled aft.
"My mind misgives me, sir, that we
Were wrong about that selvagee—
I should restore it."
"Good," said the captain, and that day
Restored it to the maintop-stay.
Well-practised sailors often make
A much more serious mistake,
And then ignore it.

Next day old Jasper came once more:
"I think, sir, I was right before."
Well, up the mast the sailors skipped,
The selvagee was soon unshipped,
And all were merry.

Again a day, and Jasper came:
"I p'raps deserve your honour's blame,
I can't make up my mind," said he,
"About that cursed selvagee—
It's foolish—very.

"On Monday night I could have sworn
That maintop-stay it should adorn,
On Tuesday morning I could swear
That selvagee should not be there.
The knot's a rasper!"
"Oh, you be hanged!" said Captain P.,
"Here, go ashore at Caribbee.
Get out—good-bye—shove off—all right!"
Old Jasper soon was out of sight—
Farewell, old Jasper!

THE CUNNING WOMAN

On all Arcadia's sunny plain,
On all Arcadia's hill,
None were so blithe as Bill and Jane,
So blithe as Jane and Bill.

No social earthquake e'er occurred
  To rack their common mind:
To them a Panic was a word—
  A Crisis, empty wind.

No Stock Exchange disturbed the lad
  With overwhelming shocks—
Bill ploughed with all the shares he had,
  Jane planted all her stocks.

And learn in what a simple way
  Their pleasures they enhanced—
Jane danced like any lamb all day,
  Bill piped as well as danced.

Surrounded by a twittling crew,
  Of linnet, lark, and thrush,
Bill treated his young lady to
  This sentimental gush:

"Oh, Jane, how true I am to you!
  How true you are to me!
And how we woo, and how we coo!
  So fond a pair are we!

"To think, dear Jane, that anyways,
  Your chiefest end and aim
Is, one of these fine summer days,
  To bear my humble name!"

Quoth Jane, "Well, as you put the case,
  I'm true enough, no doubt,
But then, you see, in this here place
  There's none to cut you out.

"But, oh! if anybody came—
  A Lord or any such—
I do not think your humble name
  Would fascinate me much.

"For though your mates, you often boast,
  You distance out-and-out;
Still, in the abstract, you're a most
  Uncompromising lout!"

Poor Bill, he gave a heavy sigh,
He tried in vain to speak—
A fat tear started to each eye
And coursed adown each cheek.

For, oh! right well in truth he knew
That very self-same day,
The Lord de Jacob Pillaloo
Was coming there to stay!

The Lord de Jacob Pillaloo
All proper maidens shun—
He loves all women, it is true,
But never marries one.

Now Jane, with all her mad self-will,
Was no coquette—oh no!
She really loved her faithful Bill,
And thus she tuned her woe:

"Oh, willow, willow, o'er the lea!
And willow once again!
The Peer will fall in love with me!
Why wasn't I made plain?"

* * * * *

A cunning woman lived hard by,
  A sorceressing dame,
MacCatacomb de Salmon-Eye
  Was her uncommon name.

To her good Jane, with kindly yearn
  For Bill's increasing pain,
Repaired in secrecy to learn
  How best to make her plain.

"Oh, Jane," the worthy woman said,
  "This mystic phial keep,
And rub its liquor in your head
  Before you go to sleep.

"When you awake next day, I trow,
  You'll look in form and hue
To others just as you do now—
  But not to Pillaloo!

"When you approach him, you will find
  He'll think you coarse—unkempt—
And rudely bid you get behind,
  With undisguised contempt."

The Lord de Pillaloo arrived
  With his expensive train,
And when in state serenely hived,
  He sent for Bill and Jane.

"Oh, spare her, Lord of Pillaloo!
  (Said Bill) if wed you be,
There's anything *I'd* rather do
  Than flirt with Lady P."

The Lord he gazed in Jenny's eyes,
  He looked her through and through:
The cunning woman's prophecies
  Were clearly coming true.

Lord Pillaloo, the Rustic's Bane
  (Bad person he, and proud),
He laughed Ha! ha! at pretty Jane,
  And sneered at her aloud!

He bade her get behind him then,
  And seek her mother's stye—
Yet to her native countrymen
  She was as fair as aye!

MACCATACOMB, continue green!
  Grow, SALMON-EYE, in might,
Except for you, there might have been
  The deuce's own delight!

PHRENOLOGY

"Come, collar this bad man—
  Around the throat he knotted me
Till I to choke began—
  In point of fact, garrotted me!"

So spake Sir HERBERT WHITE
  To JAMES, Policeman Thirty-two—
All ruffled with his fight
  SIR HERBERT was, and dirty too.

Policeman nothing said
  (Though he had much to say on it),
But from the bad man's head
  He took the cap that lay on it.

"No, great SIR HERBERT WHITE—
  Impossible to take him up.
This man is honest quite—
  Wherever did you rake him up?

"For Burglars, Thieves, and Co.,
  Indeed I'm no apologist;
But I, some years ago,
  Assisted a Phrenologist.

"Observe his various bumps,
  His head as I uncover it;
His morals lie in lumps
  All round about and over it."

"Now take him," said Sir White,
"Or you will soon be rueing it;
Bless me! I must be right,—
I caught the fellow doing it!"

Policeman calmly smiled,
"Indeed you are mistaken, sir,
You're agitated—riled—
And very badly shaken, sir.

"Sit down, and I'll explain
My system of Phrenology,
A second, please, remain"—
(A second is horology).

Policeman left his beat—
(The Bart., no longer furious,
Sat down upon a seat,
Observing, "This is curious!")

"Oh, surely here are signs
Should soften your rigidity,
This gentleman combines
Politeness with timidity.

"Of Shyness here's a lump—
A hole for Animosity—
And like my fist his bump
Of Generenerosity.

"Just here the bump appears
Of Innocent Hilarity,
And just behind his ear
Are Faith, and Hope, and Charity.

"He of true Christian ways
As bright example sent us is—
This maxim he obeys,
'Sorte tuâ contentus sis.'

"There, let him go his ways,
He needs no stern admonishing."
The Bart., in blank amaze,
Exclaimed, "This is astonishing!

"I *must* have made a mull,
  This matter I've been blind in it:
Examine, please, *my* skull,
  And tell me what you find in it."

Policeman looked, and said,
  With unimpaired urbanity,
"SIR HERBERT, you've a head
  That teems with inhumanity.

"Here's Murder, Envy, Strife
  (Propensity to kill any),
And Lies as large as life,
  And heaps of Social Villainy:

"Here's Love of Bran New Clothes,
  Embezzling—Arson—Deism—
A taste for Slang and Oaths,
  And Fraudulent Trusteeism.

"Here's Love of Groundless Charge—
  Here's Malice, too, and Trickery,
Unusually large
  Your bump of Pocket-Pickery——"

"Stop!" said the Bart., "my cup
  Is full—I'm worse than him in all—
Policeman, take me up—
  No doubt I am some criminal!"

That Policeman's scorn grew large
  (Phrenology had nettled it),
He took that Bart. in charge—
  I don't know how they settled it.

THE FAIRY CURATE

Once a fairy
Light and airy
Married with a mortal;
Men, however,
Never, never
Pass the fairy portal.

Slyly stealing,
She to Ealing
Made a daily journey;
There she found him,
Clients round him
(He was an attorney).

Long they tarried,
Then they married.
When the ceremony
Once was ended,
Off they wended
On their moon of honey.
Twelvemonth, maybe,
Saw a baby
(Friends performed an orgie)
Much they prized him,
And baptized him
By the name of Georgie.

Georgie grew up;
Then he flew up
To his fairy mother.
Happy meeting
Pleasant greeting—
Kissing one another.
"Choose a calling
Most enthralling,
I sincerely urge ye."
"Mother," said he
(Rev'rence made he),
"I would join the clergy.

"Give permission
In addition—
Pa will let me do it:
There's a living
In his giving,
He'll appoint me to it.
Dreams of coff'ring
Easter off'ring,
Tithe and rent and pew-rate,
So inflame me
(Do not blame me),
That I'll be a curate."

She, with pleasure,
Said, "My treasure,
'Tis my wish precisely.
Do your duty,
There's a beauty;
You have chosen wisely.
Tell your father
I would rather
As a churchman rank you.
You, in clover,
I'll watch over."
GEORGIE said, "Oh, thank you!"

GEORGIE scudded,
Went and studied,
Made all preparations,
And with credit
(Though he said it)
Passed examinations.
(Do not quarrel
With him, moral,
Scrupulous digestions—
But his mother,
And no other,
Answered all the questions.)

Time proceeded;
Little needed
GEORGIE admonition:

He, elated,
Vindicated
Clergyman's position.
People round him
Always found him
Plain and unpretending;
Kindly teaching,
Plainly preaching—
All his money lending.

So the fairy,
Wise and wary,
Felt no sorrow rising—
No occasion
For persuasion,
Warning, or advising.
He, resuming
Fairy pluming
(That's not English, is it?)
Oft would fly up,
To the sky up,
Pay mamma a visit.

* * * *

Time progressing,
GEORGIE's blessing
Grew more Ritualistic—
Popish scandals,
Tonsures—sandals—
Genuflections mystic;
Gushing meetings—
Bosom-beatings—
Heavenly ecstatics—
Broidered spencers—
Copes and censers—
Rochets and dalmatics.

This quandary
Vexed the fairy—
Flew she down to Ealing.
"GEORGIE, stop it!
Pray you, drop it;
Hark to my appealing:

To this foolish
Papal rule-ish
Twaddle put an ending;
This a swerve is
From our Service
Plain and unpretending."

He, replying,
Answered, sighing,
Hawing, hemming, humming,
"It's a pity—
They're so pritty;
Yet in mode becoming,
Mother tender,
I'll surrender—
I'll be unaffected—"
Then his Bishop
Into *his* shop
Entered unexpected:

"Who is this, sir,—
Ballet miss, sir?"
Said the Bishop coldly.
" 'Tis my mother,
And no other,"
GEORGIE answered boldly.
"Go along, sir!
You are wrong, sir,
You have years in plenty;
While this hussy
(Gracious mussy!)
Isn't two-and-twenty!"

(Fairies clever
Never, never
Grow in visage older;
And the fairy,
All unwary,
Leant upon his shoulder!)
Bishop grieved him,
Disbelieved him,
GEORGE the point grew warm on;
Changed religion,
Like a pigeon,[1]
And became a Mormon.

[1] "Like a bird."

THE WAY OF WOOING

A maiden sat at her window wide,
Pretty enough for a prince's bride,
Yet nobody came to claim her.
She sat like a beautiful picture there,
With pretty bluebells and roses fair,
And jasmine leaves to frame her.
And why she sat there nobody knows;
But thus she sang as she plucked a rose,
The leaves around her strewing:
"I've time to lose and power to choose;
'Tis not so much the gallant who woos
As the gallant's way of wooing!"

A lover came riding by awhile,
A wealthy lover was he, whose smile
  Some maids would value greatly—
A formal lover, who bowed and bent,
With many a high-flown compliment,
  And cold demeanour stately.

"You've still," said she to her suitor stern,
"The 'prentice-work of your craft to learn,
  If thus you come a-cooing.
I've time to lose and power to choose;
'Tis not so much the gallant who woos
  As the gallant's way of wooing!"

A second lover came ambling by—
A timid lad with a frightened eye
  And a colour mantling highly.
He muttered the errand on which he'd come,
Then only chuckled and bit his thumb,
  And simpered, simpered shyly.

"No," said the maiden, "go your way,
You dare but think what a man would say,
  Yet dare come a-suing!
I've time to lose and power to choose;
'Tis not so much the gallant who woos
  As the gallant's way of wooing!"

A third rode up at a startling pace—
A suitor poor, with a homely face—
  No doubts appeared to bind him.
He kissed her lips and he pressed her waist,
And off he rode with the maiden, placed
  On a pillion safe behind him.
And she heard the suitor bold confide
This golden hint to the priest who tied
  The knot there's no undoing:
"With pretty young maidens who can choose,
'Tis not so much the gallant who woos
  As the gallant's way of wooing!"

HONGREE AND MAHRY

A RICHARDSONIAN MELODRAMA

The sun was setting in its wonted west,
When Hongree, Sub-Lieutenant of Chassoores,
Met Mahry Daubigny, the Village Rose,
Under the Wizard's Oak—old trysting-place
Of those who loved in rosy Aquitaine.

They thought themselves unwatched, but they were not,
For Hongree, Sub-Lieutenant of Chassoores,
Found in Lieutenant-Colonel Jooles Dubosc
A rival, envious and unscrupulous,
Who thought it not foul scorn to dog his steps,
And listen, unperceived, to all that passed
Between the simple little Village Rose
And Hongree, Sub-Lieutenant of Chassoores.

A clumsy barrack-bully was Dubosc,
Quite unfamiliar with the well-bred tact
That actuates a proper gentleman
In dealing with a girl of humble rank.

You'll understand his coarseness when I say
He would have married MAHRY DAUBIGNY,
And dragged the unsophisticated girl
Into the whirl of fashionable life,
For which her singularly rustic ways,
Her breeding (moral, but extremely rude),
Her language (chaste, but ungrammatical),
Would absolutely have unfitted her.
No such intention lurked within the breast
Of HONGREE, Sub-Lieutenant of Chassoores!

Contemporary with the incident
Related in our opening paragraph,
Was that sad war 'twixt Gallia and ourselves
That followed on the treaty signed at Troyes;
And so LIEUTENANT-COLONEL JOOLES DUBOSC
(Brave soldier, he, with all his faults of style)
And HONGREE, Sub-Lieutenant of Chassoores,
Were sent by CHARLES of France against the lines
Of our Sixth HENRY (Fourteen twenty-nine),
To drive his legions out of Aquitaine.

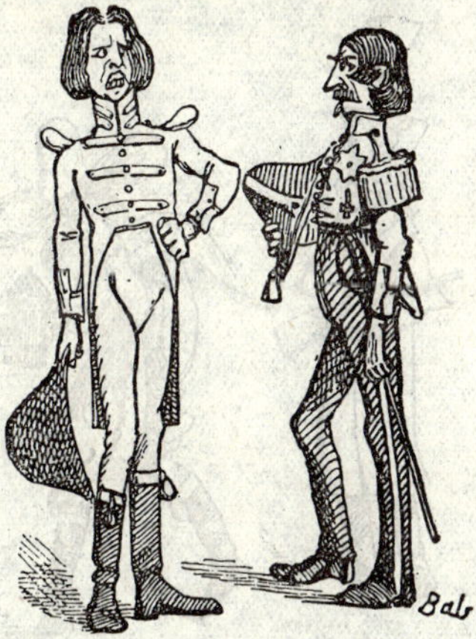

When Hongree, Sub-Lieutenant of Chassoores,
Returned (suspecting nothing) to his camp,
After his meeting with the Village Rose,
He found inside his barrack letter-box
A note from the commanding-officer,
Requiring his attendance at headquarters.

He went, and found Lieutenant-Colonel Jooles.
"Young Hongree, Sub-Lieutenant of Chassoores,
This night we shall attack the English camp:
Be the 'forlorn hope' yours—you'll lead it, sir.
And lead it too with credit, I've no doubt"
(These last words with a cruelly obvious sneer).
"As every soul must certainly be killed
(For you are twenty 'gainst two thousand men),
It is not likely that you will return;
But what of that? you'll have the benefit
Of knowing that you die a soldier's death."

Obedience was young Hongree's strongest point,
But he imagined that he only owed
Allegiance to his Mahry and his King.
"If Mahry bade me lead these fated men,

I'd lead them—but I do not think she would.
If CHARLES, my King, said, 'Go, my son, and die,'
I'd go, of course—my duty would be clear.
But MAHRY is in bed asleep (I hope),
And CHARLES, my King, a hundred leagues from this.
As for LIEUTENANT-COLONEL JOOLES DUBOSC,
How know I that our monarch would approve
The order he has given me to-night?
My King I've sworn in all things to obey—
I'll only take my orders from my King!"
Thus HONGREE, Sub-Lieutenant of Chassoores
Interpreted the terms of his commission.

And HONGREE, who was wise as he was good,
Disguised himself that night in ample cloak,
Round flapping hat, and visor mask of black,
And made, unnoticed, for the English camp.
He passed the unsuspecting sentinels
(Who little thought a man in this disguise
Could be a proper object of suspicion),
And ere the curfew-bell had boomed "lights out,"
He found in audience Bedford's haughty Duke.

"Your Grace," he said, "start not—be not alarmed,
Although a Frenchman stands before your eyes.
I'm Hongree, Sub-Lieutenant of Chassoores.
My colonel will attack your camp to-night,
And orders me to lead the hope forlorn.
Now I am sure our excellent King Charles
Would not approve of this; but he's away
A hundred leagues, and rather more than that.
So, utterly devoted to my King,
Blinded by my attachment to the throne,
And having but its interest at heart,
I feel it is my duty to disclose
All schemes that emanate from Colonel Jooles,
If I believe that they are not the kind
Of schemes that our good monarch could approve."
"But how," said Bedford's Duke, "do you propose
That we should overthrow your colonel's scheme?"
And Hongree, Sub-Lieutenant of Chassoores,
Replied at once with never-failing tact:
"Oh, sir, I know this cursed country well.
Entrust yourself and all your host to me;
I'll lead you safely by a secret path
Into the heart of Colonel Jooles' array,
And you can then attack them unprepared,
And slay my fellow-countrymen unarmed."

The thing was done. The DUKE OF BEDFORD gave
The order, and two thousand fighting-men
Crept silently into the Gallic camp,
And killed the Frenchmen as they lay asleep;
And Bedford's haughty Duke slew COLONEL JOOLES,
And married MAHRY, pride of Aquitaine,
To HONGREE, Sub-Lieutenant of Chassoores.

THE REVEREND MICAH SOWLS

The REVEREND MICAH SOWLS,
He shouts and yells and howls,
He screams, he mouths, he bumps,
He foams, he rants, he thumps.

His armour he has buckled on, to wage
The regulation war against the Stage;
And warns his congregation all to shun
"The Presence-Chamber of the Evil One."

The subject's sad enough
To make him rant and puff,
And fortunately, too,
His Bishop's in a pew.

So Reverend Micah claps on extra steam,
His eyes are flashing with superior gleam,
He is as energetic as can be,
For there are fatter livings in that see.

The Bishop, when it's o'er,
Goes through the vestry door,
Where Micah, very red,
Is mopping of his head.

"Pardon, my Lord, your Sowls' excessive zeal,
It is a theme on which I strongly feel."
(The sermon somebody had sent him down
From London, at a charge of half-a-crown.)

The Bishop bowed his head,
And, acquiescing, said,
"I've heard your well-meant rage
Against the Modern Stage.

"A modern Theatre, as I heard you say,
Sows seeds of evil broadcast—well it may;
But let me ask you, my respected son,
Pray, have you ever ventured into one?"

"My Lord," said MICAH, "no!
I never, never go!
What! Go and see a play?
My goodness gracious, nay!"

The worthy Bishop said, "My friend, no doubt
The Stage may be the place you make it out;
But if, my REVEREND SOWLS, you never go,
I don't quite understand how you're to know."

"Well, really," MICAH said,
"I've often heard and read,
But never go—do you?"
The Bishop said, "I do."

"That proves me wrong," said MICAH, in a trice:
"I thought it all frivolity and vice."
The Bishop handed him a printed card;
"Go to a theatre where they play our Bard."

The Bishop took his leave,
Rejoicing in his sleeve.
The next ensuing day
SOWLS went and heard a play.

He saw a dreary person on the stage,
Who mouthed and mugged in simulated rage,
Who growled and spluttered in a mode absurd,
And spoke an English SOWLS had never heard.

For "gaunt" was spoken "garnt,"
And "haunt" transformed to "harnt,"
And "wrath" pronounced as "rath,"
And "death" was changed to "dath."

For hours and hours that dismal actor walked,
And talked, and talked, and talked, and talked,
Till lethargy upon the parson crept,
And sleepy MICAH SOWLS serenely slept.

He slept away until
The farce that closed the bill
Had warned him not to stay,
And then he went away.

"I thought *my* gait ridiculous," said he—
"*My* elocution faulty as could be;
I thought *I* mumbled on a matchless plan—
I had not seen our great Tragedian!

"Forgive me, if you can,
O great Tragedian!
I own it with a sigh—
You're drearier than I!"

THE FORCE OF ARGUMENT

LORD B. was a nobleman bold
Who came of illustrious stocks,
He was thirty or forty years old,
And several feet in his socks.

To Turniptopville-by-the-Sea
This elegant nobleman went,
For that was a borough that he
Was anxious to rep-per-re-sent.

At local assemblies he danced
Until he felt thoroughly ill;
He waltzed, and he galloped, and lanced,
And threaded the mazy quadrille.

The maidens of Turniptopville
Were simple—ingenuous—pure—
And they all worked away with a will
The nobleman's heart to secure.

Two maidens all others beyond
  Endeavoured his cares to dispel—
The one was the lively Ann Pond,
  The other sad Mary Morell.

Ann Pond had determined to try
  And carry the Earl with a rush;
Her principal feature was eye,
  Her greatest accomplishment—gush.

And Mary chose this for her play:
  Whenever he looked in her eye
She'd blush and turn quickly away,
  And flitter, and flutter, and sigh.

It was noticed he constantly sighed
  As she worked out the scheme she had planned,
A fact he endeavoured to hide
  With his aristocratical hand.

Old POND was a farmer, they say,
And so was old TOMMY MORELL.
In a humble and pottering way
They were doing exceedingly well.

They both of them carried by vote
The Earl was a dangerous man;
So nervously clearing his throat,
One morning old TOMMY began:

"My darter's no pratty young doll—
I'm a plain-spoken Zommerzet man—
Now what do 'ee mean by my POLL,
And what do 'ee mean by his ANN?"

Said B., "I will give you my bond,
I mean them uncommonly well,
Believe me, my excellent POND,
And credit me, worthy MORELL.

"It's quite indisputable, for
I'll prove it with singular ease,—
You shall have it in 'Barbara' or
'Celarent'—whichever you please.

"You see, when an anchorite bows
To the yoke of intentional sin,
If the state of the country allows,
Homogeny always steps in—

"It's a highly æsthetical bond,
As any mere ploughboy can tell——"
"Of course," replied puzzled old POND,
"I see," said old TOMMY MORELL.

"Very good, then," continued the lord;
"When it's fooled to the top of its bent,
With a sweep of a Damocles sword
The web of intention is rent.

"That's patent to all of us here,
As any mere schoolboy can tell."
POND answered, "Of course it's quite clear";
And so did that humbug MORELL.

"It's tone's esoteric in force—
I trust that I make myself clear?"
MORELL only answered, "Of course,"
While POND slowly muttered, "Hear, hear."

"Volition—celestial prize,
Pellucid as porphyry cell—
Is based on a principle wise."
"Quite so," exclaimed POND and MORELL.

"From what I have said you will see
That I couldn't wed either—in fine,
By Nature's unchanging decree
Your daughters could never be *mine*.

"Go home to your pigs and your ricks,
My hands of the matter I've rinsed."
So they take up their hats and their sticks,
And *exeunt ambo*, convinced.

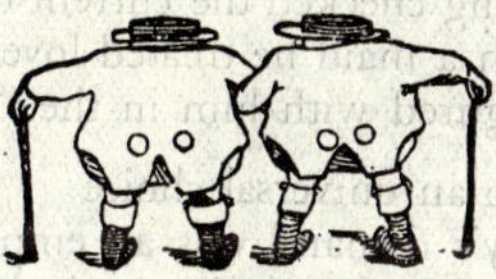

THE PHANTOM CURATE

A FABLE

A bishop once—I will not name his see—
Annoyed his clergy in the mode conventional;
From pulpit shackles never set them free,
And found a sin where sin was unintentional.
All pleasures ended in abuse auricular—
That Bishop was so terribly particular.

Though, on the whole, a wise and upright man,
He sought to make of human pleasures clearances,
And form his priests on that much-lauded plan
Which pays undue attention to appearances.

He couldn't do good deeds without a psalm in 'em,
Although, in truth, he bore away the palm in 'em.

Enraged to find a deacon at a dance,
Or catch a curate at some mild frivolity,
He sought by open censure to enhance
Their dread of joining harmless social jollity;
Yet he enjoyed (a fact of notoriety)
The ordinary pleasures of society.

One evening, sitting at a pantomime
(Forbidden treat to those who stood in fear of him),
Roaring at jokes *sans* metre, sense, or rhyme,
He turned, and saw immediately in rear of him—
His peace of mind upsetting, and annoying it—
A curate, also heartily enjoying it.

Again, 'twas Christmas Eve, and to enhance
His children's pleasure in their harmless rollicking,
He, like a good old fellow, stood to dance;
When something checked the current of his frolicking:
That curate, with a maid he treated loverly,
Stood up and figured with him in the "Coverley"!

Once, yielding to an universal choice
(The company's demand was an emphatic one,
For the old Bishop had a glorious voice),
In a quartet he joined—an operatic one—
Harmless enough, though ne'er a word of grace in it;
When, lo! that curate came and took the bass in it!

One day, when passing through a quiet street,
He stopped awhile and joined a Punch's gathering,
And chuckled more than solemn folk think meet
To see that gentleman his Judy lathering;
And heard, as Punch was being treated penally,
That phantom curate laughing all hyænally!

Now at a picnic, 'mid fair golden curls,
Bright eyes, straw hats, *bottines* that fit amazingly,
A croquêt-bout is planned by all the girls,
And he, consenting, speaks of croquêt praisingly;
But suddenly declines to play at all in it—
The curate fiend has come to take a ball in it!

Next, when at quiet seaside village, freed
  From cares episcopal and ties monarchical,
He grows his beard, and smokes his fragrant weed,
  In manner anything but hierarchical—
He sees—and fixes an unearthly stare on it—
That curate's face, with half a yard of hair on it!

At length he gave a charge, and spake this word:
  "Vicars, your curates to enjoyment urge ye may
To check their harmless pleasuring's absurd;
  What laymen do without reproach, my clergy may."
He spake, and lo! at this concluding word of him,
The curate vanished—no one since has heard of him.

THE SENSATION CAPTAIN

No nobler captain ever trod
Than CAPTAIN PARKLEBURY TODD,
  So good—so wise—so brave, he!

But still, as all his friends would own,
He had one folly—one alone—
This Captain in the Navy.

I do not think I ever knew
A man so wholly given to
Creating a sensation;
Or p'raps I should in justice say—
To what in an Adelphi play
Is known as "situation."

He passed his time designing traps
To flurry unsuspicious chaps—
The taste was his innately;
He couldn't walk into a room
Without ejaculating "Boom!"
Which startled ladies greatly.

He'd wear a mask and muffling cloak,
Not, you will understand, in joke,
As some assume disguises;
He did it, actuated by
A simple love of mystery
And fondness for surprises.

I need not say he loved a maid—
His eloquence threw into shade
All others who adored her.
The maid, though pleased at first, I know,
Found, after several years or so,
Her startling lover bored her.

So, when his orders came to sail,
She did not faint or scream or wail,
Or with her tears anoint him:
She shook his hand, and said "Good-bye,"
With laughter dancing in her eye—
Which seemed to disappoint him.

But ere he went aboard his boat,
He placed around her little throat
A ribbon, blue and yellow,
On which he hung a double tooth—
A simple token this, in sooth—
'Twas all he had, poor fellow!

"I often wonder," he would say,
When very, very far away,
"If ANGELINA wears it?
A plan has entered in my head:
I will pretend that I am dead,
And see how ANGY bears it."

The news he made a messmate tell.
His ANGELINA bore it well,
No sign gave she of crazing;
But, steady as the Inchcape Rock,
His ANGELINA stood the shock
With fortitude amazing.

She said, "Some one I must elect
Poor ANGELINA to protect
From all who wish to harm her.
Since worthy CAPTAIN TODD is dead
I rather feel inclined to wed
A comfortable farmer."

A comfortable farmer came
(BASSANIO TYLER was his name),
Who had no end of treasure.

He said, "My noble gal, be mine!"
The noble gal did not decline,
But simply said, "With pleasure."

When this was told to CAPTAIN TODD,
At first he thought it rather odd,
And felt some perturbation;
But very long he did not grieve,
He thought he could a way perceive
To *such* a situation!

"I'll not reveal myself," said he,
"Till they are both in the Eccle-
siastical arena;
Then suddenly I will appear,
And paralysing them with fear,
Demand my ANGELINA!"

At length arrived the wedding day;
Accoutred in the usual way
Appeared the bridal body;

The worthy clergyman began,
When in the gallant Captain ran
  And cried, "Behold your Toddy!"

The bridegroom, p'raps, was terrified,
And also possibly the bride—
  The bridesmaids *were* affrighted;
But Angelina, noble soul,
Contrived her feelings to control,
  And really seemed delighted.

"My bride!" said gallant Captain Todd,
"She's mine, uninteresting clod!
  My own, my darling charmer!"
"Oh dear," said she, "you're just too late—
I'm married to, I beg to state,
  This comfortable farmer!"

"Indeed," the farmer said, "she's mine:
You've been and cut it far too fine!"
  "I see," said Todd, "I'm beaten."
And so he went to sea once more,
"Sensation" he for aye forswore,
And married on her native shore
A lady whom he'd met before—
  A lovely Otaheitan.

TEMPORA MUTANTUR

Letters, letters, letters, letters!
  Some that please and some that bore,
Some that threaten prison fetters
(Metaphorically, fetters
Such as bind insolvent debtors)—
  Invitations by the score.

One from Cogson, Wiles, and Railer,
  My attorneys, off the Strand;
One from Copperblock, my tailor—
My unreasonable tailor—
  One in Flagg's disgusting hand.

One from Ephraim and Moses,
  Wanting coin without a doubt,
I should like to pull their noses—
Their uncompromising noses;
One from Alice with the roses—
  Ah, I know what that's about!

Time was when I waited, waited
  For the missives that she wrote,
Humble postmen execrated—
Loudly, deeply execrated—
When I heard I wasn't fated
  To be gladdened with a note!

Time was when I'd not have bartered
  Of her little pen a dip
For a peerage duly gartered—
For a peerage starred and gartered—
With a palace-office chartered,
  Or a Secretaryship.

But the time for that is over,
  And I wish we'd never met.
I'm afraid I've proved a rover—
I'm afraid a heartless rover—
Quarters in a place like Dover
  Tend to make a man forget.

Bills for carriages and horses,
  Bills for wine and light cigar,
Matters that concern the Forces—
News that may affect the Forces—
News affecting my resources,
  Much more interesting are!

And the tiny little paper
  With the words that seem to run
From her little fingers taper
(They are very small and taper),
By the tailor and the draper
  Are in interest outdone.

And unopened it's remaining!
  I can read her gentle hope—
Her entreaties, uncomplaining
(She was always uncomplaining),
Her devotion never waning—
  Through the little envelope!

AT A PANTOMIME

BY A BILIOUS ONE

An actor sits in doubtful gloom,
  His stock-in-trade unfurled,
In a damp funereal dressing-room
  In the Theatre Royal, World.

He comes to town at Christmas-time
  And braves its icy breath,
To play in that favourite pantomime:
  Harlequin Life and Death.

A hoary flowing wig his weird,
  Unearthly cranium caps;
He hangs a long benevolent beard
  On a pair of empty chaps.

To smooth his ghastly features down
  The actor's art he cribs;

A long and a flowing padded gown
  Bedecks his rattling ribs.

He cries, "Go on—begin, begin!
  Turn on the light of lime;
I'm dressed for jolly Old Christmas in
  A favourite pantomime!"

The curtain's up—the stage all black—
  Time and the Year nigh sped—
(Time as an advertising quack)
  The Old Year nearly dead.

The wand of Time is waved, and lo!
  Revealed Old Christmas stands,
And little children chuckle and crow,
  And laugh and clap their hands.

The cruel old scoundrel brightens up
  At the death of the Olden Year,
And he waves a gorgeous golden cup,
  And bids the world good cheer.

The little ones hail the festive King—
  No thought can make them sad;
Their laughter comes with a sounding ring,
  They clap and crow like mad!

They only see in the humbug old
  A holiday every year,
And handsome gifts, and joys untold,
  And unaccustomed cheer.

The old ones, palsied, blear, and hoar,
  Their breasts in anguish beat—
They've seen him seventy times before,
  How well they know the cheat!

They've seen that ghastly pantomime,
  They've felt its blighting breath,
They know that rollicking Christmas-time
  Meant cold and want and death—

Starvation—Poor Law Union fare,
  And deadly cramps and chills,
And illness—illness everywhere—
  And crime, and Christmas bills.

They know Old Christmas well, I ween,
  Those men of ripened age;

They've often, often, often seen
  That actor off the stage.

They see in his gay rotundity
  A clumsy stuffed-out dress;
They see in the cup he waves on high
  A tinselled emptiness.

Those aged men so lean and wan,
  They've seen it all before;
They know they'll see the charlatan
  But twice or three times more.

And so they bear with dance and song,
  And crimson foil and green;
They wearily sit, and grimly long
  For the Transformation Scene.

THE STORY OF PRINCE AGIB

Strike the concertina's melancholy string!
Blow the spirit-stirring harp like anything!
    Let the piano's martial blast
    Rouse the echoes of the past,
For of Agib, Prince of Tartary, I sing!

Of Agib, who, amid Tartaric scenes,
Wrote a lot of ballet-music in his teens:
    His gentle spirit rolls
    In the melody of souls—
Which is pretty, but I don't know what it means.

Of Agib, who could readily, at sight,
Strum a march upon the loud Theodolite.
He would diligently play
On the Zoetrope all day,
And blow the gay Pantechnicon all night.

One winter—I am shaky in my dates—
Came two starving Tartar minstrels to his gates;
Oh, Allah be obeyed,
How infernally they played!
I remember that they called themselves the "Oüaits."

Oh! that day of sorrow, misery, and rage,
I shall carry to the Catacombs of Age,
Photographically lined
On the tablet of my mind,
When a yesterday has faded from its page!

Alas! Prince Agib went and asked them in;
Gave them beer, and eggs, and sweets, and scent, and tin;
And when (as snobs would say)
They had "put it all away,"
He requested them to tune up and begin.

Though its icy horror chill you to the core,
I will tell you what I never told before—
The consequences true
Of that awful interview,
For I listened at the keyhole in the door!

They played him a sonata—let me see!
"Medulla oblongata"—key of G.
Then they began to sing
That extremely lovely thing,
"Scherzando! ma non troppo, ppp."

He gave them money, more than they could count,
Scent from a most ingenious little fount,
More beer in little kegs,
Many dozen hard-boiled eggs,
And goodies to a fabulous amount.

Now follows the dim horror of my tale,
And I feel I'm growing gradually pale;
For even at this day,
Though its sting has passed away,
When I venture to remember it, I quail!

The elder of the brothers gave a squeal,
All-overish it made me for to feel.
"O Prince," he says, says he,
"If a Prince indeed you be,
I've a mystery I'm going to reveal!

"Oh, listen, if you'd shun a horrid death,
To what the gent who's speaking to you saith:

No 'Oüaits' in truth are we,
As you fancy that we be,
For (ter-remble!) I am Aleck—this is Beth!"

Said Agib, "Oh! accursed of your kind,
I have heard that ye are men of evil mind!"
Beth gave a dreadful shriek—
But before he'd time to speak
I was mercilessly collared from behind.

In number ten or twelve, or even more,
They fastened me, full length, upon the floor.
On my face extended flat,
I was walloped with a cat,
For listening at the keyhole of a door.

Oh! the horror of that agonising thrill!
(I can feel the place in frosty weather still.)
For a week from ten to four
I was fastened to the floor,
While a mercenary wopped me with a will!

They branded me and broke me on a wheel,
And they left me in an hospital to heal;
And, upon my solemn word,
I have never, never heard
What those Tartars had determined to reveal.

But that day of sorrow, misery, and rage,
I shall carry to the Catacombs of Age,
Photographically lined
On the tablet of my mind,
When a yesterday has faded from its page!

JOE GOLIGHTLY

OR, THE FIRST LORD'S DAUGHTER

A tar, but poorly prized,
Long, shambling, and unsightly,
Thrashed, bullied, and despised,
Was wretched Joe Golightly.

He bore a workhouse brand;
No Pa or Ma had claimed him,
The Beadle found him, and
The Board of Guardians named him.

P'r'aps some Princess's son—
A beggar p'r'aps his mother.
He rather thought the one,
I rather think the other.

He liked his ship at sea,
He loved the salt sea-water,
He worshipped junk, and he
Adored the First Lord's daughter.

The First Lord's daughter, proud,
Snubbed Earls and Viscounts nightly;
She sneered at Barts. aloud,
And spurned poor JOE GOLIGHTLY.

Whene'er he sailed afar
Upon a Channel cruise, he
Unpacked his light guitar
And sang this ballad (Boosey):

Ballad

The moon is on the sea,
Willow!
The wind blows towards the lee,
Willow!
But though I sigh and sob and cry,
No Lady Jane for me,
Willow!

She says, " 'Twere folly quite,
Willow!
For me to wed a wight,
Willow!
Whose lot is cast before the mast";
And possibly she's right,
Willow!

His skipper (Captain Joyce),
He gave him many a rating,
And almost lost his voice
From thus expostulating:

"Lay aft, you lubber, do!
What's come to that young man, Joe?
Belay!—'vast heaving! you!
Do kindly stop that banjo!

"I wish, I do—O lor'!—
You'd shipped aboard a trader:
Are you a sailor or
A negro serenader?"

But still the stricken lad
Aloft or on his pillow,
Howled forth in accents sad
His aggravating "Willow!"

Stern love of duty had
Been Joyce's chiefest beauty;
Says he, "I love that lad,
But duty, damme! duty!

"Twelve months' black-hole, I say,
  Where daylight never flashes;
And always twice a day
  A good six dozen lashes!"

But JOSEPH had a mate,
  A sailor stout and lusty,
A man of low estate,
  But singularly trusty.

Says he, "Cheer hup, young JOE!
  I'll tell you what I'm arter—
To that Fust Lord I'll go
  And ax him for his darter.

"To that Fust Lord I'll go
  And say you love her dearly."
And JOE said (weeping low),
  "I wish you would, sincerely!"

That sailor to that Lord
  Went, soon as he had landed,
And of his own accord
  An interview demanded.

Says he, with seaman's roll,
"My Captain (wot's a Tartar)
Guv Joe twelve months' black-hole,
For lovering your darter.

"He loves Miss Lady Jane
(I own she is his betters),
But if you'll jine them twain,
They'll free him from his fetters.

"And if so be as how
You'll let her come aboard ship,
I'll take her with me now."
"Get out!" remarked his Lordship.

That honest tar repaired
To Joe upon the billow,
And told him how he'd fared.
Joe only whispered, "Willow!"

And for that dreadful crime
(Young sailors, learn to shun it)
He's working out his time;
In six months he'll have done it.

TO THE TERRESTRIAL GLOBE

BY A MISERABLE WRETCH

Roll on, thou ball, roll on!
Through pathless realms of Space
Roll on!
What though I'm in a sorry case?
What though I cannot meet my bills?
What though I suffer toothache's ills?
What though I swallow countless pills?
Never *you* mind!
Roll on!

Roll on, thou ball, roll on!
Through seas of inky air
Roll on!

It's true I have no shirts to wear;
It's true my butcher's bill is due;
It's true my prospects all look blue—
But don't let that unsettle you:
Never *you* mind!
Roll on!

[*It rolls on.*

ETIQUETTE [1]

The *Ballyshannon* foundered off the coast of Cariboo,
And down in fathoms many went the captain and the crew;
Down went the owners—greedy men whom hope of gain allured:
Oh, dry the starting tear, for they were heavily insured.

Besides the captain and the mate, the owners and the crew,
The passengers were also drowned excepting only two:
Young Peter Gray, who tasted teas for Baker, Croop, and Co.,
And Somers, who from Eastern shores imported indigo.

These passengers, by reason of their clinging to a mast,
Upon a desert island were eventually cast,
They hunted for their meals, as Alexander Selkirk used,
But they couldn't chat together—they had not been introduced.

For Peter Gray, and Somers too, though certainly in trade,
Were properly particular about the friends they made;
And somehow thus they settled it without a word of mouth—
That Gray should take the northern half, while Somers took the south.

On Peter's portion oysters grew—a delicacy rare,
But oysters were a delicacy Peter couldn't bear.

[1] Reprinted from the *Graphic*, by permission of the proprietors.

On Somers' side was turtle, on the shingle lying thick,
Which Somers couldn't eat, because it always made him sick.

Gray gnashed his teeth with envy as he saw a mighty store
Of turtle unmolested on his fellow-creature's shore:
The oysters at his feet aside impatiently he shoved,
For turtle and his mother were the only things he loved.

And Somers sighed in sorrow as he settled in the south,
For the thought of Peter's oysters brought the water to his mouth.
He longed to lay him down upon the shelly bed, and stuff:
He had often eaten oysters, but had never had enough.

How they wished an introduction to each other they had had
When on board the *Ballyshannon!* And it drove them nearly mad
To think how very friendly with each other they might get,
If it wasn't for the arbitrary rule of etiquette!

One day, when out a-hunting for the *mus ridiculus,*
Gray overheard his fellow-man soliloquising thus:
"I wonder how the playmates of my youth are getting on,
M'Connell, S. B. Walters, Paddy Byles, and Robinson?"

These simple words made Peter as delighted as could be,
Old chummies at the Charterhouse were Robinson and he!

He walked straight up to SOMERS, then he turned extremely red,
Hesitated, hummed and hawed a bit, then cleared his throat, and said:

"I beg your pardon—pray forgive me if I seem too bold,
But you have breathed a name I knew familiarly of old.
You spoke aloud of ROBINSON—I happened to be by—
You know him?" "Yes, extremely well." "Allow me—so do I!"

It was enough: they felt they could more sociably get on,
For (ah, the magic of the fact!) they each knew ROBINSON!
And MR. SOMERS' turtle was at PETER's service quite,
And MR. SOMERS punished PETER's oyster-beds all night.

They soon became like brothers from community of wrongs:
They wrote each other little odes and sang each other songs;
They told each other anecdotes disparaging their wives;
On several occasions, too, they saved each other's lives.

They felt quite melancholy when they parted for the night,
And got up in the morning soon as ever it was light;
Each other's pleasant company they reckoned so upon,
And all because it happened that they both knew ROBINSON!

They lived for many years on that inhospitable shore,
And day by day they learned to love each other more and more.
At last, to their astonishment, on getting up one day,
They saw a vessel anchored in the offing of the bay!

To PETER an idea occurred. "Suppose we cross the main?
So good an opportunity may not occur again."
And SOMERS thought a minute, then ejaculated, "Done!
I wonder how my business in the City's getting on?"

"But stay," said MR. PETER: "when in England, as you know,
I earned a living tasting teas for BAKER, CROOP, AND CO.,

I may be superseded—my employers think me dead!"
"Then come with me," said SOMERS, "and taste indigo instead."

But all their plans were scattered in a moment when they found
The vessel was a convict ship from Portland, outward bound!
When a boat came off to fetch them, though they felt it very kind,
To go on board they firmly but respectfully declined.

As both the happy settlers roared with laughter at the joke,
They recognised an unattractive fellow pulling stroke:
'Twas ROBINSON—a convict, in an unbecoming frock!
Condemned to seven years for misappropriating stock!!!

They laughed no more, for SOMERS thought he had been rather rash
In knowing one whose friend had misappropriated cash;
And PETER thought a foolish tack he must have gone upon
In making the acquaintance of a friend of ROBINSON.

At first they didn't quarrel very openly, I've heard;
They nodded when they met, and now and then exchanged a word:
The word grew rare, and rarer still the nodding of the head,
And when they meet each other now, they cut each other dead.

To allocate the island they agreed by word of mouth,
And PETER takes the north again, and SOMERS takes the south;
And PETER has the oysters, which he loathes with horror grim,
And SOMERS has the turtle—turtle disagrees with him.

BEN ALLAH ACHMET;

OR, THE FATAL TUM

I once did know a Turkish man
 Whom I upon a two-pair-back met,
His name it was EFFENDI KHAN
 BACKSHEESH PASHA BEN ALLAH ACHMET.

A DOCTOR BROWN I also knew—
 I've often eaten of his bounty;
The Turk and he they lived at Hooe,
 In Sussex, that delightful county!

I knew a nice young lady there,
 Her name was EMILY MACPHERSON,
And though she wore another's hair,
 She was an interesting person.

The Turk adored the maid of Hooe
(Although his harem would have shocked her).
But BROWN adored that maiden too:
He was a most seductive doctor.

They'd follow her where'er she'd go—
A course of action most improper;
She neither knew by sight, and so
For neither of them cared a copper.

BROWN did not know that Turkish male,
He might have been his sainted mother:
The people in this simple tale
Are total strangers to each other.

One day that Turk he sickened sore,
And suffered agonies oppressive;
He threw himself upon the floor
And rolled about in pain excessive.

It made him moan, it made him groan,
And almost wore him to a mummy.
Why should I hesitate to own
That pain was in his little tummy?

At length a doctor came, and rung
(As ALLAH ACHMET had desired),
Who felt his pulse, looked up his tongue,
And hemmed and hawed, and then inquired:

"Where is the pain that long has preyed
Upon you in so sad a way, sir?"
The Turk he giggled, blushed, and said:
"I don't exactly like to say, sir."

"Come, nonsense!" said good DOCTOR BROWN.
"So this is Turkish coyness, is it?
You must contrive to fight it down—
Come, come, sir, please to be explicit."

The Turk he shyly bit his thumb,
And coyly blushed like one half-witted,
"The pain is in my little tum,"
He, whispering, at length admitted.

"Then take you this, and take you that—
Your blood flows sluggish in its channel—
You must get rid of all this fat,
And wear my medicated flannel.

"You'll send for me when you're in need—
My name is BROWN—your life I've saved it."
"My rival!" shrieked the invalid,
And drew a mighty sword and waved it:

"This to thy weazand, Christian pest!"
Aloud the Turk in frenzy yelled it,
And drove right through the doctor's chest
The sabre and the hand that held it.

The blow was a decisive one,
And DOCTOR BROWN grew deadly pasty,
"Now see the mischief that you've done—
You Turks are so extremely hasty.

"There are two DOCTOR BROWNS in Hooe—
He's short and stout, *I'm* tall and wizen;
You've been and run the wrong one through,
That's how the error has arisen."

The accident was thus explained,
  Apologies were only heard now:
"At my mistake I'm really pained—
  I am, indeed—upon my word now.

"With me, sir, you shall be interred,
  A mausoleum grand awaits me."
"Oh, pray don't say another word,
  I'm sure that more than compensates me.

"But p'r'aps, kind Turk, you're full inside?"
  "There's room," said he, "for any number."
And so they laid them down and died.
  In proud Stamboul they sleep their slumber.

THE LOST BAB BALLADS

THE "LOST BABS"

The following *Bab Ballads* were printed in *Fun,* but were not included in any of the collections made by Gilbert.

PRINCE IL BALEINE

When autumn boat and train
  Bore London folk to pleasure,
The good Prince Il Baleine
He sought, across the main,
  Amusement for his leisure.

A dusty time, and long,
  He'd had at balls and races,
At crowded levee throng,
At play and concert song,
  And various other places.

But, ah! the British Snob
  Besieged that Prince, in plenty:

The Snob adores a Nob,
And follows him, to rob
His *dolce far niente*!

And finding that the Prince
Much eagerness to know them
Did not at once evince,
They did not matters mince,
But begged himself he'd show them.

"Our wishes do not baulk,
Throw off this English shyness—
And show us how you walk,
And let us hear you talk—
Now do, your Royal Highness!

"You're too reserved by half:
Begin perambulating;
We've paid to see you laugh—
We've paid to hear you chaff
Four gentlemen in waiting.

"Come sit and eat an ice,
Or drain a bumping measure;
We've practised much device,
And paid a heavy price,
To see you take your leisure."

(It grieved that Prince Baleine—
Most sensitive of fishes—
It always gives him pain
When people can't obtain
The fullness of their wishes.

But doctors grave had said,
"Hang up your stick and beaver;
You *must* have rest and shade,
Or you will soon be laid
Upon your back with fever.")

No morning when he woke
But British Snobs addressed him;
His peace of mind they broke,
So up he rose, and spoke
These words to those who pressed him:

"Oh, over-loyal throng,
  Be guided, pray, by reason:
You may encore a song
(Though that, I think, is wrong),
  But not a London Season!

"I'm told to lie me down
  And rest me at my leisure;
But here's my valet, Brown,
He's not much worked in town,
  He'll take my place with pleasure!

"I am his special care;
  He brushes, combs, and laves me,
He parts my chestnut hair—
He folds the coats I wear—
  And strops the blade that shaves me.

"He knows my little ways
  And, though it's not expected
He'll match my Royal blaze,
Yet, basking in my rays,
  He'll shine with light reflected."

"Oh, my!" the people cried,
  "To Mister Brown I'll bow me!
Oh, ain't he dignified,
Yet not a spark of pride!
  Oh, Mister Brown, allow me!

"And so you wash the Prince,
And pack his clothes for starting,
You scent with jasmine leaf
His pocket-handkerchief,
And regulate his parting!

"And that, I understand,
Is your department, is it?
And this then is the hand
That combs at his command?
Oh, please, do let me kiss it!

"Is this (oh, treat of treats!)
The bedroom that you sleep in?
When cloyed with Royal sweets,
And these the very sheets
Which every night you creep in?

"And in this bath you tub,
Ere out of doors you sally?
And do these flesh-gloves scrub—
These dainty towels rub—
The Prince's happy *valet*?"

The Snobs with joy insane,
Kotoo'd to Brown, unseemly:
And Brown does not complain,
While good Prince Il Baleine
Enjoys his rest extremely.

FANNY AND JENNY

Fanny and Jenny in Paris did dwell,
Miss Jane was a dowdy, Miss Fanny a swell—
Each went for to dine at a quarter to four—
At her own little favourite Restaura*tore*—
Fanny of Bertram and Roberts was fond,
While Jenny she worshipped her Spiers and Pond.

Fanny was pretty and piquante and pert,
Her manners were shortish and so was her skirt,
While Jenny the elder would make a man wince,
In a dress of the mode of a century since.
Bertram and Roberts's Fanny was blonde,
And dark was the Jenny of Spiers and Pond.

Jane lived in a modest and lady-like way:
To Spiers and Pond she went every day,
She'd order up beef and potatoes as well,
And cut off the joint until senseless she fell:
(She fed herself daily all reason beyond
To gaze all the longer at Spiers and Pond.)

But Fanny, that frolicsome, frivolous maid
(Whose tastes were more airy than Jenny's the staid),
To Bertram and Roberts would hie her away,
And swallow plum-pudding the rest of the day.
The best of her dresses Miss Fanny she donned
(As Jenny did also for Spiers and Pond).

The Restaurateurs didn't seem for to care
For Jenny's soft ogle or Fanny's fond stare.
Said Jenny, "Don't let us be taken aback,
We're probably on an erroneous tack,
And Bertram and Roberts of *me* may be fond,
While *you* are beloved by Spiers and Pond!"

"Oh, Bertram and R., are you dying for me,
Or am I the chosen of Spiers and P.?
Oh, which is the angel and fostering star
Of Spiers and P., or of Bertram and R.?
Which firm have I collared in Venus's bond?
Say, Bertram and Roberts—speak, Spiers and Pond!

"Perhaps if you cannot completely agree
Which of you shall have Fanny and which shall have me,
And you wish for to go for to do what is right,
You will go to the Bois de Boulogne for to fight—
It's the mode that is popular in the *beau monde,*—
Will Bertram and Roberts fight Spiers and Pond?"

But Spiers and Pond are but perishing clay,
So they gasped and they gurgled and fainted away—
The burden of Bertram and Roberts's song
Was "Goodness! how shocking! Oh, please go along!

With neither for worlds would we ever abscond!"
And "Ditto for us," exclaimed Spiers and Pond.

Said Fanny, "How bold, and how dreadfully rude!"
"Those men are too forward," said Jenny the prude,
"Such youth and such beauty as both of us own
Are safe in the walls of a convent alone,
We shall there be the coarse persecutions beyond
Of Bertram and Roberts and Spiers and Pond."

SIR CONRAD AND THE RUSTY ONE

A knight for doughty doings rife,
With falchion, lance, or bill,
Was fair Sir Conrad Talbotype,
Of Talbotypetonneville.

His parents he had never known
(The sting of many a taunt);
He had one relative alone—
A sweet, dyspeptic aunt.

A time must come when loving hearts
  Must part awhile—and lo!
Sir Conrad into foreign parts
  As errant-knight must go!

Some name to which he might be true
  He sought for near and far,
But with the maidens whom he knew
  He was not popular.

Men jeered the knight who ne'er had been
  With love of maiden blessed,
Till, mad with disappointment keen,
  His aunt he thus addressed:

"No longer shall such chaff inane
  Against my head be hurled;
If you'll allow me, I'll maintain
  Your charms against the world!

"All knights shall at thine honoured name
  In fealty bend the knee—
From every errant I will claim
  His homage, aunt, for thee!"

A tear stood in her widow'd eye,
  And thus outspoke the dame—
"Oh, don't you think you'd better try
  Some younger lady's name?

"For folks would chuckle if they should
  Discover I'm your aunt."
"I would," said Conrad, "if I could,
  But then, you see, I can't."

"Then go, my boy, with dauntless eye,
  My peerlessness maintain;
Make this your dreaded battle-cry,
  'King Harry and Aunt Jane!' "

* * * * *

"Ho! stand, Sir Knight, if thou be brave,
  And try thy might with mine,
Unless you wish this trusty glaive
  To cleave thee to the chine!"

So spake Sir Conrad as he thrust
His lance in gallant mode—
Towards a knight in suit of rust,
Who passed him on the road.

The knight at words so boldly shaped,
Stopped short and turned him round,
Then humbly touched his brow, and scraped
His foot upon the ground.

"Ha!" quoth Sir Conrad, "malpert!
Dost think with threats to brave
Sir Conrad's wrath, thou thing of dirt—
Thou braggadocio knave?

"Sir Conrad thus you may not daunt,
Or make him hold his rein—
Come—swear you never knew an aunt
So fair as my Aunt Jane!"

"Fair sir," the Rusty One replied,
"Indeed, I do not think
I ever knew but one—who died,
And all along of drink."

"Then own, thou braggart, by thy star,"
  Sir Talbotype replied,
"That my Aunt Jane is fairer far
  Than she who lately died!"

The knight rejoined, "Oh, do not cut—
  Forbear, my Lord, to strike!
I have not seen the lady, but
  I think it's very like.

"To that belief—I own it free—
  I solemnly incline—
No aunt of yours could ever be
  So great a beast as mine.

"She figured in police reports
  Along of 'heavy wet,'
And was be-known at all the courts
  As 'Coxybogy Bet!'"

"Then sign this paper," Conrad said,
  "Or there I'll stretch thee stark!"
The Rusty One inclined his head
  And made his knightly mark.

"Beshrew me! here's a dullard wight,
  Gramercy, halidame!
Thou call'st thyself an errant knight,
  And canst not sign thy name!"

"A knight?" exclaimed the Rusty one;
  "Lor bless your honour, no!
I'm only hired to set of sun
  To join the Lord Mayor's Show!"

* * * * *

Sir Conrad hied him home again
  As quickly as he could,
Right-welcomed by his kind Aunt Jane
  And all the neighbourhood.

He told them how in foreign land
  He fought that rusty buck;
And though the maidens scorn his hand,
  They do not doubt his pluck.

THE BANDOLINE PLAYER

A troubadour, young, brave, and tall,
  One morning might be seen,
A singing under Colter's Hall
  Upon the village green.

He went through all the usual forms,
  And rolled his eyes of blue,
As dying ducks in thunderstorms
  Are often said to do.

For Colter had a daughter, she
  Was barely twenty-two.
Why sang that minstrel party? He
  Adored her—so would you.

He played upon a what's-its-name—
  You know the thing I mean—
The *Pall Mall* critics call the same
  A "dainty bandoline."

And Colter's daughter, wrapt in joy
  (A sweet romantic maid),
She smiled upon that guileless boy
  As gracefully he played.

"Oh, person in the crimson legs,"
  She modestly exclaimed,
"A bashful maiden coyly begs
  You'll tell her how you're named.

"For, oh, you feed a tender flame
  In playing on the green,
And, oh, she loves what critics name
  The dainty bandoline!"

That troubadour he tore his hair
  And sent a sigh above,
To think his bandoline should share
  That maiden's wealth of love.

He hied him to his village shed,
  Wept village tears in quarts,
Then laid him on his village bed,
  And thought these village thoughts:

"I must be worshipped all in all,
  For what I've always been—
And not for what the critics call
  My dainty bandoline.

"To which of us her loving may
Be due, I'll thus detect—
Upon the fiddle I can play
With singular effect.

"To-morrow, with its graceful aid,
Her moments I'll beguile,
That maiden I will serenade
In Joachim's finest style."

And so he did, that gallant boy,
But never came the maid;
He, hoping she was only coy,
Still sang to her and played.

Beethoven, Gluck, Puccini, Spohr,
He gave her for a while,
And other masters even more
"Dot-touch-and-go" in style.

For hours that patient boy he played
At Father Colter's farm—
Behind his noble shoulder-blade,
And underneath his arm:

Below his leg—behind his back
He played till he was red—
Between his knees, with dainty knack,
And then above his head.

With musico-gymnastic tricks
He warbled forth her name:
From half-past nine till half-past six,
But, ah! no maiden came.

(For Mary had been sent away
To Weston-super-Mare—
A fact of which that minstrel gay
Was wholly unaware.)

But Father Colter rose at nine,
His wrath it also rised,
For fiddle, voice, and bandoline
He equally despised.

"I have," said he, "some bellows *here*—
A fine young noddle *there*—
It would but be politeness mere
To introduce the pair!"

No sooner was it said than done,
And as above I've shown,
Upon the sconce he fetched him one—
One for himself alone!

"Ah, Mary," said the simple lad,
"I know thy gentle touch,
Upon my word, this is too bad,
I feel it very much.

"That you don't care for me at all
Is easy to be seen—
You love what *Pall Mall* critics call
My dainty bandoline!"

(But Mary had been sent away
To Weston-super-Mare—
A fact of which that minstrel gay
Was wholly unaware.)

THE STORY OF GENTLE ARCHIBALD

WHO WANTED TO BE A CLOWN

My children, once I knew a boy
(His name was Archibald Molloy),
Whose kind papa, one Christmas-time,
Took him to see a pantomime.
He was a mild, delightful boy,
Who hated jokes that caused annoy;
And none who knew him could complain
That Archy ever gave them pain.
But don't suppose he was a sad,
Or serious, solemn kind of lad;
Indeed, he was a cheerful son,
Renowned for mild, respectful fun.

But, oh, it was a rueful day
When he was taken to the play;
The Christmas pantomime that night
Destroyed his gentle nature quite;
And as they walked along the road
That led to his papa's abode,
As on they trudged through muck and mire,
He said, "Papa, if you desire
My fondest hopes and joys to crown,
Allow me to become a clown!"
I will not here attempt to show
The bitter agony and woe,
The sorrow and depression dire
Of Archy's old and feeble sire.
"Oh, Archibald," said he, "my boy,
My darling Archibald Molloy!
Attention for one moment lend—
You cannot seriously intend
To spend a roving life in town,
As vulgar, base, dishonest clown,
And leave your father in the lurch,
Who always meant you for the Church,
And nightly dreams he sees his boy
The Reverend Archibald Molloy?"
That night as Archy lay awake,
Thinking of all he'd break and take,
If he but had his heart's desire,
The room seemed filled with crimson fire;
The wall expanded by degrees,
Disclosing shells and golden trees,
Revolving round, and round, and round;
Red coral strewn upon the ground;
And on the trees, in tasty green,
The loveliest fairies ever seen;
But one more fair than all the rest
Came from a lovely golden nest,
And said to the astonished boy,
"Oh, Master Archibald Molloy,
I know the object of your heart—
To-morrow morning you shall start

Upon your rambles through the town
As merry, mischief-making clown!"

* * * * *

Next day, when Nurse Amelia called,
To wash and dress her Archibald,
She opened both her aged eyes,
With unmistakable surprise,
To find that Archy, in the night,
Had turned all red, and blue, and white,
Of healthy colour not a trace—
Red patches on his little face,
Black horsehair wig, round rolling eyes,
Short trousers of prodigious size,
White legs and arms, with spots of blue,
And spots upon his body too!
Said she, "Why, what is this, my boy?
My gentle Archibald Molloy!
Your good papa I'll go and tell,
You must be dreadfully unwell,
Although I know of no disease
With any symptoms such as these."

The good old lady turned to go
And fetch his good papa, when lo!
With irresistible attack
He jumped upon her aged back,
Pulled off the poor old lady's front,
And thrashed her, while she tried to grunt,
"Oh, Archibald, what have you done?
Is this your mild, respectful fun,
You bad, ungentlemanly boy?
Fie on you, Archibald Molloy!"
Some dreadful power unseen, but near,
Still urged him on his wild career,
And made him burn, and steal, and kill,
Against his gentlemanly will.
The change had really turned his brain;
He boiled his little sister Jane;
He painted blue his aged mother;
Sat down upon his little brother;
Tripped up his cousins with his hoop;
Put pussy in his father's soup;

Placed beetles in his uncle's shoe;
Cut a policeman right in two;
Spread devastation round,—and, ah,
He red-hot pokered his papa!

Be sure, this highly reckless course
Brought Archibald sincere remorse.
He liked a joke, and loved a laugh,
But was too well-behaved by half—
With too much justice and good sense—
To laugh at other folks' expense.
The gentle boy could never sleep,
But used to lie awake and weep,
To think of all the ill he'd done.
"Is this," said he, "respectful fun?
Oh, fairy, fairy, I would fain
That you should change me back again;
Some dreadful power I can't resist
Directs my once respectful fist;
Change, and I'll never once complain,
Or wish to be a clown again!"

He spoke, and lo! the wretched boy
Once more was Archibald Molloy;
He gave a wild, delighted scream,
And woke—for, lo, it was a dream!

THE THREE BOHEMIAN ONES

A worthy man in every way
Was Mister Jasper Porklebay;
He was a merchant of renown
(The firm was Porklebay and Brown).

Three sons he had, and only three,
But they were bad as bad could be;
They spurned their father's righteous ways,
And went to races, balls, and plays.

On Sundays they would laugh and joke,
I've heard them bet, I've known them smoke.
At whist they'd sometimes take a hand;
These vices Jasper couldn't stand.

At length the eldest son, called Dan,
Became a stock tragedian,
And earned his bread by ranting through
Shakespearean parts, as others do.

The second (Donald) would insist
On starting as a journalist,
And wrote amusing tales and scenes
In all the monthly magazines.

The youngest (Singleton his name)
A comic artist he became,
And made an income fairly good
By drawing funny heads on wood.

And as they trod these fearful ways
(These three misguided Porklebays)
They drew not on their father's hoard—
For Jasper threw them overboard.

Yes—Jasper, grieving at their fall,
Renounced them one, renounced them all.
And lived alone, so good and wise,
At Zion Villa, Clapham Rise.

By dint of work and skilful plan
Old Jasper grew a wealthy man;
And people said, in slangy form,
That Jasper P. would "cut up warm."

He had no relative at all
On whom his property could fall,
Except, of course, his wicked sons,
Those three depraved Bohemian ones.

So he determined he would fain
Bequeath his wealth (despite mortmain),
Freeholds, debenture, stock and all,
To some deserving hospital.

When his intent was known abroad,
Excitement reigned in every ward,
And with the well-experienced throng
Of operators all went wrong.

St. George's, Charing Cross, and Guy's,
And little Westminster likewise,
Bartholomew's and Middlesex,
Combined old Jasper to perplex.

House surgeons, spite of patients' hints,
Bound headaches up in fracture splints;
In measles, strapped the spots that come,
With strips of plain diachylum.

Rare leeches, skilled at fever beds,
For toothache shaved their patients' heads;
And always cut their fingers off
If they complained of whooping cough.

Their zeal grew greater day by day,
And each did all that in him lay
To prove his own pet hospital
The most deserving of them all.

Though Jasper P. could not but feel
Delighted at this show of zeal,
When each in zeal exceeds the rest,
One can't determine which is best.

Interea, his reckless boys
Indulged in low Bohemian joys;
They sometimes smoked till all was blue,
And danced at evening parties too.

The hospitals, conflicting sore,
Perplexed poor Jasper more and more.
But, ah! ere Jasper could decide,
Poor charitable man, he died.

And Donald, Singleton, and Dan
Now roll in wealth, despite his plan:
So Donald, Dan, and Singleton,
By dint of accident have won.

Vice triumphs here; but, if you please,
It's by exceptions such as these
(From probability removed)
That every standing rule is proved.

By strange exceptions Virtue deigns
To prove how paramount she reigns;
A standing rule I do not know,
That's been more oft established so.

ALPHABETICAL INDEX

to titles of

THE BAB BALLADS

INDEX TO FIRST LINES

of

THE BAB BALLADS